FIFTH EDITION

A GUIDE TO COMPUTER USER SUPPORT FOR HELP DESK & SUPPORT SPECIALISTS

FRED BEISSE

Lane Community College

COURSE TECHNOLOGY
CENGAGE Learning®

Australia • Brazil • Japan • Korea • Mexico • Singapore • Spain • United Kingdom • United States

COURSE TECHNOLOGY
CENGAGE Learning

A Guide to Computer User Support for Help Desk & Support Specialists, Fifth Edition
Fred Beisse

Executive Editor: Marie Lee

Acquisitions Editor: Brandi Shailer

Senior Product Manager: Alyssa Pratt

Developmental Editor: Mary Pat Shaffer

Senior Content Project Manager: Cathie DiMassa

Associate Product Manager: Stephanie Lorenz

Associate Marketing Manager: Shanna Shelton

Art Director: Faith Brosnan

Cover Designer: Cabbage Design Company

Cover Image: iStockphoto.com/diane39

Senior Print Buyer: Julio Esperas

Copyeditor: Michael Beckett

Proofreader: John Bosco

Indexer: Sharon Hilgenberg

Compositor: Integra Software Services

Library of Congress Control Number: 2012931582

ISBN-13: 978-1-133-18782-0

ISBN-10: 1-133-18782-X

Course Technology
20 Channel Center Street
Boston, MA 02210
USA

Cengage Learning is a leading provider of customized learning solutions with office locations around the globe, including Singapore, the United Kingdom, Australia, Mexico, Brazil, and Japan. Locate your local office at **www.cengage.com/global.**

Cengage Learning products are represented in Canada by Nelson Education, Ltd.

To learn more about Course Technology, visit
www.cengage.com/coursetechnology.

Purchase any of our products at your local college store or at our preferred online store: **www.ichapters.com.**

Photo credits: p. 56, Figure 2-1(a) Paul Matthew Photography/Shutterstock.com; p. 56, Figure 2-1(b) vgstudio/Shutterstock.com; p. 80, Figure 2-4 © 2001–2010, Tech Support Forum; p. 155, Figure 4-6 © 2011 Microsoft; p. 157, Figure 4-7 Monkey Business Images /Shutterstock.com; p. 167, Figure 4-9 Christina Richards/Shutterstock.com; p. 190, Figure 5-2 Chris Hellyar/Shutterstock.com; p. 194, Figure 5-3 Courtesy of Fred Beisse; p. 205, Figure 5-4 © 2011 Google; p. 256, Figure 6-4 © 2010 Help Desk Technology International Corporation; p. 257, Figure 6-5 © 2010 Help Desk Technology International Corporation; p. 258, Figure 6-6 © 2010 Help Desk Technology International Corporation; p. 259, Figure 6-7 © 2010 Help Desk Technology International Corporation; p. 260, Figure 6-8 © 2010 Help Desk Technology International Corporation; p. 269, Figure 6-10 C. Kurt Holter/Shutterstock.com; p. 302, Figure 7-3 © 2010 Help Desk Technology International Corporation; p. 331, Figure 8-2 Monkey Business Images/Shutterstock.com; p. 347, Figure 8-4 Reprinted by permission of Honolulu Community College; p. 351, Figure 8-5 Reprinted by permission of Honolulu Community College; p. 350, Figure 8-6 Reprinted by permission of Honolulu Community College; p. 445, Figure 10-5 Natalia Siverina/Shutterstock.com; p. 540, Figure 12-11 © 2011 Comodo Security Solutions, Inc. All rights reserved; p. 603, Figure B-2 © 2010 Help Desk Technology International Corporation; p. 607, Figure B-3 © 2010 Help Desk Technology International Corporation; p. 610, Figure B-4 © 2010 Help Desk Technology International Corporation; p. 611, Figure B-5 © 2010 Help Desk Technology International Corporation; p. 612, Figure B-6 © 2010 Help Desk Technology International Corporation; p. 614, Figure B-7 © 2010 Help Desk Technology International Corporation; p. 615, Figure B-8 © 2010 Help Desk Technology International Corporation; p. 617, Figure B-9 © 2010 Help Desk Technology International Corporation; p. 618, Figure B-10 © 2010 Help Desk Technology International Corporation

Printed in the United States of America
2 3 4 5 6 17 16 15 14 13 12

Contents

CHAPTER 7   User Support Management **284**

CHAPTER 8   Product Evaluation Strategies and
                   Support Standards **328**

x

Preface

My goal for this fifth edition is to address the needs of readers who want to learn about the user support field and need resources to help them learn. This edition as introduction to the broad range of topics that an entry-level user support specialist is expected to know. The responsibilities of support positions vary widely; however, armed with the foundation of topics and activities covered in this book, workers entering the support industry will be better prepared to meet employers' expectations.

Learning about user support requires access to trade books, vendor manuals, and Web sites, but these materials are often not designed for students or entry-level support staff. First-time learners need textbooks with features to guide their learning, such as key term definitions, chapter summaries, discussion questions, hands-on activities, and case projects to help them practice and apply their new knowledge. In the years since the first edition of this book, many aspects of user support have remained the same; however, a surprising number of changes have occurred. I am grateful that Course Technology gave me the opportunity to update this book again to reflect recent changes in the user support field.

The Intended Audience

This book is primarily intended for three kinds of readers:

- Readers who are considering career opportunities in computer user support and who want an introduction to the field. This book describes the kinds of knowledge, skills, and abilities they need to find employment in the support industry.

- Readers who work in a related field, but find themselves in a position with growing user support responsibilities. They can use this book to acquire additional breadth and depth in the support field. This audience includes programmers, computer operators, network administrators, customer support representatives, and computer applications specialists.

- Readers who are taking a course in a user support or related degree program. They can use this book to tie together knowledge and skills introduced in other courses. These readers will especially benefit from the end-of-chapter activities and case projects that provide practice skills and experiences they will use on the job.

The Approach

A Guide to Computer User Support for Help Desk and Support Specialists is designed as an introduction to each of the topics covered. I believe that a user support textbook can introduce basic concepts and a beginning perspective, lead readers into the field, and point readers toward appropriate knowledge, skills, and resource materials. To derive maximum benefit from this book, each reader must be an active participant in the learning process.

The end-of-chapter discussion questions and hands-on activities are specifically designed to develop knowledge and skills. The hands-on activities encourage interaction with school or work colleagues to strengthen readers' learning experiences. Learning to work with others in project teams is important preparation for the collaborative work environment of the 21st century. Many end-of-chapter activities are designed to acquaint readers with information resources and technical tools that are essential to function effectively in support positions.

Assumed Knowledge

This textbook is written for readers who already have a background in the following areas, either through course work, independent study, or work experience:

- Basic computer concepts (computer literacy)

- Word processor, spreadsheet, and database applications

- Internet, email, and Web access

Overview of This Book

The organization of this book is based on the knowledge, skills, and abilities commonly found in user support position descriptions and on the tasks employers expect entry-level support staff to be able to perform.

CHAPTER 1: INTRODUCTION TO COMPUTER USER SUPPORT briefly discusses the historical context of end-user computing, how users increase their productivity with computer technology, the resources end users need, and common problems they encounter. It also covers the kinds of help that support groups provide and the variety of ways organizations have found to support end users. The chapter includes information about the knowledge, skills, and abilities a successful applicant for a support position needs, and it concludes with a discussion of alternative career paths for support workers.

CHAPTER 2: CUSTOMER SERVICE SKILLS FOR USER SUPPORT AGENTS describes the communication and customer service skills user support staff need. It also outlines ways to develop an incident management strategy and handle difficult support situations. The fifth edition includes updated material on communicating with users through support Web sites.

CHAPTER 3: WRITING FOR END USERS examines the many types of written communications a support specialist may be assigned to prepare, and explains how to plan, write, and evaluate end-user documents. It covers the strategies and tools technical writers use and discusses how to avoid common writing problems.

CHAPTER 4: SKILLS FOR TROUBLESHOOTING COMPUTER PROBLEMS discusses standard tools and methods troubleshooters use to solve computer problems. It also describes eight problem-solving strategies that a user support specialist can apply to a troubleshooting situation.

CHAPTER 5: COMMON SUPPORT PROBLEMS approaches computer problems from a practical perspective. It describes several different types of common computer problems and shows how to apply problem-solving strategies to examples of real-life situations pulled from the experiences of support workers. The end-of-chapter activities are designed to help readers build problem-solving skills and abilities.

CHAPTER 6: HELP DESK OPERATION introduces a multi-level support model and the incident management process, and provides an overview of the features of help desk software packages. The chapter includes coverage of industry best practices in help desk operation, expanded information about help desk job stress, and features the 2012 version of HelpSTAR® to illustrate typical features of help desk software.

CHAPTER 7: USER SUPPORT MANAGEMENT discusses responsibilities and perspectives of support managers and supervisors that support workers need to understand. It describes the mission of support groups and how to staff and train them. The chapter covers computer industry certification, professional associations for support workers, and standards of ethical conduct. A new section on support service budgets has been added to the fifth edition.

CHAPTER 8: PRODUCT EVALUATION STRATEGIES AND SUPPORT STANDARDS describes strategies support specialists use to evaluate computer products and define product standards for an organization. It includes updated pointers to information resources and decision-making tools for evaluating and selecting computer products. The chapter also includes an extended example of technology product standards in use at Honolulu Community College.

CHAPTER 9: END-USER NEEDS ASSESSMENT PROJECTS provides tools to help support staff analyze and assess user needs for computer hardware, software, and network products and services. An extended case study illustrates the steps in assessment projects throughout the chapter. The fifth edition includes Microsoft® Project Professional 2010 to illustrate the use of project management software tools in assessment projects. Some activities in the chapter are based on a 180-day version of the software, which is included on a CD bundled with the book.

CHAPTER 10: INSTALLING AND MANAGING END-USER COMPUTERS covers the steps to prepare an end user's site and install hardware, operating systems, network connectivity, and application software. It describes the role and contents of a site management notebook as well as tasks support workers often perform to help users manage their computers. The fifth edition updates many of the installation checklists from previous editions.

CHAPTER 11: TRAINING COMPUTER USERS explains how to plan training activities; how to prepare training materials; and how to present, evaluate, and improve training for end users. The chapter describes role-playing as a training activity. (Each chapter includes a role-playing scenario designed to give readers an opportunity to apply what they learn to a work situation.)

CHAPTER 12: A USER SUPPORT UTILITY TOOL KIT addresses the importance of utility software to diagnose, resolve, and repair the variety of problems support specialists encounter. It provides suggestions for over 30 software utilities that can be used as a starting point for building a support resource tool kit. Many of the utilities described can be downloaded, installed, and used without cost to get experience with utility software. The chapter includes an extended case study to illustrate how some of the utilities can be used in support situations.

APPENDIX A: ANSWERS TO CHECK YOUR UNDERSTANDING QUESTIONS provides answers to the end-of-chapter self-check questions.

APPENDIX B: HELPSTAR® STUDENT EDITION provides a step-by-step tutorial and hands-on activities to help readers get experience with help desk software. A 180-day version of HelpSTAR® Student Edition, developed by Help Desk Technology International Corporation, is included on a CD bundled with this book. The fifth edition features the 2012 version of HelpSTAR and access to their Web site resources.

APPENDIX C: USER SUPPORT PRESENTATIONS AND MEETINGS recognizes that, as part of their job responsibilities, support workers often need to be able to prepare and present effective presentations to users, managers, and work colleagues. The appendix is included due to requests from instructors for coverage of presentation skills. The appendix concludes with strategies for making support worker meetings more productive.

Features

Several features in this book are designed to aid readers' understanding of user support concepts and improve its value to learners.

CHAPTER OBJECTIVES Each chapter begins with a list of the important concepts presented. This list orients readers with a quick reference to the contents of the chapter and is a useful study aid.

FIGURES AND TABLES Figures and illustrations in each chapter help readers visualize concepts and examples. Tables list conceptual items and examples in a visual and readable format.

BULLETED FIGURES Selected figures contain bullets that summarize important points. They provide an overview of upcoming discussion points and help you review material when you need to recall chapter topics.

ON THE WEB These features point readers to the Web for more information about a topic, an example related to what was learned in the chapter, or additional information resources.

TIPS These features offer readers practical tips and comments from the author to supplement the information in a nearby paragraph.

NOTES These features point readers to where they can find additional material on a topic elsewhere in the book.

INFORMATION RESOURCES These features point readers to additional information resources on the book's companion Web site.

ROLE-PLAYING SCENARIOS Each chapter features a role-playing scenario designed to give readers an opportunity to apply what they learn. These scenarios are based on the experiences of actual support workers and are included to give readers an opportunity to gain insight into real-world applications of the topics and to build support skills.

CHAPTER SUMMARIES Each chapter is followed by a summary of chapter concepts. These summaries are a convenient way to recap the main ideas in each chapter and help readers review chapter contents to prepare for quizzes and hands-on activities.

KEY TERMS Each chapter includes a list of the terms introduced in the chapter and a short definition of each term. This list is a convenient way to review the user support vocabulary in the chapter.

CHECK YOUR UNDERSTANDING End-of-chapter assessment begins with a set of approximately 20 review questions that reinforce the main ideas introduced in the chapter. These questions gauge whether you have mastered the concepts and provide examples of questions you might encounter on a quiz or exam. Answers to these questions are provided in Appendix A.

DISCUSSION QUESTIONS Discussion questions are designed to supplement and extend the chapter topics and provide an opportunity for readers to formulate and discuss positions on issues they are likely to encounter in the support field.

HANDS-ON ACTIVITIES Although the vocabulary and concepts in user support topics are important, no amount of vocabulary can substitute for actual experience. To supplement conceptual explanations, each chapter has approximately ten Hands-On Activities to help readers build experience with user support tasks. Some activities involve researching information from people in the support industry, printed resources, and the Web. Others let readers work with software used by support agents in the workplace. Because Hands-On Activities ask readers to go beyond the boundaries of the text, they provide practice in real-world research as performed in a user support position.

CASE PROJECTS The end of each chapter includes several Case Projects. The projects are longer and more open-ended than Hands-On Activities and designed to help readers apply what they have learned to business situations. They provide an opportunity to independently analyze, synthesize, and evaluate information, examine potential solutions, and make recommendations—as one would in an actual business situation. The Case Projects section of each chapter has been updated and expanded in the fifth edition.

HelpSTAR® **HELP DESK SOFTWARE** A CD included with this edition includes a 180-day version of HelpSTAR Student Edition. New features include Request Document Management, Calendar Management for help desk resources, Communication Management for emails and notifications, and Recent Service Request Views for easier ticket handling. The student edition can be used to gain hands-on experience with help desk software and operational procedures such as those described in Chapter 6.

PROJECT MANAGEMENT SOFTWARE A CD included with this edition contains a 60-day version of Microsoft® Project Professional 2010, which can be used to plan user needs assessments and other special projects such as those described in Chapter 9.

Instructor Resources

The following supplemental materials are available to instructors when this book is used in a classroom setting. All of the instructor resources available with this book are provided to the instructor on a CD.

ELECTRONIC INSTRUCTOR'S MANUAL The Instructor's Manual follows the text chapter-by-chapter to assist in planning and organizing an effective, engaging course. The manual includes learning objectives, chapter overviews, lecture notes, ideas for classroom activities, and additional resources. A **sample course syllabus** is also provided.

EXAMVIEW® ExamView is a powerful testing software package that allows instructors to create and administer printed, LAN-based, and Web-based exams. ExamView includes hundreds of questions that correspond directly to the text, enabling students to generate detailed study guides that include page references for further review. The computer-based and Internet testing components allow students to take exams at their computers, and save instructor time by grading each exam automatically. These test banks are also available in **Blackboard, WebCT, and Angel** compatible formats.

POWERPOINT® PRESENTATIONS This text provides PowerPoint slides for each chapter. Slides are included to guide classroom presentation, make available to students for chapter review, or print as classroom handouts. Instructors may add to the slides to cover additional topics and customize the slides with access to **the complete figure files** from the text.

Visit this Book's Web Site

To extend the information in this book, pointers to many sites on the Web are provided throughout the book. Over time, these sites will change or be replaced with newer information. In some cases, a URL in the book may result in a "Web address not found" message. To reduce the amount of typing to enter lengthy URLs and to provide alternate Web resources for obsolete links, a Web site is available to readers at **www.CUS5e.com**. The following features can be found on the book's Web site:

- Links to Web resource URLs in each chapter
- Replacement URLs for obsolete links
- Additional Web site links and information to supplement topics within the chapters
- Errata for the book and Instructor's Resources
- An email link for readers and faculty to provide feedback and report broken links

Acknowledgments

I want to express my gratitude to the staff at Course Technology who played vital roles on the team of people who guided the development of the fifth edition. Brandi Shailer, Acquisitions Editor, got the project started, and Alyssa Pratt, Senior Product Manager, kept the project on track and consulted on production issues. So many other people worked on the production of the book. Several of them are listed on the copyright page, and each of them made significant contributions to the book you hold in your hands.

The person who labored most intently, day-by-day, during the development work on both the fourth and fifth editions is Mary Pat Shaffer. While she has the title, Development Editor, I appreciate that Mary Pat is so much more than the title Editor can describe. In the two editions on which Mary Pat and I have collaborated, her contributions to this book are enormous. She is at the same time a strategist, a professional editor, a designer par excellence, and a careful wordsmith. She never fails to encourage when I need it the most. I hope these words convey how much I appreciate our association on this book.

I also very much appreciate the faculty members who reviewed several revised chapters in the fifth edition and made useful suggestions on the organization and contents: Lisa Bock, Pennsylvania College of Technology; Gerlinde Brady, Cabrillo College; Lee Cottrell, Bradford School Pittsburgh, Judi Elmer, Ogden-Weber Applied Technology College; Brenda Phillips, Lone Star College (Tomball campus).

The software bundled with this book has the potential to materially aid the understanding and job preparation skills of readers, and I want to thank Microsoft Corporation and Help Desk Technology International Corporation for making academic versions of their products available. Rakhi Madan, Rick DaSilva, and Carlos Ferreira of Help Desk Technology provided valuable technical assistance during the development of Chapter 6 and Appendix B. Thanks, too, to the staff at Honolulu Community College for their willingness to share the product standards in effect at the college as an example of an industry best practice.

I want to dedicate this fifth edition to my sons, Eric and Dale Beyer, and their wives, Kaori and Amy. Eric and Dale are members of the current generation of hard-working technology professionals, and their mother and I are very proud of the contributions they are making to support application software and design computer hardware products.

Fred Beisse
Eugene, Oregon

CHAPTER 1

Introduction to Computer User Support

In this chapter, you will learn about:

◎ How changes in computer technology over time have affected computer use

◎ Ways to classify end users

◎ Resources computer users need and major categories of end-user software

◎ Common problems encountered by users

◎ Job market demand for user support workers

◎ Common ways to organize and provide support services

◎ Typical position descriptions for user support staff

◎ Knowledge, skills, and abilities required for an entry-level support position

◎ Career paths for user support workers

The computer industry has been changing continuously since it began over 60 years ago, and it will undoubtedly continue to change in the future. One result of this ongoing transformation is that computer industry professionals rarely work with the same hardware, software, networks, operational procedures, and job descriptions they learned about in school or training courses. To prepare for future positions in the computer industry, students today must learn more than just the current technology. They also need to learn how to keep up with constant change and how to make learning new technologies a part of their day-to-day work routine.

The purpose of this book is to help you learn about and prepare for information technology jobs, with a focus on the problems that your coworkers or clients will encounter when they attempt to make effective use of computer technology. The book includes information on what you need to know and what you need to be able to do in order to work in the field of computer user support. Chapter 1 gives you an overview of information technology from two perspectives. We will look at computer use from the perspective of end users—your coworkers and clients who use computers for work or personal activities. We will also introduce computer user support as a career field, and discuss how you may prepare for work as a computer support professional. To help you understand the context of end-user computing within the computer industry and the need for computer user support workers, we will begin with a brief overview of the past 70 years of development of computer technology.

Historical Changes in Computer Use

End-user computing refers to the use of computers for both business and personal use. At every level within organizations, workers today use personal computers (PCs) to accomplish their work. Furthermore, most people also have computers in their homes or use computers in public places such as libraries, schools, and government offices. However, when computers were first used in business, most workers did not have computers on their desks nor did they use computers themselves—at least not directly. The highlights of changes in computer technology and the developments that led to end-user computing and user support are summarized in Table 1-1.

Decade	Primary Types and Uses of Computer Systems
1940s	• Invention of central processing units and peripheral devices
1950s	• Early use of computers in large corporations
1960s	• Widespread use of large-scale computers
	• Early use of smaller, workgroup computers
1970s	• Widespread use of workgroup computers
	• Terminal access by workers to large-scale and workgroup computers
	• Early use of personal computers
1980s	• Widespread use of home and business personal computers
	• Availability of mass-market application software and GUI personal computer operating systems
	• Early use of data communications and networks to connect personal computers to each other and PCs to larger systems
1990s	• Widespread use of data communications and local area and wide area computer networks
	• Growth of distributed computing
	• Rapid growth of the Internet as a global network
2000s	• Increased use of the Internet for electronic business and business-to-business transactions
	• Availability of very low-cost PCs
	• Development of wireless communication technologies
2010s	• Integration of computer technology into a variety of business and personal devices
	• Development of cloud computing

Table 1-1   Milestones in the adoption of computer technology

ON THE WEB

A detailed time line of events in the history of computers is available at The History of Computing Project Web site (**www.thocp.net**). For a history of the Internet, view a slide show (**www.isoc.org/internet/history/2002_0918_Internet_History_and_Growth .ppt**); requires Microsoft PowerPoint, or a viewer.

Or, view a short video on the history of the Internet at **www.youtube.com/watch? v=9hIQjrMHTv4**.

*Instead of entering the lengthy Web site addresses in the On the Web features in this book, use the book's companion Web site (**www.cus5e.com**) to link to the address of each resource described in the book.*

The 1950s and 1960s: Early Computers

In the 1950s and 1960s, computer systems in business and government were highly centralized. Early computer systems were very large and very expensive to buy and operate. Because of this, they were installed in secure central locations. These systems were programmed and operated not by end users, but by computer professionals. The primary goal of early computer use was to increase business productivity by automating manual tasks. Employees used these early, large-scale systems by transporting trays of punched cards that recorded business transactions to a central site for processing.

The 1970s: The First Steps Toward Decentralized Computing

During the 1970s, computer use in many organizations gradually became decentralized. Two trends in computing encouraged the transition:

- The development of terminals (keyboards and display screens) that were located on workers' desks and could be connected directly to large computer systems.

- The development of smaller, less expensive computer systems that reduced the cost of ownership to businesses and government agencies. These systems were used by smaller businesses and by departments or workgroups in larger organizations.

The 1980s and 1990s: The Growth of Decentralized Computing

It was not until the 1980s and 1990s that large numbers of workers in many companies began to use computers directly on a daily basis—a trend that ushered in the era of end-user computing. Several trends converged in the 1980s to make the widespread transition to decentralized end-user computing possible. These trends are summarized in Figure 1-1.

- The backlog of requests for new computer applications
- An increase in the number of knowledge workers
- The availability of inexpensive personal computers
- The availability of inexpensive productivity software
- The development of user-friendly graphical user interfaces

Figure 1-1 Major reasons for the growth of decentralized computing

Applications Backlog

The **applications development backlog** refers to the excess demand for new computer applications that could not be met by the supply of computer professionals available to develop them. The widespread backlog problem was well known during this period and was a source of frustration for professional data-processing staffs and business departments that demanded new applications.

More Knowledge Workers

A **knowledge worker** is an employee whose primary job is to collect, prepare, process, and distribute information. The growth in the number of knowledge workers has corresponded with shifts in the U.S. economy from agricultural and industrial to automated work tasks that rely on computer technology.

ON THE WEB

The demand for knowledge workers continues today. An examination of the number and types of positions listed on Internet job search sites and in Sunday newspapers attests to the unmet demand for knowledge workers in many industries, even during challenging economic times. To learn more about knowledge workers, read the article "The Age of Social Transformation" by Peter Drucker (who invented the term in 1959) on the *Atlantic Monthly* Web site (**www.theatlantic.com/past/docs/issues/ 95dec/chilearn/drucker.htm**).

Declining Personal Computer Costs

Another reason for the rapid growth of end-user computing during the 1980s and 1990s was a dramatic drop in the cost of providing computer technology to workers. As computer costs were decreasing, technology capabilities (especially semiconductor power and capacity) were doubling every 18 to 24 months due to advances in microcomputer technology. A **microcomputer** is a complete computer (often called a personal computer, or PC) built on a smaller scale than large-scale or workgroup systems, with a microprocessor as the central processing unit (CPU). During the 1980s, the first microcomputers in an organization were often acquired by individual workers who made unauthorized purchases, despite warnings by computer professionals that money should not be wasted on these "toy" computers.

ON THE WEB

Moore's Law is a popular rule of thumb in the computer industry. Intel co-founder Gordon Moore predicted in 1975 that the capabilities of the technology (CPU speed, for example) would double every two years. Read a 2005 interview with Gordon Moore at **news.cnet.com/Moore on 40 years of his dictum/2008-1006_3-5657677.html**.

Inexpensive Productivity Software

While early computer hardware was expensive, developing applications software was even more costly. Many organizations reported that they actually spent more on programming custom software applications than on hardware. The development of inexpensive mass-market applications software (such as WordStar, VisiCalc, Lotus 1-2-3, and dBASE) meant that many organizations, and sometimes even individual workers, could afford not only personal computer hardware but also the software that would make workers more productive computer users. As a consequence, many end users were no longer dependent on computer professionals (and the related applications development backlog) to automate their work tasks.

User-Friendly Graphical User Interfaces

Users of early computer systems communicated with a computer's operating system by typing commands at a terminal keyboard. During the 1980s and 1990s, many of the programs written for personal computers incorporated menus and **graphical user interfaces (GUIs)**, or screen images that enable users to access program features and functions intuitively. GUIs and point-and-click devices made programs much easier to use than command-oriented software.

ON THE WEB

For more information about the development of the graphical user interface, including a time line of development highlights, see **toastytech.com/guis/guitimeline.html**.

The Late 1990s and 2000s: The Era of Distributed and Network Computing

Innovations in the way computers were used continued to develop during the late 1990s and into the 2000s. Large-scale and workgroup computers were not replaced by end-user personal computers in many organizations; rather, the two were joined through the technology of computer networks. **Distributed computing**, a term that describes an environment in which the needs of an organization and its workers determine the location of its computer resources, became common during this time. Organizations frequently require large-scale and workgroup computers, acting as network servers, to perform enterprise-wide transaction processing and information storage, as well as desktop tools to increase personal productivity at each workstation. Distributed computing relies on server, wired, wireless, and Internet network technology to link workers and clients in a small business or throughout an entire enterprise.

The 2010s and Beyond: Cloud Computing

In the early years of the 2010s, a new era of integrated and converging technologies is beginning. Computer technology is now embedded in a variety of business and personal technologies and devices, including cell phones, tablet PCs, music and video players, gaming systems, Global Positioning System (GPS) devices, televisions, digital cameras, electronic book readers, text and video messaging, and home security systems. Because computer technology now permits very small devices to store and process large amounts of information, and because wireless communication permits these devices to communicate with each other as well as to access the Internet, these devices are often referred to as smart technologies.

In addition, the trend of the 1980s and 1990s toward decentralization of computing has begun to swing back to a more centralized infrastructure called **cloud computing**. In cloud computing, powerful servers store and process data remotely—delivering information, communication tools, and powerful software applications (also called *apps*) on demand via the Internet. Computer users today may connect to the cloud from a variety of smart devices. Cloud computing will have significant impacts on the delivery of end-user support services, as we will see in Chapter 6.

Changes in computer technology over the past 70 years have been accompanied by organizational changes. What was formerly known as the Data Processing (DP) Department in the 1960s and 70s has been renamed **Information Systems** or **Information Services (IS)**, or **Information Technology (IT)**. The name change reflects a broader role for technology in organizations and an increased emphasis on providing services to knowledge workers. The IS or IT Department now operates distributed corporate networks that can include large-scale workgroup, desktop, laptop, tablet, and wireless systems as well as individual communications devices, such as cellular technology.

8

Classifying End Users

To understand the variety of environments and situations in which organizations provide technical support to their knowledge workers, it is helpful to recognize the different types of end users. Who are end users? Where are they located? Do they use computers in a business or home environment? How do they use computers? End users can be classified in many ways; Figure 1-2 lists some common classifications.

- **Environment**: Personal (home) user or work (corporate, organizational, enterprise) user
- **Skill level**: Novice, semiskilled, or expert
- **Frequency of use**: Occasional, frequent, or extensive
- **Software use**: Word processing, email, accounting, or others (see "End-User Applications Software" in this chapter)
- **Features used**: Basic, intermediate, or advanced (power users)
- **Relationship**: Internal user (coworker) or external user (client)

Figure 1-2   Common categories of end users

Environment

It can be helpful to distinguish between people whose primary use of computers occurs at home with nonbusiness-related applications and those whose primary use occurs at work with business-related applications. Of course, many users fall into both groups at different times.

Skill Level

End users span a range from novice users (who have little or no computer experience, difficulty with basic computer vocabulary, and many questions) to highly skilled users who may be largely self-sufficient. However, users who are highly skilled in one application program may be novices in another application.

Frequency of Use

Some people use computers only occasionally; they may not use a computer every day or even every week. Other users make frequent, often daily, use of a computer. Some users make almost continual use of a computer.

Software Used

Users can be classified by which software applications they use. For example, home users may primarily work with word-processing and email programs, and play computer games for entertainment. Business users often work with spreadsheet and database applications or software designed for a specific business function, such as a specialized healthcare accounting system.

Features Used

Some people may use only basic software features. They may only know how to perform a limited set of simple tasks using common features of a program. Others may use more features, including some that are intermediate in their power and complexity. Users who are comfortable with advanced software features have learned to use the full power of the software in order to be very productive; they are sometimes called *power users*.

Relationship

Another way to classify end users is by their relationship to the support provider. Some are **internal users** who work within the overall organization that provides support services. They are sometimes called in-house clients from a support perspective. In this context, a coworker who telecommutes from home is an internal end user. Others are **external users** who are clients or customers located outside of an organization. One example of an external user is an individual who purchases hardware, software, or technical services from a retail vendor. Another example is enterprise users, such as people who work for a company that purchases hardware, software, or services from a vendor. As you will learn, internal and external users can have very different demands for support services.

Any user may, of course, fall into several of these categories. For example, a specific end user may be a semiskilled, internal user in the accounting department who makes frequent use of intermediate features of QuickBooks accounting software. No matter how they are categorized, all end users need some common resources to make their use of computer technology as effective as possible.

Resources End Users Need

People who want to use computers at home, on the job, or in school often purchase their first computer on the basis of media advertising. Ads for computers may tout complete systems for less than $500. These are usable, but fairly basic, hardware configurations that may or may not include the full range of hardware a user needs to be productive at a specific task. First-time purchasers are sometimes surprised that the full cost of owning a personal computer system is often much more than the purchase price of the initial hardware. What kinds of resources do end users need, and what costs are they likely to encounter?

Basic Hardware

Hardware refers to the electrical and mechanical components that are part of a computer system. Users who want to perform even basic tasks, such as word processing or reading and sending email, need a system with a central processing unit (CPU) as well as memory, storage space, a keyboard and a mouse, a monitor, and usually a printer. The cost of the hardware is only a starting point in the cost of a complete system.

Add-on Peripherals

In addition to basic hardware, users frequently need **peripheral devices**, or hardware add-ons that plug into the computer's system unit, either internally (inside the case) or externally. For example, anyone who wants to connect to the Internet needs a dial-up or broadband modem or a wired or wireless connection to a local area network. Users who work with graphic images usually purchase a scanner or a digital camera, or both. Anyone who wants to make convenient media backups might invest in a removable disk. The list of available peripheral devices is long and can add considerable expense to a basic system.

Hardware Maintenance and Upgrades

Most PCs are sold with a basic warranty and perhaps some technical assistance to cover initial installation or operational problems. Warranties of 90 days to a year are common. During a warranty period, hardware problems are repaired or replaced without charge. A few companies also offer next-day, on-site repair services. Other companies offer a warranty that specifies that the user must pay shipping to return a defective device to the manufacturer or to a repair depot. Some companies offer extended warranties on hardware components. Because most computer components that fail do so early, during the standard warranty period, the cost of extended warranties is often very high relative to their value. In any case, computer purchasers should know the features of the warranty that comes with a new PC and whether technical assistance is available locally or via a long-distance phone call.

Even after the initial purchase of a system and peripherals, additional costs may arise. During the two- to four-year life of a typical computer system, users might need to upgrade the amount of memory, the CPU speed, the size of the hard disk drive, the speed of a peripheral (such as a modem or a printer), or other system components. As technological improvements are introduced, users may want to take advantage of new devices such as an improved graphics or sound system, a removable hard drive, or a Web-cam. Hardware upgrades help keep systems fully functional as more complex software packages with larger memory and disk space requirements become available and as hardware devices with more capabilities are developed.

Although the hardware components in most PCs are generally reliable, hardware service organizations stay busy diagnosing and repairing a multitude of malfunctions. Most organizations and even individual users with a sizable investment in computer equipment should budget for occasional hardware repairs or replacement. Although individual home users may beat the odds and never need hardware repairs, the probability is that at some point, a user will experience a burned-out power supply or a crashed hard drive, and will have to pay the cost of a replacement.

Software and Software Upgrades

Most hardware packages are bundled (sold) with a preconfigured operating system. However, some users need an alternate operating system, such as Linux, instead of or in addition to Windows. For these users, the alternate operating system often represents an added cost.

Users should anticipate their application software needs and budget accordingly, especially if they need to purchase one or more special-purpose packages. Examples of specialized software include a computer-aided design (CAD) program and a software package tailored to a specific business, such as a patient-billing system. Although mass-market software is often fairly inexpensive, specialized software can add thousands of dollars to the cost of a system. The significant cost of software is a reason users are attracted to open source software, which is often distributed free of charge.

Besides the initial purchase of an operating system and applications software, users need to budget for software upgrades. Although some software upgrades are free when downloaded from the Internet, many upgrades must be purchased. Common examples include annual fees for many virus-protection programs and annual updates to a tax-preparation program.

Supplies

When estimating the total cost of a computer system, users should be sure to include consumables, such as printer paper, mailing labels, ink-jet or laser printer cartridges, cleaning supplies, media (recordable CDs and DVDs or tape cartridges), cables, and other supplies they will need to operate their system.

Data and Information

End users who need to communicate with other users or obtain information from outside sources can incur costs for information services. The monthly cost of an Internet service provider falls into this category, as do the costs of downloading stock market, financial, or economic data from an online service. Although many information vendors initially offer free access to data to attract customers, providers of specialized or proprietary information and expert knowledge typically charge for access after an introductory period.

Technical Support

As end users buy and learn new programs and discover additional uses for programs they already own, they often need technical support. Support costs can include installation assistance, training courses, books, and magazines. Users may want to contract with a vendor to perform the initial system installation tasks, or they may need to contact a help desk to solve an installation or operational problem. When they do, they may have to pay for long-distance telephone charges in addition to the cost of the support call itself. Some computer vendors sell installation assistance and user support by the hour or for a fixed fee. In a large organization, computer support for employees is a major budget item.

Training is a good example of a technical support service that can add substantially to the cost of a computer system. Training for end users is available in a variety of formats, as described in Chapter 11. Some users try to avoid the cost of training by using a trial-and-error learning approach, which may appear to be free. However, when you factor in the cost of reduced productivity and the errors made by a poorly trained user, the hidden costs of this approach to training are significant. While the purchase of a $40 tutorial, book, or online course for a software product may seem inexpensive, a worker's time away from task must be included as a hidden cost.

Facilities, Administration, and Overhead

Both home users and businesses should budget for the cost of the facilities needed to house and operate a computer system. Facilities include furniture, ergonomic devices (such as keyboard wrist rests and antiglare screens), electricity, air conditioning, power conditioners, space, and other workplace components that are necessary to operate a computer system.

In many organizations, overhead and supervisory costs are related to the management of end-user computing systems. These costs include acquisition assistance, purchase-order processing, shipping, inventory control, insurance, security, and related costs of doing business. The cost of end-user computing must include a proportional share of overhead costs.

Total Cost of Ownership

The list of cost categories for an end-user computing system is long. Of course, not all costs apply to each user or to every system. But what costs should be anticipated, bottom line? The **total cost of ownership (TCO)**, or the total expenditures necessary to purchase, maintain, upgrade, and support an end user's personal computer over its expected useful lifetime, provides this figure. Gartner, a technology consulting company that researches trends in the computer industry, estimates that the total cost of ownership to an organization for a personal computer system over a four-year period averages over $23,000, or approximately $5800 per year. Hardware costs accounted for only about 20 percent of the total cost of ownership; software, maintenance, and support made up the remainder.

As you can see from this overview, end users need many types of resources to make their computers true productivity tools. End users who are attracted to an ad for a $500 computer should be aware that other ownership costs must be included in the total package.

ON THE WEB

To learn more about total cost of ownership and the factors that users should consider in a computer budget, see **www.federalelectronicschallenge.net/ resources/docs/costofown.pdf**.

End-User Application Software

Among the computer resources needed by end users, application software has a significant impact on user productivity. Tasks that formerly required considerable manual effort, such as preparing a budget report or maintaining a mailing list, can be done quickly and more accurately with a well-designed application software program. End users run a variety of software applications, which are grouped into several broad categories:

- **Electronic mail and instant messaging**—Electronic mail (email) enables users to communicate with other users, and it is a the most common use of computers today—for both home and business users. A popular feature of email is the ability to send attachments to a message (an attachment is a separate file transmitted with the email message that contains a document, worksheet, graphic image, video clip, or other output from an application program). Instant messaging (or "chat") is communication between two or more users who are online (connected to the Internet or to a server) at the same time.

- **Web browser**—A Web browser is a software tool that enables users to find and display information on the Internet and to perform tasks such as banking and shopping from a home computer. Pages of information in a format called Hypertext Markup Language (HTML) are stored and transmitted via Internet servers. A Web browser retrieves each page and displays it on a user's PC.

- **Word processing**—Word-processing software enables users to prepare and change text and to easily integrate graphics, numeric data, and footnotes into a document that can be printed or emailed as an attachment. Word processors are usually part of an office suite of software tools.

- **Spreadsheets**—Because office workers frequently prepare reports with numeric data values in addition to narrative text, electronic spreadsheets are close to the top of many users' software shopping lists. Spreadsheets are used to prepare budgets, sales reports and forecasts, financial statements, and management analyses. Spreadsheet software is also commonly included in packages of business software tools (also called *office suites*).

- **Database management**—End users frequently need to track information that relates to business activities and projects. Database management software is used to maintain client lists, mailing lists, personnel records, office supply inventories, and class rosters. Database software runs the gamut from easy-to-use packages that are often included in office suites to sophisticated enterprise-wide database management systems.

- **Graphics**—Users often need to summarize and present information in the form of pictures, charts, maps, or drawings. Graphics software lets a user create illustrations and charts that analyze trends, show relationships, summarize large amounts of data, and help people visualize information. Many office suites include some graphics capabilities.

- **Planning and scheduling**—Office workers spend a considerable amount of time planning and scheduling their individual tasks as well as collaborating on team projects. Software packages for planning and scheduling include personal information managers, which help business or home users maintain an electronic calendar, a to-do list, and an electronic address book. For collaborative projects, scheduling and calendar software can help users arrange meetings at an available time for all team members. In addition, project management programs allow managers to plan, schedule, and monitor the status of tasks for a project team, as you will see in Chapter 7.

- **Desktop publishing**—Desktop publishing software combines the features of a word processor and a graphics program. Desktop publishing software enables users to design, lay out, and prepare—at a relatively low cost—high-quality brochures, newsletters, posters, manuals, and other printed material that would otherwise need to be designed and typeset by a printing professional.

- **Web site development**—Web site development software is popular with professional and home users who design and maintain a business or personal Web site. **Web site development software** enable users to create, maintain, and update Web pages that include a mixture of text and graphics and incorporate features such as email links, blogs, chat rooms, File Transfer Protocol (FTP), and restricted access for security.

- **Educational and entertainment software**—Educational software provides learners with hands-on experience to supplement an instructor's lectures or course materials. Educational software can simulate real-world activities, test learner understanding, and provide feedback on a learner's progress. Computer games are, of course, a significant portion of the online entertainment industry.

- **Enterprise applications**—Corporations and business enterprises continue to run many of the same applications on their large-scale systems as they did decades ago, including payroll, accounting, inventory and asset control, manufacturing, and human resource management. Popular categories of applications software for large-scale systems include customer relationship management (CRM) and enterprise resource planning (ERP).

- **Industry-specific applications**—In addition to the general categories of applications software listed earlier, many businesses and professionals use computer applications that are specific to their specialized fields. Examples include:

  - Patient care and billing software used in medical, dental, optometric, veterinary, and other healthcare occupations for patient histories and billing

  - Geographic Information Systems (GIS) software used by governmental, urban planning, and engineering organizations to analyze geographic data and prepare maps

  - Brokerage transaction systems that allow financial institutions and individual investors to submit buy and sell orders for stocks and commodities directly to a stock exchange

  - Automated design software used by engineering and construction firms to plan structural steel and concrete bridges and buildings and to manage the details of infrastructure construction projects

These software categories describe some common personal computer applications and include many of the primary applications workers use in business, government, education, nonprofit, and other organizations. New categories of applications continue to emerge as needs develop.

 Chapter 10 lists some of the popular packages in each category.

Whether for home or business use, almost all software applications are designed to increase users' productivity. In fact, most organizations justify their computer purchases on the basis that they help make workers more efficient in their jobs. Computers can either increase the amount of output (product or service) a worker can produce based on a given amount of input (effort), or reduce the amount of input required to produce a given amount of output. In general, end-user computing has accomplished this ambitious goal, but not without problems along the way.

ON THE WEB

For some examples of how knowledge worker productivity is measured and improved, read an industry white paper prepared by the Australian company, Enabling, a provider of business management applications, at **enabling.net/download/whitepapers/ Enabling.Productivity.Whitepaper1.pdf**.

Problems End Users Experience

The productivity gains from end-user computing are often accompanied by a new set of problems that organizations must address. Although not necessarily unique to end-user computing, the problems listed in Figure 1-3 can result from an environment in which powerful hardware and software tools are used (and can be easily misused) by a large number of workers.

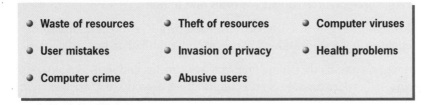

◦ Waste of resources	◦ Theft of resources	◦ Computer viruses
◦ User mistakes	◦ Invasion of privacy	◦ Health problems
◦ Computer crime	◦ Abusive users	

Figure 1-3   Common problems related to end-user computing

Every end user will likely encounter or even cause one or more of these problems in the course of their work or home computing experience.

Waste of Resources

Waste occurs when money, time, or other resources are spent in ways that do not contribute directly to increased user productivity, or that result in lower productivity. Examples include:

- A user who makes purchasing decisions about hardware, peripherals, software, and networks without the necessary expertise and experience to make cost-effective selections. For example, an inexperienced end user might purchase software that is incompatible with existing hardware.

- A user who spends excessive time trying to solve a problem with hardware or software that could be solved quickly with a phone call to a support person.

- A worker who spends time searching for information on the Internet or reading and sending email messages that are not directly job related.

User Mistakes

Users who are careless or not properly trained can easily make mistakes as they use sophisticated software. Examples include:

- A user who inadvertently enters the wrong formula or data for critical calculations while creating a spreadsheet to estimate a project's cost.

- A user who deletes or uninstalls important software while cleaning up disk space because he or she does not understand the software's purpose.

- A user who fails to make a backup copy of important information and loses the data due to a hardware failure.

Computer Crime

Computers are also sometimes used to commit intentional crimes. Examples include:

- A worker who has access to sensitive company information that would be potentially valuable to a competitor tries to profit from the sale of the information.

- A user who reveals confidential bank account information via email in response to a fraudulent request for information and becomes a victim of identity theft.

Theft of Resources

Another form of computer crime is theft of computer equipment, software, or services. Examples include:

- A user who illegally copies, distributes, or uses computer programs or information (proprietary data, videos, or music)—a practice commonly called software **piracy**.

- A worker who uses the Internet at work (contrary to company policy) to sell items online.

- A user who finds a removable USB drive in a school's teaching lab and pockets the device instead of turning it in to lost and found.

- A worker who removes a software installation CD from his/her place of employment and takes it home to install on a home computer. (This would only be legal if the employer's policies and the software vendor's license agreement permit home use.)

Invasion of Privacy

Another form of computer crime is invasion of privacy, when unauthorized parties exploit personal information. Examples include:

- A user who has access to confidential medical information at work searches the files of friends and relatives.

- A user who is unaware of the risks of spyware inadvertently downloads software that secretly records information about purchases made on Web sites. The spyware periodically sends a history of the user's purchases to a company that resells profiles of users.

Abusive Users

Worker abuse of company resources is not unique to the information age; however, workers who use computer technology in an abusive way present difficult challenges to managers. Examples include:

- A user who continues to send unwanted, personal email messages to a coworker despite repeated requests to stop.

- A user who displays offensive, off-color material on a computer screensaver, which is visible to coworkers.

Computer Viruses

A **computer virus** is a piece of software created with malicious intent that can destroy information, erase or corrupt software, or adversely affect the operation of an infected computer. Examples include:

- A user who downloads software that contains a virus, which then attacks services throughout an office network.

- A user who forwards emails to colleagues with an attachment that contains a virus.

- A user who sends information to email contacts about a suspected new virus attack. The virus is a well-documented hoax, but the message results in lost time as coworkers investigate the potential problem.

Health Problems

Every tool that can be used can also be misused. A common source of misuse that may not even be apparent to end users is the physical environment in which a computer is operated. Without proper lighting, space, furniture, and environmental safeguards, physical injury to end users can result. Examples include:

- A user who doesn't take adequate breaks loses work time due to **carpal tunnel syndrome**, which is severe hand or wrist pain due to an inflammation of the tendons in a user's hand and wrist.

- A user who experiences extreme stress due to the frustrations of working with technology and is forced into early retirement due to health problems.

- An employer who refuses to purchase ergonomic office furniture despite requests from workers risks injury to workers, lower productivity, and disability claims. **Ergonomics** is a field that studies how to design a workspace that promotes worker health, safety, and productivity. Many common ailments can be avoided by paying attention to office ergonomics.

 Chapter 10 discusses ergonomic concerns and workspace design in more detail.

Professionals who provide technical support to end users often confront these problems. A user support worker's responsibilities may include consulting with users about possible solutions to problems that arise due to the use or misuse of technology.

Addressing the Need for User Support Workers

Most manufacturing, service, or consulting organizations provide computers to their knowledge workers to help them be more productive. But an organization's commitment usually does not end with the initial purchase. Organizations understand that they must also provide some form of ongoing assistance to their workers so that the computers become tools that increase worker productivity instead of stumbling blocks and sources of frustration. Because of this, many organizations have recognized an increasing need for user support workers. With the evolution of end-user computing, along with the growth of the Internet as a way to obtain information, organizations often find themselves unable to meet the demand for user support and support workers. The U.S. Bureau of Labor Statistics (BLS) estimates that over the next 10 years, the number of computer support workers will grow from about 566,000 to over 644,000, a growth rate of nearly 14 percent. Network specialist positions are expected to grow from about 340,000 to over 420,000 (a growth rate of 23 percent) over the next 10 years. These two occupational categories are expected to account for over 1 million workers by 2018.

ON THE WEB

If you would like to know more about the BLS outlook for employment in computer and network support occupations, see the current edition of the Occupational Outlook Handbook (**www.bls.gov/search/ooh.htm**). In the search box, enter *15-1041* for computer support specialists or *15-1071* for network support occupations, and then click on the article of interest to you.

During the early part of the twenty-first century, several trends have influenced the demand for user support workers, including the following:

1. The economic recession from 2007 to 2009 caused a sharp increase in the overall U.S. unemployment rate, to over 10 percent. As a result, hiring in all information technology fields, including user support, decreased substantially when compared to the rapid growth years of the 1990s.

2. The transfer of some technical support jobs overseas (especially to India and East Asian countries), where well-trained workers are available and wages are comparably lower, has reduced the demand somewhat for IT and technical support workers in the United States.

3. Some organizations that need technical support services now contract with temporary employment agencies for the workers they need. Some of these temporary work opportunities evolve into permanent positions, so that the temporary assignment is effectively a trial period for both the employee and the employer.

ON THE WEB

To learn about temporary employment agencies in your area that are seeking computer professionals, visit the Web site of the American Staffing Association (**www.staffingtoday.net**).

4. Some organizations have experienced an increased demand for support workers due to the expansion of mobile technologies and the increased need for computer security specialists.

ON THE WEB

Computerworld, a computer industry magazine, provides an interactive salary estimator on its Web site (**www.computerworld.com/action/usertools.do? command=getSalaryInformation&yr=2011**). Enter the job title in which you are interested (for example, Help Desk/Technical Support Specialist), select your level of experience, and then select a region of the country. Note that estimates in the *Computerworld* survey are often based on small numbers of respondents and are reported as averages. Salaries for entry-level positions are much lower than average salaries.

How Organizations Provide a User Support Function

Computer user support (or simply user support) provides information and services to workers or clients to help them use computers more productively in their jobs or at home. Computer user support includes a broad spectrum of services furnished to help people resolve problems and be more productive when they use computer technology. The user support function is known by a variety of names in various organizations. Common names include customer service, help desk, service desk, technology support services, client support services, computer assistance, computer help hotline, call center, information center, or the word *support* with any modifier, such as *user*, *product*, *hardware*, *software*, or *network*. **Technical support** is usually a level of user support that focuses on advanced troubleshooting and problem solving. In some organizations, user support is called technical support, especially if the support staff consists of workers who are technicians or who have advanced technical skills. No matter what name is used, what is important are the tasks that user support performs in an organization.

Organizations provide support to their workers or clients in a variety of ways. Figure 1-4 lists the most common methods of organizing the user support function. These methods are described in more detail in the following sections.

- Peer support
- Part-time user support
- User support worker or work team
- Help desk support
- User support center
- User support as an IT responsibility
- User support outsourced to a vendor

Figure 1-4   Common ways that organizations provide a user support function

The strategy an organization selects to provide user support often depends on the organization's size, type, location, financial situation, and goals for computer support services, as well as the skill level and the support needs of workers and clients. In fact, an organization may use different support strategies at different times as the needs of its workers and clients change, and it may use more than one strategy at the same time.

Peer Support

Many small organizations and even individual departments in larger organizations provide support services with a peer support model. One or more workers, whose job titles usually have little to do directly with computers (for example, they are office managers, administrative specialists, or accounting department heads), are generally recognized as *the* person to turn to when a computer user has a question. This form of support is called **peer support**, and is often informal, because workers look to their colleagues, or peers, when they need computer assistance. For example, a sales representative with a special interest in computer technology may become the "guru" for computer problems that arise in the sales department.

ON THE WEB

Microsoft has extended the strategy of peer support to the Web in the form of virtual user groups of peers who share common interests. To learn more about Microsoft user groups, go to **www.microsoft.com/communities/usergroups/default.mspx**. Click the **Find a Community** link in the left pane to see a list of peer user groups. A vendor-neutral Web site that offers a technical support forum can be found at **www.techsupportforum.com/forums**.

An informal network of peers who provide user support to their work colleagues often precedes the formation of a more formal organizational structure. Informal peer support also occurs in colleges and vocational schools, where students quickly learn who among their classmates is a good source of information and assistance. You may have provided informal peer support in a computer or training lab when the person next to you asked for your help to solve a hardware or software problem.

Part-Time User Support

Often the first step an organization takes toward a formal computer support function occurs when some user support responsibilities are written into an existing worker's position description. This step may formalize a responsibility that existed informally for some time. The combination of user support with other responsibilities is a good way for very small organizations to meet the need for computer support when they cannot justify the cost of a full-time support position. Workers who are assigned user support responsibilities in conjunction with other duties often see the designation as a positive career step because their expertise is recognized formally and perhaps rewarded financially. On the downside, these workers can become overloaded and stressed because computer support tasks can make significant demands on their time and can interrupt or compete with other assigned tasks.

Small organizations that sell computer hardware or software often provide informal client support during the early stages of product development and sales. When the volume of sales is small, client support may be assigned to a product development engineer or a programmer along with their other duties. As sales increase, the need to provide support to a growing client base becomes greater. At that point, the support function usually becomes more formal, in the form of a full-time support position or a user support group.

User Support Worker or Work Team

When organizations find that peer support or part-time workers are no longer sufficient to handle the volume or variety of requests for computer support or that the hidden costs of peer support are growing, they have several options. One alternative is to devote a full-time position to provide support. Some organizations recognize that they have reached this point when a number of workers are engaged in informal peer support roles or when several workers provide computer support as one part of their official responsibilities. Organizations that devote a full-time position to user support tasks may seek the expertise of a support worker who has a greater breadth and depth of technical skills as well as an ability to communicate effectively with users.

A second alternative is to organize the part-time support workers into a **user support team**, a formal workgroup that is organized to provide computer support services. Depending on the needs of the organization, a user support team can consist of workers who provide support in addition to other job responsibilities. The advantage of these split positions is that the support workers can be very familiar with the day-to-day business operation of the organization. A user support team can also combine full- and part-time staff into a support group.

Another alternative open to companies that experience a growing demand for computer support is to outsource their support needs, a strategy that is discussed in an upcoming section.

Help Desk Support

When individual workers need assistance, they may turn to the staff of a user support team or they may contact a help desk facility. A **help desk** provides a single point of contact for users in need of technical support, whether they are internal workers or external clients. A help desk manages client problems and requests and provides solutions-oriented support services. A help desk may be part of a larger user support group, or it may stand alone as the primary source of user support. In a large organization with many internal users, a help desk may be one of many support services offered. In a computer products vendor organization, a help desk may be the only support service provided to customers.

A help desk facility often includes one or more of these options:

- A physical location where internal workers or external clients can go when they have a question or problem, or want to request an office visit or a field service call

- A telephone number (sometimes called a **hotline**) that external clients or internal workers can call for assistance with a hardware or software product

 Telephone help desk support is a small part of the much larger call center industry, which includes incoming, outbound, and blended telephone centers that respond to clients in a variety of industries. A user support hotline or telephone help desk is technically an incoming call center. Telemarketing and political surveys are examples of activities in outbound call centers. Blended call centers combine both incoming and outbound telephone operations.

- An email address, Web site, or online **chat service** (also called instant messaging) that workers or clients can contact for technical assistance

Help desk staff attempt to resolve problems as soon as possible. If they cannot, they may refer the problem to someone else for resolution. For example, a help desk staff member may serve as an interface between an internal user with a problem and an external vendor who can solve the problem.

 The operation of a help desk is described in greater detail in Chapter 6.

User Support Center

Another organizational model for user support services is a user support center. A **user support center** (also called an **information center**) provides a wider range of services than a help desk to an organization's internal computer users. These services can include consultation on computer purchases (the user support center may even offer computer products for purchase by workers); a training center or training program to provide learning experiences, manuals, and other documentation on supported hardware and software products; and a help desk for information, troubleshooting, and assistance. The user support center in some organizations may provide facilities management and hardware repair services as well.

User Support as an IT Responsibility

Although some organizations view computer user support as a separate, independent function, other organizations assign this responsibility to the IT department. Technical support as part of the IT department has advantages and disadvantages. On the one hand, because the IT department's primary responsibility is to design and develop application programs and operate the organization's large-scale systems and telecommunications networks, some organizations have found that the IT department is not an effective location for the end-user support function. The IT staff is often busy working on its own priorities, and may have little time to devote to work with end users. On the other hand, some organizations believe that all corporate computing activities should be organized under one umbrella (the IT department) in order to provide a single point of contact for all network, personal computer, and telecommunications users. Whether end-user support is organized separately or combined with other computer activities in an IT department depends on an organization's history, its experience with computer support, its organizational culture, and its users' needs.

ON THE WEB

Chaim Yudkowsky, a Certified Public Accountant, has written about how organizations provide user support services to their workers. Read his perspective on the pros and cons of locating the help desk function inside and outside an IT department at **accounting.smartpros.com/x33607.xml**.

User Support Outsourced to a Vendor

Outsourcing is another alternative for organizations that need to provide support services to their workers and clients. To **outsource** its user support services, an organization contracts with a vendor that specializes in user support functions to handle problem incidents. Organizations can outsource support services for both internal and external users. For example, workers may contact a support provider via a dedicated telephone line or email. Alternately, an organization's internal help desk operation may handle some incidents itself and refer difficult technical problems to an external support provider. Outsourcing can be an attractive option for an organization that wants to control its costs or take advantage of expertise it does not have among its existing support staff.

ON THE WEB

To learn more about the advantages of outsourcing help desk and user support services, visit the Web site of Convergys, a company that provides outsourced support for other organizations and vendors (**www.convergys.com/industries/ technology/technical-support.php**).

The disadvantages of outsourcing user support include the following:

1. Outsourced support usually occurs by telephone or email because on-site assistance can be prohibitively expensive and is rarely included in an outsourcing agreement.

2. Outsourced support costs are typically predictable, although not necessarily lower than internal support.

3. When an organization outsources support, it relies on a vendor's staff for an important organizational function. It does not develop its own in-house technical support expertise.

4. When support is outsourced, the support staff rarely develops a personal relationship with an organization's end users. A personal relationship between end users and support staff often means that users are more likely to report problems and request help.

ON THE WEB

Azure Knowledge Corporation is an example of a technical support vendor that reflects the trend for support providers to locate in India and East Asian countries. Visit their Web site (**www.azurecrm.com/customersupport.html**).

No single, one-size-fits-all organizational structure for end-user support works well in every situation. More often than not, an organization's approach to user support evolves over time, and is influenced by its history, goals, resources, corporate culture, expertise, and needs.

User Support Services

The user support function in an organization frequently provides a variety of services. The range of services provided depends on the goals of the organization, the specific needs of the workers or clients, and the resources the organization decides to devote to the support function. Figure 1-5 lists some common user support services.

- Staff a help desk, hotline, or chat service to provide information
- Provide technical troubleshooting assistance for hardware, software, and network problems
- Locate information to assist users
- Evaluate hardware, software, and network products
- Coordinate organization-wide support standards
- Perform needs assessment and provide purchase assistance for users
- Provide system installation assistance
- Provide training on computer systems and procedures
- Prepare documentation on computer use
- Perform computer facilities management tasks
- Assist users with software development projects

Figure 1-5   Common user support services

Figure 1-6 illustrates the wide variety of support services users need. User support, as a field within information technology, includes all of these functions. Not every organization provides all these services to its workers or clients, but organizations that provide user support offer at least some of these services to respond to worker or client needs.

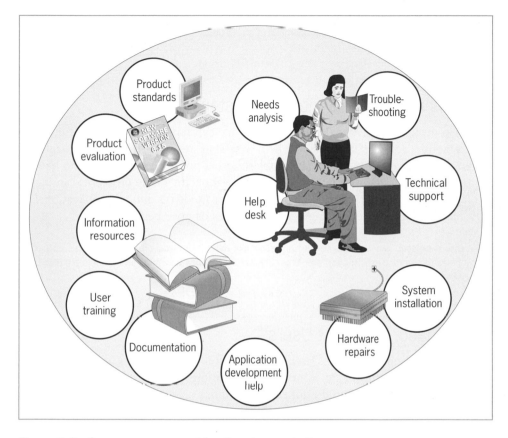

Figure 1-6   Common user support functions in organizations

Staff a Help Desk, Hotline, or Chat Service to Provide Information

Users who encounter problems with their computer system need a place to turn for information. A help desk, hotline, or chat service often meets this need. Providing information is one of the most common types of services offered by a user support organization. Agents who provide information services via a help desk, hotline, Web site, or online chat service may do the following:

- Respond to requests for product information
- Provide solutions to common problems
- Market and sell products and services, including add-ons and upgrades
- Receive and log user complaints about product features
- Handle warranty claims and authorize product returns or exchanges

Chapter 2 discusses the client service and communication skills that support staff need in a help desk environment. Chapter 6 describes the operation of a help desk from the perspective of a help desk agent.

Provide Technical Troubleshooting Assistance

Although a help desk, hotline, Web site, or chat service can handle common user problems and questions, some problems fall outside a help desk staff's expertise. Most organizations recognize the need for a level of technical troubleshooting provided by people who have the knowledge to resolve seemingly intractable problems that occur. These problems can include hardware diagnosis, repairs, or upgrades; fixes or workarounds for difficult applications software problems; and troubleshooting network crashes or poor performance.

Chapter 4 presents some strategies for troubleshooting difficult technical problems. Chapter 5 provides examples of common user support problems. Chapter 6 describes how problem incidents are managed.

Locate Information to Assist Users

A challenge that continually confronts user support staff is the need to locate information to resolve a user's question or problem. Although organizations provide their workers with computers and software, they often do not supply manuals or documentation about computer operation. In other cases, manuals get misplaced or thrown away by users, or become obsolete. Users can sometimes use online help, which can be excellent in commercial software products. But online help is often neither in-depth enough nor technical enough to help users solve every problem, especially difficult ones. And sometimes vendor documentation is just not very good. For their information needs, users often turn to support staff.

Information can be found in a variety of places: printed vendor manuals, trade books and textbooks, online help, CD-ROM databases, Web sites, and automated telephone voice-response units. User support workers need to understand the characteristics of each of these information resources and be able to use them effectively.

Check the **Additional Resources** section on this book's companion Web site (**www.cus5e.com**) for pointers to information and resources that user support staff have found helpful.

Evaluate Hardware, Software, and Network Products

Most organizations are on the lookout for new technologies to enhance worker productivity. Consequently, the user support staff frequently must research, compare, and evaluate new technology products and services, including hardware, software, and network products, against existing products. The user support staff must find answers to such questions as:

- Will a new product make workers more productive?

- Will a specific product meet user needs better than another product?

- Should some or all users upgrade from one version of an application to a newer one, or wait until the next version is released?

- What features are important to evaluate in the purchase of a new computer?

- Will a particular hardware configuration or software package be cost effective?

Individual workers do not always have the information and expertise to make these decisions wisely. When users make individual purchasing decisions, organizations can encounter incompatibilities, excessive costs, unusable products, and productivity problems that can be difficult to resolve. The evaluation of new hardware and software products is an important, challenging, and ongoing task for user support staffs.

Chapter 8 provides examples of tools to help with product-evaluation tasks.

Coordinate Organization-Wide Support Standards

A task closely related to product evaluation is the definition of product support standards. **Support standards** are lists of computer products that an organization allows or encourages its workers to use and that it will support. Support standards help limit the hardware, software, and network products that a support staff must be able to support. Therefore, standards reduce support costs. Support standards are important because it is impossible for an organization to support every hardware configuration or software package that an individual user or department might choose to purchase.

Chapter 8 describes the role of support standards in organizations.

Perform Needs Analysis and Provide Purchase Assistance for Users

In addition to evaluating computer products and defining support standards, the support staff tries to match supported products with the needs of each user. Occasionally, the match between a user's needs and specific products is obvious. In other cases, support staff may perform a user **needs analysis** (or needs assessment), which is an investigation to determine the features and configuration of hardware and software (from among those supported or available) that will best match a user's specific needs. Most support teams that offer this service also assist users with the paperwork required to purchase a system, such as forms to justify the purchase, place an order, and pay for the system.

Chapter 9 explains how to perform a needs analysis for an end user.

Provide Installation Assistance

Once an organization or individual user has purchased a system or upgrade, the support staff may offer to unpack, set up, install, and configure the system for the end user. The goal of this service is efficiency; the support staff often has the tools and expertise to make sure the installation is done correctly, and they can identify and solve many common installation problems that might frustrate an inexperienced user. Where applicable, the support staff can ensure that the appropriate network software is installed and configured to connect a computer to an organization's network. They can also install peripheral devices such as printers and scanners, and install and configure driver software for these devices. While some end users might be able to perform these tasks, user support staff can often do the work faster and with fewer errors because they usually have more experience with system installations than a typical end user.

Chapter 10 details the system installation process.

In addition to providing installation assistance, user support teams often help users with **computer facilities management** tasks such as network security, media backups, virus detection and prevention, ergonomic analyses, supplies management, preventive maintenance and repairs on hardware and peripherals, and other related tasks.

Provide Training on Computer Systems and Procedures

Users who have new job responsibilities and those with new hardware or software often require training. With proper training, users can become productive more rapidly than if they learn by trial and error. User support teams in many organizations provide end-user training. The support team may have periodic scheduled group training sessions, provide one-on-one training, or suggest ways to learn a new system that complement a user's personal learning needs and style.

Chapter 11 presents some guidelines on how to prepare effective user training materials and conduct training sessions.

Prepare Documentation on Computer Use

Although user training is a necessary and often efficient way to teach users how to effectively use the features of a system, documentation is equally important. Whereas a training session is generally a one-time event, documentation can be retained by a user to answer questions or as a reminder of how to perform a task they may perform only occasionally.

Documentation includes introductory manuals for new users, explanations of organizational computer use procedures and guidelines, as well as "how to" tutorials and reference manuals on specific software products. It also includes online documentation in the form of help files, answers to frequently asked questions (FAQs), and email responses to remote users.

Chapter 3 provides tips on how to prepare documentation and other written materials targeted to end users.

Assist Users with Software Development Projects

Most user support teams do not provide software development or programming as part of their regular services to users. Software development is usually the responsibility of an IT department, or is contracted to a vendor with software development expertise. However, in some organizations, the support staff may *help* users develop software applications to solve specific problems or meet specialized requirements for information. For example, support staff may consult with users on the most effective way to program a difficult task in a spreadsheet.

Software development has long been considered the domain of the IT department. However, with today's powerful application development tools, such as scripting languages, spreadsheets, database-management packages, and Web-page development tools, end users are able to develop some applications independent of the IT department.

Because software development is an extensive topic, no chapter in this book is devoted specifically to software development tasks for support staff. The ability to provide assistance with software development projects requires additional training or education in applications software and programming languages.

Although the mission of user support groups in organizations varies considerably, the tasks they perform define their service profile in an organization. Whereas most support groups provide help desk services and troubleshooting assistance, a smaller percentage provide documentation or product training. Few provide applications development assistance.

Position Descriptions for User Support Staff

Positions in the user support industry frequently include some combination of the tasks outlined in the previous section. A **position description** is a written description of the qualifications for and responsibilities of a job in an organization. It is a tool that reflects how an organization structures its user support function. For example, when describing the requirements for a user support position, an organization with a full-fledged support group is more likely to include the ability to analyze worker computer needs and recommend hardware and software purchases. On the other hand, an organization that primarily provides telephone or Web-based support usually emphasizes problem-solving and communication skills, and is much less likely to expect applicants to assess user needs or to be able to train end users, for example.

To understand more about the specific job of a user support staff member, let's look in detail at two position descriptions for support positions. The first position description, shown in Figure 1-7, describes the duties and responsibilities of a help desk agent who works in a company that provides IT consulting and outsourcing services. The position description in Figure 1-7 provides a picture of the wide range of activities you might encounter in user support positions in today's job market. If you are a prospective user support worker, you should be aware that managers will probably look for the kinds of capabilities listed here.

The second user support position description, shown in Figure 1-8, describes a network support technician position in a large company that operates its own local area network. Compare the responsibilities in this position, which emphasizes network support, with those in Figure 1-7, which is primarily responsible for desktop support of applications software.

Job Title: Level 1 Help Desk Agent

Position Overview: A Level 1 Help Desk Agent provides tier 1 technical support and incident and problem management to end users on technology issues—with an emphasis on good customer service skills.

Duties: A Level 1 Help Desk Agent fulfills a range of duties, including, but not limited to the following (other duties may be assigned based on company business requirements):

- Provides tier 1 technical support and incident problem management support to end users on technology use, including computer operation, network connectivity, application software support, and system installation.
- Provides support to users in face-to-face contacts, telephone calls, email messages, chat sessions, Web-based contacts, and user training sessions.
- Installs, tests, configures, and monitors hardware and software.
- Diagnoses and repairs hardware and printer problems.
- Troubleshoots and supports software applications and business processes.
- Advises users on best practices in technology use; performs user needs assessments and makes recommendations on suitability of technology solutions to meet business needs.
- Prepares reports and technical documentation as needed.

Qualifications:

- Basic knowledge of computer technology, including hardware, software, and network operation
- Working knowledge of Microsoft Windows XP/Vista/7 environments
- Expertise in system troubleshooting and problem solving
- Hands-on experience with the installation and support of PC systems
- Experience with automated help desk management systems

Skills Expectations:

- Excellent time management and multi-tasking skills
- Telephone and interpersonal skills that promote user satisfaction
- Ability to build rapport with help desk customers; escalate problems; and record, track, and document the incident problem-solving process
- Ability to use diagnostic utilities to aid in troubleshooting
- Internet search skills to locate software updates, drivers, knowledge bases, and FAQ resources to aid in problem resolution
- Handle smartphone issues, such as activation, email configuration, information transfer, and password resets; ability to troubleshoot common problems
- Develop reference sheets and FAQs for users and other support staff
- Maintain current knowledge of technology innovations in networking and computing
- Maintain an appropriate level of confidentiality with sensitive information

Education and Training:

- Minimum of two years of experience in a help desk environment; an Associate's degree in a relevant field may substitute for experience
- Certification in A+ or ability to pass certification exam required

Figure 1-7   Position description for a help desk agent

Job Title: Network Support Technician

Reports To: Manager of Network Services

Job Scope

This position is responsible for supporting a local area network operation to ensure it meets the business operation needs of the company. The position is at an intermediate support staff level and is responsible for applying some judgment to resolve routine problems and make recommendations.

Responsibilities

- Monitor the operation of the local area network to ensure minimum downtime and prompt resolution of problems.
- Identify network problems and perform corrective action; escalate issues that cannot be resolved after basic troubleshooting.
- Provide tier 1 level support to understand the nature of reported network problems; initiate troubleshooting strategies to ensure the highest quality of network services.
- Research solutions to user problems to meet employee needs.
- Prepare detailed documentation of corrective actions taken to resolve network faults in the incident management system.
- Adhere to established company procedures to ensure compliance with ITIL best practices, and to meet and exceed IT department standards.

Qualifications

- Degree or relevant industry experience
- Knowledge and understanding of local area network technology
- Accuracy, attention to detail, and ability to multi-task
- Good analytical skills
- Excellent customer service skills required
- Good written and verbal communication skills
- Demonstrated ability to manage multiple service requests at a time

Preferred qualifications

- CompTIA Network+ certification
- Working knowledge of Microsoft Office applications
- 1-2 years of experience in a technical customer support/help desk environment
- Military veteran
- Ability to communicate in Spanish

Figure 1-8   Position description for an associate network technician

Knowledge, Skills, and Abilities

One way to better understand the requirements for a specific position is to analyze them in terms of **KSAs**—the knowledge, skills, and abilities needed to perform the job. Human Resources personnel often analyze a position description and prepare a checklist of KSAs to use to screen applicants.

Knowledge

Each position includes a description of what a worker needs to know in order to do the job. The knowledge component may be stated in terms of a specific number of years of education, a degree in a specified field, a specific industry certification (such as an A+ certificate), or a list of topics a worker is expected to know.

Examples of knowledge required for the help desk agent position in Figure 1-7 include:

- Knowledge of computer technology, including hardware, software, and networking

- Knowledge of Windows operating system

Skills

Each position requires specific job skills or tasks that a support specialist must be able to perform well. User support positions may require advanced skills in one or more areas. In general, a skill is a task that a support specialist can perform better (at a higher level of effectiveness or efficiency) with practice and experience.

Examples of skills required for the help desk agent position in Figure 1-7 include:

- Skills in troubleshooting system problems

- Telephone and interpersonal communication skills

Abilities

Each position requires special tasks that a support specialist must be able to perform. Abilities are functions that an applicant either can or cannot do. For example, some positions may specify abilities such as being able to lift 50-pound boxes or communicate in Spanish.

Examples of abilities required for the help desk agent position in Figure 1-7 include:

- Ability to maintain an appropriate level of confidentiality

- Ability to prepare reports and technical documentation

If you have difficulty with the precise differences between skills and abilities, don't worry. People often use the terms interchangeably.

ON THE WEB

If you want to learn more about the KSAs required for entry-level positions for computer support specialists, visit America's Career InfoNet Web site (**www.acinet.org/ acinet/tools/tools_tech.aspx?onetcode=15-1041.00**). Click **View Occupation Profile**, and select the state you are interested in. The Web site includes a short video on computer support specialists. You can also find information on the employment outlook and typical wages for computer support specialists for your state.

How does one person ever learn to do all the tasks and acquire all the KSAs noted in these position descriptions? Actually, very few workers start in an entry-level position with all the knowledge, skills, and abilities they need to perform every task listed in the job description. Many user support positions include a training program before a support worker ever answers a live telephone call or installs and configures a piece of network hardware. Most user support positions also include a significant amount of continuing education or on-the-job learning. So don't get discouraged if you can't do everything in these job descriptions today.

If you compare the services offered by user support groups and the job duties listed in the preceding position descriptions with the table of contents of this book, you will find that this textbook is organized around these job duties—many of the primary tasks of a support staff member are described in this book.

ON THE WEB

For more information about help desk careers, use these resources:

- To view a short video on jobs in information technology, visit **www.youtube.com/ watch?v=hOOlqQ3Mk-w**.

- To read more about the computer support field, visit **www.collegegrad.com/ careers/proft45.shtml**.

- To assess your interests in an IT career, take a short inventory at the National Workforce Center for Emerging Technologies Web site (**www.nwcet.org/ programs/cybercareers/students/test/default.asp**).

- To assess some of your skills with software tools, you can try a simple assessment activity at the Web site for ACE Training, a computer training company (**www.ace.co.nz/Pages.aspx?id=161&sectionid=96**). (Registration is required, but the skills assessment is a free service.)

A ROLE-PLAYING SCENARIO

This is a transcript of a conversation between two colleagues in a user support group, Chris and Lee. If possible, have fellow students or coworkers play the parts of Chris and Lee, and then discuss your feelings about their conversation.

CHRIS: I've been working on a position description for the new help desk specialist we plan to hire. Would you like to look it over for typos?

LEE: Hmm! I see that you've listed almost all technical qualifications for the position. Everything is hardware and software and networks.

CHRIS: That isn't true! Look at item 8. I listed problem-solving ability there.

LEE: Yes, but there is nothing on the list of qualifications that mentions any people skills. You know, listening skills, communication skills, ability to explain information to users in nontechnical language, ability to work as a member of a team. That sort of thing.

CHRIS: Well, I've always felt that you can teach someone to use good communication skills, but you can't teach them the technical and problem-solving parts of a help desk job. So I emphasized technical qualifications in the position description.

LEE: I'm sorry, Chris, but I don't buy that! Given a choice between technical skills and soft skills, I'd prefer the new person come into the job with good interpersonal skills. I don't think you can teach that. But I can teach someone to use and troubleshoot the specific software features our users call us about.

CHRIS: I guess it's a question of whether you really believe you can teach someone to be a good communicator. I think I can!

LEE: Well, obviously, we'd prefer to find someone with both technical and people skills. But given a choice, I'd take the people skills as a given and teach the technical skills.

CHRIS: I think we just disagree about that.

LEE: For purposes of the position description qualifications, I think we should agree to list both, and then see if we can find applicants who have both.

CHRIS: Okay, but I want to emphasize the technical skills as being definitely more important than the interpersonal skills. Okay?

Alternative Career Paths for User Support Workers

Many user support workers select this field as an entry into other, more advanced positions. The following sections discuss some careers into which an entry-level position in user support can lead.

Programmer/Developer

User support workers who are technically oriented may want to work toward a position as a computer programmer or Web applications developer. Workers in these positions write code (instructions) in a programming language such as C++, Java, Python or Visual Basic, or in a scripting language such as JavaScript, VBScript, Perl, or PHP. Advancement into a programmer/developer position often requires coursework in programming languages and a four-year degree.

Network Technician

User support workers may also follow a career path toward more technical network positions. Network technician positions often involve tasks such as installing and configuring network servers and client systems, network cabling, troubleshooting, performance analysis and configuration, security, facilities management, and related tasks. Although many user support workers perform simple network administration and monitoring tasks, a career as a technical network support worker usually requires a two- or four-year degree with a specialization in an advanced network topic, such as network security.

Web Site Maintainer

A Web site maintainer is a worker who uses software packages, such as Dreamweaver, FrontPage, and ColdFusion, to build and maintain Web sites. These positions are less technically demanding than positions that require workers to develop large Web sites from scratch, but they do require someone who has a good eye for visually pleasing layouts and who understands Web navigational tools well enough to make Web sites usable.

Support Manager

Support workers who enjoy the challenge of user support can aspire to a lead worker or supervisory position in a support group. These workers often plan and schedule the work of other support staff as well as prepare budgets, hire and evaluate staff members, and work with user departments or groups to better understand their support needs. Many colleges and vocational/technical schools offer courses aimed at workers who want to become supervisors or managers. Courses designed for beginning supervisors or managers of technical and professional workers are especially useful for those who aspire to a support management position.

Project Manager

A career path that many entry-level support workers do not consider, but perhaps should, is project management. IT projects in both business and government often require leaders who can successfully manage other workers, as well as budgets, schedules, and deadlines.

Chapter 7 describes some project management tools you should understand if you are interested in a career in project management. Some schools and colleges offer coursework on project management and project management software tools.

Trainer/Technical Writer

Many entry-level support positions include some end-user training (described in Chapter 11) and technical writing (described in Chapter 3) responsibilities. Support workers who enjoy these tasks may want to specialize in either of these areas, which are described below:

- A full-time trainer designs, prepares, presents, and evaluates training materials not only for computer users, but also for other workers. Training topics can include company orientations for new employees, introductory supervisory training, time and project management, stress management, conflict resolution, and other subjects. A support worker who is interested in training as a career should take some "train-the-trainer" courses or courses in adult education.

- A full-time technical writer may design, write, and edit a variety of technical documentation, including brochures, newsletters, user guides, management reports, and Web-based materials. Those who aspire to technical writing careers can take additional coursework at a college or vocational/technical school to prepare.

Security Specialist

As the Internet and local networks have become an increasingly common part of technology infrastructure over the past decade, the computer security specialist job category has grown. Workers in these positions develop and implement plans to protect computer systems and both wired and wireless networks from various sources of internal and external threats that could result in destroyed, lost, or stolen information. These positions generally require additional study and specialization beyond a basic user support degree.

ON THE WEB

To learn more about the duties, knowledge, skills, and abilities associated with jobs described in this chapter, visit the Occupational Information Network Web page (**online.onetcenter.org/gen_search_page**). Enter one of these keywords:

- Computer programmer
- Computer security specialist
- Computer support specialist
- Network administrator
- Technical writer
- Training specialist
- Web administrator

Chapter Summary

- Early computer systems were primarily large, centralized corporate or government systems. They were used to automate manual tasks. The first steps toward decentralized computing were the use of terminals to connect workers to a central system, and the introduction of less powerful but less expensive workgroup computers.

- The development of end-user computing was spurred by several industry trends during the 1970s and 1980s: (1) the backlog of requests for new software applications; (2) an increase in the number of knowledge workers who work primarily with information; (3) the availability of inexpensive personal computers; (4) the availability of inexpensive productivity software; and (5) the development of user-friendly graphical user interfaces.

- End users can be categorized according to environment (personal use or business use), skill level (novice, semiskilled, or expert), frequency of use (occasional, frequent, or extensive), software used, features used (basic, intermediate, or advanced), and relationship (internal coworker or external client).

- Resources that users need to be productive include hardware, peripherals, hardware upgrades and maintenance, operating system and applications software, software upgrades, supplies, data and information, facilities, and technical support. These resources significantly affect the total cost of end-user computing for an individual or a company.

- End users operate a variety of software packages on their personal computers, including email and instant messaging, Web browsers, word processors, spreadsheets, database management, graphics, planning and scheduling, desktop publishing, Web page development, educational and entertainment software, as well as enterprise and industry-specific business applications.

- A primary goal of end-user computing is to make workers more productive in their jobs. However, productivity is not without costs, because personal computers can pose many challenges. Common problems include waste of resources, user mistakes, computer crime, piracy, invasion of privacy, abusive use, computer viruses, and health problems.

- End user assistance can be organized in several ways, including peer support from a coworker; support from a user support group; support via a help desk, hotline, or chat service; a user support center; support from technical staff in an IT department; or support from a vendor who contracts to provide outsourced support services.

- Users need a variety of support services, depending on how they use their computers and their level of expertise. User support centers frequently provide help services that may include operating a help desk, hotline, or chat service; troubleshooting difficult problems; locating information; evaluating new hardware, software, and network products; establishing organization-wide product support standards; analyzing and assessing user needs; installing systems; training users; writing user documentation; managing computer facilities; and assisting with software development projects.

- The job descriptions for support staff members reflect the variety of services a support function may offer. Many jobs require a combination of knowledge, skills, and abilities in hardware, operating systems, applications software, networks, interpersonal communication, problem solving and analysis, and supervision or leadership.

- Support workers may use entry-level support positions, along with additional education and training, as a career pathway to a position such as a programmer/developer, network technician, Web site maintainer, support manager, project manager, trainer, technical writer, or security specialist.

Key Terms

applications development backlog—The excess demand for new computer applications that outstripped the existing supply of computer professionals to develop them.

carpal tunnel syndrome—Severe hand or wrist pain due to an inflammation of the tendons in a user's hand and wrist; often a result of overuse in combination with an improper physical environment.

chat service—A Web-based interactive service that allows two or more users who are both online to communicate by alternately typing and viewing messages; also called instant messaging.

cloud computing—A type of infrastructure in which powerful servers in organizations store and process information remotely, delivering information, communications, and software applications on demand via the Internet; cloud computing is an industry trend toward centralized software and services.

computer facilities management—Support services to help users with information and questions about security, media backups, viruses, ergonomics, purchase of supplies, preventive maintenance, and other tasks required to keep a computer system operational.

computer user support—A job function or department in an organization that provides information and services to workers or clients to help them use computers more productively in their employment or at home.

computer virus—A piece of software created with malicious intent that can destroy information, erase or corrupt other software or data, or adversely affect the operation of a computer that is infected by the virus.

distributed computing—A computing environment in which the needs of the organization and its workers determine the location of computer resources; this often includes a centralized system, such as a network server, and decentralized systems, such as individual PCs on worker desks.

end-user computing—The use of computer technology for both business and personal use; it is designed to increase the productivity of workers, managers, students, and home users of computers.

42

ergonomics—The study of how to design a workspace that promotes user health, safety, and productivity.

external user—An end user who is a client or customer of an organization, such as retail customers of hardware and software vendors, or corporate users who have purchased products or services from a vendor.

graphical user interface (GUI)—Screen images that enable users to access program features and functions intuitively, using a mouse or other pointing device.

help desk—A single point of contact for users in need of support services, whether in-house employees or external clients; a help desk may provide information and problem-solving services face to face, by telephone, by email, or by an online chat session.

hotline—A telephone number that an internal or external user can call to reach a help desk service.

information center—An older name for a user support center.

Information Technology (IT), Information Systems, Information Services (IS)—The modern names of what had formerly been known as the Data Processing department; this department also may be responsible for network and distributed systems, such as user PCs and support services.

internal user—A computer user who works within the overall organization that provides support services; sometimes called an in-house client from a support perspective.

knowledge worker—An employee whose primary job function is to collect, prepare, process, and distribute information.

KSAs—The knowledge, skills, and abilities required to perform the tasks in a job.

microcomputer—A complete computer (often called a personal computer, or PC) built on a smaller scale than a large-scale or a workgroup system, with a microprocessor as the central processing unit (CPU).

needs analysis—An investigation to determine the features and configuration of hardware and software that will best match a user's specific needs; also called needs assessment.

outsource—To contract with a vendor that specializes in user support functions to handle support incidents for internal and external users.

peer support—An informal level of user support whereby colleagues in an organization or department exchange information and provide assistance about computer use and problems encountered.

peripheral device—A hardware add-on that plugs into a computer's system unit, either externally or internally; peripheral devices include input devices (keyboard, scanner), output devices (monitor, printer), input and output devices (modem, network interface card, touch display screen), and storage devices (magnetic media such as tapes and disks, and optical media such as CDs and DVDs).

piracy—Theft of computer resources such as software, services, or data; often involves illegal copying, distribution, or use of computer programs or information.

position description—A written description of the qualifications for and responsibilities of a job in an organization.

support standards—A list of computer products that an organization allows or encourages its employees to use and that it will support; product support standards limit the hardware, software, and network components that a staff supports in order to reduce support costs.

technical support—A level of user support that focuses on advanced troubleshooting and problem solving; whereas computer user support deals with a broad spectrum of support issues, technical support usually deals with more advanced and difficult problems.

total cost of ownership (TCO)—The total expenditures necessary to purchase, maintain, upgrade, and support an end user's personal computer system over its expected useful lifetime; TCO includes hardware, software, network connectivity, information, training, and technical support costs.

user support center—A group or department in an organization that provides a wide range of services to internal computer users; services may include a help desk, consulting on product purchases, training, documentation, and facilities management.

user support team—A formal workgroup that is organized to provide computer user support services; the team may include combinations of full- and part-time and peer support.

Web site development software—Software that enables users to create, maintain, and update Web pages that include a mixture of text and graphics and incorporate features such as email links, blogs, chat rooms, File Transfer Protocol (FTP), and restricted access for security.

Check Your Understanding

Answers to Check Your Understanding questions are in Appendix A.

1. True or False? The goal of early large-scale computers was to automate as much manual processing of business information as possible.

2. Which of these developments account for the trend to decentralized computers in the 1980s and 1990s?

   a. increase in the number of knowledge workers

   b. availability of inexpensive microcomputers

   c. availability of inexpensive productivity software

   d. all of these

3. Computer users can be classified by characteristics such as skill level, frequency of use, _____, and _____.

4. A modern name for the Data Processing Department is _____.

5. Widespread use of the Internet among business and home computer users first occurred during which decade?

   a. 1960s
   b. 1970s
   c. 1980s
   d. 1990s
   e. 2000s

6. An internal user is a(n):

   a. end user
   b. worker in an organization
   c. retail customer
   d. client who buys over the Internet

7. True or False? Technical support costs are generally included in the purchase price of a computer product, and therefore technical support is free to users.

8. _____ is a field that studies how to design a work environment that promotes worker health, safety, and productivity.

9. Use of a computer to obtain unauthorized access to information about a customer, student, or patient is:

   a. a waste of resources
   b. an ergonomic problem
   c. an invasion of privacy
   d. piracy

10. A(n) _____ uses pull-down menus and screen images that are easier to use than systems that require users to memorize and type lengthy commands.

11. True or False? Small companies often meet their need for computer support by combining user support with another position.

12. True or False? A help desk provides a single point of contact for computer users in need of support.

13. Help desk services can be provided via:

    a. a physical location where users can get help

    b. a telephone hotline users can call for help

    c. an email address where users can send a message

    d. any of the above

14. Which of the following statements is an advantage of using outsourcing to provide user support?

    a. Outsourcing is a low-cost support method.

    b. Outsourcing develops in-house support expertise.

    c. Outsourcing uses expertise a company may not have.

    d. Outsourcing provides on-site assistance.

15. Over the next 10 years, employment in computer and network support occupations is expected to:

    a. increase

    b. remain about the same

    c. decrease

    d. depend on the number of employees who retire

16. The process of matching a user's needs with supported computer products is called a(n) _____.

17. _____ are lists of approved and recommended computer products that an organization is committed to support.

18. Which of the following job responsibilities would you least expect to find in a position description for a user support specialist?

    a. troubleshoots problems

    b. recommends product standards

    c. operates a large-scale computer

    d. installs hardware and software

19. Printed or online tutorial or reference materials for computer users are called _____.

20. A(n) _____ outlines what you need to know or be able to do to perform a job.

21. A Web-based communication between two Internet users who are online at the same time and alternately type and view messages is called:

    a. peer support

    b. email

    c. a hotline

    d. a chat session

22. True or False? Cloud computing refers to the use of security software on the Internet to hide users' workstations from harmful computer viruses.

Discussion Questions

1. Why do you think so much of the software that ran on large-scale computers was custom-written by programmers, whereas today most personal computer software is purchased off-the-shelf?

2. Do you think the changes in the way computers are used are due primarily to advances in computer technology over the past 50 years or to demand for improvements among end users?

3. Based on your knowledge and studies of the computer industry, what other information would you add to the row in Table 1-1 for the 2010s that would help someone understand important changes in computer technology? What do you think will be the significant new developments in computer technology in the latter part of the 2010s?

4. Are the end-user problems described in this chapter inevitable or can users and support workers take steps to avoid them?

5. Do you agree or disagree with the following statement? *"Facilities management is more of a concern with large-scale computer systems than in an end-user computing environment."* Explain your position.

6. Is it more important for a user support staff member to have the ability to solve difficult technical problems or the ability to communicate with a difficult user? Why?

7. How do you think the knowledge, skills, and abilities needed for telephone support are different from the KSAs needed to provide email or online chat support? Compare these to the KSAs needed for face-to-face support.

Hands-On Activities

Activity 1-1

Interview a technical support person. Locate a technical support worker at your school, your work, or a local company and set up an informational interview. Ask the following questions to the technical support worker:

1. Using the categories of end users in Figure 1-2, how would you describe the users you support?

2. What types of software applications do you need to know in order to support users?

3. Do any users or applications present particularly difficult problems for you as a technical support worker? (Ask for a description of some typical problems.)

4. Does the organization that employs you have policies on software piracy, invasion of privacy, and virus protection?

5. Will cloud computing affect your job, and in what ways?

6. Can you provide a copy of your position description?

Write a one-page summary of the information you collect from your interview.

Activity 1-2

Predict future computing trends. Based on your knowledge of current trends in the computer industry, add more information to the decade milestones shown in Table 1-1 for the 2010s. What do you think will be the significant events and trends in the 2010s? Make predictions about computer size, cost, ease of use, primary functions, and the extent of integration with other technologies during the rest of the decade. Include both personal and business computer use in your predictions.

Activity 1-3

Identify software packages. Find a mail-order computer catalog (in your school or company's computer room or library) or an Internet site that sells applications software packages like those described in this chapter. List the names of two or three representative packages for each of the following categories: electronic mail and messaging, Web browser, word processing, spreadsheets, database management, graphics, planning and scheduling, desktop publishing, Web site software, and educational and entertainment software. Include the price range for a typical package in each category.

Activity 1-4

Identify computer users' health concerns. Interview three classmates, coworkers, or family members about their health, safety, and productivity concerns related to their use of computers. Make a list of their concerns. What similarities in concerns did you find? Did any of their concerns surprise you? Write a brief summary of your conclusions.

Activity 1-5

Evaluate total cost of ownership. A Houston, Texas consulting company, JDA Professional Services, provides an online worksheet for calculating the total cost ownership (TCO) of computer technology. Read about the factors the company thinks contribute to the TCO at its Web site (**www.jdapsi.com/client/Articles/Default.php?Article=tco**). Write a one-page report that describes how the factors JDA considers significant are different from those listed in this chapter.

Click the **JDA's Online TCO Worksheet** link, and enter the data for the following scenario: An instructional computer lab manager wants to purchase 10 computers for a new lab at a cost of $1200 per machine. The cost of a network server, laser printer, and related hardware and software is expected to be $5000. The lab will require two part-time support staff, expected to cost $15,000 each. Use the Gartner Group's recommended percentage for hidden costs (as detailed on the online worksheet). Answer the following questions:

1. What is the total cost of ownership per machine?

2. Is this a one-time cost or an annual cost?

Activity 1-6

Evaluate user support position descriptions. Use the Internet to locate position descriptions for user support jobs in government as well as other types of organizations. If possible, find information about a position in your state or local employment area, and try to find a job that might be of interest to you. How do the duties and responsibilities you found compare with those described in this chapter? What are some similarities? What are some differences?

Some Web sites you could visit are listed in Table 1-2.

48

Web Site	Description
www.dop.wa.gov/JobClasses/479I.doc	State of Washington Information Technology Specialist 1 job description
www.montva.com/filestorage/1146/98/151/644/781/ Help_Desk_User_Support_Technician.pdf	Montgomery County, Virginia Help Desk/User Support Technician job description
www.computerjobs.com Click the link for a region in which you are interested, or click the **Help Desk** link.	Job search Web site for computer professionals
www.dice.com Enter a keyword, such as **help desk** or **computer support**; use the location menu to specify a state or local area, and then click the **Find Jobs** button.	Job search Web site for computer professionals
www.JustTechJobs.com Click **Search Jobs**; enter the keyword *help desk* and select the geographic area in which you are interested.	Job search Web site for computer professionals
jobsearch.monster.com In the Job Title box, enter **help desk** or **network**; if desired, narrow the search in the Location box to your state or local area.	Job search Web site for a variety of fields

Table 1-2   Internet sites with information about user support positions

Activity 1-7

Evaluate user support positions. Select one of the user support position descriptions presented in this chapter or one you found in Activity 1-6. Answer the following questions:

1. Would you classify the job described in the position description as primarily a technical position or primarily a people-oriented position? Explain your answer.

2. Do you think the position description requires a person who is a specialist (one with depth of knowledge) or a generalist (one with breadth of knowledge)? Explain why.

3. What personal qualities do you think will be necessary for someone to be successful in the position?

If you are a member of a class or project group, meet with the other members and discuss your answers to these questions. Write a one-page summary of your conclusions.

Activity 1-8

Compare your KSAs to a user support position. Select one of the user support position descriptions presented in this chapter or one you found in an earlier activity. Make a list of the knowledge, skills, and abilities (KSAs) you would need to perform the duties in the position description. Don't worry too much about the differences between skills and abilities. Compare your own knowledge, skills, and abilities with those for the position description. Analyze your strengths as well as areas in which you need additional KSAs in order to be qualified for the position. How do the KSAs you listed correspond to courses you are taking now or have taken in the past? What additional courses could you take to satisfy some of the KSAs on your list?

Activity 1-9

Analyze your personal skills for a support position. Compare your personal skills with those of some basic job categories. Visit the Occupational Information Network (O*NET) Web site (**www.onetonline.org/skills**). In the list of skills, check the skills you have or are working on, and then click the **Go** button to learn which job categories best match your skills. Is Computer Support Specialist or a related occupation on your list? Click the **Skills Matched** column for a particular occupation to learn how the skills for a job title of interest to you match your personal skills. Or, in the Occupation Quick Search box in the top-right corner of the Web page, enter the code *15-1041* for computer support or code *15-1071* for network support to get a list of the skills required for a position of interest to you. How well do your skills match with the job title you chose?

Case Projects

1. TCO of a $500 Computer

Your friend Ron has asked for your help in buying a home computer. He is skeptical of ads for computers that cost less than $500. He intends to use the computer for word processing, email, entertainment, and Internet access, and he wants your advice about how much he should budget for a home personal computer system. What is a realistic amount your friend should expect to spend, both at the time of initial purchase and over the next four years of ownership? Use catalogs, computer magazines, or the Internet to obtain current price information. Design a spreadsheet to draw up a sample budget, showing your recommended initial expenditure and the annual cost for the next four years. Break down the costs by the categories described in this chapter. Show the total cost of ownership over the four years that Ron plans to own the computer.

2. Training Facility Problems at Cascade University

Mary Ann Lacy is the coordinator of Cascade University's computer training facility. The facility offers courses in computer applications software to Cascade's regular students and faculty, and to employees of local organizations that send their workers to Cascade's Continuing Education Division to upgrade their computer skills.

The computer training facility consists of two rooms: a training room where scheduled classes are conducted and an open lab where students can work on assignments outside class time. The entire training facility is open from 8 A.M. to 5 P.M., Monday through Friday. Each room is equipped with 24 PCs. Mary Ann operates a Windows 2008 server operating system so students can access software on the network server, store data files, and access email and the Internet. She also teaches some of the continuing education classes in the training room. Cascade University's computer faculty members teach in the training room when it is not in use for continuing education classes.

Mary Ann recently conducted a user satisfaction survey to learn how Cascade students, faculty, and continuing education students rated the entire training facility. She was pleased that users were very satisfied with the equipment because she tries to keep the systems properly maintained and gets PCs quickly repaired if a problem arises. The electronics shop at Cascade maintains the hardware. The users also expressed satisfaction with the operation of the network server and with the selection of software that is available to them. However, Mary Ann was less pleased about some of the comments users wrote on their survey forms. Here is a sample of some comments:

- *"I am an advanced user of the open lab. Some of the inexperienced students have discovered that I know quite a bit about the hardware and the network. They ask me a lot of questions. I don't mind answering them, but when I have a class assignment due, I can't take time out to help everyone who has a question. After a while, some of the questions get pretty repetitious."*

- *"The open lab runs smoothly when the coordinator is in the room. But when she is next door teaching a class in the training room, there is no one to ask for help. I feel badly when students have to interrupt her training session to report a problem like a server crash or even to get a new ink cartridge put in the printer."*

- *"The software manuals are in a locked cabinet. When I need one, I have to track down Mary Ann to get the key. Why can't the documentation cabinet be left unlocked?"*

- *"Last year, there was seldom a wait to get a computer in the open lab. This year, with more classes in the training room, the wait is longer. It would be nice if the lab were open more than 8 to 5. Some evening and weekend hours would be great."*

Mary Ann has decided to ask a small group of training facility users, consisting of students, faculty, and continuing education students, to meet to discuss the responses to her survey. If you were a member of the group, what advice would you give Mary Ann that would address the concerns described about the operation of the training facility? What user support issues have users raised? What are some other ways Mary Ann could address these issues? Are some alternatives more expensive than others?

3. Computer User Satisfaction at Indiana University Bloomington

Indiana University Bloomington (IUB) is a public university with over 40,000 students enrolled. Every year, University Information Technology Services (UITS) conducts a survey of IUB's students, staff, and faculty to measure their satisfaction with computer services on campus. A summary of the results of the UITS survey for the most recent year is available at **www.iu.edu/~uitssur**. Most questions are answered on a scale of 1 to 5, with 5 being the most favorable rating. Analyze the results of the most recent survey and answer the following questions:

1. Use responses in the "Computing and Computer Networking" section of the survey results to write a short narrative description of a typical (average) computer user at IUB.

2. Based on the responses in the "Computing and Computer Networking" section, which kinds of computers should be supported by UITS staff? Which should not be supported? Explain your decision.

3. Based on responses in the "User Support Services" section of the survey, which service provided by UITS needs the most improvement? Why?

4. Based on responses in the "General Assessment" section, which of the three groups—teaching faculty, researchers, or student learners—are the most satisfied with their computer support at IUB? Which are the least satisfied? Are the differences between the groups significant?

5. Overall, are computer users at IUB satisfied with the computer services they experience? Explain your answer.

4. User Accounts at Foothills Wood Products

Foothills Wood Products manufactures and sells ready-to-assemble furniture such as bookcases, nightstands, bed headboards, computer desks, and TV stands. The company employs several office workers using a job-share arrangement in which two or more employees work part-time and occupy a full-time position. In an attempt to reduce the total cost of ownership (TCO) of their office computers, the company encourages part-time workers to share a computer. Shihori, the computer supervisor at Foothills, would like you to prepare a document that would help its computer users set up more than one user account on a PC. The goal is to allow multiple users to have separate accounts on the same machine with different logins, passwords, and desktops.

Your task is to prepare a step-by-step procedure that each part-time worker at Foothills can use to set up his or her own account on an office PC shared with others. Research the steps required on the type of PC you use, and write up a first draft of the procedure document. Then compare your document with ones prepared by a couple of your colleagues. Make any necessary modifications to your draft and finalize the document. Remember, your goal is to prepare a document that end users can follow.

CHAPTER 2

Customer Service Skills for User Support Agents

In this chapter, you will learn about:

◎ The importance of communication and interpersonal skills and customer service relationships for support agents

◎ Reasons support agents must listen and read carefully

◎ How agents build and communicate understanding

◎ Important aspects of effective speaking and nonverbal communication

◎ How support agents develop a personal communication style

◎ Strategies support agents use for telephone communications

◎ How support agents develop an incident management strategy

◎ How developing an understanding of different personality types and work styles can help an agent

◎ Strategies support agents use to handle difficult clients

◎ Guidelines for client-friendly communications on user support Web sites

◎ How to build excellent customer service

As you learned in Chapter 1, communication and interpersonal skills are very important for help desk and user support agents. Whether they assist end users face to face, via telephone, in email messages, through a Web site, in chat sessions, via remote access, or in blog articles, all successful support staff must be able to listen, read, understand, communicate, and work effectively with people to solve problems.

Excellent communication and interpersonal skills are often more challenging for new user support workers to learn than technical or business skills. These skills are also more difficult to measure and evaluate. Practice is the key to learning how to use communication skills effectively. Experienced user support agents and their managers know that client satisfaction is directly related to how well agents listen to, understand, and communicate with users. Support agents who concentrate solely on finding the correct technical answers might be frustrated and surprised to learn that clients may be less than satisfied with their support interactions.

In this chapter, you'll learn some practical listening, understanding, speaking, and relationship-building skills. User support staff can apply these skills to almost any situation to help solve problems and achieve two crucial goals of every support request: client satisfaction and excellent customer service. Although many of the skills discussed in this chapter apply directly to telephone and face-to-face support, most of these skills also apply to written communication, such as email, online chats, and communication with end users via Web sites. In fact, written communication is often trickier than oral communication because the tone and voice intonations are missing. The important point is that strong communication and interpersonal skills are essential in any support environment.

Communication and Customer Service Skills

Communication skills are essential to providing high-quality customer service. Communication is a process that involves both listening and responding. Some communications, notably face-to-face or telephone conversations, email exchanges, and online chat sessions, are two-way interactions between a support agent and an end user. Communication on support Web sites and blogs is primarily one-way. To effectively solve end-user problems, agents must be able to hear or read and understand a user's problem or question, and then reflect their understanding in a spoken or written response. Listening, understanding, and responding are essential to solving user problems. A support organization that can solve user problems effectively and efficiently, and does so using good interpersonal skills, creates client satisfaction and demonstrates its commitment to providing excellent customer service.

Help desks and user support organizations frequently incorporate a customer-service ethic into their mission statements. A **customer-service ethic** is an organization-wide commitment—shared by everyone from top management to operational staff—that client relationships and client satisfaction are the most important aspect of a business. Many organizations aim for a target of 100 percent client satisfaction 100 percent of the time. This means that the user support staff aims to satisfy every client in every support incident.

Chapter 7 discusses user support mission statements in detail.

How important is customer service to organizations? In a classic article in *Harvard Business Review* (*HBR*), Thomas O. Jones and W. Earl Sasser, Jr. discuss "Why Satisfied Customers Defect" (*HBR*, Nov–Dec, 1995). They describe a study of Xerox company customers in which "totally satisfied" customers were six times more likely to purchase other Xerox products than customers who were just "satisfied." The authors conclude: "Merely satisfying customers who have the freedom to make choices is not enough to keep them loyal. The only truly loyal customers are totally satisfied customers." Another author, Frederick Reichheld, writes in a March 1996 *HBR* article, "Learning from Customer Defections," that "on average, the CEOs of the U.S. corporations lose half of their customers every five years." Although these articles were written several years ago, they are classic works in customer satisfaction literature, and the conclusions still apply.

Many support organizations place a greater emphasis on customer-service excellence than they did in the past. Why? First, totally satisfied clients are more likely to be repeat customers. A frequent reason that clients cite for leaving a hardware or software vendor for another is poor service. In fact, excellent service may be more important to clients than product features, price, convenience, or any other aspect of a business transaction. Second, it usually takes more support resources to handle incidents from dissatisfied clients than from satisfied ones. Dissatisfied clients are more likely to generate:

- Lengthy support incidents
- Repeated callbacks or help desk contacts
- Complaints and ill-will that are often communicated to potential clients, which can translate into a poor business image and lost sales
- Incidents that need to be rerouted to a higher-level support agent or a manager
- Product returns and requests for a refund

Because dissatisfied clients consume more support resources, any of these results reduce support staff productivity and may lead to a reputation for poor support service.

ON THE WEB

Jeff Davis, a frequent contributor to TechRepublic, shares tips on the importance of communication skills for support professionals in his article "Improve Your Communication Skills with these Techniques" (**www.techrepublic.com/article/title/1052198**).

MindTools, a Web site focused on career skills, offers several short articles on improving communication and listening skills (**www.mindtools.com/page8.html**).

What are the characteristics of a support organization that is devoted to a customer-service ethic? In the pursuit of excellent customer service, support staff members:

- Provide clients with the information, service, or solutions they need, if there is a reasonable way to do so

- Explain to a client what they *can* do for him or her if the client's problem cannot be resolved immediately

- Treat clients and potential clients with respect and courtesy

- Communicate to clients how long they are likely to be on hold, how long it will be before they receive a return call or email, and how long it may take to provide information or solve a problem

- Return phone calls or emails when promised, even if just to report that no progress has yet been made

Think of each user as a valued client. Always remember that user support is essentially a customer-service business and that the goal is to create totally satisfied clients. If users are not treated as valued clients, they may not remain clients for long. If clients have a choice of vendors, where do you think they will choose to make their next purchase? Usually, they will buy where customer service is taken seriously. Even in telephone support, users observe your attitude and react to the way you communicate and handle an incident. Support agents communicate by their voice or written responses whether they consider an incident interesting or boring and whether they value the user or view the incident as an intrusion on their time.

Treat each incident as an opportunity to build total client satisfaction. To create client satisfaction and help attain an organization's customer service goals, support agents must master the essential communication skills: listening, understanding, and responding. These skills are the foundations of the communication process between a support agent and a user, as illustrated in Figure 2-1.

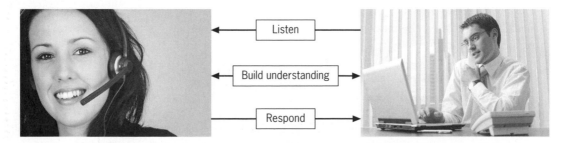

Figure 2-1   Foundations of the communication process between a support agent and a user

Listen Carefully

In any support conversation, learn to listen before you speak. Listen initially to a caller's description of the question or problem to develop a thorough understanding of it. Interrupting a caller is one indication to a customer that you are not listening carefully. In any written communication, read all of the text and try to fully understand the user's problem before you initiate a response.

 In Chapter 4, you'll learn about a technique called *active listening*, which is a way to restate and clarify what you heard to reach a mutual understanding of a user's problem.

Experts in listening skills have identified six different types or purposes of listening. These are shown in Table 2-1.

Listening Type	Purpose
Discriminative	Learn about the user • What is the knowledge level of the user? What level of technical language do they use? • What is the tone and style of the user's communication? Are they upset or angry?
Comprehensive	Understand the user's message • Do I have a complete and accurate understanding of the information the user provided?
Critical	Analyze and evaluate the user's message • Does the information the user provides make sense? • Do I need additional information from the user?
Therapeutic	Identify opportunities to provide positive support to the user • Can I find opportunities to empathize with the user's situation? • Am I listening to the user without prejudging the message?
Appreciative	Find enjoyment • Am I treating the user as a real person, not just a voice? • Does my communication treat the user with dignity and respect? • Do I have empathy for the user?
Relational	Develop rapport with the user • Am I taking advantage of opportunities to use small talk with the user to develop an effective working relationship?

Table 2-1 Six types of listening

58

ON THE WEB

To learn more about the six purposes of listening, read a paper by John A. Kline, an author who has written widely on listening and speaking skills, at **www.au.af.mil/au/ awc/awcgate/kline-listen/b10ch4.htm**.

When a user begins to describe a problem, be sure to make effective use of these discriminative listening skills:

- Listen to or observe the *language* used to describe the problem. A user's language frequently provides important clues as to whether the user is a novice or an experienced user. Support agents can then adjust the language in their response so as to avoid language that might be too complex or too technical for the user to understand.

- Listen to *how* the user describes the problem, which can provide further insight into the problem and the user. What is the user's tone of voice? Does the user sound angry or frustrated? Does he hesitate or apologize about the misuse of technical terms? Does he sound distracted or in a hurry? Subtle cues like these can provide valuable information about how to handle an incident.

Although detecting a user's "tone of voice" is more difficult in written communication, support agents can look for statements that indicate frustration. For example, a user who writes, "*This is my third chat session to try to resolve this problem*" is undoubtedly making more than a simple factual statement.

ON THE WEB

A short online article by author Lillian D. Bjorseth, "Shhh! Listen, Don't Just Hear," offers some useful strategies for becoming a better listener. Read the article at **www.selfgrowth.com/articles/bjorseth4.html**.

To view a guide to developing better listening habits, read a summary sheet at **www.scribd.com/doc/1095379/Active-Listening-A-Guide**.

While many support workers focus on comprehensive and critical listening skills, the therapeutic and relational listening skills listed in Table 2-1 are probably more important in satisfying the goal of providing excellent customer service. Figure 2-2 provides some suggestions to help you listen effectively, and it notes obstacles that can hinder effective listening.

Tips for effective listening	Barriers to effective listening
● Avoid distractions	● Focusing on your own concerns instead of the user's
● Give the user plenty of time to explain, think, and communicate	● Allocating insufficient time to a user's problem
● Summarize what the user says	● Talking too much instead of listening
● Probe for more details	● Talking to avoid silences
● Use attentive body language (face the user, maintain an open stance, establish eye contact)	● Avoiding eye contact
● View the problem from the user's perspective	● Taking user complaints or criticism personally or responding defensively
● Be positive and encouraging	● Lecturing the user
● Speak clearly and concisely	● Speaking rapidly
● Match your speech to the user's proficiency level	● Using overly technical language or jargon

Figure 2-2 Tools for and barriers to effective listening

To build listening skills, look for training courses in small group or interpersonal communication, which often place equal weight on listening and speaking skills. Many vocational-technical training programs and professional development seminars in customer service skills also include opportunities to work on listening and speaking skills. To develop your written communication skills, look for opportunities to study email messages from friends or colleagues. Practice analyzing each message to examine the language used and look for clues about how the sender feels. Ask yourself whether you can accurately restate the sender's message. If possible, ask the author of the message if your restatement is accurate.

Build Understanding

Once you have heard or read a user's problem description, try to develop an understanding of the user's situation. Ideally, you will develop some level of empathy with the user. **Empathy** is an understanding of and identification with another person's situation, thoughts, and feelings. Support agents who can empathize with a user are able to understand the problem or question from the user's point of view. One measure of empathy is whether you can express a user's problem in your own words. Another measure of empathy is whether a user agrees with your expression of their problem; in other words, have the two of you reached a consensus understanding? Empathy does not mean that you take complete ownership of and responsibility for a problem, but that you understand it and can relate effectively to the user, who does own the problem. Try to understand, for example, why the problem is important to a user, why a user might want to know a piece of information, or why a user is frustrated, upset, or angry. The following are examples of empathetic responses:

- *"Clearly, we need to get this program running again so you can create the report you need. Here's where we'll start ..."*

- *"It sounds like you've had a very frustrating morning, but I think I can help you with this..."*

- *"To help you close your accounting month on time, I can give you a workaround for this problem. Then, later, we can diagnose the problem you're having, so it doesn't happen again."*

- *"I will be here if you need any additional help with this problem."*

ON THE WEB

To view an article on empathy and trust in customer relations, visit the Web site **www.businessballs.com/empathy.htm**. Another short introduction to empathy can be found at **www.live.ac.uk/documents/intro_to_empathy.pdf** (requires a PDF viewer).

As you develop an understanding of the user and the problem, communicate to the user that you view him or her as a person, rather than as a support incident. One technique that experienced support agents use is to visualize the user. Even if you don't know the user personally, think of someone in your own experience who sounds like or is similar to the user and then communicate with that image rather than with a voice at the other end of the phone line or a chat message on your display screen. A second technique is to use inclusive language, such as *we* rather than *I* and *you*. A telephone technique you can use effectively is to smile while you are talking with a user. Even though a conversation is on the telephone, many users can tell whether you are smiling.

Respond Effectively

In a support interaction, all aspects of your speech or writing communicate your understanding of a situation, affect your progress toward a successful incident resolution, and influence the user's level of satisfaction with the incident. Four important aspects of your response are your greeting, how you use scripts, your tone and style, and your nonverbal communication.

Use a Sincere Greeting

If every journey begins with a single step, all support communications begin with a **greeting**, which can affect the course of the entire interaction with the user. The greeting is the icebreaker. Based on your greeting, users form their first impressions of the support staff person, the support service, and ultimately the entire organization that provides support. The greeting also sets the tone for the remainder of the incident. A sincere, positive greeting can be the first step toward calming a frustrated user and channeling an incident in a fruitful direction. Most support organizations train their staff members to use a standard greeting, which often includes the agent's first name and the name of the organization or other identification. Two common greetings are:

- **Phone:** *"This is Joel in Computer Support. Thanks very much for your call. How can I help you?"*

- **Email:** *"I'm Kana at the Help Desk. Thank you very much for contacting us with the problem you encountered. Here is how I understand the problem ..."*

Practice using a sincere greeting with a tone that communicates interest and enthusiasm and avoids sounding stiff, overly rehearsed, insincere, or bored. A sound recorder or colleague can help provide feedback on your telephone greeting style. By the way, the immediate thank-you in these examples communicates to the user that you appreciate and value the contact. Also, a sincere thank-you contributes to a positive first impression, even if the user is upset or frustrated. If a user gives his or her name after your telephone greeting, write it down so you can use it during the incident. Many support organizations prefer the use of Mr. or Ms. and a user's last name in preference to a first name, unless the user specifically invites first name use.

Use Scripts Appropriately

Many support groups provide their agents with a script to help handle routine aspects of an incident. A **script** is a prepared sequence of questions and statements that covers several important parts of an incident. A script can include branches and decision points; a support agent follows a path through the script that matches a user's answers. Scripts can be useful training aids for new support agents as well as helpful tools for handling complex technical problems and difficult users. However, a user should never suspect that you are simply reading a script or any other information unless you communicate beforehand that you are reading a piece of technical information to ensure accuracy. Furthermore, experienced support agents recognize situations in which they should deviate from a script, such as when the user demonstrates expert knowledge of the problem situation. Scripts can be very useful if an incident deteriorates into an argument or other inappropriate communication. Reverting to a script can help you get an interaction back on track and make sure that the incident is handled according to organizational policy.

Some help desks maintain a database of frequently asked questions (FAQs) and prepared responses to them. When using prepared responses, don't read lengthy responses, unless you make it clear that is what you are doing. Instead, restate the responses in your own words.

ON THE WEB

As part of a training program, a support agent may be asked to learn or develop model answers to questions. Experienced support staff and supervisors are useful sources of information about what constitutes a "good" response to an FAQ. For an example of an online FAQ database, read a list of FAQs about Microsoft PowerPoint at **www.pptfaq.com/index.html**.

Use Tone and Style Effectively

How you communicate with a user is often more important than the content of the communication. Your tone and style have a direct impact on a user's satisfaction with a support incident. Which of these user statements best illustrates the desired outcome of a support incident?

- *"The help desk agent provided me with adequate information, but I felt through the whole conversation that I was intruding on his time. He spoke rapidly and curtly, and wasn't very pleasant. I felt like he had 'been there, done that,' and wasn't interested in my problem."*

- *"The help desk agent couldn't tell me what I needed to know, but explained why the information wasn't available yet, when it would be, and invited me to call back. I felt like a valued client and that my call was important to her."*

Note that the first user received the information he sought, but was dissatisfied with the interaction, whereas the second user was fully satisfied even though her question was not answered.

Often, as part of help desk or user support training for a new agent, support organizations describe in detail the kind of communication style they want their agents to use—whether formal or informal, casual or professional, or somewhere in between. They realize that style is important because it communicates the organization's image. In reality, support staff members often modify the organization's desired standard somewhat, depending on their experience, user feedback, and their own personalities.

Recognize the Importance of Nonverbal Communication

Researcher Albert Mehrabian emphasizes the importance of **nonverbal behaviors**, such as facial expression, body language, and the tone and style used in the communication process. Mehrabian found that facial expression, body language, and the style and tone used are often more important than the specific words and the meanings of words in a communication. These nonverbal behaviors are described in Table 2-2.

Nonverbal Behavior	Use These Behaviors	Avoid These Behaviors
Posture	• Use an open stance • Face the user	• Folding arms • Crossing legs • Bowing head • Looking at a distant object or a clock
Facial expression	• Smile • Use a facial expression that indicates interest	• Frown • Adopting a facial expression that indicates boredom, disbelief, or impatience
Eye contact	• Establish frequent, but not excessive, eye contact	• Looking off into the distance or down at your feet • Staring at the user
Gestures	• Use head, hand, and arm movements to communicate your active involvement and to help with explanations	• Overly stiff gestures • Shifting weight from one leg to the other
Distance	• Stand or sit at a comfortable distance from the user	• Standing so close that you make a person uncomfortable • Standing at too great a distance so as to communicate disinterest
Voice quality	• Speak at a comfortable volume • Use voice inflection to add interest • Speak at a normal pitch • Speak in a tone that is upbeat and warm	• Shouting (especially if the user is not a native English speaker) • Whispering • Speaking in a monotone voice • Speaking in a sing-song voice • Speaking in a voice pitch that is too high or too low • Speaking in a tone that sounds negative, cold, unfriendly, or bored

Table 2-2 Nonverbal behaviors in communication

ON THE WEB

Vicki Ritts and James Stein offer several tips for improving nonverbal behaviors in the communication process. Although aimed at classroom teachers, their suggestions apply equally to support workers. View their ideas at **honolulu.hawaii.edu/intranet/ committees/FacDevCom/guidebk/teachtip/commun-1.htm**.

Develop an Effective Personal Communication Style

Every person's **personal communication style** is the result of decisions an individual makes about how he or she wants to communicate. You can polish your personal communication style with some practice in effective communication.

Use clear, succinct speech and match your speed to the user's proficiency level. Many inexperienced support agents have a tendency to speak too fast, which is often a natural reaction to job stress and a pressure to be productive. Practice speaking slowly, but not so slowly as to sound condescending. Remember, too, that shorter sentences are easier for a user to follow than long ones. Avoid a rising inflection at the end of sentences, which sounds like you are asking a question or are unsure. Many of the suggestions about writing for end users in Chapter 3 also apply to verbal communication style, including the use of gender-neutral language and avoiding wordiness, long words (when shorter ones will communicate the same meaning), overly technical terms, acronyms, and jargon.

Avoid using empty phrases in support incidents. Inexperienced support agents, in particular, sometimes continue to talk when they don't have anything to say, just to fill the pauses. Avoid empty phrases, such as *"Now let me see…, I think I've seen that problem before…,"* or *"I'm sure I must have that information somewhere here…"* These phrases do not convey useful information and do not instill confidence that you are on top of the problem, although they may give the appearance that communication is occurring. Instead of empty phrases, learn to be comfortable with pauses.

Phrase communications with end users positively, rather than negatively. For example, instead of saying or writing *"The problem with your document occurred because you didn't follow the procedure described in Chapter 2 of the manual,"* use a positive statement, such as *"I think the procedure on saving a document in Chapter 2 describes a way to avoid the problem with the document you experienced. Let me find the page for you."*

Although technically correct solutions to user problems are critical, they will not by themselves guarantee satisfied clients. Successful support agents use greetings, scripts, and their tone and style to communicate a willingness to help, regard for the client's value, and the organization's concern for the client's satisfaction.

ON THE WEB

LearnCustomerServiceOnline.com is a company that offers online courses in communication and listening skills geared to customer support workers. View a list of available courses at **www.learncustomerserviceonline.com/ CustServiceModules.htm**. You can try a free preview of a course on active listening skills at **www.learncustomerserviceonline.com/Preview/ ActiveListeningPF_DWtestPreviewThankU/start.htm**.

Special Challenges of Telephone Communication

While all support communication with clients is important, the challenges posed by telephone communication are unique. Many support agents use the telephone as a communication medium for both external and internal clients. All the suggestions in this chapter about the importance of the customer-service ethic and the role of communication to meet that ethic apply equally, or probably more so, to phone interactions with end users.

 To increase your skills with telephone communication, try the tutorials and exercises in the book by Jeannie Davis, *Beyond "Hello": A Practical Guide for Excellent Telephone Communication and Quality Customer Service* (Now Hear This, Inc., 2000).

Even before an agent answers a telephone support call, a client evaluates whether the telephone menu system to connect to an agent is well designed and offers meaningful choices. The client also evaluates the length of time it takes for an agent to answer the call. The initial greeting is also part of the first impression. It is worth practicing a sincere greeting until you get it down without sounding like you are reading a script.

Since a caller cannot see the agent on the other end of the phone, you might think that nonverbal aspects of communication are unimportant in a telephone support call. While there may be no direct way for a caller to measure visual cues such as body language or facial expression, new support agents are often surprised to learn how much nonverbal behavior contributes to the success of a call. Support agents need to develop effective ways to perform these standard parts of a telephone support call. Table 2-3 lists some suggested dialog for a variety of common user support telephone activities.

Telephone Activity	Example Dialog
Call greeting	*"This is the Help Desk, and I am Amy. Thanks very much for calling us. How can I help you today?"*
Put a call on hold	*"I need to research this problem to make sure I give you accurate information. Would you like me to put you on hold, or call you back when I have the answer?"* ● When a return call is promised, be sure to call back promptly.
Transfer a call	*"Since you are asking about a billing question, I am going to transfer you to the Billing Department, where Ms. Chang will help you with your question. She will be on the line in a moment."*
Terminate a call	*"It appears that rebooting your computer has reestablished your connection to the Internet. Thanks for calling us about the problem. Is there anything else I can help you with today?"*

Table 2-3   Suggested telephone dialog

ON THE WEB

For additional tips, download a reference sheet with suggested phrases to use when communicating via the telephone (**www.businesstrainingworks.com/Onsite% 20Training%20Web/Free%20Articles/PDFs/Telephone%20Ready% 20Reference.pdf**).

A ROLE-PLAYING SCENARIO

This is a transcript of a telephone support call between Wes, an end user in the Accounting Department, and Gene, a relatively new worker in a support group. If possible, have fellow students or coworkers play the parts of Gene and Wes, then discuss your reactions to this support call.

GENE: This is the problem hotline. What's your problem please?

WES: This is Wes in Accounting.

GENE: Oh, yes, I remember you. I've talked with you several times before. What's the problem *this* time?

WES: I'm having trouble printing a report this morning.

GENE: Your printer is probably out of paper.

WES: I've clicked the Print button three times and gone down the hall to get the printout, but each time there is just a stack of about 50 sheets in the printer with a line or two of junk characters on each one. But my report is not there.

GENE: Oh, we've been hoping whoever was wasting those reams of paper would call. I should send you a bill for the paper you wasted.

WES: I'm sorry, but I've never had this problem before. What am I doing wrong?

GENE: It is probably a user error. Did you reboot your computer?

WES: No. Do you think that would help?

GENE: Probably not.

WES: Can you suggest something else I should try?

GENE: What are you trying to print?

WES: The report is in a file named REPORT2011.EXE.

GENE: Well, there's your problem right there. Didn't your training course cover printing EXE files? EXE files are *programs*, not reports. You can't print an EXE file, you can only run them.

WES: Oh, I see. I guess I forgot about that. I feel like an idiot.

GENE: Yes, well, see if you can find a file on your hard drive named REPORT2011 with a different extension and call me back.

Case Project 5 at the end of this chapter is designed to provide readers with an opportunity to build interpersonal communication skills in an end-user support environment.

Develop an Incident Management Strategy

Support agents who provide telephone, email, chat session, remote access, and even face-to-face support often have many incidents waiting in their queue. At the same time that they provide correct technical answers and excellent customer service, they must also handle incidents efficiently. An **incident management strategy** is a collection of tools, techniques, and activities that successful support agents use to move through an incident effectively and efficiently, from the initial greeting to the end of the incident. The four goals of incident management are to:

1. Provide the user with the information he or she needs.

2. Manage stress levels for both the user and the support agent.

3. Ensure that the incident progresses from start to finish in an effective and efficient way.

4. Make the user more self-reliant.

All support agents develop and refine their own incident management strategy. However, new help desk agents do not have to invent a strategy from scratch. Resources you can build on and incorporate in your personal strategy include:

- Organizational policies on incident management and expectations

- Incident management strategies covered in support agent training programs

- Observation and imitation of respected and experienced support agents

- Your personal communication experience and style

- Feedback from users, coworkers, and supervisors on your incident-management strengths and areas for improvement

An incident management strategy begins with knowledge of the support organization's policies and guidelines, an understanding of the operation of automated help desk and user support tools such as the telephone and email systems and help desk software package (described in Chapter 6), and guidelines that experienced support agents have found useful. Figure 2-3 lists some examples of incident management guidelines.

- Ask goal-directed diagnostic questions

- Be honest

- Say "I don't know" when you don't

- Apologize when appropriate

- Say "Thank you"

- Use incident management, not user management techniques

- Teach self-reliance

Figure 2-3   Incident management guidelines

Ask Goal-Directed Diagnostic Questions

Each question a support agent asks should be designed to move an incident toward a successful resolution. Diagnostic questions can be embedded in a script, or they can be based on a support agent's experience.

Chapter 4 suggests several critical questions to ask in a troubleshooting situation.

Be Honest

It is better to be honest and forthcoming with users about product features, limitations, known bugs, and future product releases than to try to hide or cover up product problems and limitations. However, you must also abide by organizational policies on what information you are authorized to provide to users. For example, some vendors, for competitive reasons, will not disclose future product features or availability dates. So you may encounter situations in which you have the information a user requests, but you cannot divulge it because your employer asks you not to. Many organizations also have a policy that discourages communicating negative comments about a competitor's products, even though you may have an honestly negative opinion about them.

Say "I Don't Know" When You Don't

It is often more productive to admit that you don't know an answer than to waste both your time and the user's time trying to suggest possibilities you aren't sure of. A user rarely expects a support agent to know everything. However, never use a tone that conveys, *"I don't know, and therefore your question is stupid," "I don't know, and I don't think anybody else does,"* or *"I don't know, and I don't care."* If you honestly don't know an answer, refer the user to a colleague or other information resource where she or he can get the needed information. You can also promise to research the question and get back to the user with the needed information.

Apologize

A sincere apology to a user who feels that they have been done an injustice is never a sign of weakness. One way to defuse a potentially difficult situation is to empathize with a user's situation and offer an apology for the perceived injustice, whether a user has spent a long time on hold, been the victim of a runaround (however unintentional), or purchased a product ill-suited to his or her needs. A corollary to this guideline is to avoid being overly apologetic to the point of being patronizing.

Say "Thank You"

Thank the user for contacting the user support group at both the beginning and end of the interaction. Saying *"Thanks for contacting the Help Desk"* is a simple but effective way to communicate that the user and the contact are important. A thank-you ends the incident on a positive note, even if the problem has been a difficult one for both the support agent and the user.

Use Incident Management, Not User-Management, Techniques

Be sure to distinguish between *incident* management and *user* management: manage the incident, not the user. Do not attempt to manipulate users by, for example, judging how well they communicate their needs, criticizing how they organize their files and folders, or lecturing them on their computer use. The relationship between a support agent and a user is not a boss-to-worker relationship and should not be based on different levels of authority. Although you can recommend that a user read a helpful chapter in a manual or suggest a different way to organize their documents, you should not make accepting your suggestion a condition for helping the user. Do not communicate that you are upset or be defensive if a user chooses not to take your advice. Users who feel that a support agent is trying to manage them or their work habits will rightfully feel resentful or manipulated and are more likely to be dissatisfied with a support incident.

Teach Self-Reliance

An immediate goal of each support incident is to provide information or to solve a user's problem. A secondary, longer-term goal is to make each user more self-reliant when possible. To create **self-reliance**, support agents explain a solution so the user understands the reasons they encountered a problem and how to fix it. Agents also help create self-reliance when they refer to relevant printed or online documentation where a user can locate additional information about a problem or a question. To some extent, user support has a built-in contradiction: The support staff would like every user to call back (because their jobs depend on a flow of support incidents), but the staff hopes to resolve each user's problem so he or she does not have to call back.

In reality, users will never become completely self-reliant. As computers become even more widespread and computer use becomes increasingly complex, both new and experienced users will continue to need an increased array of support services. Even expert users and computer gurus occasionally need assistance. In addition, some users don't want to become self-reliant; they feel that it is the support staff's job to solve their problems. Recognize that you cannot force users to change their behavior. However, start with an assumption that each user is interested in understanding a problem and your solution to it until the user indicates clearly that they are not interested. Though complete user self-reliance may never be achieved, it is an important long-term goal for a support staff.

Successful incident management is rarely a skill or ability that comes easily to support workers. It takes practice to develop your own incident management strategy, and even then, some incidents still go awry. As you will see in the next section, even the best incident management approach can sometimes be derailed by the personalities or work styles of the participants.

Customer Service and Personality Types

A personality analysis commonly used in business and industry is the **Myers-Briggs Type Indicator (MBTI)**. The answers to a series of questions about work styles and preferences determine where a worker fits on four basic personality dimensions. The four dimensions of personality measured by the MBTI are:

- **Where do you direct your energy? Introvert (I) versus Extrovert (E)**—This dimension measures whether you focus your energy externally, to people, activities, and words (extroversion), or internally, to thoughts and ideas (introversion). An Extrovert is more social and expressive, whereas an Introvert is more private and quiet.

- **How do you process information? Sensing (S) versus Intuition (N)**—Sensing people work more with facts and experiences that they obtain through their senses, whereas Intuitive people tend to emphasize personal insights and reflection. A Sensing person tends to prefer direct communication, while an Intuitive person often acts on hunches and seeks creative or novel ways to process information.

- **How do you make decisions? Thinking (T) versus Feeling (F)**—Thinking people base decisions on logic, analysis, guiding principles, and objective factors, whereas Feeling people base decisions on personal values and subjective factors. Thinkers try to clarify decisions by detaching themselves from a problem, while Feelers are more likely to view themselves as inside a problem situation.

- **How do you organize your life? Judging (J) versus Perceiving (P)**—Judging people prefer a structured lifestyle in which they are well-organized and make structured decisions. Perceiving people are more open, flexible, and explore their options. Judging people like to be in control, whereas Perceiving people like spontaneity.

Each person is not a pure type of any of these descriptions, but fits somewhere along a continuum within each of the four dimensions. Furthermore, these four personality dimensions can be combined into any of 16 types. For example, one personality type is an ISTJ, while another is an ENFP. There is obviously no one, correct personality type. Most people are a mixture of these types.

One use of the Myers-Briggs personality types is to help workers understand how users and coworkers—either as individuals or in work groups—view the work world and behave differently in it. This understanding can help work groups avoid or work through conflicts and help support agents understand different approaches taken by end users and their work colleagues.

ON THE WEB

For a thumbnail sketch of each of these types, visit **www.personalitypage.com/ high-level.html**. To learn more about the MBTI personality test and the 16 personality types it measures, consult these resources:

- Jean M. Kummerow, Nancy J. Barger, and Linda K. Kirby, *Work Types*. New York: Warner Books, 1997.

- Otto Kroeger, Janet M. Thuesen, and Hile Rutledge, *Type Talk at Work (Revised)*. New York: Delta, 2002.

- David Kiersey, *Please Understand Me II*. Delmar, CA: Prometheus Nemesis Books, 1998.

- The Team Technology Web site (**www.teamtechnology.co.uk/tt/t-articl/ mb-simpl. htm**), which includes several pointers to additional information about the MBTI personality types, including articles you can download for an in-depth discussion of personality types.

As part of a larger study of the role of personality in information technology work teams, the U.S. Department of Defense studied the MBTI personality types in IT work groups compared with the general population. The results of the study apply to all workers in information technology and not exclusively to support workers. The study showed that:

- The two most common personality types among information technology (IT) workers they studied were ISTJ and ESTJ. Thirty-nine percent of the IT workers they studied were one of these two types, compared with 19 percent in the general population.

- Female IT workers were somewhat more likely to be ESTJ, whereas male IT workers were somewhat more likely to be ISTJ.

- Personality types that were less likely to be found among Information Technology workers included the Sensing, Feeling, and Perceiving types.

ON THE WEB

To read more results from the Department of Defense study, download a report at **www.sstc-online.org/Proceedings/2002/SpkrPDFS/ThrTracs/p567.pdf**.

Some communication difficulties that arise between a support agent and an end user may be traced to differences in basic personality type. For example, imagine the differences in communication style that may arise when a support agent, George, works on a problem with an end user, Hamida.

George, a support agent, is an ISTJ personality type on the Myers-Briggs scale. He is a very quiet, private person who prefers to work alone on problems by collecting data. He usually bases decisions on evidence he has carefully evaluated and analyzed. George prefers email communication with users so he has a written record of each incident.

Hamida, an internal end user, is an ENFP personality type. She is a warm, outgoing person who enjoys a collaborative, teamwork approach to problems. Hamida prefers to work on problems in person so she can see a help desk agent's facial expression and read his or her body language. She likes the challenge of problem solving by trial and error and is often willing to make guesses and take risks to try to find a solution.

George thinks Hamida is overly aggressive and disorganized. Her approach to problems seems illogical. He finds working on a problem using her hit-and-miss approach to be stressful and a waste of time. Hamida thinks George fits the stereotype of a typical computer nerd who can't see over his pocket protector. She is frustrated that he seems unwilling to engage in give-and-take about a problem. She doesn't understand why he isn't willing to work on a problem together, but instead prefers short meetings and then quickly returns to his office to work.

As a support professional, George works hard to accommodate Hamida's work style. He understands that personality type differences can help explain communication problems between himself and Hamida, but are not an excuse for a lack of cooperation or communications that aren't civil.

George and Hamida are very different personality types based on the Myers-Briggs classification scheme, but even small differences in basic personality can affect work and communication styles. In this section, we have focused on personality types as a way to help explain behavioral differences between support agents and end users. However, the application of the MBTI personality types can also help us anticipate problems that can occur when teams of support agents work on a project together and when support workers and other workers in the IT Department work together. For example, the user support field often attracts workers whose basic personality type includes a comfort level in working with groups of people (extroversion), whereas other information technology workers who are primarily technical professionals may be more comfortable working alone (introversion). IT managers often express concern about the ability of their professionals to function in work teams that include user support and end users. The more you know about basic personality types and their different work styles, the better you will be able to understand the dynamics of any work team.

Apart from differences in basic personality types, other barriers to effective communication between user support and end users occur because of difficult situations with which support agents must learn to deal. The next section describes some strategies for dealing with difficult clients and difficult incidents, whether they arise from differences in basic personality types or from situational factors.

Strategies for Difficult Clients and Incidents

Although most users are thoughtful and courteous, support agents may encounter several kinds of difficult users. A **difficult client** is one who requires special handling strategies because the user is angry, not communicative, rude or abusive, or exhibits a variety of other challenging attitudes or behaviors. The goal for a support agent is to steer a difficult situation to a successful conclusion. You will never be able to change a user's personality. Instead, focus on the specific problem, on getting the user the needed information, on providing excellent customer service in a respectful manner, and on moving to the next incident. To deal with difficult situations that might interfere with these goals, consider the strategies that experienced agents use. Table 2-4 summarizes the characteristics of difficult client communications.

Difficulty	Characteristics
Users who complain	• User is unhappy with features of products and services
	• User is rarely satisfied with an apology or an explanation
Power users	• User thinks they have more technical knowledge than they actually have
	• User indicates they should receive special treatment based on what or whom they know
Incidents that get off track	• User is confused or provides contradictory or inaccurate information
	• User is dissatisfied with lack of progress or problem resolution despite several attempts to solve the problem
Users who are upset or angry	• User expresses real or perceived grievances about product or support services
	• User indicates dissatisfaction through verbal and nonverbal communication
	• User loses the ability to communicate in a professional or productive manner
	• User continually turns the communication back to the source of the perceived grievance
Users who are abusive	• User employs inappropriate language or behavior
	• User engages in personal attacks on a company or its representatives
Users who are reluctant to respond	• User talks slowly, very little, or not at all
	• User does not answer direct questions
Users who won't stop responding	• User continues to talk well after a problem has been resolved
	• User changes the topic or relates personal experiences

Table 2-4   Characteristics of difficult client communications

Users Who Complain

Instead of simply describing a problem, some users want to gripe about an organization's products or services. Complaint handling and management is often an important function of a help desk staff. Give a user with a gripe ample opportunity to voice their complaints or concerns. Don't transition into problem-solving mode too early in an incident when a user wants to complain. Instead, use empathy:

- *"I can certainly understand why someone who has experienced this problem would be upset ..."*

- *"Let me take down the information about your experiences with this product so I can pass it along to the project manager."*

- *"Our company is willing to refund your purchase price if we can't help you make the product meet your needs."*

Many support organizations treat reasonable complaints as a valuable source of feedback and suggestions for future product and service enhancements. Try to understand that most complaints are not directed at you personally, and learn (with practice) not to be defensive about complaints.

Contacts by "Power Users"

In this context, **power users** are those who are technically very knowledgeable, or at least think they are, or who believe they warrant special attention or treatment because they have personal connections with significant people in an organization. These users often describe their powerful position early in an incident in an attempt to communicate their importance or expert knowledge (and occasionally to mask their actual lack of knowledge). They may, for example, try to impress a support agent with technical jargon to direct attention away from their lack of actual experience. One strategy for handling these users is to use inclusive language that makes them feel like a member of a team. Use pronouns like *we* to refer to the problem-solving process, such as:

- *"I think we can solve this problem if we work on it together ..."*

- *"The problem you called about is an interesting one. Will you give me some additional information so we can work on it?"*

- *"I appreciate your calling us about this problem, and I would like to work with you on it."*

Use an authoritative tone or speaking style because people who feel that they are important users like to communicate with knowledgeable agents. Remember that an agent's role is not to diminish the user's sense of self-importance, but to solve their problem.

Incidents That Get Off Track

Occasionally, in the course of resolving an incident, it becomes apparent to an agent that the process has taken a wrong turn and needs to get back on track. For example, a user might make a statement that contradicts an earlier statement. Or perhaps repeated attempts to isolate a problem have not succeeded. An incident during which a user becomes confused or one that results in lengthy, but unfruitful, problem-solving approaches indicates the process is off track. When that happens, try to refocus the process. Apologize to the user for the lack of a prompt resolution, summarize the basic incident information, and offer to continue to work toward a solution. Express confidence that, together, you will find a solution to the problem if you continue to work on it and that perhaps a different approach will achieve the results you both want:

- *"I'm sorry we haven't been able to resolve the problem yet. I think we have eliminated a hardware problem as the cause of the trouble you're seeing. I believe if we work for a while longer on why the software won't work, we'll be able to resolve this."*

- *"We haven't made any progress on this problem yet. I'd like to take a fresh approach and see if a different perspective will identify the cause of the problem you're seeing."*

Users Who Are Upset or Angry

Angry users are the most common kind of challenge. Angry users may be upset because of the way they have been treated. They may have been on hold too long, sent or received too many emails, worked with too many different support agents with contradictory suggestions, or explained the problem too many times. Or they may be upset because of real or perceived inadequacies in a product. They may also be angry due to circumstances that are totally unrelated to the incident at hand, such as a recent negative encounter with a coworker or family member.

The first principle for handling angry users is to let them vent their anger. Say little during the venting period, except to offer occasional agreement. Don't offer an explanation or switch to problem solving too early. Explanations to an angry person may sound defensive, or like an invitation to argue. The second principle is to reassure an angry user that the problem is an important one, and that you are willing to work with them to resolve it. The third principle to remember is that angry users may continue to vent several times before they work through their anger. A polite question that refocuses the angry user may be effective:

- *"What would you like me to do to help solve the problem at this point?"*

- *"How can we work together to resolve this situation to your satisfaction?"*

- *"This is an important problem, and I'm open to suggestions about how you think we can work together to resolve it."*

Remember to avoid defensiveness and don't sound patronizing. An angry user is rarely upset with you personally. As with all incidents, continue to follow up on promises made to an angry user to build trust and confidence.

Users Who Are Abusive

Abusive users are rude, use inappropriate language, or make personal attacks on a support agent. A support agent's goal is to transform an incident with an abusive user: first, into an incident where the user is just angry (and no longer abusive), and ultimately to transform the incident into one with a satisfied user. This goal is not always achievable. Some support groups assign experienced staff members with special training and skills to handle abusive users; these workers pride themselves on their ability to defuse difficult situations. In general, handle abusive users according to the support organization's policies and procedures for this type of user. For example, some support organizations instruct their agents to terminate an incident when abusive language is used. In other organizations, support agents are trained to invite the user to use more appropriate and professional language:

- *"We would like to work with you on this problem. But we need to communicate about it in an appropriate and professional way. Is that agreeable with you?"*

- *"Our company tries to use appropriate language in support calls. I'd like to continue to talk with you about the problem, but first, I need your commitment to use respectful language."*

- *"If we can't use more appropriate language, I don't believe we are going to be able to make any progress on this problem."*

Users Who Are Reluctant to Respond

Users who are slow or reluctant to provide information are often confused, lack confidence, or don't understand the questions. Many are inexperienced computer users. To obtain the information you need from these users, use very simple language and avoid technical jargon. Try different kinds of questions. For example, if open-ended questions fail to initiate a fruitful conversation, switch to questions that can be answered with *"yes"* or *"no."* Begin with very simple questions, such as:

- *"Is there a Start button in the lower-left corner of the screen?"*

- *"Can you read to me what it says in the box in the center of the screen?"*

Or, temporarily switch to discussing the problem-solving process, such as:

- *"I'll ask you some questions about what you see on the screen and you answer them, or tell me that you're not sure. Any information you can give me will help us solve the problem."*

Also give positive feedback when a reluctant user does provide useful information, such as:

- *"Thank you. I think the information you just provided will be helpful to us."*

Finally, if a user continues to be reluctant to respond, suggest exchanging information via another communication mode (such as email, chat session, telephone, remote access, or face-to-face) as a way to facilitate the problem-solving process.

Users Who Won't Stop Responding

Some users have a hard time letting go of a problem. Even after a problem is solved, they may continue to explain how bad it was or how similar it was to another problem they encountered. To deal with excessive communicators, use behavior that indicates the incident is over. For example, briefly summarize the incident and describe the conclusion. Thank the user for contacting the support group. Express your conviction that the problem is solved. Use very short answers that don't provide the user with lead-ins to additional responses. In face-to-face interactions, stand up and pack your briefcase. Use a wrap-up sentence to end the interaction:

- *"Thank you for calling about the problem today. Please call back if you encounter any further problems."*

- *"I think that solves the problem you called about. Thanks for contacting us about this problem."*

- *"I enjoyed working with you on this problem and hope it doesn't give you any more trouble. Have a good one ..."*

ON THE WEB

WikiHOW has prepared some suggestions on "How to Handle an Irate Customer on the Phone" (**www.wikihow.com/Handle-an-Irate-Customer-on-the-Phone**).

Jeff Dray, a help desk professional, has provided suggestions for dealing with abusive users at the TechRepublic Web site (**www.techrepublic.com/article. jhtml?id=r00320000726det02.htm**). He also published an article that describes 10 types of difficult users (**blogs.techrepublic.com.com/10things/?p=343**).

Lisa DiCarlo describes "The 5 Users You Meet in Hell" on the *Computerworld* Web site (**www.computerworld.com/action/article.do?command=printArticleBasic& articleId=9050878**).

Handling difficult users is never an easy task, but over time you can improve your skills with practice and patience. Inexperienced help desk and support staff can learn a great deal about difficult users from experienced support agents. Veteran agents are a good resource for organization-approved and time-tested techniques for dealing with difficult situations. Training sessions for new help desk and support agents often cover organizational guidelines for dealing with these situations.

Client-Friendly Web Sites and Web 2.0

Use of **support Web sites** to communicate with end users has increased dramatically in the last decade. Although customer service skills are obviously important in face-to-face and telephone interactions, these skills apply equally to written communication, such as email, online chat, and communication with users via a support Web site. Support Web sites are useful because users can get answers from frequently asked questions (FAQs) and problem-solution knowledge databases quickly, at any time, and from anywhere Internet access is available. Because user support Web sites are cost-effective and popular with end users, these sites are increasingly used in the support industry to augment other modes of user support.

e term **problem solving** is often used in business and mathematics to describe a proce

ON THE WEB

CIOinsight, an industry trade magazine, published the results of a survey that documented the extent to which support Web sites have become a leading method of providing support services. Of the companies surveyed, 88 percent use Web support to communicate with clients, compared with 74 percent telephone and 65 percent field service (face-to-face). View an article with additional data (**www.cioinsight.com/c/a/Research/Trend-3-The-Web-Becomes-the-Front-Line-For-Customer-Service**).

The first generation of support Web sites provided primarily one-way communication from support providers to end users. As the Web has evolved in recent years to include more interactivity and two-way communication, new methods of support are also emerging. **Web 2.0** is the development of technologies and Web applications that emphasize interactions among communities of users and the social networking aspects of collaboration and communication among users. Online social communities such as Facebook, LinkedIn, and Twitter and the online collaborative encyclopedia Wikipedia are examples of Web 2.0 applications. Web 2.0 trends have also impacted the way support services are delivered to users. For example, many vendors that formerly offered only support FAQs and knowledge bases now sponsor forums and blogs where users who share common interests or have purchased similar products can interact, share information and opinions, collaborate on mutual problems, and offer their expertise to a user community. A **user forum** is a feature of a Web site that allows for online discussions in which members of a user community may take part. Some forums organize each discussion topic as a **thread**, which is a commentary on a single topic, with comments posted in date order (oldest message first). Forums facilitate easy-to-follow navigation through the commentaries. A **blog** is a feature of a Web site where an individual (the blogger) posts messages and invites interested members of a user community to comment on them.

User support Web sites are a cost-effective way to communicate with end users, whether internal or external. To the extent that users can locate information about problems, either from an FAQ or a knowledge base, or from another user in a forum discussion or blog, the cost of customer support is reduced. An example of an interactive online user community is Tech Support Forum; the home page is shown in Figure 2-4.

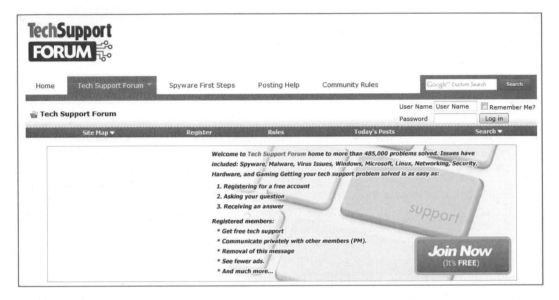

Figure 2-4   An interactive user support forum at **www.techsupportforum.com**

Customer service concerns and a customer-service ethic also apply to the design and development of support Web sites. You have probably visited Web sites that were well organized and easy to use with information and features you could locate quickly. But you've probably also visited some sites that failed the ease-of-use test. An organization that spends its resources to build a support Web site should build a client-friendly one that exemplifies the customer-service ethic described in this chapter. A support Web site is as much a reflection of an organization as are the phone contacts, email exchanges, chat sessions, and face-to-face interactions that members of the support staff have with clients.

 Simple support Web sites can be built and maintained with popular word processors as well as with more powerful Web-site-development tools such as Adobe Dreamweaver, Microsoft Expression Web, Avanquest WebEasy, Six Apart TypePad, NetObject's Fusion Essentials, and WordPress.com. Several of these development tools are open source or offer basic, free Web-authoring tools, including blogs.

Because a support Web site is an important extension of an organization, a support specialist who has the responsibility to maintain the site needs a heightened awareness of customer-service concerns as well as additional job skills to implement a successful site.

The first consideration in designing a support Web site is to clearly define the purpose. Common purposes of support Web sites include the following:

- Provide product information
- Take sale orders
- Facilitate access to technical support
- Provide software updates and downloads
- Communicate with end users
- Encourage communication and collaboration among users
- Provide user forums and blogs as communication media
- Provide links to related sites

Four general criteria apply to written communication with end users, including Web site design: content, organization, format, and mechanics. A support Web site implementer uses these criteria as tools to evaluate how a Web site measures up to the customer-service ethic.

Content

Provide accurate and up-to-date product, support, and contact information. Keep the amount of information presented at a manageable level, so it can be maintained and kept current rather than trying to present a larger amount of information that becomes out of date due to time constraints. Make the content relevant to what users need to know.

Organization

The design of the home page is critical. An effective home page is appealing and well organized, but avoids information overload and too many special graphic effects. Extensive graphics can affect download time for users with slower Internet connections. Some sites offer a text-only option to accommodate users with slow connections. The best support Web sites have menus, icons, and information "teasers" (summaries) on the home page, with navigational links to more detailed information if a user desires.

Support Web sites can be organized by product, by function, or in other ways. Sites organized by product should include search capabilities in case a user cannot find a specific product by model number. Sites organized by function may include separate pages for product features and information, an FAQ knowledge base, software downloads, a shopping cart, support contact information, a site map, and a site feedback mechanism.

Format

Information should be formatted into small units. A document that takes more than two to three PgUp or PgDn keystrokes to access should be segmented into multiple pages or easy-to-find sections.

Navigation aids expand the usability of a Web site. A well-formatted Web site includes multiple ways of accessing information, including navigation aids (to return to the top of a long page, jump to the next or previous page, or return to the home page), a search engine to help locate specific information, and menu icons to access main topics. The pages, navigation aids, and menu bars should be consistent across the site. Fonts and format features should maintain a consistent style and feel.

Mechanics

Mastering the basic mechanics of writing is an important part of effective Web site design. Check spelling and grammar on all Web documents as well as in any FAQ databases. For most Web sites, it is best to use a writing style that is straightforward and easy to read.

 Chapter 3 discusses these four criteria—content, organization, format, and mechanics—in more detail.

ON THE WEB

A good example of a support Web site that illustrates many of these design criteria is Cisco's Support and Documentation site, which was developed to support their network products. You can visit the site at **www.cisco.com/cisco/web/support/index.html**. Have you discovered Web sites that you think are easy to use and contain useful support information?

A Web site devoted to user support is useless unless users know about it and visit it. A support site can be registered with popular search engines so that Web surfers who enter relevant keywords will locate the site. A support Web site can be prominently displayed in user manuals and in online documentation (for example, a link on the toolbar of a software product). A reference to the Web site can also be included in product literature, organizational newsletters, and brochures as well as on business cards. Pointers to a support Web site can be publicized in support phone calls, emails, and chat sessions.

ON THE WEB

To learn more about Web site features that enhance usability for clients, visit **www.usabilityfirst.com**.

Many colleges and professional-technical schools offer coursework in Web site design, implementation, and maintenance. These courses are a good way to add value to a user support worker's résumé.

Comprehensive Client Services

User support communication and interpersonal skills are essential to provide excellent client services. Yet, a comprehensive approach to excellent client service is also based on specific organizational values, attitudes, and actions.

Excellent client services start when every employee, from high-level managers to the newest support agents, recognizes that the organization's clients are the primary reason for its existence. Each employee's job depends directly on client satisfaction. Most support organizations' mission statements express the commitment that each end user's enhanced productivity is a primary objective of the support staff. In a user support environment, client productivity and satisfaction are directly related to the extent to which each user is treated as a valued client.

Customer service excellence depends on whether a support staff is willing to take extra steps to make sure clients are satisfied. For example, an excellent support organization keeps its clients apprised of the progress or lack of progress toward a problem solution. It actively promotes win-win outcomes for each incident. It seeks agreement that problems have been adequately addressed, and then conducts follow-up client surveys to measure the extent of client satisfaction and identify areas where client relationships can be improved.

 Excellent customer service does not necessarily mean that the client is always right. Sometimes requests by even the most valued clients cannot be met for a variety of sound business reasons. In those situations, stress what you *can* do for a user, and look for alternate ways to meet user needs.

Outstanding customer service requires adequate support resources. Customer service excellence rarely happens by accident, but is based on advanced planning, adequate staffing, and a sufficient budget for help desk tools and information resources that encourage excellence. A sufficient support budget is not always easy to achieve because support expenses are sometimes difficult to justify, as you will learn in Chapter 7.

A comprehensive client service orientation among support staff must apply not only to every staff member in an organization, but also to every mode of communication with users. Although most of this book covers technical problem solving and operational details associated with the day-to-day operation of a help desk or support group, this chapter on communication and customer service is really the most important one in the book. Why? Because you can perform all the technical and operational duties of a support job adequately and still fail if you don't provide excellent service to your clients.

This chapter introduced customer service skills and interpersonal communication tools that support agents need to learn about and use in order to be effective in their jobs. However, reading a chapter about customer service skills or listening to a lecture on the subject, while a good beginning, is a very limited way to develop your own skills. The "On the Web" notes in this chapter contain pointers to additional information that you can use to learn more and build your own customer service and interpersonal skills. The discussion questions, hands-on activities, and case projects at the end of this chapter are especially important because they give you additional opportunities to get practical experience that will serve you well on the job.

Chapter Summary

- Communication and interpersonal relationships are the foundations of excellent customer service, which is a goal expressed in many support organizations' mission statements. Communication is a process that involves listening and reading, understanding, and speaking and writing skills.

- The most important communication skill for help desk and user support staff is the ability to listen to or read information provided by clients. In addition to a description of a user's problem, help desk staff need to evaluate a user's language level so they can target their responses to a similar level. Help desk staff need to listen or read for cues that indicate whether a user is frustrated, confused, or angry.

- Understanding a client involves being able to restate their problem, but it also means an ability to empathize with the user's situation and feelings and to understand why the problem is an important one for the client.

- Responding effectively includes using a sincere greeting, making good use of scripts as aids, and adopting a tone and style that help rather than hinder. Nonverbal aspects of communication, such as posture, facial expression, eye contact, gestures, and voice quality, may impact the success of a communication more than the meanings of words.

- Practice is the key to developing a personal communication style that adds to user satisfaction, perhaps even more than technically correct answers. Experienced agents learn to use clear, succinct speech or writing that is positive and avoids empty phrases that contribute little meaning.

- Support workers who communicate on the telephone learn effective ways to greet a user, put a call on hold, transfer a call, and terminate a call.

- Support agents should develop a personal incident management strategy. Goal-directed diagnostic questions, honesty, as well as the ability to say "*I don't know*," to apologize, to create user self-reliance, and to thank a user for contacting a support group are all components of a personal incident management strategy.

- Some barriers to communication between a support agent and a user may be related to differences in basic personality types and work styles, which can be better understood by using the Myers-Briggs classification scheme.

- Difficult support incidents can include user complaints, incidents with power users, incidents that get off track, incidents with angry or abusive users, and incidents from users who are either reluctant to respond or who won't stop responding. Skilled support agents develop specific strategies to channel difficult users into satisfied ones.

- A user support Web site is a cost-effective way to communicate with users and to encourage communication among communities of users to collaborate and share information. Web site developers need to manage information content, create an organized site, present information in a client-friendly format, and master basic writing mechanics to build a support Web site that meets the goals of a customer-service ethic.

- A comprehensive approach to client services includes not only communication skills but also an organization-wide recognition of the importance of each client, a willingness to take extra measures to satisfy users, and adequate support resources to provide client satisfaction. Comprehensive customer service applies equally to telephone, face-to-face, remote access, and written interactions with users, such as email messages, chat sessions, FAQs, and blogs.

Key Terms

blog—A feature of a Web site where a writer posts messages and invites members of a user community to comment on them.

customer-service ethic—An organization-wide commitment, shared by everyone from top management to operational staff, that client relations and client satisfaction are the most important aspects of a business.

difficult client—A user who requires special handling strategies because they are angry, uncommunicative, rude or abusive, or exhibit other hard-to-handle behaviors.

empathy—An understanding of and identification with another person's problem situation, thoughts, and feelings. A support agent who can empathize with a user is able to understand the problem or question from the client's perspective, including why it is important to the client.

greeting—The first few sentences in a support incident that introduce an agent, form the basis for the first impression of the support service by the user, and get the incident-resolution process started on a positive note.

incident management strategy—A collection of tools, techniques, and strategies that support agents use during an incident to move effectively and efficiently from the initial greeting to the conclusion of the incident.

Myers-Briggs Type Indicator (MBTI)—A personality analysis commonly used in business and industry to identify worker personality and work style preferences.

nonverbal behavior—The facial expression, body language, and tone and style of a communication. Nonverbal communication behavior may be more important than the specific words used in a communication.

personal communication style—The result of a series of decisions an individual makes about how he or she wants to communicate.

power user—A user who is technically knowledgeable (or believes that they are), or who may have a relationship with an organization that they feel warrants special attention to their incident.

script—A prepared sequence of questions and statements that support agents can use to handle parts of an incident; a script may include decision points and branches to handle different situations.

self-reliance—A goal of support service providers that seeks to increase user self-sufficiency and reduce a user's dependence on support services.

support Web site—A Web site devoted to providing clients with product information, software downloads, support staff contacts, and a sales channel. Support Web sites are a cost-effective method to communicate with users, but should be designed to be client-friendly.

thread—Commentary on a single topic posted on a Web forum to which several members may contribute comments; usually organized by date with the oldest messages first.

user forum—A feature of a Web site that allows for online discussions in which members of a user community may take part. User forums emphasize the collaborative nature of the Web as a way to encourage interaction and collaboration among users.

Web 2.0—The development of technologies and Web applications that emphasize the social networking aspects of collaboration and communication among users. Web 2.0 emphasizes interactive use of the Web.

Check Your Understanding

Answers to Check Your Understanding Questions are in Appendix A.

1. True or False? Communication skills are often more difficult for a new help desk agent to learn than technical skills or business skills.

2. A(n) _____ is a choice each support agent makes about how professional or casual, respectful or condescending, formal or informal, or terse or verbose they will be in their interactions with users.

3. A user's first impression of a support agent usually comes from the:

   a. greeting
   b. solution to the problem
   c. incident script used
   d. agent's tone and style

4. Which listening type focuses on opportunities to empathize with the user and provide positive support?

   a. Discriminative   d. Therapeutic
   b. Comprehensive   e. Relational
   c. Critical

5. Which listening type focuses on learning about the knowledge level and emotional state of the user?

   a. Discriminative   d. Therapeutic
   b. Comprehensive   e. Relational
   c. Critical

6. Which of these is not a strategy for effective listening?

   a. Avoid distractions.
   b. View the problem from the user's perspective.
   c. Talk to fill awkward silences.
   d. Probe for details.

7. Nonverbal communication behaviors include posture, facial expression, _____, and _____ .

8. True or False? Nonverbal behaviors are often more important than the meaning of words in a communication.

9. True or False? Empathy means a user support agent takes ownership and responsibility for a user's problem.

10. A support agent should make liberal use of the word:

    a. I   c. We
    b. You   d. Oops

11. One measure of whether a support agent understands a user's problem is whether they can express the problem in:

    a. the user's actual words
    b. the support agent's own words
    c. industry standard vocabulary
    d. the wording of the script for the problem

12.   True or False? Of the three essential communication skills, listening (or reading) comes before understanding and responding.

13.   True or False? Scripts designed to guide a user support agent through an incident should be memorized or read verbatim to a user to avoid mistakes.

14.   A support worker who uses a telephone extensively is likely to need to know how to put a call on hold and _____ .

15.   True or False? One of the goals of incident management is to help users be more self-reliant.

16.   Which of the following is not a primary strategy for a support organization that aims for customer service excellence?

    a.   Treat clients with respect.
    b.   Explain to clients what you can do for them.
    c.   Agree to any demand a client makes.
    d.   Return calls to clients when promised.

17.   Which of these is not a recommended incident management strategy for support agents?

    a.   Ask goal-directed diagnostic questions.
    b.   Say thanks.
    c.   Teach the user self-reliance.
    d.   Never admit that you are not sure.

18.   True or False? A successful support worker is one who has learned from experience how to manipulate a user's behavior to make the user more productive.

19.   True or False? A customer-service ethic is an organization-wide commitment that the client is always right.

20.   A support Web site implementer uses four criteria to evaluate a client-friendly site: content, _____ , _____ , and mechanics.

21.   A _____ is a way to organize the commentary on a single topic in a discussion forum from oldest to newest, in an easy-to-follow format.

Discussion Questions

1. Why are communication skills often more challenging for inexperienced support agents to learn than technical or business skills?

2. Should a support agent ever just hang up on a caller who is rude or uses abusive language? Describe some pros and cons to this approach, and explain your position.

3. Are providing excellent user support and teaching users to be more self-reliant contradictory strategies? Explain why or why not.

4. Will different work and communication styles among workers who have different MBTI personality types inevitably lead to conflict? Explain your position.

5. Describe some pros and cons to Web 2.0 interactive tools that allow users to post messages on a blog or user forum support Web site that other users can view and respond to. Do the pros outweigh the cons?

6. A sales manager made the following comment at a vendor conference: *"Good customer relationships are a worthwhile goal for us, but we usually find that it is just too expensive to provide really excellent customer service. The costs always outweigh the benefits."* Do you agree or disagree with her statement?

7. Should a support specialist who relies on a script to respond to a user's problem situation ever deviate from the script? If so, under what circumstances? What are some possible risks to deviating from an incident management script?

Hands-On Activities

Activity 2-1

Evaluate a help desk mission statement. The University of Texas Health Science Center in Houston operates a help desk for its campus users. Read the mission statement of its service desk operation (**is.uth.tmc.edu/css/mission.htm**).

Identify at least five ways in which the University of Texas help desk mission statement includes a customer-service ethic as described in this chapter.

Activity 2-2

Practice effective listening skills. The Web page **work911.com/articles/listenup.htm** describes an exercise in which you listen to the radio to practice focused listening skills. Read the article, and follow the suggested steps to improve your ability to focus on the message of computer users.

The two Web pages below each contain an exercise to help you improve your listening skills:

- **esl.about.com/library/listening/blconclusions1.htm**

- **esl.about.com/library/listening/blconclusions2.htm**

Click on the speaker icon to play a sequence of 10 audio statements. Then answer the questions about what you heard.

Activity 2-3

Interview a support agent about difficult users. Invite a help desk agent in your school or company to talk with you and your classmates. Use the following questions as a guide for your interview:

- Please tell me about some of your experiences with difficult users.

- What techniques do you use to handle these situations?

- In your experience, what is the most common kind of difficult incident?

- What kinds of incidents do you personally find the most difficult to handle?

- What policies does your support organization have to deal with difficult users?

Write a brief report that summarizes the main points of the interview.

Activity 2-4

Explore ways to improve client service. Read an article titled "Improve Customer Service— And Cut Costs" at **techupdate.zdnet.com/techupdate/stories/main/ 0,14179,2804648,00.html**. Write a short summary of the article that answers the following questions:

1.   Who should read this article (who is the intended audience)?

2.   What trends in customer service does the author describe?

3.   What will readers of this article learn? (List the main points.)

Be sure your summary includes information about the source of the article.

Activity 2-5

Evaluate your qualities as a help desk agent. Read an article on the desirable qualities of a help desk agent by Paul Chin at **www.intranetjournal.com/articles/200609/ pij_09_25_06a.html**. Make a list of the qualities of a good help desk worker described by the author. Then use Chin's criteria to evaluate your own strengths and areas where you could improve your skills. Which of the qualities would you need to improve the most to be successful in a job as a help desk agent?

Activity 2-6

Evaluate your communication skills. Take a 25-question quiz on your personal communication skills at **www.optimalthinking.com/quiz-communication-skills.asp**. Be as honest with your responses as you can. Briefly describe any of the 25 items for which you checked *sometimes* or *rarely*. Then describe any patterns or themes that you can identify in the items you checked as *sometimes* or *rarely*. Finally, what resources are available to you to address the need for skill improvements that you identified?

Activity 2-7

Learn more about effective Web site design. Read an article on effective Web site design elements by Jennifer Stewart, a professional writer who maintains a Web site devoted to improving writing skills at **www.write101.com/101web.htm**. Make a list of five design ideas or suggestions for support Web site developers that add to the guidelines provided in the chapter.

Activity 2-8

Solve a customer service crossword puzzle. Customer service week is celebrated each year in October. The Customer Service Week Web site includes a variety of puzzles to challenge customer service workers at **www.csweek.com/customer_service_week_crossword.php**. As a measure of your understanding of customer service vocabulary and concepts, try out the crossword puzzle. How many words did you need to look up in the solution?

Activity 2-9

Listen in on a support call. A user of America Online (AOL) services, Vincent Ferrari, called the vendor's hotline to cancel his account. Since he had heard rumors about the difficulty of cancelling an AOL account, Vincent recorded the call. A television interview with Vincent that includes an edited version of the call is available on YouTube at **www.youtube. com/watch?v=xmpDSBAh6RY**. View the video and answer these questions:

- List the mistakes that John (the help desk representative) made during the call.

- Describe three steps you would recommend to avoid an incident like this.

- How do you think the easy availability of this video on YouTube may have impacted AOL's business?

Activity 2-10

Working with Personality Types. In this chapter, you read about George and Hamida in the section on MBTIs. Recall that George, a user support agent, is an ISTJ personality type and Hamida, an end user, is an ENFP type. Learn more about these personality types at **www.personalitypage.com/high-level.html**, and complete the following:

1. Briefly describe the ISTJ and ENFP personality types in the Myers-Briggs categories.

2. If George and Hamida are assigned to work together on a project team, describe any problems you anticipate they might encounter working together, based on differences in work styles.

3. Describe some ways George and Hamida could function successfully working together.

4. If you joined the project team with George and Hamida, whose work style would you be least comfortable with? Explain your answer.

Case Projects

1. An Email Reply for Bug-Free Software Limited

You are a support agent for Bug-Free Software Limited, which develops customized software for businesses on a contract basis. You receive the following email message from a large client:

We received the custom Visual Basic programs from your new programmer and installed them on our system last week. It was obvious from the first time we ran the programs that the programmer was new to your organization. It was not clear the programmer had much prior experience with programming or with Visual Basic. The new programs we received converted the information from our old COBOL programs to our report formatter fairly well, according to the specifications we provided her. But we discovered that she built the specific data-conversion instructions into the Visual Basic programs. The programs lack the flexibility we need to handle all of the different data formats we have to convert. The programs should have been written with the conversion information in tables that are easily modified. The way they were written means we have to modify the programs every time we run them.

Write a reply to this email that shows empathy for the problem and a good customer-service ethic.

2. User Support Personality Types

Based on your understanding of the 16 personality types in the Myers-Briggs classification and on your knowledge of help desk communication and customer service skills described in this chapter, work with a team of three classmates or coworkers to identify which of the 16 MBTI types you think is best suited to providing excellent customer service. Would more than one of the 16 types be effective?

If you have never taken the Myers-Briggs test or have not taken it recently, check with your school's counseling department or your organization's human resources department to see if they can administer the test. If you would like to take a shorter, online version, go to The Keirsey Temperament Sorter II Web site (**www.keirsey.com/sorter/instruments2.aspx**) or the HumanMetrics Web site (**www.humanmetrics.com/cgi-win/JTypes2.asp**). While neither of these online tests are a substitute for the full Myers-Briggs test, they will give you an indication of your type.

If the results indicate that your personality type is not as well suited for help desk or user support work as other personality types, understand that the 16 MBTI personality types are not absolutes. Each person is actually a mixture of the eight pure categories in the test. The MBTI test simply measures tendencies. Most people are more adaptive than the test indicates.

Write a summary of your research into the MBTI personality types and customer service orientation among help desk staff.

3. A Complaint-Handling Script for Max Modem

Molly Jeavsey, who works in the administrative group at Max Modem, is the person to whom complaints about company products are directed. Molly has kept a running tally of which modem products generate the most complaints. She periodically passes the complaint tallies to the product design engineers and assembly line managers in the manufacturing division as feedback on problems end users or retail stores encounter with Max Modem's products.

Recently, the engineers became aware of a large volume of complaints about a new model of DSL modem, D-700i. They have asked Molly to collect more information from users and retailers about the problems with the D-700i modems.

Help Molly by writing a draft of a simple script that help desk agents could use to collect some basic information about problems users and retailers are encountering with the D-700i modems. The script you write should respond to two goals: (1) to collect basic product information that would be useful to Max Modem's engineers and managers; and (2) to exhibit a diplomatic way of asking for information that reflects an excellent customer-service ethic.

Compare your script with that of others in your class or work group to look for ideas on how to improve it.

4. Evaluate Vendor Support Web Sites

Select three or more support Web sites from among the following hardware vendors:

- Apple (**www.apple.com/support/hardware**)
- Dell (**support.dell.com**)
- Gateway (**support.gateway.com/support/default.asp**)
- Hewlett-Packard (**www8.hp.com/us/en/support-drivers.html**)

- Lenovo (**consumersupport.lenovo.com**)
- Sony (**esupport.sony.com/perl/select-system.pl**)
- Toshiba (**www.csd.toshiba.com/cgi-bin/tais/su/su_sc_home.jsp**)

You may substitute other hardware manufacturers you are familiar with if you wish. Compare and evaluate each vendor's support Web site using the customer support criteria discussed in this chapter. Limit your evaluation to the support home page and perhaps one level below the home page.

Address questions such as:

1. How easy or difficult is it to find information about a specific model?

2. Does the site provide the kind of information that a user support specialist would need to know?

3. Is the information in a format that is usable?

4. What tools are available on the Web site to allow someone to contact the vendor with a question?

5. Is it easy to navigate the Web site?

6. Based on its support Web site, how do you rate each vendor's commitment to excellent customer service?

5. Practice Interpersonal Communication Skills

The purpose of this case project is to learn about a useful malware utility program, Malwarebytes, and to develop good interpersonal communications in a support situation. First, download and install the free malware program from the Web site (**www.malwarebytes.org**). (You may substitute a different utility program if you wish.) Second, spend some time learning about the features of the program.

Then, team up with work or school colleagues to practice your interpersonal skills in a variety of support roles. Take turns with the roles of 1) end user, 2) support provider, and 3) observer/evaluator. In each role-playing session, the end user can take on a role such as:

- A novice user in a face-to-face support environment with little previous experience installing and using anti-malware software.

- An experienced user in a face-to-face support environment with a good understanding of anti-malware technology.

- A novice user in a telephone support environment with little previous experience installing and using anti-malware. If a telephone setup is not available, you may be able to simulate one using separate rooms or a barrier between the user and support provider.

- A difficult-to-handle user, such as an angry or reluctant communicator (this is a difficult user role, which may require some acting ability). The role of the end user in this situation is to challenge the interpersonal skills and abilities of the support specialist, but not to overact and provide an impossible situation for the support agent.

The goals of the support provider in each role-playing activity are:

1. Explain the problem that anti-malware is designed to address.

2. Explain how to download and install Malwarebytes.

3. Use excellent interpersonal communication skills as described in this chapter.

The role of the observer/evaluator is to provide feedback to the person playing the support provider role. If available, use a device to record the interaction so the support provider can use the recording for a self-evaluation.

Finally, when you have completed several different role-playing sessions, discuss how interactions with end users vary depending on the experience level of the user and whether the interaction is face-to-face or on the telephone.

6. Design and Build a Support Web Site

As this chapter suggests, user support information is often delivered via Web sites. The chapter describes some guidelines for client-friendly Web sites. The purpose of this case project is to give you some experience with the design and development of a simple, first phase of a support Web site. Use a PC to which you have access to host the first phase of your Web site.

- First, download and install the free Web site editor tool, KompoZer, which can be used to build and maintain your Web site. You can find a 12-page introduction to KompoZer at **ww2.nscc.edu/lyle_l/KompoZer_Instructions/Creating%20HTML% 20Pages%20With%20KompoZer.doc.** (If you have experience with a Web site editor other than KompoZer, you may use it instead.)

- Second, select a topic for your support Web site. Here are some suggested topics:

  - Links to PC vendor support Web sites, such as those listed in Case Project 4 in this chapter. You can probably think of other PC vendors to include on your support site.

  - Links to downloads of your favorite utility software useful to user support workers (see Chapter 12 for examples).

  - Links to vendors of hardware and software installed on your personal or office computer.

  - Links to tutorials for popular applications software that are available on the Web.

  - Or, your own ideas for a support Web site you and others would find useful.

- Third, design the layout of your Web site, including the home page and any other pages you will need to provide. Use the resource in Hands-On Activity 2-7 in this chapter for design elements you should consider. Draw some sketches of the layout of your site. Keep the number of pages small for this case project.

- Fourth, using your designs as a guide, develop some pages for your support Web site using KompoZer or a Web editor of your choosing.

- Finally, demo your Web site to one or more of your colleagues and get their evaluation of the content, organization, format, and mechanics, using the guidelines presented in this chapter.

Writing for End Users

In this chapter, you will learn about:

- ◎ Types of end-user documentation
- ◎ How technical writing differs from other writing
- ◎ How technical documents are organized
- ◎ How to plan effective user documentation
- ◎ The technical writing process
- ◎ Effective use of formats
- ◎ Strategies for technical writing
- ◎ Common problems in technical writing
- ◎ Tools used for technical writing
- ◎ How to evaluate documentation

For support staff members, writing for end users can take a variety of forms. Support agents may be required to prepare project reports for colleagues and create documents for use in end-user training. In addition, support groups (and hardware and software vendors) often communicate essential information to end users in writing via a variety of online documentation, such as help systems, assistants (wizards), Web pages, FAQs, email messages, chat sessions, and README files.

The creation of any document targeted for end users, whether printed or online, requires at least basic technical writing skills. The goal of technical writing is to produce documents that effectively and efficiently communicate information that a reader needs. **Documentation** is any form of written communication intended to provide user support information to end users or coworkers. Good documentation saves users and coworkers time; poor documentation can cost time and reduce productivity. This chapter provides a brief overview of several important topics in technical writing, including strategies for writing user documentation and pointers for writing successfully on technical subjects in a user support position.

Types of User Documentation

Members of a user support staff may be asked to produce written materials in a variety of situations. Although technical writing can have several purposes and can appear in very different formats, all documentation must clearly communicate a message. Figure 3-1 lists the common types of documentation, which are described in the following sections.

> - Brochures and flyers
> - Newsletters
> - Handouts and training aids
> - User guides, handbooks, and manuals
> - Online help systems
>
> - Email, chat, and text messages
> - Web pages
> - Proposals, letters, and memos
> - Procedural and operational documentation
> - Troubleshooting guides

Figure 3-1   Types of user support documentation

Brochures and Flyers

Brochures and flyers often promote various computer-related events, such as staff training sessions, computer and career fairs, hardware and software product demonstrations, and talks by guest speakers. These documents are primarily promotional and are intended to catch the reader's eye and "sell" the event. Because support staff members are often involved in organizing these kinds of events, they may need to create informational advertisements for them. To speed delivery and reduce paper use and postage costs, support groups often send advertisements for events via email or post announcements on an organizational intranet or Web portal.

Newsletters

Newsletters are an important way many support groups communicate with users. Support staff can use desktop publishing or word-processing software to create newsletters with embedded images such as diagrams, pictures, icons, and charts. User support newsletters are especially popular for large organizations in which the support staff does not come in direct contact with most employees on a regular basis. An increasing number of organizations now deliver newsletters online to their employees and customers.

ON THE WEB

For an example of an online newsletter resource targeted to the support industry, visit the TechRepublic Web site (**techrepublic.com**). Sign up to check out one or more of their newsletters. Although TechRepublic newsletters are written by a variety of writers, they generally provide examples of good technical writing.

For more information about publishing an online newsletter, visit the Web site of eBook Crossroads (**www.ebookcrossroads.com/newsletter-publishing.html**). The site includes links to several resources for newsletter writers and publishers.

Handouts and Training Aids

Handouts and training aids are primarily intended to summarize and promote recall of material covered in a training session. They may also be distributed online or via a computer documentation library of frequently asked questions. Printed handouts of PowerPoint slides with space for trainees to take notes next to each slide are common training aids. Handouts and training aids are usually short and address a single topic, such as how to perform a set of tasks in a specific software application.

 Chapter 11 covers the preparation of materials for training sessions.

User Guides, Handbooks, and Manuals

User guides, handbooks, and computer manuals are more formal examples of written documentation. For some support groups, these documents can be tens or hundreds of pages long, and are often printed in book format or created as a PDF (portable document format) for distribution via email or on the Web. They are often designed to supplement vendor documentation and trade books with information specific to an organization or computer facility. For example, an organization may issue a user handbook that specifies ground rules for computer use and abuse and details what computer facilities and services are available to workers, including information on how to access them, how to obtain software to connect to the organization's VPN (virtual private network), and how to get system support. In educational institutions, IT departments may publish similar guides for students, faculty, and administrators. Even very small organizations find a printed user guide an effective way to communicate basic information to new employees and those who are only occasional users.

Software developers and hardware vendors publish a variety of user guides and computer manuals that describe how to install and use their products. These manuals may be organized in a **tutorial format**, which guides a user step-by-step through the features of a program, with frequently used features covered first. Other manuals are organized in a **reference format**, which pulls together all the information on a specific topic in a single page, section, or chapter.

A tutorial format is convenient for new users, because it emphasizes the natural sequence for learning each step, beginning with the simplest tasks. Features are introduced as users need them for a particular task. Information about printing, for example, may be scattered throughout a tutorial manual, as various printing features and options are introduced. Basic printing features might be explained early, and more advanced or seldom-used features covered later. For experienced users, a reference format is often more useful, because all the information on printing, including a description of available options, is usually located in a single section or chapter within the manual. Some manuals combine tutorials with a reference guide to address the needs of both types of users.

Online Help Systems

Online help systems and software assistants (wizards) are common features in software packages. They are sometimes supplied on CDs, which customers can use for self-training. In other cases, help modules are available via a link to a Web site or embedded in a software product and installed at the same time as the software itself. Some online help systems are well written and can effectively rival or replace printed manuals as a source of well-organized and accurate information. Writing online documentation is an art, however, because the information must be presented succinctly. Printed training materials are usually organized sequentially with less concern about the length of each section. In online documentation, individual topics should be split into shorter sections that can appear on a single screen page; readers are not likely to spend time searching for information on a Web site where the text appears on one very long page rather than on shorter pages divided into topics.

Hypertext links and index searches in online documents are powerful tools to help users jump quickly to needed information. A **hypertext link** is a highlighted word or phrase in a document that acts as a pointer to additional information. When a user clicks a link, the software displays more detailed information about the word or phrase—by displaying a Web page, opening a different document, jumping to another location in the current document, or displaying a popup window. An index search feature permits a user to enter a word or phrase of interest; the software then searches the document and displays detailed information about the topic.

The Windows Help system illustrates the use of hypertext links and index searches and includes several examples of interactive help systems called troubleshooters. To access the troubleshooters in Windows 7, click the **Start** button, click **Help and Support** on the Start menu, type *troubleshoot* in the Search Help box, and then press the **Enter** key. In Windows Vista, click the **Start** button, click **Help and Support** on the Start menu, and then click the **Troubleshooting** icon to view a variety of troubleshooting tips. In Windows XP, click the **Start** button, and then click **Help** on the Start menu, click the **Contents** tab, click **Troubleshooting**, and then click a troubleshooter to open a page of information.

Despite the increasing popularity and convenience of online documentation, some users prefer print media when they need to read large amounts of information. Printed information is often easier to read for long periods, and it can be read even when a computer is not available. Depending on the quality and resolution of the display screen and the room lighting, lengthy online documents may be difficult to read. Some end users need extra time to become comfortable with using online documentation and to change their preference for printed materials.

Email, Chat, and Text Messages

The ability to communicate effectively via email, instant messaging (chat), and text messages is an important writing skill for user support specialists, especially those who work at a help desk that communicates primarily with online users. Many support organizations have switched their primary method of communication with end users from telephone or face-to-face interactions to email and chat sessions. Support agents who work with internal clients are also likely to make more frequent use of text messages with smartphone technology. In these organizations, support specialists who honed their verbal skills at the expense of their writing skills may find that they need to update their skills. Email, chat, and text messages may seem to be less formal methods of communication; however, any written message from a help desk staff member projects an image of an organization and should reflect good technical writing skills.

Dashing off a few disorganized phrases with typos and spelling and grammatical errors in any written message can give the recipient a poor impression of the support agent as well as the entire support organization. Writing a careful response to an end user helps a support agent to organize his or her thoughts and provides an opportunity to review and revise a response before sending it. Although internal email and other messages may be less formal than messages intended for recipients outside an organization, even these messages project an image of the sender. Remember that once you have sent an email or other message, you have no control over where it may be forwarded. Supervisors may review and evaluate the quality of support email, chat, and text messages as one measure of an agent's communication skills and promotability.

When sending text messages, support agents should generally avoid the use of abbreviations (for example, *U* instead of *you*, *BTW* as a substitute for *by the way*, or *IMHO* as a substitute for *in my humble opinion*), unless a support worker is certain the recipient understands the abbreviation.

ON THE WEB

Support staff who correspond frequently via email and instant messaging need to understand some basic guidelines called *netiquette*. A useful resource is Kaitlin Duck Sherwood's "A Beginner's Guide to Effective Email" at **webfoot.com/advice/email.top.php**.

The OWL (Online Writing Lab) at Purdue University also provides very useful suggestions on email etiquette at **owl.english.purdue.edu/owl/resource/636/01**.

For a list of common (and some uncommon) texting abbreviations, go to **www.webopedia.com/quick_ref/textmessageabbreviations.asp**.

Web Pages

Because many written materials end up on the Web, the ability to write for that medium is an important skill for support workers. Web pages need to be organized and written so users can quickly locate information. Because a Web site is usually accessible to the general public, the image of an organization is at stake. Think about how long you typically stay at a Web site that is poorly organized, contains incorrect information, or provides broken links (URLs that point to inactive Web pages). In general, materials designed for Web access should be very short, with hypertext links that lead readers to additional information. Web-based materials must be well written because Web users often do not have the patience to wade through a long document to find the information they need. They tend to skim quickly and then click a link to another site. Another challenge for support agents who maintain or contribute to support Web sites is to keep information accurate and up to date. Obsolete or inaccurate support information is often worse than no information.

ON THE WEB

You can sometimes learn useful information from studying examples of poorly executed Web sites. To find Web sites that users have nominated as among the worst on the entire Internet, go to **www.worstoftheweb.com**. The site features an archive of nominated sites along with comments from three pundits about what makes each one so bad.

On a more positive note, check out an interactive tutorial on Web site design on the University of Albany Library's Web site (**library.albany.edu/imc/webdesign/#how**).

Proposals, Letters, and Memos

Support staff members need to be able to write clear and effective proposals, reports, letters, memos, and other business documents. Support specialists who perform needs assessments for departments or individual users frequently need to present the results of their investigations in the form of a proposal or report. In addition, support staff often need to write letters, memos, and other correspondence to colleagues, end users (both inside and outside an organization), and supervisors. The ability to write standard business documents is a basic user support communication skill.

Procedural and Operational Documentation

Procedural and operational documentation includes procedure steps and checklists, usually intended for internal use. The descriptions of the steps to install hardware and software that appear in Chapter 10 are examples of technical procedural documentation. Even for internal documents such as these, technical writing skills are essential. Procedural and operational documentation that is unclear, poorly organized, or incorrect costs staff time, results in errors, and increases user frustration. Clear, well-organized documents communicate information efficiently and reflect well on the writer and the support organization. Many support specialists who have never thought of themselves as writers enjoy the challenge of writing procedural and operational documentation that is accurate and easy to follow.

Troubleshooting Guides

User support staff members often write troubleshooting guides to help other workers and clients solve problems. Common examples of troubleshooting guides include:

- A problem-solving chapter in a user guide
- An FAQ page for a Web site
- A user support script to handle a specific type of problem incident
- A problem report and solution in a help desk knowledge base

Although this type of documentation is often for internal use, it must be clear, concise, and well written.

ON THE WEB

For an example of a troubleshooting guide, see a Web page that describes the meaning of beep codes during the power-on-self-test (POST) that occurs when a PC starts (**www.computerhope.com/beep.htm**).

Each type of technical writing described above is a form of support documentation. They have more similarities than differences. The following sections discuss the similarities, including how technical writing in general differs from other types of writing.

How Technical Writing Differs from Other Writing

Technical writing is different from other types of writing—such as personal letters, research papers, or novels—in terms of the type of information communicated as well as the goals, style, and organization of the documents.

Technical Writing Style

Technical writing typically follows specific style guidelines. The goal of these guidelines is to help technical writers create documents that are clear, accurate, and accessible to most users. Keep in mind the following points as you write documentation:

- Technical writing uses short, declarative sentences, brief phrases, and lists—instead of long sentences with unnecessary words or phrases. In general, simple sentences are preferable to compound ones. A simple sentence has one subject and one verb, and expresses a complete idea. Compound sentences contain two subjects and two verbs, often include *and* or *but* as a connector, and express two complete thoughts. Avoid run-on sentences and overly complex sentence structures with multiple clauses and modifiers. Compare these examples:

    - **Simple sentence:** *Parentheses let you control how Excel uses operators in a formula.*

    - **Compound sentence:** *Parentheses let you control how Excel uses arithmetic operators in a formula, and parentheses also make equations easier to read or revise.*

    - **Run-on sentence:** *If you specify an uneven number of parentheses in a formula or a pair of parentheses that don't match, Excel displays the message, "Parentheses do not match or Error in Formula," and this highlights the location of the mistake which you can correct on the formula bar.*

Some writers believe simple sentences are not as interesting as more complex ones; however, the purpose of technical writing is not to entertain, but to communicate information vital to the reader's productivity. Also, not all readers have good reading skills; they may have a reading disability (such as dyslexia), or English may be their second language. To communicate effectively with the largest number of readers, keep sentences simple.

- Technical writing starts with the most important point at the beginning of a section or topic rather than at the end, as in other types of writing. The goal of technical writing is not to build suspense or work toward a punch line, but to communicate information as clearly and effectively as possible and help a reader make transitions between topics.

- Technical writing often communicates step-by-step sequences of events or tasks. The writing style and format used can help readers understand the sequence. For example, a sequence of steps should be listed in the order the users would perform the steps. Compare the following:

  - **Example 1:** *Click the Margin option in Page Setup under the File menu.*

  - **Example 2:** *In the File menu, click Page Setup, and then click the Margin option.*

  In the first example, the actions appear in reverse order to how they are actually performed. A user must read to the end of the sentence before they learn what action to perform first. The second example is preferable because the actions are listed in the order in which they are performed. When steps in a procedure or task must be performed in a specific sequence, a numbered list can emphasize the sequence. When information has no required order, a bulleted list is more appropriate.

- Technical writing should be concise, but not cryptic. Concise writing is short, but covers the essential information a user needs. Readers of technical documents usually want to open a document, find what they need to know, and get back to work. If they have to spend unnecessary time searching for buried information, their productivity is reduced. To include more detailed information, add **pointers**, or cross-references to the location where a user can find more information. In online documents, hypertext links effectively move a user from general to more specific information on a topic.

- The goal of technical writing is not to amuse readers with humor or call attention to the writer's personality or preferences. Humor in a technical document is likely to be misunderstood by some readers, especially those who are new to a topic or for whom English is a second language. In technical writing, the writer's personal preferences should be clearly labeled as such, enabling readers to quickly identify possible sources of bias.

Good technical writing follows these guidelines to ensure that users get the help they need from a document. If users cannot locate the information they need, the result is a higher volume of contacts with the support group, and probably a higher level of user frustration.

How Technical Documents Are Organized

Technical documents are commonly organized either sequentially or hierarchically. **Sequential organization** follows a step-by-step approach whereby information is arranged in the order in which the steps are executed. Procedural documents usually follow a sequential organization. **Hierarchical organization** flows from top to bottom, and information is arranged from general to specific. Online help systems often use a hierarchical organization.

Most successful technical documents use a combination of sequential and hierarchical organization strategies, depending on the material to be communicated, the medium of communication, and the users' needs. A common organization for a technical document is:

- **Introduction**
  - ◆ Purpose of the document
  - ◆ Who are the intended readers of the document
  - ◆ Why read the document
- **Body**
  - ◆ Specific task steps
  - ◆ Common problems users encounter
- **Summary**
  - ◆ Review of the main points
  - ◆ Pointers to additional information

The overall organization is hierarchical. At the top level, the general sections are: *Introduction*, *Body*, and *Summary*. The body in this example includes task steps, which are sequential.

The introduction begins by addressing three questions. First, "*What is the purpose of this document?*" Second, "*Who is the intended audience?*" Third, "*Why would anyone want to read this?*" In other words, readers are told up front what information they will get from reading the document. Technical writers should answer these three questions early in order to save time for those readers for whom a document is *not* intended. Even a short piece of writing, such as an FAQ or an email message, should state its purpose in the first or second sentence.

The body of a technical document should include explanatory material. Most readers want a short explanation to help them understand why something works, what result should be expected, or why the information is important. Often, technical writers include a brief explanation of what the hardware or software is capable of and how it can help readers in their work. The explanation is often followed by a detailed description of the sequential steps necessary to perform a task. Finally, the body should briefly describe common problems users are likely to encounter and how to recover from them. The summary should be brief: Review the main points and the results achieved, and direct the reader to where additional information can be accessed.

Some technical writers are tempted to include as much information as they can in a document. The writer may digress from the main points to cover material that may be of interest to only a few readers, is not critical, or is very technical. Omit less critical information or place this material in an appendix or attachment. Include a pointer to the appendix in the body so interested readers will know where to find it.

Document Planning

Planning is essential to produce high-quality documents, regardless of their length or purpose. Most planning starts with determining the characteristics of the audience and its needs, as listed in Figure 3-2.

> - Who is the target audience?
>
> - What does the audience already know?
>
> - What does the audience need to know?
>
> - What do you want the audience to be able to do when they finish reading the document?
>
> - What medium will be used to transmit the document to its audience?

Figure 3-2   Information needed for documentation planning

Asking these questions at the beginning helps prepare technical writers to create useful, well-targeted documents.

Who Is the Target Audience?

The question about the target audience is often intended to pinpoint the readers' level of technical expertise. Writing a task description for new users requires different assumptions and techniques than writing for more experienced, technically sophisticated users. The audience definition should also include an estimate of their reading level. Most newspapers, for example, are written at an eighth or ninth grade reading level, which is a good level to strive for in computer documents targeted to a general audience of end users. Documents intended for a technical audience may be written at a 10th–12th grade level, but should probably not exceed that level. Most word processors include a tool to measure the approximate reading level (readability index) of a document.

 The readability index for this chapter is 10th–11th grade level.

ON THE WEB

To quickly check the reading level of a document, visit the Web site **www.online-utility.org/english/readability_test_and_improve.jsp**. Cut and paste text from the document into the Window and click the **Process text** button to view the results. Note that the popular readability indexes do not always agree on the readability level of a document because they use different algorithms, but they provide a general indication of the level at which a document is written.

What Does the Audience Already Know?

To determine who the audience is, a technical writer should attempt to find out the readers' backgrounds, including what they already know. A statement in the introduction about what the writer assumes the readers know can help readers make an informed decision about whether the material is intended for them—whether it covers things they already know or whether it covers technical information that is beyond their ability to understand.

Example: *The information in this reference sheet is for PowerPoint users who have a basic understanding of presentation software concepts and need a reference tool for the most frequently used features in PowerPoint.*

When writing for readers who need to know a specific procedure, assessing what skills they already have is sometimes difficult. In some situations, a technical writer may be able to assess skills using a questionnaire. However, because a questionnaire is not always feasible, always cover the most basic skills first, but with appropriate section headings so more skilled users can easily skip to what they need to know.

What Does the Audience Need to Know?

Answering this question is a critical step in technical writing because it helps a writer define the purpose of a document. The purpose of technical documentation should be to move readers from what they already know to what they need to know. The purpose of a document should be stated at the beginning, within the first few sentences.

What Do You Want the Audience to Be Able to Do?

A technical writer should know what specific tasks she or he wants the audience to perform after they read the document. A task focus gives direction to the writing and helps users know when they have successfully mastered the information. Although some documents are intended for general information purposes only, most are aimed at getting a reader to a point where they can make a decision or perform a specific task.

What Medium Will Be Used to Transmit the Document to Its Audience?

The medium that will be used to transmit a document to its audience should be determined before the document is written. Common media types include print and online formats. Although some documents are written for either or both media, printed documents are often longer and therefore need transitions between topics and levels of information to help readers know where they are in the hierarchy of information. Online documents should be shorter, but can include hyperlinks and other pointers to help readers quickly navigate to the desired information. Lengthy printed documents should include a table of contents and an index to help with searches for information. Similarly, the most effective Web sites are those that include a site map to help users navigate if they can't find information in any other way.

 Over the past several years, the computer industry has experienced a transition from primarily printed documentation to almost entirely Web-based or optical media documentation.

The Technical Writing Process

After document writers have defined the audience, purpose, and medium for a document, they can then begin to write the document itself. Many writers follow the seven-step process shown in Figure 3-3.

1. Generate a list of important ideas or features to be covered.

2. Organize the list into a logical, hierarchical sequence to form an outline.

3. Expand the outline into a first draft.

4. Edit the draft one or more times for clarity.

5. Arrange for an outside review of the document.

6. Revise the draft into its final form.

7. Proofread the final document.

Figure 3-3 The technical writing process

Good technical writing follows this process. A writer may be tempted to take shortcuts because of time constraints, but once a document is published, especially in a print medium, opportunities to change it are rare. Even very experienced writers would never consider releasing a first draft to end users; they realize that the entire seven-step process is critical to producing quality documents.

Step 1: Generate an Idea List

Some writers use a word processor to generate a list of ideas; others use paper and pencil. At this stage, a writer **brainstorms** to generate as many topics as they can think of that might be useful to readers. Some ideas will become major topics, others will become minor topics, and some will be discarded. While brainstorming, the strategy is to exclude nothing; after brainstorming, the idea list can be prioritized, reorganized, and pared down to essentials.

Step 2: Organize the List into an Outline

Once writers have a topic list that includes everything they want to cover, they organize the topics into a logical order to form an outline. Most writers don't settle on a final organizational structure on the first attempt. Flexibility is important during the early organizational steps; writers often cut and paste to try out different sequences of ideas. Most word processors have an outlining feature that makes it easy to rearrange topics—to promote some in importance to major topics and demote others. As writers begin to create an outline, other topics may come to mind that can be added. The most important question an outline answers is *"In what order does the reader need to know this information?"* Cover the essential information, including qualifiers or assumptions, first.

ON THE WEB

The Outline View feature in Microsoft Word (an alternative to the more familiar Normal and Print views), allows a writer to focus on the overall structure or outline of a document. To view a short tutorial on using Outline View, visit **www.brighthub.com/ computing/windows-platform/articles/26077.aspx**.

Mind-mapping software is yet another tool some writers find useful to help organize their thoughts. Its purpose is to help with brainstorming and to provide a tool to turn random thoughts and concepts into an organized structure. To download free mind-mapping software, XMind, visit **www.xmind.net**.

Step 3: Expand the Outline into a First Draft

After creating an initial outline and checking it for logical flow, a writer expands the outline into a first draft by explaining each point in the outline. When preparing a first draft, a writer often uses the features described below to make the document readable and understandable. Although many techniques help produce understandable documentation, these four are basic.

Paragraphs with Topic Sentences

A document should be organized into paragraphs, and each paragraph should cover a different aspect of the topic. Each paragraph should have a topic sentence to introduce the topic in general terms. After the topic sentence, develop other sentences in each paragraph with details that support or expand on the topic sentence. When writing Web-based documents and email messages, the number of paragraphs on a page or in a message should be small: one or a few.

 Identify the topic sentence in each paragraph in this section of the chapter. Does each topic sentence tell you what the paragraph is about? Are some topic sentences better than others?

Transitions

Use transitional words and phrases such as *for example, therefore,* and *as a result* to help show a reader the relationship of one sentence to another. Other transitions useful for steps in a procedure are *first, second, next, then,* and *finally.* Transitions help readers keep track of where they are in a sequential organization. Numbered and bulleted lists also help show organization and transitions.

Defined Terms

Good technical writers always define the terms they use. To introduce readers to a new term, define it clearly and boldface the term where it is defined, as you have seen in this book. Be careful not to define a term using the term itself; use a synonym instead.

Formats

Writers use format features to help readers understand the organization of information. Different sized headings, for example, help clarify the overall structure. Many writers use italic type for emphasis, although italics should be used sparingly. Bulleted or numbered lists are useful to alert a reader to the structure of a long section.

A document's structure helps guide readers through the various sections. After a technical writer determines the basic structure of a document, he or she adds formats to communicate the structure to readers. The following list focuses on useful formatting tools that you can incorporate in your own writing.

- **Style elements**—When a document is organized into chapters or modules, different fonts, font sizes, boldface, capitalization, centering, indentation, underlines, bullets, and numbering help a reader understand the structure. These design elements help the reader understand what is more or less important and help identify where each topic begins and ends. They answer questions such as, *"If I am not interested in this section, where do I start reading again so I don't miss anything?"*

Although changes in font, case, indentation, and other format features can help clarify the structure of a document, some writers get carried away with the power of a word processor. Two fonts can be useful to help a reader deal with different types of material. But too many different fonts or too much boldface or italic text can be a distraction.

- **Format consistency**—Format consistency is important. Use a consistent format for headings, paragraphs, and tables. Style sheets and templates in popular word processors can help make consistent formatting easier. For technical manuals or other materials that will receive widespread commercial distribution, hardware and software organizations and publishers often hire a graphic designer to create a design for the interior of a document. For many smaller projects, however, preformatted templates, which are often created by professional designers and included with word-processing programs, are sufficient.

- **Lists and tables**—When a writer needs to present a sequence of information, a bulleted or numbered list or a table is often more understandable than a long narrative passage. Lists and tables permit readers to quickly locate the information they need. Lists are most effective when they support a generalization or summarize information presented in narrative text.

Step 4: Edit the Draft

After expanding an outline into the first draft, a writer should read and edit it. Most writers read through and edit a draft more than once, looking for particular problems on each pass. A single edit pass rarely catches all the different types of problems.

One edit pass is often used to delete extra words in order to tighten the text because a goal of technical writing is to be brief. Consider, for example, the following paragraph:

Let's spend a bit more time discussing the relationship between the automatic call distribution (ACD) system and other help desk systems. Only the more sophisticated ACDs include interfaces to other devices now, but it's clearly the wave of the future, not to mention a productivity enhancer.

The following version eliminates extraneous words while maintaining the meaning:

Let's discuss the relationship between the automatic call distribution (ACD) system and other help desk systems. Currently, only sophisticated ACDs can connect to other devices. However, future models will have connectivity to enhance user productivity.

Eliminating extra words takes practice but is beneficial because tighter prose takes less time to read. Eliminate words that are not critical to understanding your meaning.

A second edit pass that many writers perform is a format consistency check. The purpose of a **format consistency check** is to make sure that the fonts of headings and subheadings, indentation, centering, boldface, italics, and underlining are used consistently throughout a document. Do not overuse these format features. Remember that the purpose of formats is to help readers understand the structure of the document, not to show off all the features of document-processing software. Format features should guide a reader through a document without hindering understanding or becoming a distraction.

A third edit pass is a technical accuracy check, sometimes called a quality assurance pass. During a **technical accuracy check**, a writer tests any procedural or technical steps in a document by performing the steps with the hardware or software. The purpose of a technical accuracy check is to eliminate any errors in step-by-step instructions or other technical information. If a document has been written about a beta or other prerelease version of hardware or software, an accuracy check should be performed with the final version of the product. Check URLs to make sure addresses are spelled correctly, and confirm that the URLs still point to active Web sites. If a document includes screenshots to illustrate the result of steps in a procedure, each screenshot should be verified against the software to make sure it reflects the latest version of the software.

Step 5: Get an Outside Review

An outside review is a like a second opinion. A reviewer often raises questions, spots inconsistencies, finds unclear meanings, identifies poor writing techniques, and locates other problems that the writer cannot see. Getting outside criticism can be surprising, especially because writers who spend a lot of time on their first draft are often satisfied that it is just about perfect. Criticism can be especially painful if a reviewer doesn't share the same writing style and approach as the writer. But a second perspective on any written document can be helpful, especially for documents that will be widely distributed. An outside review is like a beta test of a new product. Over time, writers learn to set aside the natural defensiveness they may feel about their work and realize that a reviewer represents the potential target audience. Most writers would rather a reviewer point out problems during the writing stage than have readers do so after publication.

Step 6: Revise the Draft

After a writer edits a draft and gets feedback, he or she revises it to incorporate suggestions and corrections. If a writer is a perfectionist, one of the challenges in the writing process is to know when to stop revising. Although edit passes can serve a useful purpose up to a point, a writer must learn when to stop. Fortunately for many technical writers, publication deadlines dictate when they are finished. After a few revisions, additional edit passes may result in very small incremental improvements in a document. At the end of each edit pass, a writer should ask whether the last pass resulted in a substantial improvement, or whether the improvements were only marginal; if they didn't significantly enhance the readability or accuracy of the document, then it is time to stop reviewing and revising.

Step 7: Proofread the Document

After writing, editing, and revising a document, writers should proofread it one last time to make sure that no small errors remain. Sometimes another person, possibly a professional proofreader, copy editor, or a work colleague, can perform this task. Most technical writing benefits greatly from another proofreader's perspective. Proofreaders look for a variety of common errors, including:

- **Inconsistent capitalization and punctuation**—Are proper nouns capitalized consistently? Are words capitalized that shouldn't be? Are commas used consistently in sentences, in lists, and within large numbers?

- **Extra spaces between words and sentences**—Is the number of spaces after each sentence consistent? (Most typeset books and many desktop-published documents use only one space after periods.) Is there a single space between words?

You can use a word processor to search for two spaces and automatically replace each occurrence with one space.

- **Inconsistent font use**—Are all headings in the correct font and size? Is the body text in the same size and font throughout the document?

- **Incorrect page breaks**—Are all page breaks in logical locations? Should any page breaks be adjusted to eliminate orphaned sentences (a situation in which the first or last sentence in a paragraph or list is on a separate page from the remainder of the paragraph or list)?

If a document will be typeset or transferred to desktop publishing software, page breaks are not a concern because the length of a typeset page usually differs from a page created with word-processing software.

The seven steps in the technical writing process help both new and experienced document writers ensure that their work is both well organized and understandable.

ON THE WEB

The Web contains a wealth of useful resources for beginning and experienced technical writers. For example, David A. McMurrey, a professor at Austin Community College, provides a complete online technical writing textbook (**www.io.com/~hcexres/ textbook**). To learn more about guidelines for the use of formatting tools, click topics in the table of contents under *Document Design*.

A brief tutorial on writing user guides can be found at **www.klariti.com/technical-writing/User-Guides-Tutorial.shtml**.

Technical Writing Strategies

Although you may not have written technical documents before, you have probably used a manual, online help, or some other form of end-user documentation. Based on your experience, you might already have some opinions on what makes good or bad technical writing, and what has or has not been effective at addressing your needs as a reader and end user. Some technical writing is a pleasure to read because it is well organized and the important information is presented clearly and concisely. If you analyze successful documents, some common strategies and approaches stand out.

Analogies

Technical writers often use analogies to explain new material. An **analogy** is a comparison between an unfamiliar concept and a familiar one; an analogy highlights the similarities between things. For example, writers often use the analogy of an office filing system to explain the hierarchical structure of computer media; they draw a parallel between the information stored manually in an office filing system and the information stored electronically in a computer filing system (e.g., a hard disk is like a filing cabinet). Analogies are useful because they relate something most users are familiar with, such as an office filing system, to something they need to understand.

Repetition

Technical writers often use repetition for emphasis. Repetition is also a training strategy you will learn more about in Chapter 11. In both technical documents and user training, a useful strategy is to introduce a topic, explain it, and then summarize it. Repetition helps users learn new material and recall it later. However, excessive use of repetition can unnecessarily lengthen a document without contributing to its usefulness.

Consistent Word Use

Technical writers try to use words consistently. In creative writing, writers are taught to look for synonyms to avoid overuse of certain words and to inject variety in written work. In technical writing, however, consistent use of words can contribute to a reader's understanding. To vary word use unnecessarily may cause the reader to question whether different words signal a subtle difference in meaning. For example, a writer may use synonyms such as *CD*, *CD-ROM*, *compact disc*, and *optical disk* interchangeably to refer to the same thing, which can confuse readers. Technical writing is often clearer when one word among synonyms is selected and used throughout a document.

Many organizations maintain a **style sheet** that lists their preferences for common terms so all writers use the same terminology. Sometimes a style sheet is a simple list of preferred terms and spelling conventions. In other cases, a style sheet can be a lengthy document that lists not only terms and spelling conventions but also preferred grammatical structures, product name usage conventions, and the like. Figure 3-4 shows sample entries from this book's style sheet.

Style Sheet   *Page 3*

Item	Comment
acronyms	● at first use, either "spelled out (ACRONYM)" or "ACRONYM (spelled out)"; then use only ACRONYM
chapter references	● capitalize first letter in running text; (In Chapter 1, we discuss…)
key terms	● bold in text and end-of-chapter list
URLs	● bold in running text and tables
	● omit **http://**
	● use **www.cnn.com**, not **www.cnn.com/index.html**

Vocabulary	Comment
back up	● verb; (back up a system)
backup	● noun; (create a system backup)
check list	● two words; not checklist or check-list
coworker	● one word; not co-worker
end user	● noun; two words (Most end users need . . .)
end-user	● adjective; hyphenated (End-user computing is . . .)

Figure 3-4   Sample entries from the style sheet for this book

ON THE WEB

English Teaching Forum, a quarterly journal published by the U.S. Department of State for teachers of English, maintains an online style sheet to describe how writers should prepare documents for publication by their organization. For an example of a style sheet, see **exchanges.state.gov/englishteaching/forum/style-sheet.html**.

Parallel Structure

The concept of parallel structure is important in technical writing. **Parallel structure** is a writing strategy in which similar items are treated consistently throughout a document. Consistent formats for titles, headings, and subheadings are one application of parallel structure, as are consistent verb tenses and parts of speech. Parallel structure is also important in bulleted lists, as shown in Figure 3-5.

Problems with parallel structure	Revision to use parallel structure
Consider the following ways to measure help desk performance:	Consider the following ways to measure help desk performance:
◦ first: volume of calls	◦ call volume
◦ next: time it takes to respond	◦ call response time
◦ resolution time	◦ call resolution time
◦ how many calls are backlogged	◦ call backlog
◦ call aging	◦ call aging time

Figure 3-5   Parallel structure in a bulleted list

The bulleted list on the left side of Figure 3-5 does not use parallel structure. The list on the right side of the figure shows one way to rewrite the list using parallel structure; all the terms are nouns, and the phrasing is similar. In a parallel list structure, when a phrase introduces the list, each item in the list should make a complete sentence with the introductory phrase.

Consistent Verb Tense

Technical writers generally use a consistent verb tense throughout a document. Present tense is often preferable in technical writing unless the topic is something that clearly happened in the past. Consider the following examples:

- **Example 1:** *After you have powered up your computer and booted into Windows, the network connection wizard is used to establish a network connection.*

- **Example 2:** *First, power up your computer and boot into Windows. Then use the network connection wizard to establish a network connection.*

The first example uses the past tense unnecessarily. The second example uses the present tense, which leads the reader through the actions. Past tense may be appropriate in a problem description to indicate actions a user performed because the actions occurred in the past For example, an entry in a problem log could use past tense to describe a result such as: "*After I ran the antivirus utility, the user's PC started normally.*" In this example, use of present tense would be awkward.

Common Technical Writing Problems

Technical writers learn from experience to avoid common problems so their writing is clearer, more understandable, and easier to read. Figure 3-6 lists 10 common problems to avoid.

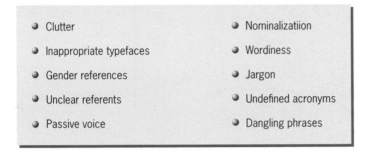

- Clutter
- Inappropriate typefaces
- Gender references
- Unclear referents
- Passive voice
- Nominalizatiion
- Wordiness
- Jargon
- Undefined acronyms
- Dangling phrases

Figure 3-6　Common technical writing problems

Clutter

The availability of powerful word processors and desktop publishing software means that even novice writers can produce professional-looking results. However, all writers need to be careful not to include too many distracting design elements. Just because graphics, clip art, shading, word art, borders, and neon printer colors can be easily included does not mean that you should use all of them. Add graphics to illustrate or highlight an important point, not just for decoration. Apply formatting sparingly and consistently, and only when it helps readers locate information or understand the subject. A user document with simple formatting is often more effective than one with too many format features.

A page chock full of text and graphics is often hard to read. The most successful documents are those that include considerable white space where readers can rest their eyes. Leave reasonable margins at the top, bottom, and sides of pages; insert spaces between paragraphs; and use a font that is large enough to be readable. The body text font size should be at least ten points or larger; don't reduce the size of a font just to fit material that is too long in the space allocated to it. Rather, edit for conciseness.

Most body text should be left-aligned. Large passages of centered text are difficult to read, as is **justified text**, which is aligned at both the right and left margins. Justified text, also called *block-justified*, sometimes contains large white spaces between words that can make text difficult to read. For example, which of these passages is easier to read?

This paragraph is left-aligned to illustrate how easily the reader's eye moves from word to word. This justification style is recommended for the body of most documents because it enhances readability.

This paragraph is block-justified to illustrate that it is more difficult to read a passage when software inserts additional spaces between words. This approach creates an artificial block style with text that extends to the right and left margins.

*This paragraph is centered
to illustrate that it is more difficult to read, and it takes
more time to read lines of text that
differ in length.*

Inappropriate Typefaces

For most readers, serif typefaces are easier to read than sans serif. **Serif typefaces** include serifs, which are fine lines that project from the top and bottom of a font's letters. These lines lead the eye from letter to letter across the line, improving readability. The font you are reading now is called Warnock Pro, which is a serif font. **Sans serif typefaces** do not have the serifs (*sans* is French for *without*). Sans serif typefaces are often used for titles and headings, whereas serif typefaces are frequently used for body text.

Most word-processing programs include several **specialty typefaces** that are intended for special uses, such as invitations, brochures, or flyers. Script fonts fall into this category. Specialty typefaces are interesting and fun, but you should save them for informal use since a script font can make text more difficult to read. Figure 3-7 shows a serif font, a sans serif font, and a specialty font. Which do you think is easiest to read?

This is an example of a 12-point serif typeface called Georgia.

This is an example of a 12-point san serif typeface called Arial.

This is an example of a 14-point script typeface called Brush Script.

Figure 3-7   Font readability examples

Gender References

In recent years, the use of gender-related pronouns has decreased. *He, she, him,* and *her* are often replaced with gender-neutral words, such as *they, their,* and *it.* This change in style means that writers sometimes use a plural pronoun where they might have previously used a singular pronoun. You can also use the phrase *he or she* (the order is sometimes reversed). Some writers use the combined form *s/he*, but this solution is usually not preferred because it is less common and more difficult to read. Others writers alternate between *he* and *she*—a strategy that can confuse a reader. Choose one of these strategies to use consistently, but try to avoid gender-related words, unless they clearly fit.

Gender-neutral words include *staff* instead of *manpower*, and *staffed* instead of *manned*. Use *chair* or *chairperson* instead of *chairman* (unless Chairman is an official title). But be consistent: Don't refer to a male as a *chairman* and a female as a *chair*; instead, refer to both genders as a *chair*. Use *supervisor* rather than *foreman*. Can you think of other common examples? Using gender-neutral language takes some practice, but the result is often clearer and less offensive than the alternatives.

Unclear Referents

Another common problem in technical writing is the use of unclear or missing referents. A **referent** is a concrete word or concept that is designated by another word. Words such as *this*, *that*, *it*, and *they* are common words used to designate referents. Consider this example:

Windows and the Office Suite use pull-down context menus. They are good examples of the power of the GUI interface.

The word *they* at the start of the second sentence designates or refers to a concept in the previous sentence. But does the writer mean that Windows and the Office Suite are examples of the power of the GUI interface, or that pull-down context menus are good examples? The concrete referent of *they* is not clear. To clarify the second sentence, replace *they* with the intended referent:

Windows and the Office Suite use pull-down context menus. Both software packages are good examples of the power of the GUI interface.

Passive Voice

Good technical writing uses the active voice instead of the passive voice whenever possible. With **active voice**, the subject of a sentence performs the action indicated by the verb; the subject is an actor. With **passive voice**, the subject of a sentence receives the action indicated by the verb; the subject is not acting. In some sentences written in the passive voice, the real subject is missing. Consider this example:

The new operating system was installed on Friday.

In this example, the subject (*operating system*) does not perform the action (*was installed*), but is the recipient of the action. Passive voice is often used to avoid naming the real subject of a sentence, as in the classic example of passive voice: *Mistakes were made*. The sentence below is much stronger in active voice:

A support specialist installed the new operating system on Friday.

In this revision, the subject (*support specialist*) performs the action (*installed*). Although some technical writers prefer passive voice because it makes the writing seem more objective, others avoid passive voice whenever possible because it can give text a stilted, awkward tone (few people talk in passive voice), and is often unclear. Active voice makes text livelier and more interesting. Compare the examples in Table 3-1 and see how much easier the active voice sentences are to understand.

 Your résumé will be more interesting and convey an action-orientation if you write it primarily in active voice rather than passive voice. The grammar checkers in some word processors alert writers to excessive use of passive voice.

Passive Voice	Active Voice
The text is highlighted by clicking the bold button.	Highlight the text by clicking the bold button.
The USB drive gets inserted into an available USB slot.	Insert the USB drive into an available slot.
The file is read from the disk.	The computer reads the file from the disk.
Touching the disk media should be avoided.	Avoid touching the disk media.

Table 3-1 Passive versus active voice

Nominalization

Nominalization is the use of *-tion, -ing, -ment* and other word endings to create nouns out of verbs. In general, avoid nominalization; verbs are easier to understand. Table 3-2 shows examples of sentences using nominalization as well as their improved forms.

Nominalization	Improved Form
Development of a JavaScript module will take three weeks.	The project team will develop a JavaScript module in three weeks.
Perform an installation of the printer driver.	Install the printer driver.
The configuration of the system should take about an hour.	The system takes about an hour to configure.

Table 3-2 Nominalization examples

Wordiness

Wordiness can lead to long sentences and hinder understanding. Avoid unnecessary words; find the shortest way to state your ideas. Table 3-3 presents several examples of how to reduce unnecessary words.

Wordy	Concise
Call customer support to raise questions about the problem you are having.	Call customer support to ask about the problem.
Prior to the actual installation of the system…	Before installing the system…
Before making an attempt to install the card…	Before installing the card…
Put the computer in a location where it will not be in danger of being harmed by anyone who might be passing by.	Locate the computer where passersby will not accidentally damage it.

Table 3-3   Reducing wordiness

To make text easier to read, use short words whenever possible. Replace long words such as *approximately* with a shorter word that means the same thing, such as *about*; replace *utilize* with *use*, and try *document* instead of *documentation*. Can you think of other examples?

ON THE WEB

For some examples of common wordiness to identify and avoid in technical writing, see an article titled "Deadwood Phrases" (**www.klariti.com/technical-writing/Deadwood%20Phrases.shtml**).

Jargon

Computer technology often intimidates end users because of the amount of jargon used to describe and discuss it. Avoid the use of **jargon**, words understood only by those experienced in a field. Instead, use simple, direct words that anyone can understand, unless you are certain the target audience will understand the jargon. For example, technical writers may write about the *cold boot process* for a computer system. However, in documents for new users, use a term like *start-up process* or *power-on step* instead.

If you must use jargon terms, define them first so you and the reader share a common understanding of the vocabulary. Writers often include a glossary at the end of a chapter or book, much like the key terms list at the end of the chapters in this book.

Undefined Acronyms

Like jargon, an **acronym**—a word formed from the initial letters of words in a phrase—can make technical writing difficult to understand. For example, *I/O* is an acronym for *input/output*; *RAM* is an acronym for *random access memory*. Writers should define the meaning of each acronym for a reader, unless the target audience will obviously understand the acronym. For example, most users today probably understand that PC stands for *personal* *computer*. Even for technical audiences, play it safe and define each acronym. The first time an acronym is used, spell out the words it represents, and then include the acronym in parentheses:

Three main types of random access memory (RAM) are in common use today: SDRAM (Synchronous Dynamic RAM), DDR-SDRAM (Double Data Rate SDRAM), and RDRAM (RAMBUS Dynamic RAM). Of the three, DDR-SDRAM is dominant in today's market.

Including acronyms in a glossary or a key terms list is another effective strategy.

Dangling Modifiers

A **dangling modifier** is a phrase (or even a single word) at the beginning or end of a sentence that adds little to the meaning and only makes the sentence longer. Sometimes, dangling modifiers can make a sentence unclear and confusing. The following four sentences include dangling modifiers:

Example 1: *The Accounting Department is eager to begin training on QuickBooks, generally.*

Example 2: *Generally, the Accounting Department is eager to begin training on QuickBooks.*

Example 3: *Mohammed turned on the LCD projector, but the image did not appear, as everyone noticed.*

Example 4: *After trying several troubleshooting approaches, the problem remained unsolved.*

Either eliminate the dangling phrase, if it makes little difference to the meaning of the sentence, or look for a way to include it in the sentence.

Revision of examples 1 and 2: *The Accounting Department is generally eager to begin training on QuickBooks.*

Revision of example 3: *When Mohammed turned on the LCD projector, everyone noticed that the image did not appear.*

Revision of example 4: *Mohammed tried several troubleshooting approaches, but the problem remained unsolved.*

This list of potential writing problems is long, and we've only covered a few common mistakes. However, many technical writers find that with practice and experience, they become adept at avoiding these problems.

ON THE WEB

Paul Brians, an English professor at Washington State University, has compiled a list of common mistakes in language use (**www.wsu.edu/~brians/errors/index.html**).

Another useful resource for information on common mistakes in technical writing is **www.docsymmetry.com/mistakes-technical-writers-make.html**.

A ROLE-PLAYING SCENARIO

The role-playing activity in this chapter is in the form of a written response to an email from a user, Erin, in the Accounting Department where you work. Your task is to prepare a response to Erin's email.

From: *Erin@Accounting.SPI.com*

To: *UserSupport@IT.SPI.com*

My computer has been running slower and slower recently. One of my coworkers in Accounting said I probably need to check my computer for something called a key logger. I know nothing about that. How can I learn how to check my PC for a key logger? Could they slow my machine down? Where can I get a program that checks for a key logger? How do I know if this will even help?

Write an email response to Erin from UserSupport@IT.SPI.com. Make your response an example of a well-written email message. Then compare your response with that of your colleagues or coworkers. Based on what you learned from the comparison, how would you improve your response to Erin?

Technical Writing Tools

Many word-processing programs include tools that support staff can use to develop useful user documentation. These include:

- An outline tool to help organize work

- A spell checker to identify and correct spelling errors

- A custom dictionary to check the spelling of jargon words, acronyms, and technical terms

- A thesaurus to help find a word that clearly expresses a concept

- A grammar checker to recommend changes in wording to improve readability

- A readability index to measure the level of difficulty of the text

- Desktop publishing features to help writers produce professional-looking documents

Even with all these built-in software tools, a good collegiate dictionary (in print or online) is also a useful tool, because spell checkers don't know the meaning of words. Be on the lookout for good examples of well-written documents. Be critical of documents you read. Ask yourself what makes a document or message useful and easy to read, and by the same token, what makes a document difficult to understand and use.

125

ON THE WEB

The Merriam-Webster dictionary is accessible online (**www.merriam-webster.com**).

One of the classic books on writing clearly in English is *The Elements of Style* by William Strunk, Jr. and E. B. White (4th edition: Longman, 1999). An earlier online version of this entire book is available on the Bartleby.com Web site (**www.bartleby. com/141**). Many writers consider *The Elements of Style* to be the bible of written communication. Another popular online resource is the *Chicago Manual of Style*, which can be found online (**www.chicagomanualofstyle.org**).

Microsoft publishes the *Microsoft Manual of Style for Technical Publications* (3rd edition: Microsoft Press, 2004).

Documentation Evaluation Criteria

All technical writers have personal preferences and writing styles. Although writers may disagree on specific style issues, the ultimate measure of user documentation is whether it effectively and efficiently communicates information the reader needs. For technical writers, *effectively* means readers get the correct information they need to master a topic or to perform a task. *Efficiently* means readers do not have to spend extra time searching for information or reading through irrelevant material to find what they need.

Four general criteria can be used as a checklist to evaluate written documents:

- Content
  - Is the information relevant?
  - Is the information timely and accurate?
  - Is the coverage of the topic complete?
- Organization
  - Is the information easy to locate?
  - Are transitions between topics identifiable?
  - Can readers get in and out quickly with the answer they need?
- Format
  - Does the layout help guide the reader?
  - Is the format consistent?

- Mechanics

  - Are words spelled correctly?

  - Is it grammatically correct?

  - Is the writing style effective?

As you plan, write, review, and revise your writing, think about how it measures up to these criteria. The principles and practices you learned in this chapter apply to all the forms of documentation a user support specialist creates. Regardless of a document's intended use, the purpose remains the same: clear communication that addresses readers' needs by giving them concise information they can use.

 The hands-on activities and case projects at the end of this chapter give you an opportunity to use the guidelines presented in this chapter in your own writing. The activities and projects are important parts of the chapter and will help you develop your writing skills.

Chapter Summary

- User support staff are frequently assigned technical writing tasks to produce brochures, flyers, newsletters, handouts, training aids, user guides, computer manuals, online help files, email, chat and text messages, Web pages, proposals, memos, operating procedure documentation, and troubleshooting guides.

- The goal of technical writing is to produce documents and messages that effectively and efficiently communicate information needed by the reader.

- A technical writing task begins by defining the characteristics of the target audience, including their background and reading level. Each document should be planned with a clear understanding of what the writer wants the reader to be able to do after reading it.

- In technical documents, short words and sentences are preferable to long ones. Information should be organized so it is easy to locate. The purpose of a document and its intended audience should be clearly stated so each reader can decide at the beginning whether to read the document.

- The process of technical writing includes organizing ideas and topics into an outline and expanding the outline into a first draft. Edit passes through a document are intended to eliminate extra words, tighten prose, and check for format consistency and technical accuracy. A review by another person is a useful check to improve a document before the final revision.

- The layout of a document should help a reader understand the organization, know what is important, and be aware when transitions between topics occur. Formatting should be used consistently to enhance the information presented, not detract from it.

- Successful technical writers use strategies such as analogies, repetition, consistent word use, and parallel structure to help the audience understand the material.

- Common problems to avoid in technical documents include clutter, inappropriate typefaces, gender references, unclear referents, and passive voice. Other common problems are nominalization, wordiness, jargon, undefined acronyms, and dangling modifiers.

- Several software tools, including an outline tool, spell checker, thesaurus, grammar checker, and desktop publishing features, are available to help technical writers produce well-organized, accurate, and professional-looking documentation.

- Writers use four criteria—content, organization, format, and mechanics—to evaluate a technical document.

Key Terms

acronym—A word formed from the initial letters of words in a phrase; for example, *RAM* is an acronym for *random access memory*; define acronyms to ensure readers' understanding.

active voice—A sentence in which the subject performs the action indicated by the verb; for example: *Mary will present a tutorial on Excel macros on Monday;* compare to passive voice.

analogy—A comparison between an unfamiliar concept and a familiar one; an analogy highlights the similarities between things; for example, a computer hard disk is like a filing cabinet.

brainstorm—A method used to generate a list of potential ideas or topics; the brainstormed list is then prioritized and pared down, as needed.

dangling modifier—A phrase (or a single word) at the beginning or end of a sentence that adds little to the meaning of the sentence; can make a sentence unclear and confusing.

documentation—Written communication intended to provide user support information to end users or coworkers; can be printed or online; includes brochures, flyers, newsletters, handouts, training aids, user guides, handbooks, manuals, online help systems, proposals, letters, memos, email and chat messages, procedural and operational documentation, Web pages, and troubleshooting guides.

format consistency check—An edit pass through a draft document in which a writer checks to make sure that the headings and subheadings, fonts, indentation, centering, boldface, italics, underlining, and other format elements are used consistently throughout a document.

hierarchical organization—A document organization style that flows from top to bottom; information is arranged from general to specific; online help systems are an example.

hypertext link—A highlighted word or phrase in a document that acts as a pointer to additional information; when a user clicks a link, the software displays a Web page, opens a different document, jumps to another location in the current document, or displays a popup window.

jargon—Words that are understood only by those experienced in a field; for example, *hacker* is jargon, whereas *unauthorized user* is more general; define jargon words to ensure that readers understand them.

justified text—A document or paragraph format in which the text is extended to both the right and left margins; commonly used in books and newspapers, but can be difficult to read.

nominalization—The use of *-tion, -ing, -ment* and other word endings to create nouns; for example, *Capitalization can be performed with the Change Case command* could be rewritten to avoid nominalization as: *To capitalize words, use the Change Case command.*

parallel structure—A writing strategy in which similar items are treated consistently throughout a document; examples include consistent verb tenses and consistent phrasing in lists.

passive voice—A sentence in which the subject of a sentence *receives* the action indicated by the verb; for example, "*The documentation was prepared by me*" is in passive voice, whereas "*I prepared the documentation*" is in active voice.

pointer—A cross-reference in a document indicating where a user can find more information on a topic; often used in technical writing to reduce the size of a document by including directions to appendices, attachments, exhibits, figures, tables, and other related materials.

reference format—A documentation style that pulls together all the information on a specific topic in a single page, section, or chapter; compare to tutorial format.

referent—A concrete word or concept that is designated by another word; for example, in "*Before you insert a CD, inspect it for scratches,*" the word *CD* is the referent of *it*; avoid pronouns such as *it*, *them*, and *their* when the referent is unclear.

sans serif typeface—A style of type that does not have fine lines (serifs) added to each character; often used in titles and headings; compare with serif typeface.

sequential organization—A document organization style that follows a step-by-step approach whereby information is arranged in the order in which the steps are executed; procedural documents are examples.

serif typeface—A style of type in which each character includes fine lines (called *serifs*) that project from the top and bottom of each letter; serifs lead the reader's eye from letter to letter across the line, improving readability; compare with sans serif typeface.

specialty typeface—A style of type that is intended for special uses, such as invitations, brochures, or flyers; draws attention to text, although it makes general text more difficult to read; script typefaces are an example.

style sheet—A list of common terms, formats, and writing conventions that describes a department's or organization's preferred usage and spelling so writers use consistent terminology and formats.

technical accuracy check—An edit pass through a draft in which a writer tests any procedural or technical steps in a document by performing them with the hardware or software; helps reduce errors in step-by-step instructions or other technical information.

tutorial format—A documentation style that guides a user step-by-step through the features of a program with frequently used features covered first; compare to reference format.

Check Your Understanding

Answers to Check Your Understanding questions are in Appendix A.

1. True or False? The primary goal of technical writing is to entertain readers and hold their interest.

2. A(n) _____ is a short document primarily intended to summarize material covered in a training session and promote recall.

3. True or False? All users prefer online documentation to printed documentation because accessing necessary information is easier.

4. Documentation that is organized as a step-by-step introduction to the features of a computer program is called a:

    a. reference manual   c. tutorial manual
    b. technical manual   d. troubleshooting manual

5. True or False? Effectively written user documents should result in a lower volume of user support calls and emails.

6. Which of the following forms of documentation often contain hyperlinks to related topics?

    a. online help systems   c. user manuals
    b. newsletters   d. troubleshooting guides

7. True or False? Good technical documents should provide a reader with everything they would ever want to know about a topic.

8. A(n) _____ is an attempt to relate something a reader may be familiar with to something they need to know about.

9. What is the correct sequence of the following steps in the technical writing process? (1) proofread the document; (2) generate a list of ideas; (3) arrange for an outside reviewer; (4) write a first draft

    a. 1 – 2 – 3 – 4   c. 4 – 2 – 1 – 3
    b. 2 – 4 – 3 – 1   d. 2 – 1 – 4 – 3

10. True or False? An outside review of a technical document serves the same purpose as a beta test of a software package.

11. True or False? Changes in case, font, indentation, and centering are format elements used to help the reader of a document understand its structure.

12. The information on a Web site should be expected to have all of the following characteristics except:

    a. complete

    b. concise

    c. includes pointers to other information

    d. well organized

13. True or False? A technical writer should use the same word to refer to an object or a concept throughout a document rather than a variety of different words that are synonyms.

14. A reading level that is appropriate for most technical documentation is:

    a. 4th–5th grade   c. 10th–12th grade
    b. 7th–8th grade   d. college level

15. Whether to use the form 'Plug-n-Play' or 'Plug-and-Play' in a document would likely be specified in a(n) _____.

16. True or False? The following example of a list illustrates good parallel structure:

    1. *Move the mouse pointer to the button of your choice.*

    2. *Next, click the button on the mouse.*

    3. *You then click on "OK."*

17. To avoid jargon, a technical writer might substitute a word(s) such as _____ for *head crash* in the following sentence: *Users frequently lose their data when there is a head crash on the file server.*

18. _____ is a method used to generate a list of potential ideas or topics to include in a document.

19. A document organization style in which all the information on a topic is pulled together in one place is called:

    a. reference format

    b. hierarchical format

    c. tutorial format

    d. sequential format

20. True or False? Because the default font in most word processors is a sans serif typeface, technical writers should use the default in the body text to improve a document's readability.

21. True or False? A hypertext link in a document is a word or phrase that uses a fancy Word Art format to draw attention to the text.

Discussion Questions

1. *"Because email, chat, and text messages are less formal methods of communication, good technical writing skills are less important for these messages."* Do you agree or disagree with this statement? Explain why.

2. In order to avoid using gender-related pronouns, some writers use a plural pronoun with a singular subject. For example: *"A technical writer should choose their words carefully"*. Other alternatives are: *"A technical writer should choose his or her words carefully"*; and, *"Technical writers should choose their words carefully"*. Which format do you prefer? Discuss these alternatives and other ways around this writing challenge.

3. All professions use technical jargon terms and acronyms. Professionals such as health care workers, accountants, and lawyers can frequently be difficult to understand. Is the rationale, "All professionals use jargon and acronyms" a good justification for computer professionals to use them?

4. Discuss some ways to determine whether the target audience for a document will understand various acronyms and jargon terms. Brainstorm some effective ways to deal with these terms if a writer is not sure whether the audience will understand them.

5. *"If one purpose of a flyer is to advertise an event, a writer should use as many design elements (fonts, bold, italic, underlining, color, shading, clip art) as possible to attract attention to the flyer."* Do you agree or disagree with this statement? Explain your position.

6. *"If a technical writer has a choice of reading levels for a document (as measured by a readability index), it is preferable to aim for a reading level that is a little too high, rather than a little too low, which might insult the intelligence of your readers."* Explain your position on this statement.

Hands-On Activities

Activity 3-1

Revise existing documents. The following sentences and paragraphs highlight some of the problems you learned about in this chapter. Use what you have learned to rewrite the examples to make them clear and readable.

1. From a one-page notice informing employees which machines they can use in a training facility:

   Employees should be well advised that they should use only the first row of machines, the HP PCs. All other machines are used only for classes for training new users. If an employee doesn't do this, he will be asked to leave the training room.

2. From an email message sent to all employees of a law firm advising them to be alert for a new virus:

   This virus has been known to cause the destruction of files, and it is very important that you perform a search of your hard drive to try and attempt eradication of it using the search feature. Search for .EDT file extensions and delete them. Then the problem will be solved.

3. From an instruction sheet that will be handed out during a training session on a new email package; this passage explains the capabilities of the package to users who have never used email before:

   Email messages are stored on a central server, and you download it every time you open one, in effect. You can save it to a local disk if you want to keep it.

4. From a booklet that a user support department will distribute to employees of an insurance organization to explain the capabilities of a new software claims management package:

   This is a new type of CMS (claims management software) that every adjuster, regardless of his level, will benefit from, greatly. This claims management software can: (1) organize claims information, (2) be used while you are on the telephone, (3) do reports by claim type, and (4) for generation of summary claims information.

Activity 3-2

Write and compare procedural documentation. Write an explanation of the steps required to insert a USB flash drive into a USB port. Your explanation should be aimed at a person who has never used a computer before.

Exchange explanations with a classmate or coworker and critique each other's draft. Did you include enough information for the user to insert the USB flash drive correctly? Is your explanation complete, or did you leave out important information about the steps? Did you include extra unnecessary information?

Find an inexperienced user to test your document. Have that person use your document without any assistance to see if he or she can perform the task using only your written documentation. Revise your instructions based on the peer and user feedback you receive.

Activity 3-3

Revise procedure documentation. The instructions below are intended to describe the steps for running a defragmentation utility under Windows. Your task is to revise the document following the guidelines in this chapter so it is a good example of technical writing.

*These instructions will run the Windows defragmenter program, which is named **defrag.exe**, once a week on Friday afternoon at 6PM. Of course, you can change the schedule to whatever time you desire.*

1. *Click on **Add a Scheduled Task** from the **Scheduled Tasks Wizzard**, which you can find in the **Control Panel.***

2. *Click **Next** and the user will see a list of programs he can schedule.*

3. *Note that the **defragger.exe** does not appear, so click on **Browse.***

4. *Browse lets you find defrag.exe in this path: **C:\Windows\System32\defrag.exe**. Click on **Open.***

5. *Next, please give the task Wizzard the name of the task, such as **defrag** and then set up the schedule.*

6. *When you click on **Weakly** and **Next.***

7. *Type in the start time, which is **6:00 PM** and click the box for **Friday.***

8. *Windows will ask you what user name and password to use to login the defragger.*

9. *You are done.*

Activity 3-4

Revise a textbook paragraph. The following document is an excerpt from a computer textbook. It contains examples of many of the common problems described in this chapter. (The line numbers are for your convenience to identify and refer to problems).

First, go through the document and note the problems that you find with it. If you are working as part of a project group, compare your list of problems with others to see where group members agree and disagree. Second, rewrite the document to correct the problems you identified. Your rewrite should make the document as clear and as easy to understand as possible. Your instructor may be able to provide you with a copy of the document in machine-readable form.

1. *MANAGING FOLDERS AND DISKS*

2.

3. *Introduction*

4.

5.   *There are many types of storage media today. Hard disks are the most*

6.   *common. It is the best of all the possible ways to save data. A hard*

7.   *drive is divided into various folders so that files can be*

8.   *saved to them. Definitely, this is the most efficient way to manage a large*

9.   *number of files stored on a disk.*

10.

11.   *Various commands, especially those dealing with disks and*

12.   *directories, produce lots of computer numbers. To get a handle*

13.   *on computer numbers, you need to get the big picture on bits, bytes,*

14.   *megabytes, and gigabytes.*

15.   *A computer may seem intelligent, but essentially it can "understand"*

16.   *only whether power is on or not. To issue an instruction to a computer,*

17.   *we need to go by 1 (on) or 0 (off). The two digits of 1 and 0 are the*

18.   *foundation of binary (base 2) math. Binary math is based on bits, which*

19.   *is a contraction of two words—binary digit. One bit can have the*

20.   *value of either 1 or 0. Bits get a little large to move around, so*

21.   *programmers combine 8 bits together to form a byte. Bytes can increase*

22.   *in number: 1 byte can store a 1; 1 KB (kilobyte) is the same as 1024; 1 MB*

23.   *(megabyte) is 1048576; and 1073742824 equals 1 GB. So, when you*

24.   *hear that a disk has a 40 GB capacity, it can store 40 × 1074742824 =*

25.   *42989712960 bytes.*

26.

27.   *Formatting of Disks*

28.

29.   *When you create a file you need to store it on a hard disc. Before that,*

30.   *it must be properly prepared to receive information (formatted). If you*

31.   *have used a disk and it has some space on it, you can not follow this section.*

32.

33.   *While it was being formatted, the disk was divided into a number of*

34.   *concentric rings or tracks. Each track was separated into a number of*

35. *sectors. Each sector stored 512 bytes. A higher capacity disk contains*

36. *more tracks and sectors; that is how they stored more data, for your*

37. *information.*

Activity 3-5

Experiment with format and font variations. Select a short description of a simple computer task, such as the procedure for inserting a USB flash drive into a USB port from Activity 3-2. The description should include at least two headings and some procedural steps. Format the document in three ways, using font and style variations. Show the three versions to three classmates or colleagues. Ask them to choose which one is easiest to read and then to explain their preferences. Write a short summary of their responses and describe the conclusions you reached about document formatting from this activity.

Activity 3-6

Evaluate and rewrite a document. Find a piece of computer documentation, a memo, or other technical writing that you wrote prior to reading this chapter. The document you select should be at least one page and contain two or more paragraphs. Apply the concepts and ideas you have learned in this chapter to critique the document; revise it to correct any problems you discovered.

If the word processor you use has a readability index feature, check the reading level of your revised document. Then revise the document to lower its readability index by at least one grade level (for example, if your rewritten document is at 10th grade level, modify the document until the readability index is at a 9th grade level).

Have a classmate or coworker review your work and make suggestions. Do you agree with her or his suggestions? Explain why or why not. Use the suggestions to revise your work.

Activity 3-7

Evaluate online documentation. Visit a Microsoft Web page that displays information about the accessibility features in Internet Explorer 9, at **www.microsoft.com/enable/ products/ie9**.

Analyze and critique the Web site based on the information you have learned in this chapter. Remember that the target audience for this site is users who have physical limitations that might affect their ability to use Web browser software. Write a one-page summary of your evaluation, with recommendations on how you would improve the documentation. Include in your analysis how the Web site document meets or doesn't meet the four evaluation criteria described in this chapter.

Activity 3-8

Revise a section in this chapter. The last section in this chapter, *Documentation Evaluation Criteria*, describes four criteria a writer can use to evaluate technical writing. Apply what you have learned about technical writing in this chapter by completing the following analysis of that section:

- With three or four of your colleagues, critique the *Documentation Evaluation Criteria* section of the chapter.

- Apply the criteria described in that section to the section itself. What are the strengths of the section? What improvements could be made?

- Based on your evaluation, write an evaluation and describe how you would modify the section for the next edition of this book.

Activity 3-9

Rewrite information in a user's manual. Some writing examples from a poorly written MP3 user's guide are posted at **web.techwr-l.com/pipermail/techwr-l/2006-April/004066. html**. Copy and paste the excerpts included on this Web page into a word-processing document. Then rewrite each instruction to make each instruction as clear to the reader as possible.

Case Projects

1. Web Search Guide for Sergio Escobar

Sergio Escobar is the supervisor of a computer facility used by trainees in a job retraining program. The computer facility has 18 Apple Mac computers, which are used by the trainees to improve their job skills and to aid them in their job search efforts. Sergio has recently connected the Macs to a network to provide Internet access. However, the trainees he serves do not have good Web search skills, and many are frustrated that they cannot find useful employment information on the Web.

Sergio posted a few URLs for various local and regional job banks, but he knows information online changes daily. He also knows that if trainees knew how, they could use the Web to research organizations in preparation for job interviews. As a support specialist, you are assigned to work with Sergio to prepare some basic documentation for the trainees on how to do information searches on the Web. Use the search engine you are most familiar with for this case project.

Create a short document titled "Guide to Web Searches" that Sergio can give to users of the facility he supervises. The document should include a description of how to use a search engine, instructions on how to enter a search term and how to narrow a search, and helpful Web search strategies. It should include some examples that relate to job search strategies. The document should be self-contained and designed for use outside a classroom environment. Use the online documentation published by one or more organizations that provide Web search engines as a resource.

If you work in a group with other workers or students, post several examples of group members' documents and let each member nominate the guide they think best meets the four criteria for good documents discussed in the chapter.

2. Orientation Guide for The Career School

As a user support specialist for a computer lab at The Career School, you have been assigned the task of developing a lab orientation guide aimed at new students who use the facility. Prepare a one-sheet (two pages printed back to back) summary of information for new users of the lab. You can use the policies of a lab environment you are familiar with, such as a facility at your school or workplace. First, describe who uses the lab. Orient your guide to those users.

Your orientation guide can include basic information about lab operating policies and procedures, instructions on logging in and out of the network, directions to access popular software packages, information on proper printing procedures, guidelines on the use of resource materials, and other general or technical information you think should be included. You may want to include short sections with information aimed at students in specific courses or training sessions.

For ideas on topics you might want to include, think about what information a new student or trainee would want to know. For inspiration, go to the lab and look at the postings on bulletin boards, whiteboards, walls, doors, machines, and tables. Rely on your own experience as a user or as a lab assistant. One of the goals of this writing project is to replace as much of the verbal instructions given by lab staff and as many printed signs as possible with an information sheet that the lab staff can distribute to new users.

3. Templates for Rocky Mountain Consultants

Erica Allan is the supervisor of documentation for Rocky Mountain Consultants, a firm that provides consulting services to engineering organizations. She recently received a request from several departments at Rocky Mountain to design a memo form that each department can adopt and use as its standard memo format. Erica wants to accommodate each department, but is short of staff she can assign to the project. Erica also feels strongly that it would be more useful to give each department the tools it needs to develop its own memo template, rather than designing a template for each department.

Erica wants you to develop an instructional document aimed at word-processor users that describes the procedure to create a simple template. (Use whichever word processor you have access to for this project.) Although each department wants a different and distinctive memo format, Erica suggests you use a simple memo like the one shown in Figure 3-8 as an example. Describe the fonts and format features necessary to create a template that looks as much like the example as possible. Your document should include the steps a user would follow to create and store a template for the memo in the figure. Prepare a document titled

"How to Prepare a Simple Memo Template" that describes the process to users at Rocky Mountain Consultants.

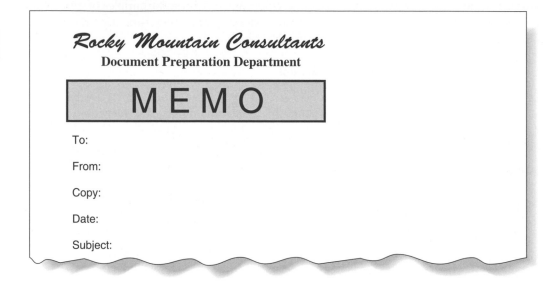

Figure 3-8   Sample memo format

4. Cartridge Recycling at Re-Nu-Cartridge

Elma McDonald works in the Production Department at Re-Nu-Cartridge, a local company that refills ink and toner cartridges for computer printers. Elma's job is to clean and inspect inkjet and toner cartridges before they are refilled. With the equipment at Re-Nu-Cartridge, Elma can clean several types of common cartridges. However, the company does not have the facilities to clean all types of cartridges, especially less common ones. Several of Re-Nu-Cartridge's environmentally responsible corporate customers have asked Elma for information about how to recycle cartridges that can't be refilled.

Elma would like you to use the Web to research companies that recycle ink and toner cartridges. See if you can find more than one company that offers a cartridge recycling service. Based on your research, write a set of instructions for recycling cartridges. Your documentation should be targeted at employees of Re-Nu-Cartridge's customers (but would probably be useful to anyone who uses printer cartridges). The information sheet should include instructions on how to package and ship used cartridges to recycle service centers, details on which cartridges the recyclers will take, where to send the cartridges, information on what the service costs (if anything), a description of the benefits of using a cartridge recycle service, and any other information someone would need to use the recycle services. Follow the guidelines for good technical writing in this chapter to make the recycling instruction sheet an example of your best professional documentation.

5. Describe a support problem you solved.

Chapter 5 in this book includes descriptions of common support problems, some of which are based on actual reports by support specialists who solved the problems. Your task in this assignment is to write a descriptive report, similar to those in Chapter 5, of a support incident or situation that you worked on and resolved. Your report should describe the situation, the end user(s), the problem you solved, the method and steps you took to solve the problem, and what you learned from the experience. Make your report an example of your best professional technical writing—write your report as if you were preparing it to include in the next edition of this textbook. If you do this exercise as part of a class or training assignment, share your report with others so they can benefit from your problem-solving and writing experience.

6. Document a utility tool for a support specialist.

Chapter 12 in this book describes several utility software tools that support specialists might use themselves or in their work with users. Select one of the utilities in Chapter 12 or a similar utility you are familiar with. Write a document targeted to other user support specialists. The purpose of your document is to describe the following:

- The purpose of the utility software tool

- Where to download the utility tool

- How to install the software

- How to use the software tool to solve a typical problem and what the output (results) of the software mean

- Any problems you think a support specialist might encounter with the download, installation, and use of the software tool

- Where to get additional information about the use of the utility software tool

After you have written your first draft, exchange it with a colleague and get his or her feedback on your document. Then revise your draft based on the feedback you receive.

CHAPTER 4

Skills for Troubleshooting Computer Problems

In this chapter, you will learn about:

◎ The troubleshooting process and the thinking skills required for successful troubleshooting

◎ Communication skills for troubleshooting

◎ Information resources to help solve computer problems

◎ Diagnostic and repair tools used to troubleshoot computer problems

◎ Strategies for troubleshooting

◎ How to develop your own approach to problem solving

Solving computer problems is one of the most critical and frequent tasks user support agents perform. End users bring a variety of issues to user support agents, including requests for information, questions about how to perform a task, complaints about a product or feature, and problems that prevent end users from operating hardware or software. Many problems are relatively easy for support agents to solve quickly. Agents may have seen the problems before and know the solution, or they may be able to find the solution quickly in a database of problem solutions.

Some problems are more challenging and difficult to solve, such as ones that support agents have never encountered and those for which the solutions are not obvious. Despite attempts to find a quick solution, the problem-solving effort may not succeed at first. On occasion, a seemingly straightforward problem report may turn out to be the first in a long series of incidents about a significant problem with a new or recently modified product.

This chapter describes the tools, methods, and strategies that support agents use to work on user problems, especially difficult ones. After examining these strategies, you will be encouraged to use these tools to develop your own problem-solving skills.

What is Troubleshooting?

Troubleshooting is defining, diagnosing, and solving computer problems. Some people think that a fixed sequence of steps can be followed to diagnose and repair any malfunction with computer hardware, software, or networks. The ability to follow a sequence of steps, such as those used to install a software package, is an important job skill for support agents. However, no single sequence of steps is likely to diagnose every computer problem. Troubleshooting computer problems is frequently more complex than that.

Troubleshooting is often an **iterative process**—a process that involves several paths or approaches to problem solving. A troubleshooter may follow one sequence of steps for a while and then loop back and perform other, perhaps similar, steps along a different path. The process can include many false starts and temporary roadblocks as a troubleshooter pursues an approach, hits a dead end, switches to an alternate approach, and makes some progress, only to hit a snag and be required to start down another path. Figure 4-1 graphically compares a sequential process with an iterative one.

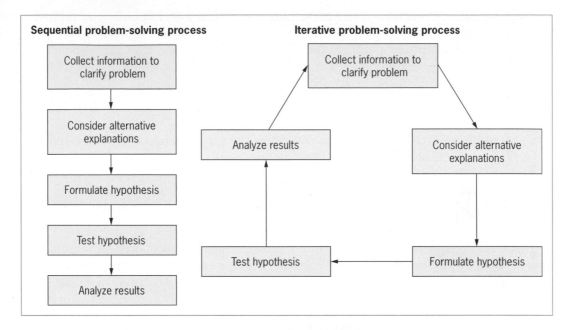

Figure 4-1   Sequential versus iterative problem-solving processes

An iterative process may seem repetitious, and in a way it is. Troubleshooting is not always a neat, linear, and orderly process. It is often both a logically structured and a creative process that requires flexibility, thinking skills, and patience. It is partly a scientific process that follows rules of logic and partly a creative process that relies on insight and ingenuity.

The approach to troubleshooting advocated in this chapter differs from two alternate approaches, the first of which treats troubleshooting as a fixed sequence of steps one follows until a problem is solved. Sometimes a predefined sequence of steps moves troubleshooters toward resolution, and sometimes it doesn't. A second troubleshooting approach might be described as a hit-or-miss strategy (sometimes called *trial-and-error*). It consists of randomly trying various things in hopes of eventually hitting on something that works. A troubleshooter who decides to "*poke around and see what I can find*" is using the hit-or-miss approach. Occasionally, a hit-or-miss approach stumbles across a solution and resolves a problem, but often it doesn't. And sometimes troubleshooters using the hit-or-miss approach try things that actually make matters worse.

Like woodworkers, computer troubleshooters use a variety of tools and skills as they try to solve a difficult problem. They may pick up one tool, work on an aspect of a problem, set that tool aside for a while, and pick up another tool, only to turn back to a tool or skill used previously. The tools user support agents employ in troubleshooting can be physical tools, such as a diagnostic program or a database of information, or they can be thinking skills, such as problem solving, critical thinking, and decision making.

143

Problem-Solving Skills

The term **problem solving** is often used in business and mathematics to describe a process of moving from the current state of events X (the problem state) to a future, desired state of events Y (sometimes called the **goal state**). Figure 4-2 illustrates this process.

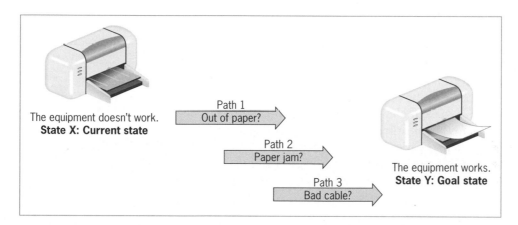

Figure 4-2   Problem-solving process

In Figure 4-2, the objective is to move from the problem state (the printer doesn't work) to the goal state (the printer works again). A problem solver is looking for a path from the problem state to the goal state that locates the correct answer. Good problem solvers are skilled at getting from problem to goal quickly, accurately, and efficiently.

Problem solvers use a variety of thinking skills. For example, a problem solver may analyze a problem on the basis of analogies or contradictions, as explained below:

- **Analogies**—In problem solving, an analogy is a comparison of the way in which the current problem is similar to other problems that have been solved previously; for example, *"This problem with the address book in Windows Live Mail is very similar to a problem with the address book I've seen in Outlook Express."*

- **Contradictions**—A **contradiction** is a fact established through investigation that rules out, or contradicts, a potential solution; for example, *"If this network card doesn't operate in one computer, but works in another one, the problem is unlikely to be a defective network card."*

Analyzing analogies and contradictions may lead a problem solver to a possible solution.

Critical-Thinking Skills

Critical thinking describes the cognitive skills a problem solver uses to analyze a situation, search for the underlying logic or rationale for it, and seek out alternate ways to explain it. To think critically is to use personal experience, the power of logical thinking, "mental models" of how things work, and various analytic tools to examine and understand a situation. To understand the possible causes for the observed behavior (or misbehavior) of a computer system, computer problem solvers often rely on critical-thinking skills such as those listed in Figure 4-3.

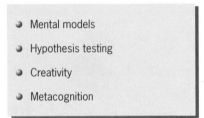

- Mental models

- Hypothesis testing

- Creativity

- Metacognition

Figure 4-3   Critical-thinking skills

Each of these critical-thinking skills is described in the following sections:

- **Mental models**—A **mental model** is a conceptual picture that a problem solver builds in order to understand how things work. Mental models are often based on education and experience. For example, when confronted with a software program that does not operate, a user support agent may construct a mental model of the sequence of steps a computer takes to find, load, and execute a program. Based on the model, the problem solver may formulate some hypotheses about which steps in the sequence could fail.

- **Hypothesis testing**—**Hypothesis testing** involves formulating a **hypothesis**—a guess or prediction based on experience—about the cause of a problem and then designing a test that will prove or disprove the hypothesis. Troubleshooters often formulate a hypothesis based on their mental model or prior experience with other problems. For example, a problem solver may make an initial guess that garbage characters output on a printer are due to a faulty signal cable from the computer to the printer, and then use critical-thinking skills to devise a series of tests to determine whether the signal cable is indeed the cause of the problem. A critical thinker may then look for another operational printer cable nearby to use in place of the original signal cable as a test.

- **Creativity**—In problem solving, **creativity** is the ability to find a novel or innovative solution to a problem. Creative troubleshooters have an ability to see a problem from new or different perspectives. For example, a computer problem solver may discover a unique solution to a problem he or she has never seen before by thinking about how a similar piece of hardware or software operates. Some troubleshooters refer to the search for a novel approach as thinking outside the mental model, or "thinking outside the box."

- **Metacognition**—The ability to think about thinking is called **metacognition**. Successful troubleshooters have the ability to step back from a problem-solving situation and analyze their thought processes. Using metacognition, for example, a troubleshooter may realize that he or she is assuming that a problem is hardware related, when, in fact, it may be software related. Metacognition is a critical-thinking skill that can help good troubleshooters become better ones, because it involves self-analysis and challenging one's assumptions.

- Examples of metacognitive questions that troubleshooters can ask themselves include:

    - What assumptions did I make that led me in the wrong direction?

    - Where did I go wrong solving this problem?

    - Why did one problem-solving approach work well in this situation when another one didn't?

    - How could I have thought differently about this problem to solve it more effectively or efficiently?

Decision-Making Skills

Decision making is the ability to select one alternative from among a number of alternatives, based on some evaluation criteria. For example, business decisions are often based on criteria such as lower cost, greater output volume, higher profit margin, improved quality, superior customer service, and better employee morale. Good decision makers often define several effective alternatives, weigh the pros and cons of each alternative against some predefined criteria, and reach a decision.

Decision making in computer problem solving is particularly important when support agents are confronted with several explanations for a problem. For example, when a number of diagnostic tests can be used to gather information, a problem solver must decide which test is most likely to produce useful and informative results. Selecting the wrong test could delay progress toward the correct solution and reduce the efficiency of the problem-solving process.

Troubleshooters routinely use skills such as problem solving, critical thinking, and decision making in their work—whether they are computer support agents, auto mechanics, clock repairers, or medical doctors. Several of the problem-solving scenarios in this and the next chapter illustrate problem-solving methods that use these thinking skills.

Tools Troubleshooters Use

Most successful troubleshooters use tools that fall into one of five broad categories, which are listed in Figure 4-4. Think about the tools you have used to work on computer problems in your own experience and try to determine how the tools fit into one of these categories.

- Communication skills
- Information resources
- Diagnostic and repair tools
- Problem-solving strategies
- Personal characteristics

Figure 4-4   Categories of problem-solving tools

Communication Skills

Communication and interpersonal skills are important troubleshooting tools, because most computer problem situations require at least some interaction with an end user, and sometimes with a computer hardware or software vendor. Troubleshooters use communication skills to get a basic description of a problem, to learn the user's perspectives on the problem, and to probe for additional information. After a problem has been solved, the troubleshooter also needs to effectively communicate the resolution to the user. The six principal types of communication skills used to troubleshoot computer problems are: basic listening skills, active listening, probes, critical questions, explanations, and verification skills. Successful support agents are adept at using these skills in almost every user support situation.

Basic Listening Skills

To start a troubleshooting challenge on the right foot, support agents try to obtain as accurate a description of the problem as possible from the user's perspective. Therefore, the foremost communication tools every troubleshooter needs are listening skills, or in some cases, reading skills.

Listen to the words the end user chooses to describe a problem. The danger of a support agent not listening carefully, or of not giving the user enough time to explain the problem, is that the agent may jump ahead of the user and begin to work on a solution before they really understand the problem. When troubleshooters turn their attention away from what a user is saying to focus on the solution to a problem, they can miss critical pieces of information. The result is a troubleshooting process that is less efficient and perhaps frustrating for the end user, who feels that he or she has to repeat information unnecessarily.

Listen to (or read) the user's description of the problem's symptoms. Some support agents take notes about the symptoms. Listen for causal, if-then statements of the form, *"If I do X, then the result is Y."* For example, *"If I try to adjust the monitor, then the screen goes blank,"* or, *"When I click Cancel, my system freezes."* User reports of computer behavior in this if-then form often provide clues that lead to a possible path toward a solution more quickly than simple statements such as, *"My LCD display doesn't work."*

Active Listening

If basic listening skills are the most important communication skill, active listening skills rate a close second place. In **active listening**, the listener is as engaged in the communication process as the speaker—rather than being a passive receiver of information. An active listening skill that is often extremely helpful to user support agents is **paraphrasing**, restating in your own words what you heard the user say. The user can then verify that you understood him or her. Paraphrasing is especially helpful to clarify a problem description and often leads to resolving misunderstandings about the nature of a problem. In describing a problem, a user might include unclear, unnecessary, or even contradictory information. As a troubleshooter paraphrases a problem statement, the user may correct the words to clarify the meaning.

 Avoid describing a problem with the user's identical words. Parroting is not a productive feedback technique and is unlikely to lead to clarifications.

The following examples show how paraphrasing can help clarify the problem definition:

- **End-user description**: *I don't know what happened, but the program doesn't work. I wonder if it is a defective program or if I am doing something wrong.*

- **Support agent paraphrase**: *Let me make sure I understand. The program used to work, but now it doesn't?*

- **End-user description**: *No, I just got the program installed, and it doesn't start up right. You would think they wouldn't sell this stuff until it operates correctly.*

- **Support agent paraphrase**: *So you installed the program following the instructions in the manual, and when you double-click the program icon, the program doesn't run at all?*

- **End-user description**: *Well, the box on the screen asks me for a file to open, but there are no files listed. Can't the program find its own files?*

- **Support agent paraphrase**: *So the program opens a window and starts to run, but when the Open Files dialog box appears, the file list is empty?*

ON THE WEB

Executive Blueprints has developed an eBook and a PowerPoint presentation (both media cover the same material) titled *Active Listening: Hear and Understand Content and Feeling in Communication*. If you would like to learn more about active listening skills, you can review their materials at **www.executiveblueprints.com/agenda/ 0306activelistening.htm**.

Probes

Follow-up questions intended to elicit more information from a user about a problem are called **probes**. Successful troubleshooters learn to ask effective follow-up questions to clarify their understanding of a problem situation. Consider the role-playing scenario that follows. See if you can identify the points at which the troubleshooter uses effective probes.

148

A ROLE-PLAYING SCENARIO

This is a transcript of a conversation between a user, Randy, and a support agent, Lou. If possible, have fellow students or coworkers play the parts of Randy and Lou, and then discuss Lou's use of probes.

RANDY: When I am in the middle of working on a spreadsheet or a text document, my computer frequently starts running another program automatically. Something just pops up in the middle of the screen and takes over my computer. Is there something wrong with the CPU or a short in the circuitry?

LOU: Maybe, but maybe not. When a program pops up in the middle of the screen, is it always the same program, or a different one each time?

RANDY: Usually it is my email program.

LOU: Does it ever automatically run any program other than email that you can remember?

RANDY: No, I guess not. Do I need to reinstall my email program?

LOU: How often does this problem happen?

RANDY: Every once in a while.

LOU: Like, once a week, once a day, or more often?

RANDY: It seems like several times a day.

LOU: Does the email program seem to pop up on a regular basis or at random times?

RANDY: Now that you mention it, it is probably about every half hour, or so.

LOU: Okay. Some email programs have a feature to automatically check to see if you have any new messages. That feature may be turned on in your email program. You can check the preferences to see if it is on, and if it is, either turn it off or set the time interval to a longer period, like one or more hours.

Notice the importance of probes as follow-ups in this scenario. Through a series of probing questions and careful listening, the troubleshooter was able to determine that what the user originally thought was a hardware problem probably wasn't, and to suggest a course of action to try to solve the problem for the user.

Critical Questions

Another helpful troubleshooting tool is a list of **critical questions**—questions designed to elicit important information from a user. These questions also serve to challenge common assumptions support agents may make (sometimes incorrectly) about a problem situation. Five examples of critical questions are:

- Has the problem system or component or feature *ever* worked?

- Have you ever had this problem before? When?

- Can this problem be replicated?

- What were you doing on your computer just before you first noticed the problem?

- Have you made any recent hardware or software changes to your system?

In their responses to critical questions, users often reveal information they perhaps wouldn't have thought to mention to a support agent. Consider several examples:

- A user might forget to say that her inability to print a specific CorelDRAW document is because she has *never* been able to print from CorelDRAW.

- A user may neglect to say that he encountered the same problem burning recordable DVDs the last time he bought a particular brand of inexpensive discs.

- A user may omit the information that a problem logging on to a network occurs in only one computer lab on campus and not in any other lab.

- A user might fail to mention that a power outage occurred immediately before she reported that her display screen no longer works correctly.

- A user may not tell a troubleshooter that his system became sluggish right after he installed a new version of the Microsoft Office software suite.

In each of these examples, responses to one of the five sample critical questions could provide important additional information, or force a support agent to challenge some assumptions he or she may have made—intentionally or unintentionally—about a problem situation. Critical questions often enable a support agent to move beyond a situation in which a problem investigation has reached a dead end.

ON THE WEB

In a course offered through the Knowledge Systems Institute, Professor C.Y. Hsieh provides his students with a list of critical questions in computer troubleshooting. View the questions at **pluto.ksi.edu/~cyh/cis370/ebook/ch13b.htm**.

All successful support agents have a checklist of favorite critical questions, such as those suggested earlier. These questions are especially useful in breaking new ground after an agent has asked every other question or probe he or she can think of, but still hasn't arrived at a solution.

Explanations

Communication skills are also important at the end of a troubleshooting session. Effective troubleshooters explain a problem's solution to the end user. **Explanations** involve a support agent describing the solution to a problem, so the user understands why the problem occurred and what steps are required to resolve it.

For many users, a word of explanation is helpful and is more satisfying than merely concluding, *"Click the Cancel button to fix the problem."* One way help desks and support groups can reduce repeated callbacks is to explain a problem solution at a level the user can understand. The user will then have some insight into the cause of the problem and into how the given solution fixes the problem. Otherwise, a user in the preceding example may incorrectly assume that the solution to every problem is to press the Cancel button.

Verification

Communication at the end of a troubleshooting process also provides important closure to the process. **Verification** is a communication skill that allows troubleshooters to confirm their perception that a problem is fixed. If the user's perception and troubleshooter's perspective are different, verification can help resolve the differences. Verification can be as simple as, *"I believe rebooting the router has restored your network connection. As a test, can you list your files in the folder on the server?"*

Information Resources

Support agents can't possibly have had prior experience with every problem situation they come across, so they must have access to information resources when they need to research solutions to problems that they have not yet encountered. Because new products and versions of software are released every day, support agents' prior experience and the information they can recall instantly are less important than their ability to use information resources effectively to locate what they need to know.

Technical information about how computer systems work—and an understanding of some reasons they don't—are invaluable in a troubleshooting situation. The more information support agents know from their experience (the better their mental models), the more likely they will be able to find a quick solution to a problem. However, all troubleshooters encounter problems they have never seen or problems with hardware or software they have never worked with. Examples of common information resources include personal experience, scripts and checklists, knowledge bases, coworkers and professional contacts, support vendors and contractors, and escalation and team problem solving.

Personal Experience

Most support agents have a personal store of knowledge—based on their education, career background, and previous experiences—that they bring to each problem-solving event. One of the first steps in any troubleshooting situation is to search your personal knowledge for information about the problem or related problems:

- Have I seen this problem before?

- How is this problem similar to or different from the problem I worked on last week?

- What did I do last time the printer beeped three times and quit printing?

- Do I have a good mental model of this problem situation?

This type of personal knowledge search usually happens almost automatically.

Successful troubleshooters often make notes after they have solved a problem. Notes can be informally organized in a loose-leaf binder or notebook or formally entered into a problem-solution database. Written troubleshooting notes can help avoid a situation in which troubleshooters too often find themselves: *"I know I've seen this problem before, but I don't remember what we did to fix it."* A notebook with reminders of past problems solved becomes an important personal resource for troubleshooters and can be used even if a help desk or support center doesn't have a formal record-keeping procedure. A troubleshooting notebook can be organized by symptoms, equipment or software category, or date or in any other logical way that makes the information easy to find.

 An alternative to an informal notebook or a more formal company-wide problem database is a personal database maintained by a support agent using Microsoft Access or another database product that can be sorted by date or product and searched by keywords.

Scripts and Checklists

Organizations that provide computer support on a contract basis and those that provide telephone help desk support often develop scripts and checklists to aid in troubleshooting. Among other benefits, these tools ensure that agents ask a standard set of questions and provide a uniform response to user questions. As you learned in Chapter 2, a script is a document that lists questions to ask, along with appropriate follow-up probes, depending on the user's response to each question. Often organized in the form of a flowchart or a decision tree, scripts are arranged in a logical sequence and cover many of the possible (known) paths to solve a problem. Although scripts tend to be oriented toward common problems, they can also contain valuable pointers to unusual problems, such as those that occur very infrequently or only in a few relatively rare configurations. Figure 4-5 shows an example of a script to diagnose problems with a hypothetical printer model based on the control panel LED lights.

 See Chapter 9 for more information on flowcharts.

151

Script: *SpeedJet Model 5 Printer Diagnostics* (revised March 8, 2012)

A SpeedJet Model 5 printer has several LEDs on its control panel that indicate its status: 1) ONLINE, 2) BUSY, and 3) OTHER LEDs. When a printer problem occurs, the behavior of the LEDs often provides important diagnostic information. Use the following script when a user calls about a problem with the SpeedJet Model 5 printer.

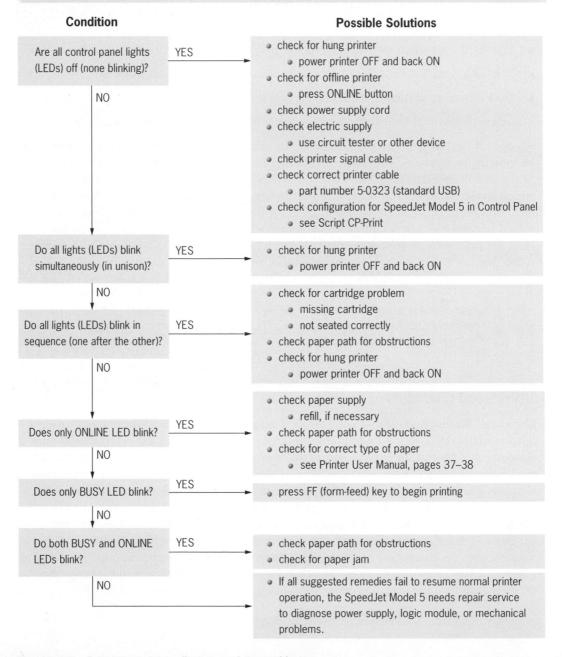

Condition

Possible Solutions

Are all control panel lights (LEDs) off (none blinking)? — YES

- check for hung printer
  - power printer OFF and back ON
- check for offline printer
  - press ONLINE button
- check power supply cord
- check electric supply
  - use circuit tester or other device
- check printer signal cable
- check correct printer cable
  - part number 5-0323 (standard USB)
- check configuration for SpeedJet Model 5 in Control Panel
  - see Script CP-Print

NO

Do all lights (LEDs) blink simultaneously (in unison)? — YES

- check for hung printer
  - power printer OFF and back ON

NO

Do all lights (LEDs) blink in sequence (one after the other)? — YES

- check for cartridge problem
  - missing cartridge
  - not seated correctly
- check paper path for obstructions
- check for hung printer
  - power printer OFF and back ON

NO

Does only ONLINE LED blink? — YES

- check paper supply
  - refill, if necessary
- check paper path for obstructions
- check for correct type of paper
  - see Printer User Manual, pages 37–38

NO

Does only BUSY LED blink? — YES

- press FF (form-feed) key to begin printing

NO

Do both BUSY and ONLINE LEDs blink? — YES

- check paper path for obstructions
- check for paper jam

NO

- If all suggested remedies fail to resume normal printer operation, the SpeedJet Model 5 needs repair service to diagnose power supply, logic module, or mechanical problems.

Figure 4-5 Example script to diagnose printer problems

ON THE WEB

For more information about the use of scripts in a call center environment, visit the Digisoft Web site (**www.crmxchange.com/whitepapers/pdf/digisoft-rfi.pdf**). Digisoft is a vendor of Telescript, a call center script-development tool.

For suggestions on developing a script for a telephone help desk, visit **www.helpdesknotes.com/2007/02/telephone_script_by_reader_request.html**.

To see examples of scripts implemented as a flowchart or a decision tree, visit **technet.microsoft.com/en-us/library/cc180183.aspx**, **www.mapitdesigner.com/examples/DemoMapit.htm**, or **support.mfm.com/support/troubleshooting/copyprot.html**.

Knowledge Bases

Good troubleshooters have at their fingertips a variety of information resources to augment their personal experience. A **knowledge base** is an organized collection of information, articles, procedures, tips, and solutions to previous problems that can serve as a resource in problem-solving situations. In effect, a support agent's personal troubleshooting notebook of previous problems and their solutions is a simple knowledge base. Knowledge bases come in a variety of other forms from several sources, including:

- **Vendor manuals**—Most hardware and software products come with tutorial or reference manuals, sometimes in print, but frequently in an electronic format, such as on a CD. Support agents who provide technical support for specific products need easy access to the vendor manuals for the products for which they are responsible. Vendor manuals often contain chapters on troubleshooting and frequently asked questions.

- **Trade books**—Because some vendor manuals are poorly written, a thriving trade book industry has developed to fill the vacuum for well-written information about popular hardware and software products. Web sites for online booksellers such as **www.amazon.com**, **www.barnesandnoble.com**, and **www.computerbooksonline.com** have search capabilities to help users locate trade books for specific hardware or software products. Computer trade books are also available at most general bookstores, large computer stores, and libraries—where you can browse the books to find one that is suitable. Over time, most successful troubleshooters build a small personal or professional library that is a convenient source of information about problems with products they support.

ON THE WEB

Microsoft Press publishes books on troubleshooting for several popular Microsoft products. To see a list of the titles in the troubleshooting series, go to **learning. microsoft.com/Manager/catalog.aspx?qry=troubleshooting**.

- **Trade periodicals**—Computer industry trade magazines and journals publish regular features on problems and solutions. These publications are available on a subscription basis, or in large book and computer stores. Some have both print and online editions; others are available only online. Examples include *Smart Computing*, *PCWorld*, *Macworld*, *PC Today*, *Redmond Magazine*, and *PC Magazine*.

- **Online help**—Most software products, and some hardware products, have an online help feature. Sometimes the online help is no more than a convenient way to access the same information covered in the vendor manual. However, online help may include interactive troubleshooting wizards that provide useful insights into problem situations. Wizards are a form of online script or flowchart that guides a user or support agent through a series of steps to diagnose a problem.

  Windows incorporates several online troubleshooters into the operating system. To access them in Windows 7, click the **Windows Start** button, select **Control Panel**, then in the System and Security category, click on **Find and fix problems**. In Windows Vista, click the **Windows Start** button, select **Help and Support**, and then click the **Troubleshooting** icon (**?**). In Windows XP, press **F1** and search for the keyword *troubleshooting*.

ON THE WEB

To view a brief video on using the Action Center in Windows 7 for troubleshooting operating system problems, go to **windows.microsoft.com/en-US/windows7/ help/videos/using-troubleshooters**.

- **Web sites**—Web sites maintained by product and service vendors are popular and widely available support information resources. Most sites provide product information and problem-solving suggestions; some sites include interactive troubleshooting assistance. Microsoft offers an extensive support Web site for its products at **support. microsoft.com/select/?target=hub**, shown in Figure 4-6. Microsoft's support site contains articles, problem reports, downloads and other support resources.

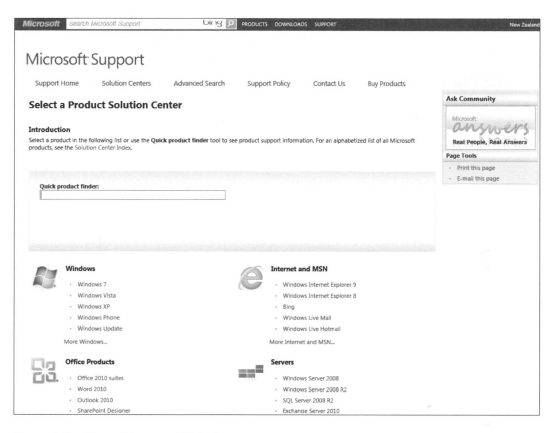

Figure 4-6 Microsoft's support Web site

- **Search engines**—When looking for information resources on a specific problem, don't forget to try a general-purpose search engine, such as **www.google.com**, **www.bing.com**, or **www.ask.com**. These search engines are likely to turn up reports, suggestions, and forum discussions from other users who have encountered a similar problem to the one you're researching. Follow these suggestions to narrow a search for information in a search engine:

  1. Use noun keyword descriptors of a problem, including the exact wording or number of any error messages, such as *DVD drive write error*.

  2. Use the present tense of verbs; avoid *-ing* and *-ed* verbs, for example, use *write error* instead of *writing error*.

  3. Include the manufacturer or vendor's name, model number of hardware, and software version numbers, such as *HP 640 Lightscribe DVD*.

  4. Include the operating system name and version, such as *Windows 7*.

  5. Put quotation marks around phrases, such as *"Apple iBook."*

6. Put + in front of essential keywords, such as *DVD +burner*.

7. Use the Boolean operator *and* to narrow a search; use the *or* operator to expand a search, such as *Vista OR XP*.

ON THE WEB

For a tutorial on Google search engine operation, visit **www.googleguide.com**.

Coworkers and Other Professional Contacts

Access to other computer professionals is an important resource for problem solving. Professional contacts can be work colleagues or other experts in the computer industry. Contact with these computer professionals can take place through Web site discussion forums, ListServs, newsgroups, RSS feeds, and social media.

COWORKERS Coworkers are an important resource for many troubleshooters. When a troubleshooter experiences a block trying to solve a problem, a different perspective or "another set of eyes" can often help break through the block. On occasion, just the process of describing a problem to a colleague may trigger new insights into a problem. When a problem is especially complex or of high priority, a meeting of the team members in a support organization may be convened to address a problem, as illustrated in Figure 4-7. Although a team approach to problem solving may be expensive because it involves several staff members, it is sometimes the only way to solve really difficult problems. Team members often bring different personal experiences and creative energies to finding a solution.

Many support agents report that informal relationships with other user support students or trainees have served them well later in their careers. It is never too early to begin networking and developing professional relationships.

Figure 4-7 A team of support agents provides varying perspectives on a complex problem

DISCUSSION FORUMS Many Web sites have discussion forums that provide access to industry professionals and experts, including these examples:

- Tech Support Guy (**www.techguy.org**)
- 5 Star Support (**www.5starsupport.com**)
- TechRepublic (**www.techrepublic.com/forum/questions**)
- Cyber Tech Help (**www.cybertechhelp.com/forums**)
- Computer Hope (**www.computerhope.com**)
- PC Help Forum (**www.pchelpforum.com**)

Some of these sites require registration, which is usually free.

LISTSERVS A **ListServ** is an automated email service that distributes all (or selected) email messages posted to the ListServ to every member who has subscribed to the ListServ. Some computer vendors operate ListServs to provide their distributors, retail resellers, and customers with information and a communication channel for technical problems. An active ListServ can be an excellent information resource but can also result in a high volume of mail in your inbox.

ON THE WEB

A searchable database of ListServs can be found at **www.lsoft.com/lists/list_q.html**. Enter keywords to describe a topic that interests you. For example, to find ListServs that address topics of interest to Macintosh computer owners, enter *Macintosh* as a keyword. Similarly, support agents interested in Microsoft Access could join a ListServ that discusses use and problems associated with the database software.

Many ListServs maintain archives of email messages that were distributed to their membership. A prospective member can use ListServ archives to get a feeling for the kinds of topics discussed on a ListServ prior to joining. You can also search the archives for answers to specific problems that were previously posted.

NEWSGROUPS **Newsgroups** are Internet discussion groups in which participants with common interests in a topic post messages. A newsgroup is like an electronic bulletin board. Participation is open to anyone who has an interest in a topic, and access is through a newsreader, which is built into most Web browsers or search engines, such as Google. Many support agents find newsgroups an effective way to ask questions and to obtain and provide information. Some newsgroups offer new participants an FAQ archive that can be a valuable resource for troubleshooters.

ON THE WEB

Tens of thousands of active newsgroups are in operation. Some are very general; others are highly specialized. Professionals with interests in a specific field are often regular contributors to newsgroups. Many Web browsers and search engines maintain lists of current newsgroups. For example, go to **groups.google.com**, and enter a topic of interest in the search box. To learn more about newsgroups, visit Harley Hawn's Web site (**www.harley.com/usenet**).

RSS FEEDS An information service that simplifies access to Web resources is **RSS (Really Simple Syndication)**. A support worker may subscribe to an RSS feed that aggregates information from several newsgroups, blogs, forums, news, and other Web sites whose content changes rapidly. The RSS feed delivers information selected by a user to his or her desktop in a convenient, single point of access, easy-to-use format. Several of the user support Web sites mentioned in this chapter include a link to RSS feeds on their Web sites. Click the RSS link (which typically appears as a symbol, such as) to subscribe to the feed.

SOCIAL MEDIA **Social media** such as Facebook, LinkedIn, Twitter, blogs, and other forms of online communication can provide interactions with people around the world who share similar interests and problems. Since the evolution of Web 2.0 described in Chapter 2, these communication media have become an important resource for computer support workers. However, not all users who represent themselves as technical support resources or experts on social media sites are trustworthy. Many ask for money or donations for their services, and some are sources of malware, viruses and misinformation. Use only those computer support resources that you know and trust.

Support Vendors and Contractors

Product vendors are often an extremely useful information resource. A vendor may have seen a baffling problem before and be able to offer suggestions on how to resolve it. Some vendors provide email access to their technical support staff or open access to their proprietary troubleshooting knowledge bases.

Alternative troubleshooting resources include companies that provide outsourcing of support services. As you learned in Chapter 1, outsourcing companies provide problem-solving assistance for a fee. These companies can provide a useful resource to augment the internal support services in an organization. For example, an organization might contract with a support service provider to handle incidents for products that are beyond the expertise of its help desk staff or to provide backup to the internal help desk when the volume of problem reports is greater than the support staff can handle.

ON THE WEB

Examples of companies that provide outsourced technical support services include:

- Convergys (**www.convergys.com/industries/technology/technology-services-support.php**)
- Stream International (**www.stream.com/industries/technology.aspx**)
- GTC (**www.ygtc.com**)

Escalation and Team Problem Solving

When all other problem-solving attempts fail, a referral to a higher support level, called an **escalation**, is often an option. Escalation usually involves referring a problem from a level 1 or level 2 support agent to a higher level of technical support. However, some support organizations de-emphasize staff levels and organize their support agents into teams where mutual assistance and group problem solving is encouraged; in these organizations, an entire team is responsible for solving problems, not just individual staff members.

Diagnostic and Repair Tools

Support agents often use a variety of diagnostic tools to detect and repair hardware, software, and network problems. Many of these tools correspond to the carpenter's hammer and saw, the auto mechanic's wrench and test equipment, and the physician's X-ray machine. Hardware repair and network technicians and engineers use hardware diagnostic tools, such as circuit testers, signal loop-back tools, and network protocol analyzers. The purpose of diagnostic software tools, sometimes called utility software, is to provide troubleshooters with information, problem diagnosis, and even repairs for common computer problems.

General-Purpose and Remote Diagnostic Tools

These tools include software utilities that aid troubleshooters with the diagnosis of computer problems. **Remote access** is a type of utility software that permits support agents to control the operation of a user's computer remotely over a network or telephone connection. Remote access tools are an economical way to provide support for users in distant locations, because a support agent does not have to be in the same physical location as the user. When a remote access connection is established, a help desk staff member can see a remote user's desktop and control the operation of the user's PC directly from a help desk system. Examples of remote control software include:

- LogMeIn (**secure.logmein.com**)
- GoToMyPC (**www.gotomypc.com**)
- RapidAssist (**www.rapidassist.com/index.asp**)
- pcAnywhere (**www.symantec.com/norton/symantec-pcanywhere**)

Windows 7 includes a feature called Remote Desktop Connection that facilitates remote access to other PCs.

ON THE WEB

For information and a video on Remote Desktop Connection, see **windows. microsoft.com/en-US/windows7/Connect-to-another-computer-using-Remote-Desktop-Connection**. For a review of several remote access products, visit **remote-pc-access-software-review.toptenreviews.com**.

Organizations that are concerned about the security of remote access to a user's PC via the Internet can adopt **virtual private network (VPN)** technology. A VPN uses the Internet to connect remote users to corporate servers, but it employs sophisticated user authentication and encryption technologies to provide heightened security when a remote user connects to a corporate server. The level of security in a VPN rivals the security in a hard-wired network, and the VPN software may include remote access tools for help desk connection to a user's desktop.

 In addition to the software tools described in this chapter, help desk agents also use problem incident-tracking software to help record, prioritize, assign, monitor, and document problem incidents. Software tools that help agents track problem incidents are described in Chapter 6.

ON THE WEB

To learn more about virtual private networks, visit **compnetworking.about.com/od/vpn/a/vpn_tutorial.htm**.

Hardware Problem Diagnosis

Tools in this category include software utilities that help diagnose common hardware problems. Many desktop and laptop systems are bundled with preinstalled hardware diagnostic utilities. Diagnostic software can detect some defective hardware components, identify performance enhancements, recover some kinds of lost data, fix problems with defective media, document hardware-configuration information and common configuration problems, and monitor the operation of a system. Examples of hardware diagnosis software include:

- PC Diagnostics (**www.pc-diagnostics.com/pc_diagnostics_tools/pc_diagnostics_pro.shtml**)
- PC-Doctor (**www.pc-doctor.com/index.php**)
- PC Pitstop (**www.pcpitstop.com**)
- CheckIt Diagnostics (**store.smithmicro.com/productdetails.aspx?id=12299**)

Software Problem Diagnosis

Software problem diagnosis tools include utilities that can identify the software configuration of desktops, laptops, and servers as well as identify and repair various kinds of software installation and configuration problems. They can detect authorized and unauthorized software installations, identify incorrect or incompatible software versions, and repair some kinds of problems with the Windows registry. Both experienced troubleshooters and novice support agents who need assistance with basic problem identification can use software diagnostic tools. Examples of problem diagnosis software include:

- Registry Mechanic (**www.pctools.com/registry-mechanic**)
- System Mechanic (**www.iolo.com/system-mechanic/standard**)

- FixIt Utilities (**www.avanquest.com/USA/software/fixit-utilities11-professional-146390**)
- LookInMyPC (**www.lookinmypc.com**)

Network Problem Diagnosis

These tools include network monitoring, remote management, and performance management utilities. Network monitoring software runs on a local area network and searches for network connectivity problems, configuration problems, unauthorized access, and performance problems. Remote management software can help manage the distribution and configuration of software to a few or hundreds of networked PCs, and can restore software and configurations on PCs that have failed for a variety of reasons. Performance management utilities track the uptime, responsiveness, and throughput of a network and identify problems as well as performance enhancement opportunities. Examples of network diagnostic tools include:

- OP Manager (**www.manageengine.com/network-monitoring**)
- OpUtils (**www.monitortools.com/diagnostics**)
- PacketTrap ptFlow (**www.packettrap.com/product/network_traffic.aspx**)
- Ionix Network Protocol Manager (**www.emc.com/products/detail/software/network-protocol-manager.htm**)
- Orion Network Performance Monitor (NPM) (**www.solarwinds.com/products/orion**)
- PRTG network diagnosis (**www.paessler.com/network_diagnostic_tools**)

Successful troubleshooters keep several of their favorite diagnostic utilities at their fingertips to aid in solving hardware, software, and network problems.

This chapter introduces several utilities to help with problem diagnosis. Chapter 12 expands the coverage of user support tools and resources.

Problem-Solving Strategies

Troubleshooters often apply one or more common strategies to solve problems. Figure 4-8 summarizes eight commonly used logical approaches to problem solving that are often effective in a variety of troubleshooting situations, even difficult ones.

- Look for a simple, obvious solution
- Attempt to replicate the problem
- Examine the configuration
- Initiate a root cause analysis
- View a system as a group of subsystems
- Use a module replacement strategy
- Apply a hypothesis-testing approach
- Restore a basic configuration

Figure 4-8 Eight common problem-solving strategies

Look for a Simple, Obvious Solution

Because most computer problems are not difficult to solve, the first problem-solving strategy in any situation should probably be to look for a simple, obvious solution to a problem. For example, if a monitor does not work, and you've tried to fix it without success, consider the possibility that it may have become unplugged. But remember that there are four possible ways for a display screen to become unplugged, as shown in Table 4-1.

	At the Display Screen	**At the Other End**
Power cord	Is the power cord plugged into the back of the display?	Is the power cord plugged into the wall outlet? Is the wall outlet working?
Signal cable	Is the signal cable plugged into the back of the display?	Is the signal cable plugged into the video card on the back of the system unit?

Table 4-1 Ways for a display screen to become unplugged

Furthermore, a power or signal cable that looks like it is securely plugged in may not be. When possible, unplug and replug a cable to verify it is connected. Experienced troubleshooters are often amazed at how frequently an inoperable system is caused by a custodian who accidentally unplugged equipment while moving furniture to clean the floor. Table 4-1 illustrates that even a simple problem-solving incident requires some logical thinking skills. The example also illustrates another simple problem-solving tool: a diagram or checklist of possible alternatives, which reduces the chance that a potential source of the problem will be overlooked.

Checklists as a problem-solving tool are illustrated in Chapter 10.

Another "old standard" in every support worker's toolkit is, "If every other obvious fix fails, try rebooting the system." This advice falls into the category of looking for a simple, obvious solution, because rebooting a system can eliminate a number of stubborn problems (low memory resources, device conflicts, application software freezes, or inoperative peripheral devices, for example). However, sometimes old standbys, such as rebooting a system to clear a problem, actually mask the real cause of the problem and will eventually result in a callback when the problem recurs.

164

ON THE WEB

Faithe Wempen wrote an article on troubleshooting entitled "Top 10 Tips for Troubleshooting PC Problems" (**certcities.com/editorial/tips/story.asp? EditorialsID=17**). Many of her suggestions fall into the category of quick and simple things to try.

If a simple, obvious fix solves a problem, that may be the end point. After all, many technology problems are so-called "N=1" problems because they never or rarely reoccur. And if a simple reboot or replugging a cable solves a problem, why spend more time on it? However, some problems that appear to be solved with a simple fix can recur, as we will see in the next chapter.

Attempt to Replicate the Problem

Replication is the process of trying to repeat a problem, either in the same or a different situation or environment, to see if the problem recurs. A user may report that a problem occurs every time she performs a specific activity or series of steps. Although most users do not intentionally try to mislead a help desk agent, their problem description may omit important pieces of information. First, support agents should try to replicate a problem on the user's computer if possible. Second, they should try to perform the same task or reproduce the same situation on another user system or on their own support system. If they can't get a problem to reoccur on the user's system, it may be traceable to a mistake the user is making. If the problem won't reoccur on another system, a difference in the configuration of the two systems may account for the problem. Then a troubleshooter can begin to look at differences between the two systems (hardware and operating system configuration differences, different software versions, and so on) to get to the root of the problem.

Examine the Configuration

Some problems with computer systems occur because a particular combination of hardware, operating system, and applications software doesn't work well together. In technical jargon, they don't interoperate well. Examining and verifying the ways hardware and software are configured may lead to an understanding of the problem or a solution. For example, failure of an image scanner to work on a user's system may be traceable to one or more of the following potential configuration problems:

- The scanner device is not supported by the operating system.

- The scanner was not configured to work correctly with the operating system.

- An up-to-date device driver was not installed and configured to support the device.

- The applications software that inputs scanned images was not correctly configured for the specific model of scanner.

- Another device conflicts with the scanner's use of system resources.

- Software has recently been installed that conflicts with the scanner or its software.

The documentation for most hardware and software packages includes a description of the configuration requirements (for example, amount of memory, type of processor, disk space, or type of video card) needed to operate correctly. A comparison of the configuration requirements with the actual installation configuration can often resolve incompatibilities.

Initiate a Root Cause Analysis

We began this list of problem-solving strategies with looking for a simple, obvious solution to a problem. Many, if not most, problems benefit from that approach as a first strategy. However, some problems cannot be solved by rebooting a system, reinstalling and configuring a software package, or rechecking the cables. In some cases, a simple, quick fix may get rid of the symptoms of a problem, but fail to get to the underlying cause of the problem. **Root cause analysis** is a strategy that requires a troubleshooter to look beyond the visible symptoms of a problem to search for its root cause (the real cause). This strategy is used primarily for problems that reoccur (and can be replicated). In most cases, root cause analysis is an iterative process that asks a series of *Why?* questions about an observable event (problem), until the root cause is identified.

The first step in root cause analysis is to identify what the problem is. Many root cause analysts say that writing a clear, complete statement of the problem helps to clarify their thinking. The second step is to ask why the problem you described occurs, and to write down the answer. If the second step doesn't identify the root cause of the problem, the next step is to ask why again, and write down the answer. This process continues until the root cause (the real cause) is identified. Root cause analysis may take five or more iterations to find the real cause.

ON THE WEB

To learn more about root cause analysis, read an article on TechRepublic's Web site (**www.techrepublic.com/blog/security/prevent-recurring-problems-with-root-cause-analysis/579**). The article illustrates the use of a fishbone diagram, which is a tool used frequently in root cause analysis.

Several of the strategies described in the following sections are useful in a search for an underlying cause to a problem that can be replicated.

View a System as a Group of Subsystems

A computer system is actually a group of subsystems linked together to form a complete system. One problem-solving strategy is to consider the subsystems as a sequence of linked components, some hardware and some software. For example, consider the problem of a user who wants to print a memo in the Courier font; however, when printed, the memo is in Arial font. Where does the problem lie? Several subsystems are involved in the process of printing the memo in the correct font. These include the following:

- The applications software module that prepares the output
- The printer driver in the operating system that adds printer control codes
- The operating system software that transmits the output to the hardware
- The BIOS operating system component that sends data to the printer
- The parallel or USB port where the printer is connected
- The cable from the port to the printer
- The firmware in the printer that translates data received from the computer into formatted characters
- The circuitry in the printer, including the print head, that transfers the formatted characters onto the paper

Some of these subsystems, such as the printer cable and the print head, may be less likely culprits in this problem situation. However, a short in one of the signal lines in the printer cable may turn out to be at fault. There is probably not enough evidence yet to eliminate this possibility.

One strategy in this situation is to break the sequence in the chain of subsystems at some point (the midpoint is often a good place to start), and determine on which side of the midpoint the problem occurs. In this example, you might select the point at which the printer cable connects to the parallel or USB port as the midpoint. A support agent could observe, perhaps with a different printer, whether the font problem is on the printer side or the system unit side of the midpoint. Another strategy is to start at one end of the sequence of subsystems and trace the problem either forward or backward. Used with the module replacement strategy described next, treating a system as a group of subsystems can serve as a strategy to help isolate a problem.

Use a Module Replacement Strategy

Hardware technicians frequently use module replacement as a tool to diagnose computer hardware problems, as shown in Figure 4-9.

Figure 4-9   A hardware technician performs module replacement to evaluate a problem

Module replacement is a problem-solving strategy that involves replacing a hardware or software component whose operational status is unknown with a component that is known to be operational. For example, if a DVD drive fails to work correctly, the problem may be the drive itself or a piece of hardware or software related to its operation. One way to determine whether the problem really is the DVD drive is to disconnect it from the computer where it is malfunctioning and connect it to a second system. If the DVD drive works correctly in the second system, then the problem is not with the drive itself, and the technician can consider other options, such as the DVD driver software or the signal cables that connect the drive. Many organizations troubleshoot hardware modules only to a field replaceable unit (FRU) level such as an expansion card, a circuit board, the motherboard, the power supply, a disk drive, and so forth, and replace the entire FRU, if necessary. It is usually not cost effective to go further to identify a defective component below the board level.

168

The module replacement strategy also works for software. In the case of malfunctioning software that worked previously, but now fails, the equivalent of rebooting a computer is to reinstall the software package. Occasionally, the image of a software package stored on a hard disk becomes corrupted when some of the bits in the instructions are accidentally overwritten. The faulty software image loads into memory when the program runs, and the software fails to perform as it did previously. Reinstalling the software package replaces the copy of the program (module) on the disk with a fresh image. Some software packages include a "repair" option. Instead of reinstalling the entire program image, only the module that is defective is reinstalled, which takes less time.

Take precautionary steps before doing a module replacement on an internal device. Draw a sketch and label cable connections before unplugging any hardware components. Back up any software prior to reinstallation in case a problem arises during the reinstallation process. Prior to reinstalling a software package, uninstall the package to avoid possible contamination between the inoperable image and the fresh installation.

Apply a Hypothesis-Testing Approach

In hypothesis testing, a troubleshooter formulates a hypothesis about the cause of a problem. Then the troubleshooter carries out an experiment to determine whether the hypothesis is true (sometimes called *confirming the hypothesis*) or false. For example, a user may report that he is unable to log on to a network server:

USER: *I type my username and password, just as I usually do. The network gives me an error message that the username and password are invalid.*

The troubleshooter listens to the problem description and may formulate some hypotheses that would explain the problem.

TROUBLESHOOTER (to herself):*This problem may be a hardware, software, or network problem. Where should I start? It is unlikely a hardware problem, so I'll assume* (hypothesis) *that it is a network problem. If it is, then the user should not be able to log on from any other workstation on the network. So I'll try an experiment to see if the problem is specific to a particular workstation.*

In this case, suppose the user can, in fact, log on from another workstation.

TROUBLESHOOTER: *If it's a network problem, it must not be on the server side. I'll look at* (hypothesis) *the client side. If there is a problem with the client software, then no one else should be able to log on from the user's workstation. Let me try* (experiment) *to log on to my own account from the user's workstation.*

In this scenario, suppose the troubleshooter was indeed able to log on to the server from the user's workstation using her own username and password.

TROUBLESHOOTER: *Interesting! We've apparently eliminated the network as a culprit. Maybe* (hypothesis) *the user is the culprit. Maybe he's mistyped his password. Let me try* (experiment) *to log on to the user's account from his workstation.*

In this case, the troubleshooter's attempt to log on was unsuccessful, too. She was able to replicate the user's problem.

TROUBLESHOOTER: *Okay! What now? Perhaps* (hypothesis) *the user's record in the database of user accounts does not have access rights defined appropriately for this user from his workstation.*

A call to the network administrator determines that the user database record for the user does include the correct username, password, and access rights for the user.

TROUBLESHOOTER: *Hmmm! I assumed* (hypothesis) *that the problem was unlikely to be hardware. Maybe I should reconsider that assumption. Suppose I plug a different keyboard* (experiment) *into the user's system and try again. Aha! Success. The problem is a defective key on the keyboard that happened to be in the user's password.*

Although this scenario is oversimplified, it illustrates the hypothesis-testing and experimental method that is at the heart of many problem-solving efforts. The ability to formulate a series of hypotheses and carry out experiments to test them is a valuable skill for any troubleshooter to develop. This skill is based in large part on a troubleshooter's experience with a number of different problem situations, the ability to devise a successful experiment to test a hypothesis, and the ability to think clearly and carefully about a problem situation. An important ingredient in hypothesis testing is critical thinking. The hypothesis-testing strategy works best when a support agent can think of several alternate explanations for a situation. Sometimes it helps to make a list of possible causes for a problem and to brainstorm alternatives with other agents in a team environment.

ON THE WEB

To learn more about hypothesis testing, also called the *scientific method*, read an article at **www.inetdaemon.com/tutorials/troubleshooting/scientific_method.shtml**.

Restore a Basic Configuration

Some problems occur when hardware or software interacts with other parts of a system. If a problem cannot be traced to a configuration problem, another problem-solving strategy is to remove components (hardware or software) to "pare back" a system to a basic configuration. This approach is suggested at the end of the list of strategies intentionally, because modifying a configuration by uninstalling components can have side effects that are unpredictable and cause other problems. The strength of this strategy is that it eliminates **variables**, or factors in a problem-solving situation. The presence of extra variables can make a problem too complex to solve easily, especially when more than one problem is present.

For example, if a piece of hardware such as an image scanner will not operate correctly when added to a system, a support technician may try removing one or more other components to see if the new hardware component will operate correctly in a stripped-down system configuration. If a technician finds that the scanner works fine when another component is removed, but fails when that component is reconnected, then incompatibility between the two devices can be researched.

In another common scenario, a software package may fail to run when installed on a computer connected to a network. One approach is to disconnect the computer from the network and observe whether the program runs on the computer in standalone mode. This experiment removes a variable (the network connection) to see whether that factor makes a difference. If the software runs on a standalone PC, but not on a networked system, then the technician can examine the network configuration requirements for the software.

The problem-solving strategies just described are critical tools in a troubleshooter's repertoire. They involve logical, organized, and critical-thinking skills and are designed to lead to a satisfactory solution. Problem solving is a skill that can be learned, but practice and experience really build problem-solving expertise. Other factors that contribute to successful problem solving include several personal characteristics.

Personal Characteristics of Successful Troubleshooters

Personal characteristics play an important role in the troubleshooting process, and some can contribute directly to one's success as a troubleshooter. These are listed in Figure 4-10.

- They are patient and persistent
- They enjoy the problem-solving process
- They like working with people
- They enjoy continuous learning

Figure 4-10   Characteristics of successful troubleshooters

To some degree, these characteristics are part of a support agent's basic personality. However, personal experience, feedback from users, and coaching by other support staff can affect the degree to which a support agent makes effective use of these characteristics.

Patience and Persistence

Problem solving is often difficult work. It is frustrating to follow a strategy, reach a dead end, admit you've hit a wall, and start over with a different approach. A certain amount of stress and frustration over an especially difficult problem is inevitable. But successful troubleshooters find ways to deal with stress and frustration. One useful strategy to regain patience and perspective is to take a break from a problem. Go for a walk or work on another task where progress is possible, and then return later to the problem for which progress seemed impossible. When you return, you can take a fresh look at the problem and perhaps see other alternative solutions you overlooked earlier.

Patience is important in two respects. First, troubleshooters must be persistent. They also need to be patient with themselves and with users. Successful support agents are able to shield users from their own frustrations. Expressing impatience with a client or a problem only impairs communication with the client, a situation that will not help resolve the problem. Users may also lack persistence. They may be too willing to give up on a difficult problem (*"Oh, it's not that important."*), and may need to be reassured that a problem is not insurmountable—that possible approaches and resources have not yet been exhausted.

Enjoy the Problem-Solving Process

Successful support agents get enjoyment from the problem-solving process. Where users may see the computer world as a never-ending sequence of technical problems and frustrations, support agents tend to see challenges and opportunities. They enjoy finding the sometimes-obscure relationship between a problem and its cause. Like physicians, who only see sick people, user support staff members are hired to solve problems for end users. If you don't enjoy the challenge of solving problems and the satisfaction when an apparently difficult problem gets solved, you should perhaps consider a career in a field other than user support.

Like Working with People

The ability to work with all types of people is critical in the user support industry. User support agents don't have to like every user they encounter, and they don't have to treat each user as a personal friend in order to solve problems successfully. But they do need to communicate effectively with users and to interact with them in a professional manner. If you don't enjoy working at a professional level with users, user support is not a field you'll likely enjoy for very long.

Enjoy Continuous Learning

Change is one of the constant features of the computer industry and the user support field. The hardware or software package you learn in school is not the one you will likely get assigned to support on the job. Last year's products you knew inside and out will become obsolete. Anyone with a serious commitment to the user support field must enjoy learning about new products.

Continual learning is an important job skill in a support position, whether it is written into a formal position description or not. Most user support agents subscribe to one or more computer industry periodicals to keep up to date with changes in the computer field and with industry trends. Support agents regularly attend training sessions and teach themselves new software packages. They look for opportunities to learn from other support agents. Some support organizations sponsor formal professional development opportunities, such as training sessions and informal sessions over lunch to encourage support staff to exchange information about products and the computer industry.

ON THE WEB

Trade publications that offer a broad perspective on trends in the computer industry include:

Computerworld (**www.computerworld.com**)

InformationWeek (**www.informationweek.com**)

InfoWorld (**www.infoworld.com**)

Developing Your Own Approach to Problem Solving

The problem-solving approach in this chapter treats troubleshooting computer problems as a process, but not a process with a fixed sequence of one-size-fits-all steps that are guaranteed to work every time. You have learned about several problem-solving tools that you can apply to many troubleshooting situations. Like a carpenter or auto mechanic, support agents reach into a tool bag, grab a tool, use it, and then pick up another tool, use it, and so on. Either a problem gets resolved, or the troubleshooter recognizes that he or she doesn't have the tools needed to solve it and begins to search for other resources.

All support agents are eventually confronted with problems they cannot solve easily. At such times, they need a personal approach to problem solving. A personal problem-solving perspective includes an understanding of the strengths a support agent brings to each problem. It is based on the experience that selected tools and skills have been successful in solving past problems. It relies on information resources that have proved useful in past situations. It is improved by the metacognition process described in this chapter, whereby problem solvers carefully examine their own thought processes. Without a personal problem-solving approach, support agents are more likely to use a random, hit-or-miss strategy instead of a logical, well-organized problem-solving approach. They are more likely to get frustrated by difficult problems or become overly reliant on others when they encounter a dead end. Successful troubleshooters recognize a dead end not as a stopping point but as an opportunity to get a fresh start, question assumptions, and try another approach, with perhaps a different tool.

How do you develop your personal approach to problem solving?

1. Use your own experience, knowledge, skills, thought processes, access to information, and communication skills as the basis for your personal strategy.

2. Improve your troubleshooting skills and learn to use the problem-solving tools described in this chapter. Begin to build your personal kit of tools and information resources to help solve problems Use the tools described in this chapter and those in Chapter 12 as a starting point.

3. Analyze your troubleshooting approach. Recognize your personal strengths and the areas in which you need to improve. For example, some support agents develop extremely good skills at finding information about a problem on the Internet. They learn to use search engines effectively and bookmark Web sites on their browser's favorites list that have been useful in the past. They pride themselves on their ability to find information quickly. Other support agents develop a network of colleagues with whom they regularly exchange email or phone calls about difficult problems. They are proud of the fact that if they don't know an answer, they know someone who does.

Of course, no one support agent is equally adept at all the strategies in this chapter. Successful troubleshooters develop a sense of what works for them (a plan of attack) and what doesn't, and they try to take maximum advantage of their strengths. A personal problem-solving approach is not necessarily something a support agent writes down. However, a personal approach to problem solving is something a successful support agent thinks about a lot and works to improve.

 Chapter 5 and the hands-on activities and case projects in this chapter provide examples of common problems you can use to help develop your own problem-solving skills.

Chapter Summary

- Most computer problems are not difficult to handle because they are requests for information, complaints, or problems with which a support staff member has previous experience.

- Troubleshooting is the process of solving more difficult computer problems. Rather than a series of sequential steps, troubleshooting is an iterative process—a creative process in which a support agent tries an approach, and if one approach doesn't work, he or she tries another.

- Troubleshooters use an assortment of skills in their work, including problem solving, critical thinking, and decision making. They also use several kinds of troubleshooting tools, including communication skills, information resources, problem-solving strategies, and personal characteristics. Troubleshooters select from among these tools, skills, and resources to tackle various aspects of a problem.

- Communication skills include listening to a user's description of problem symptoms, active listening (or paraphrasing) to verify understanding of a problem, and using critical questions to obtain information from a user and to challenge a support agent's own assumptions that may block the path to a solution. Helpful communication skills also include the ability to ask probing questions, explain a problem resolution to a user, and verify that a problem is solved.

- Information resources include a troubleshooter's personal experience with similar or related problems, prepared scripts and checklists that follow a logical path to a solution, and various knowledge bases. Vendor manuals, trade books, online help, ListServs, newsgroups, Web sites, and search engines are rich sources of information about problems. Coworkers, industry professionals, friends, and vendors are other potential information resources that may move a problem toward resolution.

- Computer troubleshooters use a variety of diagnostic and repair tools to solve problems. Remote access utilities let a support agent view and control events on a user's computer from a remote location. Other utility software is designed to diagnose and help repair hardware, software, and network problems and improve system performance.

- Problem-solving strategies include eight logical-thinking processes that are often useful to troubleshooters:

  1. Look for a simple, obvious fix.

  2. Attempt to replicate a problem.

  3. Examine the configuration.

  4. Initiate a root cause analysis.

  5. View a system as a group of subsystems.

  6. Use a module replacement strategy.

  7. Apply a hypothesis-testing approach.

  8. Restore a basic configuration.

- Personal characteristics that aid successful troubleshooters include patience and persistence, enjoyment of the problem-solving process, satisfaction in working with people, and an interest in continuous learning.

- All support agents need to develop their problem-solving skills, to think about the problem-solving process, and to develop their own approach to problem solving. A support agent's personal problem-solving perspective should include an awareness of his or her strengths and areas for improvement when working with the problem-solving tools and resources described in this chapter.

Key Terms

active listening—A communication skill that results in a listener being as involved and engaged in the communication process as the speaker; paraphrasing is an example of active listening.

contradiction—A fact established through investigation that rules out, or contradicts, a potential solution.

creativity—The critical-thinking ability to find a novel or innovative solution to a problem; the ability to see a problem from new and different perspectives.

critical question—A question designed to elicit important information from a user that may force a support agent to challenge some basic assumptions about a problem.

critical thinking—Cognitive skills a problem solver uses to analyze a problem, search for the underlying logic or rationale, or strive for alternate ways to explain an event or situation.

decision making—The ability to select one alternative from among a number of alternatives, based on some evaluation criteria; an important skill for troubleshooters.

escalation—A problem-solving tool whereby a difficult or complex problem is referred to a higher-level support person or team for resolution.

explanation—A communication skill that involves a support agent describing the solution to a problem so the user understands why the problem occurred and the steps required to resolve it.

goal state—A desired state of events or outcome; in troubleshooting, a common goal state is to diagnose or repair a computer subsystem to return it to a normal operational state.

hypothesis—An initial guess, hunch, or prediction based on experience.

hypothesis testing—Formulating a hypothesis about the cause of a problem and designing an experiment that will prove or disprove the hypothesis.

iterative process—A process that involves several paths or approaches to problem solving; steps are repeated in a loop until a fruitful path is found; troubleshooting is an iterative process in that it uses and reuses a variety of tools and skills.

knowledge base—An organized collection of information, articles, procedures, tips, and solutions to existing problems that can serve as a resource in a problem-solving situation.

ListServ—An automated email service that distributes all (or selected) email messages posted to the ListServ to every member who has subscribed to the ListServ; organized around a topic of special interest to its members.

mental model—A conceptual picture that a problem solver builds to help understand how a system works; mental models are based on education and experience.

metacognition—The ability to think about thinking; the ability of a troubleshooter to step back from a problem-solving situation and analyze his or her thought processes.

module replacement—A problem-solving strategy that involves replacing a hardware or software component whose operational status is unknown with a component that is known to be operational.

newsgroup—An Internet discussion group in which participants with common interests in a topic post messages; similar to an electronic bulletin board.

paraphrasing—A communication skill that involves someone restating in their own words what they believe they heard a speaker say.

probe—A follow-up question designed to elicit additional information from a user about a problem; a sequence of probes often clarifies a problem situation.

problem solving—A process of moving from a current state of events X (the *problem state*) to a future desired state of events Y (sometimes called the *goal state*); the objective of problem solving is to get from X to Y quickly, accurately, effectively, and efficiently.

remote access—Utility software that lets a support agent control the operation of a user's computer remotely over a network or telephone connection.

replication—The process of trying to repeat a problem either in the same or a different situation or environment, to see if the problem reoccurs.

root cause analysis—A troubleshooting strategy that requires a support worker to look beyond the visible symptoms of a recurring problem to search for its underlying cause.

RSS (Really Simple Syndication)—A Web service that aggregates selected information from various Web resources, including newsgroups, blogs, forums, and other news and information services and delivers it to a user's desktop in a convenient, easy-to-use format.

social media—Forms of online communication that provide interactions with people around the world who share similar interests and problems; examples include Facebook, LinkedIn, Twitter, and blogs.

troubleshooting—The process of defining, diagnosing, and solving computer problems; involves the use of several thinking and communications skills, information resources, strategies, and methods.

variable—A factor or aspect in a problem-solving situation that can change or be changed; eliminating variables by removing components simplifies a complex problem so it is more manageable and can be solved.

verification—A communication skill that allows a troubleshooter to confirm their perception that a problem is solved.

virtual private network (VPN)—A computer network that uses the Internet to connect remote users to a corporate network; a VPN uses authentication and encryption to enhance security on a network.

Check Your Understanding

Answers to Check Your Understanding questions are in Appendix A.

1. Which of these is not an example of a difficult support problem?

    a. a problem a support worker has not seen before
    b. a problem involving an angry caller
    c. a problem for which the solution is not obvious
    d. All of these are difficult problems.

2. True or False? Troubleshooting computer problems is a fixed sequence of steps a support agent follows from the initial problem description to the resolved problem.

3. True or False? Problem solving, critical thinking, and decision making are different names for the same skill.

4. The strategy in which the listener is as engaged as the speaker in a communication is called:

    a. probing   c. paraphrasing
    b. active listening   d. replicating

5. A mental model to help a computer troubleshooter understand and explain a problem situation is based on:

    a. metacognition   c. decision making
    b. critical thinking   d. problem solving

6. A troubleshooting process that involves selecting one alternative from among a number of possible alternatives based on some evaluation criteria is called _____ .

7. True or False? To restate a problem description using the user's exact words is called paraphrasing.

8. _____ is a problem-solving tool that involves a difficult or complex problem being referred to a higher-level support person for resolution.

9. The ability to step back from a troubleshooting situation and analyze one's own thinking process is called _____ .

10. A follow-up question a troubleshooter asks to get additional information about a problem situation is called a(n) _____ .

11. An organized collection of information, articles, procedures, tips, and problem solutions is called a:

   a. script   c. knowledge base

   b. flowchart   d. newsgroup

12. True or False? A troubleshooting strategy that involves swapping a hardware or software component whose status is unknown with one that is known to be operational is called module replacement.

13. Rebooting a system in an attempt to fix a problem is an example of which of these problem-solving strategies?

   a. Look for a simple, obvious fix.

   b. Attempt to replicate a problem.

   c. Use a module-replacement strategy.

   d. View a system as a group of subsystems.

14. A successful troubleshooter recognizes a dead end (or block in progress) as:

   a. a frustration

   b. the end of the troubleshooting process

   c. a stopping point

   d. an opportunity to look at other alternatives

15. Write a paraphrase for the following problem statement: *"The screen on my PC is blank."*

16. A troubleshooter who observes that a suspected faulty modem does not work in computer A, but operates correctly in computer B, is confronted with a(n) _____ .

17. A communication skill that confirms a troubleshooter's perception that a problem is fixed is:

   a. authentication   c. explanation

   b. verification   d. metacognition

18. True or False? Root cause analysis is a troubleshooting strategy designed to eliminate the symptoms of a problem.

19. A network technology that uses authentication and encryption to connect remote users to a company server over the Internet is a(n) _____ .

20. Simplifying a problem situation by removing components from a configuration is a strategy to eliminate or reduce the number of _____ in a problem.

21. Facebook, LinkedIn, blogs and Twitter are examples of _____ .

Discussion Questions

1. Suggest some additional critical questions that you would add to the list of five described in the chapter to help a support agent and a user who have reached a roadblock in their search for a problem solution. Are some questions more useful than others?

2. Which of the personal characteristics in this chapter is the single most important trait for a successful troubleshooter? Describe some attributes of successful troubleshooters that were not discussed in the chapter.

3. Which are more important to a successful computer troubleshooter: good technical skills or good people skills? Why?

4. Which are more important to a successful computer troubleshooter: good listening skills or good speaking skills? Why?

5. Which is more important to a successful computer troubleshooter: what they know or what they can find out? Why?

6. If you were a user support specialist who supported internal users, which tool or information resource described in this chapter would you want to have available to you if you could pick only one? Defend your answer.

7. Discuss the pros and cons of contracting with a support services vendor to provide help desk services to an organization versus in-house support. Do the advantages of outsourcing outweigh the disadvantages?

8. Are the personal traits of successful problem solvers discussed in this chapter hardwired parts of a support specialist's basic personality, or can they be learned and improved upon?

Hands-On Activities

Activity 4-1

Listen actively. Team up with another student or coworker and practice listening and paraphrasing skills. One person takes the role of the user; the other takes the role of a support person. The user describes a common problem with a computer system to the support person, who then paraphrases the problem description back to the user.

The user's role is important because he or she needs to listen for important parts of the problem that the support person omitted, that didn't exist in the original problem description, or that the support person modified. Continue the paraphrasing activity until the person in the support role can correctly paraphrase the original problem description. Then change roles and repeat the process. (Note that the purpose of this activity is to practice paraphrasing, not solve the problem.)

Activity 4-2

Ask questions. Study the following problem description. Then determine what additional information you, as a support agent, would want from this user. Develop several questions you could ask to obtain the information you would need to resolve this problem.

"My computer is hung up. I don't know what I did wrong. The screen is frozen. Nothing I try does any good. I press keys on the keyboard, and nothing happens. The mouse pointer won't move."

Activity 4-3

Provide explanations. Write an explanation to a user who wants to know why the Office 2010 software suite will not operate on a PC he purchased in 2001. The user has a PC with a 133 MHz processor, 128 MB of RAM, and a VGA monitor; the computer runs the Windows 2000 operating system. Use the Internet search tools described in this chapter to prepare your explanation.

Activity 4-4

Examine the configuration. A software package runs correctly on computer A, but the same package does not operate correctly on computer B. Make a list of basic computer system configuration information you would like to know to diagnose this problem further.

Activity 4-5

Use information resources. A user of Quattro Pro X3, which is part of the WordPerfect Office suite, installed Quattro Pro on a Windows Vista PC. When he runs Quattro Pro, he immediately gets an error message, *"Program c:\Program files\wordperfect office x3\QPW.exe abnormal program termination."* Write a brief problem report that addresses the following points:

1. Describe the approach you would take to solve this problem.

2. Based on your research, what solution would you recommend to the user?

3. Will the solution you recommend in Step 2 fix the root cause of the problem?

Activity 4-6

Develop a printer troubleshooting script. Use the Windows help system to locate the troubleshooting tools in your current version of Windows. Write a script with a minimum of five steps that documents how to diagnose and fix several common printing problems users might encounter. Don't worry about rare printer problems.

Activity 4-7

Evaluate a troubleshooting event. Think about the most difficult troubleshooting problem you've encountered in your recent experience—one where the solution was not straightforward and where the problem was not a simple request for information.

The problem you pick might be one you experienced personally, one you encountered at work or while helping in a computer lab, or one you encountered while helping a friend. Write a description of the troubleshooting event that answers the following questions:

1. What troubleshooting tools, methods, and strategies did you use? Describe them using the concepts in this chapter.

2. What subsystems were involved in the problem?

3. Which communications tools, information resources, and problem analysis/diagnosis tools did you use?

4. Were the troubleshooting methods you used effective? Why or why not?

5. How could you have improved the effectiveness of your troubleshooting strategy?

Activity 4-8

Learn about Windows system utilities. The Windows operating system includes several diagnostic utility programs that are useful to troubleshooters. Use the Windows Help system to learn the purpose of each of these utilities:

- System Information
- Performance Information and Tools
- Windows Easy Transfer
- Disk Cleanup
- Disk Defragmenter
- System Restore

Write a brief description of the purpose of each of these utilities. Include in your description an example of a situation in which a troubleshooter might need to use each tool. Finally, briefly explain the difference between Disk Cleanup and Disk Defragmenter.

Activity 4-9

Alternative system utilities. Use Google or another search engine to locate examples of software utilities that are alternatives to the Windows system utilities listed in Activity 4-8. In each case, briefly describe features of the utilities you found that differ from the comparable Windows utility. Also note whether the utilities you found are commercial products, shareware, freeware, or open source software.

Activity 4-10

Create and solve a practice problem. Based on your personal experience, write up a problem statement similar to the examples in Case Project 1, which follows the Hands-On Activities. Then, exchange problem statements with another student or coworker and see if you can solve the problem he or she described. Try to make your problem a common one you've encountered, and don't make the problem you describe too difficult. Remember, your partner is writing a problem for you to work on, too!

Activity 4-11

Adjust small print. A user complained that printed output from her Web browser and email client was very tiny. Write an explanation that could be included in an email to the user that describes how to increase the size of the print from these programs. (Assume she uses the same Web browser and email programs that you use.)

Activity 4-12

Learn about Windows processes. When the Windows operating system runs in a computer's memory, it loads into RAM and runs several small utilities called *processes*. Learn about the Windows Process Explorer utility at **technet.microsoft.com/en-us/sysinternals/ bb896653**. Then, download and install the program on a PC to which you have access. Run the Process Explorer to learn about its output.

From the list of active processes on your PC, select five processes that are NOT provided by Microsoft (as indicated in the Company Name column). Use an Internet search engine to research the processes you selected. Answer these questions about each of the five processes you selected:

- Which vendor supplied the software that runs the process?

- What is the basic purpose of the process?

- Is the process one that is required for your PC or its peripheral devices to operate? (Would stopping the process cause a major problem?)

- Is the process a potentially dangerous one (e.g., a virus, spyware, malware, or adware).

Case Projects

1. Problem Solving: Your Turn

See how many of the problems listed below you can solve working by yourself. Use books, manuals, online help, the Internet, and other resources, as necessary. Some of these problems are easier than others, so don't work too long on a problem that seems difficult; ask your work colleagues or your instructor for help. As you work on these tasks, make some brief notes that describe your experience. Do some metacognition about your problem-solving approach.

1. A user running Internet Explorer reports a message, *"Internet Explorer cannot display the web page."* What information about this problem can you provide the user?

2. A user gets an error message: *"Error Loading Kernel. You must reinstall Windows."* What is the likely cause of this message? Do you really have to reinstall Windows to fix the problem?

3. A Microsoft Excel user often selects the Shrink-to-Fit feature in Microsoft Word to force a memo that is a little too long to fit on a single page. He wants to know if Excel has a similar feature that will force a worksheet to fit on a single page without overlapping to a second page. Is there a Shrink-to-Fit feature in Excel? If so, how is it used?

4. If you have a desktop computer, unplug the keyboard from your computer while it is turned off. Then power up your system. During the power-on self test (POST) boot up diagnostic tests, one of the devices tested is the keyboard. What message appears to alert the user to the keyboard problem? If you plug the keyboard back in, will the system recover without rebooting? If necessary, plug your keyboard back in and reboot.

5. Use the operating system utilities on your computer to document the following information about your computer. For each question, indicate what tool you used to find the information.

   a. What model of processor is in your system?

   b. What type of bus architecture is used?

   c. How much total memory does your system have?

   d. Is the subdirectory C:\NET in the search path?

   e. How is the environment variable TEMP defined?

   f. For the mouse on your system, what is the IRQ address and the device driver version?

   g. What is the size of the hard drive? How much free space is available on it?

6. Find a utility program in Windows that will scan your hard drive for errors (such as chkdsk or ScanDisk). (*Hint:* Use Windows Help and search for *disk errors.*) Run the error scan utility on your computer's hard drive. What problems, if any, did the error scan find? If problems exist, what is the procedure you would follow to eliminate them? What precautions should a user take before taking action to eliminate lost disk clusters?

7. A user wants to know whether it is possible to password-protect a removable USB drive so that another person cannot intentionally or accidentally access confidential information on the drive if it is misplaced or stolen. How would you respond to the user's question?

8. A user reports that she has a program named ERU.exe on her hard disk. She doesn't know its purpose, doesn't want to try running it for fear it will damage her system, and doesn't want to erase it for fear it is necessary for Windows to operate correctly. What can you tell her about the function of ERU.exe and who should run it?

9. A user in engineering says he has a very old program on a floppy disk that he used to run 25 years ago to perform a special analysis on steel structures. He now has a project for which he needs to run the program. The program ran previously on an

operating system named CP/M. The program could be rewritten to run on a modern system, but the rewrite would take several weeks. Is there any way to run a CP/M program on today's computers?

10. A user reports that when he runs a program on his hard drive, he gets an error message about a missing VBRUN700.dll file. He has searched the hard drive and cannot find the missing file. How can he get a copy of the missing VBRUN700.dll? He mentions that his computer does have a file named VBRUN500.dll. Can he use it instead? If so, how?

11. A user who has recently changed departments from Manufacturing to Product Design says that all the email messages he sends have two lines appended automatically to the end of each message:

GRIGORY VLADNIK

MANUFACTURING DEPT, XT 555

He wants to change the department name to *PRODUCT DESIGN*, but he does not know how the automatic lines get there because he doesn't type them. How can he make the change in his email program? (Use an email program with which you are familiar to answer this question.)

12. A Microsoft Word user noticed that another user in her department has more than four files listed in the recently used files list in the Files pull-down menu. How can she increase the number of files listed on her computer? Does the answer depend on which version of Word the user has? Explain.

13. A panicked user writes the following email: *"I just accidentally deleted a Microsoft Project .mpp file from my hard drive, and I really need to get it back. My job may depend on it. Can you help me get the deleted file back?"* Describe the strategies you would use to help this user.

14. A Microsoft Excel user has a spreadsheet with a cell that contains the text: *#REF!* What does this cell entry mean? Research and prepare a list of other messages that Excel can display in a cell that indicates a possible problem with the cell contents.

15. A user discovered a program named Win32.exe on his hard drive. He would like to know if the program is required by the Windows operating system and what its function is. What advice would you give him?

16. A PC that used to operate correctly displays a message, *BOOTMGR is missing*. Research this problem and make a list of possible reasons why a PC could report this error.

2. Window 7's Problem Steps Recorder

Dale Andrews, a desktop support technician, walked into the support center late one afternoon after a busy day diagnosing PC problems. He called out to anyone who was listening, *"Help!"* Dale explained to the support agents who were in the office that he spent most of his day trying to replicate problems that several users were experiencing on their PCs. He said, *"I spent several hours trying to figure out exactly what each user had done to cause the problems they reported. In some cases, I just couldn't get the problem to reveal itself."*

As one of Dale's desktop support colleagues, you suggested the support group investigate how to use a tool in Windows 7 called the Problem Steps Recorder. Several of the support staff expressed interest in this tool because they have all had experiences similar to Dale's. Complete the following steps:

1. Research how the Windows Problem Steps Recorder works.

2. If you have access to a Windows 7 PC, set up an example of a common problem. Then use the Problem Steps Recorder (PSR) to try out the utility. For example, with the Problem Steps Recorder running, open an application program, such as Word or Excel, and try to open a document that doesn't exist on your computer. You should get an error message. Next, inspect the output from the PSR to learn about the kinds of information it captured when you tried to open a file that doesn't exist. Although PSR only works with Windows 7, if you use Windows XP or Vista, you can try out a similar tool called Screenrecorder, which can be downloaded from **technet.microsoft.com/en-us/magazine/2009.03.utilityspotlight2.aspx**.

3. Write a brief procedure targeted to end users that explains how to use the Problem Steps Recorder.

3. Diagnostic Software for Pre-Fab Engineering

Tamara Harold received the email message shown below from Fred Long, president of Pre-Fab Engineering. Tamara is busy working on another project now, and asks you to help with this assignment.

To: TamaraHarold@Pre-Fab.biz

From: FredLong@Pre-Fab.biz

I would like to help our engineering users at Pre-Fab become more self-reliant when they encounter computer problems.

Since you are one of the most knowledgeable computer users at Pre-Fab, I wonder if you would look into whether a diagnostic utility program would be useful. I am especially interested in the kinds of problems these utility programs can detect and whether the software would make our employees more productive when they have problems. Could you pull together some information about the capabilities a diagnostic program might offer us so that we can make a decision about whether to purchase one for each of our workers' use?

I will very much appreciate your advice on this one.

Download a trial or evaluation copy of a diagnostic utility such as one described in this chapter, or use another similar program with which you are familiar. Install it and try it out. Write a short description of the capabilities of the program that Tamara can send to Fred.

4. Pat Newland's Chat on OpenDNS

Here is a transcript of a chat session between Pat Newland, a supervisor in the Reference Department of the local library, and Betty Wills, the library's Director of Technology Services:

PAT NEWLAND: *I read a brief article in a computer magazine last night about the advantages of using OpenDNS for Internet access. I'm not sure I understood it all, so I wonder if anyone on your tech support staff knows anything about OpenDNS.*

BETTY WILLS: *I don't believe we currently use OpenDNS, but we'll certainly investigate it and find out if it is something our users should be using.*

PAT NEWLAND: *I'd appreciate that. The article talked about the advantages of OpenDNS, but didn't say anything about any downsides.*

BETTY WILLS: *Well, I'll find out about that, too.*

PAT NEWLAND: *Thanks. Please let me know what you find out. Apparently OpenDNS has some safety advantages for Internet users, but I don't have any idea how to set it up.*

BETTY WILLS: *I'll get back to you. Thanks for the suggestion.*

Betty asks if you could help research OpenDNS. Learn about its purpose, use, advantages, and disadvantages. Write up the results of your research in a response to Betty Wills.

5. OEM Printer Cartridges Versus Refilled Cartridges?

Pat Hughes, an employee in the production department of a large book publisher, contacted the user support team with a question about the advantages and disadvantages of using OEM (original equipment manufacturer) printer cartridges versus refilled cartridges. Pat explained that the production department uses a large number of printers and has been purchasing OEM cartridges at a considerable cost. Several of the workers in book production thought their department could save a substantial amount if they switched to refilled cartridges. Your task is to research the pros and cons of OEM cartridges versus refilled cartridges. Then, using presentation software such as Microsoft PowerPoint, or other presentation software to which you have access, prepare a presentation for users in the production department on the advantages and disadvantages of OEM printer cartridges versus refilled cartridges. Your presentation could address these issues:

- What are the relative costs of OEM versus refilled cartridges for a typical printer? (Use a printer you have experience with as an example.)

- What factors other than cost should be considered in making a decision about OEM versus refilled cartridges? What are the pros and cons in this decision?

- Do some printer manufacturers discourage printer users from purchasing refilled cartridges? How?

- How might the purchase and use of refilled printer cartridges impact the work of the support team? Are users in book production likely to experience increased problems with refilled cartridges that will result in more incidents for the user support team?

CHAPTER 5

Common Support Problems

In this chapter, you will learn about:

◎ Several categories of common end-user computer problems

◎ Problem-solving processes that can be applied to typical support problems

As you learned in Chapter 4, many problems that user support agents handle are not particularly difficult or complex. In that chapter, you learned about effective problem-solving and troubleshooting processes as well as some of the tools support agents use to solve more difficult problems. In this chapter, you will examine some actual problem-solving situations and how user support agents resolved them.

This chapter is not a comprehensive catalog of every kind of problem a user support agent might encounter; that would be an impossible task. However, experienced support agents see some categories of problems frequently, and in this chapter you will look at several examples of some of the most common kinds of problems. The examples detail how the user described the problem, what problem-solving strategies the support agent employed to solve the problem, and the agent's conclusions about the process. All of the examples are based on actual support situations.

Common End-User Problems

Although computer problems come in a variety of forms, most problems fall into one of seven categories. Figure 5-1 lists these common problem categories. The following sections discuss each category in more detail, with examples presented to illustrate typical problems support specialists may encounter. The problem details are less important than the categories they represent.

- Hardware problems
- Software problems
- User problems
- Documentation problems
- Vendor problems
- Operating environment problems
- Network problems

Figure 5-1   Seven common problem categories

Hardware Problems

Many hardware problems stem from one or more of the following four sources: improper installation, incompatibilities between hardware components, configuration problems, and hardware malfunctions.

Hardware Installation and Compatibility Problems

A large percentage of hardware problems arise when users install a new hardware product or upgrade an old one. A problem may occur because a product is incompatible with existing hardware or because the end user did not install it correctly. **Incompatible** computer components are those that cannot operate together in the same system. The following example illustrates the discovery of hardware incompatibility during installation and the user support agent's solution.

PROBLEM A user purchased a new desktop computer, which included a 1 GB memory module. The user decided to upgrade his RAM by adding a second memory module to speed up the computer. He researched the type of memory that was used in the motherboard of his desktop model and purchased a 2 GB memory module as an upgrade. However, after he installed the memory upgrade, the computer beeped several times and failed to boot up. When he removed the new 2 GB memory module, the computer booted up correctly. The user also tried removing the 1 GB memory module and using just the new 2 GB module, and the computer again booted up correctly.

SOLUTION An online chat with the desktop vendor's technical support staff confirmed that 1 GB and 2 GB memory modules do not always function correctly together on the motherboard of the user's computer model. The hardware vendor suggested that if the user needed more than 1 GB of RAM he should exchange the 2 GB module for a 4 GB module.

ON THE WEB

Some vendors provide information about compatible hardware devices. Microsoft provides a list of devices certified to be compatible with Windows 7 at **www.microsoft.com/windows/compatibility/windows-7/en-us/default.aspx**.

To check compatibility of common hardware devices with Ubuntu, a common version of the Linux operating system, visit **help.ubuntu.com/8.04/switching/preparing-hardware.html**.

Hardware Configuration Problems

Configuration problems occur when hardware (or software) options are set incorrectly for the computer environment in which a component must operate. Hardware settings may be changed by adjusting small jumper pins or DIP switches, as shown in Figure 5-2. For example, a hard drive may serve as a master drive or a slave drive, depending on how jumper pins are set.

Figure 5-2   Dip switches can be used to set configuration options on a motherboard

Hardware settings can also be modified by using a software utility program that selects among various hardware configuration options. A serial port on a communication adapter card can be addressed as COM1, COM2, COM3, or COM4, depending on how the COM address is set when the configuration software is run during installation. In some cases, the startup files on a computer must be modified by installing a vendor's software driver to get a hardware component to operate.

ON THE WEB

To learn more about the role that jumper pins and DIP switches play in hardware configurations, read about these terms in the Webopedia (**www.webopedia.com/TERM/J/jumper.html** and **www.webopedia.com/TERM/D/DIP_switch.html**).

Hardware configuration problems were much more common before the widespread adoption of **Plug and Play standards**, which are a set of protocols followed by hardware and operating system vendors relating to hardware installation. These standards specify the communication methods and rules that an operating system uses to recognize and incorporate hardware components into an operational system. With Plug and Play, an operating system can often recognize the existence of a new hardware component and select configuration options that permit the component to communicate successfully with the operating system.

ON THE WEB

To learn more about Plug and Play standards, visit the Web site of the UPnP Forum, the industry organization that works to establish standards to reduce configuration problems (**www.upnp.org**).

Although Plug and Play standards can help a user load the appropriate device drivers, Plug and Play devices do not always automatically adjust software settings to take maximum advantage of the new hardware's capabilities, as shown in the following example.

PROBLEM   A user purchased a new video graphics adapter card to increase her computer's display screen resolution from 1280 × 1024 pixels to 1600 × 1200 pixels. The card was easy to install, and the Windows 7 operating system recognized on startup that a new piece of hardware had been added to the system. The Windows Add New Hardware Wizard went through the process of installing an updated software driver to support the new video card. However, when the user restarted the computer after installation, the video image was the same resolution as before.

SOLUTION   A PC repair technician suggested that the new video graphics adapter card actually supported several different display screen resolutions, including the older 1280 × 1024 and the newer 1600 × 1200 settings. The technician pointed out that the default resolution for the operating system was probably still set at 1280 × 1024. The technician then instructed the user to right-click the desktop, choose the Graphics Properties option in the context menu, click Display Settings, and then change the Screen Resolution to 1600 × 1200. Once the user changed the operating system's settings to match the new video card's capabilities, the screen image appeared at the higher resolution.

Hardware Malfunctions

Some hardware problems result from components that have either never worked or no longer work. To cut down on this type of problem, an organization's support staff may "burn in" a new system before installing it at a user's workstation. During a **burn-in test**, a new computer or component is operated continuously over a 48- to 72-hour period in an attempt to discover obvious operational problems and to identify any marginal or temperature-sensitive components. A burn-in test gives the support staff the opportunity to identify hardware malfunctions before they become a source of frustration to a user. A burn-in test is effective because a defective component often fails during its first few hours of operation. If a component successfully completes the burn-in test, it is much less likely to fail in the future.

Electromechanical devices that have moving parts (such as hard disks, image scanners, CD and DVD drives, and printers) are much more likely to develop hardware malfunctions than components that are entirely electronic (such as CPUs, memory, bus slots, USB drives, and expansion cards).

ON THE WEB

Passmark sells utility software that performs hardware burn-in tests at **www.passmark.com**.

Vendors that sell hardware components often include a diagnostic utility to help users and support agents detect possible problem components. Many software vendors also sell hardware diagnostic software, which helps user support agents identify common hardware malfunctions. These software programs can detect problems such as a device that is not getting power, a device that is not communicating correctly with other hardware devices, or a device that has a defective logic circuit on its controller card. Although some hardware components that malfunction can be repaired after a problem is identified, the hourly charge for electronic shop labor often makes it more cost-effective to replace rather than repair faulty devices. Support specialists who work with a large population of computers often keep a small supply of spare parts on hand to use when a device needs to be replaced. Others rely on overnight shipping from hardware vendors when a replacement part is needed quickly.

PROBLEM A user called a help desk regarding a problem with an inoperative *S* key on his PC's keyboard. The user wondered if the *S* keycap could have broken and asked if he could bring the keyboard in to the Service Department to get it repaired. He also asked about the cost to repair the *S* key.

SOLUTION The user support agent at the help desk said that physical damage to a keycap is rare and that, more frequently, the contacts located underneath the keycap wear out or get sticky. The support agent explained that hardware technicians rarely try to repair a keyboard malfunction because the cost of a replacement keyboard is usually much less than a technician's time to diagnose and repair a broken keyboard.

ON THE WEB

To see an example of a hardware diagnostic utility, visit the HP support site (**h20239. www2.hp.com/techcenter/HP_SystemCheck/hp_syscheck.htm**).

Other companies that offer software utilities to help diagnose hardware malfunctions include PC-Diag Inc. (**www.pc-diagnostics.com**), AnswersThatWork (**www.answersthatwork.com**), and PC-Doctor Service Center (**www.pcdservicecenter.com**).

Effective Hardware Problem-Solving Steps

To solve hardware problems, support agents should be sure to do the following:

1. Check the hardware vendor's Web site for updated drivers or reports of hardware problems for the specific model that has encountered a problem.

2. Use the Windows troubleshooters to identify common problems. To access the troubleshooters, use the Windows online troubleshooting service at the Fix It Solution Center (**support.microsoft.com/fixit**). Some hardware vendors install additional troubleshooters and diagnostics specific to their systems, which may be located by clicking **All Programs** on the **Start** menu.

3. Look in Device Manager for possible interaction problems between hardware devices and software drivers. To access Device Manager from the Start menu, type *Device Manager* in the Search box, and then click *Device Manager* in the list of search results. Note that some operations in the device manager may be performed only by users with administrator privileges.

4. Examine any applicable README files on the distribution media that accompany the hardware component for updated compatibility information.

5. Use an Internet search engine to locate reports of hardware problems and possible fixes in forums, blogs, and technical support sites.

 The resources discussed in the previous sections often lead to solutions to hardware installation and incompatibility problems. Chapter 4 described several general diagnostic utility programs that also provide useful tools for diagnosing common hardware problems.

ON THE WEB

To find contact information for many hardware vendors, visit **support.microsoft. com/gp/vendors**.

Software Problems

Many software problems stem from one or more of the following five sources: improper installation, incompatibility, configuration problems, bugs, and poor performance.

Software Installation and Compatibility Problems

Software problems occur more frequently during the installation (or setup) process than they do after software is operational. Luckily, installation of new software products and upgrades to existing products are generally easier today than in the past. During the 1970s and 1980s, a user manually created a subdirectory (or folder) for the new software, copied files from the distribution media to a system's hard drive, and then configured software drivers and system startup files to set software options to match the hardware configuration. Because command strings were lengthy and the probability of a typing error was high, the potential for mistakes during this manual procedure was substantial.

Today, the software installation process is usually automated, and users who install software can avoid many common problems that once plagued both users and support agents. **Installation software** is special-purpose utility software used by software vendors to help users install software packages. A software vendor writes a script with the steps to perform an installation. The script can perform steps such as checking on hardware compatibility, creating folders, copying files, updating the system Registry, configuring the software based on the hardware configuration, cleaning up temporary files created during the installation process, and other related tasks. The goal of the script is to automate as many installation tasks as possible. In many cases, the user has only to choose the kind of installation she or he wants, as shown in Figure 5-3. Most steps in the installation offer defaults that a typical user can accept or an advanced user can override.

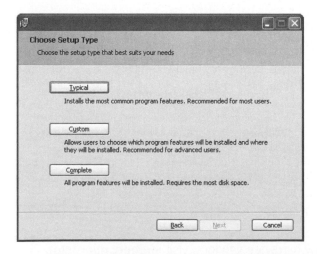

Figure 5-3 This installation utility provides users with setup options

After completing the script, a vendor creates a package that includes the software to be installed, the software installation utility, documentation (such as a user's guide), device drivers, and anything else needed to perform the installation. When a user downloads the vendor's installation package or uses physical distribution media, the user runs the installation utility provided by the vendor. The utility automatically examines the hardware configuration to determine whether the software and hardware are compatible, creates folders with correct pathnames, and sets configuration options in the software and the operating system to match the hardware.

 Chapter 10 contains additional information about software installations.

ON THE WEB

Many companies use a popular installation scripting tool called InstallShield (**www.acresso.com/products/is/installshield-overview.htm**). If you need to purchase a product for your use, some shareware vendors sell lower-cost alternatives, such as wItem Software's Installer2Go (**www.witemsoft.com/togo**).

ON THE WEB

Information about many software compatibility problems can be found in vendor manuals, in README files on distribution media, and on vendor Web sites. For example, see Microsoft's Web site that addresses application software compatibility problems with Windows and offers a compatibility toolkit (**technet.microsoft.com/en-us/library/cc722055%28WS.10%29.aspx**).

Despite installation utilities that solve many common hardware and software configuration issues, support agents still deal with installation problems. Not all software installs automatically, and end users frequently do not understand the implications of various options provided during the installation process. In addition, support agents are occasionally asked to install older software, as in the following example.

PROBLEM A support agent installed a software package—which was originally programmed to run in a Windows 2000 environment—on a Windows 7 system. Unfortunately, the Windows 2000 application did not operate correctly in Windows 7 because it was programmed to use features of Windows 2000 that are no longer supported in Windows 7. Specifically, it sent information to the display screen in ways that are incompatible with Windows 7's methods.

SOLUTION The support agent attempted to contact the software vendor but learned that the company had been sold to another vendor, and the software product was no longer supported. However, a technical support representative at the new company suggested that the support agent investigate Windows 7 compatibility mode, which allows many programs designed to run on older versions of operating systems to run under Windows 7 in compatibility mode. The support agent typed *Windows 7 compatibility mode* into a search engine and found several useful articles about setting an application to operate in compatibility mode. Fortunately, the software that was originally designed to run in Windows 2000 worked correctly in Windows 7 under compatibility mode.

A computer may be set up as a dual-boot system so it can run both a newer operating system and an older one. This solution sometimes permits legacy versions of software to operate on newer computers using an older operating system. A utility that helps set up and manage a dual-boot system is DualBootPro (**www.dualbootpro.org**).

Shareware software downloaded from the Internet can be another source of compatibility problems. **Shareware** is commercial software that users can try out with the vendor's permission during an evaluation period (usually 10 to 45 days; 30 is most common) prior to making a purchase decision. Although many shareware programs are written to industry programming standards and are designed to be compatible with operating systems and other applications, some shareware programs may produce conflicts with hardware or other software. A **conflict** is a condition in which a computer component uses system resources (e.g., CPU, memory, or peripheral devices) in a way that is incompatible with another component. Conflicts often make systems inoperable or prevent them from operating normally (for example, by slowing down performance).

Another category of software that can sometimes cause compatibility problems is **freeware**, which, as the name implies, is distributed without cost or a licensing fee. **Donationware** is a category of freeware for which there is no set purchase price but for which a donation is requested by the author to support further development of a product. A freeware license usually states that users are free to use, but not sell, the software. Some freeware runs trouble-free, but users are advised to take precautions, such as making a backup copy of the system Registry (described below), prior to the installation of freeware programs. Those who write and distribute freeware usually do not intend to provide software that is incompatible. However, shareware and freeware may not be tested for compatibility to the same extent that commercial software is.

ON THE WEB

Distributors of shareware programs include **www.tucows.com**, **www.jumbo.com**, **www.shareware.com**, and **download.cnet.com**.

A distributor of freeware programs is **www.freewarebox.com**.

Freeware and shareware are not the same as open source software. **Open source software** is developed collaboratively by a loose-knit group of programmers who agree to join efforts to improve and debug a software product and make the source code (and the program) available to anyone. Open source software is often comparable in quality to commercial software. Open source software may carry an Open Source Initiative (OSI) certification. The OSI certification means that the software has been developed under specific design principles and guidelines.

ON THE WEB

To learn more about the development of open source software, visit the Web site of the Open Source Initiative (**www.opensource.org**).

A collection of some of the most popular open source software for the Windows operating system is maintained at **www.opensourcewindows.org**.

Software Configuration Problems

Some software problems are related to the way the software is configured to run on a system. Configuration problems result when software parameters and options are not set correctly for the specific operating environment or hardware. These problems may occur when end users install or upgrade new hardware or software or attempt to use a software feature for the first time, as in the following example.

PROBLEM A Windows user installed a new software application that uses a utility program called Word Viewer 2010. After the installation, the end user could not open any Microsoft Word document by double-clicking it. When the user double-clicked a Word (DOC or DOCX) file, Word Viewer 2010 opened the document rather than Word itself. However, the user reported that if he started Word and used the File menu's Open command, he could successfully open a DOC or DOCX file in Word. For convenience, he would like to be able to double-click a Word file and have it open in Word.

SOLUTION A support worker researched the problem on the Web and found that Word Viewer 2010 is a free Microsoft utility that allows users who do not have the Word program to view, but not modify, any Word file. The support agent suggested that perhaps when the new application that uses Word Viewer was installed, it configured Word Viewer as the default application for all Word (DOC and DOCX) files. The support agent advised the user to perform the following steps: Right-click any Word file to select it, point to the "Open with" command, and click "Choose default program." In the "Open with" dialog box, select Microsoft Word, and then click the check box in front of the option to "Always use the selected program to open this kind of file."

Another source of problems related to software compatibility and configuration in the Windows operating system is the system Registry. The **Registry** file serves as a database of configuration information related to a system's hardware and software components. During normal system operation, the Registry is frequently read from and written to by applications and system software. The Registry file can also be edited with a software utility— regedit.exe or regedit32.exe (depending on operating system version). However, end users and support agents who are unfamiliar with the Registry, its entries, and how to modify the configuration information should avoid making or modifying entries in the Registry. Improper Registry information can result in an inoperable system. Due to the frequency of Registry problems, Windows includes a feature to restore a prior version of the Registry on a computer that fails to operate because of invalid changes to Registry information.

 Warning! Modification of the Windows system Registry should never be attempted by anyone who is not entirely familiar with the purpose of a Registry, how it is organized, and how to back up, restore, modify, and save it. A damaged Registry can cause serious problems. Support agents who need to learn about the Registry should consult one of the many trade books that describe its use and proper procedures for modification.

ON THE WEB

To take a tutorial on Registry basics, visit **www.pctools.com/guides/article/id/1**. A free Windows Registry editor is available at **regmagik.com/default.htm**.

Any tool that modifies or repairs the Registry should be used with care and appropriate precautions.

To guard against an inoperable system due to Registry corruption, many support specialists advise users to create an emergency system recovery CD, DVD, or USB drive for each system, and to learn to use automated Registry recovery utilities when an operating system offers these tools. For more information, use an operating system's help feature to search for detailed procedures.

Software Bugs

Bugs are errors in a computer program that occur when a programmer writes incorrectly coded instructions during program development. A bug causes the software to either not do what it is expected to do or to do things that it is not intended to do. Some bugs occur because a programmer made a mistake, but more often they occur because the programmer could not anticipate every possible situation that might arise when the program is used on various hardware platforms or with other software. Bugs are more likely to occur in freeware, shareware, and custom-developed programs than in mass-market commercial programs; they are also more likely to occur in the first version of any software than in subsequent versions. In all software, bugs are more likely to be encountered in infrequently used features of a program. Many bugs are eliminated during the testing period that occurs before a software product is released for sale. However, even the most popular software products have known bugs several years after their initial release.

In order to fix bugs and provide new features, software vendors often distribute patches, updates, service packs, new releases, new versions, and upgrades:

- A **patch** is a replacement for one or a few modules of a software package to fix known bugs.

- An **update** is a bug-fix distribution that repairs known problems in a previous version or release of a software package; some vendors include an **automatic update** feature that periodically checks the vendor's Web site for updates that are recommended to solve specific problems and bring the version of the software up to current specifications.

- A **service pack** (or **service release**) contains both updates and patches to fix documented problems with a version of a program.

- A new **release** of a program is a distribution that contains some new features not found in the original program.

- A new **version** of a software package contains significant new features and is usually the result of a substantially rewritten program.

- An **upgrade** is a new version of an existing program that is sold at a reduced cost to owners of a previous version of the program.

Although no industry standards dictate how vendors should designate software distributions, some software vendors use the version number to indicate the release type. For example, Version 2.0 is the first distribution of a new version, and Version 2.1 is an update with new features. Version 2.11 (or 2.1.1) is a bug-fix release or an update of Version 2.1 that does not necessarily include major new features. Other vendors add a service pack/ release letter to a version number. For example, Version 2.5A is the first (A-level) patch of Release 2.5.

Some vendors identify a **build number**, which designates a lower-level version number and can create a four-part identification: Version#– Release# – Update# - Build#. Some software vendors also use the year of release to number their software versions. For example, *Office 2010* is the release of the Office Suite issued in the year 2010. Although there is usually no direct correspondence between competing vendors' version-numbering schemes, vendors may intentionally skip a version number in order to maintain parity with the version number of a competitor's product.

The version number of a software product can usually be found in the Help menu by clicking on the About menu item.

The following example illustrates how one end user obtained a patch.

PROBLEM An end user experienced a formatting problem in an accounting program that occurred only with very large dollar amounts.

SOLUTION When the end user contacted the software vendor's help desk, the user learned that the problem was a known bug, that it had been repaired, and that a patch could be downloaded from the vendor's Web site. The vendor's help desk staff explained that the problem would affect very few users, provided the user with instructions on how to download the patch, and explained that it would self-install when the user double-clicked the downloaded file.

Before a user or support agent installs any patch, he or she should verify that the patch is for the software version that is actually installed on the user's system. A cautious user or support agent may choose to back up the original copy of a program before updates are installed. In addition, any software updates, service packs, or patches that are installed on a computer should be documented in the site installation notebook, as described in Chapter 10. If a patch is installed, it must be reinstalled if it becomes necessary to reinstall the original software from the distribution media. Therefore, support agents should maintain a record of all updates and patches installed on a system as a reinstallation reminder. In general, new software releases or versions incorporate all bug fixes that have been reported and fixed prior to the new release. For example, Version 3.1 of a particular program would contain all patches released for Version 3.0. However, the documentation for some patches may include a note, for example, that Patch 3.4A must be installed before Patch 3.4B can be installed.

In cases where no patch exists for a software bug, a support agent or software vendor may be able to suggest a workaround for a problem. A **workaround** is a procedure or operation that accomplishes the same result as the original feature that currently does not work due to a bug or other malfunction. Workarounds are used when it is impossible or impractical for a support agent to correct an underlying problem. For example, a command in a GUI environment can often be entered in several ways: keyboard commands, menu commands, toolbar icons, or shortcut keys. If a menu option does not work correctly, a keyboard shortcut may provide a successful workaround.

Software Performance Problems

Performance problems occur when a computer is operational but is not operating as efficiently as it should. Although performance problems are sometimes due to excessive traffic on a network, degraded performance can result from poor interaction between hardware and software. For example, a user may report that a PC's hard drive light comes on more frequently and stays on longer than it used to and that the system seems sluggish. Or the response time from when a Save command is selected to the completion of the Save task has been increasing. The user may suspect that the problem is due to hardware—perhaps the hard drive is beginning to fail. However, performance problems are usually related to how the software—the operating system, in this case—is managing the hardware. Before concluding that a hard drive failure is the likely problem, a support agent might investigate alternate explanations, such as those in the following list:

- The hard drive may be nearly full; the operating system may not have adequate unused space to write temporary files to the hard drive during its file management tasks. The user may need to back up and then delete infrequently used programs and data files, or install a second hard drive in the system.

- The hard disk may be fragmented; files written on the disk in small chunks take longer to read and write than files in contiguous sectors on the disk. A defragmentation (or defrag, for short) utility can often fix this problem, as described in Chapter 12.

- The hard drive may contain wasted space because links to free space are lost. Windows utility programs—such as Scandisk and Chkdsk—can often locate and reclaim lost space resulting from improperly linked allocation units on a disk.

- The system may not have enough RAM to run the software and may be using the hard disk as an extension of RAM (called *virtual memory* or *swap file space*) to accommodate large amounts of data. The virtual memory may need to be enlarged, or the computer may just need additional internal memory to run the software efficiently. Hardware experts often emphasize that the most effective way to improve software performance is to add RAM.

- The system may be infected with one or more kinds of malware, such as a virus, spyware, or a keystroke logger. Running a utility program to scan the hard drive for malware may improve overall system performance.

 Performance problems may also occur in a system that is not properly maintained. Users should take advantage of automatic update features in operating systems, software utilities, and application programs. Performance is usually maintained or enhanced when a system's software is kept up to date on a regular schedule by downloading updates from a vendor's Web site.

A user's ability to operate the software is often closely related to software problems.

User Problems

Users unintentionally cause many support problems. Although most users strive to be well informed and try to use hardware and software correctly, even the best-intentioned users can introduce problems.

Workers in the support industry have coined a special acronym to label user problems: *PEBSAK* is a designation that the *Problem Exists Between Seat and Keyboard*.

Mistakes

All end users, including computer professionals, make mistakes. During the initial design of a program, systems analysts may not adequately understand all the detailed aspects of a business process and may design a software solution incorrectly. Programmers may make mistakes in the code they write and introduce software bugs. A professionally trained and experienced data-entry operator may type an erroneous keystroke every few thousand characters. Even experienced user support workers make an occasional error. What can be done about user mistakes? Well-designed computer systems anticipate many potential user mistakes, alert the user, and provide corrective action. For example, an accounting program may be able to perform a validity check on input data and detect input errors. A common example is a range validity check on the number of hours each employee worked in a week to identify input that falls outside a predefined range of values. For example, an input of *400* (instead of *40*) would trigger a warning.

Despite the best efforts of software developers, users occasionally press a wrong key or click the mouse in an unintended situation and end up in a part of a program where they didn't want to be. Some inadvertent user actions are invalid and have no consequence other than a beep or a redisplayed prompt message. Other errors can have more drastic consequences. For example, in some word processors, if a passage is selected (highlighted) and the user inadvertently presses any key, the character representing the pressed key replaces the entire selected passage. Users who don't know how to recover from this situation (such as by pressing the Undo button) can easily lose some work.

Inadvertently pressing the Caps Lock key instead of the Tab or Shift key is a common keyboarding error. To hear an audible beep whenever the Caps Lock key is pressed, click on the Windows 7's **Start** button and enter *Ease* in the search box. In the Program list, click on **Ease of Access Center.** Then click on **Make keyboard easier to use**. Finally, click the option to **Turn on Toggle Keys**.

User mistakes account for a significant percentage of common problems. However, support agents need to consider carefully how to handle these problems from a client service perspective; some users do not like to be told that they made a mistake. Chapter 2 offered strategies for handling difficult interactions with users.

Misunderstandings

Other end-user problems stem from misunderstandings about product features or limitations. Users may expect a product or service to be able to perform tasks for which it was not intended. Or they may be unaware of a product's features, as shown in the following example.

PROBLEM A user complained that it took a long time to find a file on his computer. On investigation, a user support worker discovered that the user kept all his work files in the Documents directory. His Documents folder had hundreds of files in it, all at the top level. He had never created subfolders for various projects so that his work would be better organized and easier to find. When asked why, he explained that he understood the concept of subfolders but had never taken the time to learn about creating them.

SOLUTION The support worker showed the user how easy it is to create folders and subfolders for each project or routine task in Windows, and demonstrated how to drag and drop files into folders. The support worker also explained that it would take some time to reorganize all the files in the Documents folder, but that the user would reap the rewards when it was time to locate a file he needed.

 User mistakes sometimes provide an opening for a support agent to tactfully point a user toward a training opportunity, whether an in-house session, a trade book, or a computer-based tutorial.

Wrong Products

Users may purchase the wrong product to accomplish a task. For example, they may buy a software package or hardware peripheral that is incompatible with their existing system. A common problem occurs when a user of an older model PC hears about a new software product they want to use, but does not understand that the new product requires a faster processor or more memory than their computer has. Users with Windows computers may inadvertently purchase the Macintosh version of a software package because they have not read the packaging carefully.

Furthermore, users may purchase software without understanding its capabilities or without knowledge of alternatives, as in the following example.

PROBLEM A Macintosh user who wanted to create a newsletter bought a collection of clip art on a CD-ROM from an office supply store because the packaging included an illustration of clip art embedded in a newsletter. The user assumed that the software was capable of producing a newsletter like the one illustrated on the package. When the user installed the clip art on his system, he called the support number in the documentation to complain that the software did not produce the newsletter format he wanted.

SOLUTION The software vendor's customer support agent provided the user with a Return Merchandise Authorization (RMA) number and suggested that the user return to the store to look for a desktop publishing program with a newsletter template.

A similar problem can arise with the purchase of new hardware, as the next problem illustrates.

PROBLEM A user purchased an external hard drive to back up data from a computer's internal hard drive. The new external drive was designed to connect to a computer's USB port. Unfortunately, the user's computer was an older model that had only two USB ports, which were needed for his keyboard and mouse. Because the user couldn't figure out how to connect the drive to his computer, he put the external drive in his closet, awaiting an opportunity to ask for assistance.

SOLUTION Unfortunately, the user was unaware that an inexpensive USB port expansion card or external USB hub could easily be added to his system to accommodate other USB devices. Therefore, the external hard drive is still in his closet today. And, with no backup, the user still worries about what will happen if he experiences problems with the data on his internal drive.

Inadequate Information or Training

Many computer problems arise because users are inadequately trained or do not read the documentation that came with the hardware or software. A high percentage of calls to support centers can be easily answered by referring to a user manual, a tutorial, or online help. Users often do not know where to find the information they need, or they don't want to take the time to search for information. Users who have not been adequately trained or who do not recall information from a training session pose a challenge for help desk staff. Ideally, training sessions should not only provide users with the information they need, but should also include pointers to where users can locate the information later, without help desk assistance.

Quick start behavior is a tendency among computer users to skip the installation manual and attempt to get new hardware or software installed and operational as rapidly as possible. Their attitude can be summed up as: *"If all else fails, I can always read the manual later."* Many vendors include a very brief quick start guide, or "Getting Started with..." manual or instruction sheet, in an attempt to get users at least to read something before they begin to use a new product. For example, Figure 5-4 shows the first page of a getting started tutorial for Picasa, Google's photo organizing and editing software.

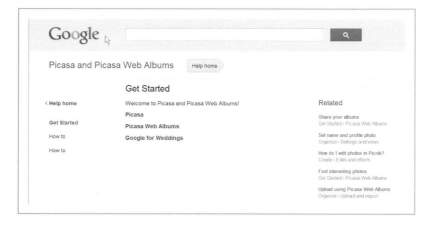

Figure 5-4 Example of a quick start tutorial for Picasa

Lack of adequate information and training ultimately translate into wasted effort and lost user productivity. For example, the Macintosh user described earlier who wanted to produce a newsletter did not realize that his word processor included many of the features he would need to produce a reasonably complex newsletter. He actually had the software he needed but did not realize it. Appropriate training or consulting with user support staff could help him learn how to use an existing program to produce newsletters.

 User problems that result from inadequate documentation and training provide both a challenge and an opportunity for support specialists who write documentation, as you learned in Chapter 3, and for those who train users, as you will learn in Chapter 11.

Forgotten Information

At times, users simply forget how to perform a task or find the information they need. For example, local area network administrators report that the single most common contact they experience is from users who have forgotten the password to their accounts. Web sites that register users receive many phone calls and emails from users who cannot remember the PIN (personal identification number) they need to log on to the site. Many Web sites that require registration have now automated the password-recovery process via an email reminder so no support staff time is required to respond to the high volume of requests for passwords.

For users who are forgetful or who infrequently use a password, one strategy is to keep a written note in an obscure location that does not contain their actual password, but contains a word or phrase that serves as a password reminder. Some operating systems and application programs include a feature to store and retrieve passwords for users or ask a prompting question to help refresh a user's recollection of a password. These features should be used with caution in an office or school environment where other users may have access to a system.

Support agents should caution users against writing their passwords on paper. One of the biggest security problems in many organizations is users who write their password on a sticky note and attach the reminder to their monitor, where anyone who walks past can easily see it.

Users who make less frequent use of their computers are especially likely to forget information. Reference sheets (formal or informal notes) and scripts or checklists are an effective aid to help users recall how to perform infrequent tasks that are difficult to remember.

Documentation Problems

Another source of end-user support problems can be traced to inadequate documentation. The readability of computer vendor documentation has generally improved in recent years. However, documentation that is poorly organized, inaccurate, and omits important points is still the direct cause of much misunderstanding, which contributes to user frustration as well as to a higher volume of help desk calls.

A complete set of user documentation can include:

- a quick start guide
- a tutorial that walks a user through the major features of a software package
- a reference manual with information organized by topic
- a troubleshooting guide
- online help, including information that users can search by keyword
- troubleshooting wizards to assist users with common problems

Well-written user documentation takes time to develop. Support staff who write documentation, whether in print or online, should make effective use of graphics. Users learn faster and retain information longer when visuals are used to supplement narrative explanations. Support staff should also consider how to address user quick start behavior when they design and develop documentation. Finally, support staff should ask coworkers and end users to review documentation and help identify points that need clarification before publication.

Support staff who prepare user documentation should follow the suggestions offered in Chapter 3 on writing end-user documentation.

Vendor Problems

Calls to a help desk or hotline may be related to vendor performance. Some vendors consistently oversell their products; they advertise or promise features that may not be delivered as part of the current version of the product. Vendors may also release a beta software version that contains known bugs that can put user data at risk or produce questionable results. Some vendors are also notorious for delivering new products long after they were promised. Help desk agents may find themselves in the uncomfortable position of handling incidents from users who are complaining about their company's performance as a vendor. Or agents may be asked to consult with internal users who have been the victim of vendor performance problems.

Vaporware refers to hardware or software products that appear in ads or press releases but are not yet available for sale. A vendor may announce a product that doesn't yet exist in order to study market reaction or to confuse its competitors. A help desk that handles incidents for external users usually establishes a policy for its support staff on how to handle clients who have questions about product announcements. Chapter 2 described some client service and communications skills that are useful in handling these incidents.

Rebates on hardware and software purchases are often a source of user frustration with vendor performance. The purpose of a vendor rebate is to encourage sales; a price with a rebate subtracted is often attractively low. Failure to provide a rebate during the time period promised in an advertisement is a client service issue, and it can have as much impact as product features or performance on a user's impression of a vendor. Some vendors are very conscientious about rebate deadlines and provide contact information so clients can check on the status of a rebate. In other cases, rebate fulfillment centers are understaffed and struggle to keep up with the volume of calls and emails related to expected client rebates. Questions and complaints about rebates are common to help desk agents in some vendors' support organizations.

ON THE WEB

To learn more about rebates and how to guard against problems, visit **www.consumeraffairs.com/consumerism/rebate_madness01.html**.

Operating Environment Problems

Some support calls are about problems in the environment in which computers are operated. The operating environment category includes:

- problems with computing facilities
  - electricity, lighting, and air conditioning
  - office furniture and related office equipment
  - workplace ergonomics and safety

- problems with the computing environment
  - data backup and recovery
  - security threats
  - disaster and contingency planning and preparation

Chapter 10 describes solutions to several problems with computing facilities and the operating environment.

Network Problems

Computer networks are a frequent source of problems that support agents encounter. However, many network problems are traceable to hardware (including servers, hubs, routers, bridges, switches, and gateways), software, operating systems, or other categories of problems discussed earlier. Network problems are often among those that are most difficult for a support staff to handle because they frequently involve the interaction of hardware, software, and other components.

PROBLEM A network administrator in a county planning office received several phone calls and emails one morning indicating that the office network was running very slowly. The network staff uses a network monitoring and performance utility distributed by ManageEngine called OpManager. This utility tool monitors several aspects of network operation, including servers, network devices, printers, and other aspects of network operation. The administrator checked on OpManager's performance indicators and learned that the server disk space was perilously full. She knew that disk space usage was tight and that the agency had discussed purchasing additional disk storage for the server. The system had been operating normally the previous day, however.

SOLUTION Upon further checking, the network administrator discovered that one of the planners had downloaded some very large files of training videos the previous evening; the files had filled up most of the free disk space on the server. She contacted the planner and offered to back up the video files onto a tape cartridge until they were needed. The planner agreed. The network administrator was able to use network monitoring software to help identify the network bottleneck. Then, she was able to troubleshoot the problem and offer a solution that permitted her to free up valuable space on the server's hard drive and return the network to normal operation.

ON THE WEB

If you would like to learn more about the network monitoring tool the administrator used, view a five-minute video overview of OpManager (**manageengine.adventnet. com/products/opmanager/OpManagerOverview.htm**).

Many print publications serve as a good resource for best practices in troubleshooting common computer problems:

- Morris Rosenthal, *Computer Repair with Diagnostic Flowcharts: Troubleshooting PC Hardware Problems from Boot Failure to Poor Performance* (Foner Books, 2008). (Preview selected flowcharts at **www.fonerbooks.com/pcrepair.htm**.)

- Jean Andrews, *PC Troubleshooting Pocket Guide for Managing & Maintaining Your PC* (Boston: Course Technology, 2010).

- Mitch Tulloch, et al., *Windows 7 Resource Kit.* (Redmond, WA: Microsoft Press, 2009).

- Ed Bott and Carl Siechert, *2010 Microsoft Office Inside Out.* (Redmond, WA: Microsoft Press, 2010).

ON THE WEB

Many sites on the Web also provide helpful information for user support staff who work on specific problems or want to know more about the troubleshooting and problem-solving process.

General troubleshooting:

- **pcsupport.about.com**—This About.com site contains a wealth of information on PCs and troubleshooting.

- **www.askdrtech.com**—Ask Dr. Tech is a fee-based site that provides 24/7 support services via phone or Web.

- **www.smartcomputing.com/techsupport**—*Smart Computing* magazine's site offers a variety of services on the Web and via phone, email, or online chat. Some services require a paid subscription to their monthly magazine.

Hardware troubleshooting:

- **www.tomshardware.com/us**—Tom's Hardware Guide contains a database of searchable articles on common hardware components.

- **www.directron.com/howtobuilyou.html**—Directron.org's site includes troubleshooting tips for several types of hardware components.

- **www.preventiveguru.com**—PreventiveGuru's computer maintenance guide provides articles on repairs for various hardware components.

- **hardwarehell.com/macintos.shtml**—This site provides links to a variety of troubleshooting resources for Mac OS systems.

(continues)

(continued)

Software troubleshooting:

- **www.helpwithwindows.com**—HelpWithWindows.com's troubleshooting tips link to articles on common problems (select your version of Windows in the tabs at the top).

- **support.microsoft.com**—This site is Microsoft's product support center for operating system and application software. In the search box, enter *troubleshoot* and the name of the product.

- **guides.macrumors.com/Troubleshooting_Software_Problems**—The MacRumors Web site includes several sections for resolving Macintosh software problems.

Other resources:

- **www.google.com**—The Google search engine can locate Web sites for specific problems; use the name of hardware and software products, as well as version and model numbers, for search keywords.

- **www.ask.com**—The Ask search engine provides information in an informal question-and-answer format.

- **www.zdnet.com**—ZDNet's extensive Web site offers product and troubleshooting information and tips; the home page includes a keyword search feature.

- **www.about.com/compute**—About.com is a collection of moderated Web sites with information on a variety of topics. The home page includes an extensive menu and keyword search feature.

Problem-Solving Processes Applied to Typical End-User Problems

As the user support staff in an organization solve the kinds of computer problems described in this chapter, the solutions become common knowledge among members of the staff. They use this ever-expanding bank of knowledge to solve new problems. The greater the variety of problems user support agents are exposed to, the more knowledge and experience they will have at their command to tackle new problems. User support agents use the problem-solving processes described in Chapter 4 to find appropriate solutions, as shown in the following accounts from support agents about how they resolved some typical support problems.

Problem 1: Sounds Like Trouble

PROBLEM A user in a remote branch office sent me an email message stating that she had lost the sound in her system. I started the troubleshooting process by asking questions about her basic configuration and some critical questions, such as, *"Has this problem ever happened before?"* and *"What programs were you running when you noticed the sound was lost?"* She wrote back that the system is a Pentium, running Windows. She indicated that the sound had been working fine, and she couldn't remember exactly which program she was running when she first noticed the sound no longer worked. She also mentioned that two other employees had access to her system.

PROBLEM-SOLVING STRATEGY My first reaction was to try some quick fixes. I suggested that she do the following:

- Reset the sound card in the expansion slot.
- Try the sound card in a different expansion slot.
- Check all the connections and cables to the sound card.
- Check the Windows device manager to see if there were any IRQ conflicts between the sound card and other devices.

The user responded that she had checked these items, but that the sound still didn't work. I discussed the problem with some support colleagues, describing what we had already tried. They came up with a few other suggestions:

- Make sure that the volume is turned up on the speakers.
- Make sure that the volume is turned up in the Windows media player.
- Check that the speakers are connected correctly.
- If the speakers require electrical current, make sure they're plugged in and turned on.

The user checked all these possibilities and reported that there was still no sound. I asked her if there were any changes made to her system recently. She wrote back that one of her work colleagues had downloaded a shareware version of an antivirus program from the Internet about the time the sound problem first occurred. The colleague said that, after several attempts, he couldn't get the antivirus program to work correctly on the system, so he uninstalled it. The fact that new software had recently been installed on her system got me thinking in a different direction. I looked on the Internet and found a Web site for her brand of sound card. They listed about 20 different models of cards, one of which was hers. I sent her the Web address where she could download the latest version of the software driver for her particular card. Later that day, I received a message that she had downloaded the sound card driver, installed it in Windows, and her sound worked again.

CONCLUSION I'm not certain of the diagnosis, but I think the shareware program may have affected the driver software used by her sound card. Once she reinstalled the driver, the problem was fixed.

I was pleased that I solved the problem. I used communications skills to get information from the end user, which was not easy using email. I also used critical questions that opened up a different avenue of investigation. I used several information resources, including my support colleagues and the vendor's Web site. I used some troubleshooting strategies, including looking for an obvious fix, some hypothesis testing, and module replacement. (*Based on an incident described by Billie Brendlinger.*)

Problem 2: The Problem with Modems

PROBLEM I work for an Internet Service Provider (ISP) as an installer/troubleshooter. I was at a client's site in a small, rural town to troubleshoot an Internet setup on their Macintosh computer. I had previously installed Internet access software and configured the client's machine for Internet access. I had also trained the user to log on and run the software to access the Internet. After the installation, everything appeared to be in working order.

The user called our trouble line about a week later, saying that she had an occasional problem with Internet access from her Mac. Her modem usually dialed our ISP's server successfully, but occasionally it would report that it couldn't get a dial tone.

PROBLEM-SOLVING STRATEGY On my follow-up visit, I asked a series of questions about her telephone service, including whether she had any features added to her basic phone service, such as caller ID, call waiting, or other services. The end user assured me that her telephone was a standard line with no frills. I checked the modem with the terminal emulation software, and the diagnostic check indicated that the modem was correctly connected. Because the setup had worked after the original installation, I had suspected the modem connection was okay, but I was glad to get the confirmation.

Then I decided to unplug the modem and connect the telephone handset directly to the phone line. My hypothesis was that there was something wrong with the telephone service that was affecting the modem. When I picked up the handset, I heard a "blip-blip-blip-blip" sound, then a long pause, and finally a dial tone. I recalled that I had heard the blip sounds before at a friend's house. I realized that it is the sound that the telephone company's voice mail system makes when the client has a message waiting. If there were no voice mail messages waiting, there were no blip sounds.

CONCLUSION I advised the user to check for voice mail messages before dialing the Internet phone number. I also found a setting in the Internet access software that controls the amount of time the software listens for a dial tone before it gives up. I increased the time to 20 seconds in case the user forgot to check for voice mail messages.

The problem was an interesting one, and I was glad I was able to solve it. I learned that users don't always know the answers to the questions I ask. In this case, the user's answers threw me off track. I also used my personal experience to identify the source of the voice mail tones on the phone line. The rest of the process involved eliminating variables (when I replaced the modem with the telephone handset) and hypothesis testing. *(Based on an incident reported by Jaime Chamoulos.)*

Problem 3: Give Credit Where It Is Due

PROBLEM I am a support person in an online ticket sales company. A computer operator within our company is responsible for running an electronic data interchange (EDI) software package to process credit card transactions. The program uploads batches of credit card transactions to a credit card processor, which then authenticates each transaction and processes it with the financial institution that issued the credit card.

The computer operator was frustrated and unhappy with the EDI software because the program would not process batches of transactions correctly, so she had to enter each transaction individually. She had contacted the EDI software vendor, who said the problem was likely on the credit card processor's end. When the operator called the processor, they pointed the finger back at the EDI software package. I was assigned the task of finding the cause of the problem.

PROBLEM-SOLVING STRATEGY Before I contacted the software company, I wanted to make sure I understood how the procedure was supposed to work and what the real problem was. I put together a list of the subsystems in the procedure:

1. Computer operator batches together credit card transactions.

2. EDI software uploads and transmits the batch of transactions to the credit card processor.

3. Credit card processor posts transactions to customer accounts.

4. Credit card processor returns a confirmation report of processed transactions.

5. Computer operator verifies the status of processed transactions.

I considered that the problem could be with the EDI software program, the credit card processor, or the computer operator's procedures. I started at the top of the list and assumed that the problem was with the EDI software. I decided to install it on my own computer, read through the manual, and use the computer operator's notes to learn how to process batches of transactions. Although the software documentation was skimpy, I eventually pieced together enough information to understand how the program worked. I put together a few sample transactions to test the system. The test cases that I constructed seemed to work fine. I decided to create better documentation for the computer operator based on the software manual, her notes, and some conversations I had with a representative from the EDI software company about the batch-processing procedure.

Then the computer operator and I went through the process of building a batch of transactions with some actual data. We used my expanded documentation as a guide and

214

a checklist. The batch file we uploaded seemed to process correctly, but we did not receive the expected confirmation that the transactions were received or accepted. According to the software manual, the credit card processor should have sent us a report file indicating a normal termination of the batch process as well as the status of each transaction. The next day, I called the credit card processor to see if they could verify that the transactions we sent had been received and approved. They had been, so I was fairly confident that the procedure documentation I wrote was accurate. We could upload batches of transactions that were received and processed by the credit card processor.

However, we still did not know why we hadn't received the confirmation. I tried to open the report file from within the EDI software, but nothing happened. I eventually found the report file on the hard drive and used a file-diagnosis utility to examine it. My examination revealed that the file contained all of the confirmations that successful batches of transactions had been uploaded and received, including the ones we had sent the previous day. For some reason, the EDI program could not display the file. Then I noticed some corrupted data at the beginning of the report file that was in a different format than the remainder of the file. I made a backup copy of the file as a precaution and then deleted the original. The next day, we ran a batch of about 200 transactions. The credit card processor received the transactions, processed them, and returned the confirmation file successfully.

CONCLUSION I think the corrupted data in the report file may have been due to an error the computer operator made because she didn't really understand all the steps necessary to transmit batches. When the confirmation for each day's transactions was added to the corrupted file, it could not be displayed. Once I removed the corrupted data, the confirmation report could be displayed correctly.

I used a list of subsystems and a lot of hypothesis testing on this problem. I also tried to replicate on my own system the problem the operator had experienced. To this day, I'm not sure I understand the exact error the computer operator made. She was very frustrated and obviously needed better documentation. Based on the documentation I prepared, she has been able to process transactions correctly ever since I worked on this problem. *(Based on an incident described by Mark Gauthier.)*

Problem 4: Antivirus Protection Worth Every Cent You Pay for It

PROBLEM A user called the help desk hotline to ask if we had ever heard of a free antivirus program called Win 7 Anti-Virus 2011. He had downloaded the program from a Web site, and it had scanned his hard disk for viruses and identified several vulnerabilities. The program listed the problems and indicated the program could remove the infected files if he updated the program by purchasing a full license on the Web. The user asked if our company would pay for a license for the program.

PROBLEM-SOLVING STRATEGY I had never heard of Win 7 Anti-Virus 2011 nor the Web site where the user downloaded the program. However, new shareware programs seem to be available daily, so I wasn't surprised—only suspicious. I checked several reputable download sites on the Web and could not find any reference to Win 7 Anti-Virus. Upon checking further, I discovered some Web sites that described the program as **malware**, which is a program with harmful or malicious intent that disrupts the normal operation of a computer or network, or attempts to steal information or money as a result of its operation.

I learned that the program is not a Microsoft product, and probably uses the name Win 7 illegally. Most legitimate antivirus programs will detect and delete Win 7 Anti-Virus. I found a Web site with instructions for manual removal (**www.howtogeek.com/57837/how-to-remove-win-7-anti-spyware-2011-fake-anti-malware-infections**). The site also includes links to programs that will detect the malware program.

CONCLUSION I was able to help the user remove the Win 7 Anti-Virus program using the instructions I found on the Web. To solve this problem, I relied on my experience with popular antivirus software and an ability to locate useful information resources on the Web. I was pleased to be able to save the user from wasting money on a useless piece of software. As a result of this incident, I wrote a short note to warn about the Win 7 Anti-Virus program for the next issue of our user support newsletter. I also sent the user a pointer to a Web site where he could download our company's recommended antivirus utility.

Problem 5: The Path Not Taken

PROBLEM The phone call came into the support center late one afternoon. A user said that one of his PCs could no longer access my company's vertical market software. The rest of our support staff was in a training seminar for the afternoon, so I had to solve the problem on my own. As a new member of the support staff, I was a little nervous. The user on the phone said that he had been able to run the software successfully earlier in the day, but the desktop icon to run our software package was no longer visible.

PROBLEM-SOLVING STRATEGY After asking a few questions and paraphrasing some of his statements, I clarified that the icon for our software was actually still on the desktop but that double-clicking it produced no results. I asked several other questions, including the critical question, *"What were you doing on the system when the icon stopped working?"* The user responded that he had been deleting some unwanted files.

My first thought was that perhaps the user had accidentally deleted the EXE file associated with the icon. I led him through the steps to see if the EXE program file was still in the correct folder—it was. My next idea was that perhaps the shortcut path from the icon to the EXE file had been destroyed. After checking the shortcut properties, we confirmed that the path was in place. Then I wondered whether the user had somehow deleted the path to some of the files the program needs to operate. I wasn't sure how to check that, but I knew that some of the files were on a server and that each client machine defines the drive mappings to the network drives when it boots up. I explained my reasoning to the user and suggested that he quit all applications and shut down his system, just as if it were the end of the day. We waited a few seconds and then rebooted his system. After the reboot, everything worked fine. Apparently, he had accidentally erased the drive mappings during his system housekeeping.

An EXE file is an executable program in a Windows system (as are COM and DLL files).

CONCLUSION I was pleased to be able to handle the call, which was one of my first as a user support agent. I used several troubleshooting strategies, including communication skills to listen to the user's definition of the problem, paraphrasing, and asking critical questions to give me the information I needed to formulate a hypothesis. I also used a mental image of the sequence from the icon to the disk files to troubleshoot the problem. *(Based on an incident reported by Andra Heath.)*

Problem 6: The Nonresponsive Network

PROBLEM I am the network support assistant for an economic research think tank. One afternoon I received a call from a staff member who reported that something was wrong with his workstation. He said it was very sluggish. I walked down the hall and looked at his workstation, which was running Excel. The user was in the process of saving a worksheet on the file server, but Excel had not yet responded to the save command.

PROBLEM-SOLVING STRATEGY I canceled the save operation. Before I investigated the problem further, as a precaution I tried to save the user's worksheet on the local hard drive instead of on the file server. This time the save operation worked fine, so I thought it was unlikely the user's PC was the problem. My attention immediately turned to the network server.

I went to the computer room where the server is located and found that the console monitor was blank. I noticed that the power lamp indicators were lit on both the server and the monitor, so I eliminated the likelihood of a power supply problem. I tried to log on to the server using a workstation that we have set up in the computer room, but the attempt failed. Then I tried to reboot the server. It did not appear to boot, but I couldn't tell much because the monitor was still blank. I thought that perhaps there was a problem with the monitor, but I wasn't sure. However, I felt that I needed to fix any problem that existed with the monitor first so that I could diagnose the situation with the server.

I disconnected the monitor from the server and borrowed a monitor and cable from a nearby workstation. After I plugged in a different monitor, the server still didn't appear to boot and the monitor was still blank. So the monitor itself was probably not related to the problem.

Because I was focused on the blank monitor screen, my next thought was to replace the video card in the server. So I pulled the video card from the nearby workstation and replaced the one in the server with one I knew was operational. When I rebooted the server, the result was the same blank monitor screen.

At this point, I stopped to think about the subsystems that were involved in the display screen problem. I sketched on a notepad the monitor, cable, video card, motherboard, and power supply. Because the power supply lamp was lit, and because I had replaced everything else, I looked at the motherboard. I could not see any visible problems with it. I decided to set up a substitute server. First I returned the borrowed video card and monitor to the workstation. I then removed the hard drive from the inoperable server and installed it in the workstation. Finally, I crossed my fingers and rebooted the substitute server. It came up okay. The motherboard apparently was the problem.

CONCLUSION I received a call from the repair shop the next day that confirmed my suspicion that the server motherboard was damaged. It had several burned-out components and needed to be replaced. I relied heavily in this situation on a module replacement strategy and on my knowledge of how the subsystems in a computer are linked together. The incident confirmed for me that users are not always capable of diagnosing the problem, which turned out to be with the server and not with the user's workstation.

Only authorized network support personnel should reboot a server.

Problem 7: The Big, Red X

A ROLE-PLAYING SCENARIO

This is a transcript of a conversation between a user, Tracy, and a support agent, Chris. If possible, have fellow students or coworkers play the parts of Tracy and Chris, and then discuss Chris's use of problem-solving tools and skills.

CHRIS: This is Chris in the support center. How can I help you?

TRACY: I am working on a Web site and found some material I want to use in a report. The material includes a graph, but where the graph should appear, all I see is an empty box on the screen with a red X in the left corner.

CHRIS: Which Web browser are you using?

TRACY: Internet Explorer version 8.

CHRIS: What happens if you click inside the box?

TRACY: I tried that. Nothing happens.

CHRIS: Perhaps a server that is transmitting Web pages to you is just slow in loading the graph, or maybe the graph is large and is a slow download. Is the mouse pointer displayed as an hourglass?

TRACY: No.

CHRIS: Does the message on the status bar line underneath the browser window indicate that the browser is waiting or that an image has not completed downloading?

TRACY: The status bar just says, "Done."

CHRIS: Okay, maybe the graphic image is being blocked by your Web browser. Is there a message on the display screen that an image has been blocked?

TRACY: No.

CHRIS: Then let's see if the Web browser you are using can display the graphic image. Right-click inside the box and click "Show Picture."

TRACY: Okay, let me try that … Well, nothing happens. Same result.

CHRIS: I wonder if the settings in your Web browser are set to display graphic images. Do other images display correctly?

TRACY: As far as I know they do.

CHRIS: Well, let's check the settings just to make sure. Click the Tools menu, and then Internet options. Then click the Advanced tab. Is the box in front of Show Pictures checked?

TRACY: Let me see. Yes, it's checked.

CHRIS: I'm just about out of ideas. But let's try another approach. Right-click inside the empty box, and click Properties. What type of image file is the Web browser unable to display? Look on the Address or URL line.

TRACY: The image file is called a TIFF file.

CHRIS: Ah, I think that your Web browser may not be able to display a TIFF file without a special plug-in.

TRACY: What is a TIFF file?

CHRIS: A TIFF is a common graphic image file, but not one that is supported by all Web browsers. Let me check on that possibility for Internet Explorer. I'll call you back to let you know if a plug-in to display TIFF images is available and how to download it.

TRACY: Thanks, I'll be waiting for your call.

After the role-playing activity, discuss these aspects of this troubleshooting incident:

1. What strategies did Chris use to determine the cause of the problem?

2. How would you evaluate Chris's use of the communication skills described in Chapter 2 in this incident?

3. Do you think Chris found the cause of the problem?

4. Should Chris consider other potential problems?

5. Is an Internet Explorer plug-in available to display TIFF images? If so, how could Tracy get and install it?

Chapter 4 and the Hands-On Activities and Case Projects in this chapter provide examples of common problems you can use to help develop your own problem-solving skills and get experience with common problems encountered by support agents.

Chapter Summary

- Although computer problems vary widely, a few categories of problems account for most user contacts with help desks, hotlines, and support centers. The categories include problems with hardware, software, users, documentation, vendors, operating environments, and network problems. Network problems are often a combination of several other categories.

- Common hardware problems include difficulties with the installation of hardware components, incompatibility of new or upgraded components with other hardware in a system, hardware configuration problems, and actual malfunctions that require repair or replacement of components.

- Common software problems include difficulties with installation (although these problems are less common today than they were with earlier generations of software), incompatibilities with hardware or other software packages, and configuration problems that prevent the software from operating correctly. Other software problems may occur due to bugs or less-than-optimum system performance.

- User problems are caused by mistakes (which all users make), misunderstandings about how a system operates to perform a task, the purchase of the wrong product, inadequate training, failure to read product documentation, and forgotten procedures or passwords.

220

- Other common computer problems include difficulties with documentation (such as poor organization and incorrect or incomplete information), vendor problems (such as a tendency of some vendors to oversell their products, misrepresent product features, deliver software with known bugs, or deliver products later than they were promised), operating environment problems (such as problems with electricity, furniture, security, data backup procedures, and disaster and contingency planning), and network problems (which can often be traced to hardware, software, systems, or other categories of problems).

- The greater the variety of problems and solutions user support agents learn about, the more knowledge and experience they will have at their command when they tackle new problems.

Key Terms

automatic update—A feature of operating systems and application software that periodically checks a vendor's Web site for updates that the vendor recommends be installed to solve specific problems and bring the version of the software up to current specifications.

bug—An error in a computer program that occurs when a programmer writes incorrectly coded instructions during program development.

build number—A low-level version number for a software program, which can add information to the version number, release number, and update number.

burn-in test—A hardware test during which a new computer or component is operated continuously over a 48- to 72-hour period in an attempt to discover obvious problems and identify any marginal or temperature-sensitive components.

configuration problem—A difficulty that occurs when the hardware or software options are set incorrectly for the computer environment in which a component must operate.

conflict—A state in which a computer component uses system resources (e.g., CPU, memory, or peripheral devices) in a way that is incompatible with another component. *See also* incompatible.

donationware—A category of freeware for which there is no set purchase price but for which a donation is requested by the author to support further development of the product.

freeware—Computer software for which no purchase price or licensing fee is charged.

incompatible—A term that describes computer components that cannot operate together successfully in the same system. *See also* conflict.

installation software—Special-purpose utility software that aids in the installation (or setup) of other software packages; it is able to detect and correctly configure software for most hardware and operating environments.

malware—A program with harmful or malicious intent that disrupts the normal operation of a computer or network, or attempts to steal information or money as a result of its operation.

open source software—Software developed collaboratively by a loose-knit group of programmers who agree to join efforts to improve and debug a software product; the source code (and the program) is available without cost.

patch—A replacement for one or a few modules in a software package to fix one or more known bugs.

performance problem—A category of computer problems in which a system is minimally operational, but does not operate as efficiently as it should; a performance problem often results from poor interaction between hardware and software.

Plug and Play standards—A set of protocols followed by hardware and operating system vendors that specify the communication methods and rules that an operating system uses to recognize and incorporate hardware components into an operational system.

quick start behavior—A tendency among computer users to skip reading an installation manual and attempt to get new hardware or software installed and operational as rapidly as possible.

Registry—A file that serves as a database of configuration information relating to a system's hardware and software components.

release—A distribution of a software program that contains some new features not found in the original program.

service pack (or **service release**)—A software revision that contains both updates and patches to fix documented problems with a version of a program.

shareware—Commercial software that users can try out with a vendor's permission during an evaluation period (usually 30 days) prior to making a purchase decision.

update—A bug-fix distribution that repairs known problems in a previous version or release of a software package.

upgrade—A new version of an existing program that is sold at a reduced cost to owners of a previous version of the program.

vaporware—Hardware or software products that appear in ads or press releases but are not yet available for sale.

version—A software package that contains significant new features and is usually the result of a substantially rewritten program.

workaround—A procedure or operation that accomplishes the same result as the original feature that currently does not work due to a bug or other malfunction.

Check Your Understanding

Answers to Check Your Understanding questions are in Appendix A.

1. True or False? Most hardware problems are the result of component failures due to incorrect voltages in a computer system.

2. During _____, a computer system is operated nonstop for a 48- to 72-hour period to give marginal components a chance to fail.

3. Most hardware problems occur:

    a. at the time a component is purchased and installed
    b. when the component becomes obsolete
    c. after the warranty period has expired
    d. hardware problems are almost nonexistent today

4. True or False? Plug and Play-compatible hardware guarantees that users will not experience installation problems with new or upgraded hardware.

5. Which of the following hardware devices is most likely to fail during the operation of a computer system?

    a. CPU   c. hard drive
    b. memory   d. peripheral adapter card

6. A mismatch between the type of printer connected to a system and the installed software printer driver is an example of a:

    a. design problem   c. bug
    b. conflict   d. configuration problem

7. A(n) _____ is a situation in which two software packages use system resources in different and incompatible ways.

8. True or False? By the time a software package has gone through extensive testing and quality assurance, all the bugs have generally been eliminated.

9. A substantially rewritten software package that contains major new features is called a(n):

    a. update   c. new release
    b. patch   d. new version

10. A procedure or method to accomplish the same result as a feature that does not work due to a bug or other malfunction is called a(n) _____ .

11. True or False? A computer system that operates at some level, but not as efficiently as it should, is called vaporware.

12. True or False? One difference between end users and computer professionals is that the latter do not make mistakes while using a computer.

13. Performance problems in a computer system are usually due to:

    a. hardware problems
    b. software problems
    c. both hardware and software problems
    d. neither hardware nor software problems

14. True or False? Freeware and shareware may cause compatibility problems when installed because they may not be tested as extensively as commercial software.

15. _____ is a tendency among users to want to get a new hardware or software product operational without reading the installation documentation.

16. List three strategies for dealing with users who forget important information.

17. True or False? *Freeware* and *open source* are two ways of referring to the same kinds of software.

18. A revision to a software package that contains a collection of patches to fix documented problems with a program is called:

    a. donationware   c. freeware
    b. a new release   d. a service pack

19. Computer components that cannot operate together in the same system are said to be:

    a. incompatible   c. shareware
    b. a bug   d. malware

20. _____ is a feature of an operating system or application program that periodically checks a vendor's Web site for modifications that can be downloaded and installed in a user's system.

21. A(n) _____ is a database of hardware and software configuration information collected into one large file in a Windows system.

Discussion Questions

1. Why do support staff members rarely know at the outset whether a specific problem is hardware-related, software-related, or network-related?

2. Consider the following statement: *"Network problems are not really a unique category of computer problems; all network problems are basically either hardware or software problems, or both."* Do you agree or disagree? Explain your reasoning.

3. Why are so many computer problems traceable to user mistakes? Describe a recent mistake you made as a computer user. Do you think your mistake is a common or rare one? What could be done in the future, if anything, to prevent the kind of mistake you made?

4. Is freeware or shareware easier or more difficult to support and troubleshoot than commercial software? Explain your answer.

5. A user made the following statement: *"With the prices we pay for software today, you would think that vendors would be able to provide programs that work correctly out-of-the-box; instead we get buggy software that requires constant updates."* Do you agree or disagree? Explain your position.

6. An engineering company has a policy that its end users should never make changes to the system Registry or perform hardware repairs of any kind on their office systems. Do you think the policy is a good one? Discuss the pros and cons of this policy.

7. A manager commented at a support staff meeting, *"What you know about how to solve computer problems is less important than the skills you have to locate information."* Do you agree or disagree?

Hands-On Activities

The Hands-On Activities in this chapter and in the preceding chapter provide opportunities to gain additional experience with troubleshooting and problem solving. The activities vary in difficulty from easy to challenging. They require a variety of problem-solving skills and information resources to find the answers. Use them as practice to build your troubleshooting and problem-solving skills. Do not spend too long on any one project. If you run into a roadblock and can't find the answer, ask your instructor or colleagues for assistance.

Activity 5-1

Find Excel's data analysis tools. A user wants to use the advanced statistical functions and features in the Excel spreadsheet program because she does a lot of statistical work in her job. She has a book that explains how to use these features. She clicked the Data tab on Excel's Ribbon menu but did not find the Data Analysis option that the book had described.

She also tried to use some of the built-in statistical functions that are included in Excel according to the book; however, whenever she entered one of the function names, the error message *"#NAME?"* appeared. Describe the steps the user would need to take to be able to use the statistical functions.

Activity 5-2

Explore the msconfig program. On a Windows system, find the utility program named msconfig. If you can find it, where is it located? Use the msconfig help system to learn about the features of the program. Write a brief description of its purpose and indicate for whom it would be useful.

Activity 5-3

Evaluate hard drive symptoms. A frantic user called a help desk to report that his hard drive did not appear to work. He related that the drive produced neither noise nor any indication of obvious activity. In fact, the drive light on the PC case was not lighting up. The user fears the worst: a hard drive failure. List as many alternative explanations you can think of for the behavior he describes.

Activity 5-4

Unresponsive software. A user contacted a help desk with a report that he has an error message on his screen that says, *"Program Not Responding."* Research possible causes of this error message, and suggest one or more ways to recover from this problem.

Activity 5-5

Low disk space. A user continually gets the following warning message that his disk space is low: *"You are running out of disk space on drive C:"*. He says he knows his disk space is low, but he doesn't have time to deal with the problem. He would like to know if there is a way to disable the message. Can this warning be disabled? If so, how? Is it advisable to do so? Write an email response to the user with your answer.

Activity 5-6

Set up an automatic time log. A user who is away from her office for much of the day wants to keep a simple log of contacts and short notes about client meetings she has throughout the day. She wants to include the current date and time for each entry in the log. She says a work colleague has an icon on her laptop that automatically opens Notepad and inserts an entry in the file that contains the current date and time. Then, it is easy for her colleague to write a short note about a meeting with a client. She wants you to help her set up her laptop with a similar feature. Write a brief piece of documentation listing the steps she should take to accomplish this task.

Activity 5-7

Recover Word's Normal.dot file. A trainer who instructs classes in Microsoft Word reports that one of her students, Robin, accidentally saved a document as Normal.dot. Each time a student at that computer in the training center opens a new Word document, Robin's document appears instead of a new, blank document. She says she has tried to fix the problem, but hasn't hit on a solution yet. What would you suggest to the trainer? Is there more than one solution to this problem?

Activity 5-8

Decipher an Internet error message. An email from a user says: *"I have been using Google to search for information on the Web. I received a message, 'Error 403: Forbidden,' when I attempted to access a Web site that interests me. What does this message mean, and how can I view the page?"* Research the problem, and write a response to the email.

Activity 5-9

Memory errors. A help desk supervisor wrote the following in an email: *"As our users' PCs age, we are seeing indications that some of the RAM modules are beginning to experience intermittent failures. Microsoft apparently has a Windows Memory Diagnostic utility program that is available free. Please research the memory utility program, and let me know whether it is easy enough to use that we could run it on all our users' PCs."* Write a response to the supervisor's request.

Activity 5-10

No volume. A user received a message: *"Windows cannot display the volume control on the taskbar because the Volume Control program has not been installed. To install it use Add/Remove Programs in Control Panel."* Describe the steps you would take to solve this problem for the user. Is there more than one solution to this problem?

Activity 5-11

What's in a Quick Start guide? LastPass is a password manager for Web browsers. It helps users maintain separate passwords for various Web sites. Study a quick start tutorial on LastPass at **www.howtogeek.com/77319/the-how-to-geek-guide-to-getting-started-with-lastpass**, and answer these questions:

1. What are the main topics covered in the LastPass Quick Start tutorial?

2. Are the topics covered sufficient to enable a user to get started quickly with LastPass?

3. What topics were not covered? How did the Quick Start tutorial handle omitted topics?

4. Briefly describe the changes you would make to the Quick Start guide to LastPass to make it more useful to users who want a quick way to get started using this service.

Activity 5-12

Improve a troubleshooting strategy. Visit the following Web site, which describes some troubleshooting strategies for common problems that users encounter: **www.directron.com/ howtobuilyou.html**. Select a category of problems with which you are familiar. Are the methods and strategies the Web site recommends effective? Based on your own experience, add two troubleshooting strategies to the category you selected.

Activity 5-13

Edit the Windows 7 Registry

Warning: This activity should not be attempted on a PC for which you do not have permission to edit the Registry. You must have administrator login privileges to perform these tasks.

1. Read a tutorial that covers the basic use of the Registry editor, REGEDIT, at **www.techsupportalert.com/content/learn-how-use-windows-Registry-editor-regedit-one-easy-lesson.htm**.

2. Complete one or more of the brief exercises at **www.computerperformance.co.uk/ windows7/windows7_registry_benefits.htm**.

3. Verify that the exercise(s) you completed in Step 2 had the intended effect on the operations of Windows 7.

Case Projects

1. Document Internet Error Messages

Find out the error messages users are most likely to encounter on the Web. Learn what the messages mean, and what users should do to work around each type of error. Then write a brief document intended for end users that lists the most common Internet error messages, provides users with information about each message, and explains how to work around each error, if possible.

2. Disk Space Management at Maps Unlimited

The user support group at Maps Unlimited, a company that makes computerized maps for urban planners, has analyzed the log of support calls it received in the past month to identify the ten most common calls. As part of a project to write model answers for end users' frequently asked questions, the support staff wants you to research and write a short document on disk space management. The support staff finds that many callers with disk space complaints say that they have run out of space on their hard drives. Most of these calls come from active email users and users who frequently download information from the Web. Other calls come from users who have older PCs that were purchased with smaller hard drives than those available today. In many of these cases, the hard drives on their Windows PCs are now full, and they are looking for a solution that doesn't require replacing the hard drive.

Investigate common ways that the space on a hard drive gets filled up. You may want to compare your ideas, experiences, and findings with those of your coworkers or classmates. Then write a document for support staff to provide to end users that briefly describes the reasons that hard drives become full and the procedures you recommend to free up disk space. Organize your document as a checklist, but include any explanations and precautions you feel are necessary before a user embarks on a procedure to reclaim disk space on a hard drive.

3. Problem-Solving Slideshow for Support Staff

Prepare a slideshow presentation that could be used to train new user support staff. The topic of your slideshow should be selected from the following list:

- Common hardware problems and how to solve them

- Common software configuration problems

- Typical user problems and ideas to prevent them

- Tools support staff can use to diagnose common problems

- The most difficult computer problem I have ever solved, and how I solved it

Make your slideshow presentation a professional one that you would be proud to show others as an example of your work. If possible, present your slideshow to your school or work colleagues. Ask for suggestions on how to improve your slideshow.

4. Check Hard Drive Health with CrystalDiskInfo

A user, Lawrence Keys, sent the following email to desktop support desk:

I am using an external hard drive to back up the C drive on my PC. The hard drive plugs in to a USB port on my PC. When I start a backup procedure, the drive periodically disconnects from Windows and then reconnects a few moments later. The backup procedure is interrupted and does not restart. Can you suggest how I can check this drive to see if there is a problem with it?

One of the support desk agents had heard about a hard disk utility program, CrystalDiskInfo, which is available for free download at **crystalmark.info/software/CrystalDiskInfo/index-e. html**. Download and install this utility on a PC to which you have access. Learn about the operation of the utility, and run it on your PC. Write a one- to two-page report that summarizes your findings. In your report, answer the following questions:

- Which aspects of a hard drive does CrystalDiskInfo evaluate?

- What is S.M.A.R.T. technology?

- Did CrystalDiskInfo identify any problems with your disk drive? If so, describe the problems.

5. Create a system recovery disk

One reason a PC can fail to boot properly is that the image of the operating system has become corrupted. A corrupted operating system may be due to physical damage to the hard drive, accidental modifications to system files (for example, a damaged master boot record, deleted critical operating system files, or incorrectly modified records in the system Registry), or a virus or other malware. The causes are many, but the end result is that the system cannot be booted through normal procedures.

Many experienced support specialists have prepared a system recovery disk to permit a PC to be rebooted when the operating system or hard drive is damaged. Booting a damaged PC is one way to assess the extent of the damage and formulate a recovery plan.

Your challenge in this case is to prepare a system recovery disk for a PC to which you have access. Complete the following steps:

1. Research the recommended procedures to create and use a system recovery disk for the operating system on your PC.

2. Follow the procedures to create a system recovery disk.

3. Test the system recovery disk to make sure your PC boots correctly from the disk.

4. Write procedure documentation on the steps to use the system recovery disk to boot your PC.

CHAPTER 6

Help Desk Operation

In this chapter, you will learn about:

◎ Help desk operational procedures

◎ The multilevel support model

◎ The incident management process

◎ Best practices in help desk operation

◎ The physical layout of help desk work areas

◎ Job stress in help desk work

◎ Hardware and software tools used by support agents, managers, and end users

◎ Help desk industry trends

Recall that an organization can choose to provide support to its employees and external clients in several ways. Some organizations opt for informal peer support for workers who use computers. Others choose a more formal structure, such as a user support group or an information center, or they delegate computer support to an IT department. Some organizations outsource all or part of the computer support function. Although the details of the structure may differ, many companies organize their user support function internally as a help desk because: (1) the help desk is usually very visible, and its services are well-publicized to employees or clients; and (2) it provides a single point of contact for users who need technical support. To make contact with a help desk, users might visit a physical location, call a hotline, send an email message, initiate a chat session, or go to a Web site. In each case, users interact with a help desk agent to ask questions or request assistance with problems.

A help desk operation, like other support methods, can be costly. Therefore, organizations that have a substantial investment in end-user computer technology or that serve many end users are continually searching for cost-effective ways to provide technical support. This chapter describes a number of strategies and tools that help desks employ to effectively and efficiently support end users.

What Is a Help Desk?

A help desk is an organization that provides a single point of contact for users in need of technical support, whether they are internal workers or external clients. Having a single point of contact streamlines the process for end users and agents. In a user support center with multiple points of contact, a user may not know whom to contact about a specific problem. For example, they may not know whether a problem is hardware-related or network-related. If hardware repairs are handled by an electronic repair department and network problems are handled by a network administrator, a user could easily make several calls before reaching the proper contact. Furthermore, the first agent who responds to an incident might not have the expertise to answer a particular question, and might have to refer the user to a different agent or department for an answer. In extreme cases, multiple points of contact may disagree about the source of a problem or the strategy to resolve it. To avoid situations like these, many organizations have consolidated their user support function into one help desk operation.

 Some help desk operations have chosen the name Service Desk to replace the older Help Desk title. The new name emphasizes the service mission of help desk operations.

Although the specifics of how support is provided differ in telephone, face-to-face, email, chat, and Web contacts, there are similarities in the way help desks organize and provide support. Some help desks provide a wide range of support services, such as those you learned about in Chapter 1. Others focus on limited services. For example, a telephone support hotline for a popular software package will probably limit its services to questions about the specific product. In contrast, the help desk in a large medical center may provide a more extensive array of computer support services to its employees. Whether a help desk includes a hotline, information center, training assistance, support consultant, or any number of other services, its purpose is the same: to keep end users productive by providing them with a single point of contact for resolving computer problems.

Organizations structure their help desks differently, depending on several factors, including whether their users are internal or external, the number of users and products they support, and the organization's goals and objectives for computer support. Organizations frequently structure their help desks into several levels (or tiers) of support, sometimes called a **multilevel support model** or frontline/backline model, shown in Figure 6-1.

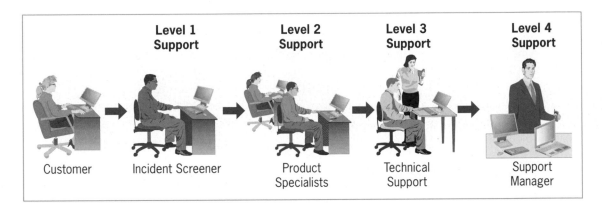

Level 1 Support   **Level 2 Support**   **Level 3 Support**   **Level 4 Support**

Customer   Incident Screener   Product Specialists   Technical Support   Support Manager

Figure 6-1   Multilevel support model

In this model, each level is staffed by a worker with different skills. The level 1 incident screener (also called an incident dispatcher or receptionist) is usually an entry-level worker. Higher levels require greater knowledge and experience. A level 2 product specialist is usually a more experienced help desk worker; a level 3 technical support position is often staffed by a programmer, product designer, or engineer; and level 4 support is typically staffed by a supervisor or manager. In small help desk organizations, external vendor support or an outsourced help desk provider may augment the services provided by the internal help desk staff.

Multilevel help desks and support groups vary in the number of levels they have. In general, help desks try to handle as many incidents at the lowest possible level in the support hierarchy in order to save their higher-level, more experienced staff resources for situations that require specialized expertise. In many organizations, lower-level help desk staff members can refer complex problems and even difficult callers to more experienced staff members.

Regardless of structure, all help desks have the same goal: to promote client satisfaction by effectively and efficiently resolving problems and questions. To accomplish this, help desk staff use well-defined operational processes, tools, and strategies.

The Incident Management Process

Incident management is a well-defined, formal process that help desk staff follow to receive and prescreen problem incidents, obtain the information requested by a user or solve a user's problem, and then close the incident. Because it refers to telephone, face-to-face, email, chat, and Web-based forms of support, incident management is a more general term than call management. **Call management** is a subset of incident management, and describes the steps in handling telephone contacts between users and support agents. Figure 6-2 shows the major steps in the incident management process. Each step is described in the following sections.

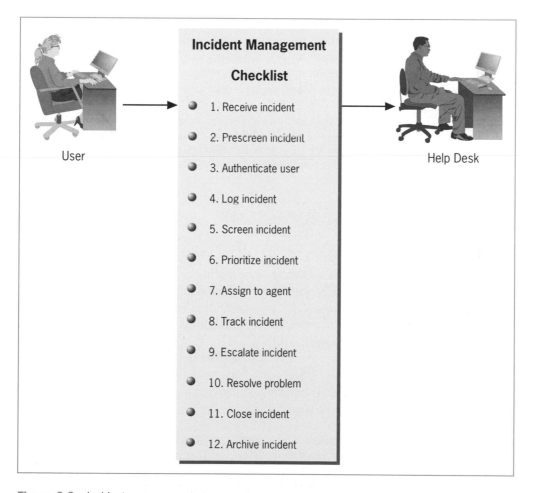

Figure 6-2   Incident management process

1. Receive the Incident

Whether an incident is received via telephone, email, in person, or through a Web-based contact (such as a chat session or a problem report form), an agent's first step is to establish a relationship with the end user. Some support groups follow a specific script when contact with a user begins. The script can be in the form of a recommended greeting in a phone conversation or a predefined introductory paragraph that is inserted in a reply to an email message or chat session. For example, in a telephone support call, the level 1 help desk agent may confirm the name of the support organization and provide their first name. The agent may ask the name of the person who is calling. Other common early incident management tasks include providing a warning that the conversation may be monitored (this is a legal requirement in most states) and an apology for any wait time. If a follow-up call or email is likely, the agent may request the caller's phone number or email address. As you will learn later in this chapter, some of these tasks can be automated. In all incident-handling situations, the guidelines for client service, communications, and interpersonal skills described in Chapter 2 apply to each step in the incident management process.

The incident management process described here applies primarily to telephone calls; however, many of the same steps apply to face-to-face, email, chat, and Web-based contacts with a help desk. Although the specific steps and tools for written and verbal communications are slightly different, the general flow and communication guidelines described here still apply.

2. Prescreen the Incident

Prescreening is a filtering process that helps agents quickly identify and respond to simple requests for information, sometimes without even initiating an official incident. Some help desks do not prescreen incidents. When incident management procedures include prescreening, a level 1 worker asks questions to determine if an incident is a simple request for information that the screener can provide. Many help desk incidents fall into this category. For example, a user may want to know when the next version of a software package will be released and whether a known problem will be fixed in the new release. The user may want to receive product information or find out where to buy the product. Information request calls can frequently be handled quickly and easily at support level 1 and then closed without proceeding to the subsequent steps.

Incidents may be prescreened manually at support level 1, or by an automated call distribution system, which you will learn more about later in this chapter.

3. Authenticate the User

If an incident is more than a simple request for information, many help desks use an **authentication procedure**. In this step, an agent determines whether the help desk is authorized to handle the incident and provide information or services to the user. Authentication (also called an entitlement verification) may involve asking a user for a product ID number, product serial number, model number, or software license number. In other situations, a screener may ask for the user's name (and perhaps department or email address or phone number) in order to query a database to learn whether the user is a registered owner of a product and which level of support services, if any, the user has purchased. If the user is a client on a pay-per-call basis, the staff member may obtain billing information from the user (usually a credit card or purchase order number). Like prescreening, authentication is a filtering process. A help desk agent determines whether a user has a legitimate claim to support services, and if so, at what service level. Once a staff member has authenticated a user, the incident-handling process can continue.

4. Log the Incident

In the incident **logging** step, an agent begins documenting the incident. The agent may make an initial entry in a problem log, on a trouble report form, or in an incident tracking database. If user information already exists in a product registration database or user support knowledge base, logging an incident may be a simple matter of clicking a button that opens a new incident record linked to the client's user record. Some incident management software packages automatically fill in the user contact information. Figure 6-3 shows an example of a help desk incident log.

Incident Tracking # [   ]

Incident Tracking Log

User: _____   Dept: _____   Phone: _____

Email address: _____

Date opened: [/ /]   Time opened: [   ]   Taken by: [   ]

Problem Category:
☐ Request for info   ☐ Question   ☐ Complaint
☐ Hardware   ☐ Software   ☐ LAN   ☐ Internet

Priority Code:[   ]

Problem Description:

Incident assigned to: _____

Action Taken:

Incident escalated to: _____   Incident escalated to: _____

Incident Resolution:

Incident closed by:_____   Date closed: [/ /]   Time closed: [   ]

Figure 6-3   Incident tracking log

5. Screen the Incident

During incident **screening**, a help desk agent asks a series of questions to categorize and describe the incident. Incidents are often categorized in one of the following ways:

- Requests for information that could not be handled during prescreening: *"Will the latest release fix my font problem?"*

- Questions: *"How do I get rid of commas in the numbers on my spreadsheet?"*

- Problems: *"My printer works with every known software package in the world except yours."*

- Complaints: *"Your software is so full of bugs it locks up my computer every time I run it."*

- Work (or service) orders: *"Will you please upgrade the operating system software on my machine so that I can use the latest version of Internet Explorer?"*

In addition, the support agent enters a brief written description of the request, question, problem, complaint, or work order into the problem log or incident tracking database. An experienced agent learns to capture the essential facts of a problem report in a few key words or phrases. Although lengthy, verbatim details of the problem description are usually not necessary, an agent should include relevant facts that might be useful in solving the problem. The following is an example of a problem description:

QuickBooks icon missing from Windows 7 desktop after reboot this morning.

When an incident is contained in an email message or received via a Web-based contact, the user's entire correspondence may be captured in a database or included in the problem log.

6. Prioritize the Incident

Based on the category and nature of a problem or request, an agent typically assigns an incident a priority code. A **priority code** indicates how serious the problem is, how many users are affected, and the consequence of not addressing the problem immediately. Help desk staff may determine that a problem affects only one user and is therefore a lower priority than an incident in which a malfunction in a network, for example, affects an entire department. Examples of priority codes used in some support organizations are: 1 – urgent; 2 – high priority; 3 – medium priority; and 4 – low priority.

For example, the network equipment provider Cisco defines these priority levels in its Technical Assistance Center:

- Priority 1—The network is down; no workaround is available; and business processes are at a critical stage.

- Priority 2—The network is badly degraded; business processes are impacted; and no workaround is possible.

- Priority 3—The network is degraded, but most business processes are working.

- Priority 4—Caller needs support for installation or configuration, or information on a Cisco product.

During their training, help desk agents are given guidelines to help them prioritize incidents. Some organizations use incident management software that automatically assigns a priority code to a problem report. The priority code is frequently based on the type of incident, its severity, the number of users affected, and the help desk's policy for handling that type of incident. For users who have purchased a service level agreement, the user's service level usually affects the priority.

When working with an internal user, a support agent may ask the user to help set an incident's priority or to agree to a priority level. Consensus about an incident's priority ensures that those involved have the same expectations for help desk performance. Some support organizations defer to a user's priority assessment if the user and agent disagree on the priority level. Furthermore, a priority level may change during the life of an incident. For example, a problem may be defined initially as priority 1 because a network is down. If a quick workaround can be implemented and the network becomes operational, the problem that caused the downtime may be reprioritized to a priority 2 or priority 3.

The type of incident and its priority often determine the queue into which an incident will be placed. A **queue** is a waiting line, like the checkout line in a grocery store. Just as a grocery store may have separate lines or queues for regular, express, and self-checkout, a help desk may have queues for different types and priorities of incidents. The incident queues in a help desk may be defined by product, by priority code, or on any other basis that the help desk uses to allocate and assign incidents to support staff.

Instead of assigning priority codes, some help desks simply assign incidents to support staff on a first-in, first-out (FIFO) basis.

7. Assign the Incident

If the level 1 help desk staff cannot resolve an incident immediately, they may assign or refer the incident to another staff member who has the technical expertise to provide the information, respond to the request, or solve the problem quickly. Help desks often maintain a list of staff members who specialize in specific products or types of problems. In some automated incident management systems, the process of assigning an incident simply moves it from one queue to another.

New help desk workers sometimes find it difficult to determine the best place to refer an incident they cannot resolve. However, entry-level staff members usually learn quickly who among the experienced technical support staff have good problem-solving skills, give quick and correct answers for a specific type of problem, and can help deal with incidents effectively so user contacts can be handled at the lowest possible support level in a multilevel structure.

8. Track the Incident

Whenever the essential facts associated with an incident change—such as when additional problem information is received, a new priority code is assigned, or the incident is assigned to a different staff member—the help desk staff update the incident information record. Incident **tracking** refers to the process of updating the incident record with information about a problem as it progresses. An automated help desk system often records in a database the date and time of each incident tracking entry. These entries provide a complete record of what happened and when. Incident tracking provides an important history of a problem, how it was handled, and how it was resolved. A record of how an incident was handled can be useful for help desk staff when they encounter a similar problem. Incident tracking information is also important input when measuring the quality of incident management, evaluating the performance of help desk workers, and identifying support staff training needs.

9. Escalate the Incident

If initial attempts to resolve a user's problem are unsuccessful, most support groups have policies and procedures to escalate an incident. As you learned in Chapter 4, incident escalation is a normal process in which a problem is transferred to a higher level of support that is better able to handle more difficult problems.

In some automated incident management systems, the escalation process is automatic. For example, help desk software can often be programmed to escalate an incident to the next level automatically if a support agent cannot resolve it within a predetermined period of time. If a problem has been active, but unresolved, for more than a defined amount of time (usually a few hours), an incident management system may automatically display it on a support manager's screen, where he or she can monitor the problem closely to make sure that staff members are progressing toward a solution.

In all escalation situations, whether formal or informal, manual or automated, assigning ownership of a problem incident is important. A problem incident can get lost as it moves from agent to agent. Help desks need to have mechanisms in place to ensure that the ownership of an incident either stays with the level 1 agent, who is responsible for follow up, or that ownership clearly passes to an upper-level staff member or supervisor as the incident is escalated. The potential to lose track of responsibility for an incident is especially high when an incident is referred to an outside vendor for resolution.

10. Resolve the Incident

Ideally, help desk staff members will be able to resolve all users' problems and questions. In the incident **resolution** step, a user's problem is solved or a complaint is noted or referred to product designers as a suggestion for the next product revision cycle. Alternately, incident resolution may involve giving the client authorization to return a product for replacement or a refund. Incident resolution doesn't necessarily mean the user or client is completely satisfied, however.

A small percentage of all calls, usually those that involve complaints about product bugs or features, may not be satisfactorily resolved. Obviously, one of the goals of a help desk is to minimize the percentage of problems that cannot be resolved satisfactorily, but the percentage is rarely zero. The help desk's goal, however, is that users receive the information or problem resolution they need and feel that the problem has been resolved to their satisfaction.

11. Close the Incident

In incident **closing**, a support agent may review the steps the help desk took to solve a problem. An agent may also get feedback from the user about her or his satisfaction level. An agent usually concludes an incident by inviting the user to contact the help desk if further problems arise or if the recommended solution does not work. Closing the incident may also involve the agent making additional entries in a problem log or database to indicate how the problem was resolved.

Incident closing can be a challenge, especially in a telephone support environment. Some users either can't accept that their problem cannot be resolved, or don't want to hang up because they enjoy talking about technology with help desk staff. These cases may fall into the category of difficult calls, which you learned about in Chapter 2.

12. Archive the Incident

Closed incidents are often retained in an incident management system for some predetermined period in case the user calls back or sends a follow-up message. A help desk's policies usually specify how long a closed incident is retained before it is archived. An incident **archive** is a database or paper file used to store and retain records relating to closed incidents. In an automated system, archived incidents are periodically deleted from the active incident management database. In a manual system that uses written problem logs or trouble reports, the resolved incident archive process may simply involve moving a folder of resolved incidents from one file drawer to another.

Incident archives provide data that can be incorporated into a help desk knowledge base. Recall from Chapter 4 that a knowledge base is an organized collection of information, articles, procedures, tips, and previous problems with known solutions that can serve as a resource for support agents. In some organizations, the closing process may require an agent to enter the incident information into a help desk knowledge base. Support staff members can then search the knowledge base to find previously solved problems with the same or similar characteristics as an active incident. Incident archives may be analyzed to produce statistical reports of the frequency of various categories of incidents.

 Reports on the frequency of solved problems are useful to managers in making staffing decisions and analyzing help desk performance trends over time, as you'll learn more about in Chapter 7.

The incident management steps described here are examples of the kinds of activities that occur during incident processing. Each organization's support policies and procedures may dictate a somewhat different sequence of incident processing events, based on unique business requirements, user expectations, help desk procedures, and an organization's resources. Training for entry-level help desk workers usually includes an orientation to and hands-on practice with the specific steps the staff is expected to follow.

ON THE WEB

Mary Baldwin College describes its user support incident management procedures for faculty and staff and explains how priorities for problem resolution are set on its Web site (**academic.mbc.edu/cis/PDF/13.4_User_Support_-_Computer_&_ Telephony.pdf**).

The University of Connecticut School of Law's Web site provides information about its help desk policies and procedures (**www.law.uconn.edu/information-systems/ computer-services/policies/general-information-about-services-and- procedures-sla**).

Best Practices for Help Desk Operations

Several attempts have been made in recent years to define a set of industry-wide best practices for organizations that provide and manage help desk and computer services. **Best practices** are procedures, tools, and methods employed by successful support groups; these practices often set apart very successful support operations from mediocre ones. One widely followed set of guidelines is the **Information Technology Infrastructure Library (ITIL)**, which is designed to help organizations align and integrate their computer services with their business objectives. The ITIL was initially published in the United Kingdom, based on earlier work on service management objectives initiated by IBM. The ITIL is intended as a "framework" rather than an industry standard in the traditional sense.

The ITIL is an extensive series of publications that document guidelines organizations should consider as they design and manage a help desk or information services function. In a full implementation of the ITIL framework, the guideline documents are often supplemented with the purchase of software products and consulting services.

The ITIL best practices describe how successful organizations handle matters such as:

- *Incident management*—The processes for handling any disruption of normal services that affects a user or the business; the goal of incident management is to restore computer services to normal operation as quickly as possible.

- *Problem management*—Proactive strategies to find and fix the root cause of problem incidents; the goal of problem management is to anticipate, repair, and eliminate the root causes of computer problems.

- *Change management*—Methods for managing the constant changes that occur due to an organization's use of technology; the goal of change management is to develop plans to minimize the business impact of technology changes (to hardware, software, networking, and operational procedures).

- *Release management*—The implementation side of change management; the goal of release management is to educate users and provide for a smooth implementation of technology change that minimizes the impact on a business.

- *Configuration management*—The maintenance of a database of hardware and software assets used in an organization; the goal of configuration management is to help an organization identify, control, monitor, plan, and audit its investment in technology.

ON THE WEB

For a brief introduction to some basic ITIL guidelines related to help desk operations, read a white paper prepared by ManageEngine, an ITIL software provider (**manageengine.adventnet.com/products/service-desk/itil-whitepaper.pdf**).

For another perspective on help desk industry best practices, read an industry white paper, "Thirty-One Best Practices for the Service Desk," based on research by Forrester Research (**whitepapers.theregister.co.uk/paper/view/149/c-forrester-white-paper.pdf**); free registration is required to download the report as a PDF file.

A full enterprise-wide implementation of the ITIL framework is an expensive, ongoing process that includes substantial software and consulting costs. However, the implementation of help desk industry best practices and comparative service benchmarks often results in a more effective and efficient help desk operation that is better integrated with an organization's business objectives.

Physical Layout of Help Desk Work Areas

In most large-scale help desk operations, each support agent works in a cubicle enclosed on three sides by carpeted wall panels. The wall panels are from four to six feet high, depending on whether visual contact with coworkers is deemed desirable and depending on the need to reduce equipment and background noise. A typical cubicle is eight to ten feet long by six to eight feet wide.

In each cubicle, a support agent sits at a desk that includes space for one or more computer systems. Agents have their own PCs on which they run incident management software as well as the specific software packages or hardware components they support. Support agents may also have other computer systems in their cubicle with different hardware and operating system platforms, which they can use to replicate a user's problem. For example, an agent who supports software that runs on Windows, Mac, and Linux systems may have access to all three platforms. In some situations, computers for problem replication may be located in a separate room where they can be shared among support staff. An agent may have access to a reference library of manuals and information on specific products, either in print or electronic form.

To answer or initiate telephone calls, most support agents prefer a wireless headset rather than a standard wired telephone handset. The headset helps prevent neck and shoulder ailments and permits considerable freedom of motion when it is necessary to confer with a coworker or supervisor about a problem. Wireless headsets, which often use Bluetooth technology, are an improvement over older model headsets that are connected by a cable to an agent's computer.

 Workplace ergonomic issues, important for end users in general, are even more critical for help desk staff members who provide telephone or Web-based support for several hours each day. Chapter 10 discusses ergonomic concerns that apply to the design of workstations for end users as well as help desk staff.

ON THE WEB

To view a tutorial by Jim Hanks on how telephone headsets can affect call center productivity, visit **telecom.hellodirect.com/docs/Tutorials/Productivity.1.080701.asp**.

Job Stress in Help Desk Work

Job stress is a common complaint of help desk workers. **Job stress** results from the physical and emotional responses help desk staff experience when the individual characteristics of a worker don't match the requirements of their position. Job stress can be exacerbated by a variety of factors, such as the following:

- Inadequate training
- Lack of qualifications or experience for a position
- Inadequate resources (equipment, software, and access to information) to perform tasks
- Lack of attention to ergonomic issues in the workplace

243

- Unrealistic management expectations (including workload volume that exceeds resources to handle it, lack of adequate breaks, long work shifts, and extensive overtime requirements)

- Abusive callers, or those with unrealistic service or product expectations

- Poor help desk management practices (including inadequate communication within an organization and unclear employee evaluation and promotion criteria)

- Involvement in office politics

- Work style differences between employees, such as those described in Chapter 2

Job stress may result in a variety of health-related problems including fatigue and insomnia, head and body aches, inability to concentrate on job tasks, expression of anger, substance abuse, low morale, and low self-esteem. Solutions to reduce the impact of job stress include personal stress management strategies and organizational change.

 Strategies for dealing with workplace stress include getting enough exercise and sleep, eating a healthy diet, reducing alcohol and nicotine consumption, and using time and work management techniques to prioritize work tasks.

ON THE WEB

The National Institute of Occupational Safety and Health maintains a comprehensive Web site devoted to job-related stress (**www.cdc.gov/niosh/docs/99-101**).

To learn more about personal stress management strategies, use the resources at Helpguide's Web site (**www.helpguide.org/mental/work_stress_management. htm**). The Web site includes several articles on reducing stress in the workplace.

The working conditions and physical environment of help desk work areas can either contribute to job stress or diminish it. Work areas should be designed to reduce distractions from excessive noise, motion, and other interruptions as much as possible. Frequent scheduled breaks are useful stress reduction tools. Some support groups provide employee lounges, cafeterias, and break rooms with refreshments, televisions, pool tables, video games, and other diversions.

ON THE WEB

To learn more about organizational changes that can help to reduce workplace stress, read "Organizational Stress Management for Managers" (**www.novanthealth.org/ eap/tools/Self-Care%20Series%20Stress%20Management%20for% 20Managers.pdf**).

244

A ROLE-PLAYING SCENARIO

This scenario is an excerpt from a meeting between an experienced help desk staff member, Lonnie, and a relatively new help desk agent, Robin. Lonnie has been assigned as a mentor to Robin and has observed that Robin seems stressed recently. If possible, have fellow students or coworkers play the parts of Lonnie and Robin, and then discuss your observations about their conversation. In several cases below, Lonnie's responses are blank. Discuss how you would respond if you were Robin's mentor.

LONNIE: I'd like to begin by asking how you feel about your work as a help desk agent after three months on the job.

ROBIN: I like having a job in the help desk, but I don't feel like I fit in very well with the group here.

LONNIE: Why do you feel you don't fit in?

ROBIN: When I can't answer a question and am forced to escalate a trouble report to a tech support person, I feel like I'm not doing my job. And the tech support people I talk to never get back to me on the solution to a problem. So I'm left in the dark about what I did wrong. It is really frustrating to me to be so out-of-the-loop.

LONNIE: (suggest a useful response here)

ROBIN: It seems to me like we get a lot of calls from confused users. I had one last week from a user who had a new PC and couldn't find the icon to run a program he needed because the icon changed slightly and was in a different place on the screen from his old PC. How stupid is that? When I pointed out that he should do a better job of getting to know his PC, he got angry. That was upsetting to me.

LONNIE: (suggest a useful response here)

ROBIN: I don't feel like my training was adequate when I started here. I've been criticized unfairly by some of my coworkers for providing information to users that they say I shouldn't give out. How am I supposed to know what I can and can't say?

LONNIE: Can you give me an example of a situation where you were criticized?

ROBIN: Well, I told one user that I didn't think we would ever upgrade our company PCs to Windows 7. Someone said I shouldn't make statements like that because it was against company policy. I feel like other members of the help desk team should support each other on things like that.

LONNIE: (suggest a useful response here)

ROBIN: I feel like I am starting to burn out in this job after just three months. At the end of the day, I feel extremely tired and achy. My eyes hurt from staring at my workstation. I feel frustrated that I'm not getting along better. Does this sound like job burnout to you?

LONNIE: (suggest a useful response here)

If you haven't already, as part of Lonnie's responses above, discuss some suggestions Lonnie, as a mentor, could offer based on the comments Robin made during the session.

Help Desk Technology and Tools

Ongoing developments in automation have significantly impacted the help desk industry in recent years. These developments include new and more advanced help desk software packages, computer telephony, and Web-based support.

Help Desk Software

The incident management process described above often results in a large volume of incident transactions being collected, processed, and stored. Some help desks organize these incident transactions in a database, in which tables contain detailed information about clients, products, computer configurations, and help desk staff as well as an archive of solved problems. Transactions are created when links in the database are established between a client and a product (such as a product registration), or between a client, a computer, and a help desk staff member (such as a problem incident report).

A large-scale help desk operation may receive and process hundreds (or even thousands) of incidents every day. A small-scale help desk may handle only a few incidents daily. Commercial software packages are available to help both large- and small-scale help desks manage the processing of support transactions. These packages typically have features and capabilities, described below, that are useful to support both internal and external users.

In the paragraphs that follow, you will learn about help desk tools for agents, managers, and end users.

Help Desk Agent Tools

Help desk agents need a variety of tools to be successful. A help desk software package can be quite useful to ensure agent productivity. These packages range from simple, open source software that small help desks can download and implement (without cost for the software itself) to enterprise-wide packages with an extensive array of tools for managing help desk activities for internal and external users in a large organization. Although help desk software applications vary considerably, many packages offer a core of common capabilities and features, as described below.

INCIDENT LOGGING AND TRACKING FEATURES Help desk software packages include features that allow agents to log and track incidents. The software packages often work in conjunction with a telephone, email, or Web-based system to manage incident queues, set priorities, assign incidents to agents, and escalate incidents when necessary. An incident tracking system is useful even in a very small support center staffed by one or a few agents. No user who needs technical support likes to "get lost in the system."

Sandy, a help desk agent for a small insurance company, says, "As the size of our help desk staff and the number of employees we were assisting grew, our manual help desk incident management system became hard to work with. We were always losing information. Our new help desk software is now my primary contact point with our users. I get tickets from users who need help. Each one has a priority code, which helps me organize my work. And I can easily check on the status of all my open tickets."

CLIENT INFORMATION DATABASES Support incidents invariably involve contacts with people. Help desk software typically includes capabilities to store, edit, and recall contact and location information about internal clients, external clients, help desk and IT staff, information resources, and vendors.

Sandy says, "Our help desk software displays information I use daily on how to contact our users and all of our hardware and software vendors. Every incident ticket I get automatically includes each user's name, job title, office location, phone number, and email address. And I no longer have to search for vendors' Web site addresses."

LINKS TO PRODUCT INFORMATION Many users contact a help desk to request product information. Help desk software that contains links to detailed information about hardware, software, networks, and services enables support staff to respond to many common questions regarding product features, limitations, new versions, system requirements, configuration constraints, known bugs, product availability, and related information. An organization's Web site may provide users with links to product information in order to reduce the level of support staff required to answer requests for information.

Sandy notes, "I used to have to hunt down a printed manual to answer an employee's question about the specialized insurance software package our agency uses. Now, we have links in our help desk software to the vendor's Web site, which has the most current information about the hardware and software products our employees use. I can display information quickly and can usually get a user the information they need.

ACCESS TO SYSTEM CONFIGURATION INFORMATION Help desk software packages typically include the ability to document hardware, software, and network information about client systems. Although system configuration information about external client systems is useful, it is difficult to collect and keep up to date, unless a service or facilities management contract covers the client users' systems. But configuration information is critical to help desk staff members who support internal clients.

 Much of the site management notebook and configuration checklist documentation you will learn about in Chapter 10 can be stored in a database.

Sandy says, "When one of our users calls with a question or problem, I can instantly display information about their workstation, such as what hardware they have and how it is configured, which software packages are licensed on their PC, and technical details about their connection to our office network. All this information, which used to be contained in a site notebook for each PC, is now available in our help desk software."

PROBLEM-SOLUTION KNOWLEDGE BASES A knowledge base (sometimes called a "smart database") can contain information about common problems and their solutions. Some knowledge bases are built over time as user problems are solved and archived. Other knowledge bases with a store of common problems and their solutions can be accessed on the Web or purchased ready-made. Because a knowledge base of support problems and solutions can be huge and grow daily, the ability to locate relevant information is critical to its effective use. Training for help desk staff often includes practice problems that require them to locate information in a support knowledge base.

The "smart" part of a knowledge base is a set of search tools to help locate past problem situations that are similar to a current problem. Some help desk knowledge bases rely on keyword search strategies to locate problem solutions. Other help desk software incorporates search strategies based on artificial intelligence tools. Expert systems (sequences of if-then rules), neural networks (automated learning systems), case-based reasoning (pattern-matching strategies), and natural language processing (the ability to formulate questions in English) may be incorporated into help desk software to help support staff quickly locate the specific information in a knowledge base they need to solve a problem.

Sandy reports, "Each problem our help desk staff receives gets logged in our help desk software. I write a brief description of each problem I get and how I solved it. Then, when a user reports a problem, I can do a keyword search on the problem database in our help desk system to see if the same problem occurred before and what our help desk agents did to solve it. That feature alone has saved me huge amounts of time. I no longer waste time looking for a solution to a problem someone else on our staff has already solved."

DIAGNOSTIC UTILITIES Some help desk software packages include utility software to assist a support agent to diagnose problems. Diagnostic software is useful for analyzing the performance of a remote system and identifying potential problem areas. As you learned in Chapter 4, some diagnostic utilities permit agents to connect directly to a remote client's system, which can facilitate the problem diagnosis and repair process.

Sandy says, "Our help desk package includes some basic diagnostic utilities we use all the time. When a user calls about a possible problem, I can open a window on my desktop that connects to their PC, which means I can start diagnosing the problem immediately—without having to take the time to go to their office. If the user's problem appears to be hardware-related, I can run a diagnostic utility that scans their PC for common problems and gives me a report. If the problem appears to be software-related, I can take the necessary steps to fix the problem on their PC. And I can do all of this from my own PC. My mouse and keyboard work just like I was sitting at the user's computer.

COMMUNICATION AND INFORMATION RESOURCE LINKS Most help desk software packages recognize that connections to communication and information resources are critical for both end users and support agents. These packages frequently include external connections to email, chat facilities, and Web resources as well as connections to internal help files, product documentation, and problem archives.

Sandy relates, "When I need to follow up quickly with one of our users about a problem they've experienced, I can open a chat session to send them a quick message directly from our help desk software. Chat sessions are quicker than email for a brief message."

PRODUCT ORDER-ENTRY CAPABILITIES Marketing is often an important help desk function, because a user's request for information about a product can lead directly to a purchase order for it. Therefore, many help desk software packages include an order-entry capability, which permits a user or a support agent to enter an order online. In some cases, a help desk system's product order-entry function is integrated directly with other business systems, such as shipping and invoicing. In this way, a help desk subsystem can be integrated with other enterprise-wide applications.

Sandy mentions, "Our agency uses the order-entry feature in our help desk system a little differently. When an employee needs a hardware or software component for their PC, I can use the order-entry feature in our help desk software to create and send a purchase request. We use that capability to quickly generate requests that are routed directly to the agency's purchasing agent, who then places the actual order."

AGENT TIME MANAGEMENT TOOLS Help desk software often includes **time management tools**, which are features designed to increase agent productivity. These tools include:

- Calendar management
- Automated reminders
- Meeting and project task scheduling
- Alarms to warn of upcoming events and deadlines
- Collaboration tools (such as the ability to work jointly on a document-writing project)
- To-do lists with priorities
- Project management tools

Sandy says, "I would be lost without some of the personal time management tools available in our help desk software. I use the calendar to record when I have an important deadline or have promised a user I'd check back with them. Our help desk team also uses the calendar to schedule meetings. And we make heavy use of to-do lists to keep track of our assignments. It really helps me manage my priorities when I get a spare moment to work on a project."

While technology has impacted the work of help desk agents, it has also impacted the way their bosses work, as described in the next section.

Help Desk Management Tools

Managers of help desk operations need tools to help them and their team members perform a variety of tasks that fall outside the standard incident management process. This section describes how software packages assist help desks in carrying out management-related functions.

ASSET MANAGEMENT Many support groups are responsible for technology asset management. They keep track of an organization's inventory of computer hardware, peripherals, software package licenses, network components, spare parts, and related equipment. Help desk packages commonly offer asset and inventory control features. These capabilities are designed to help the support staff manage an organization's fixed assets (sometimes called capital assets).

Sandy's supervisor, Leslie, says, "Our insurance agency tags each piece of computer equipment with an asset ID number. Each PC and peripheral is then recorded in an asset management database, which is part of our help desk package. The asset management system also stores information about software licenses owned by the agency. Because my help desk staff often helps with the purchase and installation of employee computer systems, our help desk software is a convenient place to record installation information. And because our help desk agents usually help if equipment needs to be moved from one office to another, they update the asset database at the time of the equipment transfer. These asset management components of the help desk software really make life easier when our annual audit of equipment and software happens."

SERVICE MANAGEMENT Organizations often outsource hardware and peripheral maintenance and repairs to outside vendors. In addition to managing configuration and asset information, some help desk packages include features to manage these hardware service contracts and agreements.

Leslie says, "One of my responsibilities is to manage the service agreements we have with our vendors. I keep track of warranty information and a service history for each computer and office product in a database in our help desk software. I also keep a schedule of when the next preventive maintenance or service is scheduled to be performed on each piece of equipment, and by whom."

SERVICE LEVEL AGREEMENT (SLA) MANAGEMENT Managers of help desk operations are often responsible for managing service level agreements. A **service level agreement (SLA)** is a contract that defines the expected performance of user support services or external vendor services. Service level agreements may specify that a help desk will respond to internal or external incidents within a defined time period and that incidents will be resolved within another defined time period. For example, an SLA may specify that 90 percent of emails will be answered within four hours of their receipt by a help desk. A help desk manager can use the tools in the help desk software to monitor performance toward meeting the objectives specified in the service level agreement. In turn, a help desk manager may have an SLA with one or more of its vendors that specifies their performance when the help desk refers a problem for resolution or outsources equipment for repair. In order to manage both internal help desk and external vendor performance expectations, many software packages include service level agreement management tools.

Leslie says, "Our agency doesn't provide computer help for external clients, but we do have internal goals for our help desk team. For example, we try to respond to 95 percent of all incidents within an hour (actually, faster if the incident is a high priority), and resolve 95 percent of all incidents within 24 hours. I use the service level management feature in our help desk system to keep statistics for our team on various performance metrics, such as response time and resolution time."

CLIENT FEEDBACK CAPABILITIES **Client feedback** typically includes evaluations of the level of user satisfaction with an organization's products or services as well as satisfaction with specific help desk services. Measures of satisfaction with products and services can range from complaints about features that don't work as advertised to suggestions for new features. Help desk staff members need a way to capture user feedback and route the information to product designers, programmers, and engineers. This feedback is often a source of useful ideas for the next round of product planning. Measures of satisfaction with help desk services can include feedback about the handling of a specific incident, the problem resolution process, or help desk services in general.

Leslie reports, "Our help desk software includes two satisfaction survey tools we use all the time. One is a short email questionnaire we send to users after an incident has closed to see if we responded appropriately and solved the problem. The other is a Web-based survey our agency employees can use to let us know their overall satisfaction with the computer services they receive from us. We do a survey twice a year."

STATISTICAL REPORTS Help desk software includes built-in statistical reports and dashboards that report on key performance indicators to meet the information needs of help desk staff and management. Reports related to the abandonment rate (callers who hang up), the number of unresolved incidents by hour and day, the average length of time telephone callers spend on hold, the average length of incident processing (from receipt to closure), the productivity of staff members (incident closure rate), inventory control, and performance compared to service level agreement expectations are examples of predefined reports that are commonly available in help desk software packages.

You'll learn more about key performance indicators that are helpful to help desk managers in Chapter 7.

Leslie says, "I get a monthly report that shows the frequency of problems in various categories, such as hardware, peripherals, office productivity software, insurance agency software, network connectivity, security, and so on. Our help desk software lets me print a monthly performance report I distribute to my staff that shows how we're doing as a team, compares our performance to our benchmark goals, and shows trends over time."

CUSTOMIZABLE INTERFACES, FORMS, AND REPORTS Some help desk software includes features that let managers and staff modify the user interface, toolbars, menus, and data-entry forms the help desk uses. Customization allows a help desk to add or modify fields in the database tables to meet site-specific needs.

A report generator that prepares custom reports from database tables is another common feature. Custom reports enable the help desk managers and staff to augment predefined reports with ones designed to address specific staff and management information needs. Some help desk packages include a programming or scripting language that managers and staff can use to write macros or code to support extensions of the basic package.

Leslie says, "Our agency uses the term "trouble ticket number" operationally, whereas our help desk package contained a field labeled as "incident identifier." One of the first things we did when we converted to the help desk program was to change that field name. It was easy to change the name on the form in the software, and our help desk staff didn't have to convert to a different term in our everyday operations. And, although I was pretty happy with the built-in performance reports in the help desk software, I asked one of our agents to learn the macro scripting language so we could create some special reports on computer use the agency management wants to receive."

TELEPHONE SYSTEM INTERFACE Another useful help desk software feature is an ability to interface with a telephone system. Because many help desk support groups deal with a large volume of incoming and outgoing calls, integrated access to an organization's telephone system is important. Automated telephone systems are described later in this chapter.

Leslie noted that the agency's help desk software has the capability to connect to an automated telephone system. However, because their agency uses primarily standard office telephone, email, chat, or Web-based communication, the help desk doesn't use the software's telephone connectivity interface.

AUTOMATED INCIDENT MANAGEMENT Some help desk software packages include the ability to define business rules to automate selected incident management tasks. For example, in conjunction with an automated telephone answering system or a Web-based trouble report form, business rules within the help desk software may automatically route an incident to a specific agent with special expertise, or to an appropriate problem queue.

Leslie says, "I want to make sure that unresolved help desk incidents don't fall through the cracks. So we use the business rules feature in our help desk software to automatically escalate any problem that has been unresolved for 24 hours. The help desk system automatically sends me an email when that happens so I can follow up with the agent or the user."

Help Desk End User Tools

Although help desk software is intended primarily for agents and their managers, an increasing number of packages include tools that end users can access directly. These tools allow users to use the Web to locate information about a product or problem, submit an incident, monitor progress on incident resolution, and submit feedback to the help desk on its performance. With these tools, a user can perform many of the tasks related to incident management without direct contact with a help desk agent.

From a user perspective, a help desk incident may be initiated face to face, via a telephone call, or, in an increasing number of cases, via email or Web access. In the latter cases, a user uses an email client or a Web browser to enter and receive incident information. In some cases, client software is installed on each user's desktop computer and is used to submit a trouble ticket directly to the help desk system, when necessary. Web access to a help desk system can enable users to find information so that simple questions get answered without direct intervention by an agent. Users can also update information about a problem and get an automated status report on the progress toward a problem solution.

The preceding list of help desk software features and capabilities is not in any implied order of importance. Each tool may have greater or lesser importance depending on each help desk group's needs. And although no single help desk package necessarily offers all of these features and capabilities, most packages offer several of them. Selecting a help desk software package from among those on the market (and there are many) is often one of the most important product evaluation decisions a help desk staff makes.

ON THE WEB

The list of companies that sell help desk software packages is long. Popular packages for large-scale help desk operations including the following:

- Help Desk Technology International's HelpSTAR (**www.helpstar.com/help-desk-technology.asp**)
- BMC Service Desk (**www.bmc.com/products/offering/service-desk-software-incident-problem-management.html**)
- Epicor's IT Service Management (ITSM) (**www.epicor.com/Solutions/Pages/ITServiceManagement.aspx**)
- HEAT Service & Support (**www.frontrange.com/help-desk-software**)
- TechExcel ServiceWise (**www.techexcel.com/products/itsm**)

The following packages are targeted primarily at small- or mid-scale help desks:

- Monarch Bay HelpTrac (**www.helptrac.com**)
- Numera Track-It! (**www.numarasoftware.com/track-it/help-desk**)
- Soffront Customer Helpdesk (**www.soffront.com/crm/solutions/customersupport.asp**)
- ScriptLogic's Help Desk Authority (**www.helpdesksoftware.com**)

Packages available without charge (or at low cost) and geared toward small help desks include the following:

- Spiceworks (**www.spiceworks.com**)
- Ilient Software's SysAid (**www.ilient.com/free-help-desk-software.htm**)
- Macs Design Studio's Web Help Desk (**www.webhelpdesk.com/free-help-desk-software.html**)

Several of these packages offer downloadable evaluation versions.

A list of other help desk software vendors can be found at **dir.yahoo.com/Business_and_Economy/Business_to_Business/Corporate_Services/Customer_Service/Software/Help_Desk**.

ON THE WEB

For additional information on selecting and implementing a help desk software package, consult these resources:

- HelpDeskSoftware.org presents a guide to help desk software solutions (**www.helpdesksoftware.org**).

- DataWatch, a vendor of IT software and services, provides a white paper on implementing a help desk and evaluating help desk software (**www.datawatch.com/whitepapers/Help_Desk_practical_guide_whitepaper.pdf**).

- TechRepublic offers a call-tracking software evaluation toolkit as a download (**www.techrepublic.com/article/evaluate-help-desk-call-tracking-software-with-these-criteria/5030618**); free registration is required.

- To view a buyer's guide to help desk software, visit **www.helpdesk-guide.com/helpdesk-software-buyers-guide.asp**.

- Cartels Consulting has prepared a help desk software evaluation checklist as an Excel spreadsheet (**www.cartelsconsulting.com/docs/Free_help_desk_evaluation_checklist.xls**).

HelpSTAR® Software

The case study in this section illustrates typical help desk software features with a package named HelpSTAR, which is developed and sold by Help Desk Technology International (**itil.helpstar.com**).

The HelpSTAR package is a commercial help desk program that includes many of the features you just learned about. Like many help desk software packages, HelpSTAR has an extensive array of built-in features and is customizable for specific situations.

A student edition of HelpSTAR is included on a CD in this book. You can install the 180-day student edition to get experience with the features of help desk software. HelpSTAR is described in more detail in Appendix B, which also includes hands-on activities for the software.

Figure 6-4 shows a sample HelpSTAR screen with a new service request (an incident report) from an internal user, Chris Green, an engineer in the Design Department at Willamette Planning. Chris is unable to print to a printer on the company's network, and he called the help desk dispatcher to report the problem. Users with Web access may also submit problem reports via email.

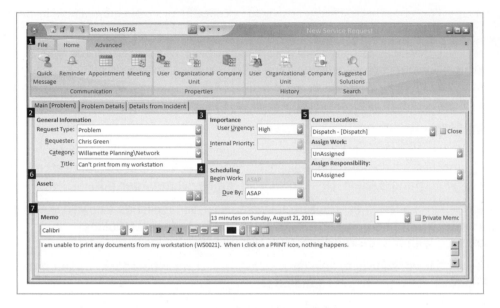

Figure 6-4   HelpSTAR service request from user Chris Green

The New Service Request screen shown in Figure 6-4 contains several important elements. The numbers in the feature list below correspond to the numbered black squares in the figure:

1. *Ribbon menu*—HelpSTAR's user interface is based on the Microsoft Windows ribbon menu, in which common tasks are represented as menu tabs and icon groups on the ribbon. For example, a help desk agent can display a user's previous incidents and requests in the History group on the Home tab.

2. *General Information*—This section identifies the request type, the requester, the category, and a request title. Because all printers are networked at Willamette Planning, the incident dispatcher selected the category "Willamette Planning \Network" and gave the request a title to further identify the nature of the problem.

3. *Importance*—These fields allow the agent to identify the priority of the incident from both the user's and the dispatcher's perspectives.

4. *Scheduling*—This feature can be used to indicate that an incident or request has a deadline or due date.

5. *Current Location*—This field indicates in which queue or status an incident is currently located. Incidents can be reviewed by a dispatcher and assigned to a specific support agent, or entered into a queue according to the category of the incident based on rules the help desk supervisor defines.

6. *Asset*—This optional field indicates whether a specific piece of equipment is involved in the request.

7. *Memo*—This section allows the agent(s) involved to provide a complete description of the problem, including any notes made by those who work on the problem during its resolution. The Memo window also includes a field showing how much time has been spent on the request.

The HelpSTAR system automatically assigns a number to Chris Green's service request. When help desk agent Beth Markham displayed her queue of assigned service requests, she learned that the incident reported by Chris Green had been assigned to her for resolution, as shown in Figure 6-5.

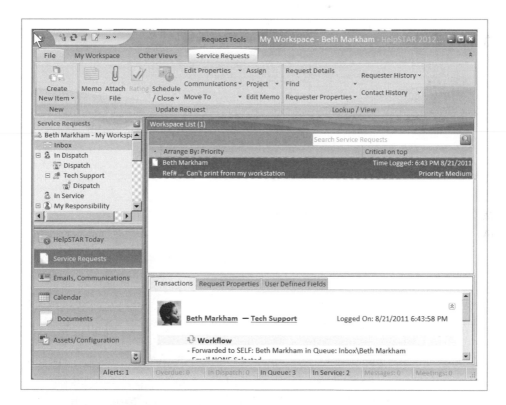

Figure 6-5 HelpSTAR lists Chris Green's request for help desk agent Beth Markham

Incidents may be assigned to agents manually by a dispatcher, or automatically by application of business rules the help desk supervisor has defined in HelpSTAR. Organizations can also specify whether an agent is allowed to manually retrieve a request from a HelpSTAR queue, or whether an incident must be assigned to an agent either automatically or by a supervisor.

If Beth doesn't know the solution to Chris's problem, she can use HelpSTAR's Best Solutions knowledge base to search for a possible solution to the problem. The Best Solutions knowledge base contains reports of previously reported problems and their solutions contributed by Beth and other agents, as shown in Figure 6-6. It may also contain articles and pointers to Web-based information and product manuals that agents can use to diagnose and solve problems.

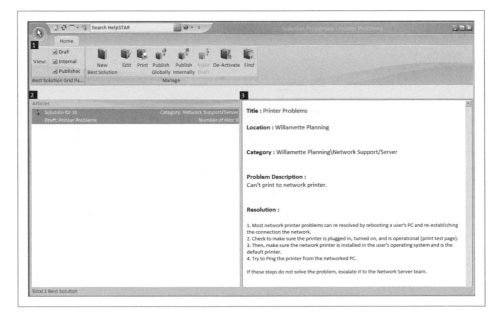

Figure 6-6   HelpSTAR's knowledge base of Best Solutions can be searched for problem resolutions

The Solutions knowledge base screen shown in Figure 6-6 is divided into three main sections. The numbers in the feature list below correspond to the numbered bullets shown in the figure:

1. *Ribbon menu*—As a help desk agent, Beth can write, edit, print, or publish a draft of a new Best Solution, or update an existing solution.

2. *Articles*—This window displays solutions from the knowledge base, which may be searched using text strings or keywords, or by browsing problem categories.

3. *Solution details*—This window displays the title, location, and category of the incident that prompted the solution entry into the knowledge base, a description of the problem, and the steps taken to resolve it.

In addition to service requests for assistance, HelpSTAR can be used to maintain a database of assets, as shown in Figure 6-7. Assets include hardware and software, but could also include office furniture and other inventory items.

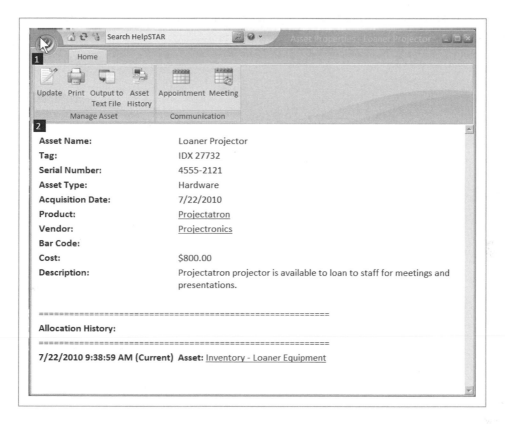

Figure 6-7 HelpSTAR's asset identification screen

The Asset Properties screen shown in Figure 6-7 has two sections. The numbers in the feature list below correspond to the numbered bullets shown in the figure:

1. *Ribbon menu*—The help desk staff or the property management department can use the ribbon menu to enter, update, or print information about an asset.

2. *Properties*—This window provides information about each asset, including a field for a narrative description of the asset (a loaner projector, in this example).

Help desk staff may search for an asset with HelpSTAR's advanced search tool, or perform an audit of networked workstations to determine compliance with software license requirements.

Figure 6-8 is an example of a management dashboard report that is predefined in HelpSTAR. A **dashboard** is a visual display of measures based on key performance indicators; it is used to quickly monitor help desk operations and identify aspects that vary from stated goals or require management attention. The dashboard displays are customizable, both with respect to content (such as which performance indicators are included) and with respect to format (bar chart, pie chart, line graph, etc.).

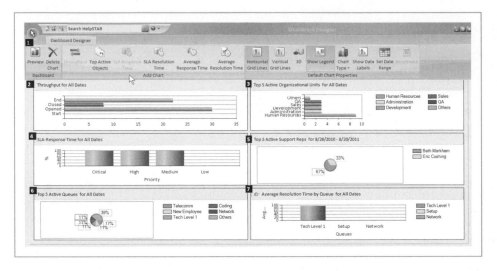

Figure 6-8   HelpSTAR's management dashboard provides a quick overview of important measures of help desk operation

The dashboard shown in Figure 6-8 provides information on several different metrics. The numbers in the feature list below correspond to the numbered bullets shown in the figure:

1. *Ribbon menu*—Help desk managers can design dashboard reports to display selected key performance indicators to alert management and staff to changes in the performance of the help desk operation. Reports can be created for a user-specified time period, such as daily, weekly, monthly, or annually.

2. *Throughput*—This bar chart displays the volume of incidents in various categories during the selected time period.

3. *Top Active Organizational Units*—This bar chart shows the volume of incidents from various departments in an organization during the selected time period.

4. *SLA Response Time*—This column chart provides a quick picture of how effectively the help desk met its response time goals as defined in service level agreements.

5. *Top Active Support Reps*—This pie chart shows the top support reps as measured by the percent of incidents handled during the selected time period.

6. *Top Active Queues*—This pie chart displays the percent of incidents in various categories of problem queues.

7. *Average Resolution Time*—This section shows the average time to resolve incidents by category of incident.

Appendix B includes a tutorial for HelpSTAR as well as hands-on activities to give you an opportunity to gain experience with the software.

Other commercial help desk software packages have similar features and capabilities to those in the HelpSTAR package. Many help desk packages can be integrated with telephone systems to provide a powerful suite of tools for help desk staff.

Computer Telephony Systems

Computer telephony is technology designed to increase help desk productivity by providing a seamless interface between telephone and computer systems. Computer telephony is popular among support organizations that make heavy use of both technologies to provide help desk services. Whereas many small support centers rely on a help desk receptionist or a call dispatcher to respond to incoming telephone calls, most large help desk facilities invest in automated telephone systems.

An **automated call distributor (ACD)** is a computer telephony system that can answer calls, greet callers, provide menus to categorize the type of call, and route each call to a specific support agent or queue. When integrated with a help desk software package, an ACD system can take incident management a step further. When an appropriate support agent becomes available, an ACD system can match the support agent with the highest priority caller, signal the support agent on his or her computer screen, and display information on the agent's monitor about the caller and the problem. The ACD then routes the call to the agent's telephone.

ON THE WEB

One vendor of call center ACD systems is Database Systems. Their call center products are described on the company's Web site (**www.call-center-tech.com/ call-centers.htm**).

Common features of ACD systems include the following:

- *Skill set distribution*—Routes each call to an agent who has expertise in a problem area
- *Overflow routing*—Sends calls to another agent queue when one queue is long or when calls have been in a queue longer than a predefined time period
- *Call accounting*—Provides statistics on the number of calls received in half-hour periods during the day
- *Lost call reporting*—Provides statistics on calls that were abandoned because the caller terminated the call before it was answered by an agent

- *Queue time*—Provides statistics on the length of time calls wait in a queue before an agent responds

- *Agent performance*—Provides statistics on each agent's call handling, including average length of calls and idle time

- *Call monitoring*—Permits supervisors to listen to or record calls for training and worker evaluation purposes

The major benefit of an ACD system is that it reduces the amount of time needed to respond to and route calls to support staff. Because ACD systems increase the efficiency of help desk staff, they are important help desk productivity tools.

Although computer telephony systems are designed to make efficient use of scarce support staff resources, many of these systems have a well-deserved poor reputation among end users. Lengthy hold times, long and complex menu options, repetitive requests for information, inability to reach a live agent, and dropped calls are common complaints of users who must navigate ACD systems. An increased emphasis on client relationship management in the support industry may eventually provide users with some relief from poorly designed computer telephony systems.

Another computer telephony product with applications in user support is an interactive voice response system. An **interactive voice response (IVR)** system allows a user to interact with a database of information by pressing keys on a telephone handset or by speaking simple words into the telephone. Based on a caller's input, an IVR unit retrieves information from its database and plays a response for the user. IVRs, which work together with ACD systems, can be programmed with decision tree logic to ask questions to narrow a search for the information the user needs.

ON THE WEB

To learn more about interactive voice response (sometimes called intelligent voice response) technology:

- Read an explanation of how IVR technology works (**communication. howstuffworks.com/interactive-voice-response.htm**).

- View a demonstration video prepared by an IVR vendor (**www.spoken.com/ conversational-ivr-demo-video**).

- Learn about some common mistakes in the design of IVR systems (**www.youtube. com/watch?v=QSpWNA8hOX4**).

Web-Based Support

As support organizations and their clients search for more efficient and cost-effective ways to provide support to technology users, the role of the Web has increased dramatically. Virtually every large hardware component manufacturer, system integrator, software developer, network services supplier, and computer support provider operates a support Web site. Vendor Web sites typically offer a variety of support services to users, including the following:

- Product information, specifications, updates, pricing, and licensing
- Product order initiation and order fulfillment status reports
- Purchase rebate status
- Automated requests for literature, newsletters, and product-related email notifications
- Online manuals and documentation
- Software downloads for drivers, patches, updates, diagnostic tools, templates, product tutorials, and demonstration versions of software
- Troubleshooting wizards
- Knowledge base access to frequently asked questions (FAQs), articles, problem reports, white papers, and technical information
- Bulletin boards and chat rooms to connect users with other more knowledgeable users
- Email and chat access to technical support staff
- Problem incident reports
- Contact information for support staff
- Feedback on client satisfaction with products and support services
- Links to other sites with information about related products and services

Although few vendor Web sites offer all these services, most vendors now see the Web as an ideal supplement to telephone, face-to-face, and email support services. One of the reasons Web support has become popular, even for small support organizations, is that the cost to provide Web support is often considerably less than that of other methods. Users find they can frequently locate the information they need on a Web site without a phone conversation or an email exchange with a support agent. When a support organization can respond to a user's needs without involving a support staff member, it saves money. And any time a user can locate information on a Web site, he or she does not have to spend time in a telephone queue waiting for the next support agent. Web-based support is another tool employed by support centers to meet the objective of making users more self-reliant.

ON THE WEB

Web Help Desk is an incident management system specifically designed for Web-based support. An online demonstration of its features, including the ability to log on as an agent or a user, is available at **www.webhelpdesk.com**.

To get experience with an example of a Web-based support site, visit IBM's support site (**www-947.ibm.com/support/entry/portal/Overview**). While you are there, take note of the various services IBM provides at its support site.

Even when an email exchange between a user and a support staff member is required, email can be more efficient and less costly than telephone support. First, email is **asynchronous**, which means that the communication between the user and support staff does not have to occur when both are available. A support agent does not have to respond to a user's email request immediately, and does not have to be available to communicate on the client's schedule, as is the case with a telephone call. Email support makes more efficient use of support staff resources than telephone support does. Second, email responses to frequently asked questions can be composed in advance, checked for accuracy, stored, and then easily pasted into a response to a user. When appropriate, use of "canned" responses to email requests is a cost-effective use of support staff time.

The potential to abuse a client relationship with canned email responses is enormous. Users who submit a question to a support site sometimes receive several pages of canned response. On occasion, when a user asks a follow-up question, the same canned response is emailed back. This problem can occur if a support agent does not read an inquiry carefully or if a support group automatically scans customers' emails and sends back canned responses based on keywords in the user's message. Neither of these practices is likely to improve the client relationship.

Increased use of the Web as a user support tool means that some knowledge, skills, and abilities that were important for a support staff member in the past are now less important, whereas other skills are becoming more valuable. Telephone support emphasizes verbal skills, pleasant voice quality, an ability to recall information quickly, and patience with clients; Web-based and email support require agents who are skilled in written and visual communications. The ability to recall information quickly is less important in an online environment than the ability to locate information from various resources. The ability to speak well is less important than the ability to write clearly. The ability to listen is less important than the ability to read and understand. However, good client service skills and the ability to ask probing questions are important in every support environment.

Web-based and email support are attractive options for small organizations and those that support primarily internal clients. Many organizations now use an intranet to deliver information and user support services to their workers. An **intranet** is a network modeled after the Internet, with information organized into Web pages, but accessible primarily or exclusively by employees within an organization. An intranet provides a way to support internal users via tools they are familiar with, such as their Web browser, but it also provides security from access by unauthorized external users. At small organizations and departments within large ones, help desk staff may need skills in Web site layout and design as well as Web applications software and programming languages in order to build pages that provide clients and employees with Web-based user support services.

ON THE WEB

For a short tutorial on intranets and their benefits to an organization, visit the Intranet Road Map Web site (**www.intranetroadmap.com**).

Trends in Help Desk Operation

Help desk operation is a field that is changing rapidly and continually. Many of the industry trends that have been described above will continue, and new trends will emerge. Some of these technology and workplace trends are summarized in Figure 6-9 and are discussed in the following sections.

Technology Trends

- Cloud computing

- Virtualization of software platforms

- Support for wireless technology

- Remote diagnosis and voice response technologies

Help Desk Workplace Trends

- Outsourcing

- Worker certification

- Telecommuting as a work style

- Industry best practices such as ITIL

- Pressure to reduce support costs

- Web based support portals

- Reliance on quantitative metrics

- Computer security

- Help desk software integration

Figure 6-9   Help desk industry trends

Technology Trends

Some trends that have impacted the help desk field are due to more general changes in technology, which affect the services required of help desks as well as the way in which those services are provided. Many of these trends will continue to influence the help desk field for the foreseeable future.

Cloud Computing

In some ways, **cloud computing** is simply a new name for an old idea: providing access to computer software, data, and services by subscription over the Internet—using a pay-for-what-you-use model. The trend toward cloud computing may result in fewer outright purchases of operating system and application software packages. Instead of purchasing, downloading, and installing software on their PCs, individual users or organizations pay a fee to license the use of software, data, and other Internet services. Some organizations have developed their own internal cloud services to support employees. Cloud computing represents a step back from distributed computing toward more centralized computer services, and in many cases is yet another step in reliance on the Internet to provide computer services.

The cloud computing shift in the software delivery paradigm has several advantages, including the instant availability on a software vendor's Web server (in the cloud) of the latest version of a software package, complete with up-to-date patches and new features. In addition to software, in cloud computing, user data is stored on Internet servers, which means it is available via any Internet connection. With applications software and data on the cloud, collaboration among members of a project team is more feasible. While cloud computing may be just the latest paradigm shift that will impact user support workers, it will not be the last. Support workers who do not anticipate and learn about technology changes will find the IT job market a challenge.

Virtualization of Software Platforms

Virtualization is a method of allocating the resources of a computer into several execution environments, in which each virtual machine, operating in its own partition (memory and disk space), has the capability to run its own operating system and application software. Each virtual machine shares the hardware resources of the host system, which permits a help desk agent to respond to questions about multiple operating systems and application programs from a single host machine. Virtualization should reduce the equipment and operational costs of help desk groups and increase the resources available to help desk workers to troubleshoot problems.

Support for Wireless Technology

The integration of wireless devices (such as cell phones, smartphones, Bluetooth devices, MP3 players, PDAs, netbooks, tablet computers, electronic book readers, Wi-Fi networks, and GPS units) with computer technology will undoubtedly continue. User support as a field will likely have to expand its mission to meet the demand for support for integrated wireless technologies.

Remote Diagnosis and Voice Response Technologies

Automation continues to impact help desk operations. Whereas many help desks in the past were based on walk-in, on-site, or telephone support, future help desks will undoubtedly rely to an increasing extent on email, the Web, chat facilities, self-help, and remote diagnosis to provide help desk services. As mentioned previously, remote diagnosis is the use of a computer system at a help desk site to connect to a client's system, and then to test the various components of the user's hardware, examine the user's software configuration, and replicate a problem scenario.

Furthermore, help desk technology in the future will likely incorporate advances in voice recognition and response in products aimed at the support industry. The key to the successful help desk of the future is to reduce users' reliance on help desk staff by helping them be more self-reliant, and to increase the productivity (often by decreasing the effort expended) of help desk staff when users cannot be self-sufficient for whatever reason.

Workplace Trends

Other trends that will impact future help desk operations are due to changes in the workplace environment within the help desk industry.

Outsourcing

As you learned in Chapter 1, an ongoing user support trend is the outsourcing of some help desk services. Outsourcing can be onshore (when companies contract with support service providers in the United States) or offshore (when companies contract with support service providers in other countries). The impact of onshore outsourcing is mixed. On the one hand, companies tend to hire fewer support employees to provide services directly to their workers and clients. On the other hand, as companies and vendors shed help desk employees, the outsource service providers they contract with then need workers to staff their help desk support positions. The upshot of the onshore outsourcing trend is that some entry-level support workers end up as employees of outsource service providers rather than as employees of the companies and vendors whose workers and clients need the support services.

268

Offshore outsourcing means that some help desk jobs that were formerly located in North American are now located in Asia (especially India)—and to some extent in Europe—because relative wages overseas are sometimes significantly less than in North America. This trend has reduced the need for support workers in the United States to answer help desk telephone calls, respond to emails from users, and operate self-help Web sites. Outsourcing help desk operations overseas raises several issues, including the long-range impact on the U.S. workforce, whether quality support standards can be maintained, and the role of help desks in building and maintaining customer relationships.

On a practical level, outsourcing help desk operations overseas means relatively fewer jobs are available for entry-level help desk agents in the United States. On the other hand, relatively more entry-level positions will be available in North America for support workers who serve internal clients. Some organizations and vendors that were quick to jump on the offshore outsourcing bandwagon to save money are also now rethinking that strategy due to feedback from disgruntled workers and clients. Complaints about communication difficulties with offshore agents have resulted in the return of some user support jobs to North America.

ON THE WEB

To learn more about trends in offshore outsourcing, read an article at **www.outsourcing-offshore.com/2007-offshore.html**. Although the article is several years old, the trends it discusses are relevant to today.

Worker Certification

Another computer industry trend that impacts help desk staffing is the increasing reliance on certifications. Not only are help desk staff in many organizations expected to pass certification exams for the specific products they support, but certifications are now available for the more general knowledge, skills, and abilities required of help desk agents. Certification is an employment and professional development tool that can enhance a support agent's job marketability and opportunities for promotion—in combination with the agent's education, training, and experience. However, industry certification is no guarantee of employment, and there is no industry-wide agreement on the need for certifications.

Chapter 7 describes the certification process in detail.

Telecommuting as a Work Style

Telecommuting is full or part-time work performed at a home office for an employer. **Voice over Internet Protocol (VoIP)** is a technology that makes telecommuting for help desk work more feasible, by transmitting voice communications over the Internet rather than via telephone lines. As the quality of VoIP has improved, it has allowed help desk workers to maintain communication with end users and work colleagues from a home office (see Figure 6-10).

Figure 6-10   Help desk agent telecommutes part-time from home office

An increasing number of help desk employers permit or encourage telecommuting as a way to reduce worker turnover and decrease office space and operational costs. Telecommuting provides workers with greater flexibility in work hours and conditions, and it reduces the amount of money employees must spend on transportation, child care, clothing, food, and other employment-related expenses. Help desk organizations that use telecommuting as an alternate work style must address concerns about worker productivity, quality control, and confidentiality. They must also tackle the challenges of having supervisors oversee agents who are located remotely.

Industry Best Practices such as ITIL

The Information Technology Infrastructure Library (ITIL), described earlier in this chapter, is one of many evolving frameworks, guidelines, and standards that continue to develop and expand as the help desk industry matures. Adoption of industry best practices should contribute to help desk staff productivity and effectiveness.

Pressure to Reduce Support Costs

Many of the help desk industry trends in this section are the result of pressures to reduce the cost of user support. Increased use of outsourcing, telecommuting, Web-based support portals, interactive voice response, and remote diagnosis are obvious examples. The challenge for the user support industry in the next decade will be to further reduce costs while increasing the quality of services provided, which are often contradictory objectives.

Web-Based Support Portals

One response to the need to reduce user support costs is to make increased use of Web sites as a medium for communicating with users. Many organizations are developing support **portals**, which provide a single point of Web access for all support services. The development of support portals is both a technical challenge and a customer-service challenge, as you learned in Chapter 2. As help desks make increasing use of the Web as a delivery vehicle for support services, the specific skills required of support workers in many organizations will change. Less emphasis on telephone help desk operations will give way to a greater emphasis on more comprehensive training to prepare workers for the broader spectrum of knowledge, skills, and abilities required to support end users.

Reliance on Quantitative Metrics

As more help desk functions become automated, help desk managers need access to high-quality reports and statistical information that will alert managers and staff to trends in the volume of incidents, the kinds of questions asked, the need for help desk staff with particular skills, and the kinds of problems about which end users are inquiring. Measuring human behavior is never an easy task. However, as help desk managers react to corporate pressures to increase agent productivity and justify the costs of help desk operations, the industry will see an expanded reliance on quantitative performance metrics.

 Chapter 7 describes some ways help desks' organizations and their agents are measured and evaluated.

Computer Security

Despite continuing efforts to develop effective tools to fight viruses, spyware, spam, rootkits, keyloggers, phishing, and other malware attacks on servers and user PCs, security threats will never be eliminated. Help desk practitioners need to keep up to date on trends in security threats and increase their knowledge of tools to manage them. Additional industry efforts at server-based security tools will continue in the future.

 Chapter 12 discusses resources help desk staff can use to increase vigilance on client systems.

271

Help Desk Software Integration

Help desks of the future will be seen as one component of a larger **client relationship management (CRM)** system. Client relationship management is a relatively new name for an old objective: meet the needs of clients by providing excellent customer service. CRM proponents view each client as the reason an organization exists. CRM is based on findings that the cost to recruit a new client is many times greater than the cost of managing a successful relationship with an existing client. Going forward, help desk agents will see increasing integration of features in software tools and alignment of their work with other business functions.

The help desk of the future will undoubtedly look very different from ones today. The challenge for support workers is to prepare for these operational changes by taking advantage of educational opportunities and professional development and by learning more about industry trends.

Chapter Summary

- Simply stated, the goal of most help desk operations is to provide clients with a single point of contact for information requests, IT services, and problem resolution.

- Many help desks are organized in a multilevel (or tier) system. The lowest level is an incident screener or dispatcher. Increased levels of technical expertise include product specialists, technical support, and support managers.

- Many help desk procedures involve the effective management of problem incidents. Incident management addresses the details of how problem incidents are received, prescreened, authenticated to determine the user's right to various types and levels of service, logged for record-keeping purposes, and screened to determine their importance. Incidents are then prioritized, assigned to an appropriate agent, tracked as they move toward a satisfactory resolution, escalated if necessary, resolved, closed, and archived in a database.

- The Information Technology Infrastructure Library (ITIL) is a compendium of best practice guidelines for support organizations that address IT service management, including how to manage incidents and technology changes in organizations.

- The physical environment of a help desk facility includes the workspace, furniture, equipment, and computer systems help desk agents use in their work. Wireless headsets that permit flexibility of movement are an important tool for telephone agents.

- Support workers are often vulnerable to job stress when the requirements of a position do not match the personal characteristics of a worker. The physical layout of a workspace and other work conditions may contribute to job stress.

- Several tools are available to assist in managing problem incidents. These include help desk software packages designed to organize and automate many incident management tasks and procedures—with tools intended for agents, managers, and users; computer telephony systems (including automated call distributors and interactive voice response systems) that automate call routing and task assignment; and the Web as a support delivery vehicle.

- Help desk operations continue to evolve. Changes in technology require that workers keep abreast of trends and developments in the computer field, including cloud computing, virtualization, wireless technologies, and remote access. Workplace changes in the help desk industry, including outsourcing of help desk services domestically and overseas, will impact industry employment trends as well as training programs. Increased use of technology and automation of help desk functions address the need to improve the productivity of help desk staff as well as the need to be more proactive by anticipating user problems. In a growing number of organizations, help desks are viewed as an increasingly important component in client relationship management.

Key Terms

archive—A database or paper file used to store and retain records relating to closed incidents.

asynchronous—A method of communication in which the communicators do not have to participate at the same time; email and Web-based communication are examples.

authentication procedure—An incident management step in which an agent determines whether a help desk is authorized to handle a call and to provide information or services to the user; authentication usually includes checking product registrations, support services licenses, or contracts.

automated call distributor (ACD)—A computer telephony system that automates many of the first steps in incident management, such as a greeting, menu options, caller authentication, call holding, queue management, and staff notification.

best practices—Procedures, tools, and methods that successful support groups employ; these practices often set apart very successful support operations from mediocre ones.

call management—A process followed by help desk staff when handling telephone contacts between end users and support staff.

273

client feedback—Evaluations collected from help desk users about their level of satisfaction with a product or service, a specific help desk incident, the problem resolution, or help desk services in general.

client relationship management (CRM)—Business processes that aim to meet the needs of and satisfy clients by providing excellent client service; CRM is based on findings that the cost of replacing a client is many times greater than the cost of managing the relationship with an existing client.

closing—An incident management step in which a support agent reviews the steps the help desk took to solve a problem, agrees with the end user that a solution has been reached, invites the user to call back (if necessary), and makes final entries regarding the incident in a database.

cloud computing—A subscription service in which computer software, data, and services are accessed via the Internet instead of residing on individual PCs.

computer telephony—Technology designed to increase help desk productivity by providing a seamless interface between telephone and computer systems.

dashboard—A visual display of measures based on key indicators; it is used to quickly monitor help desk operations and identify aspects that vary from stated goals or require management attention.

incident management—A well-defined, formal process that help desk staff follow to receive and prescreen problem incidents—via face-to-face, telephone, email, chat, or Web-based contacts—then obtain the information requested by a user or solve an end user's problem, and close an incident; compare to *call management*.

Information Technology Infrastructure Library (ITIL)—A set of guidelines designed to help organizations align and integrate their computer services with their business objectives.

interactive voice response (IVR)—A computer telephony system that allows a user to interact with a database of information by pressing keys on a telephone handset or by speaking simple words into the telephone; an IVR unit plays back a recorded response based on the user's input.

intranet—A network modeled after the Internet, with information organized into Web pages, but accessible primarily or exclusively by employees within an organization.

job stress—A physical or emotional response that occurs when the individual characteristics of a help desk worker do not match the requirements of their position.

logging—An incident management step in which an agent begins documenting the incident and its related problem.

multilevel support model—A help desk structure that organizes support staff and services into several levels, or tiers, of support; sometimes called a frontline/backline model; the goal is to handle calls at the lowest possible support level.

portal—A Web site that provides a single point of entry (or contact) for all support services.

prescreening—An incident management step in which agents identify and respond to simple requests for information, often without initiating an official incident; prescreening is essentially a filtering process.

priority code—A designation assigned to an incident that indicates how serious the problem is for users, how many users are affected, and perhaps the consequence of not addressing the problem immediately; priority codes are often the basis for determining the order in which incidents are assigned to agents.

queue—A waiting line into which incoming calls or incidents are placed when they cannot be addressed immediately; queues are often established for different types and priorities of incidents or for specific products, clients, or levels of support.

resolution—An incident management step in which a user's problem is solved, a complaint is noted or referred to product designers, or authorization is given to return a product for replacement or a refund.

screening—An incident management step in which a help desk staff member asks a series of questions to categorize and describe the incident; incidents may be categorized as a request for information, a question, a problem, a complaint, or a work (or service) order.

service level agreement (SLA)—A contract that defines the expected performance of user support services or external vendor services.

telecommuting—Full- or part-time work performed at a home office for an employer.

time management tools—Software tools designed to help support agents increase their personal productivity; time management tools include calendaring systems, to-do lists, and collaboration and project management tools.

tracking—An incident management step in which an agent updates the incident record with information about a problem as it progresses.

virtualization—A method of allocating the resources of a computer into several execution environments, in which each virtual machine, operating in its own partition (memory and disk space), has the capability to run its own operating system and application software.

Voice over Internet Protocol (VoIP)—A technology that transmits voice communications over the Internet rather than via telephone lines.

Check Your Understanding

Answers to Check Your Understanding questions are in Appendix A.

1. True or False? In a help desk that uses the multilevel support model, the goal is to handle calls at the lowest possible support level.

2. In a help desk patterned on the multilevel support model, what is the common title of workers at each level?

    a. *level 1*: assistant; *level 2*: product specialist; *level 3*: programmer; *level 4*: support manager
    b. *level 1*: incident dispatcher; *level 2*: technical support; *level 3*: product specialist; *level 4*: support supervisor
    c. *level 1*: incident screener; *level 2*: product specialist; *level 3*: technical support; *level 4*: support manager
    d. *level 1*: incident screener; *level 2*: product specialist; *level 3*: support manager; *level 4*: programmer

3. _____ is a well-defined, formal procedure that help desk staff follow to solve user problems.

4. True or False? Every help desk incident, no matter what kind, goes through all 12 steps of the incident management process described in the chapter, even if some of the steps do not apply.

5. Of the sequences listed below, which shows the correct order of the steps in the incident management process: (1) authenticate the incident; (2) archive the incident; (3) log the incident; and (4) prioritize the problem

    a. 4 – 3 – 1 – 2   c. 1 – 3 – 4 – 2
    b. 3 – 1 – 2 – 4   d. 1 – 2 – 3 – 4

6. True or False? The percentage of incidents that cannot be resolved during the incident management process is frequently zero.

7. In which category of help desk incidents does the following statement fall? *"My computer runs slowly when I connect to the Web in the evenings."*

    a. a question   c. a complaint
    b. a problem   d. a work order

8. A common strategy for assigning a priority to help desk calls is:

    a. first in, first out (FIFO)

    b. last in, first out (LIFO)

    c. in random order

    d. in the order the help desk agent prefers

9. An incident management step in which a problem is transferred to a support staff member who has greater experience or resources to handle difficult questions is:

    a. assignment   c. tracking

    b. screening   d. escalation

10. A(n) _____ is a waiting line into which incoming calls are placed when they cannot be answered immediately.

11. True or False? An automated incident tracking system is primarily useful in a large help desk operation, but is of very limited or no use in a small help desk operation.

12. True or False? Knowledge bases that have special search tools and other help desk software features are called smart databases.

13. True or False? The purpose of client feedback features in a help desk software package is to make it easier for managers to terminate support agents with poor customer service skills.

14. A(n) _____ is a telephone system that can answer calls, greet callers, provide menus, and route calls.

15. True or False? Incident management and call management are terms that mean the same thing.

16. True or False? A priority code indicates how easy or difficult a dispatcher thinks an incident will be to resolve.

17. _____ is often the result of the personal characteristics of a worker not matching the requirements of a position.

18. Help desk software packages usually include tools to help _____, _____, and _____ manage problem incidents.

19. An increasing number of help desk incidents are handled:

    a. in face-to-face situations   c. on a support Web site

    b. via a telephone call   d. using IVR technology

20. Describe a recent trend in help desk operation and briefly explain how it will impact help desk agents in the future.

21. ITIL is:

    a. a set of industry best practices
    b. a set of industry standards
    c. a set of software programs
    d. an incident management procedure

22. True or False? Telecommuting is working for an employer full- or part-time from a home office.

Discussion Questions

1. Should a help desk organization hire additional agents in order to satisfy 100 percent of its users 100 percent of the time? Explain why or why not.

2. Based on your experiences with checkout lines in grocery stores or fast-food restaurants, discuss whether the number of queues makes a difference in the level of service provided. For example, if five clerks are available, is it more effective to have one long queue, where the next customer in the queue gets served next, or five separate queues, one for each clerk, so that a customer has to decide which queue to select. Does either arrangement really make any difference? If so, to whom? Relate your discussion to managing help desk incidents.

3. Which of the help desk industry trends described in this chapter do you think will have the greatest impact on the work of future help desk agents? Explain your answer. Based on your own experience, list some additional trends you would add to the list included in the chapter.

4. Is job stress among agents in a help desk operation inevitable? Explain your answer. What characteristics of a help desk operation increase or reduce job stress?

5. Should every help desk operation use automated incident tracking software, or can some support operations use less formal, paper-and-pencil methods? Explain your position.

6. Is job stress among help desk agents caused more by the characteristics of each worker or by the working conditions in a help desk operation? Is the solution to job stress more the responsibility of each worker or the responsibility of help desk management?

7. Are the steps in the incident management process described in this chapter designed to resolve problem incidents effectively and efficiently? If the objective is effective and efficient problem resolution, what steps would you add, delete, or change?

Hands-On Activities

Activity 6-1

Interview a help desk support agent. Identify a support agent at your organization or school, or one employed in a local business. Interview the agent to find out how his or her help desk is organized and what services it provides. Ask about this person's career path; if possible, obtain his or her current position description. Write a summary of the interview highlights.

Activity 6-2

Visit a local telephone contact center. Arrange a visit to a help desk operation or contact center that provides telephone support, if one is available locally. Study how the physical workspace for contact center workers is organized to facilitate their work. Find out if the organization has a written incident or call management process, if it uses help desk or call management software, and if it uses a computer telephony system. Write a summary of your findings, including the pros and cons of working in the facility you visited. Include in your summary a sketch of the physical layout of the contact center operation you observed.

Activity 6-3

Assign priority codes to help desk incidents. Use the priority code system shown below to assign codes to various types of situations.

Code	Meaning
U	Urgent
H	High priority
M	Medium priority
L	Low priority

When setting the priority code, consider these criteria:

- The severity of the problem
- The number of users affected
- The availability of a reasonable workaround
- Your own judgment

Assign a priority code to each of the following examples:

1. A user calls with a question about how to format a chart in Excel.

2. The administrative assistant in the manufacturing division calls to report that the server in his building is down.

3. A user emails to report a suspected bug in the way a toolbar works in a software package, but she says the equivalent pull-down menu option works okay.

4. The president of the organization calls to request the latest performance statistics on the help desk operation.

5. A bug is reported in the beta release of a software package; the production version is scheduled to ship next week.

6. Several calls are received from irate users who indicate that the accounting software package they purchased 12 months ago does not handle end-of-year processing correctly and the reports prepared contain obvious errors.

7. A user calls to report that your company's Web site is having problems, including broken links, and that the shopping cart feature, among others, no longer works.

Discuss your priority code assignments with two coworkers or classmates. Explore any problem incidents where you differ by more than one priority code. Write a summary of your conclusions, and explain how much difference of opinion you found in how to assign priority codes.

Activity 6-4

Identify information in an incident management database. List the important pieces of information about a typical problem incident that you would expect to find in an incident logging/tracking system. Use a word processor, spreadsheet, or database to design a data-entry form that captures the information you identified. Compare the information you plan to collect with that of others.

Activity 6-5

Evaluate a telephone system user interface. Based on your experience as a user of a help desk or other telephone service that uses an ACD telephone system, write an evaluation of the user interface. Describe the first level of menus and at least one other menu level. Evaluate the menus and menu navigation from a user's perspective. Write at least three suggestions on how the ACD interface could be improved.

Assemble a team of at least three classmates, and compare your suggestions with those of the members in your group. What are some common design principles the members in your group agree on for an ACD system?

Activity 6-6

Learn more about help desk software. Visit HelpSTAR's tutorial Web site (**www.helpstar. com/help-desk-resources/feature-demos.asp**). Use the icons on the page to view videos that describe the software. Compare the features of HelpSTAR with the list of typical help desk software features described in this chapter. Write a report on whether HelpSTAR has each of the features listed in the chapter. Describe any major features HelpSTAR has in addition to those described in the chapter.

Activity 6-7

Learn more about the basis for setting incident priorities. Read a short article on Tech Target's Web site, "Use SLAs to Assign Help Desk Incident Priorities" (**searchwinit. techtarget.com/tip/Use-SLAs-to-assign-help-desk-incident-priorities**); free registration is required. Compare the author's description of how incident priorities should be set with the criteria described in this chapter. Write a short report on the similarities and differences you found in the two sources.

Activity 6-8

Identify help desk job stressors. Based on your understanding of help desk operations and job stress, make a list of 10 or more different factors in a help desk environment that can increase or decrease the job stress experienced by agents. Use the Web sites listed in the chapter as resources if you need ideas. Then organize the stressors into a few large categories. Compare your list with those developed by your colleagues. Do you have the same or different categories?

Activity 6-9

Analyze a problem with Web support. Read a help desk manager's report of a problem with a new incident management support site (**www.itsmsolutions.com/newsletters/ DITYvol3iss17.pdf**). Then answer these questions about this case:

1. Why do you think users bypassed the new Service Desk?

2. Do you think the manager's solution to the problem was an effective one? Why or why not?

3. Describe alternative steps she might have taken to solve the problem.

Activity 6-10

Take a job stress quiz. Take the job burnout quiz at **stress.about.com/library/burnout/ bl_job_burnout_quiz.htm**. Answer the 20 questions about your own situation as best you can. Do you agree or disagree with the result of the quiz? Go through the questions a second time, and compare each question with the help desk job stress factors described in this chapter. Do the questions suggest other factors that may be stressors that you would add to those described in the chapter?

Activity 6-11

Research help desk industry trends. Select one of the help desk industry trends described at the end of this chapter. Do research online to find information about the trend. Write a report or prepare a slideshow presentation on the trend you selected. Include in your report or presentation your ideas about how the trend will impact workers in the help desk industry.

Case Projects

1. A Support Web Site for a Training Facility

You've been hired to design a support Web site for a training facility for end users. To generate ideas, look at examples of existing support Web sites, including the following:

- Gateway's support Web site (**support.gateway.com/support**)

- Adobe software support site (**www.adobe.com/support**)

- Symantec Web support site (**www.symantec.com/support**)

- Howard Community College's student support Web site (**www.howardcc.edu/students/ helpdesk**)

Or, visit other product and services support Web sites with which you are familiar. Analyze the features that you like and the features you believe could be improved on the sites you visit. Use a word processor or other tool to lay out your basic ideas for the Home page and for two or three other important pages for the site you design. Your design layout does not have to include the information on the site, but should describe the kind of information you would include on each page. Give special attention to:

- The information users would expect to find on the Web site

- The support features you would offer on your Web site

- How the support features would be organized and presented to users

- The navigation between pages

When you have finished your design, meet with three classmates or coworkers and compare your designs. How did your designs differ? How were they similar? What features of Web site design did you learn from them?

2. An Incident Management Script for the Adair Library

The help desk staff at the Adair Library is small, but its responsibilities for providing help desk services are growing. The help desk provides support to library staff who work in multiple offices and also to the public who access email and the Web through workstations in the library building. Most contacts with library staff are on the phone; most contacts with the public, however, are face-to-face.

The current help desk procedures rely primarily on informal communication between help desk staff members:

- Scribbled notes and phone messages about requests for support assistance

- A bulletin board in the help desk office where notes about ongoing problems are posted

- A clipboard that lists pending incidents that need resolution

- The wastebasket as a closed incident archive

The help desk staff would like to transform its current method for handling support problem incidents into a more structured incident management process.

Based on what you learned about incident management in this chapter, write a first draft of a sample script that could be used to train new agents to handle incidents at the help desk in the library. Your script should cover the basic tasks in incident management that you learned about in this chapter. Your script should also cover how to close an incident. Incorporate your own ideas on effective handling of incidents and help desk client relationships.

3. A Help Desk Tool for the Library

Use your experience with a spreadsheet, database package, or programming language to design and develop a prototype for a software tool that could be used by a small help desk, such as the one at the Adair Library in Case Project 2. A prototype is not necessarily a complete system with every possible useful feature, but one that contains basic functions that could be enhanced and expanded later. The primary purpose of the help desk tool you are developing for the library is to keep track of problem incidents. A user of the help desk tool should be able to enter, store, retrieve, update, and close problem reports received from users. The system should also include the ability to create one or more reports from stored data. The report(s) should enable the help desk supervisor in the library to obtain summary information on problem status and to analyze the kinds of problems that arise, including hardware, operating system, applications software, network, user, email, Internet, and other common problem categories.

Assemble a team of three classmates or coworkers and develop design specification by answering questions such as the following:

- What are the possible features and capabilities of a simple problem-tracking system?
- What information (data elements) needs to be input and stored to meet the primary objectives?
- How will the user interface to the help desk tool be designed to facilitate efficient use by help desk staff?
- How will the data entry screens appear to a help desk agent?
- What query capabilities should the help desk system provide a staff member?
- What reports should be predefined to provide problem-tracking summary and status information?
- What are the highest priority features for development in the first version (prototype) of the help desk tool you are designing?

This project could be a large one. Whether you work alone or with a team, remember to keep the design simple and make decisions about what you can reasonably accomplish in the limited time you have to devote to this project. Additional features can be added later.

4. HelpSTAR Software Tutorial

Use the tutorial steps in Appendix B to get experience with the HelpSTAR package included on a CD in this book. Then, complete Case Project 1 at the end of Appendix B.

5. Help Desk Knowledge Base Articles

Based on an analysis of the volume of incidents reported to a company help desk, the help desk manager identified two problem incidents that occur frequently, but for which no articles are currently available in the help desk knowledge base. The two problems are:

- The shutdown command menu on my PC is missing the hibernate option.

- The volume control in the notification area on my PC's taskbar is missing.

Your task is to research these problems and then use a word processor to write drafts of two help desk knowledge base articles that explain the steps to fix each of these problems. Write your drafts so that an end user who has access to the knowledge base can follow the steps. Exchange your drafts with those of a work or school colleague, and give each other feedback on the draft articles. Incorporate any useful suggestions in your drafts so they are ready to publish in the knowledge base.

CHAPTER 7

User Support Management

In this chapter, you will learn about:

◎ The mission of a support group and the features of a mission statement

◎ Items in a typical user support budget

◎ Staffing a help desk

◎ Support staff training programs

◎ Evaluations of support staff performance

◎ Industry certifications for support professionals

◎ Professional help desk and user support associations

◎ Ethical principles that guide the professional behavior of support workers

Some workers in the user support field aspire to become user support or help desk managers; others do not. Whether or not their career plans include a future management position, all user support workers can benefit from a basic understanding of the managerial perspective. When applicants interview for a user support position, the interviewer will likely be a user support manager or supervisor. If hired as a user support worker in a very small company, workers may be expected to perform some tasks that require management, supervisory, lead worker, or project coordinator skills.

User support management encompasses a variety of positions. In many organizations, a help desk or user support manager directly manages the user support staff. Managers of large support groups may oversee one or more supervisors or team leaders who in turn supervise a team of support agents. For example, an organization that provides several levels of support, as described in Chapter 6, may have a level 1 (call screening) supervisor, a level 2 (product specialist) supervisor, and a level 3 (technical support) supervisor. Even small support groups may assign occasional project leader or coordinator responsibilities to user support workers. For example, a user support worker might be asked to coordinate a project to evaluate a new software or hardware product and prepare relevant documentation, training materials, and information on anticipated user problems to other support staff.

When searching for additional information on user support management, be aware that some organizations use alternate terms, such as *help desk management*, *client support management*, *call center management*, and *customer support management*. These terms are usually interchangeable.

Although most of this book focuses on the knowledge, skills, and abilities required for an effective user support worker, this chapter examines some of the particular tasks and issues that user support and help desk managers might face. The tasks discussed include developing a mission statement, budgeting for support services, staffing and evaluating a user support operation, and training team members. The section on certification describes the ways support workers can add to their professional credentials by taking certification exams. The final section of this chapter focuses on user support as a profession and provides information on employment in the field and on IT and help desk professional associations, including a discussion of how association members are expected to follow codes of ethical conduct in their work.

Managerial Concerns: Mission, Budgets, Staffing, Training, and Performance

From the moment you decide to pursue a help desk or user support career, you should be aware of the perspectives of the managers of support services. Every decision a help desk manager makes affects the people on his or her team. The more support staff members know about their manager's concerns and priorities, the better equipped they will be to understand the need for certain task assignments and to focus their efforts on completing them, which will improve client satisfaction and help the support team succeed. Understanding the managerial perspective also helps prepare entry-level staff to advance into positions with more responsibilities and higher salaries.

This chapter is not intended as a comprehensive introduction to user support or help desk management. Instead, the chapter focuses on five areas of user support management that directly affect members of a support staff: the support mission, budgeting, staffing, training, and performance measures. The objective is to give you an understanding of some of the issues user support managers face so you will be better prepared to obtain and work effectively in a user support position.

To further investigate help desk management, refer to Phil Gerbyshak and Jeffrey Brook's *Help Desk Manager's Crash Course* (BookSurge Publishing, 2009). It describes organizing, staffing, evaluating, and marketing a help desk operation. An older but classic book on help desk management is Barbara Czegel's *Running an Effective Help Desk, 2nd edition* (Wiley, 1998).

User Support Mission

Support groups often develop a **mission statement**, which is used to communicate a set of guiding principles to support team members, end users or clients, and management. It says, in effect, *"Here is what we think is most important to our support group."* Support groups also use their mission statement as a yardstick against which they measure progress toward their goals. Figure 7-1 shows an example of a user support mission statement. The example primarily addresses support for internal employees, but it could be modified to apply to external clients. The italicized terms highlight important concepts.

User Support Mission Statement

The mission of the user support group is to:

(a) maximize *operational efficiency* among users in the organization by providing timely resolution to *technology use questions*, and

(b) effectively *manage problems* to continuously improve the:

- *quality* of support services to users
- *usability* of information systems
- *effectiveness* of documentation and training
- *users' satisfaction* with support services

Figure 7-1   Example of a user support group mission statement

Several points in the sample mission statement in Figure 7-1 directly address end users' productivity. Increased worker (or client) productivity is usually a primary goal, because every support group or help desk must justify its existence based on the services it provides to other workers or clients. The support group must prove to the parent organization that the benefits it provides outweigh its operational and administrative costs. Other mission statements may include goals relating to user self-sufficiency, ethical professional conduct of staff members, increased company profitability, and career path development for user support workers.

 A mission statement that includes a laundry list of goals is often less effective than a shorter, more focused, list of guidelines.

ON THE WEB

To see an example of a mission statement, visit the Web site of the University of Texas Health Science Center (**is.uth.tmc.edu/css/mission.htm**).

For guidelines on writing a help desk mission statement, read an article on TechRepublic's Web site (**articles.techrepublic.com.com/5100-10878_11-5032967.html**).

Budgeting for User Support Services

Two important tasks for support managers depend heavily on the support group's mission statement: developing help desk budgets and writing employee position descriptions. A help desk or support group budget is a financial plan a manager prepares to translate the goals in a mission statement into a concrete strategy to meet those goals. For example, if a help desk mission statement includes a goal to provide a series of three training sessions for all new employees on how to use company software, then the budget needs to answer the question, *"What is the cost to prepare and present the training sessions for new employees?"*

New help desk workers and new managers may be surprised at the total cost of support services. As you learned in Chapter 1, the total cost of ownership (TCO) of a computer system can be considerably more than the initial purchase cost. Likewise, the total cost of a help desk worker is usually considerably more than simply the salary or wages paid to the worker.

The actual dollar amounts included in a help desk budget vary depending on several factors, including:

- The kind of users the help desk supports (for example, internal users may be more expensive to support because they need a greater variety of services, whereas external clients may make fewer demands for help desk services)

- The ways in which help desk services are provided (face-to-face contacts are usually more expensive to provide than telephone or email services; Web support tends to be less expensive because it is often largely self-service)

- The range of services provided (full support services, including user needs assessment, system installation, and user training, can be very expensive to provide, whereas a telephone hotline for problems usually costs much less)

- The number of support employees and how they are supervised influence the need for management staff (for example, a few support workers in a small company supervised by a manager who has other responsibilities may cost less than a help desk operation where several workers on a support team are managed by a full-time manager and perhaps a shift supervisor)

- The method of budgeting for facilities costs, such as office space, furniture, hardware, software, and communication costs (facilities costs may be included in a help desk budget or may be covered elsewhere in a company budget)

- The method of covering specific cost categories (capital costs are one-time expenses, such as the purchase of equipment or furniture; lease costs are ongoing expenses, such as facilities or equipment rental; operating expenses are ongoing monthly costs of operation, such as salaries, office supplies, and maintenance)

Because support service costs vary considerably, depending on these and other factors, the budget categories are described below in general terms as a brief introduction rather than as a definitive budget that fits all situations.

Help desk budgets are often divided into two large categories: revenue and expenses, as shown in Figure 7-2. As you will see later in this chapter, many help desk managers do not have a revenue budget, especially if the help desk does not receive income for the services it provides. The expense side of the budget usually includes personnel and facilities expenses.

Budget Category	Examples

Revenue	● Fees for services
	    ● Per-incident or per-hour fees for computer installation, training, and troubleshooting
	● Subscription fees
	    ● From users who pay a regular fee (monthly or annually) for support services
	● Per-seat fees
	    ● A fixed fee per each user to cover all of a company's employee support services
	● Negotiated service level agreement (SLA) fees
	    ● One fee to cover an entire company's support services
	● Bundled support revenue
	    ● The cost of support is included in the price of hardware, software, or other services
	● Hardware repair income
	● Other revenue
	    ● Charges for user training classes, including purchases of materials, hardware, and software
	    ● Miscellaneous fees
	
	This list is incomplete. A support services manager who maintains a revenue budget to cover some or all support costs is constantly searching for both direct and indirect (hidden) sources of income.

Expenses:
  Personnel
	● Staff salaries and wages
	    ● Help desk/user support agents
	        ● Level 1 agents
	        ● Level 2 technical support
	        ● Level 3 team leaders/supervisors
	    ● Trainers
	    ● Technical writers
	    ● Web site maintainers
	    ● Administrative assistants
	● Other staffing costs
	    ● Benefits (health insurance, transportation subsidies, and retirement contributions)
	    ● Paid leave (vacations, sick leave, and family leave)
	    ● Payroll taxes
	    ● Staff recruiting costs
	    ● Professional education and development
	        ● Books, in-house training, conferences, courses, and necessary travel

Figure 7-2　Examples of categories included in a user support group budget plan (*continues*)

(continued)

Budget Category	Examples

Expenses:
    Personnel
    (continued)
	• Other benefits
	    • Employee recognition programs and break room refreshments
	• Staffing overhead costs
	    • Supervision and management
	    • Accounting and payroll
	    • Benefits administration
	    • Human resources
	
	Not all of these categories apply to every situation, but for most support organizations, personnel costs are the single largest category in a budget. A quick glance at some of the above categories of personnel expenses helps to explain why a help desk agent with an annual salary of $35,000, for example, could actually cost his or her employer more than $50,000.

Expenses:
    Facilities
	• Office space
	    • Furniture
	    • Utilities (electricity, heating, air conditioning, and phone service)
	    • Janitorial services
	• Equipment
	    • Help desk agent's workstation (hardware)
	    • Maintenance, repairs, and upgrades
	• Software
	    • Office applications
	    • Help desk software
	    • Web development
	    • Email/chat hosting
	    • User billing software
	• Office and computer supplies
	• Communications costs
	    • Office network installation, operation, and maintenance
	        • Network server(s)
	        • Network software
	        • Connectivity (routers, hubs, gateways, and wiring)
	        • Network backup (including off-site backup services)
	    • Internet connection fees
	    • Telephone access charges
	    • Automatic call distribution (ACD) equipment
	        • Call recording and monitoring equipment
	    • Mobile technology

Figure 7-2   Examples of categories included in a user support group budget plan (*continues*)

(continued)

Budget Category	Examples
Expenses: **Facilities** **(continued)**	*The cost of facilities to house and enable help desk workers to do their jobs varies. For example, a small help desk located in a company's IT department will likely have low facilities costs. In contrast, facilities costs may be a sizeable part of the budget for a standalone support organization whose sole function is to provide support services.*

Figure 7-2   Examples of categories included in a user support group budget plan

Rarely does a help desk manager build a budget from scratch. Even in a growing help desk organization, some financial history is usually available to serve as a guide for developing a budget for future years. And even a new help desk manager with no previous budgeting experience would not be completely on their own when confronted with the task of planning a first-time budget. Internet information resources such as employment Web sites can help with salary estimates. Human resource and payroll departments can help estimate staffing and overhead costs in addition to direct salary expenses. And vendors are usually more than willing to provide estimated costs of facilities and equipment for help desk operations.

ON THE WEB

To learn more about user support budgets and categories, view a 15-minute video titled, "The Complete Contact Center Budget" (**www.youtube.com/watch? v=EuJvBDyyill**).

Staffing the Help Desk

Based on the goals in the help desk mission statement, support managers are responsible for determining the number of agents required, writing position descriptions, and selecting staff members.

Help Desk Staffing Levels

An ongoing challenge for many user support and help desk managers is determining how many support agents are needed to meet the expected service levels. Support managers must employ and schedule sufficient staff to meet the performance expectations detailed in the help desk's mission statement. On the other hand, support managers do not want to hire staff beyond the level needed to be responsive to users' needs. If they hire excess staff, the department's performance statistics when compared to staff expenses will suffer.

So how many support staff workers are required to meet a targeted service level? This problem is similar to determining the number of cashiers a grocery store needs to keep checkout lines from getting too long (which frustrates customers) or too short (which leaves cashiers idle). A calculation tool called an Erlang unit can be used in these situations. An **Erlang** is a unit of traffic (or a user incident, in the case of support groups) processed in a given period of time. The Erlang calculation is used in a variety of situations in which queues (such as clients waiting on hold or customers waiting for grocery store cashiers) need to be handled. Managers may also use trial and error, previous experience, or a sophisticated calculator or estimation spreadsheet to assist them in making help desk staffing decisions.

ON THE WEB

Westbay Engineers provides an online Erlang calculator to estimate support center staffing needs. See its Web site (**www.erlang.com**), click **Free calculators**, and then click **Call Centre Calculator**.

Help Desk Position Descriptions

An applicant for a help desk or user support position should be aware of the support manager's staffing priorities. User support staffing decisions often begin with the support group's mission statement. Based on the mission statement, a manager writes one or more position descriptions: one if the user support operation is small, and several for a help desk operation that has a large staff or a multilevel structure. The position descriptions (like those you examined in Chapter 1) are also based on an analysis of the knowledge and skills user support staff members need. The mission statement, position descriptions, and a list of the specific knowledge, skills, and abilities (KSAs) required for a user support operation are important resources for managers who must staff a help desk or support group.

A KSA analysis for a user support position begins with a written list of technical, business, and communication qualifications required for a position. These qualifications spell out the position's requirements in terms of the following:

- Hardware, operating systems, and application software proficiency
- Technical skills
- Network knowledge and experience
- Internet and Web expertise
- Troubleshooting and problem-solving capabilities
- Communication, listening, reading, writing, and telephone skills
- Work experience as a project team member
- Understanding of business information systems and business perspectives

Support managers use these types of qualification categories as a checklist for developing detailed job-related requirements for specific positions. For example, a support position may require a person to work with Intel-compatible hardware platforms in a local area network (LAN) environment and to have Windows operating system experience along with a working knowledge of Microsoft Office applications software. A help desk manager might emphasize the importance of communication skills and interpersonal relationships for an entry-level position in a help desk that provides primarily telephone support, but would probably place greater emphasis on technical knowledge and troubleshooting skills when hiring for a position that provides more advanced technical support.

After a support manager has developed a detailed list of KSAs, the next step is to develop a position description. Well-written position descriptions, such as those in Chapter 1, contain a clear explanation of the staff member's duties and responsibilities. A support manager then uses the position description and KSA checklist to prepare a job posting (for a newspaper classified ad section or a Web-based job board) or a position order (for an employment or temporary worker agency). However, the position description and KSA checklist are really wish lists. A manager of support services may or may not find applicants who possess 100 percent of the desired characteristics and skills.

Because help desk managers often do not find job candidates with all the KSAs they are seeking, job applicants should not rule out positions for which they meet most, but not all, of the desired qualifications.

An increasing number of user support positions are advertised on Web employment sites. However, only a fraction of job openings are advertised publicly in any medium. Many job seekers learn about open support positions through informal channels, such as a current employee in an organization or through an instructor in a vocational/technical school or community college who has contacts with support employers. Thus, building relationships with classmates, work colleagues, friends, and relatives can be a more important job search tool than traditional job search methods.

Screening Applicants

The search for a new staff member continues when a support manager receives applications. The next step often involves a selection team comprised of members who represent the current support staff, user support management, IT department (if applicable), and human resources department. This team screens résumés and applications to narrow the list of candidates. Applicants whose personal KSAs most closely match the position requirements advance to the next stage in screening—the interview. Some selection teams check applicants' employment and academic references prior to an interview; others check these references after the interview.

Interviewing Applicants

During an interview, managers may use a variety of selection tools, such as the following:

- Knowledge and skills tests
- Traditional interview questions, including directed and nondirected questions
- Behavioral questions
- Scenario questions
- Stress tolerance assessment
- Illegal questions

A **knowledge and skills test** is a paper-and-pencil, verbal, or online test that measures a prospective worker's knowledge and problem-solving abilities. These tests may include written, verbal, and/or hands-on components. The tests may be supplied from a vendor that provides testing materials, or they may be developed by a support group specifically for its job applicants.

ON THE WEB

An example of a vendor that sells help desk aptitude and skills tests is Expert Rating (**www.expertrating.com/employers/employers.html**).

Employment interviews often include traditional questions about an applicant's résumé and qualifications. Some questions are **directed questions**, which are focused on specific job requirements and are intended to help the interviewer determine whether an applicant has specific educational or work experiences. An example of a directed question is:

"What courses have you taken to prepare yourself to support desktop operating systems?"

Other questions are **nondirected questions**; they are open-ended and are intended to give an applicant an opportunity to talk in general terms about their qualifications for a position. For example:

"Tell me about your customer service experience."

ON THE WEB

To view some sample help desk interview questions, visit **www.best-job-interview. com/help-desk-interview-questions.html**.

For some examples of general job interview questions and suggested answers, see **jobsearch.about.com/od/interviewquestionsanswers/a/interviewquest.htm**.

Interviews for help desk positions may also include **behavioral questions**, which give an applicant an opportunity to describe the actions she or he took in a specific situation. For example:

"Describe the most difficult user you've had to deal with and how you interacted with that person."

ON THE WEB

Examples of behavioral interview questions can be found on the Web site **blog. emurse.com/2007/05/21/complete-list-of-behavioral-interview-questions**.

Help desk applicants should also be prepared for scenario questions, which help the interviewer identify candidates' strengths and weaknesses. A **scenario question** gives an applicant a specific problem (or set of problems) representative of the situations user support agents actually encounter. A scenario might be a written exercise (sometimes provided as a supplemental questionnaire when an applicant first applies) or a problem-solving exercise during an interview. Interviews for a telephone support position often include an activity that requires an applicant to answer questions in a simulated telephone environment so the applicant's telephone skills can be evaluated. Scenario questions provide insights into an applicant's problem-solving, conflict-resolution, and communication skills as well as his or her ability to perform in stressful work situations. When combined with traditional interview questions, the scenario approach is often more effective than traditional interview questions alone in identifying staff who can work well under pressure. Here is a sample scenario question:

"Suppose a user in the manufacturing division approaches you and wants to bend your ear about the endless network problems that have been affecting the productivity of manufacturing workers. The user relates that manufacturing workers have experienced an increasing number of network crashes in recent weeks. The user says that it takes forever to get the network restarted when it crashes and the downtime affects the workers' productivity. The user also mentions that other manufacturing workers feel that they would be better off scrapping the network and working with the system they used to have. As a user support staff member, how would you respond?"

 Scenario questions can often be answered from a number of perspectives. Some applicants might treat the scenario question in this example as an opportunity to display their technical knowledge about networks. Others might discuss the problem-solving and communication skills they would use to address the problem within the organization.

As if employment interviews are not stressful enough, some hiring managers also use a stress tolerance assessment to evaluate potential employees. A **stress tolerance assessment** is an interview tactic that helps employers evaluate how well a job applicant works or thinks under pressure. Elements that can add stress to an interview situation include a very noisy interview environment (perhaps with interruptions), questions from several interviewers, some of whom seem to have different agendas, overly technical questions, and similar tactics.

Finally, both the selection team and job applicants need to be alert to **illegal questions**, which are designed to obtain information about an applicant's characteristics that are not specifically job related. Examples of illegal questions may include those intended to ascertain an applicant's age, ethnicity, marital status, sexual orientation, political views, or religion; some questions regarding disabilities are also illegal.

ON THE WEB

To learn more about illegal interview questions and how to handle them, visit **www.ehow.com/how_2140042_handle-illegal-interview-questions.html**.

For many entry-level job applicants, the employment interview is one of the most anticipated and daunting parts of a job search. However, many professionals say that the more experience with interviews they have, the more comfortable they become and the more confident they are about their interviewing skills. The following role-playing scenario is designed to help you prepare for job interviews.

 Many career centers in colleges, universities, and vocational/technical schools offer practice job interviews (as well as résumé preparation) as a part of their services.

A ROLE-PLAYING SCENARIO

The purpose of this role-playing activity is to help prospective job applicants prepare for future employment interviews.

- Select a job description for a typical help desk or user support position. Use a position description from Chapter 1, or find another one that interests you.

- Work with a team of three or four colleagues or fellow students to discuss and prepare some sample interview questions for the position you identified. Limit the number of questions to a few that could be answered in 10–15 minutes.

- Discuss some effective answers to the sample questions with members of the team.

- For some ideas on possible questions to use, download a PDF from TechRepublic's Web site (**i.i.com/cnwk.1d/i/tr/downloads/home/10_questions_help_desk_hires.pdf**). If you use questions from the TechRepublic Web site, reword them so they apply directly to the specific job description you are using.

- Arrange some practice interview situations in which one team member plays the role of the interviewer and another plays the role of a job applicant. Other team members can observe the interview and evaluate how well the job applicant did.

- After each role-playing interview, the interviewer and observers should give the job applicant feedback on what he or she did well, and how his or her interview skills could be improved. The feedback could include an evaluation of factors such as the following:

  - Eye contact

  - Body language

  - Facial expression

  - Tone of voice

  - Choice of words

  - Level of interest displayed

  - Content of answers

- Remember that the purpose of this activity is to get interviewing experience and to help team members improve their interviewing skills. If possible, give each team member more than one opportunity to be interviewed. Participants in similar role-playing activities have said that it often feels like an actual interview, and that they feel more confident about their skills after just one or two practice interviews.

User Support Staff Training

One of the most important aspects of user support and help desk management is user support staff training. Support **staff training** includes new worker orientation as well as ongoing training that allows experienced staff to update their knowledge and keep their skills current. A well-trained support staff is a critical component of success for a help desk operation. Without a well-trained staff, a help desk can rarely meet its performance objectives. Both management and staff need to recognize that training is a two-way street. Help desk managers need to provide training and professional development opportunities for staff members, including time away from routine responsibilities to participate in training activities. And help desk professionals need to seek out and take advantage of ways to keep their job skills up-to-date in an industry that is constantly changing.

 Many of the end-user training methods and strategies you will learn about in Chapter 11 are also effective for training user support staff.

Orientations for New Staff

Some support organizations assume that help desk agents will somehow learn on the job everything they need to know about the organization, the products supported, and the help desk's policies and procedures. However, a more common practice is for an organization to conduct one or more training sessions for new support employees, which often include topics such as:

- Organizational structure, including important managers

- Organizational culture, policies, and procedures

- Payroll and employee benefits

- Specific job skill training

- Available help desk tools, including the phone system and incident management software

- Support group policies and procedures

- Performance appraisal criteria and procedures

- Professional development and career path opportunities

Of these training topics, information about support group policies and procedures is especially important. New employees need to have specific job skills to function effectively, but they also need to learn where to find answers to questions such as, *"What is the company's policy if a client insists on a refund?"* or *"What is the recommended procedure if a client demands to speak to a supervisor or the company president?"* Although it is not possible to learn about every organizational policy or procedure during an orientation period, it is important that training sessions cover basic information about the organization's general user support philosophy and procedures.

ON THE WEB

TechRepublic's Web site frequently carries articles on the training needs of new help desk workers. For example, read Jeff Davis' article, "Training Tips Can Jump-Start Your Help Desk Team" (**www.techrepublic.com/article/training-tips-can-jump-start-your-help-desk-team/1034678**), or Jeff Dray's article, "Create Structured Training for Help Desk Staffers" (**www.techrepublic.com/article/build-your-skills-create-structured-training-for-new-help-desk-staffers/5034674**).

Ongoing Help Desk Training

Often, the biggest challenge in support staff training is scheduling training time for staff members who are in constant demand. To allow support staff members enough time for training—and for special projects and paperwork—many managers schedule agents for only a portion of their total work shift (for example, six hours of an eight-hour shift).

Training programs for user support workers should help keep support staff current with changes in computer technology and the way in which the changes affect their client base. Support managers and help desk agents should work together to identify appropriate training and professional development opportunities. The training should serve a dual purpose: first, to address any opportunities for improved performance as identified in the worker's performance appraisal (discussed in the next section) that will enable the worker to do an even better job; and second, to help the support employee grow as a professional and prepare for career advancement opportunities. Common ongoing training and professional development opportunities include the following:

- Attend an industry conference (for example, **www.hdiconference.com**)

- Participate in advanced technical training (for example, **www.microsoft.com/learning/en/us/training/windows.aspx**)

- Read a trade publication (for example, **www.icmi.com**)

- Read a technical publication about a subject of support interest (for example, **technet.microsoft.com/en-us/library/cc303401.aspx**)

- Study for and take a certification exam (such as one described later in this chapter)

- Become active in a local chapter of a professional organization (for examples, see those described later in this chapter)

- Learn about alternate career paths for support workers (such as those described in Chapter 1)

As you will see in the next section, performance appraisals are often used to identify training needs for help desk staff.

User Support Performance Evaluation and Justification

In order to improve support services, help desk managers continually measure and evaluate several aspects of user support. The performance of each help desk agent is periodically evaluated, and the services provided by the entire help desk staff may also be evaluated.

Performance Appraisals

An activity important to both support supervisors and workers is the periodic employee performance appraisal process. A **performance appraisal** is an evaluation of a user support worker according to established achievement criteria. The performance appraisal criteria should be based on the following:

- the support group's mission

- the worker's position description

- the worker's individual professional growth objectives

- the specific goals and objectives from the worker's prior performance appraisal

If performance statistics, such those described in the next section, are used as part of the performance appraisal process, the manager should communicate to team members the way in which those statistics are collected, interpreted, and used in the evaluation process.

Support managers often use recordings of monitored support calls to help workers identify areas where performance improvement is needed. In many support groups, performance appraisals are important tools for identifying worker training needs.

Performance appraisals are not always a satisfying activity for either help desk agents or their supervisors. Often, that is because the evaluation criteria are not made explicit, or the evaluation process occurs annually (rather than as part of an ongoing process), or the evaluation is based on numeric scores, when written comments are preferable. In addition, many performance appraisals are set up so the help desk worker is the recipient of the evaluation rather than a participant in the process. An effective performance appraisal process often begins with the worker completing a self-evaluation.

 Self-evaluations are often difficult to write. The process may be easier for workers who maintain a running log of accomplishments, such as employee recognition awards, significant project milestones completed, and exceptional performance results.

ON THE WEB

To learn more about successful performance appraisals for support workers, visit **www.callcentrehelper.com/how-do-i-give-top-notch-performance-appraisals-171.htm**.

For a legal perspective on performance evaluations, visit **www.laborlaws.com/block4/item421**.

And for tips on ways both managers and workers can improve performance appraisals, read Jonathan Farrington's suggestions (**ezinearticles.com/?How-To-Plan-And-Prepare-For-An-Effective-Appraisal&id=480071**).

In addition to the performance of individual staff members, support managers also evaluate the services provided by the support team as a whole. Performance statistics and measures of client satisfaction are two ways to evaluate, document, and justify the value of user support services.

Performance Statistics

Performance statistics are objective data collected to evaluate a user support or help desk operation. Managers track performance statistics to measure their teams against specific goals, which are often stated in the group's mission statement. For example, a mission statement might include a goal of responding to 90 percent of incoming telephone calls within 60 seconds. If the help desk actually responded to 88 percent of the calls in 60 seconds or less last week, then the help desk team fell short of that objective and should investigate ways to improve response times. Performance statistics can help a support group measure how effectively and efficiently it responds to incidents. Examples of common help desk performance measures include:

- Average time to respond to incidents (sometimes called **wait time**)

- Percentage of incidents that were abandoned (user hung up or gave up before the support staff responded); also called the **abandonment rate**

- Average resolution time for incidents that required problem solving

- Percentage of problems that could not be resolved

- Percentage of closed incidents that had to be reopened

- Number of incidents currently in an unresolved status (perhaps a separate count for each priority code)

- Cost per incident (based on support expenses and the number of incidents handled)

 Performance statistics are sometimes also called metrics, indices, benchmarks, critical success factors, or key performance indicators (KPIs). These statistics are often displayed in a dashboard, as you learned about in Chapter 6.

Performance statistics should be related to goals highlighted in the support group's mission statement or to specific problem areas a help desk group manager wants to address. These statistics can be collected and reported for a point in time, but they are more useful when compared across various times of the day, days of the week, or months. Trends in performance are often more meaningful to managers and workers than isolated measurements. Performance statistics can be reported for an entire support team or for individual workers. These statistics are often used to answer the questions, *"Is the help desk operation more (or less) productive or responsive over time?"* and, *"How does Emily's productivity or accuracy compare with other help desk workers?"*

 Many automatic call distributor (ACD) systems collect the raw data from which reports on these and other support performance statistics can be prepared.

Performance measures may be presented in a table of statistical results but are often more useful when presented as a graphic, as shown in Figure 7-3. A user support manager used HelpSTAR help desk software to prepare the chart in Figure 7-3 to show the source of incidents opened last week. She learned that the category with the highest number of incidents last week was the PC Support Level 1 category.

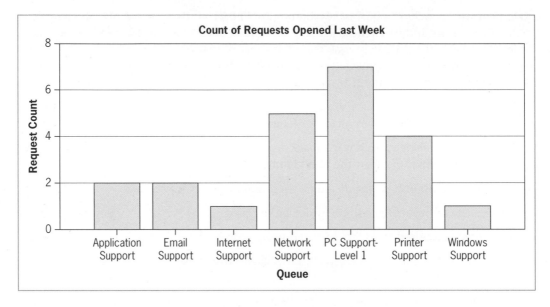

Figure 7-3   A histogram prepared with HelpSTAR software shows the distribution of categories of support incidents

    HelpSTAR software was introduced in Chapter 6.

User Satisfaction Surveys

In addition to objective, statistical measures of user support performance, support groups may periodically collect subjective information from users via a user satisfaction survey. A **user satisfaction survey** is a questionnaire that attempts to measure how satisfied users are with the support services they have experienced. Questions are often used to prepare a report card for the user support group by measuring its performance against its mission statement goals. Examples include the following:

- On a scale from 1 (very satisfied) to 5 (very dissatisfied), how would you evaluate the overall user support services you receive as a computer user in this organization?

- On a scale from 1 (very satisfied) to 5 (very dissatisfied), how would you rate the knowledge of the help desk staff?

User satisfaction surveys may ask users to evaluate a wide range of issues, including:

- Availability of help when it was needed

- Responsiveness of support staff

- Ability of support staff to communicate effectively with users
- Usefulness of online information resources
- Technical knowledge of support staff
- Ability of support staff to resolve problems

Satisfaction surveys may also ask users to identify a support staff member who has been especially helpful to them. A help desk that provides external support may ask similar questions of a selected sample of clients. Data from external clients is often collected after an incident has been closed in a follow-up phone call or via a mail or email questionnaire. Organizations that provide Web-based support may include an online feedback mechanism to help evaluate the quality of information and client services their Web site and support team provide. For example, information on a Web page may be accompanied by a question such as, *"Did you find this information useful? Click YES or NO."*

ON THE WEB

A Web service that offers both free and fee-based online questionnaire and survey tools is **www.surveymonkey.com**. The site also offers suggestions on effective ways to ask survey questions.

Justifying Support Services

A user support group can be treated as a cost center or a profit center in an organization. In a **cost center operation**, the cost of providing user support services appears as an expense in an organization's budget, without a corresponding revenue source. In a **profit center operation**, user support costs are also treated as expenses, but those expenses are offset by revenue generated by the user support group. In a profit center operation, a user support group might charge fees to clients or other departments who make use of support services (sometimes called a **chargeback**); the fees might be designed to totally or partially offset the expenses of the support group.

Support operations that use the cost center approach can find it difficult to justify support expenses solely on the basis of performance statistics or client satisfaction, because there is no direct revenue stream to offset the costs. One reason many hardware and software manufacturers now charge clients for help desk services is the need to relate the support services they provide to the costs associated with providing the services. Product vendors may offer several levels of user support services, including a free level, a standard (fee-for-service) level, and a premium level, for clients who want immediate service. Although the premium service level may be more responsive to users than the free or standard service, it also costs more to provide.

Support workers at all levels, even in entry-level positions, need to understand the importance of performance measures and the need to justify support services. Performance statistics impact user support management decisions, which directly affect support workers. A support worker who ignores performance and the need to justify support services may end up without a job.

 In order to justify user support operations, managers often perform a cost-benefit analysis, a tool you will learn about in Chapter 9.

ON THE WEB

To learn more about performance statistics and see some benchmark results, view an industry white paper prepared by one vendor, MetricNets (**www.thinkhdi.com/ hdi2009/files/MetricNetsSevenImportantKPIs.pdf**).

User Support Certification

In the last decade, an important trend in education, training, and employment in the computer field has been the increasing reliance on certification to evaluate knowledge, skills, and abilities. **Certification** is an assessment process designed to measure and document worker knowledge and skills in a specialized segment of the information technology field. The role that industry certification plays in the user support field is like one leg of a three-legged stool: education, experience, and certification. Certification offers several benefits to both employers and support workers, as we will see later in this section.

Several kinds of certification are common, including the following:

- Formal education that results in a certificate, diploma, or degree

- Vendor-specific product knowledge and skills certification

- Industry-standard knowledge and skills certification in a specific area, such as hardware, networking, or support

- Certification that measures the fitness of a support group against industry-standard criteria

Formal Education Certification

Community colleges and vocational/technical schools have been in the certification business for many years. After a student has successfully completed a well-defined program of courses, the student graduates with a certificate, diploma, or degree. However, certification based on formal education or training from a degree or certificate-granting educational institution may document only general knowledge and skills. In addition to the knowledge gained through class work, many schools offer internships or cooperative education opportunities for students about to graduate. These internships match students with local employers to provide on-the-job work experience. Internships provide graduates with experience they cannot get in classroom learning alone, and give students some work experience to include on a résumé for employment after graduation.

Employers are often also interested in a job applicant's specific expertise. For example, a degree in computer user support, or a related field, does not necessarily guarantee that a job applicant has specialized or technical expertise in, say, Windows 7—although many user support degree programs today include coursework in that operating system. Similarly, coursework in *operating systems* does not guarantee that a graduate can apply what he or she has learned specifically to the Linux operating system, for example.

Vendor-Specific Certification

Partly in reaction to the industry-wide need to certify product-specific knowledge and skills, vendors in the computer industry offer a variety of certificates that assess knowledge and skills in a specialized product. One of the first vendor-specific certifications was Novell's Certified NetWare Engineer (CNE), created in the early 1990s. The CNE certification process resulted in thousands of network specialists who were certified as specialists on Novell network products. Because the CNE was vendor-specific, however, it did not indicate that a certificate holder necessarily knew anything about the network products of other vendors such as Microsoft or Cisco. As a result, other network vendors began to offer certifications in their specific product lines.

 Some job applicants who excel at studying a body of material and passing a test discovered that they could study a CNE preparatory book, pass the certification exam, and advertise that they were qualified CNEs. They had a paper to certify their expertise, but no real expertise. Employers coined the term *paper CNE* to describe a person who had passed the CNE test, but did not have any practical knowledge or hands-on networking experience.

Today, certification is available for many vendor-specific products. Some examples of vendor certifications are described in Table 7-1.

ON THE WEB

To see a more complete list of hardware, software, and networking product vendors' certification Web sites, visit **www.mcmcse.com/othercerts.shtml**.

Vendor	Certification Overview	Certification Titles	Knowledge Areas
Microsoft	www.microsoft.com/learning/en/us/certification/view-by-name.aspx	• Microsoft Office Specialist (MOS)	• Microsoft Office applications such as Word, Excel, Access, Outlook, and PowerPoint, as well as Windows operating system
		• Microsoft Certified Technology Specialist (MCTS)	• Windows Server and Microsoft network support
Cisco	www.cisco.com/web/learning/le3/learning_career_certifications_and_learning_paths_home.html	• Cisco Certified Entry Networking Technician (CCENT)	• Installing, operating, and troubleshooting a small Cisco network, including basic network security
		• Cisco Certified Network Associate (CCNA)	• Cisco network installation, configuration, operation, and troubleshooting
Novell	www.novell.com/training/certinfo	• Certified Novell Administrator (CNA)	• Basic networking and user support skills
		• Certified Novell Engineer (CNE)	• Advanced Novell networking and support project skills
Apple	images.apple.com/education/docs/Apple-TrainingCertificationCatalogWeb.pdf	• Apple Certified Support Professional (ACSP)	• Mac OS X operating system, including the ability to configure, troubleshoot, and support Macintosh systems

Table 7-1   Examples of vendor-specific certification programs

Industry-Standard Certification

An alternate kind of certification is one that is not specific to an individual vendor's products but rather aims to measure industry-standard knowledge and skills. Because it is not tied to a specific vendor or product line, this kind of certification is more general and is vendor-neutral. In addition to hardware, operating systems, and troubleshooting skills, industry-standard certifications cover a variety of specialized skills, such as network administration, Web design, and project management. Examples of certification targeted at an industry-wide audience of employers and workers are listed in Table 7-2.

Organization	Certification Overview	Certification Titles	Knowledge Areas
Computer Technology Industry Association (CompTIA)	**certification.comptia. org/home.aspx**	• A+	• Hardware and operating systems, including basic knowledge of configuring, installing, diagnosing, repairing, upgrading, and maintaining computers
		• Network+	• Network architecture and operating systems, including installing, configuring, and troubleshooting a network client
		• Security+	• Enterprise security, including access controls, authentication, infrastructure, and operational security
		• Project+	• IT project management skills
Institute for Certification of Computing Professionals (ICCP)	**www.iccp.org/ iccpnew/acp.html**	• Associate Computing Professional (ACP)	• Knowledge and skills earned primarily through academic or vocational degree programs
Internet and Computing Core Certification	**www.certiport.com/ PORTAl/desktop default.aspx? tabid=229**	• IC^3 Certification	• Fundamental, entry-level knowledge and skills on computer hardware, software, and Internet use

Table 7-2   Examples of industry-standard, vendor-neutral certification programs (*continues*)

(continued)

Organization	Certification Overview	Certification Titles	Knowledge Areas
Linux Professional Institute	**www.lpi.org**	• Linux Professional Institute Certification (LPIC)	• Linux operating system administration skills
Certified Internet Web Professional	**www.ciwcertified.com**	• CIW Web Foundations Associate	• Basic knowledge of Internet technologies, network infrastructure, and Web authoring

Table 7-2   Examples of industry-standard, vendor-neutral certification programs

Project management is covered in Chapter 9, where you will also learn about Microsoft Project, a software tool used to manage special support projects.

User Support and Help Desk Certification

In addition to certification in a technical specialty (either vendor-specific or vendor-neutral), user support specialists and help desk staff can also get their support skills certified. Help Desk Institute (HDI) is a professional organization that certifies support professionals. Microsoft also provides certifications targeted at the technical skills of desktop support workers. User support certifications vary in terms of the topics they cover.

Visit the Web sites listed in Table 7-3 for current details on available user support and help desk certifications, including topics covered, preparation suggestions, and costs.

Organization	Certification Overview	Certification Titles	Knowledge Areas
Help Desk Institute (HDI)	**www.thinkhdi.com/ hdi.aspx?c=563**	• Support Center Analyst (SCA)	• Skills for help desk agents who are the primary contact for customers
		• Desktop Support Technician (DST)	• Skills for user support workers who provide face-to-face technical support
			• Other HDI certifications are available for:
			◆ Customer service representatives (CSR)
			◆ Help desk team leads
			◆ Help desk managers
Microsoft	**www.microsoft. com/learning/en/ us/certification/ mcdst.aspx**	• Microsoft Certified Desktop Support Technician (MCDST)	• Supporting and troubleshooting Windows 7 and Windows 7 applications

Table 7-3   Examples of user support and help desk certification programs

User Support Center Certification Programs

Some certification programs are aimed at organizations, rather than individuals. For example, as part of the professional services it provides to members, the Help Desk Institute offers programs to certify entire help desk groups. Some of these certification programs include consulting services on support industry best practices, such as the Information Technology Infrastructure Library (ITIL). As you learned in Chapter 6, best practices are procedures, tools, and methods employed by very successful support groups.

The Benefits of Certification

For help desk and user support specialists, the benefits of certification include:

- A recognized benchmark of minimum-level job skills and expertise in the area covered by certification
- A justification for receiving higher pay, as a new or experienced worker
- Career advancement opportunities based on documented knowledge and skills

- A way for an employer to document an employee's efforts to keep up-to-date in the computer field

- A feeling of pride of accomplishment and increased job satisfaction upon passing a certification milestone

Although certification expectations differ for various jobs in the user support and IT fields, the most popular certifications for recent graduates of community college and vocational/technical degree programs are CompTIA's A+ and Network + certifications, Microsoft's MOS and MCDST certifications, and Help Desk Institute's DST certification.

Is certification a requirement for a support position? Some employers specify in job announcements and ads for support positions that they expect applicants to be certified, perhaps in addition to their formal education. However, many employers do not expect or require applicants to be certified. Even these employers, however, may view an applicant's certification as additional evidence of qualification for a support position. Organizations that require prospective support employees to be certified as a help desk professional are not yet common, because the skills required for help desk positions vary considerably between organizations, and certification exams are not yet standardized nor universally recognized.

ON THE WEB

Since the names and details of each certification program change frequently, you can get up-to-date information about computer industry certification and exam procedures by following the links in this chapter or those in Wikipedia's article on certification (**en.wikipedia.org/wiki/Professional_certification_%28computer_technology%29**).

Certification Exam Preparation

Many college and vocational/technical schools now match the curriculum in their courses with the most common certifications. For example, an introductory spreadsheet course may be targeted at students who wish to prepare for Microsoft's MOS exam in Excel. An advantage of a preparatory course in a college or vocational/technical school is that assistance is usually available when a student has questions about the course material.

Other common ways to prepare for a certification exam include crash courses, e-learning tutorials, and self-study courses. **Crash courses**, sometimes called boot camps, are intensive classes designed to prepare participants in a short period of time (usually a week or less) to take a certification exam. Crash courses are expensive, and a student usually must travel to the site where the course is offered. However, for professionals who have experience in a subject area, crash courses are a quick way to review material and prepare to get certified. Several training vendors offer **e-learning tutorials** in either computer-based training (CBT) or Web-based training (WBT) formats. CBT and WBT preparatory courses usually cost substantially less than crash courses, but rarely include an option for a student to obtain help with course materials. Finally, **self-study courses** are preparatory materials, usually in book format, that readers complete at their own pace. The books are often a thousand or more pages. Some are packaged with CBT tutorials and with practice exam questions. Although generally less expensive, self-study courses rarely provide assistance to students who have questions. The market for certification preparatory courses is large, and both product vendors and third-party training vendors offer materials and services to meet the growing interest in industry certification.

311

 Many computer industry professionals believe they should be able to pass a certification exam based on their professional experience. However, these exams are not easy to pass, especially for those who do little to prepare. Some exam providers permit exam retakes with no additional fee or a reduced fee after additional preparation.

ON THE WEB

Organizations that offer certification exam preparation courses include:

- MindLeaders (**link.mindleaders.com/e-learn/courseprice.jsp**)
- Netwind Learning Center (**www.netwind.com**)
- Aaron's Computer Training (**www.aarons-computer-training.com**)
- Learnthat.com (**www.learnthat.com/courses**)

Many of these training vendors offer a free sample lesson on their Web sites. For other training and certification vendors, see a compiled by the Open Directory Project **dmoz.org/Computers/Education/Certification**.

Prometric is an organization that offers many types of certification tests in testing centers throughout the United States. Prometric's Web site (**www.prometric.com/default.htm**) is a good certification resource because it includes links to Web sites where various certification programs are described. Another organization that offers similar services is Pearson Vue (**www.vue.com**).

Most certification exams are administered on a computer workstation. Some are traditional tests, which ask test takers a fixed-length sequence of questions similar to the final exam in a college course. In the traditional format, each test taker answers the same set of questions. However, certification exams often use a type of test called a **computer adaptive test**, which asks questions selected from a test database to try to quickly estimate the test taker's ability. The test database for an adaptive test consists of questions that are graded from easy to moderate to difficult. The first question asked in an adaptive test session is of moderate difficulty. As the test taker answers each question, an adaptive test uses a mathematical formula to estimate the test taker's level of ability. Subsequent questions asked are either easier or more difficult, based on the pattern of previous right and wrong answers. An adaptive test continually selects questions from the test database and revises its estimate of the test taker's ability until it is relatively certain that it has an accurate measure. Sometimes the estimation process requires as few as 15 questions. Thus, some test takers may answer more questions than others. Some may respond to easier questions; others may respond to more difficult ones, as an adaptive test hones in on the test taker's ability. Adaptive testing saves time because fewer questions are asked; it reduces boredom from too many easy or repetitive questions; it reduces intimidation from very difficult questions; and ideally, it makes the testing process shorter and less stressful.

Some certification tests include scenario questions that require the test taker to answer questions using a simulated version of a product. Certification exams also frequently include a hands-on component to eliminate the "paper CNE" phenomenon described earlier.

ON THE WEB

For a brief introduction to computer adaptive testing (CAT), and an opportunity to try out a computer adaptive test, go to **echo.edres.org:8080/scripts/cat/ catdemo.htm**. (Note the server for this Web site is slow.)

ON THE WEB

For information about various certification pre-tests, visit the following vendors' Web sites:

- Pearson's Exam Cram 2 (**www.pearsonitcertification.com/imprint/series_ detail.aspx?ser=340082**)

- Transcender (**www.transcender.com**)

- Brainbench, which offers a free certification exam for a Computer Technical Support agent (**www.brainbench.com/xml/bb/common/testcenter/ taketest.xml?testId=68**).

User Support as a Profession

The number of user support and help desk positions in the United States and worldwide increased significantly in the 1990s. However, recent recessions in the United States in 2001-2003 and 2007-2009 reduced employment in the user support industry, as did the trend to outsource some low-level support positions overseas. These recessions have undoubtedly had a more significant impact on support industry employment than jobs outsourced overseas.

The U.S. Bureau of Labor Statistics estimates that over 900,000 workers were employed as computer support specialists and system administrators in 2008, as shown in Table 7-4 below. Most of these were employed as user support workers, help desk agents, and network administrators.

	Employment in 2008	Projected Employment in 2018	Net Increase in Employment	Percent Increase in Employment
Computer Support Specialists (*BLS code 15-1041*)	565,700	643,700	+78,000	+14%
Network and Computer System Administrators (*BLS code 15-1071*)	339,500	418,400	+78,900	+23%
Total	905,200	1,062,100	+156,900	+17%

Table 7-4   U.S. employment in user and network support positions (*all numbers are rounded*)
SOURCE: Bureau of Labor Statistics, "Occupational Outlook Handbook, 2010–11 Edition"
(**www.bls.gov/oco/ocos306.htm#projections_data** and **www.bls.gov/oco/ocos305.htm# projections_data**)

The 2007-2009 recession and the slow subsequent recovery in employment may have an impact on the long-term projections in Table 7-4. However, the category of Computer Support Specialists is expected to increase faster than average over the next decade when compared with most U.S. employment fields, and the category of Network and Computer System Administrators is expected to grow at an even faster rate.

Examples of related occupations not reported in Table 7-4 include technical writers, trainers, project managers, and Web programmers who may have user support responsibilities.

ON THE WEB

To learn more about these employment categories and employment projections, visit the U.S. Bureau of Labor Statistics (BLS) Web site (**www.bls.gov/oco**). Search for code *15-1041* for Computer Support Specialists and *15-1071* for Network Administrators. A detailed breakdown of employment on the BLS Web site reports on the distribution of workers by industry and by state.

As a result of the large number of people employed in the user support field, several groups have organized to provide professional associations for these workers. A **professional association** is a formal organization that represents the interests of a group of professionals and provides services to its membership. Professional associations that are targeted to user support and help desk managers and staff are listed in Table 7-5.

Association	URL
Help Desk Institute (HDI)	**www.thinkhdi.com**
Association of Support Professionals (ASP)	**www.asponline.com**
Network and Systems Professionals Association (NaSPA)	**www.naspa.com**
Association of Information Technology Professionals (AITP)	**www.aitp.org**
Women in Technology (WIT)	**www.womenintechnology.org**

Table 7-5   User support and help desk professional associations

Professional associations perform a number of functions for their membership. They often publish journals or magazines with articles of interest to the support profession. These associations encourage their members to enhance their professional knowledge by offering books, seminars, conferences, and other learning and development activities. Some associations offer certification programs for their membership. All associations maintain Web sites with links to other sites of interest. Some offer chat rooms, forums, newsgroups, local chapters, and email services with industry news.

One important activity a professional association may undertake is to adopt a **code of ethical conduct** or principles to guide its members' professional behavior. Examples of ethical standards to which professional associations might expect their members to adhere are shown in Figure 7-4.

1. Adhere to federal, state, and local laws, including those that govern information technology, workplace and public health and safety, and the environment.

2. Keep abreast of developments and trends in technology and participate in professional growth and development activities in your area of specialization.

3. Advocate for a better understanding of technology among end users and the public.

4. Act with integrity and honesty in dealing with the public, end users, coworkers, management, and competitors.

5. Avoid conflicts of interest, abuse of power and use of position for personal gain; exhibit fairness in relationships with others.

6. Avoid workplace discrimination based on gender, ethnicity, sexual orientation, marital status, age, religion, or disability.

7. Respect the intellectual property and copyrights of end users, coworkers, vendors, and competitors, and give credit for others' work.

8. Protect the privacy and reputations of end users.

9. Perform job-related responsibilities in accordance with company policies and industry best practices.

10. Adhere to acceptable technology use policies and do not make unauthorized or personal use of property or resources.

11. Report violations of ethical principles of conduct.

12. Report all security vulnerabilities and work to eliminate harmful uses of technology.

Figure 7-4   Example principles of ethical conduct for IT professionals

ON THE WEB

Web sites where you can view examples and learn more about guidelines for ethical professional conduct include:

- Association of Information Technology Professionals (AITP) (**www.aitp.org/organization/about/ethics/ethics.jsp**)

- Canadian Information Processing Society (CIPS) (**www.cips.ca/about?q=ethics**)

- The SANS Institute (**www.sans.org/resources/ethics.php**)

The purpose of this chapter has not been to provide a comprehensive primer on user support management, but rather to discuss selected aspects of support management with an emphasis on information that is likely to be of interest and useful to job applicants and entry-level support workers. If you are interested in career advancement into a user support management position, consider taking community college or vocational/technical school coursework on business management for a comprehensive look at tasks that challenge managers.

ON THE WEB

Two "hot topic" user support management issues not included in this chapter are salaries and employee retention.

Each year, *Computerworld* conducts an annual salary survey of the information technology field. The survey includes job titles such as help desk/technical support specialist. The survey results for 2011 are available online (**www.computerworld. com/s/article/9214739/Salary_Survey_2011**). The survey is nationwide, but it includes some breakdowns that reflect regional differences in salaries.

For another perspective on salaries, consult **www.salary.com**. In the Salary Wizard box, enter a job title—such as *help desk*, *user support*, or *network support*—and your zip code, and then click the **Search** button. In the list of search results, click an occupation title, and then click **View Salary Info**. Note that the Salary Wizard reports the median (average) salary as well as the range. Entry-level workers with no experience in a job category are likely to start in the lower 10 percent of the range.

Support managers concerned with employee retention should consult a TechRepublic article, "Strategies to Boost Morale and Retention in Call Center Environments" (**techrepublic.com.com/5100-6269-5088913.html**).

Chapter Summary

- People in user support and help desk management positions include those who work as supervisors, lead workers, and project coordinators.

- Many support groups develop a mission statement to describe the guiding principles, objectives, and goals against which the support group can evaluate its performance.

- One challenge for help desk managers is to develop a budget for their department or work group. The budget usually includes categories such as revenue from fees and expenses for help desk staff and facilities.

- Support managers with a position to fill analyze the knowledge, skills, and abilities (KSAs) needed for the position and then prepare a position description listing the job qualifications required of applicants.

- The interview process for support positions may include a knowledge and skills test, traditional directed and nondirected interview questions, behavioral and scenario questions, and even stress tolerance questions to gauge an applicant's ability to think under pressure and solve problems. Interviewers and job applicants need to be aware of questions that are illegal to ask during an interview.

- Training programs for support staff include new employee orientation and ongoing professional development. Performance appraisals of user support workers provide important input into professional development activities for workers.

- Performance statistics are used to measure the extent to which a support group and its staff members meet the objectives described in its mission statement. Support groups also use satisfaction surveys to collect data on individual and group performance. Performance measures are often used as part of a periodic performance appraisal of support workers.

- Certification in the information technology industry includes college degrees, vendor-specific certification, and industry-standard certification programs. Support professionals can earn certifications in specialized products as well as certifications of their support skills. Computer adaptive tests are often used in the certification exam process.

- Associations of support professionals have evolved to meet the needs of workers in IT and the support field. Some professional associations publish codes of ethics and standards of conduct to guide their members.

Key Terms

abandonment rate—The percentage of calls in which the user hangs up before support staff respond.

behavioral question—An interview question that gives a job applicant an opportunity to describe how she or he behaved in a specific work situation.

certification—An assessment process designed to measure and document a professional's knowledge and skills in a specialized segment of the information technology field.

chargeback—A fee charged by a support group to clients or end users to offset the cost of providing support services.

code of ethical conduct—Principles to guide a worker's professional behavior; a code of conduct is often distributed by a professional association for its membership.

computer adaptive test (CAT)—A certification testing method in which a computer presents questions that are graded in difficulty from easy to moderate to difficult; the test is designed to quickly estimate a test taker's ability.

cost center operation—A user support operation for which the cost of providing services appears as an expense in an organization's budget without an offsetting revenue stream.

crash course—An intensive class, sometimes called a boot camp, designed to prepare students in a short period of time (usually a week or less) to take a certification exam.

directed question—An interview question about a specific job requirement; directed questions are intended to help the interviewer learn whether an applicant has specific educational or work experiences.

e-learning tutorial—Computer-based training (CBT) or Web-based training (WBT) designed to prepare participants for a certification exam.

Erlang—A unit of traffic (or a user incident, in the case of a support group) processed in a given period of time; it is used to estimate the number of support staff required to respond to an expected volume of incidents in a given time period.

illegal question—An interview question that is intended to obtain information about an applicant's characteristics that are not specifically job related, such as age, ethnicity, marital status, sexual orientation, political views, religion, and some information about disabilities.

knowledge and skills test—A paper-and-pencil, verbal, or online test that measures a job applicant's knowledge and problem-solving abilities.

mission statement—A set of guiding principles that communicate the goals and objectives of a support group to its staff, end users or clients, and management.

nondirected question—An interview question that is open-ended and gives an applicant an opportunity to talk in general terms about their qualifications for a position.

performance appraisal—An evaluation of a user support worker according to established criteria; criteria should be related to the support group's mission, the worker's position description, and the worker's individual professional development objectives.

performance statistics—Objective data collected to evaluate a user support or help desk operation; often directly related to the user support mission statement.

professional association—A formal organization that represents the interests of a group of professionals and provides services to its membership.

profit center operation—A user support operation for which the cost of providing services is treated as an expense that is completely or partially offset by revenue generated by the group.

scenario question—A type of interview question in which a job applicant is given a specific problem (or set of problems) representative of the kinds of situations user support staff actually encounter; scenario questions are used to measure an applicant's problem-solving skills and ability to work under pressure.

self-study course—Preparatory materials, usually in book format, that readers complete at their own pace to prepare themselves for taking a certification exam.

staff training—Training designed to orient new support workers to their jobs, as well as ongoing training to update the skills and encourage professional growth of experienced support staff.

stress tolerance assessment—An interview tactic that helps employers evaluate how well a job applicant works under pressure; elements of the assessment may include a very noisy interview environment, questions from several interviewers, and overly technical questions.

user satisfaction survey—A questionnaire that attempts to measure how satisfied users are with the support services they have experienced.

wait time—The average time it takes a help desk to respond to calls.

Check Your Understanding

Answers to Check Your Understanding questions are in Appendix A.

1. True or False? The employee selection process for a help desk position can be described as an attempt to find applicants with the knowledge, skills, and abilities that most closely match the position's requirements.

2. True or False? Unlike a question in a knowledge and skills test, there is only one correct answer to a scenario question in a job interview.

3. A primary purpose of help desk performance statistics is to:
   a. respond to computer auditors' information requirements
   b. justify the value and expense of help desk services
   c. report to company stockholders
   d. respond to complaints from angry users

4. True or False? Organizations that treat user support as a profit center may have difficulty justifying the cost of support services.

5. Which of the following aspects of help desk operation would you least expect to be covered in a help desk mission statement?
   a. operational efficiency of users
   b. help desk fees for services
   c. customer satisfaction
   d. effectiveness of help desk services

6. A(n) _____ is a process to evaluate a help desk or support worker according to established criteria.

7. A measure of the number of support calls that can be processed in a given time period, often used to determine staffing levels in a help desk operation, is:

   a. a statistical unit   c. an MOS

   b. wait time   d. an Erlang

8. True or False? Support managers often use recordings of monitored support calls to help workers identify areas where performance improvement is needed.

9. True or False? A cost center is a help desk operation that has an expense budget, but no offsetting income budget.

10. True or False? Help desk industry certification is now essentially a requirement for any user support position.

11. Which of the following testing methods is commonly used in industry certification exams?

   a. computer adaptive test   c. traditional fixed-length test

   b. scenario test   d. best practices test

12. Which kind of interview question gives a job applicant an opportunity to describe what he or she did in a specific job situation?

   a. knowledge and skills question   c. scenario question

   b. behavioral question   d. illegal question

13. A(n) _____ is a set of behavior guidelines that a professional organization expects its members to follow.

14. *"Tell me about your educational background."* is an example of:

   a. an illegal interview question   c. a directed question

   b. a stress tolerance question   d. a nondirected question

15. Briefly list three examples of interview situations that could be used to test a job applicant's stress tolerance.

16. In the next decade, the U.S. labor market demand for user support workers is expected to:

   a. increase   c. decrease somewhat

   b. remain about the same   d. decrease dramatically

17. A(n) _____ is a plan prepared by a help desk manager to describe the costs to provide support services.

18. A questionnaire designed to measure the effectiveness of services among a sample of users is called:

    a. a user satisfaction survey   c. a performance appraisal

    b. a statistical analysis   d. an Erlang assessment

19. The percentage of calls in which a user hangs up before support staff respond is called:

    a. wait time   c. stress statistic

    b. frustration index   d. abandonment rate

20. A(n) _____ is a formal organization that represents the interests of a group of help desk professionals.

Discussion Questions

1. Is it ethical for a company that operates a telephone help desk to monitor its agents? Under what circumstances should this practice be permitted? Under what circumstances should this practice not be permitted?

2. Will industry certification ever become a minimum job requirement for employment in the user support field? Why, or why not?

3. Is a code of professional ethics, such as the one presented in this chapter, useful for a field as diverse as user support, in which there are so many different kinds of jobs? How would you make the ethical principles more specific to a help desk or user support worker?

4. *"A mission statement for a user support group is worthless. It is just a statement of platitudes that are so general that they are almost meaningless."* Do you agree or disagree with this statement? Explain your position.

5. What are the pros and cons of using a stress tolerance test as part of a job interview? In what cases should one be used? When should one not be used?

6. Is professional growth and development for a user support worker primarily the worker's responsibility or primarily the responsibility of the organization for which the employee works? Explain your position.

Hands-On Activities

Activity 7-1

Evaluate a user support mission statement. Locate the mission statement for the help desk or user support group at your school or organization, or use the mission statement for The University of Texas Health Science Center (**is.uth.tmc.edu/css/mission.htm**). Compare the mission statement with the sample in this chapter. List the similarities and differences you find.

322

Activity 7-2

Design criteria to evaluate a help desk or support group. Using the mission statement you worked with in Activity 7-1, write three measurable criteria that a manager could use to evaluate the performance of the help desk or support group.

Activity 7-3

Develop a professional growth plan. Write a one-page professional development growth plan for yourself. Base your plan on your personal assessment of your strengths and areas in which you would like to improve, either as a student and future job applicant, or as a current worker. In your development plan, describe the kinds of training, courses, seminars, books, or other learning experiences that would make you a more attractive job applicant or more valuable employee. List any industry certification exams you believe would enhance your employability or promotability. Compare your plan with ones developed by three classmates or coworkers. What useful ideas did you get from them?

Activity 7-4

Write an advertisement for a user support position. Find one or more ads online or in your local newspaper for information technology and user support positions. (These ads are usually located under *Computers* or *Information Technology* headings.) Note the format and content of a typical help wanted ad in the IT field. Select one of the user support position descriptions in Chapter 1. Write a classified ad that could be used to attract job applicants for the position whose description you selected.

Activity 7-5

Write a scenario question for an interview. Develop a scenario question for a user support or help desk position that measures whether a job applicant is a good problem solver. Start by brainstorming some ideas with three classmates or coworkers. Select a scenario that is feasible for an interview. Remember the objective is to measure problem-solving ability. Work with your team to refine the wording of your scenario question to make it as useful as possible. Exchange your scenario question with another team, and write a model response to their question.

Activity 7-6

Online training course evaluation. Use the Web-based resources described in this chapter to locate an online training course that you can try out at low or no cost. After you have worked on the course, answer the following questions:

- Did you finish the course? Why or why not?

- Did you find the course materials easy to use? List examples of any problems you encountered.

- Is an online learning environment effective for your personal learning style? How could the course be improved?

- How could the course be used as part of a training program for end users or support specialists?

Activity 7-7

Take a certification exam. Visit the Brainbench Web site (**www.brainbench.com/xml/bb/common/testcenter/freetests.xml**) to learn about the advantages of online certification. Then pick one of the free exams Brainbench offers, and take the exam. Do not worry if you don't pass. The Brainbench tests are not easy, and the passing rate is low for some exams. The purpose of the exercise is to give you experience with a typical certification exam. Was the exam in a traditional format, or was it a computer adaptive test? Write a summary of your experience, and explain how you could improve your performance on the next certification exam you take.

Activity 7-8

Evaluate help desk performance statistics. Read a paper titled "How to Measure Helpdesk Performance" (**www.techsupportalert.com/pdf/m0165.pdf**). Make a list of at least eight measures the author describes that could be used to evaluate a help desk operation or a help desk worker. From your list, pick the three measures you think are the most important ways to evaluate a help desk operation and three that you think are critical measures of a help desk worker's performance. Write a brief description of the measures, and explain why they are valuable. Would you want to be evaluated using the measures you selected?

Activity 7-9

Design a short user satisfaction survey. Working with a team of colleagues, design a short questionnaire that could be used to measure user satisfaction with the performance of a help desk or computer teaching/training lab facility. Design at least five questions, one of which should ask about users' overall satisfaction with the help desk services or lab facility. Use the free service at Survey Monkey's Web site (**www.surveymonkey.com**) to build a survey that is accessible on the Web. If possible, get a group of typical users to take your survey so you can analyze the results.

Activity 7-10

Improve a performance appraisal form. Download an example of a commonly used employee performance appraisal form (**www.billthecomputerguy.com/itsupport/help%20desk/IT%20Employee%20Evaluation.doc**). Then read some guidelines for the employee performance appraisal process (**www.squidoo.com/employeeperformancereview**). Does the example appraisal form follow the guidelines described on the Squidoo Web site? If not, modify the appraisal form so it would be useful as a tool to evaluate a help desk employee based on the guidelines you learned about on the Squidoo Web site. Compare your modification with those made by your colleagues.

Activity 7-11

Develop a training travel budget spreadsheet. Training travel expenses, which are incurred when one or more workers are sent to a training session or conference in a remote city, require careful planning and monitoring. Common expenses for training travel include round-trip airfare, hotel room rates, rental car or taxi, meal allowances, training or conference tuition, and incidental expenses (such as copying, phone calls, Internet access, parking, materials, etc.). Design a spreadsheet a support supervisor could use to prepare a budget for training travel for one or more employees. Add any expenses you can think of to those described above. Format the spreadsheet with formulas and totals, and be sure to include the fields for the name, location, and dates of the training or conference.

Case Projects

1. Help Desk Performance at Virtual-Soft

Beth Goldman, supervisor of Virtual-Soft's Help Desk service, gets weekly data from a help desk software package on her support specialists' performance. She wants to use the data to measure her staff members' productivity. Use a spreadsheet program to enter the data for Beth's staff from last week shown in the table below.

Support Specialist	Calls Handled per Week	Available Hours per Week	Average Minutes per Call
Susan	112	31.5	14.2
Jose	127	31.0	11.3
Sue	0	0.0	0.0
Barbara	87	25.1	15.9
Ekaterina	151	30.0	9.2
Shere-Kahn	63	24.2	13.6
Dennis	77	29.6	11.9
Kristen	63	27.1	10.6

Beth thinks that productivity should be measured as *amount of work accomplished* divided by *effort expended*. Think about this definition of productivity. Then use your spreadsheet to calculate a measure of productivity you think would be appropriate for these workers. Who is the most productive agent on Beth's staff? Is there more than one right way to approach this problem? Print your spreadsheet, and explain your results.

2. Help Desk Staffing at Game Shack Software

Game Shack Software develops and sells computer games and related products. Ronald Liew has recently been hired to manage Game Shack's help desk operation. The management at Game Shack is concerned about the best way to schedule help desk agents. They want to employ enough help desk agents to respond to the calls they receive from users, but they cannot afford to have an excess of agents scheduled to work when relatively few calls are expected.

Ronald wants your advice about the size of the help desk staff that Game Shack needs as well as tips on the best way to schedule agents during the day. Ron has collected data for a couple of weeks on the number of calls the Game Shack help desk receives. The busiest time of the day is from 9 A.M. to 4 P.M., during which time the help desk receives an average of 155 calls. The calls average about 12 minutes, and it takes an agent an average of 2 additional minutes to finish a database entry and terminate the call. The current help desk guidelines at Game Shack state that 85 percent of the calls should be answered in 30 seconds or less. (No more than 1 percent of the calls should be lost because of insufficient available phone lines.)

The 155 calls each day are distributed approximately, as shown in the table below.

Hour	Calls
9 AM	10
10 AM	25
11 AM	25
12 PM	35
1 PM	20
2 PM	15
3 PM	15
4 PM	10

Use the Call Centre Calculator at **www.erlang.com** to advise Ronald about the following questions:

1. How many agents does Game Shack need to handle the volume of calls listed above?

2. How many telephone lines are required to meet Game Shack's objectives?

3. When is the peak call volume? How long will an average caller wait during the peak hour?

4. What is the impact on staffing and number of lines Game Shack needs if the policy guideline on the percentage of calls answered in 30 seconds or less is increased to 95 percent?

3. A Slideshow on Help Desk Employee Retention

Use a variety of online resources to learn about employee retention of help desk and user support workers. You could research questions such as:

- What are common reasons help desk employees leave their positions?

- What is the average annual turnover rate among help desk workers?

- What kinds of programs do successful employers offer to retain help desk workers?

- What kinds of worker benefits would make help desk workers more likely to stay in an existing position?

- Are help desk employee retention programs effective?

Prepare a slideshow presentation that you could use to highlight your findings and suggestions. Make your slideshow an example of your best professional work.

4. A Budget Template for XL-1000 Support Costs

Jack Holt is a support manager for McKenzie Dynamics, a local software company that has a new product it expects to release for sale in about four months. Jack has begun to rough out some expense estimates for the support team that will be handling the increased volume of problem incidents that are expected with any new software release. He has given you a sample of the format he uses to prepare a product support budget, as shown in Figure 7-5.

XL-1000 Product Support Budget Plan
Prepared by Jack Holt   2- Dec-2011

Category	Qty	Monthly rate or each	Annual cost	ECL code
Staffing Expenses				
Level 1 Agent	2	2600	62400	E
Level 2 Agent	1	3000	36000	E
			98400	E
Facilities Expenses				
PC Workstation	3	879	2637	C
			2637	C

Figure 7-5   Sample budget format for XL-1000 product support team

While Jack works on position descriptions and recruiting for the support staff, he would like your help to develop a spreadsheet template for the complete support budget. Use the budget expense categories described in Figure 7-2 and the format shown in Figure 7-5 to design a spreadsheet Jack can use to prepare a product support budget plan for presentation to McKenzie Dynamics' management team.

Your task is to develop a spreadsheet template for Jack with the following features:

- Use appropriate budget expense categories from Figure 7-2 in the chapter. The cost of support will be included in the price of the software, so you don't need to include income in your template. Also, don't worry if you include expense categories Jack doesn't need because they can be deleted and others can be added later as needed.

- You do not have to include details such as actual quantities and dollar amounts in your budget spreadsheet (unless you wish to do so to test it). Jack will input the actual data later. However, you should include all the headings and the formulas needed to calculate the annual cost of each category and category subtotals.

- Jack uses the following codes in the *ECL code* column: *E* for ongoing operating expenses, *C* for one-time capital equipment expenses, and *L* for monthly or annual lease costs.

Design your budget plan spreadsheet so it is in a format that can be presented to the management team at McKenzie Dynamics.

CHAPTER 8

Product Evaluation Strategies and Support Standards

In this chapter, you will learn about:

◎ How product and support standards emerged

◎ Common tools and methods for evaluating and selecting computer products

◎ Information resources and decision-making tools for evaluating and selecting computer products

◎ Typical product support standards

◎ How organizations develop and implement support standards

In addition to the help desk support tasks described in earlier chapters, user support workers are often responsible for evaluating computer products and services and setting product standards for end users in their organization. These tasks are more common for support groups that provide services to internal users; however, some support workers occasionally work on product evaluation and standards for external users, often in the role of a consultant.

User support groups spend time and resources on product evaluations and standards for several reasons. First, support workers often have expertise in these areas that end users do not have. (Although support specialists may have greater expertise than end users, it is still vital that end users be involved in the process.) Second, assigning support staff the responsibility for product review and evaluation can eliminate duplication of effort. If each end user researches and evaluates products of special interest to him or her, the result can be wasted time as well as deviations from an organization's product standards. Third, support groups are often able to play the role of liaison between end users, IT staff, and vendors to ensure that all viewpoints are represented when computer products are evaluated and selected.

In this chapter, you will learn about several methods that support specialists use to evaluate computer products and services and how product evaluations influence support standards. These standards are important for a variety of reasons, not the least of which is to reduce the burden on the support staff. Support staff resources are not unlimited; agreeing to support a specific set of standard products is more realistic than attempting to support any product an end user might choose.

 At the end of this chapter, you will examine one organization's product support standards.

How Product Standards Emerged

When the era of end-user computing began, few organizations had established product standards. **Product standards** are lists of hardware, peripheral, operating system, network, and application software products that have been approved for use within an organization. In the early 1980s, even users within the same department often used several different hardware platforms. Some of the first PC hardware manufacturers included Apple, KayPro, IBM, RadioShack, Commodore, Osborne, AlphaMicro, and Atari—each of whom claimed a share of the PC market. Each PC manufacturer touted the advantages of its system for users in specific application areas in which its hardware had competitive strengths. Because manufacturers believed that significant differences between their products and competing products represented a marketing advantage, they felt little pressure to move toward an industry standard in PC hardware.

As widespread as the problem of incompatible and competing hardware platforms was at that time, the situation was even worse in the software market. Owners of identical hardware models of IBM PCs, for example, could select a word processor from a long list that included

WordStar, Microsoft Word, DisplayWrite, WordPerfect, PerfectWrite, and PFS Write. Because word processing was the most popular application for business use, many products competed for market share. The list of competing spreadsheet and database software was shorter, but several popular choices were available in those application areas, as well.

It might appear that product incompatibility and competition simply reflected a healthy, competitive market environment. However, from the perspective of an organization purchasing hardware and software products in the 1980s, the lack of product standards caused several problems, which are summarized in Figure 8-1.

Limited opportunities to transfer and share information among users
Incompatible hardware and software products meant that two coworkers might have difficulty sharing data. The primary method of exchanging data files was by transfer on a floppy disk. A floppy disk written on one manufacturer's computer frequently could not be read or modified on another manufacturer's hardware.

Large inventories of parts were required to repair incompatible PCs
To repair the various makes and models of computers its workers had purchased, an organization needed to maintain a large inventory of parts. Hardware incompatibilities substantially increased the cost to make even simple component repairs.

Increased challenges in training and equipping hardware service technicians to repair different hardware platforms
Technicians had to be trained to understand, diagnose, and repair many different kinds of computers. The architecture of each platform was frequently different.

User skills were difficult to transfer from one system to another
Workers could operate their own desktop system, but often knew little about the computers on their colleagues' desks. The lack of a standard operating system and applications software meant that workers often had difficulty filling in for an absent colleague, which reduced overall worker productivity.

Increased costs as support groups struggled to assist users with many different types of PCs and software
Support groups in large organizations were confronted with the need to provide training, documentation, troubleshooting assistance, hardware problem diagnosis, and software support and upgrades for a large number of incompatible hardware and software products.

Figure 8-1   Problems caused by computer product incompatibility

ON THE WEB

The History of Computing Project (THOCP) presents information about many early hardware and software vendors on its Web site (**www.thocp.net**).

As computer use expanded during the 1980s and 1990s, organizations with large investments in computer hardware and software realized that a policy (or lack of one) that permitted employees to purchase any desktop computer they chose imposed significant additional support costs on the organization. To help control and reduce costs, many organizations developed product standards. First, they selected a small number of hardware platforms and configurations to meet their users' needs. Second, they adopted a standard operating system and, in the 1990s, a standard network operating system. Third, they limited the choice of application software to one or at most a few standard packages in each software category.

Organizations handle the responsibility for setting company-wide support standards in various ways. In many organizations, the head of the IT department, sometimes called the chief information officer (CIO), is ultimately responsible. The CIO may, in turn, delegate the responsibility to a committee composed of end users, support staff, and technical IT staff. In other organizations, the task of establishing and enforcing computer product standards is a responsibility of the user support staff.

You will learn more about product standards later in this chapter. But first we will look at how organizations evaluate products so they can set effective standards.

Methods for Evaluating and Selecting Computer Products

To establish standards, the staff evaluates competing products, as shown in Figure 8-2. During **product evaluation**, the staff researches and analyzes computer product features, capabilities, and suitability for specific uses. In the evaluation process, staff members collect product information, conduct performance tests, compare competing products, make decisions or recommendations, and communicate the results of their work throughout the organization. Recommendations and decisions about which specific products to support are often made with input from end users, the user support staff, technical IT staff, and the organization's management team.

Figure 8-2 User support staff evaluate competing software products to set organizational product standards

The user support staff evaluates new hardware and software products and upgrades to existing products. When the support staff considers a new product, they are guided by questions such as:

- Does the product or upgrade perform as advertised?

- Is a competing product significantly better than the one currently in use?

- Is a new product or upgrade compatible with the organization's existing hardware, network, and operating system configurations?

- Does the new product meet the needs of the organization's users?

- Will the product help increase user productivity?

- Is the product cost-effective to purchase and support, and will it help reduce the total cost of ownership of technology to the organization?

- Is the product likely to become an industry standard?

- Is upgrading to the product now preferable to waiting for a later release?

- Is the product stable enough that it will solve more problems than it creates?

Members of the user support staff who are familiar with the needs of the end users, computer products, and industry trends can research these and related questions. They can interview end users, observe their work habits, collect relevant product information, and ask critical questions to identify the advantages and disadvantages of competing products. Staff members who evaluate products also conduct product tests, which often take place under controlled conditions.

If each user in an organization performed his or her own product tests, their efforts would likely be repetitious and not very cost-effective. In addition, an end user who attempted to become knowledgeable about even a few new products could lose focus on his or her primary job.

Information Resources

Typically, the user support staff has several tools and information resources at its disposal to help evaluate computer products. These resources include:

- Vendor literature, marketing information, Web sites, and user manuals

- Demonstration and evaluation versions of products

- Product reviews and comparison articles in computer periodicals and on the Web

- Opinions of industry experts published in trade periodicals and Internet newsgroups

- Opinions of colleagues who have experience with a product

Examples of some of these resources are shown in Table 8-1. Although all are useful resources, independent tests and reviews with side-by-side comparisons of several competing products are often more helpful to evaluators than vendor-supplied information about a single product.

Category of Product Information Resources	Example
Vendor literature and marketing information	● Download a sample product data sheet on Adobe Acrobat X Pro (**images01.insight.com/media/pdf/0411_AcrobatXProDSue.pdf**)
Vendor Web sites	● Visit the section of Toshiba's Web site that features their laptop computers (**explore.toshiba.com/laptops**)
User manuals	● Download a PDF file of any one of several vendors' user manuals on Retrevo's Web site (**www.retrevo.com/samples/index.html**)
Demonstration and evaluation software	● Request a free, 60-day trial copy of ArcGIS (geographical information system) software (**www.esri.com/software/arcgis/arcview/eval/evalcd.html**)
Product reviews	● Read product reviews for several monochrome laser printers on *CNET*'s Web site (**reviews.cnet.com/laser-printers**)
Product comparisons	● Read a product comparison of several leading Windows Web browsers on *TopTenREVIEWS'* Web site (**internet-browser-review.toptenreviews.com**)
Industry expert opinion	● Read editorial opinions on several categories of computer products (hardware and software) on *PC Magazine*'s Web site (**www.pcmag.com/category2/0,2806,198,00.asp**)
User forums and blogs	● Read a forum exchange on alternatives to Adobe products for editing PDF files on the Warrior Forum (**www.warriorforum.com/main-internet-marketing-discussion-forum/324388-how-edit-pdf-without-using-adobe-acrobat.html**)

Table 8-1   Sources of product information

Several industry trade publications provide comprehensive, up-to-date product comparisons, both in print and **ezine** (an electronic magazine or Webzine) format on the Web, including those shown in Table 8-2.

Publication	URL for Product Information and Reviews
CNET	**reviews.cnet.com**
ComputingREVIEW.com	**www.computingreview.com**
InfoWorld	**www.infoworld.com/test-center**
Macworld	**www.macworld.com/reviews.html**
MaximumPC	**www.maximumpc.com/articles/reviews**
PC Magazine	**www.pcmag.com/reviews**
PC World	**www.pcworld.com/reviews.html**
Smart Computing	**www.smartcomputing.com/editorial/reviews.asp?atypeid=1**
Tom's Hardware	**www.tomshardware.com/reviews**
TopTenREVIEWS	**computers.toptenreviews.com**
ZDNet	**www.zdnet.com/reviews**

Table 8-2   Computer industry periodicals and Web sites that publish product reviews and comparisons

The product information examples in Table 8-2 are resources primarily within the computer industry. Alternately, many trade publications publish articles that review and evaluate hardware and software products in specific industries such as accounting, manufacturing, transportation logistics, office administration, marketing, medicine, finance, law, and education. Product comparisons in industry-specific publications are especially useful because they often address issues unique to each application area.

ON THE WEB

For a list of popular computer trade publications, see **dir.yahoo.com/ Business_and_Economy/Business_to_Business/Computers/ Industry_Information/Trade_Magazines**.

For a list of ezines targeted at the computer field, visit **www.hitmill.com/internet/ magazines.html**.

Examples of articles and Web pages that compare and evaluate computer products are listed below. For each, note the evaluation criteria used, compare how competing products are rated against the criteria, and look for ways the evaluators highlight the pros and cons of each product. Some articles provide numerical evaluation scores or "best buy" designations for products the evaluators prefer.

- "2011 External DVD Burners Product Comparisons" on *TopTenREVIEWS'* Web site (**external-dvd-burner-review.toptenreviews.com**)

- "Wireless Networking: Nine 802.11n Routers Rounded Up" on Tom's Hardware Web site (**www.tomshardware.com/reviews/802.11n-wireless-router-access-point,2605.html**)

- "Best 5 Laptops" on *CNET*'s Web site (**reviews.cnet.com/best-laptops**)

- "Battle of the Web Browsers" on *InfoWorld*'s Web site (**www.infoworld.com/d/applications/battle-the-web-browsers-091**)

- "The Best Security Suites for 2011" on *PC Magazine*'s Web site (**www.pcmag.com/article2/0,2817,2369749,00.asp**)

- "Top 7 Tax Software" on About.com's Web site (**taxes.about.com/od/taxsoftware/tp/taxsoftware.htm**)

ON THE WEB

For advice about how to read computer product reviews with a critical eye, read an article on TechSoup's Web site (**www.techsoup.org/learningcenter/software/page7379.cfm**).

In addition to studying reviews in periodicals, support staff can frequently request or download demonstration or evaluation copies of software products. A **software evaluation copy** is a limited, trial copy of a software product that permits an end user or support staff to try out a product's features and assess its ability to meet an organization's needs. Evaluation copies are frequently advertised through the mail or on vendor Web sites; they usually are provided on a CD or through a download from a vendor's Web site (when the size of the demo version is not prohibitive). An evaluation copy may not have all the features of a full commercial version, or it may operate only for a limited trial period (often 30 or 60 days), or for a limited number of launches or file-save operations.

ON THE WEB

Another way to try out commercial software prior to purchase is to use a software-as-a-service (SaaS) vendor that delivers software applications via the Internet. For a directory of SaaS vendors, visit the Cloud Computing Showcase (**www.saas-showplace.com/home.php**).

Although demonstration and evaluation copies of software packages are freely distributed, vendors usually do not offer hardware products for evaluation. Typically a vendor will only provide components for evaluation if a potential sale to an organization is of a substantial dollar value. In those cases, support groups routinely and successfully request evaluation copies of hardware components, or even complete systems, that they are seriously considering.

Decision-Making Tools

When decision makers need to decide which of several products they will select to purchase and support, they can use several tools, methods, and strategies as aids. These decision tools are listed in Figure 8-3 and are described in the upcoming sections.

- Industry standard or bestselling products

- Products used by competitors

- Benchmarks

- Weighted point evaluation method

- Request for proposal (RFP)

- Acknowledged subjective criteria

Figure 8-3   Product evaluation decision-making tools

Industry Standard or Bestselling Products

When user support staff members need to make recommendations for administrative and office automation applications, they often select **industry standard products**, which are hardware, software, and peripherals that are market leaders in sales. Industry standard software products are designed to meet the needs of a broad spectrum of end users across a wide variety of industries and are sometimes called **horizontal market applications**. Few organizations devote much staff time to evaluating popular word processors or spreadsheets, for example, because the best-selling products usually have competitive features and perform most of the functions commonly required by end users.

Many so-called "standards" in the computer industry are not true standards because no industry-wide group has agreed to the specifications. Often products become standards based on sales leadership and market share.

However, when an organization has specialized needs, such as software to prepare a significant volume of legal documents or process medical insurance claims, product evaluators often look beyond mass-market leaders. In these cases, evaluators may need to research features available in lesser-known products that are targeted at users with specialized needs. Mass-market products may lack the industry-specific features that some organizations require. As an example, the way that accounting software is evaluated typically depends on the size and scope of an organization. The evaluation process may be a simple task for a small business, because any of several mass-market accounting systems targeted at small businesses will probably meet its needs. Medium- to large-scale businesses often undertake a more extensive evaluation of accounting packages because off-the-shelf products vary considerably in how they handle more complicated circumstances. Most very large businesses develop their own accounting systems or modify a commercial package to obtain the level of customization they need to meet their unique requirements.

ON THE WEB

During a product evaluation process, some businesses (even small ones) also consider the option of outsourcing selected applications. Payroll processing is a common example. The complexity of and frequent changes in payroll laws and accounting standards mean that small businesses may find it difficult to hire the expertise to operate and maintain an up-to-date payroll system. Service providers such as PayChex (**www.paychex.com**) offer outsource services to provide payroll processing.

Selecting industry standard hardware and software products can reduce an organization's support costs. Popular software products are more likely to be the target of trade books, third-party training courses and materials, and support service vendors. However, market-leading products do not necessarily match the specific and perhaps unique requirements of some end users. Furthermore, market leadership changes over time. A product that appears to be a safe purchase today may soon become obsolete, and therefore a poor choice. For example, at one time, WordPerfect was an obvious pick as a word processor, Lotus 1-2-3 was the leading spreadsheet package, and dBASE IV was often the database software of choice. None of these packages is the bestseller in its category today.

Before recommending application software for organization-wide purchase and support, a support group should always seek input from users. Product evaluators should find out which products end users have experience with, what users feel are the advantages and disadvantages of competing products for specific tasks, and whether users have preferences among products. Support groups that fail to seek user input during the selection process can make an expensive mistake if the software they select is not a good match with user needs or is too difficult to learn and use.

Products Used by Competitors

In addition to industry standard and bestselling products, support specialists who do product research and evaluation should consider products used by an organization's competitors, especially within a vertical market. A vertical (or niche) market is one that is highly specialized, such as the automobile insurance industry, hair salons, or beer distributors. A **vertical market application** is software designed for one of these specialized industries. Vertical market software often contains features that would not be useful in other industries. An organization's competitors often have thoroughly researched the market and identified strategic reasons for adopting certain computer products, even if those products are not market leaders. If the information can be obtained legally, a product evaluator should attempt to learn which products are used by competing organizations. Then the support staff can evaluate the strengths and weaknesses of computer products the competitors use. Evaluators who consider products used by the competition are not "copycats"—they simply recognize the fact that organizations in the same industry often have very similar technology needs.

Trade publications in a specific industry are often a good resource for product ideas and reviews because vendors with targeted products are more likely to advertise and provide feature articles on their products.

Benchmarks

A **benchmark** is an objective test or measurement used to evaluate the speed, capacity, capabilities, or productivity of competing products. Evaluators can use benchmarks to compare two or more rival products. Benchmarks are a popular way to compare hardware products; they are also useful for software packages or even entire systems. The benchmark method of product comparison begins when an evaluator defines one or more criteria as critical success factors for a specific product. Examples of common benchmark criteria include processing speed, storage capacity, software performance, and user productivity.

Benchmarks are based on **objective evaluation criteria**, which are factors used in a product selection procedure that are relatively unbiased. After a benchmark evaluation has been completed, any neutral evaluator should be able to use the same objective criteria to reach the same conclusion because the criteria and measurement methods are less influenced by personal opinions and preferences. An evaluator often uses a controlled test environment to measure competing products against the same objective criteria, such as transaction processing speed. In the test, the evaluator attempts to control all variables that do not relate to the product being evaluated. For example, in an evaluation of software performance, the same user operates two or more competing software products on identical hardware, in identical operating environments, with the same workload. **Extraneous variables**, those that could bias the results of a benchmark test in one direction or the other, such as different hardware platforms, have been eliminated. Therefore, observed differences in test results are most likely due to real differences in product capabilities.

 When selecting criteria for a benchmark test, an evaluator should use criteria that will make a difference in an end user's operating environment. For example, the performance of a system's graphics display adapter may not be especially important in a word-processing environment, but the performance of a printer might be.

ON THE WEB

To see a bar graph of the results of benchmark tests on the latest models of CPUs (central processing units), visit **www.cpubenchmark.net**.

An evaluator who wants to use benchmarks to compare the speed of competing printers, for example, may define a constant unit of work, such as printing 100 pages. The pages are selected to represent different examples (text and graphics, color and black-and-white, heavy and light ink coverage) from among those that users frequently print. Then, the evaluator runs a series of tests, using competing vendors' printers that run at comparable speeds, in which the sample of 100 pages is printed. (Due to product design, performance differences are possible, even among printers that advertise the same relative print speed specifications.) As part of the tests, the evaluator attempts to eliminate other variables that could affect the benchmark results. The evaluator uses the same computer system, operating environment, application software, network environment, test documents, and paper type. The only variable that is different from one trial to the next is the printer itself. In this controlled test environment, an evaluator can determine whether one brand of printer has a significantly faster print speed than competing printers.

An evaluator can also use benchmarking to evaluate software. As with hardware benchmarks, the evaluator defines a constant unit of work—for example, the time it takes a data-entry clerk to enter and process 100 typical accounting transactions. Then the evaluator measures the amount of time the data-entry operator takes to enter the same 100 transactions using rival accounting packages, and perhaps the data-entry operator's error rate. A high error rate could indicate that a software package has a user interface that is difficult to use or that its data validity checks do not catch common errors. Finally, the evaluator compares the benchmarked times and error rate for each package.

ON THE WEB

In addition to evaluator-defined benchmarks in product evaluations, vendors and users can use several common industry standard benchmarks to evaluate competing products. To learn more about benchmarking computer products, read an article on Wikipedia's Web site at **en.wikipedia.org/wiki/Benchmark_(computing)**.

Benchmark comparisons are helpful because they are designed to use objective criteria and eliminate vendor or user bias in the evaluation of a hardware or software product. Companies that provide hardware and software benchmarks include the following:

- Business Applications Performance Corporation (BAPCO) (**www.bapco.com**—click **Products,** and then click **SYSmark)**

- PassMark Software (**www.passmark.com**)

- Standard Performance Evaluation Corporation (SPEC) (**www.spec.org**)

- PC TechBytes' Web site lists several popular free and shareware benchmark tools (**www.pctechbytes.com/tools/computer-benchmark-tools**)

 Benchmarks are often used to help evaluate computer products, but they are seldom the only factor considered. In the selection of a printer, accounting software, or any other product, factors other than performance should also be considered, as you will see in the next section.

Weighted Point Evaluation Method

Product reviews in computer periodicals sometimes use a weighted point evaluation method, a strategy that support staff can use in their own evaluation projects. The **weighted point evaluation method** is a product comparison tool that uses several key criteria of predetermined importance to evaluate competing products or services and arrive at a numerical score, which is then used as the basis for product selection. This method is also called the Kepner-Tregoe method, after two authors who described methods rational managers can use to make decisions. As with benchmarks, the goal of the weighted point method is to make the evaluation and selection process as objective as possible. It attempts to treat competing products equally, to eliminate possible favoritism or bias among evaluators, and to force evaluators to specify in advance the important factors in the evaluation of competing products. Because weighted point evaluation is an objective procedure that requires the use of well-defined criteria, public agencies are often legally required to use this method or a variant of it.

ON THE WEB

For more information about this method and an example of a weighted point evaluation of software options, see Michael S. Bandor's article, "Quantitative Methods for Software Selection and Evaluation" (**www.sei.cmu.edu/library/abstracts/reports/06tn026.cfm**).

Next, you will learn some mechanics of the weighted point evaluation process. You can apply this method to selecting a 1000-user computer network or to selecting a home personal computer. To perform a weighted point evaluation, evaluators follow these steps:

1. Decide on the evaluation criteria.

2. Determine the importance of each criterion.

3. Rate each competing product against all the evaluation criteria.

4. If more than one evaluator rates products, compute the average rating for each criterion for each product.

5. Weight the product ratings for each criterion by importance.

6. Compute the total rating for each product.

7. Compare product ratings.

The evaluation criteria selected for use in the weighted point method are based on several important factors, including:

- The specific type of hardware or software product to be evaluated

- The needs of end users

- Support issues

- Cost

Evaluation articles in periodicals are an excellent source of ideas for criteria to use to evaluate specific products. Table 8-3 provides some examples of criteria in several categories.

ON THE WEB

To learn about the extensive evaluation criteria used by the Information Technology Planning Board at UCLA, visit **www.itpb.ucla.edu/Documents/2001/Jan/Matrix-ComputerPrinterSrvcsRFP.htm**.

Category	Examples of Criteria
Hardware or software	• Processing speed
	• Storage capacity
	• Capabilities and features
	• Transaction volumes
	• Compatibility with existing systems
	• Upgradeability (scalability)
End-user needs	• Ease of learning
	• Ease of use
	• Mandatory features (must have)
	• Desirable features (nice to have)
Support availability	• Technical support services
	• Installation assistance
	• Training
	• Documentation
	• Troubleshooting
	• Maintenance and repair
Cost	• Total cost of ownership (see Chapter 1)

Table 8-3   Examples of criteria used in the weighted point evaluation method

Consider the following example of a simple weighted point evaluation method. Suppose an organization wants three evaluators in the user support group to rate two computer systems for purchase. The evaluators first decide on the comparison criteria to use, as shown in Table 8-4. They also discuss and agree on the relative importance of each criterion based on its significance to the organization, the end users, and the support group. For example, a relatively unimportant criterion might receive a weight of 5 to 10 percent. The sum of the criteria weights should total 100 percent.

Criterion	Criterion's Importance (Weight)	System X Evaluation	System Y Evaluation
Hardware configuration	25%		
Software bundled	35%		
Vendor reputation	10%		
Vendor support	30%		
TOTAL	**100%**		

Table 8-4   Example criteria and weights for evaluating two computers

Each evaluator then rates the proposed products and assigns points (usually between 1 and 100) to each criterion for each product. For example, an evaluator could learn from a survey of a vendor's current clients that the vendor is very well regarded and might assign the vendor a score of 95 out of 100 on the vendor reputation criterion. The evaluators work independently to rate each system.

Next, the three evaluators consolidate their results. They could average the points earned for each criterion. Or, the evaluators might discuss their preliminary ratings to identify and negotiate any large discrepancies and arrive at a consensus rating. For example, if one evaluator rated the System X hardware configuration at 60 and the other evaluators rated it at 100, the three evaluators can discuss the discrepancy to determine why there was such a significant difference and to arrive at a mutually acceptable rating of perhaps 80 out of 100. Small discrepancies of a few points are ignored. In this example, after discussion, the evaluators agreed that the hardware configuration for System X was worth 90 points (out of 100), and the competing System Y was worth only 70, as shown in Table 8-5.

Criterion	Criterion's Importance (Weight)	System X Evaluation	System Y Evaluation
Hardware configuration	25%	90	70
Software bundled	35%	70	70
Vendor reputation	10%	50	95
Vendor support	30%	60	90
TOTAL	**100%**		

Table 8-5   Weighted point evaluation method example with points assigned to each criterion

In the next step, the number of points assigned to each system is multiplied by the weight of each selection criterion. The resulting points for each system are then summed to arrive at a total number of points, as Table 8-6 shows. The system with the larger number of total points is the system that best meets the selection criteria.

Criterion	Criterion's Importance (Weight)	System X Evaluation	System Y Evaluation
Hardware configuration	25%	90 × 25% = 22.5	70 × 25% = 17.5
Software bundled	35%	70 × 35% = 24.5	70 × 35% = 24.5
Vender reputation	10%	50 × 10% = 5.0	95 × 10% = 9.5
Vendor support	30%	60 × 30% = 18.0	90 × 30% = 27.0
TOTAL	**100%**	**70.0/100**	**78.5/100**

Table 8-6   Weighted point method example with evaluation points

In this example, System Y's higher scores on vendor reputation and vendor support offset its lower score on hardware configuration. The weighted point method can be used to evaluate more than two products, and it can accommodate as many criteria as evaluators think are important. For simple product evaluations, a product evaluation worksheet can be prepared using a spreadsheet program.

ON THE WEB

JaxWorks, a supplier of spreadsheets for small business use, provides an Excel worksheet for vendor evaluation analysis, which uses the weighted point evaluation method. You can download a free version of the spreadsheet (**www.jaxworks.com/ library.htm**). From the list of available templates, click on the link to download the Vendor Evaluation Analysis spreadsheet. (While you're on the JaxWorks site, note the extensive list of free spreadsheet templates available for various business applications.)

One advantage of the weighted point evaluation method is that it forces evaluators to address two important questions early in the evaluation process:

- Which criteria are important in the product purchase decision or recommendation?

- How important is each criterion relative to other criteria?

Some argue that this method applies numeric values to criteria where numbers have little meaning. However, the weighted point method forces evaluators to look at measurable criteria when they might be tempted to rely on more subjective beliefs and preferences. Sometimes the objective results of a weighted point method conflict with an evaluator's subjective feelings. If a product evaluator finishes the process and receives the "wrong" result according to his or her "gut" feelings, the evaluator may be able to reexamine the criteria and the weights and ask why he or she got those results. Sometimes it is the "gut" that is wrong.

Request for Proposal (RFP)

A **request for proposal (RFP)** is a product selection tool or competitive bidding process that uses objective criteria, such as benchmarking and the weighted point evaluation method, to choose among products proposed by competing vendors. By law, many public agencies are required to use an objective evaluation process, such as a bidding process or a request for proposal procedure. A successful RFP process can assure that vendors are evaluated fairly, according to established rules; this tool helps reduce the likelihood of a lawsuit as the result of perceived or real procurement problems.

ON THE WEB

To learn more about the legal aspects of RFPs, read an article by two attorneys who suggest strategies for successful bidding procedures (**www.metrocorpcounsel. com/pdf/2005/December/06m.pdf**).

Because the RFP process is objective, many businesses also use RFPs or a similar procedure to aid in making purchase decisions. For example, an organization might issue an RFP that invites competing vendors to submit product and price proposals for an office network system. As a result of an RFP process, an organization usually designates the successful bidder as the sole authorized vendor for the office network products covered in the RFP.

To complete the RFP process, an organization follows these eight primary steps:

1. Conduct a user needs assessment (discussed in Chapter 9).

2. Based on the needs assessment, develop a purchase specification for the equipment or software to describe the technical characteristics and features required.

3. Define the decision criteria that will guide the selection process and determine the importance of each criterion. Many criteria are based on mandatory (must have) or desirable (nice to have) product features; other criteria include technical support, vendor stability, product costs, and compatibility with existing systems.

4. Write an RFP document that describes the user requirements, bidding procedure, and decision criteria.

5. Send the RFP document to prospective vendors (some organizations maintain a list of vendors who are prescreened to meet minimum financial stability criteria).

6. Receive vendors' written proposals; each proposal should address how that vendor's products meet or exceed the user requirements and include a bid price at which the vendor can supply the products or services.

7. Analyze and evaluate the responses to the RFP—using weighted point evaluation or other objective methods.

8. Select a vendor and award the purchase contract.

ON THE WEB

To learn more about the RFP process, read suggested guidelines for purchasing technology equipment published by the International Foundation for Electoral Systems (**www.ifesbuyersguide.com/resource_center.php?article=cornish**).

Or read an RFP to acquire computer systems for the city of Dayton, Minnesota (**www.cityofdaytonmn.com/RFP/2010/New%20Computer%20RFP.pdf**). Note the extensive technical specifications on pages 3 and 4 and the evaluation criteria on pages 5 and 6.

Another RFP resource is an article on the important steps involved in selecting software on Infotivity's Web site (**www.infotivity.com/selection_steps.html**).

The RFP process is a commonly used objective decision-making tool. Because RFPs include several lengthy steps and considerable staff time, they are used primarily for purchases of significant dollar value, rather than for purchases of off-the-shelf products.

Acknowledged Subjective Criteria

The evaluation tools and methods described above are primarily based on objective criteria. Using these tools, any neutral observer should be able to reach the same conclusion as the primary evaluator. Either a product performs as well on a benchmark comparison as another product or it doesn't. Although product evaluators base many hardware and software purchase decisions on objective criteria, they sometimes use criteria that are known to be subjective. **Subjective evaluation criteria** are nonobjective factors used in a product selection procedure that are not directly related to the fit between a product's features and end users' needs. Subjective factors can include a previous working relationship with a vendor, convenience, personal preferences, and reliance on traditional or historical purchasing channels. (A comment such as, *"We've always bought network equipment from that vendor"* is a good indication that subjective criteria are in use.) Subjective criteria are neither measurable nor repeatable from one evaluator to another, and two evaluators may well disagree on the result.

Legitimate reasons may result in a purchase decision based on a personal relationship between an organization and a vendor; an organization and its supplier may have a lengthy business or personal relationship or a partnership agreement that overrides all other evaluation criteria. Occasionally an organization may refuse to consider any products from a particular vendor because it has a low regard for the vendor's product reputation, business ethics, or customer-service standards. When an organization has a special relationship with a vendor based on prior experience, reputation, location, or a personal contact, other factors, including price, are often less important.

Large organizations, both public and private, often use an objective evaluation or selection procedure for computer products. Smaller organizations often use more subjective criteria. Support specialists who evaluate and select computer products may use both objective and subjective methods, depending on their employer's guidelines. However, the purpose of all product evaluation and selection strategies is to arrive at the best product choice for each user. Once an organization has researched and selected products and vendors, the next step often is to develop product support standards.

347

Product Support Standards

As you learned in the first part of this chapter, organizations often try to control support costs by establishing computer product standards to limit the number of hardware and software options users can choose. Although establishing product support standards may sound like a "one-size-fits-all" approach, it doesn't have to be. Within the standards adopted by an organization, alternatives are often permitted. Most organizations try to strike a reasonable balance between the two extremes of "Select only this product" and "Select anything you want."

Honolulu Community College in Honolulu, Hawaii, has adopted computer product standards and support policies to minimize the drain on college resources in providing user support to its faculty, staff, and students. Figure 8-4 contains several excerpts from the college's policy that describe the limits placed on hardware and software acquisitions.

Honolulu Community College Policy on Desktop Computing

The intention of this policy is to provide a standard base-line hardware and software configuration for all HCC campus desktop computers. The Supported Products List will include Workstations, Operating Systems, and Application Software for use by faculty, staff, classrooms, and student labs. The current Supported Products List will include hardware and software specifications for both Windows-based computers and Macintosh computers.

The Supported Products List will be published on the ITC web site and updated quarterly. This will allow departments to plan fiscal year budgets based on the published standards.

The Supported Products List will serve to set standards for the campus community for desktop hardware and software as well as network operating systems. Members of the campus community will then follow the published standards or understand that they may not receive support from HCC Technical Desktop Support to solve problems they encounter using non-standard hardware and/or software.

An HCC standardized base configuration will be provided by ITC through HCC Technical Desktop Support, to the faculty and staff of Honolulu Community College.
Only fully licensed software and freely distributed software products will be part of the desktop configuration.

In keeping with industry best practices, it is mandatory for all HCC-owned desktops to be configured with the HCC configuration. End users of these desktops shall have only operator access to these machines as opposed to administrative access.

All new purchases of computers and desktop workstations must conform to the current Supported Products List. Specifications will be for approved system configurations.

Figure 8-4 Computer product support policies at Honolulu Community College (*continues*)

(continued)

The HCC standardized base configuration is mandatory for all new systems connected to the HCC Campus Internet. Additional software to the base configuration is permitted provided they do not compromise the integrity of the desktop configuration.

The benefits of this policy are:

- Simplify the hardware acquisition and upgrade process;
- Provide an HCC customized base configuration for all computer users;
- Improve support services by promoting migration to selected technologies and concentrating on these limited products in greater depth;
- Plan effectively for introducing new products and phasing out older products; Develop precise goals and objectives for the Technical Desktop Support office to optimize staff training and development in order to offer reliable, high-quality services;
- Encourage a more consistent environment through the use of a standard suite of appropriate technologies.

If a product is on the Supported Software List, faculty and staff can get assistance with problems related to the use of those products. If a product is not on the list, those who need assistance will receive consultation as resources allow.

The Desktop Computing Policy is accompanied by the following list of responsibilities:

Technical Desktop Support (TDS) Responsibilities with regards to Providing Support for Supported Products

- Maintain expertise for supported products.
- Provide or facilitate support.
- Work with the Information Technology Center to coordinate support, training, and documentation for the supported product.
- When appropriate and cost effective, recommend site or volume licensing for supported products.

TDS Responsibilities in Providing Assistance with Unsupported Products

- Limited support is available.
- One hour of courtesy consulting may be provided to help requestor assess options to migrate to supported alternative.
- Referrals to vendors or other sources may be provided, when available.
- Neither training nor documentation will be available.

Customer Responsibilities for Support

- Be familiar with basic desktop skills, attend available training, and read available documentation as appropriate.
- Have valid licenses for supported products (TDS cannot provide support in case of invalid licenses).
- Be able to provide the following information when requesting support: name, campus location, telephone number, email address, type of computer in use, software and version in use, the desired outcome, and a description of the problem encountered.
- Work with TDS staff in troubleshooting problems.
- Run diagnostics provided by TDS or manufacturer.
- Maintain regular backup procedures for their desktop system.

Criteria Used to Evaluate Products for Supported Status

- Industry-wide acceptance and/or standard
- Number of customers who require the software
- Number of departments represented by customers requiring software

Figure 8-4 Computer product support policies at Honolulu Community College

Honolulu Community College's list of supported products includes both PCs and Macintosh computers. The list of approved products specifies selected software packages in several categories. The college's lists of recommended and supported hardware and software products are described in Figures 8-5 and 8-6, respectively.

ITC Windows-Based Microcomputer Approved Hardware Specifications
May - July 2010

The following approved systems will meet the needs of Honolulu Community College's faculty and staff for email, MyUH Portal, Web browsing, word processing, spreadsheet, graphics, and database functions. HCC approves purchasing the specified systems listed below.

Desktops:

Dell OptiPlex 780 Mini-Tower

Intel Core 2 Duo Processor (3.0GHz, 6M, 1333MHz or higher)
4 GB RAM or higher
160 GB Hard Drive or higher
DVD+/-RW Drive
10/100 Mbps Ethernet Connection
Windows XP Professional, SP3, x32, or Windows 7 Professional
4-year On-site Warranty (Recommended)
Surge Protector
Resource CD, which contains Diagnostics and Drivers for the System

Laptops:

Laptops should *not* be purchased as a Desktop replacement.

Dell Latitude E6410

Intel Core i5-520M Processor (2.4GHz, 3M cache or higher)
4 GB RAM or higher
160 GB Hard Drive or higher
DVD+/-RW Drive
Wireless LAN (802.11) Mini Card (Compatible with 802.11b and 802.11g networks)
Windows XP Professional, SP3, x32, or Windows 7 Professional
4-year On-site Warranty (Recommended)
  ● Warranty does not cover consumables such as batteries
Resource CD, which contains Diagnostics and Drivers for the System
  ● Finger Print (Biometric) Reader is not recommended or supported

Notes:

1. **Antivirus software:** UH Site License Department offers McAfee VirusScan free of charge for UH faculty and students for your home and office computers. Please do not obtain the antivirus software from Dell.

2. **Microsoft Office 2007 Professional:** UH Site License Department offers Microsoft Office 2007 Professional Plus, which is downgradable to Microsoft Office 2003 for office use, at a volume discount.

Updates to these specifications are posted on HCC's Web site (**itc.honolulu.hawaii.edu/?q=node/13**)

Figure 8-5 Honolulu Community College's list of supported Windows hardware products

HCC Technical Desktop Support (TDS) Supported Software May - July 2010				
Supported Software List Software not listed will be provided best effort support. During that time we will suggest you upgrade to the updated version of the software or make recommendations for the purchase of new software and/or hardware.				
Microcomputer Operating Systems and Applications				
	Macintosh Computers		**MS Windows-Based Computers**	
Category	*Product*	*Versions Supported*	*Product*	*Versions Supported*
Operating System	Mac OS	10.4, 10.5	Windows	XP Pro
Word Processing	Word	2004, 2008	Word	2003, 2007
Spreadsheets	Excel	2004, 2008	Excel	2003, 2007
Presentation Packages	PowerPoint	2004, 2008	PowerPoint	2003, 2007
Virus Protection	McAfee Virex McAfee VirusScan for Mactel	7.x 8.x	McAfee VirusScan	Ent. 8.5i, Ent. 8.7i
Web Browser	Firefox	3.x	Firefox	3.x
FTP Client	MacSFTP	1.x	SSH Secure File Transfer Client	3.x
Email Client	Thunderbird	2.x	Thunderbird Pine via SSH Secure Shell	2.x 3.x
Disk Utilities	Norton Utilities		ScanDisk	
Document Browser	Acrobat Reader	8.x, 9.x	Acrobat Reader	8.x, 9.x

Updates to these specifications are posted on HCC's Web site (itc.honolulu.hawaii.edu/?q=node/14)

Figure 8-6   Honolulu Community College's list of supported Macintosh and Windows software products

ON THE WEB

Updates to Honolulu Community College's product support policies and supported products lists are posted at **itc.honolulu.hawaii.edu**. The online version of these support standards describes the reasons each recommended product was selected over other products.

Not every organization spends the resources to thoroughly research and evaluate products and develop the type of standards described in this chapter. However, larger organizations with a substantial investment in computer technology tend to devote staff time to evaluating products and setting purchase standards because the potential for waste is high. Based on the results of product research and evaluation, user support specialists can prepare lists of approved and supported computer products. Armed with a list of approved products, they can more easily answer questions such as, *"Which kind of computer should an employee buy?"* and, *"Is this printer model compatible with the organization's computer systems?"*

How Computer Product and Support Standards Develop

An organization's computer product and support standards can emerge from a variety of sources. In some organizations, product standards evolve over time as a "computer culture" develops. For example, an organization might have adopted the standard that primarily models of Macintosh computers are supported simply because the early adopters of technology in the organization were predominantly Macintosh users. Alternately, organizations that adopted Netscape as their preferred Web browser during the 1990s may be reluctant to change to a different one, even though Netscape is no longer the most popular browser product and official product support for it ended in 2008.

Although organizational culture and traditions are one source of product standards, some organizations assign the task of developing and maintaining standards to the user support group or to a product standards committee. A **product standards committee** is a group of support specialists, end users, technical IT staff, and managers who develop and maintain a list of organization-approved standard products and services. Once established, standards must be effective; that is, they must help end users get their work done. They must be evenly administered and enforced. If end users have to work around the standards to get the equipment, software, and services they need to do their jobs, the organization's computer standards will be widely viewed as ineffective. Some organizations recognize that a "one-size-fits-all" standard is counterproductive in special situations. While standards are generally enforced, a caveat may be added: *"Standard products will be purchased and supported, unless a compelling business reason requires an exception to the standard."*

 Software standards are typically defined before hardware standards. If a standards committee defines a hardware standard first, it may later discover that one or more software packages it wants to select will not run on the hardware standard it defined earlier. Software products determine the minimum hardware requirements in most cases, not vice versa.

A change in standards for supported computer products can be an emotional time for users who are comfortable with the old standards. Resistance to changes in standards can result in statements such as: *"This technology has worked fine for many years. Why change it now?"* Whenever changes in standards are contemplated, new products should be thoroughly tested, following procedures described earlier in this chapter. The need for a change in standards should be discussed with employees, and their feedback should be sought on how current hardware and software products meet, or fail to meet, users'

needs. Changes in product standards tend to be implemented more smoothly when end users are consulted and included in the decision-making and implementation processes.

A ROLE-PLAYING SCENARIO

This is a transcript of a conversation between Kerry, a user in the Legal Research Department, and Morgan, a support specialist. If possible, have colleagues play the parts of Kerry and Morgan, and then discuss your reaction to their conversation.

MORGAN: I understand that you are in the market for a new laptop computer.

KERRY: Yes. My Toshiba is starting to have problems. The CD drive no longer works all the time, and the machine is slow by today's standards. I have been thinking about getting a new Toshiba.

MORGAN: The laptop the law firm currently recommends and supports is a Dell Latitude.

KERRY: Well, I like my Toshiba a lot, and I am familiar with Toshiba features, so that is the kind of laptop I'd like to get as a replacement.

MORGAN: The only way the company would permit you to buy a Toshiba is if you could make a business case for why a Dell Latitude would not meet your needs.

KERRY: But I've always had Toshiba laptops since I was in school. In fact, my home computer is a Toshiba laptop. They are very reliable and don't need a lot of repairs.

MORGAN: The problem is the company has standardized on the Dell Latitude running Windows 7. No Toshiba laptops are on our list of supported computer models.

KERRY: That's another thing. I have heard it's a lot of work to convert from XP to Windows 7. Some friends say it's a steep learning curve, so I'd like to stay with XP. I am more productive with XP than I would be with Windows 7.

MORGAN: Unfortunately the company made the decision to move to Windows 7 on all new computer purchases. I don't think you can even buy a laptop that runs XP today.

KERRY: Yes, I know that Microsoft wants the world to migrate to Windows 7, but I still have an installation disk for XP, so I would plan to install it on whatever machine I get.

MORGAN: But the firm could not provide tech support for XP. If you had problems with it, you would be on your own.

KERRY: If the company won't buy me a Toshiba laptop and let me run Windows XP on it, then I'll have to go out and get one myself to use here at work.

MORGAN: But if you connect a new Toshiba to the company LAN, we run the risk of you infecting the network with a virus or worm. I doubt we'd let you connect it to the network because we wouldn't want to risk the problems it might cause.

KERRY: Sounds like I am stuck. How did we ever end up with these kinds of policies, anyway?

After the role-playing activity, discuss the following questions:

1. Did Kerry make a strong business case for purchasing a Toshiba running XP instead of the company-supported Dell laptop running Windows 7?

2. Did Morgan do an effective job of explaining the reason for the product standards to Kerry? If not, continue the conversation with points you would make as an explanation.

How Organizations Implement Computer Product and Support Standards

In many organizations, two forces often influence the adoption and implementation of computer product and support standards. One factor is an organization's existing inventory of hardware and software products. Unless it is very small or has a very large computer budget, an organization could probably not afford to discard its entire investment in computer systems and adopt a new standard overnight. When they define support standards, product support groups often take into account the predominant hardware, software, and network architecture that currently exist in an organization. Support for obsolete computer products may be phased out over time, with ample notice to end users, to minimize inconvenience. To deviate substantially from what employees currently use can result in a large, one-time expense as end users convert to equipment or software that meets a new standard.

A second force that drives changes in product and service standards is the continual introduction of new products, services, and product upgrades. An important task of a user support group is to learn about and evaluate new products that have the potential to replace existing standard products. The decision to modify and update existing product support standards is usually based on criteria such as the following:

- New products offer technical improvements over older products.

- New products have features with the potential to improve employee productivity.

- End-user product preferences have changed over time.

- New products and services are available at a lower cost than existing products.

- New products may be compatible with changes in industry standards, unlike older products.

- New products have become more popular than the products they would replace.

However, the decision to replace an existing product or service standard is often difficult to make because organizations may have a sizable investment in the existing standard. Similarly, end users have invested the time to learn how to use the current products and may be reluctant to change because the conversion means retraining, which often results in reduced productivity while the end users are learning the new product. For these reasons, organizations that want to move to a new standard may decide to phase it in over time.

A transition period can occur when both old and new products are permitted and supported under the standards policy. Of course, transition periods can strain the support staff, because they must provide support for both old and new products. During the transition period, increased support costs are often incurred, as support and maintenance of existing hardware, software, and network products continue for some users, while other users convert to and are trained in the use of new products.

For example, when the Windows Vista operating system first became widely available in 2007, many organizations chose not to convert from Windows XP to Windows Vista. Their analysis included some of these points:

- Reasons to convert to Vista:
  - Vista has new features.
  - Vista is the latest technology.
- Reasons to stay with Windows XP:
  - The new features in Vista are not worth the cost to convert (Vista licenses, training for users, and implementation costs).
  - The organization has a substantial investment in Windows XP software, some of which will not work in Windows Vista.
  - The organization has a substantial investment in peripheral devices, some of which will not work in Windows Vista because vendors chose not to release updated device drivers.
  - Windows Vista is not as stable an operating system as XP.

Consequently, some organizations stayed with the Windows XP operating system as a standard. Other organizations included both Windows Vista and earlier Windows versions as standard during an extended transition period.

When Windows 7 was introduced in 2010, many organizations were still running XP. Although their XP operating system was effectively 10 years old at that point, their position can be summed up as, *"If XP does what our users want it to do, why change, just for the sake of change?"* Partly to address the concerns of users in some organizations, some versions of Windows 7 have a Windows XP compatibility mode to accommodate software that will not run under Windows 7. Acceptance of Windows 7 as a standard operating system has far surpassed adoption of Vista, but reluctance to convert to new industry standards explains why some organizations are still running even older Windows 98/Me/2000 applications.

ON THE WEB

To test a PC to find out if it can support Windows 7, use PC Pitstop's readiness evaluator (**techtalk.pcpitstop.com/2009/05/20/windows-7-readiness-test**); this requires Internet Explorer. Or use Microsoft's Windows 7 Upgrade Advisor (**windows.microsoft.com/upgradeadvisor**).

Product and support standards will continue to change in the future. In the second decade of the 21st century, organizations will face decisions about when to convert to and support new peripheral devices based on the Universal Serial Bus 3.0 standard, when to upgrade to 802.1N wireless network devices, and when to adopt voice recognition input technology. Some Windows users are still unsure whether to make the move to Windows 7, or to await Windows 8 (expected in 2012). Users of the Microsoft Office suite are confronted with the choice between learning to use the new ribbon interface in Office versions 2007 and 2010, or staying with the familiar 2003 version. Every decision to modify an existing technology standard or adopt a new one requires analysis and evaluation of products and services by the user support group. It also triggers potential support cost increases for installation, upgrades, training, documentation, troubleshooting, and help desk services.

ON THE WEB

To keep up with rumors about Windows 8 and its product features, visit the Windows 8 News Web site (**windows8news.com**).

Acceptable Use Guidelines

The same committee that sets standards for supported computer products, or a different group, may address organizational standards in another area: acceptable computer use guidelines. **Acceptable use guidelines** are adopted by organizations and publicized among their employees to clarify which types of computer use are permitted and not permitted on school or work systems. These use guidelines often describe how users are permitted to use their computers, what they are not allowed to do, and the consequences or penalties for unauthorized or illegal use. The guidelines may cover activities that are illegal according to federal or state law (such as accessing confidential information) or violations of licenses and agreements (such as copying commercial software), and activities that are prohibited by organizational policy (such as use of organizational email for personal messages).

ON THE WEB

For an example, see the University of Oregon's "Acceptable Use of Computing Resources" guidelines (**it.uoregon.edu/cio/acceptable_use.shtml**).

A template for an acceptable use policy is available at **www.sans.org/resources/ policies/Acceptable_Use_Policy.pdf**.

Chapter Summary

- During the 1980s, organizations with a substantial investment in desktop computer technology recognized the need to evaluate computer products and move toward product and support standards. Because few widely recognized industry standards existed, incompatible hardware and software increased the cost of computer technology and reduced productivity among users. Today, many organizations lower their support services costs by restricting purchases to a limited list of approved products.

- User support workers often evaluate computer products and services so they can recommend to end users and organizations the products that will meet their needs. Support workers may help an organization set standards for computer hardware and software products. Standard products help increase the compatibility among various hardware and software components and help to reduce the expense to support end user systems.

- Support staff members use a variety of information resources to evaluate hardware and software products, including vendor literature, Web sites, and user manuals; product demonstration and evaluation versions of software; product reviews and comparison articles in computer periodicals; and opinions of industry experts.

- Decision aids can help support specialists make selection choices among competing products and services. These tools and strategies include selecting industry standard or bestselling products, evaluating products used by competitors, assessing products against benchmarks, comparing alternatives using the weighted point evaluation method, using the request for proposal (RFP) procedure, and weighing acknowledged subjective criteria.

- Many organizations adopt industry standard and bestselling products. These products are in widespread use and make the selection decision appear very simple. However, simply because a product is a bestseller does not mean that it is necessarily the best fit for a user's specialized needs. A less popular product may have unique features that are actually a better match for a specific user's needs.

- Benchmarks are an objective way to compare two or more products by observing them perform a standard, predefined set of tasks. The weighted point evaluation method forces a product evaluator to make a list of important criteria and assign a weight to each criterion that reflects its importance. Competing products are evaluated against the criteria, and the product that best matches the criteria is selected. Common criteria include product features, ease of learning, ease of use, compatibility with existing products, availability of technical support, and total cost of ownership.

- Hardware and software standards are important to organizations because standards help control user support costs. Although some support standards are based on organizational culture and historical use patterns, many standards are the result of systematic analysis and evaluation of new products. The decision to adopt or modify a standard is often made by a group or committee with representatives from the end-user group, user support staff, technical IT staff, and management. Implementation of new standards is influenced by the investment in existing hardware and software and the potential loss of employee productivity during the conversion to the new products.

- Organizations also define acceptable use guidelines, which describe activities users are permitted and not permitted to do with computers in an educational or business environment.

Key Terms

acceptable use guidelines—Standards adopted by an organization and publicized among its employees to communicate policies about activities that end users are permitted and not permitted to do with their computer systems, as well as the consequences or penalties for unauthorized or illegal use.

benchmark—An objective test or measurement used to evaluate the speed, capacity, capabilities, or productivity of rival products.

extraneous variable—A factor that could bias the results of an objective benchmark test; product evaluators try to eliminate these factors to isolate and measure a product's performance.

ezine—An electronic magazine organized like a print publication, but distributed via a Web site or email; ezines (or Webzines) aimed at the computer industry often feature product reviews and comparisons.

horizontal market application—A software product designed to meet the needs of a broad spectrum of end users across a wide variety of industries (as opposed to a vertical market application).

industry standard product—Hardware, software, or a peripheral that is a market leader in sales; standards in the computer industry are often not true standards, however, in the sense that typically no industry-wide group participated in the specification.

357

objective evaluation criteria—Factors used in a product selection procedure that are relatively unbiased; any neutral observer should be able to apply the same objective evaluation criteria and reach the same conclusion.

product evaluation—A process in which staff members research and analyze computer product features, capabilities, and suitability to meet specific end-user needs.

product standard—A list of hardware, peripherals, operating system, network, and application software products that have been approved for use within an organization; standards are often enforced to reduce the cost of acquiring and supporting computer systems.

product standards committee—A group of user support specialists, end users, technical IT staff, and managers who develop and maintain a list of organization-approved standard products and services; these products are recommended for purchase and are supported by the user support staff.

request for proposal (RFP)—A product selection or competitive bidding process that uses objective criteria to choose among products proposed by competing vendors; a request for proposal process is often used as the basis for awarding a contract to provide computer products.

software evaluation copy—A limited, trial copy of a software product that permits end users and support staff to try out a product's features and assess its ability to meet an organization's needs.

subjective evaluation criteria—Nonobjective factors used in a product selection procedure that are not directly related to the fit between a product's features and end users' needs; subjective factors can include a previous working relationship with a vendor, convenience, personal preferences, and reliance on traditional or historical purchasing channels.

vertical market application—Software designed for a highly specialized industry; vertical (or niche) market software often contains features that would not be useful in other industries.

weighted point evaluation method—A product comparison method that uses several key criteria of predetermined importance to evaluate competing products and arrive at a numerical summary score as a basis for selection; also called the Kepner-Tregoe method.

Check Your Understanding

Answers to Check Your Understanding questions are in Appendix A.

1. True or False? By the early 1980s, hardware and software for personal computers were standardized in most organizations.

2. True or False? The larger the number of incompatible software packages an organization owns, the greater the cost to train and retrain workers.

3. _____ are an attempt to strike a reasonable balance between "select only this product" and "buy anything you want."

4. True or False? In order to avoid bias and favoritism, product evaluation and selection decisions are usually made by user support staff working independently of other workers.

5. _____ adopted by organizations often describe how users are permitted to use their computers, what users are not allowed to do, and the consequences or penalties for unauthorized or illegal use.

6. _____ copies of new software packages may have limited features or operate for a limited trial period, and are used to assess products.

7. True or False? Industry standard computer products are those selected by a panel of industry experts for use in most organizations.

8. True or False? As a general rule, dominance in the software industry does not change over time; the best-selling products in the early 1980s are still the best-selling products today.

9. A(n) _____ is an objective test or measurement used to evaluate the speed, capacity, capabilities, or productivity of competing computer products.

10. Which of the following product evaluation methods uses several criteria of predefined importance to arrive at a numerical summary score for each competing product?

    a. industry standard method   c. subjective criteria method
    b. benchmark method   d. weighted point method

11. A(n) _____ is a purchasing procedure that invites competing product vendors to submit product and price proposals for a system that meets specified needs.

12. When support staff select office productivity software such as word processors or spreadsheets, they often use which decision strategy?

    a. weighted point evaluations   c. request for proposals
    b. industry standard products   d. benchmarks

13. Which of the following letter sequences represents the order of steps in the request for proposal process? (A) send RFP to vendors; (B) develop product specification; (C) evaluate RFP responses against criteria; and (D) define selection criteria

    a. A – B – C – D   c. D – A – C – B
    b. B – D – A – C   d. A – D – B – C

14.   _____ are selection criteria that are neither measurable nor repeatable in an evaluation of competing computer products.

15.   True or False? A benchmark test of competing products is designed to use objective evaluation criteria instead of an evaluator's personal opinions.

16.   Computer product standards are often defined by:

   a. an organization's computer culture

   b. early adopters of technology

   c. a product standards committee

   d. any of these

17.   A(n) _____ is a factor that an evaluator tries to eliminate from a side-by-side test of competing products because it could bias the test results.

18.   Which of these is not an objective evaluation method for selecting a computer product?

   a. benchmark   c. user preferences

   b. request for proposal   d. weighted point evaluation method

19.   List three resources a product evaluator might use to locate information about competing products.

20.   True or False? Computer product standards originally emerged in order to reduce the cost to provide support for end users.

Discussion Questions

1.   Describe a product standard issue or concern you think will confront organizations (perhaps one where you work or attend school) during the next 12 months. How will the issue impact end users? How will the issue impact the user support staff?

2.   Based on your personal experience, what do you think about monopolies in the hardware and software industries and their impact on end users? Is it preferable to have a single vendor who has a substantial monopoly in a specific hardware or software product and therefore sets a standard, or is it preferable to have several competing, possibly incompatible products? Why?

3.   How would you design an effective benchmark test to evaluate competing brands of document scanners?

4.   What is the role of end users when an organization selects new hardware and software products and updates its list of supported products? Describe some strategies for overcoming user resistance to changes in standards.

5. Which do you think are most effective when making a hardware or software purchase decision: objective criteria or subjective criteria? Explain your answer.

6. Consider the following statement: *"The weighted point evaluation method forces evaluators to attach numeric values to criteria that cannot and should not be measured numerically. These supposedly objective numbers are essentially meaningless as a basis for making purchase decisions."* Do you agree or disagree? Explain your position.

7. Explain your reaction to the following statement: *"End users should not participate in product evaluations because they cannot be objective about computer products and standards."*

Hands-On Activities

Activity 8-1

Investigate product comparison information. Locate a magazine or Web site that contains one or more articles that present a side-by-side comparison of two or more products. (Use resources listed in the chapter, if you like.) Evaluate the effectiveness of the product comparison by considering the questions listed below, and then write a summary of your findings.

- Which criteria are used to compare the products?

- What additional criteria could have been used?

- Describe the evaluation method used to do the product comparisons.

- Did the method(s) produce an objective or subjective result?

- Do you agree with the results? Why or why not?

Activity 8-2

Compare computer product support standards. Locate the computer product support standards for your workplace or school, or find another organization's computer product support standards online. Write a short comparison between those you find and the support standards at Honolulu Community College described in this chapter. How are they similar? How are they different?

Activity 8-3

Try a benchmark utility program. Several benchmark utility programs are available online, including the ones listed below. Download one of these utilities and run it on one or more different systems to which you have access. Compare your results with those obtained by others. Write a brief summary of your findings.

- System Analyser (**www.sysanalyser.com**)

  System Analyser, developed by Hans Niekus, is a system information utility that measures the speed of a system's CPU, hard drive, and other components.

- PC Wizard (**www.cpuid.com/softwares/pc-wizard.html**)

  PC Wizard, developed by CPUID software, is a system analysis and benchmark utility that evaluates a system's performance.

- Fresh Diagnose (**www.freshdevices.com/benchmark_software.html**)

  Fresh Diagnose is designed to analyze and benchmark various computer components.

Activity 8-4

Identify industry standard products. Choose a category of computer products from among the following: hardware, peripherals, operating systems, application software, and local area networks. Make a list of at least three computer products you think would be described as an industry standard in the category you selected. Compare your list with the list of a team of three classmates or coworkers. Do your team members agree or disagree about the industry standards? Write a one-page paper that lists the agreed-upon standards, products over which there are disagreements, and your explanation of the reasons for any disagreements.

Activity 8-5

Compare evaluation criteria for Web browsers. Find two frequent Web users: one who uses Internet Explorer and another who uses Firefox or Chrome. Ask each user why they prefer their browser choice over the other. What criteria do they use? Are they subjective or objective criteria? How do their evaluations compare with your own choice? Write a summary of your findings.

Activity 8-6

Plan a product standards committee meeting. Suppose that you are the leader of a product standards committee whose assignment is to develop a product standard for your organization. Write an agenda for the first committee meeting that lists the high-priority tasks the committee should undertake. (*Hint:* Think about the information the committee will need, the decisions it will need to make, and what the end result will look like.)

Activity 8-7

Develop a weighted point evaluation worksheet model. Use spreadsheet software to develop a worksheet that product evaluators can use for the weighted point evaluation method. Set up columns and formulas that will make the worksheet easy to use. To test your worksheet, enter the data from the example presented earlier in this chapter. Design your worksheet to be as general as possible to make it simple to add more products or evaluation criteria. Save and print your worksheet.

Activity 8-8

Interview a product standards committee participant. Interview a support specialist or other member of a product standards committee in your school or work organization. Learn about the process the committee uses to set and maintain product and service standards. How does the committee ensure that it gets input from end users? Ask about difficult decisions to include or exclude products that the committee had to address at recent meetings. Also ask how the committee resolves conflicts when disagreements arise. Write a short summary of what you learned about product standards and committee meetings from the interview.

Activity 8-9

Evaluate an acceptable use policy. Learn whether the organization where you work or attend school has an acceptable computer use policy for employees or students. Make a list of activities that are permitted and those that are not permitted. Identify on your list those activities that are illegal and those that are not permitted according to organizational policy. Compare your organization's computer use policy with the University of Oregon's policy referenced earlier in the chapter. Describe the similarities and differences.

Case Projects

1. Antispyware Utility Evaluation at Les Deux Vaches

You are a user support specialist at Les Deux Vaches, an organization that publishes a trade publication for the dairy industry. Several managers have approached you about a problem they want help with. Each of the managers has a laptop computer they use to connect to the company's intranet and to the Internet. They use their laptops to access email and certain accounting information in the evenings and on weekends. They are concerned about the possibility of accidentally downloading spyware that could be used to obtain proprietary corporate information or slow the speed of their laptop computer.

Investigate some free antispyware utility programs that are available for download from the Web, and make a recommendation to the workers about which program to use. Complete the following tasks:

1. Create an evaluation criteria checklist for an antispyware utility. Develop as complete a list as you can, keeping in mind the problem the managers want you to help them solve. You can also consider any software support issues or other factors you think are relevant.

2. Develop evaluation criteria for an antispyware utility.

3. Select two or three freeware utilities you find online (or in Chapter 12). Download and install the utilities on a computer to which you have access.

4. Read the documentation and try the features of each program you downloaded.

5.   Evaluate each of the programs you downloaded in terms of the criteria you established.

6.   Write a short summary report for the managers detailing the antispyware utilities you evaluated and include your recommendation about which utility you would suggest the managers at Les Deux Vaches use.

2. Evaluate Online User Satisfaction Survey Web Services

The supervisor of the help desk where you work has asked for your help with a small user satisfaction survey project. The supervisor wants to get some experience with online surveys as a way to measure client satisfaction with help desk services. Your task is to evaluate the following two Web services that facilitate collecting survey information:

- SurveyMonkey (**www.surveymonkey.com**)

- Free Online Surveys (**freeonlinesurveys.com**)

Each site requires a valid email address to register, but offers a free or evaluation service as an alternate to its fee-based services. Limit your evaluation to the free services, and complete the following steps:

1.   Develop evaluation criteria for an online user satisfaction survey. (You may want to brainstorm criteria with your colleagues.)

2.   Read the documentation and view the demo survey to get experience with the features each service offers.

3.   Create an evaluation criteria checklist for an online survey tool. Develop as complete a list as you can, keeping in mind the problem the help desk supervisor wants you to help solve. You can also add to your checklist any technical support issues or other factors you think are relevant.

4.   Evaluate the two services in terms of the criteria you established.

5.   Write a summary report about the survey tools you evaluated. Include your recommendation about which service you would recommend to your supervisor.

3. Invoicing Software for Columbia Sand & Gravel

Mark Allen, owner and operator of Columbia Sand & Gravel, needs some computer advice and wants to hire you as a consultant. Due to several large construction projects and subdivision developments, Columbia has grown in recent years, and needs to replace its soon-to-be-obsolete computer billing system. The existing software runs on an older PC system and was purchased more than 12 years ago. Although Mark is still very pleased with the features of the company's existing billing system, the hardware and software no longer have the capacity and speed to process invoices and record payments for Columbia's client base. Unfortunately, the company that sold the software to Mark is no longer in business, so an upgrade of the existing system is not an option.

Mark is aware of two software companies, Digital Rock and Extractasoft, that sell invoicing applications specifically tailored for use in the sand and gravel industry. Both companies claim to have the best-selling software available for sand and gravel invoice applications. Mark wants you to evaluate these two competing products and make a recommendation on which software invoicing package Columbia should adopt as its new standard.

Mark is also aware that his company will have to purchase new hardware to run the selected software. In recent years, Columbia Sand & Gravel has developed a good working relationship with Modular PC, a local company that sells and services computer hardware products. The owner of Modular PC is a close personal friend of Mark's, but Modular PC does not sell invoicing software as specialized as Mark needs. Although Mark has already decided to purchase the computer hardware from Modular PC, and is ready to cut a purchase order for it, he wants an outside perspective to help evaluate the software products.

Using what you have learned in this chapter as well as the information described above, write a letter to Mark in which you:

1. Describe any problems you have identified with the approach Columbia plans to take in the selection of replacement hardware and invoicing software, as described above.

2. Outline your suggestions for the software and hardware product evaluation approach and the selection criteria you would recommend to Columbia Sand & Gravel.

4. An RFP Checklist for Chocoholic Specialties

Reilly Lane at Chocoholic Specialties wants to develop a Web site to sell the company's chocolate candy and cooking products directly to online customers in the United States and Canada. Reilly would like your help with the preparation of a request for proposal (RFP) to local vendors who design and develop commercial Web sites.

Reilly wants you to research what should go into the RFP and to make a list of topics the Web site development RFP should cover. Reilly asked you to submit a checklist of topics or questions that should be included in the written Web site RFP. You do not need to write the RFP, but Reilly will use your list of suggested topics and questions to make assignments to staff members who will pull together the information needed to produce a written RFP.

Begin by doing some research on the content of an RFP. One place you could look is on Web sites that contain guidelines on RFP preparation. These sites often include lists of topics or information that should be included in an RFP. Some online articles you might consult are:

- *How to Write a RFP for Your Web Project* (**www.flex360.com/flexappeal-blog/how-to-write-a-rfp-for-your-web-project**)

- *How to Write a Request for Proposal (RFP)* (**www.internettraining.com/6art2.htm**)

- *Client 101: How to Write an RFP* (**www.clickz.com/933951**)

- *RFP Development Guide* (**www.aristotlewebdesign.com/pdfs/RFP%20Guide.doc**)

The following site contains links to several different examples of Web site design RFPs:

- Municipal Research and Services Center of Washington provides examples of municipal government Web site RFPs (**www.mrsc.org/Subjects/InfoServ/webdesignrfp.aspx**).

Or, you may be able to find a book on RFPs, such as:

- Porter-Roth, Bud. *Request for Proposal: A Guide to Effective RFP Development.* Boston: Addison-Wesley Professional, 2001.

Of course, feel free to search for additional resources to help locate information on the contents of an RFP for a Web site for Chocoholic Specialties.

5. Criteria for Wireless, All-In-One Printers

The Rogue River Auto Store is a new and used car dealership that also sells parts and service. The company wants to replace eight older model printers with new models located in various departments in the dealership.

The staff at Rogue prints large volumes of predominately black and white documents. They would like printers with multifunction (all-in-one) capabilities, such as scanning, printing, faxing, and copying. The management at Rogue would also like to be able to connect the printers to the wireless network recently installed in their store. Wireless printers would have the advantage of being moveable to any part of the store as their staff and needs change.

The management at Rogue would like you to investigate the characteristics of wireless all-in-one printers and design a spreadsheet with evaluation criteria for selecting the new printers. Design your spreadsheet so you can evaluate several models of printers. You can use Internet resources or other resources, such as those described in this chapter, to help you develop the evaluation criteria. For instance, one criterion could be related to the cost of supplies (such as the per-page cost of a printed sheet). When you have a tentative list of factors to evaluate, compare the criteria you developed with those of your school or work colleagues. Did they suggest criteria you could add to your spreadsheet?

When you have a final list of criteria, choose some weights for each criterion. Before finalizing your spreadsheet, compare your weights with those identified by your colleagues. Are the weights they chose similar to yours? Where are they significantly different? Try to narrow the differences in weights.

Finally, pick a couple of models of printers to research that you think will meet Rogue's needs and fill in as much of your spreadsheet as you can. If possible, pick the same printer models as your colleagues so you can compare your results with theirs. Discuss any significant differences in results.

CHAPTER 9

End-User Needs Assessment Projects

In this chapter, you will learn about:

◎ Basic strategies for performing end-user needs analysis and assessment

◎ Steps analysts undertake to analyze and assess a user's needs

◎ Common tools that help support specialists to conduct a user needs assessment project

◎ Tasks in managing a user needs assessment project

◎ Project management software tools

User support specialists are often assigned to help end users select computer products and services. Sometimes that selection must be made from a limited array of products and services, especially if an organization maintains lists of standard, supported products—as you learned in Chapter 8. This chapter describes how to analyze and assess end-user needs and help organizations and users choose the best options among competing products and services. User needs analysis involves thoroughly investigating a situation and problem; assessment involves evaluating the results of the investigation and making a recommendation or a decision.

The chapter applies primarily to user support specialists who work with internal users rather than those who work on help desks or provide telephone support to external users. Support specialists who work with internal users in small and medium organizations are often involved in assessing end-user needs and recommending products for purchase. If the scale of an assessment project is large, it may be conducted by a team that includes a senior support staff member or supervisor and one or more junior-level support staff. Although the role of an assessment project investigator or manager is usually filled by a more experienced member of the support staff, even entry-level support workers may be assigned to work on a project team.

In larger organizations, IT staff members are likely to have primary responsibility for needs assessment projects.

If you have taken previous coursework in computer systems analysis and design or information systems, you will probably recognize some of the issues, resources, and tools described in this chapter. In some academic programs, students study systems analysis or information systems before they take courses in end-user computing support. Experience in systems analysis and design provides a good background because the role a support specialist plays in end-user needs assessment is very similar to the role of a systems analyst in an IT department. However, the tools that support specialists use may be different from those used by systems analysts whose primary focus often is to design a new application program for a programmer to code. This chapter focuses on analysis and assessment tools that support specialists use to match an end user's needs to available products and services.

Overview of User Needs Analysis and Assessment

Support staff often analyze and assess user needs to determine which hardware and software products or computer services will best meet an end user's requirements. These tasks may be performed by any support staff member who has special skills, and possibly the title of support analyst. Once a support analyst understands an end user's environment and work situation, the analyst can investigate various products and services. The analyst can then work with the end user to determine which solution will best meet the user's needs and then decide whether to purchase or build that solution.

An end-user needs analysis and assessment project can take many forms. An assessment project can result in the selection of a product, such as a new computer or software package. It may result in selecting a service, such as a training program or a hardware repair vendor. An assessment project can be informal, such as a friend or colleague who asks for help with the purchase of computer hardware or software for home or work use. Or a project can be formal, such as when a supervisor asks a support specialist to work with end users in a department to select a new Internet service provider (ISP), a new printer, or even a new office network. No matter the scale or purpose, most needs assessment projects follow the same sequence of steps, which are summarized in Figure 9-1.

I. Preparation Phase Activities

1. Understand the end user's and the organization's goals
2. Understand the decision criteria and constraints
3. Define the problem clearly
4. Identify the roles of stakeholders
5. Identify sources of information

II. Investigation Phase Activities

6. Develop an understanding of the existing system
7. Investigate alternatives to the existing system

III. Decision Phase Activities

8. Develop a model of the proposed solution
9. Make a build-versus-buy decision

Figure 9-1   Phases and activities in the needs analysis and assessment process

Because each needs assessment project is unique, support analysts don't always perform every step listed in Figure 9-1, and each step is not always of equal importance. But analysts must start with a checklist of activities to guide a needs analysis project to a satisfactory conclusion. To unintentionally omit one or more of these steps can risk basing a decision on incomplete or inaccurate information. Similarly, experienced support analysts know that user needs analysis and assessment is neither a perfect process nor one that always results in an obvious solution. End users are rarely certain of their exact needs and may not know how to translate their requirements into words. They may also have unrealistic expectations about the capabilities of computer technology at an affordable price. However, a support specialist should begin with a list of well-planned questions—even if the answers are sometimes inexact.

End-User Needs Analysis Steps and Tasks

As shown in Figure 9-1, the steps in an end-user needs analysis project can be grouped into three phases: preparation, investigation, and decision. In the **preparation phase**, analysts try to understand the end user's and the organization's goals as well as the decision criteria and project constraints; they try to define the problem, identify the roles of stakeholders, and identify potential sources of information. In the **investigation phase**, analysts try to understand the present system or workplace situation and identify potential alternatives to it. Finally, in the **decision phase**, analysts develop a model of the proposed solution and decide whether to build it or buy it.

Within each phase, analysts take specific steps and use tools that allow them to obtain information and propose a solution. By performing certain tasks for each step, analysts ensure that they have considered relevant sources of information in order to arrive at an appropriate solution for each unique situation. The following sections describe the major tasks of each step of the analysis and assessment process.

CASE STUDY: THE TRAINING TEAM WEB DEVELOPMENT PROJECT

The case study in this chapter illustrates the steps in a typical needs analysis project. The case is based on The Training Team, a local company that provides custom training solutions to other businesses. After you have read about each step in a user needs assessment project, you will learn how the step applies to solving a current problem at The Training Team.

The Training Team prepares custom training materials and services for other organizations. For years, it provided primarily printed training workbooks, tutorials, and other materials to its clients. However, an increasing number of clients are now requesting Web-based training courses for their workers. The Training Team has responded to these requests by offering Web-based materials as an alternative or supplement to printed training materials. Let's meet some of the employees of The Training Team:

- **Lindsey Dell** is a training course designer and developer. She is part of a small group at The Training Team who interview clients to learn about their training needs. Lindsey's group also designs training curriculum and materials to address those needs, and prepares workbooks, tutorial material, and some Web-based training for clients.

- **Sarita Oeste** provides technical support and some programming services to The Training Team staff. She is responsible for network administration and maintains the company's application software for sales processing, billing, course registration, and accounting transactions.

- **Margaret Rose** is a relatively new employee at The Training Team. Margaret provides desktop support to employees, and she has some experience with project management and user needs assessment from a position at a previous employer.

- **Fred Hoh** is the company president. He has identified a potential problem with the way The Training Team prepares training material for delivery on the Web. Fred has assembled an assessment project team of Margaret, Lindsey, and Sarita to discuss the Web development problem.

Step 1: Understand the End User's and the Organization's Goals

Before support analysts can recommend new computer products and services, they must develop an understanding of the individual purchaser's objectives as well as the organization's goals. Many medium to large organizations have a strategic business plan or mission statement that describes the goals and objectives of the organization. Some organizations also have business plans devoted specifically to information technology. If a business plan, mission statement, or IT master plan is available, it can serve as useful background material for a support analyst at the beginning of a project. If these documents are not available, support analysts can interview managers, supervisors, and individual purchasers to learn about their vision, goals, and future plans.

Regardless of whether support analysts obtain the information through written documents or interviews, they should learn the answers to the following questions:

- What are the goals of the organization, department, or individual purchaser that will affect the need for computer products or services?

- Is the organization for-profit or not-for-profit?

- What plans does the organization have to grow or expand?

- What is the organization's attitude about technology?

- Does the organization have a history of successful experiences with adopting changes in technology?

- What is the organization's current budget for computer systems and services?

- Does the organization's staff or the individual purchaser have the experience and expertise to operate, maintain, and support a computer system?

The purpose of these questions is to understand the big picture—the environment and culture into which the future system or service will fit. Growth forecasts and expansion plans are especially important to consider during the assessment process. The solution an analyst might recommend to an organization that is growing 5 to 10 percent per year would probably be very different from the solutions he or she would recommend to an organization that expects to grow 25 to 50 percent per year. Similarly, a smaller organization or an individual purchaser might not be able to operate, maintain, or support a sophisticated system with a lot of features and flexibility; a more straightforward package might be a better choice.

CASE STUDY: THE TRAINING TEAM WEB DEVELOPMENT PROJECT

In a preliminary meeting with the Web development project team, company president Fred Hoh gave his perspective on the company's problem with developing Web-based training materials. He told the project team that the number of requests for these materials has been increasing, and he expects that trend to continue. At some point soon, the sales of Web-based materials will exceed those of printed materials. Fred noted that clients seem to be delighted with Lindsey's course materials and the results produced by her coworkers on the design and development team.

Fred went on to say that the bottleneck in Web-based projects appears to be getting the training modules programmed and operational on The Training Team's Web site after they are designed. Because Sarita Oeste has some experience with HTML and JavaScript, she has done the programming for the Web-based projects. However, her primary responsibilities are network administration and technical support, so the time she has available to develop training materials is limited. As a consequence, a backlog of Web programming projects currently exists. In addition, Sarita often feels that she is stealing time away from her other responsibilities when she is working on a training module programming project.

Fred went into detail about the nature of this problem for Margaret's benefit, since she is a relatively new employee. He asked Margaret to lead a needs assessment project team to analyze the Web development bottleneck problem because of her previous needs analysis and project management experience. Fred closed by saying that he did not have any preconceived ideas about how to solve this problem. But he felt that because of the industry trend to Web-based delivery of training, The Training Team needed to become more responsive to client needs in order to remain competitive. The project team spent a few minutes brainstorming various options, including hiring a Web development programmer to work with Sarita to implement projects, outsourcing the programming projects to a software development company, using project management software to increase the productivity of development projects, and finding a replacement for Sarita so she could devote more of her time to Web development programming.

Step 2: Understand the Decision Criteria and Constraints

Support analysts also need to understand the criteria an organization will use to make decisions on proposed solutions. Although analysts usually recommend solutions to end users or managers rather than deciding on a solution themselves, the more support analysts understand about the decision criteria, the more they can focus on realistic alternatives.

Support analysts need to clarify what is feasible, or possible, in terms of time, money, and technology. A **feasibility study** is an investigation into the economic, operational, technological, and timeline constraints that will impact a user needs analysis and assessment project. Analysts typically consider several types of feasibility issues, including:

- *Economic feasibility*—What budget constraints will influence the final decision?

- *Operational feasibility*—With what other systems or procedures does this system need to mesh? What personnel will be required to operate this system? Do the personnel have the necessary knowledge, skills, and abilities?

- *Technological feasibility*—What limitations or constraints does the organization's current technology impose on possible solutions?

- *Timeline feasibility*—Do time constraints rule out some potential alternatives?

Support analysts also need to understand the business culture factors that will influence the final decision. Does the organization pride itself on doing business with well-known and reputable vendors, so that solutions from established vendors should be considered more seriously than those offered by relatively smaller, unknown vendors? Does the organization try to stay on the leading edge of technology, or does it take a relatively conservative view of new, and perhaps untried, products? Are users and managers comfortable with the introduction of new technology? What priority does the organization place on vendor support? For example, some organizations rely on their own support staff and don't need extensive outside support, while others are very dependent on vendor support. The answers to feasibility and business culture questions help define the criteria and constraints that support analysts must consider in order to make a recommendation about an appropriate solution.

ON THE WEB

David Allen has developed a project planning guide that lists several kinds of questions an analyst can ask about the feasibility of a project (**www.projectkickstart.com/ downloads/project-planning-checklist.cfm**).

CASE STUDY: THE TRAINING TEAM WEB DEVELOPMENT PROJECT

The user support specialist, Margaret, inquired about the financial resources available to solve the Web development problem. Fred indicated that no budget had been allocated, but that the problem clearly needed to be solved, and the sooner the better. He said there is currently a backlog of promised development projects. He expressed the belief that if The Training Team couldn't respond to requests for Web-based materials in a timely way that it would lose business to competitors and eventually go out of business.

Margaret also asked about the time frame for the project. Fred indicated that he would like the project team to make a recommendation to him and the other managers in two to three weeks. Lindsey, the design and development team member, asked whether it would be feasible to hire someone either to do Web development or to replace Sarita so she could handle the programming. Fred indicated that if hiring someone was the best solution, he would consider that option, but he expressed concern about finding a new employee who could join the company and be productive in a short period of time.

Sarita asked whether the company had ever considered adopting a Web development software package to develop the online training materials. She said the HTML and JavaScript programs she had been writing were probably not the most productive way to develop Web-based training modules. Lindsey said they had discussed Web development software tools in the past, but no one had the time to learn a new software package.

Step 3: Define the Problem Clearly

The problems user support staff attempt to tackle in assessment projects come in a variety of forms and sizes. Some are well defined, while others are not. Support analysts who work on user needs assessment projects must dig for details in order to identify the root or underlying problem they are trying to solve. Not all problems are technical; some "computer" problems turn out to be organizational, personnel, workflow, user-training, office politics, management, or resource problems. Experienced analysts look beyond the obvious symptoms of a problem to search for its root causes, whatever they may be.

Throughout a needs assessment project, a support analyst should continually ask the question, *"Do I really understand the dimensions of the problem I'm trying to solve for this user?"* For example, an end user may complain that the accounting application he uses does not work and that he wants to replace it with a new one that is more flexible. The user may have correctly concluded that he needs new software. However, the problem could also be related to the way the existing program is configured. To recommend replacing expensive hardware or software when the real problem is something else can be a costly mistake. Therefore, clearly defining the root or underlying problem is critical to any user needs analysis.

CASE STUDY: THE TRAINING TEAM WEB DEVELOPMENT PROJECT

At the next meeting of the needs assessment group, Margaret initiated a discussion that she hoped would lead to a better definition of the problem with Web module development projects. She asked whether the problem was a technical one that could be solved with better technology and more effective software, a staffing problem that could be solved by adding programming resources, or a project management problem that could be solved by adopting better coordination and supervision, and perhaps using project management software. The team discussed each of these perspectives on the problem and agreed that it was unlikely to be solved by better technology or improved project management methods. However, the team members suggested that Margaret talk with two other managers at The Training Team to get their perspectives before reaching any conclusions.

- **Zed Langers** is the coordinator of the design and development team, and Lindsey's supervisor. He has extensive curriculum development experience and a background in corporate training.

- **Naseem Rhea** is the head of the accounting and information technology group at The Training Team; she is Sarita and Margaret's supervisor. Naseem's background is in office management, but she has become very knowledgeable about technology during several years of employment at The Training Team.

Step 4: Identify the Roles of Stakeholders

Stakeholders are the participants in an end-user needs analysis and assessment project who might gain or lose from its success or failure. Four kinds of stakeholders are important in a needs analysis project: end users, managers, technical support staff, and the needs assessment analyst. Some stakeholders participate in every step of an assessment project. Others may contribute their expertise and support in only one or a few of the project steps and then leave the project, perhaps to rejoin it at a later step.

End Users

Support analysts should learn which users will be affected by a project. What are their job responsibilities? What computer experience do they have? What training have they received? What is their background? How long have they worked for the organization? What role will they play in the project?

Managers

After identifying end users and their roles, support analysts should identify the manager who will be involved in the decision to purchase a computer system or service, or implement another solution. This manager is sometimes called the project sponsor. In some cases, the project sponsor may be a board of directors in a nonprofit agency or an executive committee in a for-profit company. In any case, support analysts should determine who will make the final decision and what computer knowledge and experience the decision makers bring to the process.

If the final decision makers on a project lack technical expertise, a support analyst may need to spend project time to educate them so they can make an intelligent decision.

The management perspective is vital for the success of any assessment project. Managers provide important information about the background and priority of the problem, insights into possible solutions, and support for a project—as well as financial and decision-making expertise. Experienced support analysts know that one of the biggest mistakes they can make in a needs assessment project is to ignore the management perspective.

Information Technology or Technical Support Staff

If an organization has an IT or technical support staff, these stakeholders are often important participants in a needs assessment project. IT staff members may be ultimately responsible for installing, configuring, maintaining, and troubleshooting the solution a support analyst recommends. They may have important perspectives on possible alternate solutions and technical feasibility.

Support Analysts

Support analysts who coordinate and conduct needs analysis projects are obviously key participants in the process. As important as it is to understand the roles of other participants, analysts also need to clarify their own role. Is the analysts' role to assist existing company staff with the needs assessment, to perform the analysis and describe the pros and cons of various alternatives, to make a recommendation, or to make the final decision? How much analyst time is the organization willing to allocate to the project, and how will that time commitment affect the analysts' work on this project as well as other work responsibilities?

In some needs assessment projects, one or more vendor representatives may be key project participants. Vendor representatives can play a role if they have insights into the problem or will provide part of the eventual solution. Obviously a vendor's role may be limited by a bias toward his or her own products or services.

Support analysts who work on a large project that involves several users, managers, and IT or technical support staff may develop a brief written profile that summarizes information about each key participant in a project. A profile can include contact information such as phone numbers and email address, position title, background, primary job functions, and notes on each person's interest in the outcome of the project.

CASE STUDY: THE TRAINING TEAM WEB DEVELOPMENT PROJECT

During the initial meeting of the assessment group, Margaret had started making a list of stakeholders in the project. She knew about the current roles of Lindsey and Sarita in Web development projects. But now she also added Zed, the design and development coordinator, and Naseem, the head of the IT group, to her list of project stakeholders.

Margaret asked Fred whether the assessment team should include one of The Training Team's clients as a representative of its user community. Fred thought the idea was an interesting one, but said that their clients were focused on the end product of a development project and would probably not have much input into how the development work got accomplished. And he noted that a smaller needs assessment group could probably develop a recommendation faster than a larger one. Fred instead suggested that Margaret simply interview a client to get feedback on The Training Team's process and performance. Margaret then asked who would eventually make the final decision about the project team's recommendation. Fred said he would make the final decision after discussing it with other managers whose groups would be affected.

Step 5: Identify Sources of Information

Support analysts must also determine the sources of information necessary to complete a project successfully. The following list contains several potentially useful sources of information for a needs assessment project:

- Interviews with end users and managers

- Surveys or questionnaires completed by end users who will be most affected

- Procedure manuals that detail how to operate the current system (if one exists)

- Direct observation of the existing system

- Forms used for input into the existing system

- Reports created using the existing system

- Problem-report histories or help desk logs for the existing system

- Diagrams of workflow

- Equipment inventories

- Reports and recommendations from consultants, vendors, or auditors who have studied the existing system

Analysts often start with a checklist of resources to help them gather information about the system or situation they have been asked to analyze. They then add to or subtract from the checklist as needed.

CASE STUDY: THE TRAINING TEAM WEB DEVELOPMENT PROJECT

Margaret told the assessment team she would like some time to think about the Web development problem and the possible solutions. On her way back to her desk, she began to compile a list of information-gathering steps she wanted to undertake next:

1. Interview Zed and Naseem to get their perspectives on the backlog problem and possible solutions.

2.   Review the results of a recent Web-based training project.

3.   Interview a representative client of the company.

Margaret sent an email to Lindsey and Sarita to ask for a copy of the design specifications for a recent Web-based training project. She also asked Fred if she could interview the client for whom the recent training module was developed.

Step 6: Develop an Understanding of the Existing System

During the investigation phase, support analysts must learn as much as possible about the existing system—whether it is manual or computer-based. In this step, analysts collect and examine important documents (examples of forms, reports, and documentation), interview key participants (users, managers, and technical support staff), observe the operation of the existing system, and develop a clear understanding of what the existing system does and how it works.

Analysts should organize the information they collect so they can easily locate what they need. Analysts often use a project notebook or file folders to keep records of various forms, reports, meetings, and interviews.

 One way to organize project information is according to the steps in the analysis process described in this chapter.

The primary objective of this step is to build a model that describes the existing system. A **model** is a narrative description or graphic diagram, such as a flowchart or an organization chart, that represents a business activity (such as paper workflow), a computer system, or a network. Sometimes both a written description and diagrams are used. Analysts can also create a model by using analytic and planning tools, such as software designed specifically for systems analysts.

ON THE WEB

A popular tool support analysts use to diagram a model of an existing business system is Microsoft Visio. To learn more about Visio and take a tour of the product, visit the Visio Web site (**visio.microsoft.com**).

A shareware product that has similar capabilities is Novagraph's Chartist (**www.novagraph.com**), which offers a free 30-day trial copy.

After constructing a model, analysts can share it with other project participants to make sure the model accurately represents the existing system. Sharing a model with users, managers, and other project participants often uncovers misunderstandings about the capabilities or features of the existing system.

At the end of this step, support analysts should be able to answer *"yes"* to the following questions:

- Do I understand the existing system well enough to explain to other participants how it operates?

- Do I understand which features of the existing system users like?

- Do I understand the problems users have identified with the existing system?

Without an understanding of each of these aspects of the existing system or situation, analysts may be unprepared to consider alternatives with which to replace or repair it.

CASE STUDY: THE TRAINING TEAM WEB DEVELOPMENT PROJECT

During that week, Margaret interviewed Zed and Naseem. They both expressed a need to solve the Web development backlog problem for the future of the company. However, neither ventured an opinion about the best way to do it. Naseem said she could give up a little more of Sarita's time to work on the current development backlog. However, she warned that Sarita has other responsibilities that, in the long run, would limit the time she could spend on programming projects. Zed indicated that his design and development team members were often frustrated because the programming work on Web pages frequently lagged the design and curriculum development work on a module. He said his team wasted time waiting for a Web development module to be programmed so that it could be tested and implemented.

During the week, Margaret had an opportunity to review the sample Web-based training module she had requested, and she studied the design specifications that Sarita used to write the HTML code for the module. When she contacted the client for whom the module was developed, the client offered effusive praise for the quality of the training module, but complained that the project had been delivered after the agreed-upon date—and only after several calls to Fred to urge that it be completed promptly.

Step 7: Investigate Alternatives to the Existing System

In previous steps, the analyst's goal was to understand as much as possible about the existing system, including its purposes, features, users, advantages, disadvantages, problems, and other important characteristics. In this step, the analyst's attention shifts to ways to fix the problems with the current system or situation. Analysts often consider several kinds of alternatives:

- *Additional resources*—In order to operate effectively, the existing system may need additional resources such as personnel, equipment, budget allocation, time commitment, or a higher priority for attention by the organization's staff and management.

- *Changes to existing resources*—The existing system may be able to meet the needs of the organization if changes are made to it. Common changes to existing systems include reconfiguring software and identifying additional training that may make users more productive.

- *Upgrades*—An organization may need to upgrade hardware or software components to improve processing speed, increase storage capacity, ensure compatibility, or add new features that address identified problems.

- *New hardware*—New hardware may be necessary to address capacity constraints, run software efficiently, or operate new software with features that solve end users' problems.

- *New software*—New software may be necessary to address problems, increase user productivity, or expand business opportunities.

When developing a list of alternatives to consider, analysts often investigate the tools used by comparable users who perform similar tasks successfully in other organizations. These solutions may not solve all the identified problems, but an analyst should investigate them nonetheless, rather than risk spending scarce resources to reinvent a solution someone else has already devised. As you learned in Chapter 8, trade magazines targeted at a specific industry are often a good source of information about products that address specific needs. Articles in trade publications may report on successful computer system implementations in similar organizations. Some trade magazines publish articles that evaluate and compare technology options. Finally, advertisements in trade periodicals often identify vendors that supply hardware, software, and services aimed at a specialized market niche.

A support analyst looking for software for a specific business, such as a real estate company or a veterinary clinic, might also find useful leads online.

CASE STUDY: THE TRAINING TEAM WEB DEVELOPMENT PROJECT

At the next meeting of the assessment team, Margaret shared her recent findings with the other team members. She invited Zed and Naseem to join the group for this meeting to add their management perspective. The expanded group concluded that the development backlog problem was not a hardware or project management problem. The discussion turned to staffing as a solution. The staffing alternatives appeared to be the following:

1. Hire an additional programmer to work on Web module programming projects.

2. Hire a technical support worker to replace Sarita, who could then be assigned to work on Web development projects.

3. Outsource Web programming projects to a software developer that specializes in Web-based projects.

As supervisor of information technology, Naseem described the difficulty of hiring an additional programmer in a short time frame and getting them to be productive quickly.

She also reported that outsourced programming projects are very expensive and pose difficult timeline and coordination challenges. In response to the second alternative, Sarita indicated that she was personally more interested in network administration and technical support than in Web programming, and would prefer an alternative that reduced her role in programming projects. She added that, for the short term, she would be willing to continue to program training modules to help reduce the backlog.

Margaret was concerned that the team was about out of options but then Naseem and Sarita again raised the alternative of purchasing and adopting a Web development software tool. Naseem and Sarita reported that they had researched this segment of the software market and found several packages, such as Adobe Dreamweaver, that were designed to develop and maintain Web sites. This kind of tool could serve as a development platform for The Training Team to adopt for future projects. Naseem described Dreamweaver as a higher-level development tool compared with HTML and JavaScript. She said this kind of tool could make a Web developer more productive and potentially reduce both the time to program a training module and the current development backlog. The project team agreed to add a fourth alternative:

4. Acquire and adopt a Web development software tool for future training module projects.

Step 8: Develop a Model of the Proposed Solution

Once analysts have completed the project preparation and investigation phases of a needs assessment project, they reach the decision phase. With a clear description of the problem, an understanding of the existing system, and a list of possible alternatives, analysts can develop a model of the proposed solution to recommend to users and management.

The model that support analysts build often includes a narrative description of the proposed system or solution and one or more graphic aids to help users and managers understand the proposal. The narrative should include a description of each of the alternatives the analysts considered as well as the pros and cons of each alternative. The model should answer the questions, *"Why is the proposed solution an improvement over the present system?"* and *"Why is it the best available alternative?"*

A final decision on which of the various alternatives to recommend may be obvious. One solution may be clearly an **optimal solution**, one that is the most feasible, has the lowest cost, and offers the most benefits. However, cost is frequently a major concern, and the best solution may be the most expensive. In this case, the analyst may recommend a **satisficing solution**, one that solves the problem in a reasonable way, but is not necessarily the optimal solution.

When one solution is not obvious, or when legally required to do so, analysts may do a cost-benefit analysis of several options to help them choose from among the alternatives. A **cost-benefit analysis** compares the expense of a potential project solution with the solution's expected payoffs. A cost-benefit analysis often looks like a balance sheet (a sheet of paper divided into two columns) with the costs of a proposed system or solution on one side and the benefits on the other. Later in this chapter, you will look more closely at the factors to consider in a cost-benefit analysis.

A cost-benefit analysis is not an exact science. For a cost-benefit analysis to be most useful, alternatives in the same general category and with the same features should be compared. For most small projects, a detailed cost-benefit analysis may not be necessary, but even an informal analysis will increase the likelihood that analysts have considered the significant costs and benefits of each alternative.

When a needs assessment project results in a decision to purchase a new computer, end users' needs should drive the specifications for the new system. End users frequently believe hardware is the most crucial component of a system; however, when users' needs determine the specifications, software solutions should be considered paramount. Software requirements should drive the hardware selection. Only when software is being specified for an already-existing hardware platform should the software selection depend on the hardware configuration.

CASE STUDY: THE TRAINING TEAM WEB DEVELOPMENT PROJECT

Margaret prepared for the next meeting of the assessment team by researching the capabilities of Dreamweaver and other Web development tools. She found that the acquisition cost for these packages is around $400 per license. When the group reassembled, Margaret reported on her research. The group agreed a Web development tool seemed like a promising option; however, several issues with this proposed solution remained:

- Who would use the development tool?

- How would they learn to use it?

- What would be the total cost of this solution?

- And how fast could it happen?

Margaret then related a comment Zed had made in their initial interview: His curriculum designers often waste time awaiting the delivery of a programming project. She asked if any of his group might be interested in learning Dreamweaver as a development tool. Zed said he remembered that a couple of his curriculum designers had expressed an interest in learning Dreamweaver or a similar product as a training module prototyping tool. He offered to discuss whether they would be interested in learning Dreamweaver as a professional development opportunity. Lindsey said she might even be interested in learning Dreamweaver.

Margaret reported that her research into Dreamweaver had turned up several tutorials and trade books that could help Zed's staff members learn to use the product at a very reasonable cost.

She concluded that she would write a draft of a report to Fred and the other managers that recommended the use of Dreamweaver by a couple of members of Zed's design and development staff on future Web development projects. The team suggested several items for a proposed budget, including software licenses, training materials, and the cost of staff time to learn the new tool. Margaret felt that a project report was beginning to take shape.

383

Step 9: Make a Build-Versus-Buy Decision

A significant decision for many organizations is the **build-versus-buy decision**—that is, whether to build a custom solution or purchase one off the shelf. The build-versus-buy decision can apply to building computer hardware, developing software, and providing services. In most cases, however, the build-versus-buy decision applies to software and services. Although many projects result in a decision to purchase off-the-shelf software, the alternative of custom-developed software may better meet an end user's or an organization's exact requirements. For other organizations, acquiring a turnkey system is more appropriate. A **turnkey system** includes an integrated package of hardware, software, and support services purchased from a single vendor, and may include a combination of off-the-shelf and customizable components. Table 9-1 summarizes some of the advantages and disadvantages of building versus buying a system.

Building a Custom Solution	Buying an Off-the-Shelf Solution
• System can be custom designed to meet end-user needs; it can be tailored to exact specifications • System may provide strategic business advantages over competitors	• Lower acquisition cost due to market competition • Faster implementation • Better documentation may be available • Standard user interfaces and components • Fewer bugs due to more exhaustive testing • Ongoing technical support may be available

Table 9-1 Advantages of building versus buying a solution

Developing a complete custom system or solution is prohibitively expensive for many organizations, especially those that do not have an in-house programming staff. Even for organizations with staff members who have programming expertise, the costs of custom software development often outweigh the benefits when reasonable preprogrammed (off-the-shelf) alternatives are available. Some off-the-shelf software also includes features that permit a limited degree of customization to meet a purchaser's specific and perhaps unique needs.

Another financial decision in which a support analyst may become involved is buy-versus-lease. Especially in situations in which the purchase of equipment of substantial value is involved, an organization may consider leasing as an option to outright purchase. Because the details of buy-versus-lease options (and the pros and cons of each) vary considerably and can be complex, buy-versus-lease is not normally a decision a support analyst makes, but is a decision properly left to an organization's financial officer or advisor.

384

CASE STUDY: THE TRAINING TEAM WEB DEVELOPMENT PROJECT

At their next meeting, the needs assessment project group reviewed Margaret's draft proposal. The group agreed with the recommendation to purchase software licenses and to use an in-house resource (designer/developers in Zed's group) to learn to use the new software. However, given the current backlog of Web training module programming, the group suggested that the staff members in Zed's group who expressed an interest in Dreamweaver be sent to an intensive industry seminar at Adobe Software or a third-party training vendor to get them up-to-speed more quickly. Although the cost of this option would add substantially to the total project cost, the future of The Training Team seemed to be riding on the outcome of this project. Margaret said she would revise the draft budget to include the seminars and travel costs before presenting it to Fred.

At the final meeting of the needs assessment team, Margaret presented the group's recommendations and budget to Fred. He said that he and the other managers would discuss the proposed solution, but that he was inclined to support it because it fit well with the company's culture, mission, and resources. Fred thanked Margaret and the team members for their leadership and service on the assessment team, and they celebrated the successful completion of their project.

Each needs assessment project is unique, which means that the steps in this chapter should be tailored to each specific situation. In some instances, budget constraints may limit the possible options that can be considered. In other situations, more subjective factors, such as a long-term relationship with a vendor, may outweigh other factors.

Needs analysis and assessment projects can be used for purposes other than selecting hardware, software, or network systems. Some projects are focused on problems that have organizational rather than technological solutions, such as a training program or redesigned position descriptions.

A print resource on needs analysis and assessment is: Kavita Gupta, *A Practical Guide to Needs Assessment*, 2nd edition. San Francisco; Pfeiffer (Wiley), 2007.

ON THE WEB

To learn more about needs analysis and assessment projects, complete an online tutorial on the National Oceanic and Atmospheric Administration (NOAA) Web site (**www.csc.noaa.gov/needs**).

Needs Analysis and Assessment Tools

The needs analysis steps presented in the previous section mentioned several tools that analysts may use as aids in the assessment process. The next part of this chapter describes some of these tools (which are listed in Figure 9-2) in more detail.

Some of these tools are relatively easy for analysts to create, whereas others require more extensive effort and, in some cases, special software.

 Two tools you learned about in Chapter 8 are also useful to analysts who do needs assessments: benchmarks and weighted point comparisons. These tools are especially helpful when analysts need to compare two or more products, services, or approaches to solving a problem.

- Project charter
- Cost-benefit analysis
- Data-collection instruments
- Charts and diagrams
- Prototyping software
- Project management software

Project Charter

Figure 9-2   Needs assessment tools

All stakeholders should understand basic information about a needs analysis and assessment project. One way to ensure a common understanding is to develop a project charter. A **project charter** is a short narrative that answers basic questions, such as:

- What are the objectives of the assessment project? What will be achieved if the project is successful?

- What is the scope of the needs assessment project? What is included in the project and, sometimes more important, what is excluded?

- What methods will be used to achieve the project's goals? What tools and resources will be used?

- Who are the key project participants? What are their roles?

- What are the project deliverables? (A **deliverable** is the end result of an assessment project, such as a written report or a recommendation to purchase, modify, upgrade, or build a system, or to acquire a service.)

- What are the major steps in the needs assessment project?

- What is the project timeline? What are the significant project milestones that indicate whether the project is ahead of or behind schedule?

- How will the project's success be measured?

A charter need not be a detailed document, but rather should present a high-level overview of the project. Some organizations use a project request form (more like a work order) instead of a charter, but its contents are similar to a charter and it serves a similar purpose. An important step in the adoption of a project charter is a sign-off by major shareholders, including the project manager and project sponsor (this is usually the manager with decision-making authority over the project and in whose budget the cost of the project appears). The form shown in Figure 9-3 is an example of a simple project charter template that you can modify or use as is, depending on the needs of a project.

Project Charter

Project name:

Membership:

Contact person:

Purpose:

Steps:	Deliverables/Success Measures:

Project scope:

Implications for other projects:

Figure 9-3   Project charter template

ON THE WEB

To learn more about project charters, read an article, "How to Write a Project Charter," by Michael D. Taylor, who offers courses on project management (**www.projectmgt.com/Files/Article-How%20to%20Write%20a%20 Project%20Charter.pdf**).

An alternate project charter template in a narrative format is available at **www.projectmanagementdocs.com/templates/project-charter.html**.

You can also read a project charter prepared by the University of Minnesota's Library to select a help desk software package (**wiki.lib.umn.edu/wupl/Staff. ProjectCharters/hd-charter.pdf**).

Cost-Benefit Analysis

As you learned earlier in this chapter, a cost-benefit analysis is a tool to help identify the costs and the corresponding benefits of a proposed problem solution. A cost-benefit analysis is often prepared in the form of a side-by-side comparison or balance sheet that lists costs on one side of the sheet and benefits on the other.

Table 9-2 lists items that might appear in a cost-benefit balance sheet. As the table shows, costs can be categorized as either **acquisition costs** (whether built or purchased) or **operating costs** (ongoing costs). Benefits can include reduced expenses, increased revenue opportunities, and intangible benefits.

Costs of Alternative	Benefits of Alternative
Acquisition costs	**Reduced expenses**
• Purchase computer equipment	• Less expensive hardware and software
• Purchase software packages or licenses	• Fewer personnel required to operate system
• Software development costs (programming)	• Lower manufacturing or inventory costs
• Purchase computer services	• More efficient use of staff time or equipment (productivity)
• Purchase supplies and materials	
• Time to implement alternative	• Faster response to client needs
• Administrative costs	
• Unanticipated costs	

Table 9-2 Cost-benefit balance sheet (*continues*)

(continued)

Costs of Alternative	Benefits of Alternative
Operating costs	**Increased revenue opportunities**
• Equipment lease or rental	• New products or services for clients
• Personnel (salaries and benefits)	• Expanded markets (new clients)
• Computer supplies and materials	• Increased volume of business transactions
• Hardware and software maintenance	• Ability to raise prices due to higher quality of products or services
• User training	
	Intangible benefits
	• Ability to take advantage of new technology
	• Improved image of the organization
	• Improved service to clients
	• System easier to learn and use
	• Higher employee morale

Table 9-2   Cost-benefit balance sheet

The goal of a cost-benefit analysis is to weigh the benefits of proposed alternatives against the costs of each alternative. However, cost-benefit analyses are not always easy to do because some benefits may be difficult to quantify. **Intangible benefits** are expected results from a project that are difficult to quantify or measure. Although increased user productivity may be measurable (tangible), increased employee morale is intangible. Analysts should try to produce a best-guess estimate of intangible benefits of various alternatives, if possible.

Experienced analysts recognize that if most of the benefits of a proposed alternative are intangible, and if few quantifiable benefits will reduce expenses, improve productivity, or increase revenue, they should seriously consider other alternatives.

Companies with a longer-term perspective on investments may include estimated data for more than one year in a cost-benefit analysis. Such companies may choose to invest resources in a project for which the costs outweigh the benefits in the first year because the benefits pay off in subsequent years (often due to cost savings over a longer term). Especially for technology projects whose first-year costs include the purchase of expensive equipment or software, the cost savings may not be realized until the second year or even later. In these cases, companies are interested in the **payback period**, which is the amount of time it takes for the benefits of a project to exceed its costs.

ON THE WEB

For a more in-depth understanding of cost-benefit analyses with an example, read an article about this tool at the Mind Tools Web site (**www.mindtools.com/pages/article/newTED_08.htm**).

Data-Collection Instruments

Several steps in the needs analysis process depend on analysts' abilities to collect relevant information. When analysts gather information, they often use sources such as those summarized in Figure 9-4. The sections that follow contain a brief overview of each data-collection instrument.

- Input forms
- Output forms
- Procedure documentation
- Operating or problem logs
- Interviews and questionnaires
- Direct observation

Figure 9-4 Data-collection instruments

Input Forms

An **input form** (sometimes called a **source document**) is a paper document or display screen used to collect information about a business transaction. Because business transaction processing is the purpose of many computer systems, input forms are often important sources of information about an organization's business activities. For example, a copy shop might use a form like the sample shown in Figure 9-5 to collect information about an order for each client. In a needs analysis project focused on automating order processing at the copy shop, a support analyst would need to understand how workers use the form and what problems occur when they do.

ORDER   Date _____

the print works
1473 Main St.
Stamford, CT 06902
PHONE 555-2697
FAX 555-2698

Sold to _____

Paid By ☐ Cash ☐ Check # _____

FAX Send _____ pgs Receive _____ pgs	
Photocopies	
Taken By: **TOTAL**	

Figure 9-5   Example of an input form for a copy shop order

Output Forms

Output forms contain the results of a business transaction or process. Examples include a sales receipt from a grocery store or restaurant, a paycheck stub, and a report card at the end of a school term. In the copy shop example, once a worker fills in the input form shown in Figure 9-5 and records the prices of each item, the form also serves as an output form, or receipt, for the client.

Procedure Documentation

Written instructions about how to perform a business transaction or follow a routine organizational procedure are called **procedure documentation**. Procedure documentation is written for an organization's workers. In the copy shop example, procedure documentation might describe the steps to fill out the order form accurately for various types of copy orders, how to price each item on the form, what to do with the form after it is filled out, and where to file the form when the transaction is completed.

Procedure documentation is often used to train new workers or to answer questions about how to handle infrequent tasks.

Operating or Problem Logs

A **log** is a list of events or activities recorded in the sequence in which the events occurred. Logs can be used to record routine, periodic information about events that occur normally, such as when the hard drive on a PC was backed up. Logs can also be used to capture unusual events, errors, problems, shortages, or complaints. Analysts can make use of logs as a supplement to direct observation to collect information about business activities.

Interviews and Questionnaires

Analysts often use interviews and questionnaires to collect relevant information from end users about the work they do, the problems they encounter, and how an existing or proposed computer system might affect their work. The advantage of a face-to-face interview is that the interviewer can ask probing questions, where appropriate, to learn the details of issues that are of special interest. The ability to probe is especially useful because it is frequently difficult to anticipate every possible question one might like to ask on a printed questionnaire. However, analysts may need to obtain information from many users; therefore, they often use a questionnaire to save time. An alternative when many end users are potentially impacted is a **focus group**, which is a small, representative group of selected users. A focus group often generates ideas that may not occur in a one-on-one interview, as focus group members interact with each other.

To ensure that they have effective questions, analysts who design interview and survey questions may ask other analysts for help. Questions designed by a team are often better than those written by one investigator. Another strategy is to field-test questions on a small group of users who can give feedback on which questions were confusing or difficult to answer.

ON THE WEB

To learn more about interview and questionnaire methods for user surveys, visit a Georgia Tech Web site that describes in greater detail how to design questionnaires and interview questions (**www.cc.gatech.edu/classes/cs6751_97_winter/ Topics/quest-design**).

Direct Observation

Support analysts can often gain critical insights into end-user needs by simply watching users work. Notes taken by an analyst during direct observation can be a powerful method of collecting data in situations in which procedure documentation, questionnaires, interviews, and other forms of data collection aren't possible, or as a supplement to other methods.

Data-collection instruments help analysts find useful, relevant information about an existing system that they can then use not only to evaluate how the system functions, but also to determine its strengths and weaknesses.

Charts and Diagrams

A chart or diagram can illustrate the flow of information within an organization, relationships between workers, or the connection between parts of a networked information processing system. Because they are visual, charts and diagrams are often easier for users to read and understand than lengthy narratives written in technical language.

Analysts create charts and diagrams either manually or with a variety of graphic design tools. Some of these tools are highly specialized and take training to use effectively; books on systems analysis describe these tools in detail. Other graphic design tools are more accessible and allow analysts with a minimum of experience to create charts and diagrams. Analysts can use relatively simple tools to create two common types of charts: flowcharts and I-P-O charts.

Flowcharts

A **flowchart** is a schematic drawing that uses symbols to represent the parts of a computer system or the steps in a procedure. In a flowchart, rectangular boxes often represent departments in an organization, nodes on a network, or processing tasks that a worker performs. Diamond-shaped symbols usually represent decision points or questions that need to be answered. Lines connect various symbols in a flowchart to illustrate how the parts of the diagram are related or the sequence of processing steps.

ON THE WEB

In addition to the Visio 2010 and Chartist tools described earlier, you can view example flowcharts and a video comparison of SmartDraw and Visio (**www.smartdraw.com/videos/specials/visio/movie.htm**). You can also download a trial version of the SmartDraw flowcharting tool from that site.

I-P-O Charts

Most manual procedures or computer processing tasks can be described as some combination of input, processing, and output steps. An **I-P-O chart** is a diagramming tool that represents the input, processing, and output steps required to perform a task. An I-P-O chart answers three fundamental questions about a procedure that a user or computer performs:

- *Input*—Where do I get the information with which to work?

- *Processing*—What tasks do I perform to process or transform the information?

- *Output*—What happens to the information when I am finished?

Figure 9-6 shows a simple I-P-O chart that describes a procedure in a brokerage firm to prepare a stock portfolio report for a client.

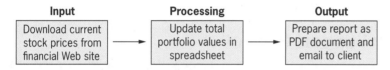

Figure 9-6   I-P-O chart to prepare a stock portfolio report

ON THE WEB

RFFlow–a vendor of professional software for preparing charts, diagrams, and flowcharts–provides examples commonly used in needs analysis projects (**www.rff.com/samples.htm**). RFFlow's process mapping chart type is similar to the I-P-O chart. Click on the links on the samples page to view these tools and enlarge the images. A 30-day trial of RFFlow's product is available.

Prototyping Software

A **prototype** is a working model that support analysts build to let end users experience and evaluate how the finished product of an analysis project will eventually work. The purpose of a prototype is to provide an easy, quick, low-cost way for end users to view the characteristics an operational system will have when one is built.

When an application design project involves software development, prototyping tools can be used to build a working model. For example, programming and database languages such as Microsoft Access, Microsoft Excel, Visual Basic, and JavaScript can be used to build a working prototype of the menus, data input screens, processing steps, output forms and reports, and user interface for a system.

Although prototype systems can give users a realistic preview of how a new system might operate, prototypes usually operate slowly and have limited data storage capacity. These limitations can be reduced or eliminated when a programmer converts a working prototype into a production system written in a programming language.

ON THE WEB

An open source prototyping tool that works with Firefox to create program menus, Web pages, and other user interface mock-ups is Pencil Project (**pencil.evolus.vn/en-US/Home.aspx**).

Managing a User Support Project

User support work can be divided into routine operational tasks, such as staffing a help desk, and special project work. Much of the work a support group performs falls into the category of routine tasks and everyday activities. A **special project**, on the other hand, is a user support task that does not happen regularly. A special project is often based on less well-defined steps and procedures, usually takes longer to accomplish, and is frequently more complex than routine support work. Factors that can contribute to a special project's increased complexity include the involvement of several staff members (perhaps along with external vendors or consultants); a time commitment of several days, weeks, or even months; and substantial expenditures in terms of staff time, equipment, software, supplies, and other resources.

In a user support environment, staff members may be assigned to work on special projects such as:

- Performing a user needs assessment project involving upgrading an organization's PCs
- Selecting and installing a new network server or enterprise-wide application software
- Developing or updating an organization's computer product standards or support policies
- Planning and implementing a new training program
- Selecting and implementing an automated help desk management system
- Developing end-user documentation or a user training session for new software

Depending on their work responsibilities, some support specialists may receive more special project assignments than others. As organizations rely increasingly on teams rather than individual workers to accomplish tasks, the ability to manage and work as part of a project team has become an increasingly important skill.

Project Management Steps

Support specialists who are assigned a special project, such as a user needs assessment, should know the basics of project management, even if they are only a team member. **Project management** is a detailed, step-by-step work plan and process designed to reach a specific goal. Project management usually involves five distinct steps, as shown in Figure 9-7.

Step 1. Project definition

Step 2. Project planning

Step 3. Project implementation

Step 4. Project monitoring

Step 5. Project termination

Figure 9-7 Steps in project management

Step 1: Project Definition

Project definition includes the preliminary work to define the scope of a project, including its goal(s), a tentative project calendar (beginning and ending dates and important due dates), and a project budget. The project definition also identifies the project participants, including users, support staff, technical staff, management, and a project manager (or project lead, or coordinator—the specific title varies). A **project goal** is a specific, measurable end result that is the ultimate target or outcome of a project. The project goal should be very specific and measurable, even if the calendar and budget are rough estimates at this first step. Compare these two goals:

- Improve user satisfaction with help desk services

- Evaluate, select, install, and implement a help desk management software package and begin operation by the first day of the next fiscal year

The first goal is neither specific nor measurable. It does not specify how user satisfaction will be improved or even measured. Ask yourself, *"How will I know that we have achieved this goal?"* For the first goal, the answer is not obvious. The second goal is more specific. It describes the scope of the project (evaluation, selection, installation, implementation), and specifies a measurable result by a specific date. A successful project will result in an operational help desk management package. Although the second goal is more specific, it could be further improved by specifying a timeline, budget limit, level of staff participation, and other project specifics.

Step 2: Project Planning

After a project's scope is carefully defined, project planning activities include dividing the project into specific tasks (or objectives), estimating a time (or duration) for each task, identifying available resources and the cost of each, and assigning resources to tasks. Typical project resources are staff time, budget, space, equipment, supplies, support services, overhead, and management support. During the planning step, the project manager or team defines each project task. A **project task** is a specific activity or objective (outcome) that must be met in order to meet an overall project goal. Examples of tasks include writing a handout for a training session, evaluating three help desk software packages for possible purchase, or installing a DSL modem in four office computers. A **project plan** pulls together all project tasks into one document that answers the questions:

- What tasks will be accomplished?

- What is the sequence of tasks?

- Who will perform each task?

- How long will each task take?

- What resources will each task require?

During the project-planning step, the project schedule (calendar) and costs become more definite. Earlier, during project definition, the project manager may have received information from organizational management or users such as, *"It would be really great if this training session was ready by the second week of next month"* or *"Our drop-dead date for installation of Office 2010 in all offices is the end of the year."* However, until each project task has been identified in detail, assigned to a staff member, and given a time and cost estimate, the project manager cannot make firm delivery commitments. After a thorough project planning process, a project manager should be able to make statements such as, *"If the staff and budget resources we have identified in the project plan are available, we estimate the project can be completed by the second week of next month."* Detailed project planning hones the preliminary estimates of schedule, resources, and costs that were prepared during the project definition step.

When developing time and cost estimates, experienced project managers know that many things can throw a project off its planned schedule. A project's **risk factors** are the unexpected problems that could arise during the life of a project. Risk factors include poor initial estimates of schedule, costs, or resources as well as unexpected incidents that may occur during the project. Common risk factors include a sick team member, a task that takes longer to complete than estimated, a team member who lacks the skills required by the project (or who is unreliable), a hardware component that is unavailable when needed or costs more than expected, and a conflict between two team members over the best way to accomplish a task. Do risk factors such as these mean it is useless to try to manage a project, or that it is better to "wing it" without a project plan? No. Experienced project managers anticipate risks like these and try to estimate their impact on the project. They set preliminary time estimates to complete a task to reflect a completion time somewhere between the minimum, best-case scenario and the maximum, worst-case scenario. They factor in time and resources for unexpected incidents that conspire to throw a project off its plan.

Step 3: Project Implementation

The implementation phase of a project is where the real work gets done. During **project implementation**, team members perform the work on each task or objective according to the schedule in the project plan and their task assignments. The project manager's responsibility shifts during Step 3 from project planning to task coordination. When tasks are interrelated, the project manager often spends time resolving conflicts between staff members over project design or resource allocation, and dealing with the issues and problems that invariably arise during any moderately complex project. During implementation, project managers must also be able to answer questions such as:

- Will the project get completed on time?
- Will the cost of the project stay within its budget?

During implementation, issues of converting from the previous system to the new system become important. The project team needs to make a decision about whether to perform a **direct conversion** (the plug is pulled on the existing system when the new system becomes operational), a **parallel conversion** (both old and new systems are run for a period of time to gain confidence in the new system), a **phased implementation** (workload is removed from the old system in stages as workload is transferred to the new system), or a **pilot project** (the replacement system is used in selected situations to gain confidence that it can be implemented organization-wide). Each of these implementation strategies has strengths, and each poses unique challenges for the project team.

Step 4: Project Monitoring

Parallel to the implementation step is an important project management task: project monitoring or tracking. **Project monitoring** involves assessing the ongoing status of all project tasks to determine whether they are on target in terms of time and budget estimates. Ideally, if every project task came in on time and under budget, monitoring would not be necessary. Because that seldom happens, project managers need to evaluate each project task regularly to determine:

- How much work has been completed?
- What remains to be done?
- How should staff or other resources be adjusted or reassigned?
- What impact will changes in tasks have on the completion date?

 Project managers need to be able to quickly answer questions such as, *"Will this project task, which is behind schedule, benefit from additional staff for some time period?"* and *"How will adding resources affect the project's completion date?"*

Another management responsibility during project monitoring reflects a reality that experienced project managers understand: Projects often change during their implementation to meet new or unexpected demands. In other words, the project's goals or objectives sometimes need to be adjusted. Modifications during a project's implementation are another risk factor that must be managed. **Scope creep** is the tendency for a project to grow or change in unexpected ways, which increases the time frame, resources, and cost required to complete the project.

During project monitoring, managers often implement **change management procedures** to analyze and approve "change orders" and communicate with stakeholders (managers, users, support staff, and vendors) about the impact of changes on schedule and costs. Project managers may periodically prepare project reports to communicate the results of project monitoring and tracking to all stakeholders.

Step 5: Project Termination

The final stage in a project, **project termination**, may include communicating its completion to stakeholders, preparing a final project report, and evaluating the performance of the project and its participants. The project termination activities help project managers and team members to learn from the mistakes of past projects and use their knowledge to improve performance on future projects. During project termination, a manager should answer questions such as:

- What did we learn in the course of this project that will help us better manage future projects?

- How well did the project team members complete their assigned tasks?

Some projects, because of their complexity, lengthy implementation time, sizable resource requirements, team coordination, or large budget, require more project management effort than others. For example, the preparation of a new training session for a software product, such as Windows Live Mail, is a relatively straightforward project. The project plan may be as simple as the example shown in Figure 9-8.

Based on the time estimates in Figure 9-8, a support manager or training supervisor can quickly determine that about a week and a half of trainer time will be required for this project. In this example, if the cost of a trainer's time is estimated at $46 per hour (including salary, benefits, and overhead costs), then the estimated total cost of the training session is $46 per hour × 58 hours = $2668, which covers the cost of preparing and presenting one training session. This project is not complex, although even a simple project like this one makes some assumptions about the availability of resources, such as the training facility and personnel other than the trainer.

	Project: Windows Live Mail Training Session	
Step	**Task**	**Time Estimate**
1	**Plan training session** Analyze position descriptions for job skills required Interview supervisor and two trainees to learn backgrounds Document skill needs of trainees Define learning and performance objectives (scope) of training	8 hours
2	**Prepare training materials** Develop outline of topics covered Schedule trainees and training facility Locate or develop Windows Live Mail demonstration examples Develop hands-on activities Develop reference sheet of Windows Live Mail features	30 hours
3	**Prepare evaluation materials** Develop hands-on performance test Prepare training session feedback form	4 hours
4	**Beta test training materials** Present training to two support colleagues (2 hours each) Analyze results and revise as needed	12 hours
5	**Present Windows Live Mail training session** Present two-hour session Evaluate and revise as needed	4 hours
	Total:	**58 hours**

Resources Required

Software
   Windows Live Mail (available)
   PowerPoint (available)
Facilities
   Training Room (schedule 2 hours)
Materials
   Position descriptions of trainees (from Human Resources)
Personnel
   Access to supervisor and two trainees for interviews
   Two beta testers (2 hours each)
Miscellaneous supplies (available)

Figure 9-8   Example project plan for Windows Live Mail

Even a simple project may have risk factors that a project manager needs to evaluate. The project manager may also want to include a contingency factor of, say, 10 to 15 percent ($300–400 in the example) to account for the fact that the completion times in the plan are estimates. In general, the more experience with similar projects a manager has, the more confident in time estimates he or she can be, and the lower the contingency factor can be.

Project Management Tools

Projects become more complex when they involve additional staff members (and therefore greater coordination), more resources, a bigger budget, a longer calendar, and additional risk factors. In these situations, a one- or two-page project plan is not sufficient. Fortunately for managers of larger-scale user support projects (or several smaller ones), **project management software** is available to assist with the management tasks described above. For example, project managers who want to automate some project management tasks can use one of several kinds of software tools:

- Microsoft Project Professional 2010 is a project management tool compatible with the Microsoft Office suite (**office.microsoft.com/en-us/project-help**). A 60-day trial version of Microsoft Project Professional 2010 is included on a CD accompanying this book.

- Milestones Simplicity 2008 is a project scheduling tool, one of several sold by Kidasa Software (**www.kidasa.com/Simplicity/index.html**). The Kidasa Web site includes a video introduction to project scheduling.

-]project-open[is an open source project management tool that is available for free (**www.project-open.com/index.html**).

Project management software tools are no substitute for careful project planning, good time estimates, accurate budget and resource forecasts, thorough analysis of project risks, and other human inputs to the project planning process.

To learn more about project management skills, see: Kathy Schwalbe, *Information Technology Project Management*, 6th edition. Boston: Course Technology (Cengage Learning), 2010.

Figure 9-9 shows a Microsoft Project 2010 screenshot of a plan with the required tasks to complete the sample Windows Live Mail Training Session project described in Figure 9-8.

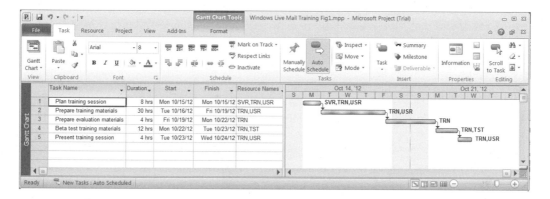

Figure 9-9   Steps in the Windows Live Mail Training Session project in Microsoft Project 2010

A **Gantt chart**, which appears in the right pane in Figure 9-9, is a common project planning tool that shows the basic information about each project task as a horizontal bar on a graph. The Gantt chart identifies each task, its relationship to other tasks, the expected calendar for task and project completion, and task participants. The left pane, in spreadsheet format, shows the input information that produced the Gantt chart. The two leftmost columns list the steps (Task Name) and estimated times (Duration) for each activity. The Resource Names column lists the four participants: the training supervisor (SVR), the trainer (TRN), the beta testers (TST), and the users (USR).

 Although the ribbon menu was introduced in Office 2007, Project 2007 retained the older menu bar command mode. However, Microsoft has introduced the ribbon user interface in Project 2010. See Case Project 4 at the end of this chapter for some learning resources for Project 2010.

The Gantt chart reflects the time spent by user support staff on this project, but it does not reflect the time spent by trainees or their supervisor.

Suppose the project team examined the draft Gantt chart in Figure 9-9 and asked questions, such as, *"What if additional support staff is added to this training project?"* In other words, *"Could we shorten the project if we identified some tasks that other support staff members could accomplish by working simultaneously with the original project trainer?"* What-if questions are often easier to answer with a project management or scheduling software tool.

Figure 9-10 shows a modification of the original Microsoft Project 2010 draft plan.

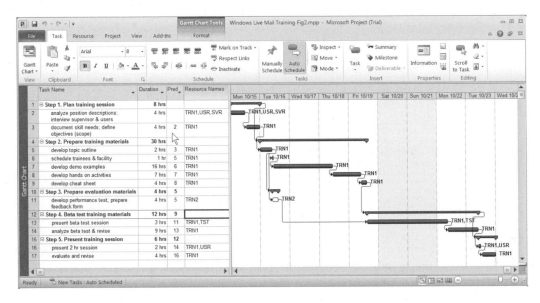

Figure 9-10   A revised Windows Live Mail training project showing the critical path

The five steps in Figure 9-9 have been expanded into more detailed tasks. In addition, some tasks are listed as predecessor tasks for other tasks (see the new Pred (predecessor tasks) column in the spreadsheet). A **predecessor task** is an activity that must be completed before another task can begin. For example, Step 1 is a predecessor task to Step 2 because the training session must be planned before the training materials can be prepared. In other words, Step 2 cannot begin until Step 1 is completed. Arrows have also been added to the Gantt chart to show the predecessor tasks on the diagram. Finally, instead of assigning one trainer to the entire project, as in the first draft plan, the revised plan includes two trainers, (TRN1) and (TRN2); the second trainer (TRN2) is assigned to help with a task in Step 3. In the revised plan, Step 3 can be completed by the second trainer while the first trainer is working on Step 2 tasks. By adding a second trainer to work on tasks that can be performed at the same time as another task, the project completion is moved up from Wednesday morning to Tuesday afternoon.

The dark bars in Figure 9-10 show this project's critical path. A **critical path** is the sequence of project tasks that must be completed on time to meet the project's completion deadline. The critical path establishes important milestones in a project's calendar. Steps 1, 2, 4, and 5 are critical path steps that are important milestones. If any one of these milestones is missed, the project's completion target is in jeopardy. However, the task for the second trainer in Step 3 in Figure 9-10 is not on the critical path. If the expected completion time for Step 3 slips, the completion of the project will not necessarily be affected.

These examples provide a brief introduction to illustrate various aspects of project management, such as project tasks, task time duration, assignments to staff members, what-if analyses, the critical path, and estimated completion time, but they barely scratch the surface of project management tools. Many project management software programs offer features to help a manager with other important project management tasks, including:

- Monitoring partial completion of project tasks and updating the Gantt chart to produce a progress report

- Identifying project tasks that are behind schedule and that might require additional resources

- Assigning personnel, facilities, equipment, supplies, and overhead costs to prepare a project budget

- Defining alternative report formats, including project calendars, budget and variance reports, PERT diagrams (also called network diagrams), and emails to staff members regarding project assignments

Many project management software packages now incorporate features that permit project work team members to view not only the overall project plans, but also detailed project task information, each team member's individual assignments, an updated project calendar, and a revised budget. In addition, the software packages enable work team members to communicate online via email or project Web pages.

ON THE WEB

To locate additional information about project management, visit the Web site of Project Management Institute (PMI), a professional organization of project managers (**www.pmi.org**). PMI offers a certification program for professional project managers.

For a brief tutorial on project management, view a slideshow presentation prepared by the Project Management Office at Massey University in New Zealand (**projectoffice. massey.ac.nz/massey/fms//Projects%20office/Documents/PM% 20Tutorial.pps**).

Other Needs Assessment and Project Management Tools

The needs analysis and project management tools discussed in this chapter are among those that support analysts find helpful when they undertake user needs assessment and other projects. However, the tools described here just scratch the surface of the information resources and tools available. New tools, especially automated ones, become available every year.

Not all needs assessment and user support projects require all of the steps described in this chapter; neither do all projects require every resource and tool discussed. In an actual project, support analysts choose from among the approaches described here to make the resources and tools fit the task. The most important fact to remember is that end-user needs analysis and assessment is a process, and the process and tools analysts choose to solve one problem will likely be different from the process and tools for another.

404

Support analysts who spend a significant amount of time on user needs assessment projects may benefit from a course on systems analysis and design. Similarly, those with project management interests and assignments may benefit from a formal course on project management.

Chapter Summary

- User support analysts who undertake a needs assessment for end-users follow a sequence of steps designed to obtain relevant information and help users make an informed decision. In the needs assessment process, support analysts may use several of the tools and information resources described in this chapter to aid them in their task.

- Steps in a user needs assessment follow three distinct phases:

  - *Preparation phase*—Before the detailed work on an assessment project begins, analysts should learn about the project's goals, decision criteria and constraints, stakeholders, and potential information resources.

  - *Investigation phase*—Analysts examine the current system or situation and evaluate possible alternatives that will improve it.

  - *Decision phase*—Analysts create a model of the proposed system and decide how the new system will be obtained.

- Decision and documentation tools are available to support analysts who work on needs assessment projects. Popular tools include project charters; cost-benefit analyses to weigh the cost of alternative solutions against their payoffs; several data-collection instruments (including input and output forms, procedure documentation, interviews and questionnaires, and direct observation); graphic design tools to draw flowcharts, I-P-O charts, and related schematic representations of systems; and prototyping tools to model the operation of software systems.

- Large needs assessment projects and other special projects often follow a sequence of steps during which a project team defines, plans, implements, monitors, and terminates the activities and tasks to successfully complete a project.

- Project managers and their team members can benefit from the planning, monitoring, and communication tools included in a project management software package.

Key Terms

acquisition costs—A category of project costs to build or purchase the initial components of a computer system or solution (compare to operating costs).

build-versus-buy decision—The decision an organization makes about whether to build a custom solution or purchase one off the shelf; build-versus-buy can apply to hardware, software, complete systems, or services.

change management procedure—Steps project managers use to document requested and approved changes in a project's design or goals; project participants submit "change orders," which managers use to communicate with stakeholders about the impact of changes on schedule and costs.

cost-benefit analysis—A comparison of the expenses of a potential project solution with the solution's expected payoffs; organizations are reluctant to spend resources on projects for which the costs outweigh the benefits.

critical path—The sequence of project tasks that must be completed on time to meet a project's completion deadline; the critical path defines important milestones in a project's calendar.

decision phase—The third phase of a user needs analysis and assessment project, in which analysts develop a model of the proposed solution and decide whether to build or buy it.

deliverable—The end result of a needs assessment project, such as a written analysis of alternatives, a feasibility report, a recommendation, or a decision to build, buy, or upgrade a system.

direct conversion—A project implementation strategy in which the existing system ceases operation at the time the new system becomes operational.

feasibility study—An investigation into the economic, operational, technological, and timeline constraints that will impact a user needs analysis and assessment project.

flowchart—A schematic drawing that uses symbols to represent the parts of a computer system or the steps in a procedure.

focus group—A small group of selected users who represent a larger group of users in a needs assessment project; a focus group may be used when interviewing every user is impractical.

Gantt chart—A common project planning tool that shows the expected start and end dates for each task and the staff resources assigned as a horizontal bar on a graph.

input form—A paper document or display screen used to collect information about a transaction; also called a *source document*.

intangible benefit—An expected result from a computer or services acquisition that is difficult to quantify or measure.

investigation phase—The second phase of a user needs analysis and assessment project, in which analysts try to understand the present system or situation and specify alternatives to it.

I-P-O chart—A diagramming tool that represents the input, processing, and output steps required to perform a task.

log—A list of events or activities recorded in the sequence that the events occur; a log is used to record information about routine, periodic events or unusual events, such as errors or problems.

model—A narrative description or graphic diagram, such as a flowchart or an organization chart, that represents a business activity in an organization (such as paper workflow), a computer system, or a network.

operating costs—A category of project costs—which are incurred after the initial acquisition costs—that includes the costs to operate a computer system or solution on a continuing basis.

optimal solution—The solution among several alternatives available in a project that is the most feasible, lowest cost, and most beneficial (compare to *satisficing solution*).

output form—A document that contains the results of a business transaction or process.

parallel conversion—A project implementation strategy in which both old and new systems are run for a period of time to gain confidence in the new system.

payback period—The amount of time it takes for the benefits of a project to exceed its costs; for some technology projects with high equipment and software costs in the first year, the payback period may be several years.

phased implementation—A project implementation strategy in which workload is removed from an existing system in stages as workload is transferred to a replacement system.

pilot project—A project implementation strategy in which a replacement system is used in selected situations to gain confidence that it can eventually be implemented organization-wide.

predecessor task—A project activity that must be completed before another task can begin.

preparation phase—The first phase of a user needs analysis and assessment project, in which analysts try to understand the end user's and the organization's goals as well as the decision criteria and project constraints; analysts define the problem, identify the roles of stakeholders, and identify potential sources of information.

procedure documentation—Written instructions about how to perform a business transaction or handle a routine organizational procedure.

project charter—A short narrative statement that describes the objectives, scope, methods, participants, deliverables, steps, timeline, and measures of success for a needs assessment or other support project.

project definition—The preliminary work to define the scope of a project, including its goals, a tentative project calendar, a project budget, and the project participants, including users, support staff, technical staff, management, and a project manager.

project goal—A specific, measurable end result that is the ultimate target or outcome of a project.

project implementation—The third step in a project during which team members perform the work on each task or objective.

project management—A detailed, step-by-step work plan and process designed to reach a specific goal; project management involves project definition, plan, implementation, monitoring, and termination steps.

project management software—An application software tool to help project leaders and workers organize the steps in a project, set priorities, establish and monitor project tasks and costs, and schedule staff and activities.

project monitoring—An ongoing assessment of the status of all project tasks to determine whether they are on target in terms of time and budget estimates.

project plan—A document that describes all project tasks; it answers questions such as what will be accomplished and by whom, how long each task will take, and what resources will be required.

project task—A specific activity or objective (outcome) that must be met in order to meet an overall project goal.

project termination—The final stage of a project, which includes communicating its completion to stakeholders, preparing a final project report, and evaluating the performance of the project and its participants.

prototype—A working model that analysts build to let users experience and evaluate how the finished product of an analysis project will actually work; a prototype contains enough features of an actual system that users can visualize or operate the model to evaluate its ability to meet their needs.

risk factors—The unexpected problems that could arise during the life of a project that would impact the project plan, costs, outcomes, or timeline.

satisficing solution—An alternate solution that solves a problem in a reasonable way, but is not necessarily the optimal solution; satisficing solutions are often adopted when an optimal solution is too expensive or impractical.

scope creep—The tendency for a project to grow or change in unexpected ways, which increases the time frame, resources, and cost to complete the project.

source document—Any form used to collect information about a business transaction for input into a business process or computer system; examples include payroll timecards, a problem log, a membership application, and an expense account record.

408

special project—A user support activity that happens infrequently; a special project is typically based on steps and procedures that are not as well-defined as those in regular support tasks.

stakeholder—A participant in a user needs analysis and assessment project who might gain or lose from its success or failure; stakeholders may be end users, managers, technical support staff, and/or support analysts.

turnkey system—An integrated, packaged solution of hardware, software, and support services purchased from a single vendor.

Check Your Understanding

Answers to Check Your Understanding questions are in Appendix A.

1. True or False? The goals and objectives of an organization are usually long-term and do not normally impact decisions about a user's immediate needs for computer systems and services.

2. Which of the following is not a primary step in the needs analysis and assessment process?

   a. preparation   c. decision
   b. investigation   d. purchase

3. True or False? A payroll clerk should make the final decision about whether or not a new payroll software package is needed.

4. In a user needs assessment project, the fact that an organization is uncomfortable with risks due to reliance on a new, untested software package would be considered as part of:

   a. economic feasibility   c. technological feasibility
   b. operational feasibility   d. timeline feasibility

5. True or False? Some problems that user support analysts investigate turn out to be organizational problems instead of technology problems.

6. Which sequence of numbers represents the correct order of the following four steps in the user needs analysis process? (1) investigate alternatives to the current system; (2) make a build-versus-buy decision; (3) identify sources of information; (4) understand the organization's goals

   a. 1 - 2 - 3 - 4   c. 3 - 1 - 4 - 2
   b. 4 - 3 - 2 - 1   d. 4 - 3 - 1 - 2

7. True or False? When making a decision about a new computer system or service, an organization must consider what is feasible in terms of time, staffing, money, and technology.

8. True or False? In an end-user needs assessment project, software requirements should generally be considered first, followed by hardware needs.

9. A(n) _____ considers whether to purchase a system off-the-shelf or construct one from scratch.

10. A narrative or diagram that explains the structure and operation of a new or existing computer system is called a:

   a. prototype   c. model
   b. layout   d. report

11. A(n) _____ is the end result of an analysis project that recommends purchase, modification, upgrade, or construction of a system.

12. True or False? A turnkey system is a package that includes hardware, software, and support services from a single vendor.

13. True or False? The build-versus-buy decision in a needs analysis project applies primarily to computer hardware.

14. True or False? A cost-benefit analysis is often in the form of a side-by-side comparison of the expenses and payoffs associated with a potential solution.

15. In a cost-benefit analysis, the development or purchase of software is generally considered a(n):

   a. acquisition cost   c. reduction of expenses
   b. operating cost   d. intangible cost

16. A(n) _____ is a written narrative that describes the objectives, scope, methods, participants, deliverables, and timeline for a needs assessment project.

17. A(n) _____ is a schematic diagram that uses symbols to represent the parts of a computer system.

18. True or False? A Gantt chart allows a project manager to ask what-if questions about how changes in resources impact the timeline of a project.

19. A(n) _____ is a project activity or step that must be completed before another task can begin.

    a. Gantt task   c. satisficing task

    b. successor task   d. predecessor task

20. Stakeholders in a needs assessment project are most likely:

    a. end users   c. support analysts

    b. managers   d. all of these

Discussion Questions

1. Do you agree or disagree with the following statement: *"Because a small dollar amount is involved, a needs assessment to purchase a $600 PC for an employee is overkill."* Explain your answer.

2. Why is it important for a support analyst to learn who will make the final decision on a needs assessment project and what decision criteria they will use?

3. In a cost-benefit analysis, which are more difficult to measure, costs or benefits? Explain why.

4. In order to save time and money in a user needs analysis project, if you could choose to omit one of the steps described in the chapter, which step would you omit, and why?

5. How could project management software tools, such as those illustrated in the chapter, be useful to even the smallest project team?

6. What are the advantages and disadvantages of purchasing a turnkey system from a single vendor versus buying components from several vendors?

Hands-On Activities

Activity 9-1

Assess the need for a personal computer. Think about how you would modify the steps described in this chapter if you were asked to recommend a personal computer to a friend for home use. Which steps would you omit? Which steps would be most important? Write a two-paragraph summary of your conclusions.

Activity 9-2

Avoid needs assessment problems. Some support analysts have expressed the view that the steps in a needs assessment project really should be described as:

1. Unbridled euphoria
2. Questions about the feasibility of the project
3. Growing concern about the project results
4. Unmitigated disaster
5. Search for the guilty
6. Punishment of the innocent
7. Promotion of the uninvolved

Behind each piece of humor may be some grain of truth. Write a two-page report that describes specific steps a support analyst can take to prevent a needs assessment project from turning into the disaster described above.

Activity 9-3

Analyze costs and benefits for a home computer. Study the categories included in the cost-benefit analysis described in Table 9-2. Think about how these categories apply to the purchase of a home computer. What additional categories of costs or benefits would you add to Table 9-2 for a home computer? Which cost categories do you think are most important in the purchase of a PC for home use? Are the benefit categories you listed tangible or intangible benefits? Explain why.

Activity 9-4

Develop a project charter. Think about the last time you purchased a PC, cell phone, MP3 player, or other electronic equipment, or helped a friend or relative purchase one. Write a project charter that describes the purchase process you followed. Use the project charter form in the book as the basis for your charter or create a project charter form of your own.

Activity 9-5

Develop an I-P-O chart and a flowchart. Select a common sales transaction, such as an automobile gasoline purchase or a grocery store purchase. Analyze the transaction and make a list of the pieces of information that are input, the processing that takes place as part of the transaction, and the resulting output. Record your analysis in the form of an I-P-O chart as shown in this chapter. Then sketch a flowchart of the transaction. Compare the information communicated in the I-P-O and flow diagrams. Which do you prefer? Explain why.

Activity 9-6

Perform a cost-benefit analysis for DVD burners. Research the relative advantages and disadvantages of internal and external DVD burners, using the library or online resources. Although internal DVD burners are generally less expensive, are there reasons why a user would want to pay more for an external DVD burner? Using the format in Table 9-2, develop a simple cost-benefit analysis for internal and external DVD burners.

Activity 9-7

Use project management software to plan a project. Use the Microsoft Project 2010 software included with this book, or download]project-open[or another project management software package. Enter the project steps in Figure 9-8 into the software to prepare a Gantt chart. Print the Gantt chart.

Activity 9-8

Prepare a Gantt chart using Excel. Although application software packages such as Microsoft Project 2010 are specifically designed as project management tools, a spreadsheet program, such as Excel, can also be used to perform some project planning tasks—such as preparing a Gantt chart. Watch a YouTube video on the steps to prepare a simple Gantt chart in Excel (**www.youtube.com/watch?v=HQwE0Xv1lAA**). Perform the steps in the tutorial and print your Gantt chart. Write a brief comparison of the Excel Gantt chart you prepared in the tutorial with the examples presented in the chapter. Which features from Project 2010's Gantt chart format would you like to incorporate in your Excel Gantt chart?

Case Projects

1. Feasibility Analysis of a Computer Facility Problem

Based on your personal experience or on conversations with work or school colleagues, select a current problem in a computer facility at work, in a lab at school, or in a training facility. The problem you choose could be with hardware performance, software availability, network connectivity, operating policies, staffing, or services. Meet with a group of your colleagues to perform the first several steps in a needs assessment project aimed at solving the problem you selected. First, make sure your group has a clear definition of the root problem. Then, identify the stakeholders and sources of information available to you. Brainstorm alternative solutions to the problem. Finally, analyze the feasibility of each alternative.

- Are some alternatives more feasible than others? Explain why.

- What additional information resources would you need to complete the analysis?

- Did your group reach consensus on a recommendation it would make to management? Why, or why not?

Write your conclusions in the form of a two- to three-page feasibility report.

2. Needs Assessment for Coastal Tool Rental

Kathleen Marsh is a recent community college graduate who plans to open an equipment and tool rental store in the next couple of months. The store will target do-it-yourselfers who need gardening and home improvement implements that may be too expensive to purchase for a limited project.

Kathleen majored in small business management, but also took a number of computer courses as electives in her community college degree program, including:

- Introduction to Business Information Systems
- PC Operating Systems
- Spreadsheets (Excel)
- Database Management (Access)
- Introductory and Advanced Visual Basic
- Systems Analysis and Design
- Introduction to Computer Networks

Kathleen did well in these courses and feels very comfortable with computer technology, but she wants an independent perspective on the feasibility of a computer system for her equipment and tool rental company. That is why she has asked for your advice. Although this is her first real venture as an entrepreneur, Kathleen worked in a tool rental shop during high school and college.

Kathleen's store, Coastal Tool Rental, will be in a new shopping center. Kathleen chose the location because a sizable bedroom community of family homes is nearby, and because no major competition is located in the area, which is about 15 miles from the nearest large town. She has arranged to rent 2500 square feet of space in the shopping center.

Kathleen has located a wholesaler who can provide her with a start-up inventory of common garden and home improvement tools. The wholesaler can also serve as a supplier for new and replacement tools, equipment, and consumables.

Kathleen has identified her major expenses, both start-up and ongoing, which are shown in Table 9-3.

Start-Up Expenses	Ongoing Expenses
• Furniture	• Rent & utilities
• Customer service counters	• Payroll & taxes
• Equipment storage bins	• Equipment and tool replacement
• Initial inventory of equipment and tools	• Consumables for resale
• Computer system (?)	• Advertising

Table 9-3 Coastal Tool Rental's expenses

Kathleen's initial thinking about a computer system is that she probably cannot afford one in her start-up budget. Instead, she had worked out a simple manual system for keeping track of her equipment and tool inventory and client rentals. In her system, each tool and piece of equipment will have an ID number recorded on a sticker attached to the item and on a card she would keep in a *Tool* card box on top of the counter. In a separate *Client* box, she would keep a card for each client. The client cards would be filed by telephone number, which she would use as a client ID number.

When a client rents one or more tools, she will clip the tool card(s) to the client card, and put them together in a third box labeled *Rentals*, which would be organized by the return date. When a rental is returned, Kathleen will unclip the tool and client cards and return them to their respective card files. At 6 P.M. each day, if there are cards in the rental box for tools that were not returned when expected, Kathleen will phone the client and assess a late charge.

Kathleen thinks this simple manual system would work until her business volume grows and she could afford a computer system. But she wonders whether a computer system would be feasible immediately, when she opens the doors in a couple of months. She even thought that perhaps she could buy a PC and write a simple program in Access, Visual Basic, or Excel to replace the manual card system. Kathleen would appreciate your advice.

1. Prepare a list of interview questions for Kathleen that would help you make a recommendation to her.

2. After you have a list of potential questions to ask in an interview, compare your questions with those of three classmates or coworkers. Merge your questions into a single list from your group. Try to arrange the questions into categories with other similar questions.

3. When you have completed the list of interview questions, your instructor will provide you with Kathleen's responses to several of the questions from an interview with her. Based on her responses, answer these questions:

   - If Coastal Tool Rental decides to purchase a computer system, what major decisions will the owner need to make?

   - Would you recommend that Kathleen Marsh build her own software or purchase a package? Explain your reasoning.

   - Make a list of the software Coastal Tool Rental will need to meet the needs Kathleen Marsh described in the interview.

   - In order to build or buy a transaction-processing program to handle equipment rentals and returns, Coastal Tools Rental would probably need a database of all rental items and a database of clients. List the fields you think Coastal would need to include in either the tools database or the client database.

- A word processor or a database language such as Access can be used as a tool to build a prototype (model) of a report. Use one of these tools to design a prototype of the equipment rental agreement that would be printed for clients to sign each time they rent a tool.

- Given what you know of Coastal Tool Rental's business plan and needs and its financial situation, do you think a computer system is feasible? Explain why or why not.

3. Computer Recommendation for Amy Lee

Amy Lee was recently hired as a personnel assistant in the Human Resources Department where you work. Because you are the user support specialist, she has contacted you for some help choosing the computer she will use in her job in employee benefits administration. You want to make sure that she gets the computer tools she will need to be productive.

Amy says that she will need an Office suite and that her boss gave her a choice of Microsoft Office 2010 or WordPerfect Office X5. Because she has previous work experience with the WordPerfect word processor, which is part of WordPerfect suite, she would like to use it. The WordPerfect suite includes most of the tools Amy needs, so her other software requirements are minimal. In addition to WordPerfect Office, Amy needs the Windows operating system. She also needs a Web browser because most information about benefits and employee compensation is available on the Web.

Amy really needs your help with the decisions on hardware. Amy's boss said she has very little money left in this year's department budget for hardware. So she suggested that Amy try to find a basic starter system, but one that could be upgraded next year when there will be more money available for computer equipment. Amy wants you to recommend a hardware configuration that meets her immediate needs, is reasonably priced, and can be upgraded next year. It needs to be able to run the software Amy has selected. Whatever hardware she buys must also be compatible with the Human Resources Department's local area network (LAN), which operates on a Windows 2008 server. The network server can provide Amy with access to one of two laser printers, so the hardware system she buys need not include a printer. However, Amy wants to be able to scan documents into her system, and no scanner is available on the network.

Analyze Amy's situation and recommend a specific hardware configuration that will meet her immediate needs. In addition, find equipment for sale in a trade magazine or advertised online or in a local newspaper that you believe is the appropriate configuration for Amy. When you are finished, prepare a recommended list of hardware specifications (and prices, if available) that Amy could take to her boss.

4. LAN Selection for Geo-Habitus

Geo-Habitus is a company that sells kits used to build vacation cabins shaped like geodesic domes. The company has identified a need for a local area network (LAN) to facilitate communication among workers and permit collaboration on tasks. Bridgette Petrang, the technology supervisor at Geo-Habitus, has asked you to develop a project plan with Microsoft Project 2010. To learn the basic features of project management software, you will input the tasks for a LAN acquisition project at Geo-Habitus, shown in the outline below. The goal of the project is to select a new LAN for the company.

Project Plan: Geo-Habitus LAN Selection Project

Step	Task	Time Estimate
1	Conduct a user needs analysis among the Geo-Habitus managers and employees for a new LAN system.	8 days
2	Develop a specification of the required LAN features.	4 days
3	Define the selection criteria based on mandatory and desirable features, vendor support, costs, and compatibility with existing equipment; decide on a weight for each criterion.	2 days
4	Write a Request For Proposal (RFP) document for vendors that describes LAN operating requirements, bidding procedures, and decision criteria.	4 days
5	Send RFP document to LAN vendors.	1 day
6	Allow time for vendors to prepare written responses to RFP.	14 days
7	Analyze vendor responses to RFP and evaluate bids.	5 days
8	Select a vendor and award the contract for the LAN installation.	1 day

First, learn about the basic features of Microsoft Project Professional 2010 from a series of online video tutorials (**office.microsoft.com/en-us/project-help/overview-RZ101831071.aspx**). The online tutorial course takes about 30 minutes and covers these Microsoft Project tasks:

- Create a new project
- Add tasks to a project
- Add links between tasks in a project
- Create an outline for tasks in a project

The tutorial also offers the following options:

- Practice (requires a Web browser with ActiveX controls)
- Test yourself

The Quick Reference Card, which can be downloaded from the tutorial site, is a very useful tool that you can print out as a reminder of basic Project 2010 features. The online version of the Quick Reference Card includes pointers to other tutorial topics for Project 2010.

An alternate learning resource for Project 2010, for those who prefer a tutorial guide in PDF format, is available from HP (**h30187.www3.hp.com/courses/overview/p/courseId/39880/Microsoft_Project_2010_introduction.htm**). Registration, which is free for this course, is required.

After completing one of the tutorials, install the 60-day trial version of Microsoft Professional Project 2010 from the CD that accompanies this book. Start Microsoft Project 2010 and enter the project planning steps for the Geo-Habitus LAN selection project above.

Remember that Project 2010 is part of the Microsoft Office suite. Many menu commands and icons in Project have the same functions as in other Office programs, including the Undo icon on the Quick Access toolbar.

Your task is to learn enough about Microsoft Project 2010 to prepare a Gantt chart similar to the ones illustrated in the chapter. Experiment with the other features of Project 2010 if you would like, but keep focused on the objective to prepare a project plan so the management at Geo-Habitus can understand the project timeline.

5. Printer Cost-Benefit Analysis for Micro Dings

Micro Dings Insurance is a local company that writes automobile insurance policies. Several years ago, Micro Dings purchased five black-and-white ink-jet printers for their agents to use to print policies, renewals, and billings for their customers. The printers are fairly good quality (600 dots per inch), but they are slow (10 pages per minute) and the ink cartridges are expensive. Each printer prints about 6000 pages per month and uses one black ink cartridge per month, which costs $30 at a local office supply store.

The printers have started to reach the end of their useful life, and last year, Micro Dings spent $1000 on printer repairs. Because of the frequency of repairs, the lead agent at Micro Dings, Rick Berry, has been approached by a sales representative for the computer shop that repairs their current printers. The sales rep has recommended the company invest in replacement printers. He suggested a model of higher quality (1200 dots per inch) color printers that sell for $400 each. The new printers can easily accommodate the page volume per month and are considerably faster at 25 pages per minute.

Because of the faster speed, the sales rep recommended that Micro Dings purchase three new printers to replace the five current printers. Black ink cartridges for the new printers cost $25 each and are expected to print about 10,000 pages, so they should last about one month. Rick Berry thinks their use of color for the insurance policies would be limited. Color cartridges for the new printers cost $30 each, but would probably last for six months before they needed to be replaced.

Rick sees additional advantages of the new printers, including the following:

- The ability to print the Micro Dings Insurance Company logo in color would enhance the company's image in its communications with customers and prospects.

- The ability to print in color could be used to highlight important information on policies and billing forms.

- The speed of the new printers means agents would wait less time for lengthy policies and renewals to print.

- The print quality of the new printers should be better than the old printers.

- Micro Dings can save on printer repair bills, at least for the first few years.

- The new printer cartridges will last longer and need to be replaced less frequently.

But Rick also has some concerns about purchasing new printers:

- The agents will have to share three printers instead of five.

- The reliability of the new printers is described as good in reviews, but printers aren't usually tested at the high rate of use that Micro Dings would require (10,000 pages per month).

Rick Berry would like you to prepare a spreadsheet that analyzes the costs and benefits of the new printers compared with the old ones. Use the guidelines and categories for cost-benefit analyses described in the chapter. (*Hint*: This case includes a lot of numeric data and other information, some of which may not be directly relevant to a cost-benefit analysis. Part of your task as an analyst is to determine which information is relevant.)

- Will any of the pay-offs to the company (cost savings) occur in the first year?

- Is the payback period longer than one year?

- Do the cost savings justify the $1200 Micro Dings will pay for the new printers?

Write a brief cover memo to accompany your spreadsheet that communicates your conclusions to Rick as well as any assumptions you made when you prepared the cost-benefit spreadsheet.

Installing and Managing End-User Computers

In this chapter, you will learn about:

◎ Major site preparation steps for computer installations

◎ Preinstallation site preparation tasks

◎ The purpose and contents of a site management notebook

◎ Tools needed to install hardware

◎ Steps to install and configure hardware, operating systems, networks, and application software

◎ Common installation wrap-up tasks

◎ Ongoing site management tasks

After a support specialist has evaluated computer products, conducted a needs assessment, and perhaps even helped end users complete the necessary procedures to purchase computer products, the next step is to install the system. Installation can include hardware, peripherals, operating systems, network connectivity and utility software, application software, and even office supplies and equipment—either packaged together as a turnkey system or sold individually.

During the installation process, a support specialist may also need to handle user training, which you will learn about in Chapter 11, and documentation issues, which you learned about in Chapter 3.

The system installation process can easily intimidate end users, especially those who are less experienced. Support specialists are often able to set up a system and get it operational in a fraction of the time it would take an end user to figure out the correct steps and resolve any problems that arise. This chapter describes typical tasks that are a part of many personal and office computer installations, although every installation poses different challenges. You will learn about site preparation tasks as well as the tools and steps necessary to install hardware, operating systems, network connections, and application software.

In addition to system installations, support specialists often have responsibility for ongoing site management tasks including media backup, system security (such as access authorization), disaster preparation (such as creating contingency plans), and related operational tasks.

System Installation Overview

User support specialists are often responsible for installing computer systems. In an efficient installation, a computer system will be up and running with a minimum of interruption to an end user's work. Adequate preparation, proper tools, and an established process for tracking important details help ensure that system installations run smoothly. Whether an installation is for a single home computer, a small office system, a training lab, or hundreds of networked computers, experienced system installers know that important details can be easily overlooked—whether at the time a system is installed or later when the system needs to be repaired or upgraded. This chapter emphasizes the importance of using installation checklists and system documentation as a way of ensuring that all the necessary steps are completed properly for the installation, as well as for future maintenance tasks.

The major installation tasks are summarized in Figure 10-1 and discussed in detail throughout the chapter.

Support specialists may not be involved in all of the tasks listed in Figure 10-1. For example, they might not need to install or configure an operating system if one is preinstalled. Or a specialized network technician may be responsible for connecting a system to a network and configuring it. The checklists in this chapter are generic; you should consider them a starting point and modify them to fit specific situations. In some cases, you may need to add steps; in other cases, some steps may not directly apply. For example, if a new or upgraded software package needs to be installed on an end-user system, the checklists for hardware, operating system, and network connections will not apply.

- Preinstallation site preparation
  - Location
  - Ergonomic planning
  - Power requirements
  - Telephone and network access
  - Air conditioning
  - Lighting
  - Fire suppression
- Site management documentation
- Hardware installation tools
- Hardware installation
- Operating system and network installation
- Application software installation
- Installation wrap-up tasks

421

Figure 10-1 Overview of system installation tasks

Preinstallation Site Preparation

Before installing a system, support specialists often visit an end user's location for a preinstallation inspection. The purpose of a site visit is to anticipate problems that may arise so an installer can address them prior to the installation. Many installers use a written checklist to make sure that they address a range of critical questions during the visit. A typical site installation checklist would contain the following queries:

- What space requirements apply to this computer system or workstation?
- What space constraints are potential problems at the user's work site?
- Is any special furniture needed to make computer use more productive?
- What materials need to be stored for convenient access near the computer?
- What ergonomic issues need to be addressed?
- Do ADA (Americans with Disabilities Act) or OSHA (Occupational Safety and Health Administration) issues or accommodations apply to this installation?
- Is the power supply accessible and adequate for the system?
- Is power conditioning required?
- Where is the nearest network, wireless, and/or telephone access?

- Is air conditioning required?

- What lighting problems may need to be addressed?

- Is a fire-suppression system installed and operational?

Experienced installers may not carry an actual checklist. Observation of the site may be sufficient to determine what problems exist, if any. However, if they have several installations to perform at different sites, a site installation checklist can help installers keep track of the conditions and special requirements of each location.

Location

When support specialists plan a new computer installation, they must determine the best location for the desktop or portable unit, display screen, printer, keyboard, mouse, and other peripherals and accessories. A system that has properly located components will be easy and efficient to use, will not cause discomfort for the user, and will ensure the physical safety of both the user and the system itself. Each installation site poses unique challenges, and support specialists try to adapt the installation to the space and layout constraints of the site.

System Unit Location

A desktop system unit is usually located within four to five feet of a user's work area—a distance dictated by the length of signal cables between the system unit and the display screen, keyboard, mouse, and other peripherals. If a system unit is a desktop model, a table or desk surface is often the most convenient location, especially for users who frequently access peripherals located in the system unit case (such as USB ports, removable hard drive, or CD/DVD drive). However, a standard ATX desktop case's **footprint**, which is the number of square inches (length × width) of usable space the computer case occupies, can be large, and may significantly reduce the work area on a desk. Space-saver cases (also called *small form factor cases*) or all-in-one units (where the system unit is part of the display screen) are popular because they have a smaller footprint. To save space, a system unit may be located off of the work surface on a bookshelf or even on the floor. If a desktop unit must be located at a distance from a user's workspace, extender cables or wireless devices for the keyboard, mouse, and display screen may be used. Laptop computers (also referred to as *notebooks*) are increasingly popular as desktop replacements; the location of the system unit is not a primary factor in these installations.

Small form factor (SFF) cases may be designated as MicroATX towers, Slimline, BTX, or DTX cases, depending on the manufacturer.

Desktop system units and older CRT monitors produce considerable heat when they operate. The vent holes in the cases of these units should not be blocked by office or bookcase walls or by shelves. Air should be able to circulate around the cases of all computer peripherals.

Although installation on an office floor reduces the desk space that a computer occupies, floor installations are not without problems. First, most floors are dusty, and internal fans may pull dust into the computer case. In order to avoid this problem, arrange for the case to be installed at least six inches above floor level on a shelf or raised platform. Second, desktop unit cases located on the floor can be accidentally kicked or may obstruct foot traffic. Cases should be located in such a way as to prevent these problems. Third, for some users, frequent bending to reach a floor unit can cause back strain. Wherever possible, ports and peripherals should be located within arm's reach of a user's normal working position.

You'll learn more about the ergonomics of computer use later in this chapter.

Keyboard and Mouse Location

Ideally, a desktop or laptop computer should be installed in a work area where the table or worktop surface is 26 to 28 inches from the floor, which is a comfortable keyboard and mouse height for most users. A typical office desk surface is 30 inches from the floor; a keyboard or mouse used on a regular office desk or table at 30 inches can cause users discomfort because the angle of their wrists at the keyboard is unnatural. To prevent wrist and finger pain, make sure that when a user's hands rest on the keyboard or mouse, they extend in a relatively straight line, or slightly downward, from the forearms. If a 30-inch office desk or table is the only possible keyboard location, one of the following adaptations may be possible:

- Shorten the desk or table legs to get the keyboard to a comfortable height.

- Adjust the chair height so the user's wrists are in a comfortable position.

- Attach an adjustable keyboard shelf to the underside of the desk or table.

The solution to one problem can cause another. In some cases, when a chair seat is adjusted high enough to enable wrist comfort, the user's feet may no longer rest comfortably on the floor, which can result in leg problems. An adjustable footrest may help in this situation.

As laptop computer models increase in popularity, support specialists need to be aware of the special ergonomic challenges they present. Because laptops are often transported from one location to another and may be used with docking stations or port replicators, the height of a laptop keyboard varies according to the location where it is used. A laptop should ideally be used on a surface that is at the lower end of the 26- to 28-inch recommended height range because the thickness of the laptop itself can add slightly to the keyboard height.

Display Screen Location

Position the display screen so a user can view it by looking straight ahead or down slightly. The most comfortable angle for viewing a display screen is usually the same angle at which a user would hold a book to read at their workspace. A user should not have to look up at the display screen. Tilt the display so the user can view it with a natural head position, without neck strain.

Printer Location

A printer does not have to be placed in the valuable real estate on a user's work surface but can instead be located on a separate table or bookshelf or, where available, on a printer stand. A printer should be in a convenient location where users can easily load paper and cartridges and where the case can be opened to remove paper jams. Extender signal cables from a desktop unit to the printer—or a wireless printer—can provide additional flexibility in printer location. Be sure to check the printer manual because some printer models will not operate reliably when lengthy extender cables are used or beyond the recommended distance from a wireless access point. The location of networked printers that will be shared among several users in an office is an important decision. Printers located some distance from frequent users can result in lost productivity as users retrieve their output.

Supplies

Users frequently want certain supplies located conveniently near their computer equipment. These supplies may include printer paper, mailing labels, photo stock, ink or toner cartridges, magnetic or optical media, computer manuals, cleaning supplies, tools, and other accessories. Supplies can usually be stored in an office file drawer, bookcase, or closet. Some supplies need to be stored in a special location to avoid certain problems. For example, paper should be stored where it is not exposed to excessive moisture, and optical media should be stored where it is not exposed to extreme heat.

Computer Furniture

An end user's desk chair often has more impact on his or her comfort, health, and safety than any other piece of office furniture, the workspace layout, the computer features, or other ergonomic factors. Adjustability is a desirable feature in an office chair: adjustable seat height, seat swivel and tilt, backrest, and arm rests. The seat height should be adjusted so the user's feet rest comfortably on the floor. Seat swivel and tilt features permit a user to vary his or her position with respect to the computer system and work area to avoid the monotony of sitting in a single position for long periods. The seat backrest should be adjusted so it supports the user's lower back. The armrests should be adjusted so the user's elbows rest comfortably on the tops of the armrests when a user is seated in the chair. Most ergonomic chairs have a "waterfall" front edge designed to reduce the pressure on the back of a user's legs. Other chair selection features include a five-leg base (rather than a less stable four-leg base), rollers that permit easy movement, and padding that is supportive and comfortable. In a carpeted office, a plastic floor pad permits a chair to roll smoothly. When possible, a user should have an opportunity to try out an ergonomic chair because chair comfort is a very individual judgment.

425

Space Constraint Solutions

Where space permits, a separate computer worktable or an extension to a user's office desk can be used to increase a user's work space. In addition, a monitor arm can be attached to the desk or a wall to move an older CRT monitor off the desktop. Some newer flat-panel LCD screens can be mounted directly on a wall to free up desk space.

Many ergonomic desks have keyboard shelves attached under the work surface. These shelves can usually be added to standard office desks and worktables. Keyboard shelves are often adjustable. In addition to saving desk space (because the keyboard can be stored out of the way when not in use), adjustable keyboard shelves enable a user to position the keyboard at a comfortable height. They are especially useful when multiple users share a work area, such as at a shared desk or in a computer lab or training facility.

With careful planning, desk space can be conserved by locating the desktop unit, display screen, printer, and other peripherals close to the user's desk area but not actually on it.

 In some executive offices, users want systems installed on furniture never intended for computers, such as an antique desk or a credenza. In these cases, furniture may need to be significantly adapted to avoid ergonomic problems later. Be sure adequate knee room is available, especially if a user is tall.

ON THE WEB

Many office supply and computer vendors carry furniture and other products designed to address the issues discussed in this section. To see examples of products described here, check the online catalogs of K-Log (**www.k-log.com**) or Anthro Technology Furniture (**www.anthro.com**).

Ergonomics

As you learned in Chapter 1, ergonomics is the study of the design of computer systems (both hardware and software) and workspaces to minimize health problems and maximize worker safety, productivity, comfort, and job satisfaction. Some large organizations employ a safety engineer whose job responsibilities include office and factory floor ergonomics.

In smaller organizations, workers may turn to user support specialists for advice about ergonomic issues.

 Software ergonomics deals with usability factors such as legible screen displays and user interfaces that incorporate consistent navigation aids, data-entry processes that eliminate unnecessary keystrokes or mouse clicks, and natural sequences of human-computer interactions.

A well-planned computer installation can help users avoid several common ergonomic problems, described in the following sections.

Back or Neck Muscle Pain

Pain in the back or neck muscles can have more than one source. A user may strain neck muscles to see a display screen that is placed too high. If a user's chair is too low, it can force a user to look up to view the screen. The user's chair may not be designed for computer use. Poorly designed chairs can cut off circulation in legs or force a worker to use back and neck muscles excessively when they should be more relaxed. The keyboard may be too high, so that a user's arms are angled in an unnatural position. And a user, despite a correctly designed workspace, may work too long without adequate breaks or without shifting body position to relieve monotony.

Solutions to back or neck muscle pain include keyboard height adjustments, a chair with both back and seat adjustment levers, better back support, adequate cushioning, and a "waterfall" seat design that takes pressure off the back of a user's legs and promotes better circulation. Some users find that a pillow or other support in their chairs at the curve of their backs helps them sit more comfortably. Users should be reminded to take stretch breaks at least once an hour. Frequent finger, hand, wrist, and neck stretches during breaks can be effective to prevent and sometimes cure pain, as can isometric exercises.

ON THE WEB

For suggested ergonomic exercises for computer users, visit **www.officefurniture. org/GuideDetail.aspx?GuideID=6&TopicID=5**.

Some users report good results with a mesh back support product; view an example at **www.travelonbags.com/pages/xxxxx/1900/1918.html**.

Leg Pain

Leg pain can result from an office chair that is too high for the user's feet to touch the floor or one that is improperly designed and impairs leg circulation. The seat height on an office chair should allow a user to comfortably rest his or her feet flat on the floor; a user's lower legs should be at a 90 degree or greater angle to their upper legs. Leg pain can also result from a work area with too little knee room or one that forces a user to sit in an uncomfortable position for extended periods.

Solutions to leg pain include ergonomically designed office chairs with back and seat adjustment levers, sufficient back support and adequate cushioning, and a "waterfall" seat design. A footrest placed at a 15-degree angle may be necessary to support the user's legs and reduce strain.

Eyestrain and Headaches

Eyestrain and headaches can result from screen glare. A user's display screen may reflect sunlight or room lights, which is one of the primary causes of eyestrain. (See the "Lighting" section later in this chapter for more details.) Glasses and contact lenses can also contribute to eyestrain and headaches if they are not appropriate for the distance at which the end user sits from the computer screen.

Solutions to eyestrain and headaches include changing the orientation of the display screen to the light source, or using window shades to reduce glare. The level of lighting in the computer area may need to be reduced. Antiglare screen filters, available from office and computer supply stores, can also alleviate eye strain. Users should make an effort to take a break at least once an hour, and they should look away periodically from the display screen at a distant object to minimize eyestrain. Users should also ensure that eyeglass prescriptions are correct for extended computer use.

Wrist and Finger Pain

Wrist and finger pain usually results from a keyboard that is too high or too low. Hand and wrist muscles and tendons should not be tense or strained at a keyboard; a user's arms should be angled slightly downward, and the wrist should have support. Physical problems called **repetitive strain injuries** result from continuous use of joints in a limited range of motion. The symptoms of repetitive strain injuries include swelling, numbness, tingling, and stiffness in joints. The most common form of repetitive strain injury is carpal tunnel syndrome, which affects wrists and fingers.

Techniques for reducing the risk of repetitive strain injuries include placing the keyboard at the optimal 26 to 28 inches from the floor, using an adjustable keyboard shelf, a wrist rest, and a chair with arms, and taking stretch breaks at least once an hour. An ergonomic keyboard—which splits the right- and left-hand keys in an inverted V shape so the user's hands, wrists, and forearms are in a more natural and comfortable position—may help reduce strain. Ergonomic keyboards take some time to acclimate to, but those who have used them generally do not want to return to a conventional keyboard.

Figure 10-2 illustrates some of the important workstation dimensions that will help ensure user comfort and eliminate many ergonomic problems. These potential ergonomic problems as well as possible solutions are summarized in Table 10-1.

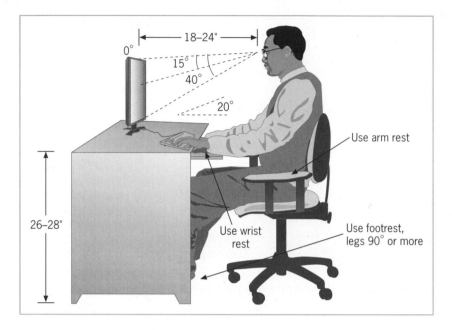

Figure 10-2　Workstation ergonomics

Ergonomic Problem	Possible Solutions
Back or neck muscle pain or numbness	• Replace office chair with one that is adjustable.
	• Adjust keyboard height.
	• Install adjustable keyboard shelf.
	• Take frequent breaks and perform exercises to reduce repetitive motion and stress.
Leg pain or numbness	• Replace office chair with ergonomic model.
	• Place footrest on floor.
Eyestrain and headaches	• Reorient computer to reduce screen glare.
	• Reduce office lighting.
	• Install display screen antiglare filter.
	• Check eyeglasses for proper fit and prescription.
	• Replace display screen with larger size and better resolution.
	• Take frequent breaks and perform exercises to reduce stress.

Table 10-1　Ergonomic problems and solutions (*continues*)

(continued)

Ergonomic Problem	Possible Solutions
Wrist and finger pain or numbness; carpal tunnel syndrome	• Adjust keyboard height. • Install adjustable keyboard shelf. • Use keyboard wrist rest. • Take frequent breaks and perform exercises to reduce stress and repetitive motion strain.

Table 10-1   Ergonomic problems and solutions

With the amount of attention that repetitive strain injuries and other ergonomic problems have received in recent years, it is no surprise that many devices designed to avoid or reduce the impact of extended computer use are on the market. These devices include:

• Adjustable tables and work surfaces

• Adjustable chairs

• Footrests

• Keyboard shelves

• Alternative ergonomic keyboards

• Alternative pointing devices (trackballs and touchpads)

• Wrist rests

• Mouse support rests

• Document holders

• CRT monitor arms

• Task lighting

• Antiglare screen filters

• Assistive devices

Assistive devices are computer peripherals and software applications that adapt a computer system so that users with various physical limitations can be more productive. For example, users with visual impairments may be able to use special software that displays extra-large type fonts on a screen. Users who cannot see a display screen may be able to use hardware and software devices that verbalize the contents of a screen for a user. Users who do not have the motor skills to type may use a keyboard alternative such as a stylus pointer or voice-recognition software.

430

ON THE WEB

If a support specialist is asked to make a recommendation on the purchase of an ergonomic device, both the support specialist and the end user should understand the advantages and disadvantages of the devices. A Web site that explains the pros and cons of several types of ergonomic devices is **office-ergo.com/about/pros-cons-many-common-ergonomic-items**.

Or, read an excerpt from *Your Guide to Office Ergonomic Furniture and Accessories*, by Alison Heller (**www.worksiteinternational.com/downloads/excerpt.PDF**).

Microsoft publishes a free monthly newsletter titled *Accessibility Update*; visit its Web site to subscribe and access archived issues (**www.microsoft.com/enable/news/subscribe/default.aspx**).

Support specialists should treat end-user ergonomic concerns seriously. Many computer users have experienced painful repetitive strain injuries that require medical treatment. Some repetitive strain injuries can disable a user for an extended period or even permanently, and some users even require a job change to compensate for injuries resulting from ergonomic problems that were not addressed promptly or properly. Employers that have ignored state and federal (OSHA) rules and regulations that cover worksite ergonomics have been the target of legal action by disabled workers.

ON THE WEB

Several Web sites contain useful information about ergonomics, including the latest research findings, specialized products, and treatment options. For example, see the UCLA Ergonomics Web site (**www.ergonomics.ucla.edu**) or the Cornell University Ergonomics Web site (**ergo.human.cornell.edu**).

OSHA also publishes information on computer workstation ergonomics (**www.osha.gov/SLTC/etools/computerworkstations**).

 Ergonomics is an area in which user support specialists can develop special expertise that adds value to their employment. Extra effort is required to keep up with the latest research and products in ergonomics, but support specialists who devote the time can become recognized as an important resource.

Power Requirements

Most small computer systems do not pose unusual electrical power problems. They plug into standard three-prong outlets. However, before installing a computer, several electrical power situations should be checked.

Electrical Power Checklist

- **Outlets**—If an installation is in an older building with two-pronged outlets (that is, those without the third ground prong), rewiring or installation of grounds may be necessary. Avoid "cheater" plug adapters, which convert two-pronged plugs to three-prong, because they defeat the ground feature that protects electronic circuits. Instead, recommend upgraded wiring.

- **Outlet wiring**—Test three-prong outlets to make sure the hot, neutral, and ground prongs were correctly wired when the outlet was installed. Incorrect wiring is uncommon, but it can cause problems if a computer system is plugged into an outlet that was improperly wired. A simple, inexpensive outlet tester is available from most electrical suppliers and hardware stores.

- **Circuit amperage**—If a computer with a significant number of peripheral devices is installed in an environment with other office equipment (copiers, fax machines, printing calculators, coffeemakers, radios, refrigerators), add up the amperage currently drawing on the circuit to determine whether it can handle the total load. Most appliances, including computers, display screens, and printers, have an information plate that displays the number of amps of current they draw. If a circuit breaker at the electrical distribution box is 15 amps, the total amperage of devices on the circuit should be less than 15. Otherwise, a separate electrical circuit should be installed for the computer and peripherals.

 During startup, some appliances draw more amps than their stated operational rating.

- **Shared circuits**—A computer should not be installed on an electrical circuit that supplies a generator, air conditioner, or a device with a heavy motor. These devices can, at times, draw large quantities of power, which may reduce the available amps on a circuit to less than that required for the proper operation of computer devices. For example, disk drives rely on electrical current for timing during read and write operations. Inadequate power during one of these operations could cause loss of data on the drive media.

- **Power stability**—In some areas, the quality of the electric supply varies considerably, even during normal operation. When installing computer equipment in areas with unstable power, consult with the local electric utility to determine whether special equipment is recommended to protect computer hardware. The electric utility may recommend a **power conditioner,** which is an electrical device installed between a computer and its power source to regulate the electrical power to ensure it stays within acceptable limits. A power conditioner draws in electrical power, makes sure that the frequency, voltage, and waveform are within acceptable specifications, and then outputs stable, "clean" power to the computer. Electrical contractors or electricians can test whether or not a power conditioner is required by monitoring a circuit with a special metering device for 24 to 48 hours. Metering devices print a statistical summary of electrical quality and the number and duration of spikes, surges, or brownouts that occurred during the test period.

- **Multiple computers**—If multiple computer systems will be installed in one location, such as an office, training room, or computer lab facility, the total electric power requirements need to be planned in advance, and an electrical contractor should be consulted to verify that the power is adequate and well conditioned. The installation of network servers and high-end workstations, whose power requirements can be unusual, may also require the help of a qualified electrician.

Electrical power and peripheral signal cables should be installed so they will not be damaged or stressed by stretching. When computer wires are installed in an existing building, surface-mounted cable conduits (or runways) can be installed along an office or computer lab wall. These conduits provide access to the cables if they need to be upgraded or repaired, but they protect the cables from potential problems due to shorted or broken cables. Avoid running power cables or signal cables over a tile office floor or under a carpet. If power or signal cables must run over or under any kind of flooring, purchase rubber conduits to protect the cables from the wear and tear of traffic. Plastic cable ties can be used to bundle cables and secure them to furniture or walls in order to get them off the floor or out of the way, and to avoid stress on the cable runs.

In work areas where power and signal cable management is a significant problem, wireless devices should be investigated as an alternative.

Specialized Power Devices

In a standard computer installation, electrical power strips are convenient because a user can flip one switch to turn on an entire system. The system unit, display screen, printer, and other peripheral devices can all be plugged into a power strip. However, power strips should not be used as electrical extension cords. Each power strip should be plugged into an electrical outlet—not into another power strip. This requirement is part of the electrical code in many areas and makes good sense even where it is not. The best power strips, **surge protectors** (or **surge suppressors**), include protective circuitry that helps prevent damage to computer equipment due to power surges and spikes. Surge protectors may also include filters that reduce radio frequency interference.

Some surge protector manufacturers offer a warranty that pays a user if computer equipment is damaged while plugged into one of their devices—if the surge protector was installed and operated according to the manufacturer's recommendations.

ON THE WEB

Not all surge protectors provide adequate safeguards from power surges and spikes. Inexpensive models may not have robust circuitry to protect against extremely powerful surges, such as a lightning strike. Electric utilities generally recommend a surge suppressor with the following minimum specifications:

- UL 1449 (second edition) listed
- 40,000 amps or more peak protection
- 330 volts or less clamping voltage level
- 1 nanosecond or less clamping response time
- 750 joules or more energy rating
- Diagnostic LED status lamps

For more information about surge protectors, read a 24-page guide prepared by NIST (**www.nist.gov/public_affairs/practiceguides/surgesfnl.pdf**).

In environments in which power problems exist or computer downtime is unacceptable, several tools are available to address specific issues. **Downtime** is a measure of the number of hours (per week or month) that a computer system is unavailable for use because of power failures or other problems; **uptime** measures the number of operational hours. Obviously, uptime for a computer system in a hospital's critical care unit is more important than uptime in a school classroom.

Uptime and downtime measurements are often converted into percentages of time to standardize these measures. For example, a system that is down 2 hours during a 30-day month has an uptime measure of 99.72 percent.

When a power conditioner is used, the device must have the capacity to condition power for the total load it is expected to service. For example, the load on a circuit may include the system unit, display screen, printer, scanner, other computer peripherals, and additional office and lighting equipment.

An **uninterruptible power supply (UPS)** is an electrical device that includes power conditioning circuits as well as a battery backup. The battery backup begins operating when the UPS senses that the electrical power supply is interrupted (or reduced during a brownout) and then provides power to the computer equipment for a limited period of time, hopefully until full power can be restored. The battery power rating of a UPS indicates how long a computer system will be able to continue operation after a power failure. A higher-power battery is more expensive; therefore, most UPS devices in use allow for the operation of a computer for a few minutes, or up to an hour at most. The battery capacity in a UPS is intended primarily to provide time for users to properly shut down their computer equipment so application software and operating systems can empty memory buffers, close files, and terminate operation, and hardware can power down normally. Without a UPS, power loss could cause hardware or software to terminate abnormally, which may cause equipment damage or unpredictable problems when the system is powered on later.

Many modern UPS devices automatically shut down a computer system to protect it from data loss if a user is not available to do it manually.

ON THE WEB

To learn more about electrical power problems, conditioning equipment, and UPS devices, visit the NetworkClue.com Web site (**www.networkclue.com/hardware/ power**). The site includes pointers to resources for selecting devices to solve various power problems.

Network and Telephone Access

Few computers today are standalone installations. Most office computer systems require connection to a local area network, and home computer systems are usually connected to the Internet. Internet access can be provided by one of the following options:

- A telephone line can be used for dial-up access to an Internet Service Provider.

- DSL (digital subscriber line) connections (available in some service areas) provide fast data and voice connections over a single telephone line.

- Cable television companies frequently offer broadband Internet service.

- Satellite television providers may offer Internet connection along with television service.

Each of these connection methods requires a modem for data transmission. After establishing the connection requirements for a specific installation, you should locate the nearest telephone, cable, or network access points to determine if extension lines are necessary, or determine whether wireless access is available.

Air Conditioning

Just as many computer installations do not require additional electrical wiring, most do not require air conditioning beyond what is necessary for end-user comfort. However, in locations where a large number of computer systems will be installed in close proximity, such as in a small office, training facility, computer lab, or network server room, additional air conditioning may be required. An engineer or consultant who specializes in heating, ventilating, and air conditioning (HVAC) can help determine the requirements. HVAC specialists use a formula that considers the total wattage of electrical devices and the heat generated by people to compute the number of BTUs (British thermal units) of air conditioning capacity required to maintain the temperature within a predetermined range.

Servers and high-end workstations are more likely to require air conditioning than small office computers. However, the total wattage within a space determines air conditioning requirements. Even a few computers in a very small office can create a need for air conditioning, especially during summer months.

Lighting

Incorrect office lighting can cause significant ergonomic problems. The lighting level can be too intense, come from the wrong source, or be the wrong type of lighting. The result can be lower worker productivity due to eyestrain or headaches.

Light Intensity

Many offices are over-lit for computer use. Too much light on a user's work surface can cause glare on a display screen. One solution is to turn off or remove some light fixtures to reduce the amount of glare. In cases where four fluorescent bulbs are housed in a fixture, for example, an electrician may be able to remove two of the four bulbs by making a simple modification to the fixture. If it is not possible to adjust the amount of light in an office, consider an antiglare filter that covers the entire display screen area.

Light Source

In addition to the amount of light, the source of light may cause problems. For example, in an office or training room with windows, computer display screens should be positioned so they are at a 90-degree angle (perpendicular) to the light source. This position is preferable to a light source that hits the screen directly, which can happen when the screen is positioned directly opposite a light source. A user generally should not face a light source, because direct light could cause eye strain if the user has to squint in order to control the amount of visible light.

Light Type

Finally, the type of lighting can cause problems with certain types of monitors. Some fluorescent bulbs flicker at the same frequency as the refresh rate on older CRT-type monitors. The result is a noticeable flicker or visible moving horizontal scan line on the screen. In these situations, an electrician or lighting consultant may be able to recommend a fluorescent bulb that flickers less or at a different rate than the monitor.

 Screen flicker is not a problem with LCD flat-panel displays.

Fire Suppression

Fortunately, computer systems rarely burst into flames. However, computer equipment *is* electrical and mechanical, and electromechanical devices can cause smoke or fires, primarily due to problems with power supplies. Devices that have moving parts or generate excessive heat, such as disk drives or printers, can also cause fires, although fires from these sources are unusual. While forecasting when a fire may occur is impossible, it is possible to be prepared for one. If an office does not have an existing fire-suppression system, place portable fire extinguishers near the equipment. Choose a fire extinguisher that is rated for electrical fires, because an extinguisher that is designed for wood or paper fires contains a dry chemical that can further damage electronic equipment.

The most effective fire extinguishers for use on and around computer equipment contain halon gas. However, the Environmental Protection Agency (EPA) has made the manufacture of new halon systems illegal because halon depletes ozone gas in the atmosphere. Existing halon systems can continue to be used; however, manufacturers have developed effective alternative fire extinguisher gases, such as Halotron, Inergen, and FE-36.

ON THE WEB

For additional information about halon, see the EPA Web site (**www.epa.gov/Ozone/ snap/fire/qa.html**).

To learn more about alternatives to halon for computer installations, read an article on BFPE International's Web site (**www.bfpe.com/fe_cleanagent.htm**).

Figure 10-3 is a checklist of issues that should be considered during the installation planning stages. As with the other checklists in this chapter, it is a summary of issues, designed as a starting point. Not all issues apply to every installation, nor are all issues of equal importance.

Site Preparation Checklist

❏ Perform preinstallation site inspection

    ❏ Electrical power access

    ❏ Network, wireless, telephone, or cable access

    ❏ Space for desktop or laptop unit, keyboard, mouse, display screen, printer, and other peripherals

        ❏ requires keyboard shelf or accommodation

        ❏ requires monitor arm

        ❏ requires space-saver case

        ❏ requires printer stand

    ❏ Furniture adequately accommodates computer equipment or user

    ❏ Power and signal cables reach system unit and peripherals

    ❏ Ergonomic issues

        ❏ height of work surface and keyboard location

        ❏ location and viewing angle of display screen

        ❏ lighting source and location

        ❏ adjustable seating

        ❏ footrest

        ❏ wrist wrest

        ❏ other ergonomic accommodations

    ❏ Ventilation and air circulation

    ❏ Location of nearest fire extinguisher rated for electrical fires

    ❏ Special site problems

        ❏ static electricity ❏ moisture ❏ dust ❏ humidity

        ❏ temperature   ❏ accommodations for physical limitations

        ❏ storage space for manuals, supplies, and site management notebook

❏ Arrange time for system installation

Figure 10-3   Site preparation checklist

A ROLE-PLAYING SCENARIO

This scenario occurred when Daren, a user support specialist, arrived at the workstation of Sean, a new employee in the Human Resources Department. If possible, have fellow students or coworkers play the parts of Daren and Sean, and then discuss your reaction to their conversation.

DAREN: Good morning. I have a work order to help you install your new computer. I see you have a laptop model.

SEAN: Yes. In my job I will be traveling occasionally and would like to be able to take my computer with me into the field.

DAREN: Good choice. We'll set it up on your desk. Can you move the phone a little, please? By the way, is there a connection to the company network anywhere around here?

SEAN: I don't know. I've just moved in, and I think this is a new cubicle. I'm not sure I've seen a connection, come to think of it.

DAREN: Well, I know there is a network drop on that load-bearing wall over there, but that must be 30 feet away. I don't have any cables that long. I can order one though.

SEAN: How long will that take?

DAREN: Only a couple of days. Until then, we can get the software you requested installed and you can use your computer now, but you won't be able to access the local area network or receive email.

SEAN: Well, if that's the best you can do…

DAREN: I did bring along the install CDs for the Office Suite.

SEAN: Is that for Office 2010?

DAREN: Yes, the company converted to 2010 a few weeks back.

SEAN: My manager says my department, HR, is still on 2007. Apparently HR has been busy with end-of-quarter processing and hasn't had the training on 2010 yet. I actually used Office 2003 at my old job, so I'm not used to the new menus in 2007 and 2010.

DAREN: Well, I'll install 2010 today, and then you'll be ready when you've had the training. You'll probably be able to pick up the Office menus quickly anyway.

DAREN: Now I just need to know where you want your printer.

SEAN: Well, I don't have much furniture yet, so I don't really have a place to put it. Could it go on the floor?

DAREN: It probably could, but the cable wouldn't reach. So we'll just put it on your desk for now, until you get something better. Could you move your phone over a little more? Oh, and call me anytime you have any problems with your new laptop.

Describe the problems you identified in this scenario. What suggestions do you have to avoid problems like the ones you identified?

Site Management Documentation

The primary goal of any installation is, of course, to achieve an operational system that enhances user productivity. However, support specialists may want to accomplish other goals during a system installation. A common goal is to build a **site management notebook**, which is a binder that consolidates important information about a system's hardware, operating system, network connection, and application software configurations, as well as facilities management information, in one location.

A site management notebook contains much of the information a support specialist might need in the future to operate, diagnose, troubleshoot, reconfigure, upgrade, and repair the system and its components. A site management notebook is also a useful resource to make sure important steps are not omitted when installing one or several systems.

The site management notebook documents important details about an installation, including:

- Hardware configuration
- Operating system configuration
- Network connectivity configuration
- Software licenses
- Application software configuration
- Special operating procedures
- Warranty and repair information
- Problem log
- Backup media log

A site management notebook may be overkill for a simple installation of a home or small office computer; however, one is often a necessity for systems installed in larger offices, training facilities, and computer labs. Even some personal computer users have found a site management notebook a useful tool and worth the time it takes to file and maintain the information. A site management notebook is especially critical in locations where a large number of computers are installed, systems are configured differently, or multiple support staff members work on various parts of a system from time to time. The notebook acts as a one-stop source of information to answer questions support specialists may have, such as:

- From which vendor was the PC purchased and when?
- When was the PC installed and by whom?
- What changes to the standard operating system configuration were made on this machine?
- What software is legally licensed to be installed on this system?
- What are the system's IP and MAC addresses?
- Who should the user contact when the display screen doesn't work?
- Where are the media backups and when were they created?
- Has the printer problem we're seeing today happened before?

Figure 10-4 shows examples of the kind of information often included in a site management notebook, including hardware and software information sheets and configuration details.

440

PC Hardware Configuration Sheet

SYSTEM _____   Serial # _____

Purchase Date ___ /___ /___   Vendor _____

Installation Date ___ /___ /___   Installer _____

1. System Unit

❑ Desktop   ❑ Laptop   ❑ Netbook   ❑ Tablet

Manufacturer _____   Model _____

Power supply _____ watts

2. CPU

❑ Intel _____   ❑ AMD _____

Bus type _____   Motherboard type _____

BIOS Manufacturer _____   Version _____

3. Internal memory

RAM _____ GB   Type _____   Pins _____   Slots _____

Cache memory   L1 _____ KB   L2 _____ MB   L3 _____ MB

4. Storage

Controller card ❑ IDE   ❑ EIDE   ❑ ATA   ❑ SATA

Hard drive _____ GB TB   Secondary drive _____ GB TB

Solid-state drive (SSD) _____ GB TB

External hard drive   Manufacturer _____   _____GB TB

❑ Optical CD _____ X   ❑ CD±RW _____ X   ❑ DVD _____ X   ❑ DVD±RW_____ X

5. Input

❑ Keyboard   ❑ Standard   ❑ Ergonomic

❑ Mouse   Type _____

❑ Scanner   Manufacturer _____   Model _____

6. Output

❑ Graphics/video adapter   Type _____   Memory _____ MB

❑ Display screen manufacturer _____   Model _____

Size _____   Resolution _____

❑ Printer   Manufacturer _____   Model _____

❑ Inkjet ❑ B/W _____ ppm _____ dpi   ❑ Color _____ ppm _____ dpi

❑ Laser ❑ B/W _____ ppm _____ dpi   ❑ Color _____ ppm _____ dpi

Cartridge # _____   Cartridge # _____   Cartridge # _____

7. Networking

❑ Ethernet _____

❑ Modem Manufacturer _____   Model _____   Speed _____

❑ Workstation ID _____   IP address _____ . _____ . _____ . _____ . _____ . _____

MAC address ____-____-____-____-____-____

❑ Wireless adapter _____

8. Expansion

❑ Ports   ❑ Serial _____   ❑ Parallel _____   ❑ Mouse

❑ USB _____   ❑ 1.1 ❑ 2.0 ❑ 3.0

❑ Bus Slots ❑ 8-bit _____   16-bit _____   32-bit _____   64-bit _____

❑ Media adapter _____

9. Other

Figure 10-4   Sample pages from a site management notebook (*continues*)

(continued)

PC Software Configuration Sheet

SYSTEM _____   **Serial #** _____

Purchase Date ___ / ___ / ___   **Vendor** _____

Installation Date ___ / ___ / ___   **Installer** _____

1. Application needs checklist

❑ Word processing	❑ Desktop publishing	❑ Web authoring	❑ Spreadsheet
❑ Accounting	❑ Database management	❑ Financial	❑ Project management
❑ Presentation	❑ Multimedia	❑ Graphics	❑ CAD
❑ GIS	❑ Statistics	❑ Decision support	❑ Forecasting

2. Operating system   **VERSION**

   ❑ Windows (Service Pack _____)   _____

   ❑ Linux   ❑ Unix   ❑ Mac OS   _____

3. Tools and Utilities   **VERSION**

   Programming languages   ❑ Visual BASIC   ❑ C/C++   _____

                              ❑ Java   ❑ Other _____   _____

   Utilities   ❑ Antivirus _____   _____

                              ❑ Firewall _____   _____

                              ❑ Antispyware _____   _____

                              ❑ PDF reader _____   _____

                              ❑ Media backup _____   _____

                              ❑ _____   _____

                              ❑ _____   _____

4. Application software installed   **VERSION**

   ❑ Office suite _____   _____

   ❑ Word processor _____   _____

   ❑ Spreadsheet _____   _____

   ❑ Database _____   _____

   ❑ Presentation _____   _____

   ❑ Accounting _____   _____

   ❑ Financial _____   _____

   ❑ PIM _____   _____

   ❑ Desktop publishing _____   _____

   ❑ Web development _____   _____

   ❑ Communications

       ❑ Email client _____   _____

       ❑ Web browser _____   _____

       ❑ FTP _____   _____

   ❑ Internet Service Provider _____   _____

   ❑ _____   _____

   ❑ _____   _____

Figure 10-4   Sample pages from a site management notebook (*continues*)

(continued)

Furniture/Supplies/Accessories

❏ desk (26–28" height)	❏ cleaning supplies:	❏ bookshelf/rack
❏ printer stand	❏ compressed air	❏ mouse pad
❏ LCD projector	❏ vacuum	❏ footrest
	❏ wipes	
❏ media	❏ cleaner	❏ tool kit
❏ power strip	❏ chair (ergonomic)	❏ printer forms
❏ documentation	❏ printer paper	❏ microphone
❏ wrist rest	❏ headset	❏ digital camera
❏ antiglare screen	❏ media storage	❏ extender cables
❏ security lockdown	❏ surge protector	❏ antistatic mat

Figure 10-4   Sample pages from a site management notebook

ON THE WEB

For additional details and information on the terms used in the PC Hardware Configuration Sheet, see the following Web sites:

- Webopedia (**www.webopedia.com/Hardware**)

- TechTerms.com (**www.techterms.com/hardware.php**)

- Javvin Company (**www.javvin.com/hardware**)

Follow links on these Web sites to learn more about each hardware option.

Several free system information utilities can be downloaded to capture and present PC configuration information, including Belarc Advisor (**www.belarc.com/free_download.html**) and SiSoftware's Sandra (**www.sisoftware.net**).

In situations where a complete site management notebook isn't practical for whatever reason, a printout of configuration information from one of these resources is better than nothing when it comes time to reconfigure, upgrade, troubleshoot, or repair a PC.

Activity 10-4 at the end of this chapter gives you an opportunity to run one of these system information utilities and learn more about the kind of information they provide.

In Windows 7 and Vista, you can explore many of the configuration options for a PC by accessing the System Information Tool (SIT). It is located on the **Start** menu, under **All Programs**. Click **Accessories**, then **System Tools**, and finally, **System Information**. Or, click the **Start** button, and then enter the command **msinfo32** in the **Search** box.

443

Hardware Installation Tools

User support specialists who frequently install and make common hardware repairs can purchase or assemble a kit with the basic tools needed to perform simple tasks with computer equipment (see Figure 10-5).

Figure 10-5 A typical hardware installation tool kit

Computer, electronic supply, and mail order vendors sell tool kits, which start at about $15. Most basic kits contain the following:

- **Screwdriver set**—Used to remove and insert screws; the set should include both a slotted blade and a Phillips-head screwdriver. The heads on the screwdrivers should be smaller than general-use screwdrivers because computer screws are often small. Some hardware technicians prefer a socketed screwdriver with interchangeable heads.

- **Nut driver**—Used to remove the case from a system because the screws on a case are often six-sided nuts. (Nut drivers come in several sizes; get one designed for computer equipment.) Some socketed screwdrivers are the correct size for a nut driver when the screwdriver heads are removed.

- **Pliers**—Used to hold and clamp parts; the kit should include both regular pliers and needle-nose pliers for working with small parts.

- **Parts-picker** (retractable claw)—Used to pick up small screws, nuts, and bolts in a tight work space; some kits contain tweezers and a magnetic parts grabber for small parts.

Tools for use around computer equipment should be nonmagnetic.

In addition, support specialists who work frequently on hardware installations or end-user problems may want to augment a basic tool kit with one or more of the following:

- **Pocketknife**—Used for tasks when perhaps no other tool will do the job. (Victorinox makes a version of the Swiss Army Knife, called the CyberTool, which is specifically designed for work with computer hardware.)

- **Small parts container**—Used for keeping track of screws, nuts, washers, and other small parts while working on a computer system (a recycled pill container is useful for this purpose).

- **Mirror**—Used to see in tight spaces and behind components that are difficult to move (an angled dental mirror is a good choice).

- **Small flashlight**—Used to illuminate hard-to-see places.

- **Isopropyl alcohol**—Used to clean electrical components, display screens, keyboards, and mouse parts. Isopropyl alcohol should be handled with care, like any chemical; it should not be consumed or inhaled under any circumstances. Alternatives include spray cleaners and packaged wipes. While the CRT screen on older PC monitors can be cleaned with isopropyl alcohol, in general, laptop display screens should be cleaned with a milder solution such as eye glass cleaner or packaged wipes, which are less likely to damage the surface than chemical cleaners.

- **Lint-free cloth or foam-tipped brush**—Used to apply isopropyl alcohol for cleaning; antistatic wipes are also recommended.

- **Microfiber cloth**—Used to clean dust from display screens, keyboards, and computer cases.

- **Antistatic wrist strap**—Used to ground a technician to the computer power supply or case whenever a need arises to handle components inside a desktop case. A strap reduces the risk of damaging a component with an accidental static charge. Inexpensive antistatic wrist straps sell for $6 to $10.

- **Cable ties**—Used to bundle together cables to keep them well organized and out of the way.

- **Electrical tape**—Used for simple repairs or in lieu of cable ties.

- **Masking tape**—Used to label cables prior to unplugging them.

- **Compressed air**—Used to blow dust out of computer cases, keyboards, printers, and other equipment. An alternative is a small vacuum cleaner designed for electronic equipment, available in many parts supply catalogs.

- **Circuit tester**—Used to determine whether an electric outlet has been properly wired (tests hot, neutral, and ground); inexpensive models are simple plug-in devices.

- **Multimeter**—Used to determine whether an electric circuit is active, whether a cable has a short, or whether a battery still has a charge; a multimeter is sometimes called a VOM (volt-ohm-meter). For many tasks, inexpensive analog multimeters can be purchased for $10 to $15; for work on motherboards, a digital multimeter is recommended.

- **Notepad and pencil**—Used for taking notes on cable connections, parts to order, reminders, and other to-do tasks.

 Some of the small tools recommended for an installer's tool kit can be obtained inexpensively at a dollar store.

Once you have inspected the installation site and are sure you have the proper equipment and tools, you can proceed with installing the hardware components.

Common Hardware Installation Steps

For most users in homes and organizations, installing computer hardware includes unpacking, connecting, and testing the basic components. Basic components usually consist of a system unit, display screen, keyboard, mouse, and perhaps a printer. An installation process can also include installing additional memory, expansion cards for peripheral devices, and network connections.

An important first step is to plan an installation. In addition to the preinstallation site checklist and steps described earlier in this chapter, planning also includes a review to make sure you have all the components and tools you will need. An installation time that is convenient for the user should also be arranged in advance. Technicians who install a large volume of systems usually develop a checklist to make sure they bring all the necessary components with them and perform all the steps required. The checklist later becomes a form of documentation that they did so. Figure 10-6 shows a typical hardware installation checklist.

Hardware Installation Checklist

BEFORE INSTALLATION:

❑ Review safety checklist

❑ Get tool kit and spare parts container

❑ Unpack hardware components and note any missing or damaged parts

❑ Save boxes and packing material in case components need to be returned

BASIC INSTALLATION:

❑ Connect basic components, power, and signal cables

❑ Perform basic system boot test

❑ Remove case cover and inspect components for proper installation

❑ Fill out hardware configuration sheet in site management notebook

    ❑ Record serial numbers in site management notebook

    ❑ File warranty information

OPTIONAL INSTALLATION:

❑ Install any memory upgrade and expansion cards:

❑ Multi-function I/O	❑ Sound card
❑ Graphics adapter	❑ Network interface
❑ Internal modem	❑ Other: _____

COMPLETE INSTALLATION:

❑ Connect peripherals

❑ display screen	❑ keyboard	❑ mouse
❑ printer	❑ external modem	❑ telephone
❑ external hard drive	❑ speakers	❑ scanner
❑ microphone	❑ digital camera	❑ _____

❑ Connect power and signal cables

❑ Attach network cable to Ethernet connector

❑ Install power strip, surge suppressor, or UPS power unit

❑ Power up system and adjust display screen

❑ Run diagnostic tests on hardware devices

❑ Install ergonomic devices (screen glare filter, copy holder, wrist rest)

❑ Check cables for excess tension and install tie-wraps to bundle cables

❑ Attach security cables for theft prevention

❑ Record vendor contact numbers and email addresses in site management notebook

Figure 10-6 Hardware installation checklist

The purpose of this sample checklist, and the others in this chapter, is to provide a starting point for support specialists who want to develop their own checklists and procedures specific to each organization and situation.

The checklists in this chapter are available as editable Word documents on this book's companion Web site (**www.cus5e.com**).

Support specialists who install systems don't necessarily perform all the steps shown in Figure 10-6 at every installation. To make the checklist more useful, installers can delete steps they never perform or insert additional steps that apply to their installations.

The checklist in Figure 10-6 assumes a support specialist is installing a preassembled system. Sometimes an installer assembles a system from basic components or installs additional equipment in a preassembled system. Trade books on installing or upgrading a computer system describe in detail the steps involved in assembling a system starting at the individual component level.

Whenever installers remove the case from a computer system to make a repair or replace a component, they should follow the basic safety precautions described in Figure 10-7.

Guidelines for Working Inside a System Unit

Before you begin . . .

☐ 1. Understand what tasks you are going to do and how you are going to do them.

☐ 2. Get documentation on how to complete each task or step you are going to perform.

☐ 3. Clear an adequate work space. Remove food and beverages from the work area.

☐ 4. Get the hardware components, tools, and software you will need to complete each task (include paper and pencil for notes).

☐ 5. Get a collector container for small parts, such as screws.

Before you remove the case . . .

☐ 6. Turn off the power switch (Is there more than one power switch?).

☐ 7. Unplug the power cord (Is there more than one power cord?).

☐ 8. If in doubt, check for electric current with a tester or turn off the power at the breaker box.

☐ 9. Work with at least one other person in the vicinity of where you are working.

☐ 10. Remember: You should not take off the case from a power supply or a CRT monitor, or try to repair those devices.

☐ 11. Avoid loose clothing while working around mechanical parts, such as printers.

After the case is removed . . .

☐ 12. Observe proper handling procedures and warnings for chemicals, such as isopropyl alcohol and printer ink.

☐ 13. Before you begin work, attach an antistatic wrist strap, especially if you are working on memory components, IC chips, the motherboard, or adapter cards.

☐ 14. Before you unplug any component, make notes or a diagram of how it is mounted and how cables are connected to it (or use tape to label cable connections).

Before you restore power to test a component or system . . .

☐ 15. Double-check signal cable connections and power connections to make sure they are secure.

☐ 16. Before you test the system, check inside the system case and around the work area to make sure you can account for all components and tools.

☐ 17. Before you complete installation or troubleshooting, thoroughly test both the components you worked on and other system components.

After you have tested a component or system . . .

☐ 18. If you restored power to the system to test the components, turn off the power switch and unplug the power cord before you resume work inside the case.

After you are finished . . .

☐ 19. Put away your tools.

☐ 20. Document any changes you made to a system or its components in the site installation notebook.

Figure 10-7 Hardware installation safety precautions

Typical Operating System and Network Installation Steps

After a hardware installation is completed, the next steps may involve the related tasks of installing and configuring an operating system and a network connection.

Operating System Installation

Support specialists do not always install an operating system. Most preassembled computer systems have an operating system already installed on the hard drive. In situations that do require support specialists to install an operating system, most are supplied on a CD or DVD. Some vendors provide operating system updates, patches, service packs, and special drivers that users can download from a Web site. In cases where support specialists install identical operating system configurations on a large number of machines, an image of the system can be written on a removable hard drive or optical media and installed with a reimaging utility. Alternately, images or updates for an operating system on computers that are connected to a network can usually be installed on a large number of machines from a copy on the network server.

The installation process is usually not complicated, but it can take an hour or more from beginning to end. The steps to install operating system software might include partitioning the hard disk, installing the operating system software and any necessary device drivers, and installing the network operating system client. After the operating system and network client have been configured for the hardware peripherals and to meet site-specific standards, support specialists perform updates and install other necessary software, including virus protection, antispyware, screen savers, company templates, and security and utility software.

Many PCs use a version of the Windows operating system, which reduces the need to install special device drivers. For the most part, Windows automatically recognizes devices that conform to Plug and Play standards. In these cases, Windows installs a default driver for devices it recognizes during the boot process. However, recent versions of Windows may not recognize some older peripheral devices, and device drivers may need to be installed manually in those cases, if they are available. Each peripheral vendor's Web site should be checked to see if an updated device driver is available for download, because bugs may have been discovered in earlier versions or performance enhancements may have been introduced. Installers of Macintosh systems usually have an easier task, because the Mac OS automatically recognizes most peripheral devices; however, some peripheral devices are sold that require specialized device drivers for the Mac OS.

Experienced installers know that incompatibility between hardware, operating systems, and device drivers can cause many hours of lost time during installations. These installers check system requirements and vendor Web sites prior to installation to reduce the probability that time will be lost due to incompatible components.

ON THE WEB

To learn more about device drivers and how to check versions and problems with device drivers, read an article on PCAuthorities' Web site (**www.pcauthorities.com/ drivers/device-drivers-explained**).

Several vendors provide a free scan of device drivers on a user's PC, report out-of-date drivers, and provide access to a database of updated device drivers for a paid registration. Two options are Driver Guide's DriverScan (**www.driverguidetoolkit. com**) and Drivers.com (**www.drivers.com**).

In many cases, replacements for out-of-date drivers identified by one of these scans can be downloaded free from a vendor's Web site.

Vendor manuals are a good source of specific information about how to install an operating system. However, the process has been highly automated in recent releases, so little printed documentation may be available. User manuals may be included on distribution CDs or on a vendor Web site. Trade books, journals, and online publications also often cover how to install and configure popular operating systems.

ON THE WEB

To view the steps Microsoft recommends to install Windows 7, visit **windows. microsoft.com/en-US/windows7/Installing-and-reinstalling-Windows-7**.

To learn about installing Linux operating systems, consult Norm Matloff's Guide (**heather.cs.ucdavis.edu/~matloff/Linux/LinuxInstall.pdf**).

Network Installation

Network connectivity is implemented with a combination of hardware, software, and operating procedures. The role of a support specialist in network installation is usually concerned primarily with the client or user workstation components. A support specialist may perform tasks such as:

- Install client software

- Configure network connectivity

- Perform network administrative tasks:

  - Administer user accounts (login IDs and passwords)

  - Grant rights to access network resources such as application software, disk space, peripheral devices, and shared printers

  - Perform periodic server media backups

  - Monitor network performance

  - Monitor network security

  - Report problems to the network support staff

In situations where a support staff has primary network installation and configuration responsibility, such as in a small organization, a network vendor or consultant often provides assistance with network server installation and configuration details.

Figure 10-8 is a checklist installers can use as a starting point when installing an operating system and network connection. The steps to install and configure network software are specific to each type of network and each user's specific needs. For installation of a standalone system, the steps related to network connectivity can be skipped; however, a typical network installation involves many of the steps described in Figure 10-8.

**Operating System and
Network Installation Checklist**

PRELIMINARY STEPS (as necessary)

☐ Make backup copy of existing operating system (if applicable)

☐ Make backup copy of any user data files (if applicable)

☐ Run FDISK to partition hard drive (if necessary)

BASIC INSTALLATION

☐ Install operating system software

☐ Install device drivers required by peripherals

☐ Configure operating system and startup files (consistent with organization standards)

☐ Modify startup and configuration files

OPTIONAL INSTALLATION

☐ Install and configure antivirus, media backup, utilities, security software, and screen savers

DIAL-UP NETWORK INSTALLATION

☐ Verify that modem hardware is operational

☐ Configure dial-up networking client and communication protocols

☐ Test dial-up network connectivity

NETWORK CLIENT INSTALLATION

☐ Verify that network hardware connection is operational

☐ Verify that PC can connect to network server

☐ Install client software on workstation

☐ Modify startup files and login scripts to connect to network

☐ Log on to network server

☐ Download any additional required network software

☐ Configure client software

☐ Test network connectivity

NETWORK ADMINISTRATION

☐ Create the user account and initial password

☐ Grant user rights to access shared network resources, such as network drives, printers, and shared folders

COMPLETE INSTALLATION

☐ Update operating system and network configuration information, node addresses, and startup file modifications in site management notebook

Figure 10-8   Operating system and network installation checklist

A network administrator often builds a disk or optical media image that contains preconfigured network client software so it can be copied easily to a computer during installation. Vendor manuals and trade books are available that describe the details of specific network client software installation.

Typical Steps to Install Application Software

Before installing an application software package, a support specialist needs to verify that the software is compatible with the hardware and network on which it will be installed. Ideally the application software's compatibility with the hardware and network should be verified before any software is purchased. Before support specialists install software, they should determine the following:

- The CPU types the software runs on

- The amount of memory the software requires

- The amount of disk drive space the software requires for a full installation

- Whether the software is compatible with hardware peripherals

- Whether the software operates in a networked environment compatible with the user's

- Whether the company or user has a license or site license for the software

Software vendors usually distribute application software on **distribution media**, such as CDs or DVDs. However, application software packages are often available to download, in compressed format, from a network server or the Internet. Before any application software is downloaded from the Internet, a support specialist should consider the available connection speed. When a user has a slow dial-up connection to the Internet, a large software package (larger than a few megabytes) can sometimes be downloaded on another system that has a broadband link to the Internet. Then the software can be transported on a USB drive, optical media, or via a local area network connection to the end user's computer, where it can be installed. Because application programs often automatically update Registry and configuration files maintained by the operating system, application software packages should be installed directly on the computer on which they will be used. Problems can arise when an attempt is made to install a program by simply copying its image from another computer, which bypasses the steps to update the system Registry with information about the program.

Whatever the distribution media, the installation steps for most application packages are generally simpler than they were several years ago. Many packages auto-install after the user double-clicks an install icon. Most computers are equipped with a CD or DVD drive that has an Autoplay feature enabled. In these cases, a system can usually recognize that media containing a software installation has been inserted in the drive, and it will automatically begin the installation process. In other cases, the Computer (or My Computer) icon in the Windows operating system can be used to examine the installation media for a setup.exe or install.exe program.

Immediately before installing a new program, all open data files and programs should be closed to make sure that operational programs do not interfere with the installation process. Prior to installing a large application on a system with limited disk space, an installer may want to perform a hard disk defragmentation to ensure that an application's image will be written on contiguous disk blocks (which increases execution speed). The first step in an application software installation is often the execution of an installation utility program, such as InstallShield. The install utility guides the installer through the process and provides prompts about available user options. An example of a topic frequently covered during installations is whether the user wants a shortcut icon to run the program placed on the desktop, in the system tray, or on a toolbar.

 During the installation of some software, it is advisable to disable security features such as antivirus programs and firewalls that could prevent a successful installation. As a precaution, the PC can be disconnected (unplugged) from the Internet during the time that the security software is disabled.

The most common software installation options allow an installer to select from among the following choices:

- **Express installation**—Sometimes called a typical or common installation; an **express installation** installs the most frequently used program functions and features as determined by the manufacturer, and asks the fewest questions during installation.

- **Custom installation**—Sometimes called an expert or special installation; a **custom installation** lets a user select specific components or features to install. A custom installation requires an installer to answer more questions than in an express installation.

- **Minimal installation**—Sometimes called a laptop or space-saver installation; a **minimal installation** installs the fewest functions and features for users with limited hard drive space available.

- **Full installation**—Sometimes called a maximum or complete installation; a **full installation** installs all program functions and features, asks few questions, and takes the maximum amount of disk space and time.

It is a good idea to ask each end user about the type of installation required to meet his or her needs. However, users are generally not familiar with the terms *express* or *minimal* and may not understand the implications of the various installation choices from this shorthand list. A support specialist may need to translate these options into lists of specific features for an end user (i.e., what features will and will not be available for each installation choice). For example, some users may need specific software functions or features that are not included in a minimal installation.

Support specialists are also responsible for verifying that a user has the appropriate software licenses to permit an authorized installation. Some organizations maintain a software license database that needs to be updated as part of the installation process. Installing application software may also involve installing organization-specific options, document templates, style sheets, macros, or device drivers.

After installation, a support specialist should test the software and make sure it runs properly. Figure 10-9 shows a sample checklist that installers can use to guide software installations.

Application Software Installation Checklist

PRELIMINARY STEPS
❒ Close all open applications
❒ Make backup copies of any user data files that could be affected by the installation process

INSTALLATION
❒ Install standard application software packages (such as an Office suite)
   ❒ Express ❒ Custom ❒ Minimal ❒ Full
❒ Install and configure email and Web browser applications
❒ Install special-purpose software (such as accounting, marketing, manufacturing, or other organization-specific applications). Reboot system as needed after each installation.
❒ Install any device drivers required by application software. Reboot system as needed after each installation.
❒ Configure application software to meet the user's needs and conform to organization standards
   ❒ Adaptive options: _____
❒ Create desktop shortcuts to applications or add to startup menu as appropriate
❒ Add any organization-specific templates or style sheets for word processing or spreadsheets
❒ Reboot system
❒ Test all application software

COMPLETE INSTALLATION
❒ Fill out software configuration sheets in site management notebook
❒ File software licenses in site management notebook
❒ Register software with vendor (via mail-in card or online registration)
❒ Verify that user knows how to start the application
❒ Verify that the user is satisfied with the installation and knows how to get help if needed

Figure 10-9 Application software installation checklist

Typical Installation Wrap-Up Tasks

The previous sections described common steps and procedures to install hardware, operating systems, networks, and application software. Depending on the kind of installation and on organizational policy, a support specialist (or an end user) might undertake several additional steps. These are steps in which an installer documents software settings, backs up critical files, creates rescue disks, fills out warranty and registration cards, documents installation problems, addresses ergonomic concerns, and makes sure the user is able to operate the system productively. Support specialists can also perform "housekeeping" tasks such as storing documentation and disposing of shipping containers. Some of these tasks can be described as facilities management or installation documentation tasks, whereas other activities involve some user orientation or training. Most installers think of these as wrap-up tasks, because they are generally performed at the end of an installation.

Keep in mind that an installation doesn't end as soon as the hardware or software is installed. Support specialists who install or upgrade a system should always check with each user to make sure they can operate the new system correctly, or know where to get the training they need. Review any new equipment with users, and ensure that they can start, operate, and shut it down properly. Then, alert users to training opportunities and alternatives. Finally, verify that each user is satisfied with the installation and that his or her questions were answered. The ultimate measure of any installation procedure is the answer to the question: *"Is the user 100 percent satisfied?"*

Figure 10-10 shows a checklist for some of these wrap-up tasks. Not every step in the checklist applies to every installation. The tasks vary depending on the type of installation and the needs of each user.

Wrap-Up Checklist

HOUSEKEEPING

❐ Store or recycle shipping containers

SECURITY

❐ Make backup copies of Registry, configuration, and startup files

❐ Create bootable rescue or boot disk and store in site notebook

USER ORIENTATION

❐ Check system with user for any ergonomic problems

❐ Brief user on basic system operation

   ❐ Walk through system startup procedures

   ❐ Provide network user ID and password

   ❐ Provide reference sheets to document common operating system and application software tasks

   ❐ Describe antivirus, backup, and security procedures

   ❐ Review printer operation, paper loading, and cartridge or ribbon change procedures

   ❐ Go over operating procedures for peripherals

   ❐ Walk through system shutdown procedures

❐ Brief user on:

   ❐ Organization policies regarding acceptable computer use and abuse

   ❐ Importance of not consuming food and beverages around computer equipment

   ❐ Preventive maintenance procedures

   ❐ User support and help desk contacts

❐ Discuss training needs and opportunities with user

SITE MANAGEMENT NOTEBOOK

❐ Document system configuration (configuration printouts, startup file settings) and file in site management notebook

❐ Complete warranty and registration cards or online registration procedures

❐ Document any installation problems or special configuration specifications in site management notebook

❐ Store user and system documentation in convenient place

❐ Store software distribution media, drivers, and backups

COMPLETION

❐ Verify that user is satisfied with installation

Figure 10-10 Installation wrap-up checklist

Installing systems is often a smooth and relatively error- and stress-free process that serves its main purpose—to get a user's system up and running efficiently as soon as possible. In some cases, a system installation may become frustrating for both the installer and the end user because an unexpected incompatibility or defective hardware or software suddenly terminates an installation before it is complete. In some instances, installers may have to uninstall or reinstall components to get them to work correctly. Installers must be sure that they plan carefully for each installation, have the appropriate tools, follow step-by-step procedures, and are alert to the issues and potential problems that each installation can present. Although proper advanced planning does not guarantee a smooth and successful installation, poor planning almost always guarantees the opposite.

Ongoing Site Management Responsibilities

Even after an installer has completed all the checklists in this chapter and repacked his or her tool kit, ongoing administrative and support responsibilities continue in order to keep users productive. Those who support end users are likely to encounter user site management challenges, such as those listed in Figure 10-11.

- Media backup
- Monitoring potential security threats
- Disaster and contingency planning
- Other site management activities
  - Preventive maintenance
  - Computer supplies
  - Recycling computers and peripherals

Figure 10-11   Typical ongoing user site management responsibilities

Media Backup

A **media backup** is produced by copying the files and folders of software and data from a PC's hard drive onto a separate medium, to preserve them in case the original data is damaged or accidentally deleted. Media backups on a network system can significantly reduce site management costs and problems. In many network environments, an administrator can schedule automated backups of server software applications and user file space. And because network servers often operate 24 hours a day, 7 days a week, media backups can be scheduled at times when the load on a system is at its lightest, such as at night or on weekends. The storage media on a server, which is accessible via an office network, also provide convenient storage space and a method for users to back up any data files stored on their individual hard drives. For example, a backup utility on a user's system can often access a network server's hard drive as a backup medium. This capability means the user does not need magnetic or optical backup media on her or his PC, and does not need to remember to manually back up files. Backup storage for user data files is also available on the cloud, as described in Chapter 2. Many Internet service providers and other vendors offer limited free or extensive paid backup file storage where user files can be encrypted for security.

ON THE WEB

An example of a vendor of cloud backup services is IDrive.com (**www.idrive.com**), which offers 5 GB of free storage, along with several subscription plans for individuals and small businesses that require more backup storage space.

 Support specialists should also encourage users to make effective use of automatic backup procedures in application software packages. Many word processor and spreadsheet programs, for example, can be configured so the current document or worksheet is saved periodically on a local hard drive or network drive.

 Chapter 12 includes a description of media backup utility software that support specialists can use to help with this user site management responsibility.

Finally, while regular backups of important files should be made, documented procedures also should be available in the event a user needs to restore files from backup media. **File restoration** is a procedure to copy one or more files from backup media to the original or a replacement disk when data or programs have been erased or destroyed—the opposite of a media backup operation. File restorations are necessary when a hard drive fails or when a user accidentally deletes one or more files and needs to recover them. A support staff member may be assigned the responsibility of restoring backup files based on requests from users. The file restore procedure often involves using the same backup utility program that made the backup, only in restore mode. In all media backup situations, periodic tests of file restore operations should be conducted to verify that backup media is viable and restore procedures work as designed.

 In large organizations, the file restoration procedure can pose security or confidentiality problems. Users are normally permitted to restore only files that they themselves created or for which they have user rights. Users need special permission to restore a file that is owned by another user.

Monitoring Potential Security Threats

Support specialists may also have ongoing responsibilities for monitoring network performance and identifying network problems, including security and denial of service interruptions.

Access security in a network environment is a significant concern. Users (both authorized and unauthorized) can potentially access data and resources anywhere on a network, and sometimes from outside the network. However, network operating systems provide additional security features that are often more sophisticated and reliable than those available in nonnetworked systems. A network administrator plays a key role in the control of access to network facilities, because the administrator controls the user account management process.

Security problems can be classified based on the kind of threat (electronic or physical) and on the origin of the threat (internal or external):

- Electronic threats arise from attempts to breach the information or resources in a computer system.

- Physical threats arise from attempts to damage, disrupt, or gain access to computer facilities.

- Internal threats arise from inside an organization, including employees.

- External threats arise from outside an organization, including clients, hackers, and the public.

Electronic Threats to Security

The list of potential security problems that affect computer facilities from external sources via electronic or remote access is long and grows every year, but the most common sources of problems include:

- Proliferation of malicious software—including worms, viruses, and Trojan horses—that overloads networks and denies service to legitimate traffic

- Spam email attacks on network servers and end-user computers

- Attempts by unauthorized users to gain access to or control over computers and information

- Operating system software vulnerabilities that permit unauthorized access due to bugs in distributed software

- Proliferation of malware software that spies on the habits and behavior of end users or targets users for pop-up advertisements

- Lack of secure data transmission using encryption features

 Chapter 12 includes a description of security utilities that support specialists can use to help with this user site management challenge.

To deal with threats from electronic access, useful tools such as passwords, antivirus software, Internet firewalls, utility software, callback modems, and other online security measures are common precautions taken in installations of every size.

Physical Threats to Security

Physical access tools are designed to reduce threats from both unauthorized access and sabotage. Computer facilities are often a target of people looking to commit theft. They are also targets of workers or the public who are disgruntled with technology or with the way they have been treated by a bureaucracy (of which computer systems are a visible symbol). To address physical threats, computer facilities that have a large investment in equipment in a central location take steps to limit physical access to their facilities. Access management tools that are used to prevent information and equipment loss include:

- Keypad entry locks

- Identification badges and ID cards that function like entry keys

- **Biometric readers** (hardware devices that can uniquely identify a user through analysis of eye patterns, hand geometry, fingerprints, or voice and signature recognition)

- Motion sensors and heat-detection devices

- Camera systems to monitor facilities

- Reception desks

- Metal detectors

- Physical barriers (walls and windows)

 In very small facilities, locked doors are typically the primary means to control physical access to computer facilities.

ON THE WEB

In an era of identity theft, the field of biometric access controls is becoming increasingly important. To learn more about the basics of this technology, read an introduction to the topic in an article by Bryan Feltin titled, "Information Assurance Using Biometrics" (**www.giac.org/paper/gsec/2052/information-assurance-biometrics/103538**), or view a video tutorial (**www.biometrics.dod.mil/References/Tutorial/1.aspx**).

ON THE WEB

Support staff who have major responsibilities for security are the target audience for two print publications that address security concerns. *SC Magazine* is available for subscription (**www.scmagazineus.com**). *CSO*, a resource for security executives, is also available for subscription (**www.csoonline.com**). Both publications are available free to qualified professionals who have security responsibilities.

While many kinds of threats to computer facility security are intentional, other threats come in the form of natural disasters and accidents.

Disaster and Contingency Planning

Support specialists cannot prevent events such as power failures, floods, fires, storms, earthquakes, terrorist attacks, and sabotage from affecting computer services. But they can help plan to manage the consequences of unpredictable events by using risk management strategies. **Risk management** is the use of strategies and tools to reduce the threat to an organization from uncontrollable disasters or accidents and to help the organization recover from a disaster, with minimal financial impact or customer service loss. Some common risk management tools include the following:

- **Insurance**—An organization can purchase **business interruption insurance**, which helps offset the cost of returning to normal operation after an unforeseen event occurs.

- **Inspections**—Organizations can obtain an **engineering inspection** to help identify the potential for damage to computer equipment and facilities due to natural disasters and accidents. An engineering inspection report may recommend that an organization modify building structures or recommend detection devices, such as fire alarms and moisture sensors.

- **Media Backups**—Media backups of important data and programs are a critical component of any disaster/contingency plan. Media backups may be stored off-site, at a separate facility from the primary work location so that data can be replaced in the event of a major disaster such as a fire.

- **Disaster/Contingency Plans**—A disaster/contingency plan is a useful planning tool for both large and small computer installations. A **disaster/contingency plan** is a document that describes various activities that will occur if a computer facility experiences a temporary disruption of service. Disaster plans often address such events as fires, earthquakes, power outages, water damage, and sabotage. An effective plan should answer the question: *"What specific steps will our organization take in the event a disaster occurs?"*

A disaster/contingency plan is effective only if workers are aware of its existence and are trained in its procedures. Support specialists responsible for disaster planning should find the most effective way to communicate these plans to workers to ensure that recovery procedures can and will be carried out.

ON THE WEB

Computing and Network Services at the University of Toronto has developed an outline for organizations that want to prepare a disaster recovery plan. Their guidelines, checklists, and eight-step action plan emphasize the importance of business continuity. See the guidelines at **www.utoronto.ca/security/ documentation/business_continuity/dis_rec_plan.htm**.

An example of a disaster/contingency plan prepared at Adams State College is available at **www2.adams.edu/administration/computing/dr-plan100206.pdf**.

Other Site Management Activities

User support specialists who support internal workers may also be asked questions about or have responsibilities that include preventive PC maintenance, acquiring computer supplies, and recycling used computer systems and components.

Preventive Maintenance

Although most personal computer equipment is primarily electronic and does not require a great deal of preventive maintenance, some moving parts do benefit from periodic attention. **Preventive maintenance** involves using tools and procedures to reduce the likelihood of computer component failure and expensive repair costs. Preventive maintenance steps focus on cleaning and adjusting equipment to prolong its useful life and enhance operational efficiency.

System Unit

Most components inside a system unit either cannot be maintained by an end user or do not require preventive maintenance. However, in a dusty environment, the life of a PC can be increased by periodically vacuuming the inside of the case to reduce dust buildup on the components. A low intake vacuum cleaner with an antistatic plastic (not metallic) nozzle is preferable to cans of compressed air, which tend to blow dust around, rather than sweep it up. Use of a standard shop vac should be avoided. After vacuuming inside a case, compressed air can be used while the vacuum cleaner is running to remove any residual dust. The system unit case and other plastic or painted parts can be cleaned with isopropyl alcohol and a lint-free or microfiber cloth, or with pretreated wipes designed for that purpose.

Prior to removing the case on a PC for any reason, turn off the power and unplug the electrical supply as a precaution.

Disk Drives

For the most part, hard drives, CD and DVD devices, and removable drives do not include user-serviceable components; when these devices fail, they are replaced, rather than repaired. Check the manufacturer's Web site for troubleshooting options or refer problems to a qualified hardware technician.

Printers

The biggest enemies of most printers are paper dust and ink buildup. Even printer paper that looks clean can attract and carry dust particles. A good preventive maintenance strategy for a printer is to dust it periodically using a nonstatic vacuum cleaner. The insides of a printer should also be kept free of ink and toner spills, because these chemicals attract dust particles. Spilled toner should be cleaned up with a vacuum designed for PC use (ideally, one that is equipped with a toner filter).

Keyboards

Vacuum a keyboard or spray it with compressed air periodically to remove dust and dirt particles from between the keys. A buildup of dust can make the keys stick or wear out the mechanism that makes contact with the membranes in the keyboard. Dirty keyboard keys can be cleaned with a lint-free cloth moistened with isopropyl alcohol.

For especially dirty keyboards, a small brush, such as a toothbrush, dipped in isopropyl alcohol can be an effective cleaner.

Mouse/Trackball Parts

Both the rubber ball inside an older mouse or trackball and the mouse case can become dusty and grimy with use. In order to clean a mouse, unplug it (if necessary) and remove the rubber ball by twisting or pushing on the plastic restrainer in the direction indicated by the arrow on the underside of the mouse. Remove the ball; clean it, the metal contacts inside the mouse cavity, and the mouse case with isopropyl alcohol and a lint-free cloth. Then reassemble the mouse and plug it in, if necessary.

The case and glides on an optical (laser) mouse can also be cleaned with isopropyl alcohol and a cloth, but avoid using excess chemicals around the optical eye opening.

Display Screen

Clean dust and smudges on a computer screen regularly with a special pretreated cloth designed for that purpose, with a microfiber cloth, or with isopropyl alcohol and a lint-free cloth. Isopropyl alcohol should not be used to clean laptop screens. Eye glass cleaner, which is milder, is an acceptable substitute for chemical cleaners.

 Preventive maintenance on a CRT or LCD monitor is limited primarily to external cleaning and adjustment. There are no user-serviceable parts inside a monitor.

ON THE WEB

To view a video on preventive PC maintenance, visit **reviews.cnet.com/4520-11319_7-6240575-1.html?tag=nav**.

For more information on preventive maintenance, see a guide on the *PCWorld* Web site (**www.pcworld.com/article/116583/hardware_tips_complete_pc_preventive_maintenance_guide.html**).

Preventive maintenance can extend the useful life of many components in a computer system. Support specialists should try to help users understand the importance of maintenance in increasing both the life expectancy of the PC and its operating efficiency.

Computer Supplies

Another user site management task that often gets delegated to support specialists is the purchase or recommendation of computer supplies. Alternately, support specialists may be asked for advice about where to find specific supplies or where to get the best prices on them. Sources of supplies range from local office supply stores to electronics specialty stores to suppliers that do business primarily on the Internet.

ON THE WEB

Vendors that specialize in selling computer and office supplies on the Internet include:

Vendor	URL
Amazon.com	**www.amazon.com**
Cheap Office Supplies	**www.cheapofficesupplies.com**
Clean Sweep Supply	**www.cleansweepsupply.com/pages/category0003.html**
Global Computer	**www.globalcomputer.com**
Keysan	**www.keysan.com/indh106.htm**
Office Depot	**www.officedepot.com**
Office Max	**www.officemax.com**
Quill Office Supplies	**www.quill.com**
Staples	**www.staples.com**

Local computer supply stores can be found in the Yellow Pages of most telephone directories under headings such as *Computers and Computer Hardware – Parts & Supplies* and *Office Equipment & Supplies.*

Managing the Recycling of Computers, Peripherals, and Supplies

Any organization with a turnover in computer equipment faces the challenge of how to dispose of used systems and peripherals. Many organizations practice a hand-me-down strategy, in which users who receive new computers and peripherals pass their older systems to other users; one user's obsolete computer may be another user's upgrade. In other situations, obsolete computers and peripherals may be donated to schools, religious groups, charities, or other nonprofit organizations; however, very obsolete equipment should probably be recycled.

ON THE WEB

Before a computer system is handed down or donated, the hard drive should be removed and destroyed, or should be erased with a special utility program, to protect the confidentiality of personal or corporate data. A free utility for this purpose is Darik's Boot and Nuke program (**www.dban.org**).

ON THE WEB

The EPA's Web site lists links to community and vendor programs that recycle used computer and electronic parts (**www.epa.gov/osw/conserve/materials/ ecycling/donate.htm**).

Direct disposal of used computer equipment into a garbage landfill should be avoided, and is illegal in many areas. Some recycling organizations take processing units, monitors, and printers for the salvage value of the raw materials, such as metals, although many charge a nominal fee to dispose of electronic equipment.

In addition to computers and peripherals, some types of supplies are recyclable. Printer paper is an obvious example. Some ink-jet and laser printer cartridges can be mailed to a recycler to be remanufactured and refilled. Postage-paid mailing envelopes for empty cartridges are available in many large office and computer supply stores and online; many of these retailers will also accept used ink and toner cartridges in-store.

Chapter Summary

- The basic steps for installing a computer system include site preparation, hardware installation and configuration, operating system and network installation and configuration, installation and configuration of application software, and wrap-up tasks.

- During the site preparation step, support specialists deal with several issues, including:

  - Locating the computer system and devising strategies to conserve space

  - Ergonomic concerns, including ways to adapt the computer system and work environment to maximize user comfort, productivity, safety, and health

  - Power requirements, which address the need to provide a convenient and reliable electric power supply

  - Connectivity issues relating to network and telephone access

  - Air conditioning, which is usually not a concern for standalone personal computers but can be an issue in offices, training facilities, and server rooms

  - Lighting problems, which are the source of several potential productivity and ergonomic concerns

  - Fire-suppression precautions

- One of the secondary goals of the system installation process is to collect a notebook of information about the computer system being installed. A site management notebook is a convenient way to organize information that support specialists may need in the future to operate, diagnose, troubleshoot, restore, reconfigure, upgrade, and repair a system.

- Tools needed to work with computer hardware include a variety of screwdrivers, a nut driver, pliers, a parts-picker, a pocketknife, a small parts container, a mirror, isopropyl alcohol or other liquid cleaner, a lint-free cloth or foam-tipped brush, an antistatic wrist strap, cable ties, electrical tape and masking tape, compressed air or a vacuum cleaner, a circuit tester, a multimeter (VOM), and a notepad and pencil for note taking.

- Installation of hardware and related peripherals includes unpacking the system, connecting power and signal cables, installing any upgrades, and testing the system. Installing an operating system and setting up network connectivity includes installing the software and device drivers if needed, configuring various options and startup files, and installing network client software. Application software installation usually involves a choice of the kind of installation: express, custom, minimal, or full. Support specialists may also install organization-specific utilities, templates, macros, or style sheets.

- The final steps in the installation process include briefing the user on various operational aspects of the system and other activities that wrap up the installation, including updating information in the site management notebook. Wrap-up tasks also include a transition into the user training process. The ultimate installation question is: *"Is the user 100 percent satisfied?"*

- Support specialists are often asked to manage or provide advice on other aspects of users' ongoing activities, including media backups, network performance, security threats, disaster and contingency planning, preventive PC maintenance, purchasing computer supplies, and recycling used computers.

Key Terms

assistive device—A computer peripheral or software application that adapts a computer system so that users with various physical limitations can be more productive.

biometric reader—A computer hardware device that can uniquely identify a user through analysis of eye patterns, hand geometry, fingerprints, or voice and signature recognition.

business interruption insurance—A type of business insurance policy that helps offset the cost of returning an organization to normal operation after an unforeseen event, such as a natural disaster or accident.

custom installation—A software installation option that lets the installer select which components and features to install; also called an expert or special installation.

disaster/contingency plan—A document that describes various activities that will occur if a computer facility experiences a temporary disruption of service; disaster plans often address such events as fires, earthquakes, power outages, water damage, and sabotage.

distribution media—Media, such as CDs, DVDs, and Internet download files, which contain the original copies of operating system, network, or application software.

downtime—A measure of the number of hours (per week or month) that a computer system is unavailable for use because of power failures or other problems; compare to uptime.

engineering inspection—A study by an engineering firm to help identify the potential for damage to computer equipment and facilities due to natural disasters or accidents.

express installation—A software installation option that installs only the most frequently used functions and features as determined by the manufacturer; also called a typical or common installation.

file restoration—A procedure to copy one or more files from backup media to the original or a replacement disk when data or programs have been erased or destroyed; the opposite of a media backup operation.

footprint—The amount of desktop space a system unit occupies; measured in square inches (length of case × width of case).

full installation—A software installation option that installs all program functions and features; usually requires the most disk space of any installation type; also called a maximum or complete installation.

media backups—A file (or files) produced by copying files and folders of software and data from a PC's hard drive onto a separate medium to preserve them in case the original is damaged; media backups are commonly written on magnetic disks or tapes, or on optical media.

minimal installation—A software installation option that installs the fewest functions and features possible to minimize the system resources required to run the software; also called a laptop or space-saver installation.

power conditioner—An electrical device installed between a computer and its power source; it draws in electrical power, makes sure that the frequency, voltage, and waveform are within acceptable specifications, and then outputs clean power to the computer system.

preventive maintenance—Tools and procedures used to reduce the likelihood of computer component failure and expensive repair costs; preventive maintenance steps focus on cleaning and adjusting equipment to prolong its useful life and enhance operational efficiency.

repetitive strain injury—A physical problem that results from continuous use of joints in a limited range of motion; symptoms include swelling, numbness, tingling, and stiffness of joints.

risk management—The use of strategies and tools to reduce the threat to an organization from uncontrollable disasters and to help the organization recover from a disaster, with minimal financial impact or customer service loss.

site management notebook—A binder that consolidates important information about a computer system's hardware, operating system, network connection, and application software configurations, as well as facilities management information, in one location; contains information needed to upgrade, maintain, restore, diagnose, or repair the system.

surge protector (surge suppressor)—A power strip that includes special circuitry to help protect against damage to computer equipment due to electrical power surges and spikes.

uninterruptible power supply (UPS)—An electrical device that includes power conditioning circuits and a battery backup to supply electricity during power outages of short duration.

uptime—A measure of the number of hours when a computer system is operational; compare to downtime.

Check Your Understanding

Answers to Check Your Understanding questions are in Appendix A.

1. The purpose of a preinstallation site visit is to:
    a. anticipate possible installation problems
    b. get acquainted with the user
    c. train the user
    d. complete a wrap-up checklist

2. The length times the width of a computer case is called its _____.

3. True or False? A keyboard placed on a standard height office desk (30") can cause user discomfort because the angle of the user's wrists at the keyboard is unnatural.

4. The display screen connected to a computer system should be located so a user looks:
    a. up slightly   c. down slightly
    b. straight ahead   d. Any of these positions is okay.

5. _____ deals with how to design computer equipment and workspaces to minimize health problems and maximize worker safety, productivity, and job satisfaction.

6. True or False? Wrist and finger pain is usually the result of a mouse that needs maintenance.

7. True or False? Most computer hardware components function well, even if the quality of electrical power is very poor.

8. A(n) _____ is an electrical device that permits a user to power on a computer system with one switch.

9. True or False? To calculate the air conditioning requirements for computer equipment, an HVAC specialist considers the heat generated by both the computer equipment and its users.

10. Before a computer is plugged into an outlet for the first time, the outlet should be checked:

   a. by a licensed electrician   c. by the local electric utility
   b. with an LED tester   d. all of these

11. A light source that may flicker at the same rate as a CRT display screen is a(n):

   a. incandescent light   c. LED light
   b. fluorescent light   d. halogen light

12. True or False? Support specialists may need to add to or delete from site installation checklists, such as those in the chapter, because user and support needs change over time.

13. A site management notebook is especially useful in:

   a. a home computer installation
   b. a standalone computer installed in an office
   c. multiple systems installed in an office or training facility
   d. none of these

14. An antistatic wrist strap is designed to:

   a. protect the safety of a support technician
   b. reduce the risk of damage to computer components
   c. reduce the risk of fire due to a static spark
   d. reduce the risk of shock if the computer is not unplugged

15. _____ is an industry standard that helps the Windows operating system automatically recognize the configuration and operating characteristics of many hardware devices.

16. True or False? A support specialist who installs an application software package must edit the system Registry and configuration files manually before the software will operate correctly.

17. A software _____ is required to ensure that a software package can be legally installed on a system.

18. A(n) _____ tries to answer the question: *"What steps will an organization take in the event an emergency occurs?"*

19. Which of the following electrical devices contains a battery backup?

a. a PC power supply

b. a power conditioner

c. a surge protector

d. an uninterruptible power supply

20. True or False? An end user who encounters a malfunctioning CRT monitor should be encouraged by a support specialist to remove the case to check the fuse.

Discussion Questions

1. Who should perform a basic computer system installation, an end user or a support specialist? Discuss the pros and cons of each before you make a decision.

2. Do you agree or disagree with this statement? *"Because they are portable, laptops are very flexible and do not create the same ergonomic problems as desktop computers."* Explain your position.

3. Which kind of support specialist would need a simple, basic hardware tool kit described in this chapter? Which kind of support specialist would need a more complete tool kit? Would a support specialist under any circumstances need a soldering gun?

4. Are computer ergonomics primarily the responsibility of employees, support specialists, or managers? Explain your reasoning.

5. A user support specialist said, about end users, *"I can't be responsible for users who don't back up their data files. It's their problem if they lose data due to a disk crash."* Do you agree or disagree with the statement? Explain your position.

6. Which do you think poses greater problems for a network support specialist: the extensive cables required in a wired network or the security problems associated with a wireless network? What are some common tools for dealing with each problem?

Hands-On Activities

Activity 10-1

Design an ergonomic checklist. Based on the description of ergonomic issues in this chapter and Web resources related to computer ergonomics, design a checklist like the ones in this chapter that could be used by a support specialist to evaluate an end user's work area for possible ergonomic problems. Compare your checklist with your colleagues' lists. Use their ideas to improve your checklist, or come up with a single, combined checklist that represents the group's consensus.

Activity 10-2

Perform an ergonomic analysis. Use the ergonomic design checklist you developed in Activity 10-1 to conduct an ergonomic analysis of your home, office, or school computer site. List any problems with the site you identified based on the ergonomic issues described in this chapter. As a support specialist, what recommendations would you make to address the ergonomic problems you identified? If possible, compare your findings with those of your colleagues. Write a summary of your recommendations.

Activity 10-3

Locate ergonomic products and prices. Find two mail-order or online catalogs for computer equipment or supplies, such as CDW, Global Computer Supplies, Office Depot, PC Connection, PC Mall, Staples, or TigerDirect. Look at the computer supplies sold. Which products are available to address specific ergonomic problems such as those described in this chapter? Make a list of at least five examples of ergonomic products and their price ranges. Are some ergonomic products more cost-effective than others? Explain your answer.

Activity 10-4

Prepare a configuration report for a PC. Use Belarc Advisor, the Sandra utility, or the System Information Tool (msinfo32), described in this chapter, to prepare a configuration report for a PC to which you have access. Perform the following steps:

- List the major categories of information reported by the software.

- Describe any additional configuration information you would like to see included in the report.

- Did any of the configuration information surprise you? Explain.

- If the PC you are using is not running the most recent version of Windows, research the hardware requirements for the latest version of Windows or the next release of Windows if one has been announced. Highlight the configuration information on the report that indicates whether or not the PC will support the most recent version.

Activity 10-5

Analyze computer tool kit contents. Find a mail-order or online catalog for computer equipment or supplies (see Activity 10-3 for suggestions) that sells tool kits for working on computer hardware. How many tool kits does the supplier sell? What is the price range? Pick one of the tool kits and describe how the contents of the kit differ from the list of tools in this chapter. Create a list of the tools you would want to add to the kit, and explain why you would add each tool.

Activity 10-6

Outline a site management notebook. Write a detailed table of contents for a site management notebook. Think about the best way to organize the site information so a support specialist who needs to find information about a specific system quickly can locate the information.

Activity 10-7

Observe a system installation. Find a facility at your organization or school where you can observe or participate in the installation of a typical system. Make a list of the installation steps you observe. Be sure to ask about steps you don't understand, and find out why they are necessary. Compare the steps you observed with those described in this chapter. What similarities and differences did you find?

Activity 10-8

Update configuration checklists. Checklists of hardware and software configurations, such as those included in this chapter, can quickly become outdated as hardware and software technology changes. Review the hardware and software configuration checklists in this chapter. Select one of the checklists and update it based on changes in technology since the lists were created for this book; you should also incorporate your own ideas into the checklist. You can find versions of the checklists in this chapter as Word documents on this book's Web site (**www.cus5e.com**).

Activity 10-9

Define technical terms. The hardware and software configuration checklists in this chapter contain technical material and product descriptions. Depending on your experience in the computer field, you may not have previously encountered some of the technical terms, product names, and specifications used in the chapter. Make a list of any technical words used in the chapter that are unfamiliar to you or that you want to learn more about. Select five terms to research further. Use the Webopedia Web site (**www.webopedia.com/Hardware**), TechTerms.com Web site (**www.techterms.com/hardware.php**), and Javvin's Web site (**www.javvin.com**) to find definitions of the terms you'd like to know more about. Do these resources agree on the definitions?

Activity 10-10

Locate local recycling options. Use the EPA's Web site (**www.epa.gov/epawaste/conserve/materials/ecycling/donate.htm**) to find recycling centers in your area that specialize in computer and electronic components. Prepare a list that you could provide to end users who inquire about the local recycling options. Include any agencies that may be looking for donations of used computers. Create a list of items that can be recycled as well as those than can't, along with any fees charged.

Activity 10-11

Research out-of-date device drivers. Download and install the free version of DriverScan at the Driver Guide's Web site (**www.driverguidetoolkit.com**), or find a similar program. Run a scan for out-of-date drivers on a PC to which you have access. Prepare a brief report of the results of the scan. You do not need to actually update the drivers that DriverScan identifies, unless you want to. Compare your results with your work or school colleagues. Were their results similar to yours? Select one obsolete device driver from your report and find the vendor's Web site where a new version can be downloaded.

Activity 10-12

Work with electrical values. A formula used frequently by electricians is: watts = volts × amps. (Alternately, amps = watts/volts.) Assume an installer determines that a dedicated electrical circuit has a capacity of 15 amps and the computer and peripherals connected to the circuit are currently rated at up to 1000 watts. At best, how much spare capacity does the electrical circuit have? Would it be possible to add a printer that operates at 100 watts without overloading the circuit? Develop a simple spreadsheet to make this calculation for you.

Activity 10-13

Write a disaster/contingency plan. Review the materials in this chapter on disaster/contingency planning. Prepare a contingency plan for a typical home computer installation or another installation you have responsibility for. Your plan should:

1. Identify any important risks to the ongoing operation of the installation. (How likely is each risk you identified?)

2. Describe any applicable insurance that would cover replacement costs if the installation was damaged, stolen, or destroyed.

3. Identify any security vulnerability or security devices (including detectors and alarms) that apply to the installation.

4. Describe the location of media backups (including both on-site and off-site backups), detail how frequently backups are created, and specify the restoration procedures.

5. Outline the major steps necessary to get the installation operational again after any kind of disaster.

Activity 10-14

Inventory printers on a network. As a network administrator in a job with a new company, you attend a meeting in which a manager asks, *"How many printers do we have in this company?"* You answer that you don't know the number, but will find out. After the meeting, you discover that no one else really knows the number of printers, which models the company owns, or where they are located. Write a memo to the manager that explains how you will go about finding this information and what tools you will use. (*Based on an activity suggested by Ron Koci, Madison Area Technical College.*)

Case Projects

1. Windows 7 Installation for Brianna Mishovsky's Training Facility

Brianna Mishovsky is the training coordinator for a large national insurance company. The company has recently agreed to purchase a new software package that will substantially increase worker productivity in its Claims Processing Department. The new software represents a major change for the company, and it is scheduled to come online in a month. The implementation schedule presents problems for Brianna's training group because several weeklong training sessions on the use of the new software must be scheduled to accommodate all the workers in the Claims Processing Department. To meet the need for the additional training classes, Brianna has to install computers in a training room where none exist now.

Brianna has purchased 20 refurbished computer systems that can be used for the training activity, but they do not currently have an operating system installed (the hard drives were replaced with larger drives). Brianna learned that the new claims processing software is designed to run on Windows 7, so you will need to assist Brianna with the installation of Windows 7 on the 20 training systems.

Your first task is to prepare an installation procedure for installing Windows 7 on the training machines. First, research the steps in the Windows 7 installation procedure. (If possible, go through an actual Windows 7 installation to identify the steps in the procedure, the key decision points, and the installation options available.) Next, write a first draft of the installation procedure for the Windows 7 installation. As you work on your draft, make a list of some questions you will need to ask Brianna to clarify how she wants Windows 7 configured on the training machines. Brianna has asked you to make the procedure steps brief, but as complete as possible. Write a draft of the Windows 7 installation procedure steps and prepare a list of questions for Brianna that you need answered before you can finalize your draft.

2. The UPS and Downs of Electrical Power at Cascade University

Mary Ann Lacy, a training facility coordinator at Cascade University, plans to install a new network server for her training facility. Mary Ann has been advised by the local electric utility that provides power to Cascade University that she probably also needs to install an uninterruptible power supply (UPS) for the new server. Mary Ann likes the idea that a UPS would help protect the university's investment in server hardware and reduce user frustration if a power outage occurs. She wants your help with the UPS part of the installation project.

The consultant at the electric utility mentioned that articles online and in computer periodicals sometimes describe UPS equipment. Many organizations that sell UPS devices for computers have Web pages that describe their products. The consultant pointed Mary Ann to an online video tutorial on UPS devices (**www.youtube.com/watch?v=pRiLgc4nd_Y**), and a Web-based tutorial at the PC911 Web site (**pcnineoneone.com/howto/ups1**). The consultant also recommended an article in PDF format (**www.falconups.com/pdf-04-2004/sbs_ups_tutorial.pdf**).

Mary Ann would like you to first learn about some of the important features to consider when purchasing and installing a UPS, and then write a one- to two-page summary of the issues the university needs to consider in the purchase and installation of a UPS for its new network server.

3. Utility Software to Automate System Installation Tasks

Suppose you work as a user support specialist for an engineering company, and you receive the following email:

From: Kozuma

To: User Support

Date: 28-Aug-2011

Subject: Installation tasks

I am concerned about the amount of time our support group spends with system installations for new employees and the occasional errors that occur in the process when we omit a step or enter the wrong information. I would like to try to automate some of the manual system installation procedures we currently use. I am thinking, for example, about the process of installing various software packages and network client software on engineering workstations. I'd like to find a utility program that would allow us to define an installation script.

By the way, would such a utility also permit our users to write a short script to define hot keys and hot strings of text? If so, we could reduce the amount of repetitive key entry work users have to do, for example, to enter a standard phrase or paragraph into an email message or a document.

Thanks very much for your help with this task.

Go to the AutoHotKey Web site (**www.autohotkey.com**), and download the program to your computer. Study the installation and configuration options for this program. Then write an installation checklist that describes how to obtain, install, and configure the program. Write your checklist so other support specialists who work with Kozuma can follow the steps. Also provide an example of how an end user can write a short script to display their name, department, email address, and telephone number whenever they press a predefined key.

4. Installation Troubleshooting at North Jetty Manufacturing

North Jetty Manufacturing makes windows and doors for local building contractors. Several of North Jetty's workers have received new computers in recent weeks, and they need your advice about how to deal with the problems described below:

1. **Jose Fonseca, production scheduler**—The desk space for Joe's workstation is very limited.

2. **Ralph Emerson, accounting specialist**—Because of carpeting, static electricity is a problem in the office area where Ralph's computer was installed.

3. **Anna Liu, marketing database coordinator**—Anna has experienced problems with eyestrain, headaches, back strain, and sore wrists.

4. **Alyssa Platt, employee benefits coordinator**—Alyssa has to squint at the display screen in the computer late in the afternoon because the windows in her office face west and the sun shines in.

5. **Mary Pat Schaeffer, Webmaster**—Mary Pat would like to minimize the number of power switches required to turn on her computer and peripherals (system unit, display screen, printer, and scanner).

6. **Lou Campanelli, shipping and receiving**—Lou's system is installed in an unusually dusty shop environment.

Write a memo to Holguer Vasconez, CEO at North Jetty Manufacturing, that recommends how you would deal with each of these specific problem areas.

5. Prepare an Installation Guide for Picasa

2B Construction Company has purchased digital cameras so its site managers can document progress on building projects. The company has decided to use the free Picasa photo editor to help 2B's site managers download and organize their photos. You have been asked to prepare a document for the site managers that details how to download, install, and use Picasa as a photo organizer. (Note that Picasa, when first installed, finds all photos currently saved on a computer, so it may take some time to install. Picasa can be uninstalled easily when this case is completed.) Complete the following steps:

1. Download and install the current version of Picasa (**picasa.google.com**).

2. Write a document on the download and installation process aimed at 2B's site managers.

3. To get some practice with Picasa, download a few sample construction site photos from **www.free-pictures-photos.com/construction/index.htm**. (These photos can be used free of charge for this case project.)

4. Research how to set up separate folders in Picasa to store pictures for each project.

5. Learn how to add captions to pictures in Picasa so site managers can label their photos with location and date information. Create some sample captions from the photos you downloaded in Step 3 for practice.

6. Add information to your installation document on how to set up folders and add captions.

7. Learn how to create a collage of pictures in Picasa. Practice making a collage from some of the pictures you downloaded in Step 3, and add the steps for creating a collage of pictures to your document.

8. Finally, learn how to email a picture from Picasa, and add that task to your documentation.

Picasa is an extensive program with many features. Focus the document you prepare for 2B Construction on the specific steps in this case.

CHAPTER 11

Training Computer Users

In this chapter, you will learn about:

- ◎ Goals of training activities
- ◎ Steps in the training process
- ◎ How to plan a training session
- ◎ How to prepare a training session
- ◎ How to present a training module
- ◎ How to progress toward higher-quality training

480

Most organizations find that providing user support is expensive. As a result, many organizations try to make end users as self-reliant as possible in order to reduce the demand for support services. Every problem that users can solve by themselves is one fewer problem the support group must resolve. Every question end users can answer on their own further reduces the burden on the support group. Ultimately, user self-reliance shrinks an organization's total support costs.

Training is one of the most effective ways to make users self-reliant. A Chinese proverb says, *"Give a person a fish and you provide a meal; teach a person to fish and you provide food for life."* That principle certainly applies to the relationship between an end user and a user support center: *"Answer a question for a user and you have solved a problem; teach users to find their own answers and you have solved many problems."*

Many support specialists who work with internal users spend a significant amount of time on training-related activities. Some user training occurs in formal classes, but much more occurs during one-on-one interactions and when users rely on self-study materials, which are sometimes written by support specialists. Many people who have been primarily on the receiving end of the training process (as trainees or students) are often surprised at the amount of work that goes into a successful training activity. This chapter takes you step-by-step through the training process. It describes how to plan a training session as well as how to prepare, present, and evaluate training materials. The end-of-chapter materials are designed to help you think further about the training process and give you an opportunity to plan, prepare, present, and evaluate your own training activities.

What is Training?

Training is a teaching and learning process that aims to build skills that are immediately useful to the trainees. Sometimes the terms *training* and *education* are used interchangeably. Although training and education are related, the terms sometimes mean different things.

Education is a teaching and learning process that aims to provide conceptual understanding and long-term thinking skills. Especially in introductory courses, the goal of education is to build a basic vocabulary and understanding of general principles. In education, teachers commonly test learners' understanding by measuring their ability to explain concepts and principles. The effects of education are intended to be long lasting.

Training focuses on performing tasks and building expertise that will be immediately useful. Trainers often test the success of a training session by measuring a learner's ability to perform a specific task. Although the results of training may be long lasting, a worker might be trained to perform a task that she or he will do only once or a few times.

People sometimes associate education with a school environment and training with an industrial or organizational environment. However, some schools, such as vocational-technical schools and community colleges, have a mission that specifically emphasizes training. Furthermore, education often occurs outside a school environment, because skills training is usually based on a firm foundation of conceptual knowledge. For example, workers need to learn basic vocabulary and computer operating principles before they can become skilled users. The ability to troubleshoot and solve problems is often closely related to one's understanding of computers and one's facility for applying general knowledge to a specific task. Although this chapter focuses primarily on user training, it assumes that all training is based on a solid foundation of vocabulary and concepts.

ON THE WEB

Educators and trainers often use a specialized vocabulary. Donald Clark has prepared an online glossary of vocabulary used in the training field (**www.nwlink.com/ ~donclark/hrd/glossary.html**).

The Training Process

Trainers can use a four-step process to successfully teach users. The four Ps of the training process are listed in Figure 11-1. In the planning step, the trainer gathers information about the objectives of the training. In the preparation step, a trainer collects and prepares materials and organizes them into modules. In the presentation step, a trainer presents the training modules to users, who then help evaluate the training process in the progress step.

- Step 1. Plan the training
- Step 2. Prepare the training
- Step 3. Present the training
- Step 4. Progress toward higher-quality user training

Figure 11-1 Steps in the training process

Step 1: Plan the Training

Experienced trainers know that planning is essential to a successful training activity. Trainers must learn who the trainees will be, what their current skill levels are, what the trainees need to know, and what skill levels the trainees need to achieve as a result of the training. Once trainers have assembled this background information, they can set learning and performance objectives.

Determine the Trainees' Backgrounds

Perhaps the most obvious detail a trainer needs to understand is who the trainees are. Are they children, young people, adults, or seniors? Adult workers who need specific job-related training usually require different content and training techniques than younger users or schoolchildren. Workers are often highly motivated to learn new skills because they already understand the benefits of applying new technology to their jobs and careers. Adults bring their personal work experiences to a training session, which can be very useful because a trainer can build on prior experiences and use analogies and metaphors to introduce new material. For example, a trainer might point out that an unfamiliar software feature or procedure is similar to one in a program the users already know. Although not all adult workers are equally motivated, the characteristics of adult learners can often be used to good advantage in a training situation. Adults are usually better able to form generalizations based on examples, and to articulate what they do and do not understand. It is also worth noting that adult trainees are often less willing to put up with an ineffective trainer than are younger trainees.

Trainers should be aware that some trainees do not attend training voluntarily, but rather do so as a job requirement. Required attendance can affect a trainee's motivation level. And some adult learners may be more likely to think that the current ways of doing things work just fine; as a result, they may be less open to training on new methods or tools. In these cases, a trainer may have to spend extra time and effort to convince attendees of the training's benefits and find creative ways to engage the trainees in order to overcome their initial resistance to being there.

Determine What Trainees Already Know

Successful trainers also establish in advance the trainees' current level of knowledge, so they do not waste learners' time. For adult trainees, training should begin with a brief review of how the training material fits with what they already know, in order to establish a context for the training; the training should then move quickly to new material. One way to gauge what trainees already know is to interview several workers or their supervisors about the trainees' backgrounds and current skill levels. Another strategy is to administer a short pretest to determine more precisely the trainees' baseline skill levels.

As industry certification tests become more widespread, training session pretests that attempt to measure what a trainee already knows will become more common. Online tests can be a good way to gauge what a trainee "brings to the table."

If a wide disparity in backgrounds exists among a group of trainees, a trainer runs the risk of covering introductory material too quickly for some and too slowly for others. Both novices and more advanced users may be equally dissatisfied because the training is not targeted at the level they need. When trainees have different interests or ability levels, trainers can provide background materials or arrange a special introductory session or activity before the actual training session begins to help less-experienced users feel more comfortable with the basic vocabulary and concepts. For example, prior to a training session on Microsoft Word, a trainer could hold a brief training session on basic computing skills for novice users to ensure that all trainees have basic keyboarding, mouse, and Windows skills; otherwise, those users may struggle with the Word training and slow down other learners with their questions.

Even with extra preparation, trainers almost always find that a group of trainees has a wide range of skill and interest levels. Trainers must find an "average" level of instruction that addresses the needs of as many trainees as possible. Trainers handle this in different ways. Some trainers aim to teach to the average level of a class, with occasional asides to provide extra explanations for those below the average and to offer more in-depth material that will challenge those above the average. Other trainers target the level of instruction somewhat below the class average level; they believe a somewhat slower pace for a training session is preferable to leaving half the trainees behind with a quicker pace. Practice and experience are the best teachers in handling this classic training challenge.

When planning a training program for an audience with a wide variety of skill levels and job functions, a trainer should try to focus on materials and examples that are common to that varied group of users. For example, a session on basic word-processing skills for a divergent group of trainees (such as department heads, administrative assistants, and engineers) might focus on the skills needed to produce basic office communications such as memos or simple correspondence, rather than technical reports.

Many trainee groups bring not only a variety of skill levels, but also a diverse range of cultural and language backgrounds. A trainer needs to recognize these situations and be sensitive to the audience's needs. For example, if some learners are nonnative English speakers, avoid idioms and jargon, and use vocabulary that is as straightforward as possible. A trainer also needs to be sensitive to cultural mores. For example, in many cultures, touching another's arm in a friendly way, as one might do to motivate a colleague or a trainee in the United States, is considered too familiar and is unacceptable behavior for a trainer. Learn to observe trainees' body language as a guide to what behaviors are acceptable to them.

 If you have an opportunity to talk with veteran trainers, ask them about their experiences with cultural differences and benefit from their observations.

Determine the Trainees' Content Needs

Once a trainer has determined who the trainees are and what they already know, the next step is to ascertain what the trainees need to know as a result of the training. This step often requires some research. A trainer usually tries to discover the kinds of jobs or tasks users will be asked to perform and what specific skills they will need. Trainers sometimes review workers' position descriptions to obtain information about their job, task, or skill objectives. In other cases, trainers must interview workers or their supervisors (or both) to determine the training objectives. For example, a trainer who prepares a session on building Access databases may discover that the trainees really need to learn how to prepare reports based on data in existing databases. Specifically, the trainer may discover that the trainees already know how to use basic features of the Access Report Wizard, and now need an introduction to custom reports.

Determine the Skill Level Trainees Need

After trainers define the required content, they need to determine the skill level the trainees need to achieve. To determine an appropriate target skill level, a trainer should have a basic understanding of skill levels and how they are classified. One way to classify skill levels in education and training, from lowest to highest, is:

1. Concepts level—an ability to use basic vocabulary

2. Understanding level—an ability to explain concepts

3. Skills level—an ability to perform a basic task

4. Expertise level—an ability to perform a task effectively and efficiently

In this skill classification, the first two levels, concepts and understanding, are conceptual. A training activity often begins with vocabulary; trainees first learn to use the language necessary to communicate with others about a topic. They need to know the meanings of the words others use to exchange information about a subject. Then trainees can begin to build an understanding of how things work, why things work (or don't work) the way they do, and the relationships between things. Once trainees understand new material at a conceptual level, they can then build a mental model of how things work and explain it to others. Analogies are especially useful during the vocabulary and conceptual learning levels. For example, a trainer could explain that a computed field in a database is like (analogous to) a formula in a spreadsheet cell.

Once trainees have a conceptual understanding, they can move on to build skills and abilities to perform tasks. At the skill-building level (level 3), users learn the steps to perform a basic task. Basic tasks may take a while to learn, and trainees may not get them exactly right at first. Trainees need to develop an ability to perform a task at a basic level before they can become proficient. Then, trainees can work on building speed, accuracy, and expertise. For example, trainees with word-processing expertise can not only embed a graphic object in a document (a basic ability or skill), they can do so quickly and without prompting; they can also easily control the placement, size, and design of the result.

Armed with a knowledge of who the trainees are, what they know, and what they need to know, trainers can begin to plan a training session. At this point, trainers often find it useful to ask, *"How do I effectively move the trainees from where they are now to where they need to be?"*

Define the Training Objectives

In the final planning step, trainers should specify the learning and performance objectives for the training. A **learning objective** is a statement of the knowledge or skill trainees need to learn. To determine learning objectives, trainers answer the question, *"What do these trainees need to learn?"* For example, one learning objective for this chapter is: *Explain the activities that occur during each of the main steps in the training process.*

A **performance objective** is a statement of what tasks the trainees should be able to perform at the end of a training session. To determine performance objectives, trainers answer the question, *"What should these trainees be able to do as a result of this training activity, and how well?"* For example, a performance objective for this chapter is: *Plan and present a successful training session.* (The end-of-chapter activities are designed to help you achieve this objective.)

The best performance objectives are measurable; they specify how well the trainees need to be able to perform a task. A training session on search engines, for example, might include a performance objective such as: *Use the Google search engine to locate a specific piece of information on the Web within five minutes.* Training objectives (both learning and performance objectives) should begin with an action verb, which makes them easier to evaluate later on. Avoid training objectives that begin with the words *understand* or *know*, because *understanding* and *knowing* can be difficult to measure or evaluate. Better verbs include *plan, describe, explain, perform, evaluate, analyze, repair*, or *prepare.* Be as specific as possible about the tasks learners should be able to perform after the training. Also specify how the performance objectives will be measured. The Google search engine example above uses time as a measure. Other common measures include answering questions correctly, writing an accurate explanation, performing a specific task, participating in a team activity with a specific objective, or producing some other measurable outcome.

ON THE WEB

To learn more about how to design training sessions with specific performance outcomes, consult a book by Ruth Stiehl, *The Outcomes Primer: Reconstructing the College Curriculum, Third Edition* (Corvallis, Oregon: The Learning Organization, 2008). Although Stiehl's book is aimed at college instructors, the learning-centered performance outcomes she advocates are equally useful in planning technology training sessions.

To learn more about Stiehl's approach, visit **www.outcomesnet.com/ OUTCOMES_PRIMER/outcomes_primer.html**.

Trainers often summarize the results of the planning steps described above in a goal statement. Identify the concepts, understanding, abilities, skills objectives, and learning and performance objectives in the training plan shown in Figure 11-2.

Notice that the training plan is short and describes the objectives in general terms. It does not describe *how* the training will be presented (for example, self-guided tutorial, classroom demonstration, face-to-face tutorial, televised demonstration, or Web-based training) or list specific topics (for example, which "basic Explorer operations" will be covered). The details of training topics, methods, and organization occur during the second step: training preparation.

485

Windows 7 Introduction

Training Objectives

Goal: Provide workers who are new computer users with an introduction to the Windows 7 end-user environment.

Audience: Designed for computer users who have little or no previous experience with Windows 7.

Prerequisites: Trainees should have some keyboarding skills and a basic understanding of vocabulary and concepts relating to office computing.

Methods: The training will include hands-on experience with basic Windows 7 operations so trainees learn to use the Windows 7 user interface. Exercises will focus on common mouse operations, window management, the Recycle Bin, the Start Menu, the Task Bar, and use of the Search tool and Explorer to locate files. With practice, trainees should be able to perform basic Windows 7 tasks with little help or prompting.

Learning and Performance Outcomes: At the end of the training, participants will be prepared to take a basic word-processing or spreadsheet course and know enough about the Windows 7 operating system to perform basic tasks such as the following:

- Start a PC
- Start an application program
- Use the Windows Task Bar to manage applications
- Create, move, and delete file folders
- Store, move, delete, and use files
- Use a printer in the Windows environment
- Use Windows Explorer, Libraries, and the Recycle Bin to locate and manage files and folders
- Use the Windows 7 help system

The session will introduce terms used frequently in the Windows 7 environment including: desktop, window, menu, icon, shortcut, file, folder, path, dialog box, cursor, mouse keys, task bar, and Recycle Bin. The training will not provide a complete understanding of the organization and operation of Windows 7, but will focus on the use of Windows 7 to run applications and the use of Windows Explorer and Libraries to manage files and storage space. Because the training session is intended to be short, it will not attempt to build skills or expertise in the use of Windows 7 beyond a basic level.

Performance Measures: Trainees should be able to define 70% of common terms in a simple test. Trainees should be able to demonstrate use of the Start Menu to run applications, as well as use of Windows Explorer, Libraries, and the Recycle Bin to locate and manage files.

Figure 11-2   A sample training plan for Windows 7

A ROLE-PLAYING SCENARIO

In Case Project 4 at the end of this chapter, Andrew Nussbaum asks you and Randy, another user support specialist, to prepare a training module for users in a company that will be converting from Office 2003 to Office 2010 in the next few weeks. Here is a transcript of an interview with Andrew conducted by Randy. If possible, have fellow students or coworkers play the parts of Andrew and Randy, and then evaluate the interview.

ANDREW: I'm pleased you agreed to help prepare one of the training modules for the Office 2003 to 2010 conversion project.

RANDY: Well, I have some questions about the project before I get started.

ANDREW: Okay, what questions do you have?

RANDY: First, I understand the trainees need to know how to use the ribbon menu interface in 2010. What experience with Office 2003 do these trainees have?

ANDREW: The trainees are all experienced 2003 users. We expect about 20 of them for the training session. The training does not need to cover features of Office 2010 products such as Word and Excel. What they need to know is how to find the features and functions they are familiar with in Office 2003 in the new version of Office. We skipped the Office 2007 version, so they do not have that background, which would have made the transition to 2010 much easier.

RANDY: Is the purpose of this training to get them to a level where they are comfortable and productive with the Office 2010 ribbon menu?

ANDREW: No, I think that is too ambitious a goal for one training session. I think we need to introduce them to the look and feel of the ribbon interface, perhaps with a brief demo of the 2010 versions of Word and Excel—just so they know what to expect. Then, perhaps we could do a PowerPoint slide show that says, for example, if you know what formatting option you would use in Office 2003, here is where you can find it on the ribbon menus.

RANDY: Would it be useful if we created a handout or reference sheet for each package (Word, Excel, etc.) that trainees could take away from the training?

ANDREW: Yes, I think that would be a great idea.

RANDY: Maybe I can find some materials online that cover the correspondence between Office 2003 menus and the Office 2007 and 2010 versions. If I can find something, I could adapt it for our needs. How will we know if the training session has been successful?

ANDREW: These are all experienced Office suite users, and this is primarily a "get acquainted with 2010" session, so I don't think a hands-on test is necessary. What I would suggest is that you give them a challenge problem or two and see if they can solve it. And leave plenty of time to answer their questions. Maybe give them a short training-evaluation questionnaire to let them say whether the training session and materials met their needs.

RANDY: Okay, I'll see if we have an evaluation form we've used before that I can modify for this training session. Thanks very much for helping me get started on this assignment.

Can you think of other questions Randy should have asked Andrew in order to be able to plan and prepare a training module for the Office 2010 ribbon menu interface? At what points in the interview should Randy have probed with follow-up questions to clarify Andrew's answers? How would you evaluate the success of the interview from Randy's perspective? From Andrew's perspective?

Step 2: Prepare for the Training

During the preparation step, a trainer develops more detail about the specific topics that will be covered and how these topics will be organized in a sequence. This step also addresses the types of training methods and how the training will be accomplished.

Specify Which Topics Will Be Covered

Based on the learning and performance objectives defined in Step 1, a trainer decides next which topics to cover. Even with very clear learning and performance objectives, deciding on specific training content may not be easy.

Most trainers do not start from scratch, however. They begin by brainstorming a long list of possible topics. Usually a preliminary list comes from several sources, including a trainer's knowledge of what is important, the learning and performance objectives defined in Step 1, and topics covered by other trainers and writers. In order to reduce the cost of training preparation, trainers should review topics covered by other trainers in existing training materials for ideas on topics to include. While trainers should never simply copy verbatim training ideas, topics, and examples from other sources, neither should trainers feel that they must start from scratch when preparing for each training session. The process of selecting specific topics from among the preliminary list is like setting priorities. When considering the list of possible topics, a trainer tries to select topics that are most useful to trainees. Consequently, the decision about what *not* to cover is just as important as the decision about what to cover. Most trainees prefer a session that devotes adequate time to fewer topics instead of a rush job that tries to cram two hours of material into one hour. Good trainers prefer to include a little less material rather than too much.

Organize the Topics

Training topics should be organized to begin with lower-level skills and progress to higher-level skills. To enhance trainee understanding, introduce concepts and vocabulary terms first, followed by explanations of concepts. Then focus on building basic skills and abilities. Finally, use exercises to build expertise. Following this strategy, a template for a training session might look like the following:

1. Introduce the trainer

2. Review previous topics, if applicable

3. Introduce the new topic

4. Establish motivation for the new material

5. Present the new material

   - Concepts

   - Explanations

6. Perform training activities

   - Teach basic skills and abilities

   - Build skills and develop expertise

7. Summarize and review the main points

8. Describe next steps and resources

9. Obtain evaluation and feedback

In Step 4 of this training outline, a trainer establishes motivation by reviewing with the trainees why they are there and what they will be able to do by the end of the training. Establishing motivation early in a training session is important because trainees who understand the need for the training and its objectives are more likely to participate in the training activities.

Trainees remember better how to perform tasks they have heard about and executed more than once. Recall the adage, *"First, tell them what you're going to tell them. Second, tell them. Third, tell them what you told them."* While this advice, if taken too literally, could lead to overly repetitious training sessions, it underlines the importance of introducing (Step 3 above), presenting (Steps 5 and 6), and summarizing (Step 7) the training material.

Step 8 in the outline, in which a trainer describes where to go from here, is an opportunity to point out additional information and resources, to recommend other training opportunities that logically build on this one, or to suggest how to build additional expertise, if that is a user's goal.

Select an Effective Training Format

Training occurs in a variety of formats, depending on the type of training, its objectives, the needs of the trainees, and the available facilities. Each format has advantages and disadvantages. The following training formats are the most common:

- Classes (15–25 trainees)
- Small groups (12 or fewer trainees)
- One-to-one training
- Self-guided tutorials

Classes

Classroom training is usually more cost effective than other formats because the ratio of trainees to trainers is high. A single trainer can instruct a large group of trainees, sometimes in a special training facility that includes a computer projection system, audiovisual equipment, and possibly computer workstations for hands-on activities. Classroom training can also take advantage of **social learning**, which is learning that takes place during interactions among trainees in a classroom or other collaborative learning environment.

What is an ideal training class size? No one class size is appropriate for every situation. Some introductory materials, vocabulary, concepts, demonstrations, and explanations can be presented in very large training groups. However, training that includes a substantial hands-on component, especially training designed to teach basic skills, should take place in sessions no larger than 15 to 25 trainees. Large classes do not permit instructor attention when individual trainees need assistance. If a training session will exceed 25 trainees, try to arrange for additional trainers or experienced users to mingle among trainees to assist when help is needed. Another factor that influences the class size a trainer can reasonably handle is the skill level of the trainees: more highly skilled trainees usually require less individual attention than beginners.

Some trainees don't perform as well in large training group settings, however, because they are uncomfortable asking questions or asking for help in a large group. Furthermore, if a trainer stops to help a couple of trainees, the rest of the trainees may be left idle. If some trainees learn at a slower pace than others, they are either left behind or they slow down the rest of the session. With practice, trainers can learn to effectively handle a large group in a classroom environment, present material at a comfortable pace for nearly everyone, and provide adequate feedback to trainees.

Small Groups

Trainees in a small group format of up to 12 trainees have an advantage over classroom sessions in that they may receive more individual assistance. Small group training also permits more interactions among trainees, which promotes social learning. However, the lower the number of trainees per each trainer, the higher the cost per trainee.

One-to-One Training

One-to-one training is the ultimate small group, and it offers the most effective format for many trainees. A trainer can closely monitor a trainee's learning curve and provide help and feedback in a timely way. **On-the-job training** is a form of one-to-one training in which a work colleague or supervisor plays the role of coach and mentor to a trainee. On-the-job training ranges from informal coaching while performing a task to a more formal apprenticeship or internship relationship.

Obviously, the cost of one-to-one training is higher than other formats, and social learning among peers is rarely possible in this format. And while one-to-one training is a very flexible format for both trainer and trainee, the advantages of informality and flexibility should not be an invitation to provide a poorly planned or executed training session.

In reality, many user support workers are always in "training mode." Many of the interactions that support staff have with end users are directly or indirectly educational. This discussion of one-to-one training focused on more formal training situations rather than the informal training opportunities that can occur every day. However, many of the principles of formal training, such as awareness of differences in learning styles, also apply to informal training situations.

Self-Guided Tutorials

Self-guided **tutorials** permit trainees to work through an interactive learning session at their own pace. Self-guided training, in which each trainee works alone without a trainer, would appear to be the most cost-effective training format because once the materials have been prepared, trainer cost is negligible. Another plus: trainees can cover material at an individualized pace. However, in self-guided tutorial programs, a trainee may not be able to obtain the assistance and feedback they need. Self-guided training and very large class sessions are similar training formats in this respect. If help can be provided when needed during self-guided training (a possible role for a user support center), then self-guided tutorials can be among the most effective learning and cost-effective training formats.

How Learners Learn

To select an effective training method, a trainer needs to consider how trainees learn. A **learning style** is the way an individual learns most effectively. Trainers who take into account learning style differences recognize that individual trainees perceive and process information in different ways. Not every trainee has the same learning style. Learners do not all learn in the same way or at the same pace. While trainees can learn something from almost any training method, each trainee has a preferred learning style. Some learners are self-motivated and self-reliant. Others need prodding and the structure and motivation that a formal training session can provide. Some workers learn concepts easily; others need several examples to understand a concept thoroughly. Some trainees learn most effectively working alone; others benefit from working in a group.

492

Three common learning styles are listed below:

- **Visual learner**—A trainee who learns most effectively by *seeing* new material, reading about it, working through a self-guided tutorial, looking at a picture or a chart, or watching a demonstration or a video.

- **Auditory learner**—A trainee who learns most effectively by *listening* to someone talk through the new material.

- **Experiential learner**—A trainee who learns most effectively by *performing* a task (also called a kinesthetic learner).

Trainers believe that the most effective learning methods are those that are targeted at two or more of these learning styles, such as interactive, multimedia presentations.

ON THE WEB

For more information about learning styles, including descriptions of visual, auditory, and experiential learners, visit a Web site sponsored by the Canadian government (**www.jobsetc.gc.ca/pieces.jsp?category_id=325&lang=e**).

Take an online survey to learn more about your predominant learning style on Diablo Valley College's Web site (**www.metamath.com/lsweb/dvclearn.htm**), or the Paragon Learning Style Inventory (PLSI) (**www.oswego.edu/plsi/taketest.htm**). The PLSI relates learning styles to the Myers-Briggs MBTI personality types you learned about in Chapter 2.

Another Web resource on learning styles is **www.learning-styles-online.com**.

In general, information retention and learning performance improve with activity and repetition. Figure 11-3 shows several learning methods and how they relate to retention.

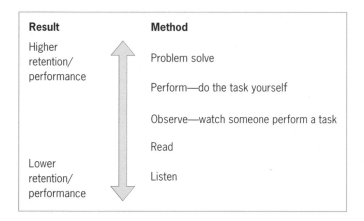

Result	Method
Higher retention/ performance	Problem solve
	Perform—do the task yourself
	Observe—watch someone perform a task
	Read
Lower retention/ performance	Listen

Figure 11-3   Learning methods and retention

Training methods toward the top of the continuum in Figure 11-3 increase the likelihood that information presented will be retained and that job skill performance will improve. In other words, the more that trainees are active participants in the learning process—rather than passive recipients of information—the better they will retain knowledge.

To understand the relationship between learning methods and retention, think about the different learning outcomes that would result if you simply read this book from cover to cover versus both reading each chapter and completing several of the end-of-chapter projects.

The continuum in Figure 11-3 is based on a popular approach to learning called Bloom's Taxonomy. Benjamin Bloom described six major categories of cognitive skills, ranging from simple to complex behaviors:

1. *Knowledge*—Ability to remember facts or information (can describe, identify, list, or recognize data or information)

    ♦ **Example:** Read and quote from a help desk incident-handling database.

2. *Comprehension*—Ability to understand meaning (can summarize, paraphrase, interpret, or explain information)

    ♦ **Example:** Paraphrase a help desk problem incident in an agent's own words.

3. *Application*—Ability to use information in a new situation (can evaluate, solve, demonstrate, or apply what was learned to a problem in a work environment)

    ♦ **Example:** Use information in a help desk database to resolve a new and different problem incident.

4. *Analysis*—Ability to break down information into understandable parts (can separate, contrast, troubleshoot, or draw inferences based on facts and information)

   • **Example:** Use multiple pieces of information in a help desk database to troubleshoot a problem incident.

5. *Synthesis*—Ability to reconstruct a new pattern or meaning from facts and data (can reorganize, categorize, integrate, or compile data into information)

   • **Example:** Rewrite information in a help desk database to make it clearer and more understandable.

6. *Evaluation*—Ability to judge ideas or information (can critique, interpret, select, or defend methods or procedures)

   • **Example:** Review incidents in a help desk database to identify those that remain relevant and need to be retained, as well as those that are obsolete and can be archived.

 Based on Bloom's Taxonomy from simple to complex cognitive skills, what conclusion do you reach about the effectiveness of classroom education experiences based almost entirely on listening to lectures and reading a textbook?

ON THE WEB

To learn more about Bloom's Taxonomy of cognitive skills, see **krummefamily.org/ guides/bloom.html**. The site includes links to additional Web resources and printed materials.

Learning is often a social phenomenon. The trainer-trainee relationship is an essential human relationship, as is the trainee-trainee relationship. Learning from peers in a group can augment the training process and is also a good way to build teamwork skills. The ability to work with a team is a required skill in today's business world, where the size and complexity of projects often require group effort and expertise.

ON THE WEB

For more information on the benefits of peer learning, read an article by Alice Christudason (**www.cdtl.nus.edu.sg/success/sl37.htm**).

A paper by Dana Black advocates a combination of computer-based and peer learning (**chil.rice.edu/research/pdf/HFES-ESTraining-Paper%20Final% 20Revisions%20Submission.pdf**).

Select Delivery Methods for the Training Materials

When a trainer decides how to present training materials, they can consider a number of alternative delivery methods. A **delivery method** is a choice among several instructional technologies, media, or approaches to presenting information. Most presentations use one or a combination of the delivery methods listed in Figure 11-4; these methods are described in more detail in the paragraphs that follow.

495

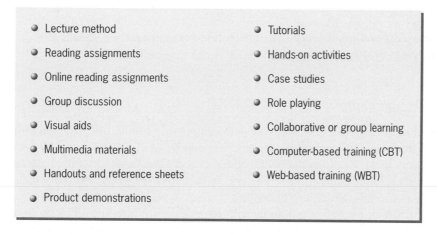

- Lecture method
- Reading assignments
- Online reading assignments
- Group discussion
- Visual aids
- Multimedia materials
- Handouts and reference sheets
- Product demonstrations
- Tutorials
- Hands-on activities
- Case studies
- Role playing
- Collaborative or group learning
- Computer-based training (CBT)
- Web-based training (WBT)

Figure 11-4   Common training delivery methods

Lecture Method

The lecture method is a familiar way to communicate information from an instructor to a learner. It makes effective use of an instructor's time, which is one reason lectures remain popular in higher education. However, the learner's role is often very passive, which is why some experts question the effectiveness of this method. Lectures can often be used effectively in combination with other delivery methods to introduce topics and materials, motivate trainees, and guide trainees toward a useful learning experience.

Reading Assignments

Some trainers believe that reading is preferable to lectures because a trainee is more actively involved in the learning process. Reading a textbook, trade book, or vendor manual is often an effective way to define vocabulary and explain concepts. However, a trainer needs to select materials carefully so the amount of assigned reading is reasonable given the time available. Materials should be selected to match the reading ability of the trainees. Some textbook and trade book materials are written at too high a reading level for trainees to understand easily.

Trade books may cover materials thoroughly but often are not appropriate for use in training sessions. Because trade books are usually designed for professionals in a field, they are less trainee-friendly; they frequently lack such features as learning objectives, chapter summaries, glossaries, comprehension self-tests, and hands-on activities or projects that are often needed by both trainers and learners.

Vendor manuals may seem very authoritative because product manufacturers publish them. However, vendor manuals vary considerably in quality. Some are well organized and well written; others are so poorly written they actually hinder effective learning. Vendor manuals are often prepared in a reference format, rather than as tutorials that guide learners through an effective step-by-step learning process.

In addition to giving trainees specific reading assignments, trainers should encourage users to access a variety of supplementary resource materials. Point trainees to high-quality supplementary materials and ensure they know how to use them effectively.

Online Reading Assignments

An increasing number of hardware and software vendors provide online tutorials and help systems with their products. Online reading assignments can be an effective training-delivery method. Some vendors include help systems embedded in software; others provide materials on a CD or on the Web. Online materials today tend to be better designed and written than many printed vendor manuals, which are becoming scarcer as vendors try to save on production costs. Furthermore, online materials with hyperlinks are interactive, so users can search for the information they need, which promotes more effective learning. However, anyone who has spent considerable time searching a CD or the Web for information knows that not all online information is equally accessible, useful, or even accurate. Some users have difficulty reading lengthy documents online, especially if the resolution of their display screens is low. And, of course, online documents may not be as portable as printed materials.

ON THE WEB

For an example of an online tutorial that also provides a print option, see Microsoft's tutorial on PowerPoint 2010 (**office.microsoft.com/en-us/powerpoint-help/ create-your-first-powerpoint-2010-presentation-RZ101848193.aspx**).

Group Discussion

For some types of training, group discussion is an improvement over the lecture method because trainees are more actively engaged. Group discussion is most effective for sharing experiences related to training topics such as user needs assessment training, help-desk incident-handling procedures, design issues in desktop publishing, and dealing with ethical issues. Beginning trainers are sometimes reluctant to use group discussion as a training method because they fear they will lose control of a training session. However, many experienced trainers have learned that group discussions are often one of the most effective approaches to training.

Visual Aids

Visual aids are a popular supplement to lectures and readings because they take advantage of the adage that *"a picture is worth a thousand words."* Pictures, charts, diagrams, and other images are useful training aids because most trainees tend to retain visual information better than information they have only heard or read (as noted in Figure 11-3). Visual aids should be large enough to be visible to everyone in an audience. The most effective visual aids have simple designs with judicious use of color and fonts for emphasis.

 Visual aids are an important component of many presentations. Parts of Appendix C in this book are devoted to the effective design of visual presentation aids.

ON THE WEB

For guidelines on the preparation and use of visual aids, consult a Web site developed by the U.S. Occupational Safety and Health Administration (OSHA), called "Presenting Effective Presentations with Visual Aids" (**www.osha.gov/doc/outreachtraining/ htmlfiles/traintec.html**).

Multimedia Materials

Visual aids are effective presentation tools, and multimedia materials can be even more effective learning aids. **Multimedia materials** are a combination of text, still images, animation, and sound. Each form of media can reinforce other forms to provide a powerful presentation, which increases the amount of material learned as well as the ability to recall material at a later time. However, the cost to develop effective multimedia materials is greater than the cost of many other delivery methods. The cost may be especially prohibitive for a one-time training session, but affordable when spread over multiple sessions.

ON THE WEB

To see an example of a multimedia presentation, view a tutorial on how to build a basic Web site on the Virtual Training Company's Web site (**www.vtc.com/products/How-To-Build-A-Basic-Website-Tutorials.htm**). Or choose one of VTC's other

(continues)

498

(continued)

multimedia presentations from their extensive library. Select topics in the first three modules to view a free demonstration of a multimedia approach to training.

The demonstration tutorials require QuickTime or Flash Player (either is a free download); a PC equipped with a sound card and speakers or a headset is generally required for multimedia presentations.

Handouts and Reference Sheets

Training sessions are, by their nature, generally a one-time event. When users return to their workstations, time passes, and they often forget important parts of the training. Training sessions, especially short ones, are more effective if they include printed materials users can take with them. Handouts and reference sheets should contain enough information that users can recall important facts or steps in a procedure. They should not contain extensive detail, or trainees will be less likely to use them. When a trainer prepares a handout or reference sheet, simplicity is more important than comprehensiveness.

ON THE WEB

For an example of a reference sheet designed for end users who already know HTML, but need a short list of available tags, go to **www.webmonkey.com/reference/ HTML_Cheatsheet**.

An example of a helpful reference sheet of commands for the UNIX operating system is on University of Washington's Web site (**www.washington.edu/computing/unix/ unixqr.html**).

Product Demonstrations

Although hands-on use of an actual software or hardware product during a training session is usually desirable, lack of equipment, insufficient copies of software, inadequate training time, or other logistical problems sometimes dictate that a training session include only a product demonstration. LCD or DLP projectors, which feature liquid crystal display (LCD) or digital light processing (DLP) projection technology, have improved so dramatically that even a large group of 50 to 75 trainees can effectively "look over the shoulder" of a trainer to view a demonstration of an operating system or application software package. The cost of many LCD and DLP projectors has dropped from $6000–$8000 to $2000–$3000 in recent years; many basic models are available for $500–$1000, or less, so these units are more affordable for training facilities even in small organizations.

ON THE WEB

To learn more about the role of LCD and DLP projectors in product demonstrations and other training activities, visit the portable projector buyer's guide at the Projector Central Web site (**www.projectorcentral.com/buyers_guide.htm**).

A demonstration of a computer product should be carefully paced. A trainer must not overwhelm trainees by going so fast that the audience cannot follow or understand the material. The pace of a demonstration is especially important in a GUI (graphical user interface) environment, in which a trainer can point and click so rapidly that trainees may be unable to follow the sequence of steps. Experienced trainers learn to pause between mouse clicks to give each trainee's eyes and brain an opportunity to assimilate the procedure. They talk through a procedure to add verbal explanations to the visual display and give adequate time for each trainee to absorb the sequence of steps.

Tutorials

Tutorials are one of the most effective ways for computer users to learn how to perform basic tasks. Trainees who are self-motivated gain the most from tutorials. Trainees who lack motivation to learn new materials often benefit from more structured training methods, such as classroom lectures or group activities.

In some tutorials, trainees use the actual hardware or software products they are learning about as they step through the tutorial. Other onscreen tutorials merely simulate hardware or software products. In either case, trainees have an opportunity to learn new materials in an environment that is very close to the one they will use when the training is completed.

ON THE WEB

For an example of an online tutorial, view an Albany University Library tutorial on evaluating Internet sites (**library.albany.edu/usered/wwwdex**). Note the overall organization of the tutorial, the effective use of interaction and feedback, and the ease of navigation.

Many trainees like the self-guided nature of tutorials as well as the opportunity to repeat difficult lessons or take a refresher course. Although the cost to develop an effective tutorial is very high, once it is developed, hundreds or even thousands of users can benefit from it at little additional cost per user.

Hands-On Activities

Because task performance leads to skill development and better information retention, hands-on activities are an especially effective delivery method for many kinds of computer training. Hands-on activities (sometimes called lab exercises) and practice projects let trainees try out what they have learned, build skills and expertise, and learn to become independent users. Well-designed activities can be a significant step toward user self-reliance.

Hands-on activities and projects should begin with easier tasks and gradually progress to more difficult ones so trainees can experience initial success before trying more complex tasks and projects. Trainees should receive immediate feedback during hands-on activities, because unlearning a skill is difficult, even if it's an incorrect or counterproductive way to perform a task. For example, many new users meticulously tap the arrow keys to move the cursor across an entire line of text to the end when a single keystroke or mouse click would accomplish the same result.

Case Studies

Larger hands-on or teamwork projects called **case studies** are designed to encourage trainees to make the transition from the artificial environment of the training room to the realities of the business world. Usually based on real business situations, case studies are a popular teaching method in higher education because they simulate the kinds of experiences learners will encounter on the job. Case studies are usually more involved than a simple step-by-step, hands-on activity or a small project, and they require trainees to apply and integrate the skills they have learned. The Case Projects at the end of each chapter in this book are examples of this integrative method of skill building.

ON THE WEB

The case study method was originally developed at Harvard Business School, and is widely used in higher education. To learn more about the goals of the case study method and how to benefit from them, visit **www.uiweb.uidaho.edu/ag/agecon/391/casestudmeth.html**.

Role Playing

A useful strategy to develop effective communication and customer service skills is **role playing**, in which trainees participate in a rehearsal of a work environment situation. Role playing permits trainees to try out their skills in a situation in which trainees can at various times take the roles of trainer, trainee, client (user), support provider, project leader, or project team member. Although a role-playing situation might be artificial, it can allow trainees to build skills and to experience some of the emotions of a particular situation before confronting something similar in their work environment. Some people love role-playing activities; others are less comfortable participating. The latter group may benefit from being an observer at first, and by giving feedback to others in the role-playing activity. Role playing can be an effective way to build actual experience with skills required as a support agent and as a trainer.

 The role-playing scenarios in each chapter of this book are designed to give readers an opportunity to experience role playing as a learning method.

501

ON THE WEB

For a description of some benefits and tips for role-playing activities, see **www.businessballs.com/roleplayinggames.htm**.

Collaborative or Group Learning

Collaborative learning is learning that occurs among members of a group or team who work together on a learning activity. Collaborative (or cooperative) learning activities include group discussions, hands-on activities for work teams, group problem solving, role playing, participation in online forums, and involvement in joint case study teams. Once called group learning, collaborative learning is based on the experience that learning is often a social activity and that trainees can learn a great deal from other trainees independent of the trainer. Collaborative learning challenges obsolete learning models that say all useful information must flow from a trainer to trainees. The roles of trainer and trainee blur in a collaborative environment. In many collaborative learning environments, the trainer is a facilitator who can also be a learner in a joint learning experience.

ON THE WEB

A Web site devoted to collaborative learning is hosted by the University of Wisconsin–Madison (**www.wcer.wisc.edu/archive/CL1/CL/doingcl/DCL1.asp**). The site includes descriptions and examples of collaborative learning activities, such as "Think – Pair – Share."

Computer-Based Training

A growth industry within the technical training field is computer-based training. **Computer-based training (CBT)** includes tutorials, multimedia presentations, product demonstrations, and hands-on activities that use a computer as an automated training system. Some CBT systems provide features that handle administrative tasks, such as registering trainees, controlling access to course materials, presenting information, assessing trainee learning, and monitoring trainee progress. Most CBT products today are downloaded or distributed on CD/DVDs, but older systems used audiocassettes and videotapes as delivery media. CBT training can be cost effective for large groups, but high-quality, instructionally sound CBT materials are usually very expensive to develop. Existing CBT products vary considerably in quality from very poor to excellent. An important role for trainers is to help evaluate the suitability, quality, and effectiveness of CBT materials. Because trainees can learn at their own pace and repeat difficult material, CBT is a popular delivery method among trainees.

Web-Based Training

A recent development in automated training systems is use of the Web as a delivery vehicle. **Web-based training (WBT)** is very similar to computer-based training, except that the Internet is the delivery vehicle. Because the development cost can be spread over many trainees, WBT allows low-cost training modules to be readily available anywhere in the world. Web-based materials are also easier to update when changes need to be made, and because the delivery vehicle is a browser, WBT presents fewer compatibility issues across hardware and operating system platforms. Many education and training institutions use WBT to deliver distance learning in an effective way. Unfortunately, quality control is sometimes missing in the development of Web-based materials. User support staff who are responsible for providing training should preview and evaluate prospective WBT training modules for quality, relevance, and cost-effectiveness.

ON THE WEB

To experience an example of a WBT training lesson, try one of the sample video lessons available on the GCF LearnFree.org Web site (**www.gcflearnfree.org/computers**).

Does the popularity of self-guided training materials such as online tutorials, computer-based training, and Web-based training mean human trainers are obsolete? Will human trainers eventually be replaced by computer technology? Probably not. Although delivery system technology continues to evolve in the training industry, the trainer's role will likely not disappear. Trainers can contribute their wealth of experience in ways that self-guided training materials cannot. And trainers add a social element so important in collaborative learning. In many organizations, training continues to be a responsibility of the user support group, even though the popularity of various training delivery methods changes over time. However, the training role will surely change. In the future, trainers will likely spend relatively more of their time on the following tasks:

- Assess the training needs of workers

- Plan and design training programs

- Evaluate and recommend training materials from among those already available

- Motivate trainees

- Help trainees make transitions between modules

- Assess training performance and effectiveness

- Assist trainees when individual attention is needed

These are not tasks that automated CBT or WBT delivery systems can perform very well, if at all. Future trainers are less likely to develop and present training materials, except where specialized materials are needed for small training audiences. The mass market for user training will undoubtedly be satisfied in part by automated training delivery systems.

ON THE WEB

For another perspective on trends in training and worker development, read the article "Trends in Training and Development" by Sandy Dutkowsky (**careers. stateuniversity.com/pages/852/Trends-in-Training-Development.html**).

Develop Specific Training Materials

Most trainers do not prepare lectures, reading materials, demonstrations, tutorials, and other materials from scratch for every training session they develop. Successful trainers rely heavily on existing material in vendor manuals, trade books, industry training packages, and other resources when possible. Why reinvent the wheel if good ideas are already available? Examples of successful training materials used elsewhere can provide a good starting point as trainers develop their own materials. However, trainers should respect copyrighted material and avoid copying verbatim from a single source. Successful trainers also try to relate the training topics to the trainees' specific interests, and develop examples that trainees are likely to relate to and encounter in their own work. Imagine, for instance, the differences in examples that could be used to teach Web search engine basics to a group of accountants versus a group of product design engineers.

503

Use Web searches to locate examples of training materials that can be tailored to meet the specific needs of a group of trainees. For example, to locate introductory materials for training on Excel 2010, enter a keyword search such as: *introduction tutorial guide excel 2010*.

504

Design Training Evaluation Methods

The final task in training preparation is **assessment**, which measures whether the training activities have met the intended learning and performance goals. Trainers usually plan two separate assessment activities during the preparation: trainee assessment and trainer assessment.

Trainee assessment provides feedback to the trainees on how well they met the learning objectives. Feedback can be in the form of a test or quiz that covers concepts and vocabulary. Trainee feedback can also include hand-on activities, exercises, or projects that require the trainee to use a computer to perform a task that measures mastery of the performance objectives.

Trainer assessment is feedback to the trainer on his or her instruction. Trainees' performance on quizzes, tests, and hands-on activities also provides feedback to the trainer. If trainees don't do very well on the tests and hands-on activities, however, does that say more about the performance of the trainee or the trainer? Test results actually provide feedback to both trainees and trainers. Trainers should analyze the results of tests, quizzes, hands-on activities, and exercises to see where trainees succeeded and where they didn't. Armed with that knowledge, trainers can adjust training modules to improve the results of future training activities.

Trainer evaluation forms are another way for trainers to obtain feedback on their performance. Evaluation forms provide an opportunity for trainees to comment on the trainer's strengths and to provide feedback on portions of the training that need improvement. Figure 11-5 shows a sample training evaluation form that can be filled out by both the trainee and the trainer (as a kind of self-evaluation).

A common practice is to assign weights of 5 points for "Agree," 4 points for "Somewhat Agree," and so on, and then calculate an average score for a trainer for each item on the Training Evaluation form in Figure 11-5.

Training Evaluation

☐ Trainer: _____   ☐ Trainee: _____

Place a check mark (√) in the column that represents your reaction to each statement.

	Agree	Somewhat Agree	Somewhat Disagree	Disagree	Does Not Apply
1. The objectives of the training were clear.					
2. Terms used in the training were defined.					
3. The training was organized in a step-by-step approach.					
4. The training included useful examples.					
5. The trainer made effective use of time, and the pace was about right.					
6. Training aids were useful.					
7. Overall, the training was done well.					

What was the best part of the training?

What could be improved?

Figure 11-5   A sample training evaluation form

To analyze feedback on evaluation forms, trainers should look for patterns of responses instead of the occasional very high or very low score. Although trainees may not agree in their responses to all questions, look for items that receive lower ratings from several trainees. Trainers should pay particular attention to these items, because they identify the most obvious ways to improve the training activity. Some trainers dislike trainee evaluations because they feel trainees are not qualified to evaluate trainers. However, most trainers consider trainee evaluations an important source of feedback. Professional trainers or support staff who do a lot of training also rely on peer evaluations from other experienced trainers or work colleagues to identify problem areas in their material or delivery and to make constructive suggestions for improving their performance as a trainer.

Training evaluation is a useful tool to help trainers constantly improve their skills at planning, preparing, and presenting training sessions. An evaluation strategy should be designed during the training preparation phase.

Step 3: Present the Training

The training presentation should follow the structure the trainer planned during Step 2. If a trainer has done a good job in the planning and preparation steps, the actual presentation of the training is likely to be effective and satisfying to both the trainer and the trainees. Figure 11-6 lists 10 training presentation guidelines you should observe in your role as a trainer. These guidelines are described in the following sections.

1. Practice the presentation
2. Arrive early to check out the facility
3. Don't read notes and PowerPoint slides verbatim
4. Don't try to cover too much material
5. Teach the most important skills
6. Use humor sparingly
7. Pause for comprehension checks
8. Monitor the training environment
9. Provide frequent breaks
10. Obtain professional feedback

Figure 11-6   Training presentation guidelines

Practice the Presentation

Most trainers find it helpful to practice a training session with one or more colleagues to evaluate materials and identify problem areas prior to the actual training session. Some trainers call this practice session a **beta test run**, a term borrowed from software beta tests, in which companies distribute prereleases of their software to potential users and ask them to note any problems they find as they work. A training beta test gives a trainer feedback from a neutral perspective. With a beta test run, you learn how the materials work with the intended audience, whether the topics can be delivered in the allotted time, if transitions between topics are smooth, whether PowerPoint slides and handouts are effective, and whether the equipment and facility work as planned.

Arrive Early to Check Out the Facility

A trainer should arrive at the training facility early enough to check out the physical environment. Experienced trainers always do a dry run to make sure their equipment works (including trainer and trainee computers, projection and overhead equipment, lights, sound, and other aspects of the training environment). Make sure participants can see you and your materials from everywhere in the room. You may need to reconfigure the room setup, such as the table and chair layout or the equipment location, so it meets your needs and is more comfortable for trainees.

 If you are presenting a training session at an unfamiliar site, find out in advance who the facilities manager is and how that person can be contacted in case of problems.

Don't Read Notes or PowerPoint Slides Verbatim

If you have prepared detailed notes to use during the training, avoid reading them or reciting lengthy materials from memory. Have a general familiarity with what you want to say and use your own words to present the material in a conversational manner. Most successful trainers find that using an outline is more effective than writing out or memorizing what they want to cover. Reading material on an overhead or PowerPoint slide verbatim is an insult to the intelligence of the audience and one of the fastest ways to put trainees to sleep. The admonition against reading slides verbatim has even earned its own reproach among trainers: "Death by PowerPoint."

Don't Try to Cover Too Much Material

Trainers who have too much material for the allotted time should eliminate some less important topics and cover the rest thoroughly. When a trainer tries to review or cover too much material, they often rush through it, which results in training that is not well paced; this can make it difficult for trainees to keep up. Similarly, don't let trainees' questions force you too far from the planned material. Although trainee questions should be answered immediately if possible, experienced trainers make notes of user questions that aren't directly relevant and answer them, if time is available, at the end of the presentation; or they give pointers to resources where trainees can find more information themselves.

 One strategy successful trainers use is to prioritize topics and examples prior to a training session. With a clear understanding of the priority of topics, a trainer can quickly cut less important material if necessary due to time constraints.

Teach the Most Important Skills

When trainers know a piece of hardware or a software package thoroughly, they are sometimes tempted to augment the training with **bells and whistles**, or features of hardware or software that may be interesting but that are used infrequently, especially by beginning users. Bells and whistles might impress and entertain an audience, but they often distract from the primary training objectives. They may even confuse new users who are struggling to understand what is important from among all the new material. Remember to focus on the needs of the learners, not on the trainer's ego.

A corollary to teaching the most important skills is to teach a single way to accomplish a task. For example, if a task can be accomplished with a keyboard shortcut, a menu option, a function key, and a toolbar icon, trainees rarely need to be shown every possible method. Trainees will be less confused if a trainer demonstrates and sticks to one method.

Use Humor Sparingly

Humor during a training session can make the session more enjoyable for trainees, but trainers should be careful about the amount and type of humor they use. The best humor is self-directed because it shows trainees you are human. Ridicule, which is humor directed at someone else, is never acceptable. Avoid making negative comments about vendor products, even in jest. If you are a naturally humorous person, you may need to rein in your talent and recognize the important difference between training and entertainment. Some trainers, mindful that the trainees will evaluate them, cross the line between training and entertainment. Use humor effectively, but recognize that the tradeoff between short-term entertainment and long-term training results should err on the side of training.

Pause for Comprehension Checks

During a presentation, pause periodically to gauge whether trainees are following the material. Many trainers plan in advance to break at predetermined points for a few "quick check" questions. Use a variety of question styles, including direct questions about the material that has been covered (such as, *"What keys would I press to select this text?"*), open-ended questions (such as, *"What is the fastest way to locate a file using Windows Explorer?"*), or group questions (such as, *"Get together with your group and take five minutes to list what you think are the most useful features of the grammar checker."*). Periodic comprehension questions will help keep trainees alert and involved because they know they might be called on to discuss what was covered.

Monitor the Training Environment

A trainer should always keep an eye on the training environment to make sure that users are comfortable and focused on the training. Is the room temperature too hot or too cool? Is the room too noisy because a door or window is open? Learn to read your audience. Watch for signs that tell you whether trainees are uncomfortable or interested, bored or attentive. Successful trainers often check their perception with the trainees: *"It seems like a lot of noise is coming from the hallway. Can you all hear the presentation?"* or, *"Can those in the last row see the screen?"*

509

Provide Frequent Breaks

In a lengthy session, recognize that trainees can become tired, which can affect their concentration. Plan the training to include frequent breaks. Trainers usually find that more frequent short stretch breaks are preferable to a few long breaks. A good guideline is to schedule a break after about 45 minutes, and every 30 to 45 minutes thereafter.

Obtain Professional Feedback

After a new trainer gets some initial experience with the training process, a professional evaluation from other trainers is often helpful. Colleagues can frequently spot even very small mannerisms that may distract trainees. Another excellent training improvement tool is to videotape a training session. Although a videotape of your own training session can be difficult to watch, all trainers can learn something from the experience that will improve their training proficiency.

The following two books provide additional material on delivering successful training sessions:

- Stephani Gerberding, *The Accidental Technology Trainer* (Medford, NJ: Information Today, 2007).

- Terrance Keys, *How to be a Successful Technical Trainer: Core Skills for Instructor Certification* (McGraw-Hill Osborne Media, 2000). This book is geared to CompTIA's Certified Technical Trainer certification exam.

Step 4: Progress Toward Higher-Quality User Training

The final step in the approach to user training described in this chapter is perhaps the most important. After each training session, a trainer should review the feedback and evaluate his or her performance. Trainers can then modify their presentation style or training materials if necessary to correct any problem areas they identify. Professional trainers and especially user support staff who do occasional training sessions are always on the lookout for ways to continually progress toward providing higher-quality user training.

The following inputs can help a trainer improve the quality of his or her training sessions:

- the results of training beta tests with colleagues as trainees

- the results of performance tests of trainees

- feedback from trainees

510

- feedback from colleagues who observe a training session

- an evaluation of videotape recordings of training sessions

Each of these tools provides useful information to trainers who want to improve the quality of their training sessions. For example, an analysis of which questions on a quiz or which steps in a hands-on exercise caused trainees the most difficulty can point to needed revisions in the training materials for subsequent training sessions. Or perhaps some test questions or exercises aren't very good measures of trainee performance. In either case, a trainer should look for clues that modifications to the training materials need to be made.

Another aspect of training materials that should be evaluated whenever a training session will be repeated is whether the information is accurate and up to date. Because hardware, software, network, and operational procedures change frequently, technical details and training materials prepared just a few weeks or months ago may be out of date today. Don't assume that the screens, icons, menus, keyboard shortcuts, and program features that worked in version 2 of a software package will work the same in version 3. Review all topics, procedures, slides, demonstrations, handouts, reference sheets, and other training materials prior to the next presentation.

ON THE WEB

Trainers and support specialists who are interested in improving the quality of their training should take advantage of the many useful training resources on the Web. To get started, review the training resources listed below.

Resource	URL
ItrainOnline's *Topic-Specific Resources for Trainers*	www.itrainonline.org/itrainonline/english/trainers_topics.shtml
The United States Navy's *Train the Trainer Guide*	www.au.af.mil/au/awc/awcgate/edref/traingde.htm
IntraHealth International's *Learning for Performance* (a health-oriented Web site with some useful downloadable resources)	www.intrahealth.org/lfp/tools.html
British Columbia Public Service Agency's *Facilitator's Train-the-Trainer Handbook*	www.scribd.com/doc/19167795/4612050-Facilitators-Train-the-Trainer-Handbook
The Bob Pike Group's collection of training articles	www.bobpikegroup.com/articles.asp?columnid=2746
NATE Network's *The Assistive Technology Trainer's Handbook*	www.natenetwork.org/manuals-forms/at-trainers-handbook

While not all of the above resources are specifically targeted at technology training, all are useful resources for those who want pointers to improve their training courses as well as their performance as a trainer. Many of these sites have links to other resources.

In addition to the training tools described in this chapter, trainers who have primary responsibility for a training program in a large organization may want to investigate a learning management system. A **learning management system (LMS)** is a software tool that automates many tasks associated with running a training program. Most learning management systems include the following:

- Authoring tools (especially for Web-based interactive multimedia training sessions)
- Features to promote online interactive learning and collaboration—such as chat sessions, discussion forums, and blogs
- Training session management tools, including facilities, equipment, and trainee scheduling
- Trainer access to libraries of instructional and reference materials and media
- Trainee testing and exam management features
- Trainee progress tracking and record keeping tools, including skills and certification databases

Learning management systems are usually not appropriate for an organization that conducts only occasional, small training sessions. They are targeted at organizations that make a substantial ongoing commitment to worker training and career development, and need help with program administrative and instructional tasks.

ON THE WEB

To learn more about learning management systems, read an evaluation of open source LMS software (**www.iadis.net/dl/final_uploads/200501C014.pdf**). The paper discusses the features of learning management systems, including Moodle (**moodle.org**), which is a popular system in many universities and community colleges. For a video introduction to Moodle prepared for instructors at Cal State LA, visit **www.youtube.com/watch?v=6ihOd-pEI_s**.

Finally, remember that the goal of all training is to meet users' needs and help them become more self-reliant, which reduces an organization's overall user support costs.

Chapter Summary

- Training is an important part of user support because it makes users more self-reliant. A well-trained user is more productive and less likely to need support services than one who has not been adequately trained. Training is based on a solid foundation of vocabulary and concepts.

- The training process is a four-step approach:

  - **Step 1. Planning**—This step identifies who the trainees are, what their background is, what they need to know or be able to do as a result of the training, the level of skills the trainees need to obtain, and the specific learning or performance objectives for the training. Plans should address several levels of training skills, including concepts (vocabulary), understanding (explanatory ability), skills (basic task performance), and expertise (highly skilled performance).

  - **Step 2. Preparation**—Preparation for training answers questions such as:

    - Which specific topics will be covered, and how will they be organized?

    - What training format will be most effective (classroom, small group, one-to-one, or self-guided)?

    - How will the training be delivered? (Alternatives include lectures, readings, discussion, visual aids and multimedia materials, handouts, demonstrations, tutorials, hands-on activities, case studies, role playing, collaborative learning, and automated learning systems such as CBT and WBT.)

    - How will the trainee and the trainer be evaluated?

  - **Step 3. Presentation**—A successful training presentation depends on adequate planning and preparation. Ten guidelines are included in the chapter to help new trainers make more effective presentations.

  - **Step 4. Progress**—Evaluation of training sessions is an important way trainers improve their skills and continually progress toward providing higher-quality presentations.

- Organizations that operate an extensive training program for end users often invest in a learning management system to automate many instructional and administrative tasks.

Key Terms

assessment—A process that measures whether training activities have met the intended learning goals; two common assessment activities are trainee assessment and trainer assessment.

auditory learner—A trainee who learns most effectively by listening to someone talk through new material.

bells and whistles—Features of hardware or software that may be interesting or entertaining to include in training materials, but are used infrequently, especially by beginning users.

beta test run—A practice training session to evaluate materials and identify problems; a dry run with colleagues rather than trainees as the audience.

case study—An extensive hands-on or teamwork project designed to encourage trainees to make the transition from the training room to the business world; case studies are based on real business situations that simulate experiences learners will encounter on the job.

collaborative learning—Learning that occurs among group or team members who work together on a learning activity; collaborative learning activities include group discussions, collective hands-on activities, group problem solving, role playing, participation in online forums, and involvement in joint case study teams.

computer-based training (CBT)—An automated training system in which learners use a computer system; includes tutorials, multimedia presentations, product demonstrations, and hands-on activities.

delivery method—An instructional technology, media, or approach to presenting information or training materials, such as a lecture, group discussion, hands-on activity, or computer-based tutorial.

education—A teaching and learning process that aims to develop conceptual understanding and long-term thinking skills; the goal is to provide basic vocabulary and understanding of general principles.

experiential learner—A trainee who learns most effectively by performing a task (also called a kinesthetic learner).

learning objective—A statement of the knowledge or skill trainees need to learn.

learning management system (LMS)—A software tool that automates many tasks associated with running a training program.

learning style—The way an individual learns most effectively.

multimedia material—A combination of text, still images, animation, and sound used as part of a presentation.

on-the-job training—A type of one-to-one training in which a work colleague or supervisor plays the role of coach and mentor to a trainee; may include informal coaching or a more formal apprenticeship or internship.

performance objective—A statement of the tasks trainees should be able to perform at the end of a training activity; objectives should be measurable, and usually start with an action verb, such as *plan, change, describe, explain, perform, evaluate, analyze, repair,* or *prepare.*

role playing—A training delivery method in which trainees participate in a rehearsal or practice of a simulated work environment situation by taking the roles of users, support staff, trainers, and trainees.

social learning—Knowledge or job skills learned during interactions among trainees in a classroom or collaborative learning environment.

training—A teaching and learning process that aims to build skills that are immediately useful to trainees; focuses on performing tasks and building expertise; can be short term and is often tested by measuring a learner's ability to perform specific tasks.

tutorial—An interactive learning technique in which a trainee works through learning tasks step-by-step, usually at their own pace.

visual learner—A trainee who learns most effectively by seeing new material, reading it, working through a self-guided tutorial, looking at a picture or a chart, or watching a demonstration or video.

Web-based training (WBT)—A form of computer-based training in which the Web replaces CDs or DVDs as the delivery medium; highly interactive and available wherever Internet access is available.

Check Your Understanding

Answers to Check Your Understanding questions are in Appendix A.

1. True or False? One goal of end-user training is to make users as self-reliant as possible in order to reduce their need for support.

2. True or False? Training is a teaching and learning process that aims to develop conceptual understanding and long-term thinking skills.

3. _____ is a skill level in which a trainee learns the basic vocabulary needed to communicate with others.

4. Which one of the following is not a step in the training process described in this chapter?

   a. plan   c. perform
   b. present   d. progress

5. True or False? The best performance objectives for a training session specify how well a trainee needs to be able to perform a task.

6. True or False? Experienced trainers agree that most trainees learn best by watching a demonstration.

7   Which of the following skill levels deals with performing a task effectively and efficiently?

a. concepts and understanding   c. expertise
b. basic skills   d. all of these

8. In the classification of skill levels listed below, what is the sequence in which the skills are usually built? (1) basic skills, (2) concepts, (3) expertise, (4) understanding

a. 1– 2 – 3 – 4   c. 1– 4 – 2 – 3
b. 2– 4 – 1 – 3   d. 2– 1 – 3 – 4

9. _____ materials combine text, images, animation, and sound in a training delivery system.

10. True or False? Due to the popularity of self-guided training materials and online interactive training delivery systems, the role of support specialists as trainers is likely to disappear in the next few years.

11. Which of the following training environments is generally the most cost-effective because the ratio of trainees to trainers is highest?

a. classes   c. one-to-one training
b. small groups/teams   d. role playing

12. Which of the following learning methods results in the highest retention and trainee performance?

a. listen   c. observe
b. read   d. problem solve

13. True or False? Trainers often discover that more short breaks during a training session are preferable to fewer long breaks.

14. Which statement accurately describes the costs associated with computer-based delivery methods?

a. The development cost is high, but the cost per user is low.
b. The development cost is high, and the cost per user is high.
c. The development cost is low, but the cost per user is high.
d. The development cost is low, and the cost per user is low.

15. Printed materials designed to be taken away by trainees from a training session to refresh a user's memory are called _____ .

16. True or False? Effective trainers often cover bells-and-whistle features in a software package to pique trainees' interests.

17. Which of these assessment tools is aimed primarily at evaluating a trainer's effectiveness?

    a. quizzes

    b. tests

    c. hands-on activities

    d. training evaluation surveys

18. _____ is a training approach that matches the needs of each individual trainee with an information-acquisition strategy in order to achieve the most effective training results.

19. _____ is an activity in which trainees participate in a rehearsal or practice of a simulated work environment situation.

20. True or False? A first-time trainer should read notes and slides to trainees in order to avoid making a mistake or omitting important material.

Discussion Questions

1. Why does higher education generally rely so heavily on the lecture method? Is the reliance on lectures appropriate? What are effective alternatives to the lecture method in training environments?

2. Do you think trainees have the knowledge and perspective to effectively evaluate the performance of a trainer? Explain why or why not.

3. How will the availability of high-quality training materials on the Web affect the need for user support workers to provide training as part of the user support role?

4. Can visual aids actually detract from learner understanding in a training activity? Give some examples to support your opinion.

5. Do the advantages of one-to-one or on-the-job training outweigh the added costs to train a new employee using these methods? Explain your reasoning.

6. What are some ways to make role-playing activities more useful as a training activity for user support workers?

7. Based on your own experiences, describe some advantages and disadvantages of the case study method described in this chapter. Do you prefer it to other learning methods?

Hands-On Activities

Activity 11-1

Analyze trainee backgrounds. Suppose you are assigned to prepare an introductory training module on a scripting language, such as JavaScript, VBScript, or Python. Develop a brief questionnaire to use with your classmates or work colleagues to learn about their background knowledge and experience for such a training session. Analyze their responses to your questionnaire. Do they all have similar experience and interest levels? Are they from diverse backgrounds? What problems would differences in education or experience among your classmates or colleagues pose for a trainer who is planning an introductory training module on scripting for the group? Write a one-page summary of your analysis of how the background of your classmates or colleagues would prepare them for a training activity on scripting.

Activity 11-2

Analyze learning levels. Choose a software package you know well, such as Windows, one of the Microsoft Office applications, or a Web browser. For the package you select, show that you understand the four skill levels introduced in the chapter by providing one or two examples of the following:

1. The definition of an important *concept* or vocabulary term

2. An *explanation* of the concept or vocabulary term that aids in understanding it

3. A *skill* or task related to the concept that a user should be able to perform at a basic level

4. A measure of *expertise* that a highly skilled user would be expected to perform

Finally, explain how you would measure whether a trainee has acquired the level of expertise you described in #4 above.

Activity 11-3

Write measurable performance objectives. Suppose that a trainer has identified as a general goal for a training module, *"Able to format printed output according to a specification sheet."* First, rewrite this goal statement so it specifies a measurable performance objective. Then, write three additional measurable performance objectives for printing in an application program.

Activity 11-4

Research and discuss resources for training materials. Discuss this statement with a small group of coworkers or classmates: *"Using existing materials from a vendor's user manual, textbook, or trade book as a source of training ideas violates the original author's copyright, and therefore should never be done."* If you need more information on copyrighted materials, use a search engine to locate information online or study the University of Texas tutorial on copyrights (**www.lib.utsystem.edu/copyright**). Write a summary of your reaction to the statement after the discussion with your colleagues. Note any points of disagreement among members of your group.

Activity 11-5

Compare training formats. Do you personally prefer classroom training, small group sessions, one-to-one training, or self-guided tutorials? Why? Are there circumstances in which you feel a one-to-one training format is more effective than another? Interview two or three classmates or coworkers and get their answers to these questions. Write a summary that compares your answers to the responses of those whom you interviewed.

Activity 11-6

Evaluate CBT or WBT materials. Locate a training module that uses computer-based or Web-based training. (This chapter lists several examples.) The module you select can be in a format such as a video, a CD/DVD, or a Web site. Try out the CBT or WBT approach, either alone or with a group of colleagues. Write a critique of the module in which you discuss the following questions:

- How well does it achieve its goals?

- What improvements would you suggest?

- What are the advantages and disadvantages of CBT or WBT delivery systems for training modules in the subject area?

Activity 11-7

Analyze training evaluation forms. List some additional aspects of training that could be evaluated in the training evaluation form in Figure 11-5. Locate one or more training evaluation or assessment forms used at your school or workplace, or examine sample evaluation forms on the Web:

- **it.toolbox.com/blogs/enterprise-solutions/training-course-evaluation-form-template-instructorled-29507**

- **www.go2itech.org/HTML/TT06/toolkit/evaluation/forms.html**

Compare the forms you found with the one in Figure 11-5. Describe the similarities. What are the major differences? Describe the changes you would make to improve the evaluation form in Figure 11-5 based on your research.

Activity 11-8

Develop training guidelines. Based on your personal experiences as a trainee or student (a recipient of training), describe some common mistakes you have observed trainers or instructors make that you would add to the suggestions for trainers listed in Figure 11-6. Which of the guidelines in the chapter or ones you added do you think will be the most difficult for you when you lead a training activity?

Activity 11-9

Experience a learning management system. Moodle is a popular Web-based learning management system used in many higher education institutions in the United States. You can take a sample course to get a flavor of Moodle as a learning management system:

- Course on Moodle (**demo.moodle.net**)

- Teaching online courses (**moodle.remote-learner.net/login**)

- Course on Java Programming (**www.examulator.com/moodle/course/view.php?id=2**)

Explore one or more of the sample courses and make a list of at least five features in Moodle that a trainer would find useful when preparing training for end users. Include your own reaction to this method of training.

Case Projects

1. Learn About Learning Styles

Barbara A. Soloman and Richard M. Felder at North Carolina State University have researched different learning styles. They created an instrument to assess learning styles on these four dimensions:

- Active/reflective

- Sensing/intuitive

- Visual/verbal

- Sequential/global

Find out more about each of these learning styles at their Web site (**www.engr.ncsu.edu/ learningstyles/ilsweb.html**). Answer their Index of Learning Styles (ILS) questionnaire (there are no right or wrong answers) to learn more about your preferred learning style. Compare your scores on the ILS questionnaire with the scores of three coworkers or classmates. Write a summary of the results you observed and what the results mean for you as a trainee. In your summary, answer this question: *"Does any one of the training methods described in this chapter meet the needs of all the different learning styles that Felder and Soloman describe on their Web site?"* Explain why or why not.

2. Design a Training Module

Choose a topic on which you could train others. Plan, prepare, and present a training module on the topic. Examples of possible topics include the following:

- How to do a mail merge in a word-processing application

- How to install a CD or DVD drive in a PC

- How to use a switchboard in Microsoft Access

- How to use one or more of the basic features of a help desk software package, such as HelpSTAR, BMC Service Desk, HEAT, HelpTrac, or Spiceworks (see Chapter 6 for ideas)
- How to use advanced features of an online search engine to perform more effective searches
- How to use the Mac OS (aimed at Windows users)
- How to write simple scripts using the Windows Script Host
- How to import tabular data from the Web into a Microsoft Excel worksheet

The training module you prepare should include all of the following elements:

Planning

1. Analyze job skills required
2. Analyze the trainees
3. Assess the needs of the trainees
4. Set training objectives

Preparation

5. Select and organize training content
6. Select training methods, techniques, and aids
7. Prepare training module
8. Decide how to evaluate training

Presentation

9. Present training module
10. Evaluate the training

Progress

11. Review and revise training materials and methods, as necessary

First, work on a plan for a sample training module for your topic. Cover Steps 1 through 6 and Step 8 in planning and preparation first. For some of these steps, such as analyzing the trainees, your instructor may give you some background information or ask you to make some assumptions. Work with other class members to brainstorm topic priorities. What could be included and what could be omitted from your training module?

Next, based on the results of brainstorming with class members, work independently to prepare a 20- to 30-minute training module for one-to-one delivery (Step 7). The module should include a hands-on component, a short quiz, and time for a brief evaluation.

Then, present your training module (Step 9) to another class member. At the end of the training session, both the trainer and the trainee should fill out a short evaluation (for the trainer it will be a self-evaluation). Use the evaluation form from this chapter, the one you produced in Activity 11-7, or write one of your own specifically for this training activity. Then reverse roles, so your partner can present his or her training module to you. (If you are working alone, ask a friend or colleague to help you evaluate your training module as a training beta test.)

When your training beta test is finished, write a short summary of what you learned from the experience that would improve the training module, or your presentation of it, the next time you present it. If possible, after you have refined the quality of your training module, present it to your entire class or work team. Use the evaluation form you prepared for the beta test to get feedback from your colleagues.

3. Present Someone Else's Training Module

In corporate training, a trainer is often provided with preplanned and prepackaged training materials to present. Repeat presentation Steps 9 through 11 from Case Project 2 using the training materials a classmate has planned and prepared. After the training activity, provide feedback to the original developer about what worked well and what could be improved.

4. A Training Module for Office 2010 Users

Andrew Nussbaum is the Director of Training Services. The company where Andrew works is planning to convert from Office 2003 to Office 2010 in the next few weeks. Andrew's company bypassed Office 2007. Andrew would like to offer a training session for about 20 experienced Office 2003 users to acquaint them with the changes to the user interface they will encounter when they convert to Office 2010. Andrew has asked you and Randy, another user support specialist, to design one training module for Office users. You may select the Office 2010 program of your choice. Then plan and prepare a training module on the Office 2010 ribbon menu for the program you selected. Assume the trainees are already acquainted with the basic features of the software features in Office, so the user interface is the focus of the training. *(The Role-Playing Scenario presented earlier in this chapter relates an interview between Andrew and Randy, your coworker on the project. It will give you additional background information for this case.)*

The training module you prepare should include all the following elements:

Planning (make assumptions where necessary)

1. Analyze job skills required
2. Analyze the trainees
3. Assess the needs of the trainees
4. Set training objectives

Preparation

5. Select and organize training content

6. Select training methods, techniques, and aids

7. Prepare training module

8. Decide how to evaluate the training

Write a brief description of your plan to address Steps 1 through 6 and Step 8 above. Then prepare training materials (Step 7 above) you would use to introduce users to the Office 2010 ribbon menu for the program you selected. One objective is to answer the trainees' question, *"If I know how to accomplish a task in Office 2003, where will I find the comparable tool in Office 2010?"* Develop training materials that could be presented by another trainer. Create a PowerPoint slide presentation and any handouts you believe would be useful during the training activity.

5. Design a Facility for the Office 2010 Training

Review the information in Case Project 4. Draw or describe an ideal room configuration for this training session. Show or describe the location of chairs, tables, presentation equipment, computers, and a whiteboard or flip charts. If it is available, use Visio, Dia (an open source alternative to Visio, available at **dia-installer.de**), a CAD program, or similar software to prepare your training room design.

6. Prepare a Slideshow for a Discussion Group

The office staff at Columbia Controls makes extensive use of computer technology. As part of their orientation program for new employees, the company assigns newly hired workers to view some free videos on LearnFree.org's Web site (**www.gcflearnfree.org/computers**) related to the software they will use in their work. The employees view the videos on their own, and then participate in a discussion group to review the materials and ask questions. Your task is to prepare a slideshow with presentation software that can be used in the discussion group meetings. Assume the discussion group meetings will last 30-45 minutes. Complete the following steps:

- First, on LearnFree's Web site, select one of the topics with which you are familiar. Choose a topic that includes one or more videos.

- Second, watch the video(s) and take notes on the material covered.

- Third, design and develop a slideshow that includes these elements:

    - A review of the major points covered in the video tutorials

    - Some discussion questions to reinforce what the new hires learned in the videos

    - Time for the participants to ask questions

If you have an opportunity, preview your slideshow with some colleagues and get their feedback on the content, design, and presentation of the material. Then revise your slideshow based on the feedback you received.

CHAPTER 12

A User Support Utility Tool Kit

In this chapter, you will learn about:

◎ Software utilities and information resources used by support specialists

◎ Categories of common user support utilities

◎ Some useful support utilities

Support specialists use a variety of software, information resources, and tools to perform their assigned tasks. Some tools are software utilities that help diagnose and resolve problems encountered by users. Other tools are information resources used by support specialists to locate information about common problems or about products and services. Yet another category consists of tools that can help users prevent common problems, including threats to security and invasion of privacy. These tools also include utilities designed to increase the productivity of support specialists.

This concluding chapter returns to the problem-solving process discussed in Chapters 4 and 5, and provides a beginning tool kit to tackle many of the user support problems described in those chapters. The following sections cover several software utilities and information tools that can help support workers to do their jobs—with a focus on common tools that many support specialists find useful in their work. In some cases, the software described may be most useful to support specialists; other software could be recommended to users to solve common problems. The chapter will not cover the much larger categories of application and personal productivity software aimed at end users.

Introduction to Utility Software and Information Resources

The tools described in this chapter are representative of several categories of utility programs and information resources. Their inclusion in the book is not intended as a recommendation or an endorsement, and in no case should a utility be used without a clear understanding of its effects on a PC or on a user's productivity. In many cases, other utilities and resources perform similar tasks or provide comparable information. Alternatives to those described in detail are included for many of the utilities; however, the alternatives listed may provide different features. Details about specific products and services discussed in this chapter, including their costs and features, may change as providers update their offerings. Examine vendor Web sites for details prior to using these utilities and resources.

 The utilities presented in this chapter were selected based on the author's experience, recommendations of colleagues, lists of highly rated utilities, and online reviews. Table 8-2 in Chapter 8 lists several industry publications that review software, including support utilities.

Many of the utilities listed here are open source, freeware, or shareware—which means they are typically free or low-cost (or are offered as free trial options). The utilities frequently provide features and functions similar to commercial software; that does not mean commercial products are less desirable. You can expect to encounter commercial versions of utility software on the job. In fact, many vendors of free versions of utilities also sell enhanced business versions with additional features or functionality. In an educational or training environment, the opportunity for learners to experience a variety of products is important. Free versions are listed here to encourage you to get experience with a variety of support tools.

Some of these resources are specifically designated for personal rather than commercial use. Observe any restrictions on use before downloading or accessing any of these resources. Open source, freeware, and shareware should not require payment, except for continued shareware use after a trial period. However, vendors of utility software often require users to register prior to downloading their product. Unfortunately, some vendors use free product registrations as a way to accumulate and sell lists of email addresses to their business partners or third parties. Users who register to download software should check the vendor's **privacy policy**, the **end-user license agreement (EULA)**, and information explaining any **opt-in check boxes** on each registration form to determine whether registration implies an agreement to receive email offers. Some users maintain a separate email address specifically for product registrations in order to avoid receiving spam offers at their primary email address.

Several caveats about the use of utility software are summarized in Figure 12-1.

This chapter is intended to provide a brief description of some popular and affordable tools and information resources that can be used to build a tool kit to help solve a variety of user support problems. Many of the tools described below are useful primarily to agents who provide support for internal end users in a face-to-face or on-site environment.

Before downloading and using any software utilities, be aware of the following:

- Information about specific utilities (including features, costs, download instructions, and documentation) often change from version to version; check online software specifications and reviews for changes and suitability before downloading or purchasing any utility.

- Open source, free, and shareware utilities may not include all the functionality and features of their better-known, commercial counterparts.

- Vendors who offer a trial or demonstration version of a software utility may disable some features or enforce other limitations, including limiting use to a specific time period; for example, a "free" utility that scans a PC for problems may offer to repair the problems only in a paid version.

- Some companies that offer free versions may limit their use to noncommercial, personal use. Use by nonprofit organizations, corporations, educational institutions, and government agencies may fall under a commercial license for which a fee is charged.

- Vendors that offer both free and commercial versions of utilities encourage users to buy their commercial versions in a variety of obvious and less-than-obvious ways, including advertisements on their Web site or during the operation of a utility; some vendors use misleading links to induce users to download commercial versions instead of free ones.

- Web sites that advertise a "free download" do not necessarily mean use of the software is free (only that it doesn't cost anything to download the software).

- While most utility software vendors are reputable and up-front about their use of registration information, some use various means, which are often buried in privacy policies, end-user license agreements (EULAs), and opt-in check boxes, to accumulate and sell registration information to third-parties.

- Some vendors of "free" software make money by including a variety of other software and toolbars along with their utility software. Be alert to check boxes on a download dialog screen relating to other Web browsers, toolbars, and software utilities; you may assent to download these extraneous items if you do not check or uncheck certain boxes.

- Some vendors of "free" software request a donation to help support product development. A donation is a suggestion, should be optional, and should not be a requirement to download a free utility (called donationware).

- Not all software utilities run on every version of an operating system. Check the system requirements for hardware and software prerequisites for each utility.

- Utilities that modify the setting or contents of a system (such as performance enhancement settings and Registry or disk cleaners) should be used with caution and only after backing up the parts of a system that will be modified so settings or content can be recovered in case of a malfunction.

- Some organizations, agencies, and educational institutions do not permit unauthorized software to be downloaded, installed, and used in a network environment in which security and support issues are common. Learn about restrictions on the use of utility software in your environment.

Figure 12-1   Warnings about utility software

Categories of Utility Software Tools

The variety of available utility software tools mirrors the variety of tasks performed by support agents. Figure 12-2 lists the categories of tools described in this chapter. In some cases, the utilities described may not be useful to all agents. For example, a support specialist who primarily provides application software or training support may not have immediate use for utilities to diagnose operating system configuration problems—however, jobs and responsibilities in the support industry are subject to change. Support agents are also computer users themselves, and may be interested in additional tools as they make software recommendations to others or maintain their own computers, or those of family, friends, and colleagues.

- Hardware Support
- System Information
- Software Support—Operating Systems
- Software Support—Applications
- System Problem Diagnosis
- Network Support
- Internet Support
- File Management Tasks
- Performance Enhancements
- Security Solutions
- User Support Tools

Figure 12-2 Categories of support utilities

 Throughout this chapter, some technical terms that may be unfamiliar are highlighted with bold text. These terms are defined in the Key Terms section at the end of the chapter, rather than in the chapter text or figures.

Hardware Support

Support agents often solve hardware problems with tools that **stress test** hardware during a burn-in period, update drivers for peripheral devices, and test a PC's hardware components.

 Each utility is described in this chapter on a standard form. The form includes information about the utility's purpose, features, download information, other alternatives, and, when available, pointers to documentation and other information.

- Figure 12-3 describes a tool that helps evaluate hardware reliability and stability during a burn-in period. This type of tool is useful for support specialists who assemble or install hardware systems.

- Figure 12-4 describes a utility that can be used to find and download updated device drivers.

- Figure 12-5 describes a utility that performs diagnostic tests of hard drives to evaluate the likelihood of drive failure.

- Figure 12-6 describes a utility that tests internal RAM to identify problems caused by memory modules that may need to be replaced.

Utilities in the System Problem Diagnosis and Performance Enhancement categories also perform related tests on hardware components.

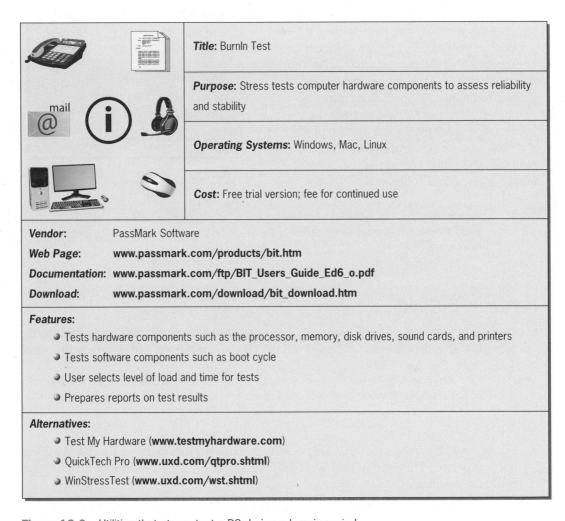

Title: BurnIn Test
Purpose: Stress tests computer hardware components to assess reliability and stability
Operating Systems: Windows, Mac, Linux
Cost: Free trial version; fee for continued use

Vendor:	PassMark Software
Web Page:	www.passmark.com/products/bit.htm
Documentation:	www.passmark.com/ftp/BIT_Users_Guide_Ed6_o.pdf
Download:	www.passmark.com/download/bit_download.htm

Features:
- Tests hardware components such as the processor, memory, disk drives, sound cards, and printers
- Tests software components such as boot cycle
- User selects level of load and time for tests
- Prepares reports on test results

Alternatives:
- Test My Hardware (**www.testmyhardware.com**)
- QuickTech Pro (**www.uxd.com/qtpro.shtml**)
- WinStressTest (**www.uxd.com/wst.shtml**)

Figure 12-3 Utilities that stress test a PC during a burn-in period

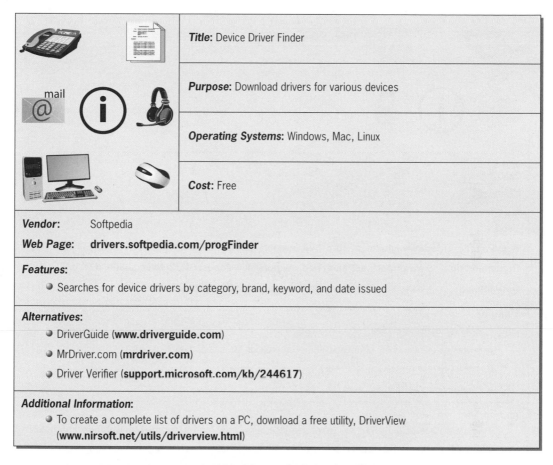

Title: Device Driver Finder

Purpose: Download drivers for various devices

Operating Systems: Windows, Mac, Linux

Cost: Free

Vendor: Softpedia

Web Page: **drivers.softpedia.com/progFinder**

Features:
- Searches for device drivers by category, brand, keyword, and date issued

Alternatives:
- DriverGuide (**www.driverguide.com**)
- MrDriver.com (**mrdriver.com**)
- Driver Verifier (**support.microsoft.com/kb/244617**)

Additional Information:
- To create a complete list of drivers on a PC, download a free utility, DriverView (**www.nirsoft.net/utils/driverview.html**)

Figure 12-4　Resources to help locate and download updated device drivers

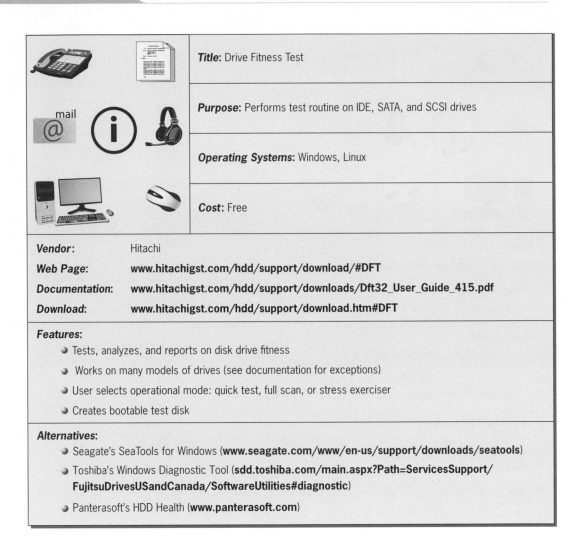

	Title: Drive Fitness Test
	Purpose: Performs test routine on IDE, SATA, and SCSI drives
	Operating Systems: Windows, Linux
	Cost: Free

Vendor:	Hitachi
Web Page:	**www.hitachigst.com/hdd/support/download/#DFT**
Documentation:	**www.hitachigst.com/hdd/support/downloads/Dft32_User_Guide_415.pdf**
Download:	**www.hitachigst.com/hdd/support/download.htm#DFT**

Features:
- Tests, analyzes, and reports on disk drive fitness
- Works on many models of drives (see documentation for exceptions)
- User selects operational mode: quick test, full scan, or stress exerciser
- Creates bootable test disk

Alternatives:
- Seagate's SeaTools for Windows (**www.seagate.com/www/en-us/support/downloads/seatools**)
- Toshiba's Windows Diagnostic Tool (**sdd.toshiba.com/main.aspx?Path=ServicesSupport/ FujitsuDrivesUSandCanada/SoftwareUtilities#diagnostic**)
- Panterasoft's HDD Health (**www.panterasoft.com**)

Figure 12-5   Utility tools to test hard disk devices

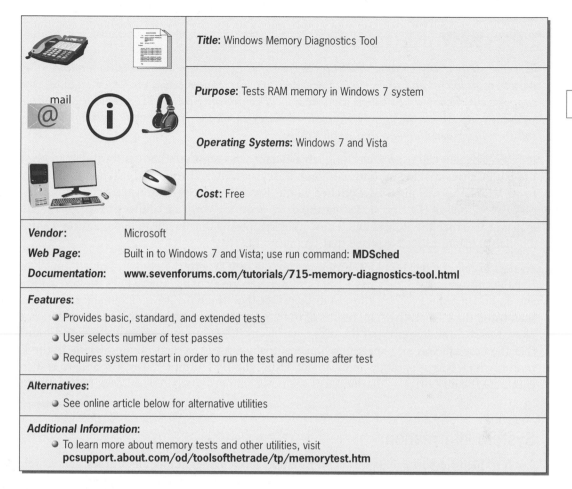

	Title: Windows Memory Diagnostics Tool
	Purpose: Tests RAM memory in Windows 7 system
	Operating Systems: Windows 7 and Vista
	Cost: Free

Vendor: Microsoft

Web Page: Built in to Windows 7 and Vista; use run command: **MDSched**

Documentation: **www.sevenforums.com/tutorials/715-memory-diagnostics-tool.html**

Features:
- Provides basic, standard, and extended tests
- User selects number of test passes
- Requires system restart in order to run the test and resume after test

Alternatives:
- See online article below for alternative utilities

Additional Information:
- To learn more about memory tests and other utilities, visit
  pcsupport.about.com/od/toolsofthetrade/tp/memorytest.htm

Figure 12-6   Utility tools to test internal memory

CASE STUDY: UTILITIES FOR USER SUPPORT TASKS

The case study in this chapter illustrates the use of utility software to troubleshoot and resolve a variety of problems end users encounter every day. The case is based on Kasey Fuentes, who supports instructors and student users at a local community college. Throughout the chapter, you will learn about the variety of problems Kasey encounters in her work and how utility software helps her diagnose and resolve them.

Kasey received a call from a teaching lab assistant who reported that the hard disk in one of the lab PCs was making an unusual noise. Kasey arrived at the lab and listened to the hard drive, which was making a high-pitched whine. Kasey knew that an unusual noise from a hard disk can be one of the first signs that the drive is on the verge of failure. She asked the lab assistant whether the PC exhibited any other symptoms that might indicate a drive failure. The lab assistant said, "No, none that I'm aware of."

As part of her standard tool kit, Kasey carries a boot CD with the Hitachi Drive Fitness Test (DFT) utility described in Figure 12-5. First, Kasey made a change to the PC's BIOS settings so she could start the PC from the CD drive rather than the hard drive. Then she ran a quick scan using the DFT utility. The results of the fitness test indicated the disk drive media tested okay. Kasey carefully removed the case cover from the PC to investigate further and found that the case fan was extremely hot. She eventually traced the high-pitched whine to the fan motor, which was apparently about to fail. Using the DFT utility, Kasey was able to test and eliminate the disk drive as the source of the noise, and ordered a replacement fan for the PC.

System Information

Tools to help support agents locate information about a system include utilities that search a PC and report on configuration information, and those that monitor and prepare a log of activities during a system's start-up process.

- Figure 12-7 describes a tool that prepares reports on installed hardware, software, and configuration information. These reports are useful additions to a site installation notebook, described in Chapter 10.

- Figure 12-8 describes a utility that monitors the start-up process and lists device drivers and system services identified during start-up.

Utilities in the System Problem Diagnosis and Performance Enhancements categories may also report some configuration information.

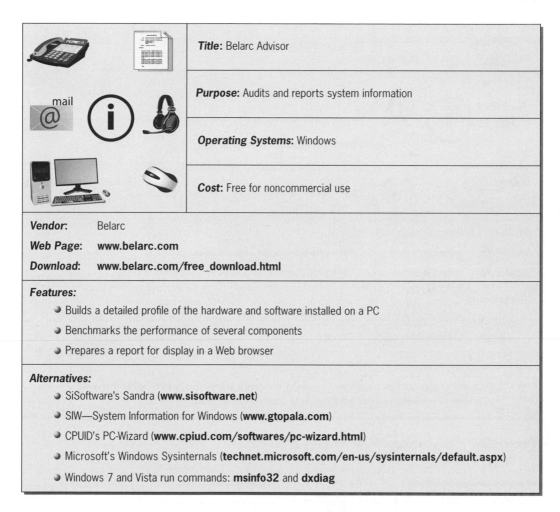

Title: Belarc Advisor

Purpose: Audits and reports system information

Operating Systems: Windows

Cost: Free for noncommercial use

Vendor: Belarc

Web Page: www.belarc.com

Download: www.belarc.com/free_download.html

Features:

- Builds a detailed profile of the hardware and software installed on a PC
- Benchmarks the performance of several components
- Prepares a report for display in a Web browser

Alternatives:

- SiSoftware's Sandra (**www.sisoftware.net**)
- SIW—System Information for Windows (**www.gtopala.com**)
- CPUID's PC-Wizard (**www.cpiud.com/softwares/pc-wizard.html**)
- Microsoft's Windows Sysinternals (**technet.microsoft.com/en-us/sysinternals/default.aspx**)
- Windows 7 and Vista run commands: **msinfo32** and **dxdiag**

Figure 12-7   Utility tools to report on system configuration information

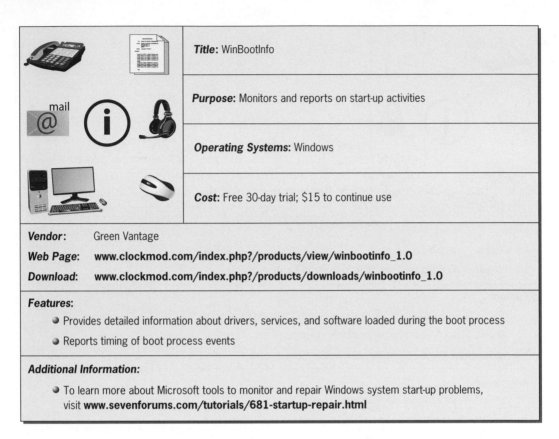

Title: WinBootInfo	
Purpose: Monitors and reports on start-up activities	
Operating Systems: Windows	
Cost: Free 30-day trial; $15 to continue use	

Vendor: Green Vantage

Web Page: **www.clockmod.com/index.php?/products/view/winbootinfo_1.0**

Download: **www.clockmod.com/index.php?/products/downloads/winbootinfo_1.0**

Features:

- Provides detailed information about drivers, services, and software loaded during the boot process
- Reports timing of boot process events

Additional Information:

- To learn more about Microsoft tools to monitor and repair Windows system start-up problems, visit **www.sevenforums.com/tutorials/681-startup-repair.html**

Figure 12-8   Utility to report on system start-up activities

CASE STUDY: UTILITIES FOR USER SUPPORT TASKS

Kasey checked her work orders and found that today's schedule includes an installation of a new PC for a Science Department instructor. Kasey had visited the instructor last week for a preinstallation site visit and learned that he purchased the PC through an instructional grant for a new data analysis and visualization course. Kasey loaded the PC and her tool-kit onto a cart and headed off to the 10 a.m. installation appointment.

After installing and testing the new PC, Kasey downloaded and installed the Belarc Advisor utility described in Figure 12-7. She ran Belarc Advisor on the PC, prepared a Computer Profile Summary report, and reviewed the report with the instructor. They were both amazed at the amount of detailed information the report included on hardware devices, the operating system, and software installed. The instructor noted that a specialized data analysis program he wanted for the curriculum project was not listed among the installed software. Kasey asked whether he had the installation disk for the software. Since he did, Kasey installed the package and re-ran Belarc Advisor. Kasey included the updated Belarc profile summary report in the PC's site installation notebook in case questions arose in the future about its original configuration.

535

Software Support—Operating Systems

Tools to help support agents diagnose problems with operating system software include utilities that permit an agent to modify the programs loaded during system start-up and utilities that delete unused and obsolete information in the Windows Registry. Other useful tools include an information resource that describes utilities and commands that can be entered into the **Windows command-line** interface, a procedure to prepare a Windows **recovery disk** to start up an inoperative system, and a variety of other Windows utilities.

- Figure 12-9 describes a tool to identify and modify the software that gets launched automatically during system start-up.

- Figure 12-10 describes a utility that cleans debris from a system Registry to improve its efficiency.

- Figure 12-11 shows a report from Comodo's Registry Cleaner (part of the Comodo System Cleaner suite), which checks for several common Registry problems.

- Figure 12-12 describes a utility tool to perform Registry management tasks, including editing Registry keys and values.

- Figure 12-13 describes a resource with information on Windows command-line utilities (sometimes still referred to as DOS commands or utilities).

- Figure 12-14 describes a tool to create a Windows recovery disk, which can be used to start up a system that has an inoperative hard drive or a corrupted operating system. An agreement between Microsoft and Neosoft permits the latter to distribute an image of Windows as a part of their recovery disk tool. The Microsoft Web site in Figure 12-14 points to a tutorial on how to make a free Windows system boot disk.

Utilities in the System Problem Diagnosis, Software Support—Applications, and File Management categories also contain tools to manage operating system tasks.

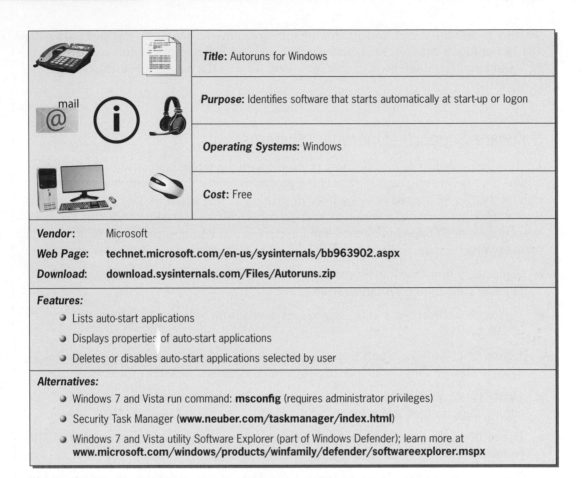

| **Title:** Autoruns for Windows |
| **Purpose:** Identifies software that starts automatically at start-up or logon |
| **Operating Systems:** Windows |
| **Cost:** Free |

Vendor: Microsoft

Web Page: technet.microsoft.com/en-us/sysinternals/bb963902.aspx

Download: download.sysinternals.com/Files/Autoruns.zip

Features:

- Lists auto-start applications
- Displays properties of auto-start applications
- Deletes or disables auto-start applications selected by user

Alternatives:

- Windows 7 and Vista run command: **msconfig** (requires administrator privileges)
- Security Task Manager (**www.neuber.com/taskmanager/index.html**)
- Windows 7 and Vista utility Software Explorer (part of Windows Defender); learn more at **www.microsoft.com/windows/products/winfamily/defender/softwareexplorer.mspx**

Figure 12-9   Autoruns utility to manage Window's start-up software

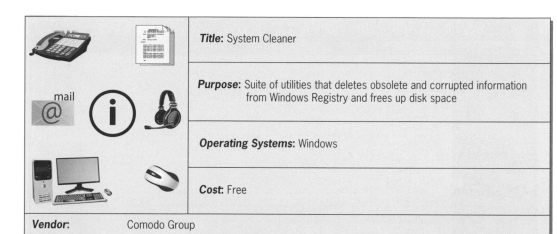

	Title: System Cleaner
	Purpose: Suite of utilities that deletes obsolete and corrupted information from Windows Registry and frees up disk space
	Operating Systems: Windows
	Cost: Free

Vendor:	Comodo Group
Web Page:	www.comodo.com/home/support-maintenance/system-cleaner.php
Documentation:	system-cleaner.comodo.com/Comodo_System_Cleaner_User_Guide.pdf
Download:	system-cleaner.comodo.com

Features:

- Deletes Windows Registry entries that are no longer needed
- Optimizes Windows Registry for improved performance
- Reduces system crashes caused by invalid Registry entries
- Deletes temporary and unused files left behind during software installations and removals, as well as those created during regular use
- Provides system configuration information
- Provides user control over start-up programs

Alternatives:

- Eusing Registry Cleaner (**www.eusing.com/free_registry_cleaner/registry_cleaner.htm**)
- Wise Registry Cleaner (**www.wisecleaner.com/download.html**)
- Glary Registry Repair (**www.glarysoft.com/products/utilities/glary-utilities**)
- ReviverSoft's Registry Reviver (**www.reviversoft.com/registry-reviver**)

Additional Information:

- Several commercial Registry cleaners are available; some perform free Registry scans, but require payment to clean problems found
- Read reviews of commercial Registry cleaner utilities at (**registry-repair-software-review.toptenreviews.com**)

Figure 12-10 Utility tools to clean and repair Windows Registry

538

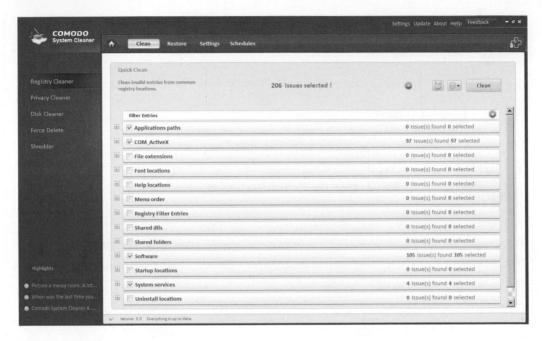

Figure 12-11   Comodo's Registry Cleaner checks several common Registry problems

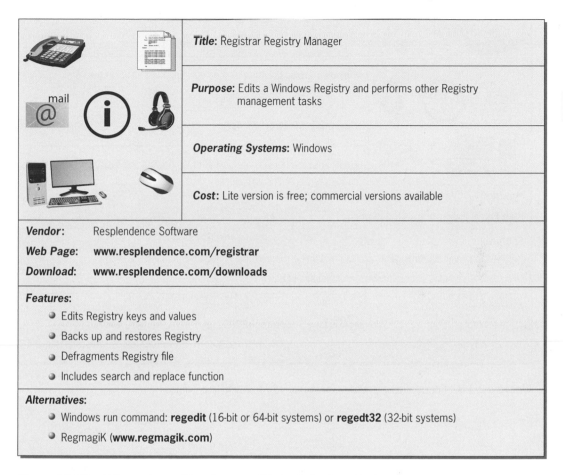

Title: Registrar Registry Manager

Purpose: Edits a Windows Registry and performs other Registry management tasks

Operating Systems: Windows

Cost: Lite version is free; commercial versions available

Vendor: Resplendence Software

Web Page: **www.resplendence.com/registrar**

Download: **www.resplendence.com/downloads**

Features:

- Edits Registry keys and values
- Backs up and restores Registry
- Defragments Registry file
- Includes search and replace function

Alternatives:

- Windows run command: **regedit** (16-bit or 64-bit systems) or **regedt32** (32-bit systems)
- RegmagiK (**www.regmagik.com**)

Figure 12-12 Utility tools to edit and manage Window's Registry database

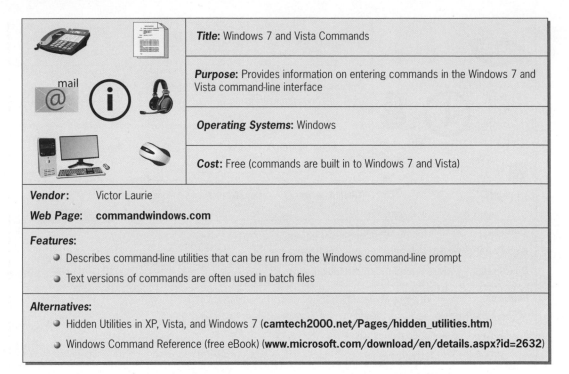

	Title: Windows 7 and Vista Commands
	Purpose: Provides information on entering commands in the Windows 7 and Vista command-line interface
	Operating Systems: Windows
	Cost: Free (commands are built in to Windows 7 and Vista)

Vendor: Victor Laurie

Web Page: **commandwindows.com**

Features:
- Describes command-line utilities that can be run from the Windows command-line prompt
- Text versions of commands are often used in batch files

Alternatives:
- Hidden Utilities in XP, Vista, and Windows 7 (**camtech2000.net/Pages/hidden_utilities.htm**)
- Windows Command Reference (free eBook) (**www.microsoft.com/download/en/details.aspx?id=2632**)

Figure 12-13 Information resources for Windows command-line utilities

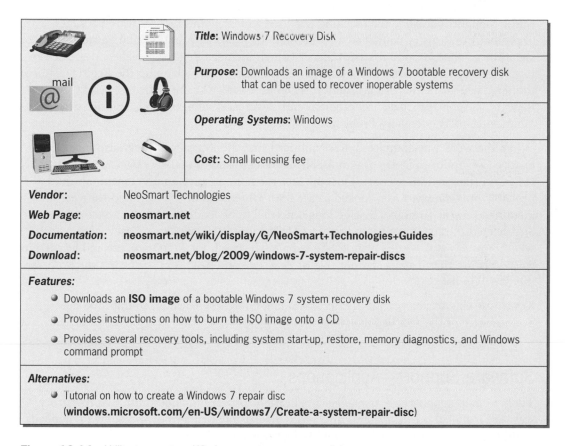

	Title: Windows 7 Recovery Disk
	Purpose: Downloads an image of a Windows 7 bootable recovery disk that can be used to recover inoperable systems
	Operating Systems: Windows
	Cost: Small licensing fee

Vendor:	NeoSmart Technologies
Web Page:	**neosmart.net**
Documentation:	**neosmart.net/wiki/display/G/NeoSmart+Technologies+Guides**
Download:	**neosmart.net/blog/2009/windows-7-system-repair-discs**

Features:

- Downloads an **ISO image** of a bootable Windows 7 system recovery disk
- Provides instructions on how to burn the ISO image onto a CD
- Provides several recovery tools, including system start-up, restore, memory diagnostics, and Windows command prompt

Alternatives:

- Tutorial on how to create a Windows 7 repair disc
  (windows.microsoft.com/en-US/windows7/Create-a-system-repair-disc)

Figure 12-14   Utility to create a Windows system recovery disk

CASE STUDY: UTILITIES FOR USER SUPPORT TASKS

Kasey and her coworkers use a PC in the support team office as a test bed for nonstandard software that needs to be downloaded, tested, and checked for viruses and compatibility with the college's network. Recently Kasey's coworkers have complained that the operation of the PC has slowed considerably. Since Kasey has a break in her schedule today, she decided to perform some standard maintenance operations on the test bed PC to see if she could improve its performance.

She first did a hard disk backup, which is standard procedure among the support team members prior to any maintenance work. The backup program established a recovery point she could return to in case any of the maintenance tasks caused operational problems for the test bed PC. Then she ran the Uninstaller utility described in Figure 12-17 and a disk cleanup utility, CCleaner, which is described later in the chapter in Figure 12-31; she also defragged the drive using Disk Defrag, described in Figure 12-32.

Kasey thought that since the machine was used to install and test software packages, it was likely that the Registry contained a lot of temporary, obsolete, and invalid entries. Therefore, she also ran the Comodo System Cleaner (which includes Registry Cleaner) described in Figure 12-10. The Registry Cleaner gave her the option of backing up the Registry before the scan, which she did as a precaution. Then Kasey ran a scan on the test bed PC's Registry. Registry Cleaner identified 455 problem entries across several of the categories. She clicked a button to fix the Registry Problems.

When the work was completed, Kasey noticed that the Registry Cleaner also includes a feature to examine Start Up programs. She knew that if some software packages that had been tested on the machine were still loading into memory at start-up, the machine would probably boot slowly. Kasey looked at the Start Up entries in the Comodo software and identified several programs that no longer needed to be loaded when the system was started. She deleted these. One entry in the Start Up list was RtHDVcpl.exe. Kasey was unsure whether it was still needed or not. She did a Web search for *RtHDVcpl.exe* and learned it is valid software that installs components of RealTek's audio system, so she left the program in the Start Up list.

Kasey was able to use several utilities, including a Registry Cleaner, to improve the performance of the test bed machine.

Software Support—Applications

Tools to help support agents manage application software include those that inventory software installed on PC systems and verify the existence of authorized **software licenses**, utilities that report on the update status of software, and those that perform tasks to uninstall a software package.

- Figure 12-15 describes a utility that **audits** installed software on a PC to help verify that only licensed software is in use.

- Figure 12-16 describes utility tools that report on the **patch status** of installed software and assist with obtaining necessary updates.

- Figure 12-17 describes utility tools to uninstall software when the Programs and Features uninstall tool in Windows does not do a thorough job.

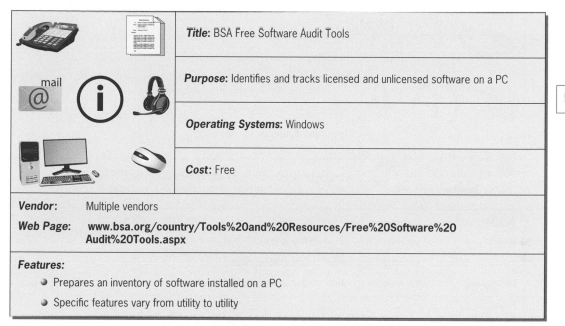

	Title: BSA Free Software Audit Tools
	Purpose: Identifies and tracks licensed and unlicensed software on a PC
	Operating Systems: Windows
	Cost: Free

Vendor: Multiple vendors

Web Page: www.bsa.org/country/Tools%20and%20Resources/Free%20Software%20
Audit%20Tools.aspx

Features:

- Prepares an inventory of software installed on a PC
- Specific features vary from utility to utility

Figure 12-15   Utility tools to audit and manage application software

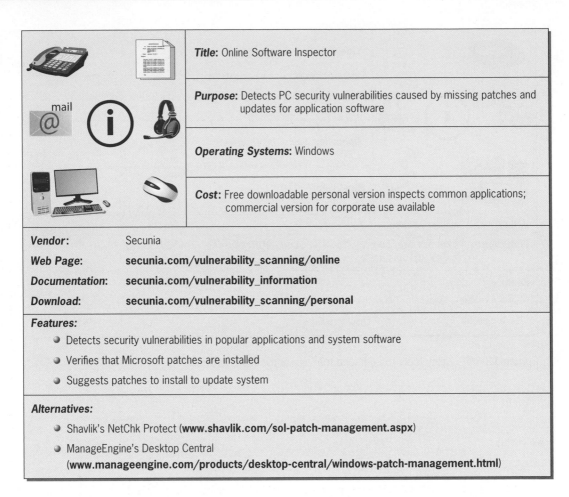

Title: Online Software Inspector	
Purpose: Detects PC security vulnerabilities caused by missing patches and updates for application software	
Operating Systems: Windows	
Cost: Free downloadable personal version inspects common applications; commercial version for corporate use available	

Vendor:	Secunia
Web Page:	**secunia.com/vulnerability_scanning/online**
Documentation:	**secunia.com/vulnerability_information**
Download:	**secunia.com/vulnerability_scanning/personal**

Features:
- Detects security vulnerabilities in popular applications and system software
- Verifies that Microsoft patches are installed
- Suggests patches to install to update system

Alternatives:
- Shavlik's NetChk Protect (**www.shavlik.com/sol-patch-management.aspx**)
- ManageEngine's Desktop Central (**www.manageengine.com/products/desktop-central/windows-patch-management.html**)

Figure 12-16   Utilities to report on the patch status of application and system software

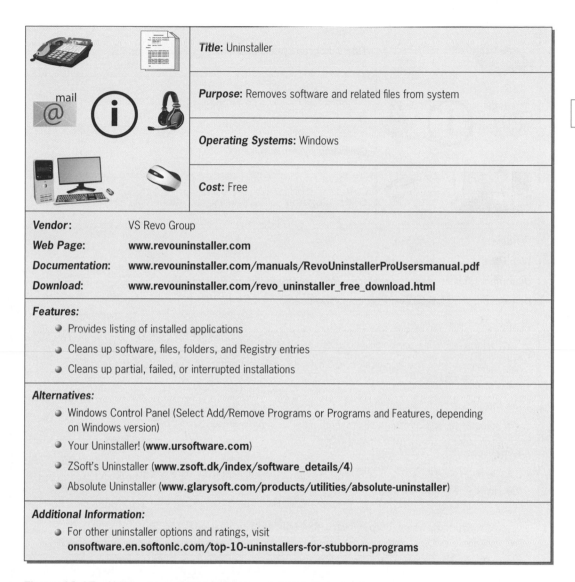

	Title: Uninstaller
	Purpose: Removes software and related files from system
	Operating Systems: Windows
	Cost: Free

Vendor:	VS Revo Group
Web Page:	**www.revouninstaller.com**
Documentation:	**www.revouninstaller.com/manuals/RevoUninstallerProUsersmanual.pdf**
Download:	**www.revouninstaller.com/revo_uninstaller_free_download.html**

Features:

- Provides listing of installed applications
- Cleans up software, files, folders, and Registry entries
- Cleans up partial, failed, or interrupted installations

Alternatives:

- Windows Control Panel (Select Add/Remove Programs or Programs and Features, depending on Windows version)
- Your Uninstaller! (**www.ursoftware.com**)
- ZSoft's Uninstaller (**www.zsoft.dk/index/software_details/4**)
- Absolute Uninstaller (**www.glarysoft.com/products/utilities/absolute-uninstaller**)

Additional Information:

- For other uninstaller options and ratings, visit
  onsoftware.en.softonic.com/top-10-uninstallers-for-stubborn-programs

Figure 12-17 Utilities to complete software uninstall tasks

System Problem Diagnosis

In addition to individual utilities that help support agents diagnose problems involving hardware, operating systems, and application software, many suites bundle several utility tools together in a package. Some of these packages are described below.

- Figure 12-18 describes a diagnostic tool to find, analyze, and, in some cases, repair hardware and software problems in computer systems.

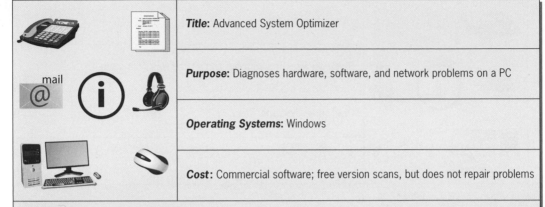

Title: Advanced System Optimizer

Purpose: Diagnoses hardware, software, and network problems on a PC

Operating Systems: Windows

Cost: Commercial software; free version scans, but does not repair problems

Vendor:	Systweak
Web Page:	**www.systweak.com/aso**
Documentation:	**www.systweak.com/ASO/ASOHelp/Smart-PC-Care.asp**
Download:	**www.systweak.com/Downloads**

Features:

- Performs several common diagnostic and repair tasks
- Tests processor, memory, disk drives, keyboard, mouse, monitor, adapter cards, ports, and bus
- Optimizes PC operation
- Provides security tools
- Prepares report on findings

Alternatives:

- IoBit's Advanced SystemCare (**www.iobit.com/advancedsystemcareper.html**)
- HWiNFO (**www.hwinfo.com**)
- Advanquest Software's Fix-It Utilities
  (**www.avanquest.com/USA/software/fixit-utilities11-professional-146390**)
- Windows 7 and Vista System Health Report (In the Windows 7 search box, enter **perfmon /report**)

Additional Information:

- Read a review of diagnostic software utilities at **pc-system-utilities-software-review.toptenreviews.com**

Figure 12-18   Utilities to analyze and diagnose PC system problems

- Figure 12-19 shows a sample System Health Report from the Windows 7 Reliability and Performance Monitor, which helps identify problems in PC systems.

- Figure 12-20 describes a utility suite that bundles several of the utility tools described individually in this chapter into an integrated suite of related tools.

Individual utilities in the Hardware Support, Software Support—Operating Systems, Software Support—Applications, and Network Support categories perform similar tasks.

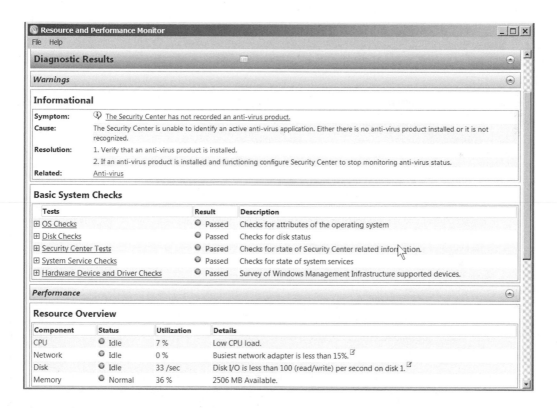

Figure 12-19   Sample output from a Windows 7 System Health Report

548

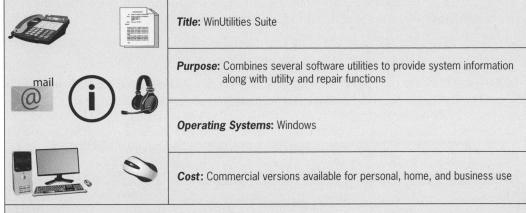

mail

Title: WinUtilities Suite	
Purpose: Combines several software utilities to provide system information along with utility and repair functions	
Operating Systems: Windows	
Cost: Commercial versions available for personal, home, and business use	

Vendor:	YL Software
Web Page:	**www.ylcomputing.com**
Documentation:	**www.ylcomputing.com/content/blogcategory/5/36**
Download:	**www.ylcomputing.com/content/view/12/31**

Features:

- Tools include: file undelete, disk cleaner, duplicate file finder, secure file eraser, Registry cleaner, Registry backup and restore, start-up file manager, history cleaner, memory optimizer, system information, uninstall manager, task scheduler, and Windows utilities launcher

Alternatives:

- Macecraft Software's jv16 PowerTools (**www.macecraft.com**)
- SystemSuite (**www.avanquest.com/USA/software/systemsuite11-professional-146483**)
- Norton Utilities (**us.norton.com/norton-utilities**)
- Wopti Utilities (**download.cnet.com/Wopti-Utilities/3000-2094_4-10821937.html**)
- iolo Technologies System Mechanic (**www.iolo.com**)
- Microsoft's Windows Sysinternals (**technet.microsoft.com/en-us/sysinternals/default.aspx**)

Additional Information:

- For a review of several Windows utility suites, see **reviews.cnet.com/4566-3690_7-0.html? filter=500343_5852202_&tag=mncol;dir3** or go to **www.utilitysoftwarereviews.com**

Figure 12-20   Description of suites of utility software to perform a range of support tasks

CASE STUDY: UTILITIES FOR USER SUPPORT TASKS

Kasey's support team has adopted a goal for the current year to be more proactive in anticipating problems with end-user systems. They have decided to recommend that users in the college periodically run a diagnostic utility program to help identify possible hardware, software configuration, or network performance problems. The team's plan is to email the college's user base a monthly reminder to run a System Health Report, which is part of the Windows operating system. The email reminders will invite users to report to the support team any problems identified on the System Health Report, especially if any of the warnings in the Basic System Checks and Resource Overview sections of the Diagnostic Results window (shown in Figure 12-19) are red.

The full System Health Report includes an analysis of the network, as well as the PC's software and hardware configurations (CPU, disk, and memory); the report also includes various performance statistics. At the end of the year, the support team plans to evaluate whether the monthly reminders and the Windows 7 diagnostic utility tool have improved the group's ability to anticipate users' PC problems.

Network Support

Tools to help support agents diagnose problems with computer networks include tools to trace and locate the source of network outages, as well as those designed to monitor network performance. Since poor performance can indicate problems with the hardware, software, or configuration settings of a network, many network utilities monitor performance, detect **service faults**, and perform other diagnostic functions. Network utilities often provide administrators with a convenient **dashboard** of performance statistics and fault alerts.

- Figure 12-21 describes a tool to monitor network performance and help identify **throughput bottlenecks** as well as other problems.

- Figure 12-22 describes a utility tool to diagnose and troubleshoot network operation to identify faults in network infrastructure.

Utilities in the Internet Support and Security Solutions categories address other network management tasks.

550

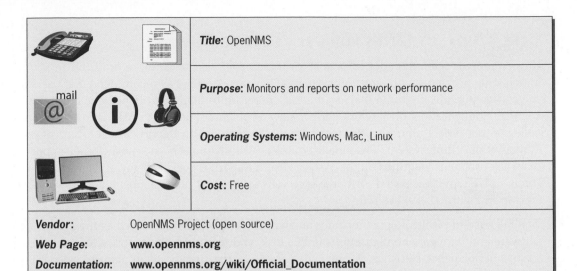

	Title: OpenNMS
	Purpose: Monitors and reports on network performance
	Operating Systems: Windows, Mac, Linux
	Cost: Free

Vendor:	OpenNMS Project (open source)
Web Page:	**www.opennms.org**
Documentation:	**www.opennms.org/wiki/Official_Documentation**
Download:	**www.opennms.org/wiki/Download**

Features:
- Monitors and reports on network system performance
- Administrator-customizable performance thresholds
- Notifies network administrator of events and problems

Alternatives:
- Spiceworks' Network Monitor (**www.spiceworks.com**)
- SNM—System and Network Monitor (**snm.sourceforge.net**)
- OpenSMART (**opensmart.sourceforge.net**)
- Total Network Monitor (**www.softinventive.com/products/total-network-monitor**)
- GroundWork Monitor (**www.gwos.com/products**)
- NetMeter (**www.hootech.com/NetMeter**)
- Alexandre Fenyo's GnetWatch (**gnetwatch.sourceforge.net**)

Additional Information:
- For listings of free and low-cost network performance and monitoring tools, visit:
  - **www.manageengine.com/products/opmanager/network-monitoring-tool.html**
  - **www.slac.stanford.edu/xorg/nmtf/nmtf-tools.html**
  - **www.netmon.org/tools.htm**

Figure 12-21 Utilities to monitor and report network performance

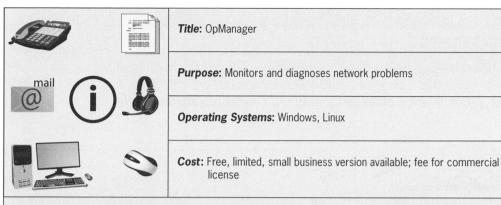

	Title: OpManager
	Purpose: Monitors and diagnoses network problems
	Operating Systems: Windows, Linux
	Cost: Free, limited, small business version available; fee for commercial license

Vendor:	Zoho Corporation
Web Page:	**www.manageengine.com/network-performance-management.html**
Documentation:	**www.manageengine.com/productdocument.html#network-performance-management**
Download:	**www.manageengine.com/network-monitoring/download-free.html**

Features:
- Automates network device discovery and mapping
- Monitors network traffic and throughput
- Monitors server operation and performance
- Detects network faults and provides alarms
- Provides a customizable report dashboard

Alternatives:
- Colasoft's Capsa Free Network Analyzer (**www.colasoft.com/capsa/capsa-free-edition.php**)
- OpUtils (**www.manageengine.com/products/oputils**)
- SolarWinds' Free Network Flow Manager
  (**www.solarwinds.com/products/freetools/netflow_analyzer.aspx**)
- FreeNATS Network Monitor (**www.purplepixie.org/freenats**)

Additional Information:
Network diagnostic tools cover a wide range of capabilities, including tools intended for end-user PCs to those designed for large enterprise networks; they range from free to very expensive. Stanford University maintains a comprehensive catalog of network tools (**www.slac.stanford.edu/xorg/nmtf/nmtf-tools.html**). The site includes links to many useful and free tools.

Figure 12-22 Utility tools to diagnose and troubleshoot network operation problems

552

ON THE WEB

For information on the basics of network monitoring and performance, see *An Introduction to Computer Network Monitoring and Performance* by A. C. Davenhall and M. J. Leese (**www.eslea.uklight.ac.uk/cookbook/intronet.pdf**).

CASE STUDY: UTILITIES FOR USER SUPPORT TASKS

One afternoon, Kasey received a call from an end user in the college's Business Department who stated that her PC was running but she was suddenly unable to access the Internet. She had been able to use the Internet earlier that morning. Kasey's support group runs OpManager, a utility described in Figure 12-22, to monitor and diagnose network problems. Kasey's first thought was to check OpManager to see whether any network problems had been identified. She looked at the OpManager dashboard, and noted that none of the network devices on the Business Department's side of the gateway—or network connection point— were responding to pings. (A ping is a brief transmission sent to a network device to determine whether the path to the device is available and the device is operational.) Because the ping failed, Kasey concluded that the network was down in the entire Business Department building. The phone would soon be ringing off the hook.

Kasey contacted one of her support colleagues, Randy. After discussing several options, Kasey suggested that Randy go to the network equipment closet in the Business Department office and reboot the gateway to see whether that would make a difference. Kasey's reasoning was that hardware devices, such as gateways, often respond to a reboot (this is an example of a simple, obvious fix you learned about in Chapter 4). Kasey continued to monitor OpManager and noted that when Randy restarted the Business Department gateway, the PCs in the department began to respond to OpManager's pings. Kasey called the faculty member back to verify that her PC was able to access the Internet and to thank her for the call. She also made an entry in the support team's problem database to record the incident in case further problems with the gateway device were reported.

Internet Support

Tools to help support agents monitor and identify problems with Internet use include utilities to test and report on Internet connection bandwidths as well as those that identify potential security problems due to Internet connectivity.

- Figure 12-23 describes a tool to test a PC's Internet connection bandwidth, including download and upload speeds.

- Figure 12-24 describes a utility tool to identify possible connectivity **vulnerabilities** due to an external Internet device's ability to penetrate a connected PC.

Utilities in the Security Solutions category address other Internet challenges.

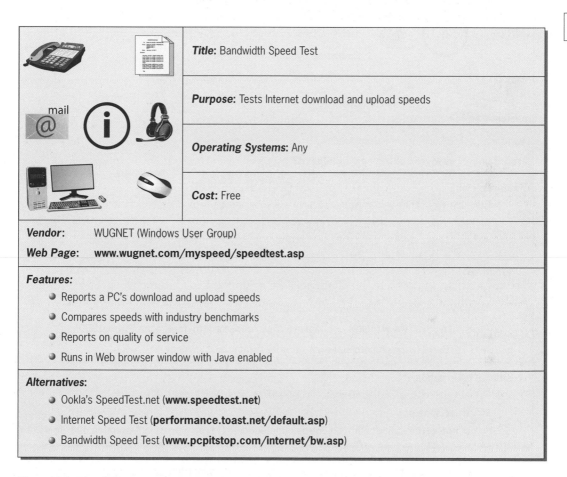

	Title: Bandwidth Speed Test
	Purpose: Tests Internet download and upload speeds
	Operating Systems: Any
	Cost: Free

Vendor: WUGNET (Windows User Group)

Web Page: **www.wugnet.com/myspeed/speedtest.asp**

Features:
- Reports a PC's download and upload speeds
- Compares speeds with industry benchmarks
- Reports on quality of service
- Runs in Web browser window with Java enabled

Alternatives:
- Ookla's SpeedTest.net (**www.speedtest.net**)
- Internet Speed Test (**performance.toast.net/default.asp**)
- Bandwidth Speed Test (**www.pcpitstop.com/internet/bw.asp**)

Figure 12-23   Utility tools to test the speed of a PC's connection to the Internet

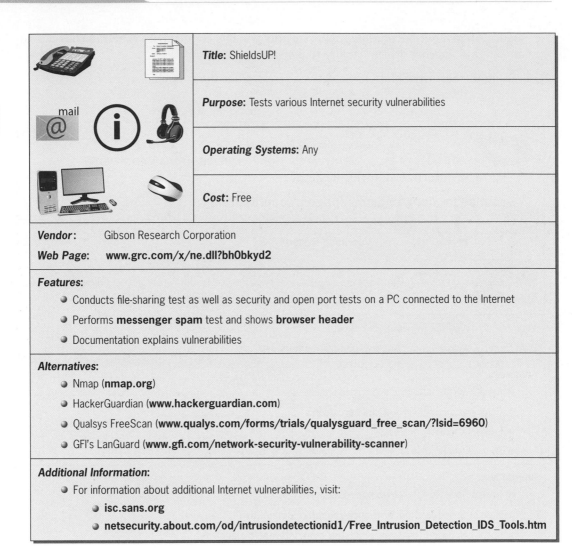

	Title: ShieldsUP!
	Purpose: Tests various Internet security vulnerabilities
	Operating Systems: Any
	Cost: Free

Vendor: Gibson Research Corporation

Web Page: **www.grc.com/x/ne.dll?bh0bkyd2**

Features:

- Conducts file-sharing test as well as security and open port tests on a PC connected to the Internet
- Performs **messenger spam** test and shows **browser header**
- Documentation explains vulnerabilities

Alternatives:

- Nmap (**nmap.org**)
- HackerGuardian (**www.hackerguardian.com**)
- Qualsys FreeScan (**www.qualys.com/forms/trials/qualysguard_free_scan/?lsid=6960**)
- GFI's LanGuard (**www.gfi.com/network-security-vulnerability-scanner**)

Additional Information:

- For information about additional Internet vulnerabilities, visit:
  - **isc.sans.org**
  - **netsecurity.about.com/od/intrusiondetectionid1/Free_Intrusion_Detection_IDS_Tools.htm**

Figure 12-24   Utility to test and identify vulnerabilities in a PC's Internet connection

ON THE WEB

To learn more about Internet security and vulnerabilities, use one of these tutorial resources:

- **www.gcflearnfree.org/internetsafety**
- **www.suite101.com/content/beyond-antivirus-sandbox–hips-web-browser-internet-security-a223227**
- **scottsecor.com/consult//pages/security.html**

File Management Tasks

Tools to help support agents manage files and folders on a PC include utilities to back up disk media, back up data to an Internet service, convert files from one format to another, and recover files that were accidentally deleted.

- Figure 12-25 describes a utility to back up files and folders from a disk to a local or network device, such as a hard drive, optical disk, removable disk, or USB drive. Backups can be scheduled to run on a predefined schedule.

- Figure 12-26 describes an Internet service that provides file and folder backup storage on an Internet server. Backups can be scheduled to run automatically.

- Figure 12-27 describes a tool to convert a file from one format to another; for example, JPG format to TIFF format.

- Figure 12-28 describes a utility tool that attempts to recover deleted files from disk media.

Utilities in the Hardware Support and Software Support—Operating Systems categories provide related file management tools.

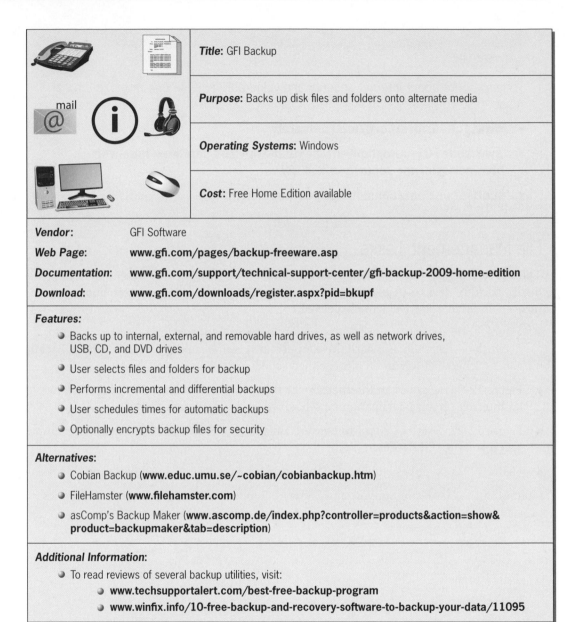

Title: GFI Backup

Purpose: Backs up disk files and folders onto alternate media

Operating Systems: Windows

Cost: Free Home Edition available

Vendor:	GFI Software
Web Page:	**www.gfi.com/pages/backup-freeware.asp**
Documentation:	**www.gfi.com/support/technical-support-center/gfi-backup-2009-home-edition**
Download:	**www.gfi.com/downloads/register.aspx?pid=bkupf**

Features:

- Backs up to internal, external, and removable hard drives, as well as network drives, USB, CD, and DVD drives
- User selects files and folders for backup
- Performs incremental and differential backups
- User schedules times for automatic backups
- Optionally encrypts backup files for security

Alternatives:

- Cobian Backup (**www.educ.umu.se/~cobian/cobianbackup.htm**)
- FileHamster (**www.filehamster.com**)
- asComp's Backup Maker (**www.ascomp.de/index.php?controller=products&action=show& product=backupmaker&tab=description**)

Additional Information:

- To read reviews of several backup utilities, visit:
  - **www.techsupportalert.com/best-free-backup-program**
  - **www.winfix.info/10-free-backup-and-recovery-software-to-backup-your-data/11095**

Figure 12-25 Utility software to perform media backups onto other local media

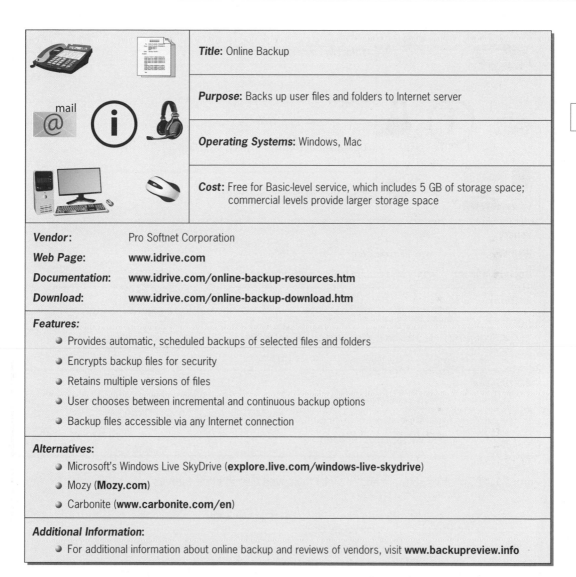

Title: Online Backup

Purpose: Backs up user files and folders to Internet server

Operating Systems: Windows, Mac

Cost: Free for Basic-level service, which includes 5 GB of storage space; commercial levels provide larger storage space

Vendor: Pro Softnet Corporation

Web Page: www.idrive.com

Documentation: www.idrive.com/online-backup-resources.htm

Download: www.idrive.com/online-backup-download.htm

Features:

- Provides automatic, scheduled backups of selected files and folders
- Encrypts backup files for security
- Retains multiple versions of files
- User chooses between incremental and continuous backup options
- Backup files accessible via any Internet connection

Alternatives:

- Microsoft's Windows Live SkyDrive (**explore.live.com/windows-live-skydrive**)
- Mozy (**Mozy.com**)
- Carbonite (**www.carbonite.com/en**)

Additional Information:

- For additional information about online backup and reviews of vendors, visit **www.backupreview.info**

Figure 12-26 Services that provide for media backups onto an Internet server

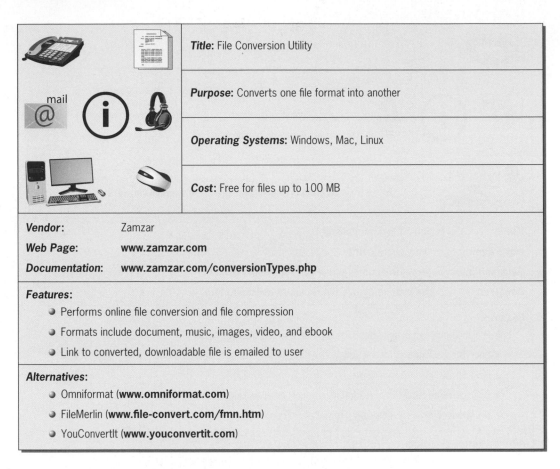

Title: File Conversion Utility

Purpose: Converts one file format into another

Operating Systems: Windows, Mac, Linux

Cost: Free for files up to 100 MB

Vendor: Zamzar

Web Page: www.zamzar.com

Documentation: www.zamzar.com/conversionTypes.php

Features:

- Performs online file conversion and file compression
- Formats include document, music, images, video, and ebook
- Link to converted, downloadable file is emailed to user

Alternatives:

- Omniformat (**www.omniformat.com**)
- FileMerlin (**www.file-convert.com/fmn.htm**)
- YouConvertIt (**www.youconvertit.com**)

Figure 12-27   Utility software and services to convert files to other formats

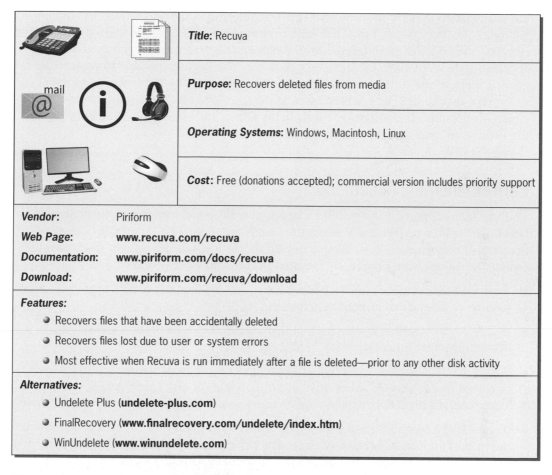

	Title: Recuva
	Purpose: Recovers deleted files from media
	Operating Systems: Windows, Macintosh, Linux
	Cost: Free (donations accepted); commercial version includes priority support

Vendor:	Piriform
Web Page:	**www.recuva.com/recuva**
Documentation:	**www.piriform.com/docs/recuva**
Download:	**www.piriform.com/recuva/download**

Features:

- Recovers files that have been accidentally deleted
- Recovers files lost due to user or system errors
- Most effective when Recuva is run immediately after a file is deleted—prior to any other disk activity

Alternatives:

- Undelete Plus (**undelete-plus.com**)
- FinalRecovery (**www.finalrecovery.com/undelete/index.htm**)
- WinUndelete (**www.winundelete.com**)

Figure 12-28 Utilities to recover deleted files

CASE STUDY: UTILITIES FOR USER SUPPORT TASKS

A student with a USB flash drive in hand approached the walk-in help desk while Kasey was on duty. The student was obviously upset and explained that he had been working on a spreadsheet assignment for an accounting class. The spreadsheet was open on the USB drive when the PC he was using in the teaching lab mysteriously shut down. After the PC restarted, the student discovered that the spreadsheet file had disappeared from the USB drive and several hours of work had been wiped out. The student reported that he had searched the drive, but could not locate the missing spreadsheet file. Kasey asked whether he had written any other files on the USB drive since the incident. The answer was, "No way!"

Kasey suggested they try to recover the file using Recuva, a file undelete utility described in Figure 12-28. They plugged the USB drive into the help desk's PC and started Recuva. It searched the USB drive and located several files and file fragments, a couple of which appeared to be versions of the missing spreadsheet file. Recuva was able to reconstruct the missing file, and the student was delighted to find that only the last few edits to the accounting assignment had not been saved in the recovered file. He promised to save multiple copies of spreadsheets on alternate media in the future, and asked if he could obtain a copy of the Recuva utility program for his personal use.

Performance Enhancements

Tools to help support agents monitor and improve PC performance include utilities to benchmark a PC's performance, adjust the configuration settings on a PC to improve operational performance, erase files to free up disk space, and defragment disk space to reduce the number of disk accesses required to read and write programs and data.

- Figure 12-29 describes a utility that evaluates and benchmarks a PC's operating speed against other systems or known standards.

- Figure 12-30 describes a software tool that adjusts the configuration and settings of a PC to optimize performance.

- Figure 12-31 describes a tool that erases temporary, unused, damaged, obsolete, and archived files from a PC's disk drive in order to free up disk space. A disk cleanup operation is a procedure support agents often perform prior to defragmenting a drive.

- Figure 12-32 describes a utility tool that defragments disk space to reduce the number of input/output operations required to read or write a file and speed up accesses to the drive. Defragmented disks often perform better than those with heavily fragmented files.

Utilities in the Hardware Support and System Problem Diagnosis categories provide related performance-enhancement tasks.

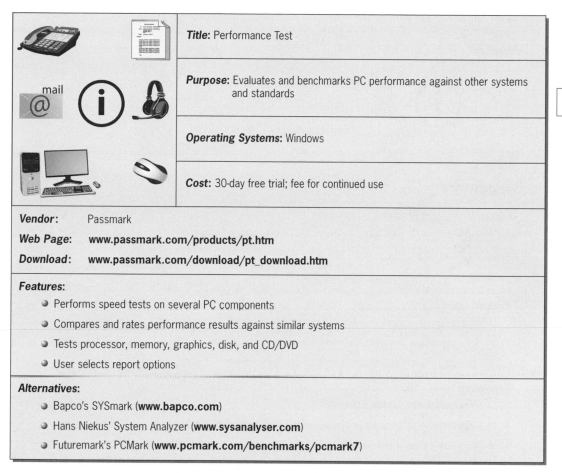

Title: Performance Test	
Purpose: Evaluates and benchmarks PC performance against other systems and standards	
Operating Systems: Windows	
Cost: 30-day free trial; fee for continued use	

Vendor: Passmark

Web Page: www.passmark.com/products/pt.htm

Download: www.passmark.com/download/pt_download.htm

Features:

- Performs speed tests on several PC components
- Compares and rates performance results against similar systems
- Tests processor, memory, graphics, disk, and CD/DVD
- User selects report options

Alternatives:

- Bapco's SYSmark (**www.bapco.com**)
- Hans Niekus' System Analyzer (**www.sysanalyser.com**)
- Futuremark's PCMark (**www.pcmark.com/benchmarks/pcmark7**)

Figure 12-29 Utilities to benchmark PC operating speeds

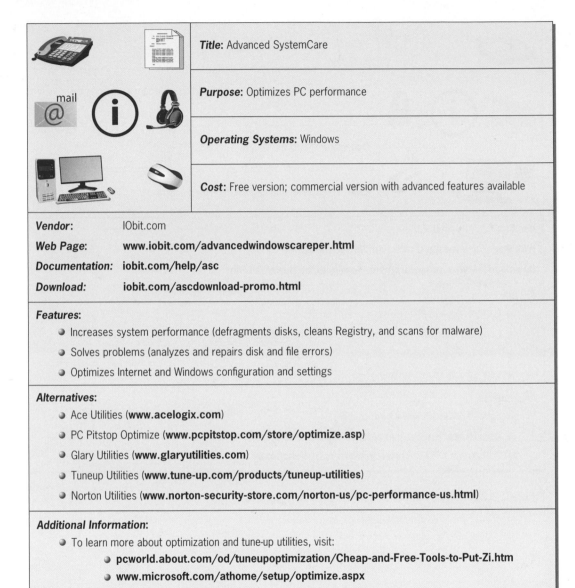

	Title: Advanced SystemCare
	Purpose: Optimizes PC performance
	Operating Systems: Windows
	Cost: Free version; commercial version with advanced features available

Vendor: IObit.com

Web Page: www.iobit.com/advancedwindowscareper.html

Documentation: iobit.com/help/asc

Download: iobit.com/ascdownload-promo.html

Features:
- Increases system performance (defragments disks, cleans Registry, and scans for malware)
- Solves problems (analyzes and repairs disk and file errors)
- Optimizes Internet and Windows configuration and settings

Alternatives:
- Ace Utilities (**www.acelogix.com**)
- PC Pitstop Optimize (**www.pcpitstop.com/store/optimize.asp**)
- Glary Utilities (**www.glaryutilities.com**)
- Tuneup Utilities (**www.tune-up.com/products/tuneup-utilities**)
- Norton Utilities (**www.norton-security-store.com/norton-us/pc-performance-us.html**)

Additional Information:
- To learn more about optimization and tune-up utilities, visit:
  - **pcworld.about.com/od/tuneupoptimization/Cheap-and-Free-Tools-to-Put-Zi.htm**
  - **www.microsoft.com/athome/setup/optimize.aspx**

Figure 12-30   Software tools to increase system performance

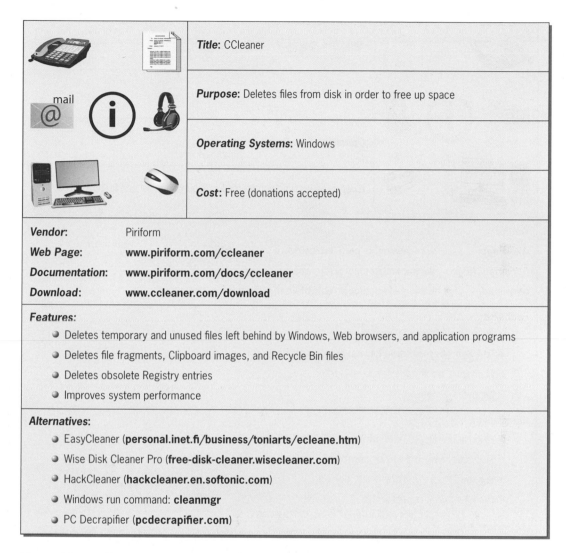

Title: CCleaner

Purpose: Deletes files from disk in order to free up space

Operating Systems: Windows

Cost: Free (donations accepted)

Vendor: Piriform

Web Page: **www.piriform.com/ccleaner**

Documentation: **www.piriform.com/docs/ccleaner**

Download: **www.ccleaner.com/download**

Features:

- Deletes temporary and unused files left behind by Windows, Web browsers, and application programs
- Deletes file fragments, Clipboard images, and Recycle Bin files
- Deletes obsolete Registry entries
- Improves system performance

Alternatives:

- EasyCleaner (**personal.inet.fi/business/toniarts/ecleane.htm**)
- Wise Disk Cleaner Pro (**free-disk-cleaner.wisecleaner.com**)
- HackCleaner (**hackcleaner.en.softonic.com**)
- Windows run command: **cleanmgr**
- PC Decrapifier (**pcdecrapifier.com**)

Figure 12-31 Utility tools to clean disk space of unused files

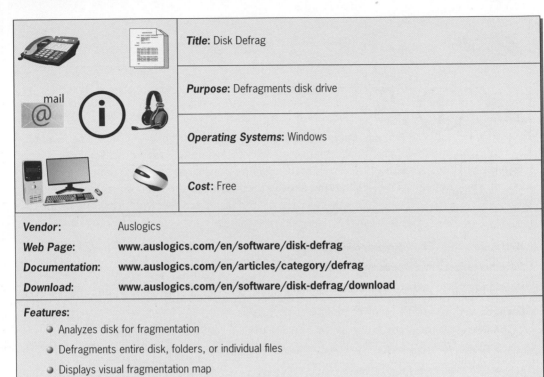

Title: Disk Defrag

Purpose: Defragments disk drive

Operating Systems: Windows

Cost: Free

Vendor:	Auslogics
Web Page:	www.auslogics.com/en/software/disk-defrag
Documentation:	www.auslogics.com/en/articles/category/defrag
Download:	www.auslogics.com/en/software/disk-defrag/download

Features:

- Analyzes disk for fragmentation
- Defragments entire disk, folders, or individual files
- Displays visual fragmentation map
- Improves system performance

Alternatives:

- Piriform Defraggler (www.piriform.com/defraggler)
- MyDefrag (www.mydefrag.com)
- Windows Vista 7 run command: defrag
- Commercial defrag utilities:
  - Diskeeper (www.diskeeper.com/defrag.aspx)
  - Diskeeper Lite (free) (www.toggle.com/lv/group/view/kl35682/Diskeeper_Lite.htm)
  - Raxco's Perfect Disk (www.raxco.com)

Additional Information:

- For an explanation of defragmentation and changes to defragmentation in Windows 7 from earlier versions, visit blogs.msdn.com/b/e7/archive/2009/01/25/disk-defragmentation-background-and-engineering-the-windows-7-improvements.aspx

Figure 12-32   Utilities to defragment disk space

CASE STUDY: UTILITIES FOR USER SUPPORT TASKS

Kasey was asked to serve on a college-wide committee to develop a recommendation for a standard PC, which the college would purchase for its use and sell to students through the bookstore during the next two years. Kasey was appointed to a hardware benchmark subcommittee. Kasey had previously used a PassMark utility to evaluate hardware for purchase and suggested the benchmark subcommittee use the software, described in Figure 12-29, to rate the three machines they were asked to evaluate. Kasey ran PassMark Performance Test on each of the three machines and compared each to a standard model PC with an Intel dual core CPU. When presenting the results to the subcommittee, Kasey noted that PCMark Basic benchmarks several very specific aspects of a computer's operation, but that she had recorded only the summary results in a spreadsheet, shown in Table 12-1.

Component	System A	System B	System C	Benchmark (Intel Dual Core)	Maximum Points
CPU	2039.6	1924.0	2104.4	1611.8	3000
Graphics	451.3	480.7	467.0	466.7	500
Memory	801.5	813.8	813.1	788.4	900
Disk	482.0	491.1	516.7	344.4	600
Overall	1024.4	992.2	1059.1	846.8	2000

Table 12-1 Summary results of benchmarking test

Based on the raw data from PassMark's Performance Test utility in Table 12-1, Kasey and the members of the hardware benchmark subcommittee compared the strengths and weaknesses of each machine.

Which system do you think they recommended, based on the results of the hardware benchmark? Why?

Security Solutions

Tools to help support agents provide users with Internet security solutions include utilities to protect against viruses, spyware, firewall penetration, and rootkit violations, as well as tools to evaluate the strength of user passwords and utilities to securely erase files from a hard drive.

- Figure 12-33 describes a utility that scans hard drives, memory, incoming and outgoing email messages, attachments, data files, and Internet pages for viruses.

- Figure 12-34 describes a software tool that scans a PC's memory and media for spyware and other malware that could compromise the identity, privacy, or confidentiality of an end user and affect PC performance.

- Figure 12-35 describes a tool to monitor **firewall** breaches and identify software that requests an open port to the Internet, which may serve as a target for Internet security attacks.

- Figure 12-36 describes a utility to detect hidden files and folders, which may indicate the presence of **rootkit** software on a PC.

- Figure 12-37 describes a utility tool to evaluate the strength of a user's password and make suggestions on how to improve passwords so they are less susceptible to **password guessers**.

- Figure 12-38 provides an example of a utility that performs a **secure erase** operation (also called a *file shred* or *destructive delete operation*) on files, folders, or an entire drive. These utilities are useful for protecting confidential information before a PC is recycled, donated, or handed down to another user.

Utilities in the Network Support, Internet Support, and System Problem Diagnosis categories provide related security solutions and tools.

Computer viruses are now a part of almost every end user's vocabulary, and the news media often report on new potential threats that attract user and media attention. An end user may also become the victim of a **virus hoax**, which is a seemingly authentic email message (or other communication) about a possible virus threat that turns out to be a deceptive or inaccurate warning about a nonexistent threat. Virus hoaxes are often forwarded as a chain letter by well-meaning users to warn their friends and colleagues about a dire problem on the horizon.

Figure 12-33 includes a pointer to a Sophos Web site where information about virus hoaxes can be found.

ON THE WEB

Microsoft provides a Web site devoted to security problems and information about tools to enhance the security of its software products; visit the site at **www.microsoft.com/security**.

Microsoft also offers a software tool, Microsoft Baseline Security Analyzer (MBSA), to analyze a Windows system for security vulnerabilities; MBSA can be downloaded from **technet.microsoft.com/en-us/security/cc184924**.

	Title: Microsoft Security Essentials
	Purpose: Protects a PC against viruses and other malware
	Operating Systems: Windows
	Cost: Free for home users and small businesses

Vendor:	Microsoft
Web Page:	www.microsoft.com/en-us/security_essentials
Documentation:	www.microsoft.com/en-us/security_essentials/ProductInformation.aspx
Download:	www.microsoft.com/en-us/security_essentials

Features:

- Protects against operating system and application software viruses
- Protects against spyware and rootkit violations
- Updates threats database automatically every day

Alternatives:

- Avast! Antivirus (**www.avast.com**)
- AVG Technologies AVG (**free.avg.com**)
- Avira AntiVir (**www.avira.com/en/avira-free-antivirus**)
- Panda Cloud Antivirus (**www.cloudantivirus.com/en**)
- Commercial antivirus software is available from:
    - Norton AntiVirus (**us.norton.com/antivirus**)
    - McAfee AntiVirus Plus (**home.mcafee.com/store/antivirus-plus**)
    - Trend Micro AntiVirus + AntiSpyware (**us.trendmicro.com/us/products/personal/antivirus-plus-anti-spyware**)
    - Kaspersky Anti-Virus (**usa.kaspersky.com/products-services/home-computer-security/anti-virus**)
    - F-Secure Anti-Virus (**www.f-secure.com/en_US/products/home-office/antivirus**)
    - Sophos Endpoint (**www.sophos.com/en-us/products/endpoint.aspx**)

Additional Information:

- Read reviews of free antivirus software at **www.free-antivirus.info**.
- To learn more about virus hoaxes, visit the Sophos site on hoaxes (**www.sophos.com/en-us/threat-center/threat-analyses/hoaxes.aspx**)

Figure 12-33 Antivirus software tools

	Title: Malwarebytes
	Purpose: Searches and deletes malware spyware software such as key loggers, adware, spyware, and hijackers
	Operating Systems: Windows
	Cost: Free to scan PC systems and eliminate malware; Pro version provides real-time monitoring

Vendor: Malwarebytes

Web Page: **www.malwarebytes.org**

Documentation: **www.bleepingcomputer.com/virus-removal/how-to-use-malwarebytes-anti-malware-tutorial**

Download: **www.techspot.com/downloads/4716-malwarebytes-anti-malware.html**

Features:
- Scans PCs for malware
- Deletes or quarantines spyware upon user command
- Updates malware database automatically

Alternatives:
- LavaSoft's Ad-Aware (**download.cnet.com/Ad-Aware-Free-Internet-Security/ 3000-8022_4-10045910.html**)
- Spybot—Search & Destroy (**www.safer-networking.org/en**)
- SUPERAntiSpyware (**www.superantispyware.com**)
- Microsoft Windows Defender (**www.microsoft.com/windows/products/winfamily/defender**)
- Spyware Terminator (**www.spywareterminator.com**)

Additional Information:
- Read reviews of commercial antispyware products (**anti-spyware-review.toptenreviews.com**)
- Read review of free antispyware products (**www.consumersearch.com/anti-spyware-reviews/free-anti-spyware**)

Figure 12-34   Tools to protect against spyware and other malware

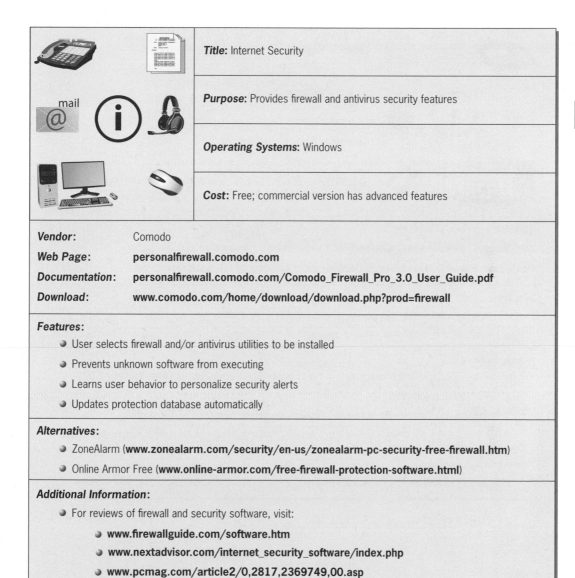

Title: Internet Security

Purpose: Provides firewall and antivirus security features

Operating Systems: Windows

Cost: Free; commercial version has advanced features

Vendor:	Comodo
Web Page:	**personalfirewall.comodo.com**
Documentation:	**personalfirewall.comodo.com/Comodo_Firewall_Pro_3.0_User_Guide.pdf**
Download:	**www.comodo.com/home/download/download.php?prod=firewall**

Features:
- User selects firewall and/or antivirus utilities to be installed
- Prevents unknown software from executing
- Learns user behavior to personalize security alerts
- Updates protection database automatically

Alternatives:
- ZoneAlarm (**www.zonealarm.com/security/en-us/zonealarm-pc-security-free-firewall.htm**)
- Online Armor Free (**www.online-armor.com/free-firewall-protection-software.html**)

Additional Information:
- For reviews of firewall and security software, visit:
  - **www.firewallguide.com/software.htm**
  - **www.nextadvisor.com/internet_security_software/index.php**
  - **www.pcmag.com/article2/0,2817,2369749,00.asp**

Figure 12-35   Firewall software utilities

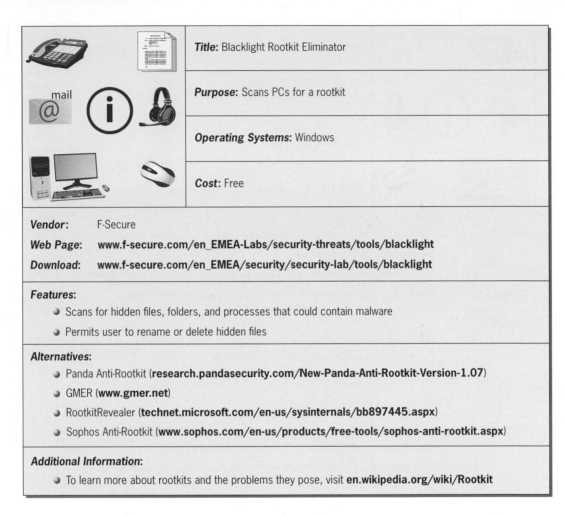

	Title: Blacklight Rootkit Eliminator
mail @ (i)	**Purpose:** Scans PCs for a rootkit
	Operating Systems: Windows
	Cost: Free

Vendor: F-Secure

Web Page: www.f-secure.com/en_EMEA-Labs/security-threats/tools/blacklight

Download: www.f-secure.com/en_EMEA/security/security-lab/tools/blacklight

Features:
- Scans for hidden files, folders, and processes that could contain malware
- Permits user to rename or delete hidden files

Alternatives:
- Panda Anti-Rootkit (**research.pandasecurity.com/New-Panda-Anti-Rootkit-Version-1.07**)
- GMER (**www.gmer.net**)
- RootkitRevealer (**technet.microsoft.com/en-us/sysinternals/bb897445.aspx**)
- Sophos Anti-Rootkit (**www.sophos.com/en-us/products/free-tools/sophos-anti-rootkit.aspx**)

Additional Information:
- To learn more about rootkits and the problems they pose, visit **en.wikipedia.org/wiki/Rootkit**

Figure 12-36   Utilities to scan PCs for evidence of a rootkit

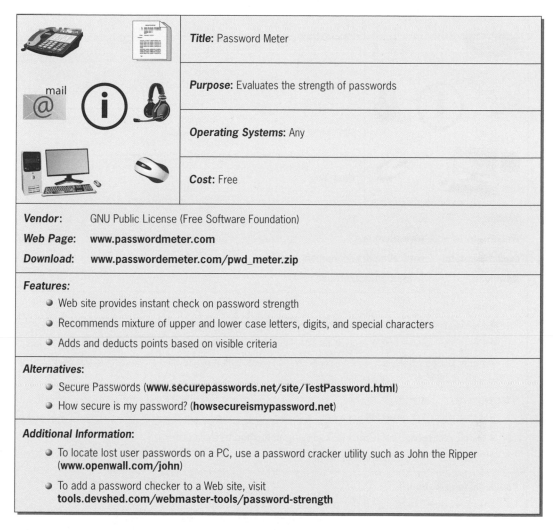

	Title: Password Meter
	Purpose: Evaluates the strength of passwords
	Operating Systems: Any
	Cost: Free

Vendor: GNU Public License (Free Software Foundation)

Web Page: **www.passwordmeter.com**

Download: **www.passwordemeter.com/pwd_meter.zip**

Features:

- Web site provides instant check on password strength
- Recommends mixture of upper and lower case letters, digits, and special characters
- Adds and deducts points based on visible criteria

Alternatives:

- Secure Passwords (**www.securepasswords.net/site/TestPassword.html**)
- How secure is my password? (**howsecureismypassword.net**)

Additional Information:

- To locate lost user passwords on a PC, use a password cracker utility such as John the Ripper (**www.openwall.com/john**)
- To add a password checker to a Web site, visit **tools.devshed.com/webmaster-tools/password-strength**

Figure 12-37   Tools that evaluate the strength of user passwords

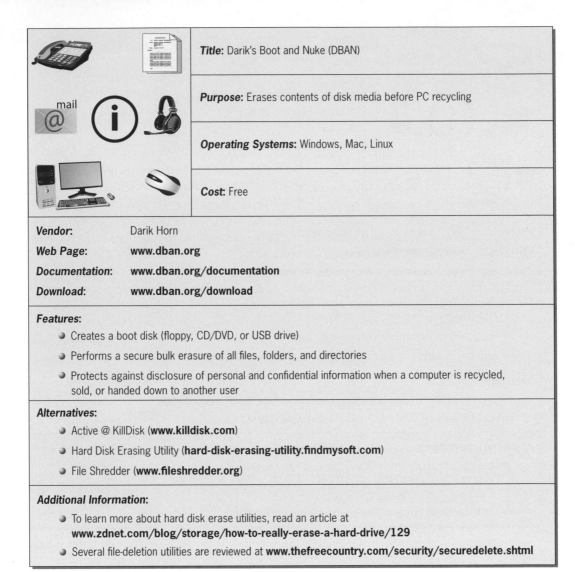

	Title: Darik's Boot and Nuke (DBAN)
	Purpose: Erases contents of disk media before PC recycling
	Operating Systems: Windows, Mac, Linux
	Cost: Free

Vendor:	Darik Horn
Web Page:	**www.dban.org**
Documentation:	**www.dban.org/documentation**
Download:	**www.dban.org/download**

Features:

- Creates a boot disk (floppy, CD/DVD, or USB drive)
- Performs a secure bulk erasure of all files, folders, and directories
- Protects against disclosure of personal and confidential information when a computer is recycled, sold, or handed down to another user

Alternatives:

- Active @ KillDisk (**www.killdisk.com**)
- Hard Disk Erasing Utility (**hard-disk-erasing-utility.findmysoft.com**)
- File Shredder (**www.fileshredder.org**)

Additional Information:

- To learn more about hard disk erase utilities, read an article at **www.zdnet.com/blog/storage/how-to-really-erase-a-hard-drive/129**
- Several file-deletion utilities are reviewed at **www.thefreecountry.com/security/securedelete.shtml**

Figure 12-38   Software to protect a user's information with a secure media erase

---

CASE STUDY: UTILITIES FOR USER SUPPORT TASKS

The support group at the college receives many questions about passwords. Kasey and her team usually recommend a utility such as Password Meter, described in Figure 12-37, to help users evaluate the security of their passwords. Kasey always warns users about the dangers of using a password that is easy to guess.

A faculty member reported that he was taught in school to use a long word that is easy to remember and then drop all the vowels to form the password. For example, *elephant* (easy to remember) becomes *lphnt* as a password. However, when Kasey asked the user to enter *lphnt* into Password Meter, the resulting score was 7 percent. Kasey suggested that the user add some digits to the letters, so the user tried *lphnt1988* and received a score of 50 percent. In an attempt to obtain a perfect score, Kasey suggested he capitalize the first letter: *Lphnt1988*, which received a score of 78 percent. Then the user added a special character (*!*) between the letters and digits and received a score of 96 percent for *Lphnt!1988*. Kasey suggested that, with this example in mind, and Password Meter as a tool, the user build a password that gets a Very Strong rating. The support group at the college includes a link to Password Meter (**www.passwordmeter.com**) on their Web site.

User Support Tools

Tools to help support agents perform their work include utilities that manage help desk operations and those that enable remote access to an end user's PC to diagnose and troubleshoot problems. Help desk software is covered in detail in Chapter 6 and in Appendix B, and will not be described further here.

- Figure 12-39 describes a utility that permits a support specialist to access a user's PC to perform diagnostic tests, troubleshoot problems, install software, and configure settings without the need for a face-to-face visit to the user's work site. Some utilities use the Internet as a remote access medium; others use a local area network or a virtual private network to enable communication between a help desk agent and a user. Remote access is an especially useful productivity tool when users are geographically dispersed.

Many utilities in other categories in this chapter are also designed to make support staff and end users more productive.

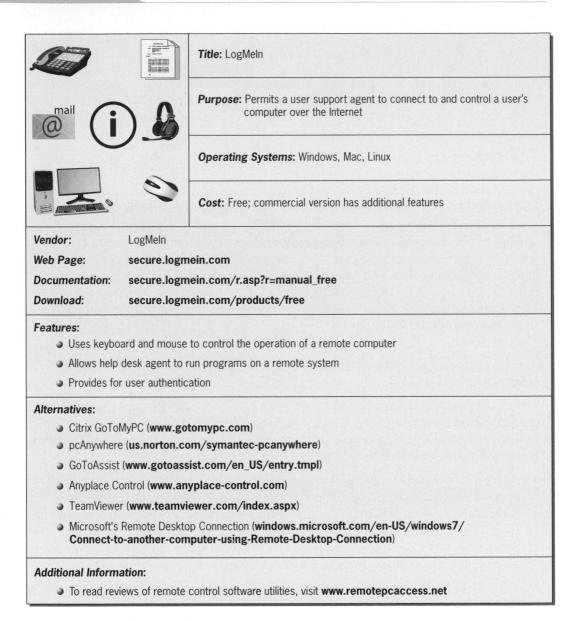

Title: LogMeIn
Purpose: Permits a user support agent to connect to and control a user's computer over the Internet
Operating Systems: Windows, Mac, Linux
Cost: Free; commercial version has additional features

Vendor: LogMeIn

Web Page: secure.logmein.com

Documentation: secure.logmein.com/r.asp?r=manual_free

Download: secure.logmein.com/products/free

Features:

- Uses keyboard and mouse to control the operation of a remote computer
- Allows help desk agent to run programs on a remote system
- Provides for user authentication

Alternatives:

- Citrix GoToMyPC (**www.gotomypc.com**)
- pcAnywhere (**us.norton.com/symantec-pcanywhere**)
- GoToAssist (**www.gotoassist.com/en_US/entry.tmpl**)
- Anyplace Control (**www.anyplace-control.com**)
- TeamViewer (**www.teamviewer.com/index.aspx**)
- Microsoft's Remote Desktop Connection (**windows.microsoft.com/en-US/windows7/ Connect-to-another-computer-using-Remote-Desktop-Connection**)

Additional Information:

- To read reviews of remote control software utilities, visit **www.remotepcaccess.net**

Figure 12-39   Remote access software to control a user's PC over a network

The software tools described in this chapter serve as examples for readers to evaluate for possible inclusion in a tool kit of utilities and information resources that can be applied to diagnose and solve problems and to increase a support worker's productivity. These utilities should be considered a starting point; support workers will investigate and evaluate various tools, depending on their job responsibilities—adding and replacing resources as better tools are discovered or as job responsibilities change. Table 12-2 summarizes the tools in the utility tool kit described in this chapter.

575

Utility Category	Utility Name	Purpose	Fig. #
Hardware Support	BurnIn Test	Stress tests hardware to assess reliability and stability	12-3
	Device Driver Finder	Downloads drivers for hardware devices	12-4
	Drive Fitness Test	Performs test routine to evaluate IDE, SATA, and SCSI hard drives	12-5
	Windows Memory Diagnostics Tool	Tests RAM memory in Windows systems	12-6
System Information	Belarc Advisor	Audits and reports system configuration information	12-7
	WinBootInfo	Monitors and reports on system start-up activities	12-8
Software Support— Operating Systems	Autoruns for Windows	Identifies software that starts automatically at start-up or logon	12-9
	System-Cleaner	Deletes obsolete and corrupted information from Windows Registry	12-10
	Registrar Registry Manager	Edits Registry keys and values and performs Registry management tasks	12-12
	Windows 7 and Vista Commands	Provides information resources on entering commands in the Windows 7 and Vista command-line interface	12-13
	Windows 7 Recovery Disk	Downloads an image of a bootable recovery disk to recover inoperable systems	12-14
Software Support— Applications	BSA Free Software Audit Tools	Identifies and tracks licensed and unlicensed software on a PC	12-15
	Online Software Inspector	Detects security vulnerabilities on a PC due to missing patches	12-16
	Uninstaller	Removes software and related files from a PC	12-17
System Problem Diagnosis	Advanced System Optimizer	Diagnoses hardware, software, and network problems on a PC	12-18
	WinUtilities Suite	Combines several software utilities to provide system information along with diagnosis and repair functions	12-20
Network Support	OpenNMS	Monitors and reports on network performance problems	12-21
	OpManager	Monitors and diagnoses network problems	12-22

Table 12-2   Summary of utility software tools described in this chapter (*continues*)

(continued)

Utility Category	Utility Name	Purpose	Fig. #
Internet Support	Bandwidth Speed Test	Tests Internet download and upload speeds	12-23
	ShieldsUP!	Tests various Internet security vulnerabilities	12-24
File Management Tasks	GFI Backup	Backs up disk files and folders onto alternate media	12-25
	Online Backup	Backs up user files and folders to an Internet server	12-26
	File Conversion Utility	Converts one file format into another	12-27
	Recuva	Recovers deleted files from media	12-28
Performance Enhancements	Performance Test	Evaluates and benchmarks PC performance against other systems and standards	12-29
	Advanced System-Care	Optimizes PC performance	12-30
	CCleaner	Deletes files from disk in order to free up space	12-31
	Disk Defrag	Defragments files and folders to make disk accesses more efficient	12-32
Security Solutions	Microsoft Security Essentials	Protects a PC against viruses and other malware	12-33
	Malwarebytes	Searches for and deletes malware software	12-34
	Internet Security	Provides firewall and antivirus security features	12-35
	Blacklight Rootkit Eliminator	Scans PCs for a rootkit	12-36
	Password Meter	Evaluates the strength of passwords	12-37
	Darik's Boot and Nuke (DBAN)	Securely erases files on disk media before PC recycling	12-38
User Support	LogMeIn	Provides remote access to a user's PC for support tasks	12-39

Table 12-2   Summary of utility software tools described in this chapter

---

A ROLE-PLAYING SCENARIO

This scenario is based on situations in which working support specialists regularly participate in meeting and discussions.

Your role-playing assignment is to participate in a panel discussion with three or four of your work or school colleagues. The group should begin by selecting a position description for an actual help desk or user support position. You could use a position description included in Chapter 1 or one in use at your organization.

The panel should develop a list of the top five utility tools a worker in the selected position would probably find most useful in performing their job duties. The panel should start by giving each participant a few minutes to nominate their personal top five utilities. (The nominated utilities do not need to come from those discussed in this chapter.) Then the panel should discuss the pros and cons of each utility nominated. Try to reach a consensus on the panel's top five.

 The companion Web site for this book, **www.CUS5e.com**, contains updates and further suggestions to augment the information in this chapter. The Web site also includes a link to the author's email address, where readers are invited to send recommendations for useful support utilities for publication on the Web site.

Chapter Summary

- User support specialists employ a variety of software tools and information resources to perform their work responsibilities. As with all tools, care must be exercised by support specialists to ensure that only appropriate, up-to-date, tested, and authorized tools are downloaded and used. The tools in this chapter are examples of those commonly available.

- Categories of user support tools include utilities to resolve hardware problems, provide system information, configure and troubleshoot operating system and application software, diagnose system and network problems, test and identify Internet connection speeds and vulnerabilities, manage files and disks, provide solutions to security threats, and increase the productivity of support specialists.

Key Terms

audit—A process to determine which software versions are installed on a PC or a network server; an audit may be conducted for inventory purposes (asset management), to gauge compliance with the terms of a software license or EULA, or to identify use of unauthorized software by end users.

browser header—Identification information about a user's PC that is sent to an Internet server by a Web browser whenever a request for information is transmitted; results in a potential vulnerability related to Internet connectivity.

dashboard—A real-time display of statistical performance information and service fault alerts in a visual, graphical format; a network administrator may view a dashboard on a monitor that reports the performance of the network operation and sounds an alarm or alert during a service interruption.

end-user license agreement (EULA)—A legal contract between a vendor and a user that governs the use of a software package or information service; in order to use a software package, an end user must agree to the terms of the license agreement. EULAs often state that an end user does not own a software package, but is allowed to use it following the terms and conditions of the agreement.

firewall—Hardware or software designed to intercept and prevent unauthorized attempts to access a computer system from an external network, such as the Internet. *See also* vulnerability.

ISO image—An archive file format that contains software modules in a form that can be burned (copied) onto a CD or DVD; the ISO format is based on industry specifications of the International Standards Organization and is often used to distribute software for installation on a PC.

messenger spam—An attack that uses a common network communication service to broadcast multiple and continuous messages to users, each of which opens a pop-up window on a user's screen and requires a user response.

opt-in check box—An input form on a Web site that permits a user to agree to specified services and provisions (a check box to accept the terms of an end-user license agreement is a common example); check box responses are not always prominently displayed and may default to a positive agreement to accept a service (periodic email ads, for example) or even a subscription to a fee-based service, unless a user unchecks the box.

password guesser—Software that attempts to discover a user's online password either by making repeated, obvious guesses based on the user's name, address, and other known information, or by using a brute force guessing method, which employs repeated tries of words in a dictionary or database of common passwords.

patch status—An evaluation of whether all current updates have been downloaded and applied to a software package to fix one or more known bugs; includes an evaluation of service packs, security fixes, and feature releases.

privacy policy—A statement describing how an organization collects, maintains, and uses information provided by and about its customers or users; a privacy policy may authorize certain uses of information—such as its sale to a business partner or other third parties.

recovery disk—A disk medium that contains software images to reinstall, repair, or restore an operating system on a PC's hard drive to its original condition; most recovery disks are optical media and are designed to start a PC when an installed operating system has been damaged or corrupted.

rootkit—Malware that permits viruses and spyware to be installed on a user's PC without their knowledge or consent; a rootkit can be activated during a system's start-up process and may capture keystrokes and mouse clicks. Rootkits are difficult to detect because rootkit files and folders are hidden from normal view.

secure erase—An operation that obliterates data in disk files and folders by repeatedly writing random bit patterns on disk media; often used before a PC is recycled, donated, or handed down to another user to erase sensitive personal or corporate information.

service fault—An interruption of service in a network environment; may appear as a performance degradation or as a complete disruption of normal service. A server crash or an inoperative network device (such as a router or gateway) are common causes of service faults.

software license—A legal contract between a vendor and a user that governs the use of a software package or information service; a user is provided with a license to use a software package according to the terms and conditions of the license agreement by paying a fee (for commercial software) or by agreeing to the terms of an end-user license agreement (for freeware, open source, or trial shareware). The license may be in the form of a purchase receipt, an online registration with email confirmation, or a product activation key.

stress test—A repetitive operation performed to evaluate the ability of a PC system to operate at peak efficiency for a defined time period under a maximum processing load; a burn-in test of new hardware components is an example of one use of a stress test.

throughput bottleneck—An interruption of normal network traffic that reduces or halts the flow of data on a network; common bottlenecks include heavy packet volumes, external denial-of-service attacks, huge volumes of spam emails, processor or memory overload, and contention for disk accesses.

virus hoax—A seemingly authentic email message or other communication a user receives about a possible virus threat that turns out to be a deceptive or inaccurate warning about a nonexistent threat.

vulnerability—Any weakness in a system that is connected to the Internet or other network that permits an attacker to violate the integrity of the system. Common vulnerabilities include the transmission of viruses, spyware, and other executable code and scripts; open firewall ports that permit external access; software design flaws that open a back door into a system; and security breaches such as easily guessed passwords.

Windows command-line interface—A mechanism for accepting keyboard commands entered as text by a user at a command-line prompt—as an alternative to the Windows GUI interface; the Windows Run command window is one method to access the command-line interface in Windows. Early versions of Microsoft operating systems used text command strings exclusively.

ON THE WEB

Definitions of many of the technical terms used in the chapter can be found in one of these resources:

- **www.webopedia.com**
- **www.wikipedia.org**
- **whatis.techtarget.com**
- **www.techterms.com**
- **www.netlingo.com**
- **www.techdictionary.com**

Check Your Understanding

Answers to Check Your Understanding questions are in Appendix A.

1. A system problem diagnosis utility suite is designed to identify problems with:

    a. hardware   c. operating system software

    b. application software   d. all of these

2. True or False? Disk fragmentation indicates that a PC's hard drive may be about to fail.

3. True or False? Open source, freeware, and shareware utilities are not commercial products.

4. A(n) _____ is a legal contract between a vendor and a user that governs the use of a software package, such as a utility.

5. True or False? A software utility advertised as a "free download" is freeware that can be used without paying a license fee.

6. A software utility tool of primary use to a support specialist who assembles or installs hardware systems is:

    a. a network performance monitor

    b. a software audit tool

    c. a file backup utility

    d. a burn-in utility

7. Which category of utility tools prepares documentation that would likely be included in a site installation notebook?

   a. System Information   c. Bandwidth Tester

   b. Rootkit Monitor   d. Network Analyzer

8. Which of these actions should be performed on a PC prior to using a Windows Registry edit utility?

   a. Defragment the hard drive.

   b. Back up the Registry onto a hard drive.

   c. Temporarily disable the system's firewall.

   d. Verify that the system patch status is up-to-date.

9. A type of utility tool that can modify which software is launched automatically at system start-up is:

   a. a benchmark utility   c. an audit utility

   b. an autoruns utility   d. a bootinfo utility

10. True or False? Versions of the Windows operating system after Windows 2000 do not have a command-line prompt feature.

11. True or False? A dashboard is a display of network performance information and fault warnings that a network administrator uses to monitor network operation.

12. A(n) _____ tool is a utility that inventories the software versions installed on a PC to determine compliance with licensing agreements.

13. True or False? A PC may be vulnerable to attacks from the Internet if some patches have not yet been downloaded and installed.

14. A utility software tool designed to clean up a failed software installation is:

    a. an undelete utility   c. an uninstaller utility

    b. a disk clean utility   d. a diagnostic utility

15. List two examples of common network bottlenecks that utility software tools might be able to detect.

16. True or False? Before a user recycles a PC, he or she must physically destroy the hard drive in order to obliterate sensitive personal information.

17. A backup utility can write copies of important data files and folders on:

    a. an internal hard drive   c. an Internet server's disk drive

    b. a network server's disk drive   d. any of these

18. A(n) _____ utility rewrites all the files and folders on a disk drive so they are stored in contiguous sectors in order to improve disk performance.

19. A(n) _____ is software that can attach itself to other software or to disk media and cause harm to the programs and data stored in a computer.

20. List three activities that can be performed by a system tune-up utility to improve system performance.

21. True or False? A firewall is hardware or software designed to prevent unauthorized attempts to penetrate a computer system from outside a network.

Discussion Questions

1. An experienced user support specialist made the following statement: *"I'm not very interested in PC performance tools. It is not our job to be concerned about the operational performance of our users' PCs. That is the users' responsibility."* Explain why you agree or disagree with the statement.

2. What do you think is the motivation of computer hackers who write virus programs and disseminate them, or who spam other users with unwanted email messages? Are their motives understandable? Are they justified?

3. If you have previous experience with utility software, describe the pros and cons of free, open source software utilities versus commercial versions of tools that perform similar tasks. In your view, should a for-profit business enterprise ever use free, open source utilities? Why or why not?

4. Which utility tools described in this chapter should be scheduled to run on a user's PC on a regular basis? Which should be run only as the need arises? Compare your answers to these questions with your colleagues' answers.

5. Based on what you know and have read about security software, do you believe it is ever possible to completely protect the data files, programs, and confidential information on a user's PC from malicious attacks and external threats, such as those launched via the Internet? Explain your viewpoint on the effectiveness of security software.

6. *"When I download software, I always check the 'I agree' box on an end-user license agreement or software license. Who needs to read all that legal mumbo-jumbo, anyway?"* Do you agree or disagree with this statement? If you disagree, how would you respond to it?

Hands-On Activities

Activity 12-1

Add a utility to the list of those described in the chapter. Based on your personal experience with user PCs, add a utility tool to the list of examples described in the chapter. The tool you describe could be one with which you have personal experience, or one that addresses a support need that the tools detailed in this chapter don't address adequately. In which category does the tool you selected fit best? Prepare a form like those used in this chapter to describe the tool you selected.

Activity 12-2

Get experience with a utility tool. Select a utility described in this chapter. If possible, download and install the utility. Learn about its operation and features. Then write a short report on your experiences. Describe the tool you investigated in terms of ease of use, purpose and features, performance in the tasks for which it is designed, and any difficulties or surprises you encountered when using it. Compare your experiences with your fellow students or work colleagues.

Activity 12-3

Compare the features of two utility tools. Examine the features of one utility tool described in this chapter. The one you select to examine could be one you used in another activity. Then, from the *Alternatives* section for that utility, pick another tool that performs similar tasks. Use a checklist to compare the features of both tools. Briefly explain which utility you prefer and why.

Activity 12-4

Make a Windows Recovery Disk. For a PC to which you have authorized access, make a Windows recovery disk following the procedures in a brief tutorial on pcsupport's Web site (**pcsupport.about.com/od/windows7/ht/system-repair-disc-windows-7.htm**). An alternate resource on Microsoft's Web site is listed in Figure 12-14. Research the various recovery options on the disk you created. Then demonstrate the use of the recovery disk to a small group of your colleagues. Explain the recovery options to them and describe when you'd need to use each option.

Activity 12-5

Evaluate user passwords. Ask each of several colleagues to think up two or three passwords (the passwords should not be ones they currently use, but could be ones they have used in the past). Use the Password Meter utility described in the chapter (see Figure 12-37) to evaluate each password suggested by the group. Which passwords received the highest score in Password Meter? Which ones received the lowest score? Explain why. Design an information sheet that could be given to end users with some guidelines on creating effective passwords. Include on your information sheet instructions on how to use Password Meter.

Activity 12-6

Audit the software on a PC. Download and install one of the audit tools described on the BSA Web site (see Figure 12-15). Perform an audit of the software on a PC to which you have authorized access. Prepare a summary report on the installed software. Describe any surprises that the audit software identified. Was the audit utility able to properly identify all of the software on the PC? Explain why or why not.

Activity 12-7

Recover a deleted file. Download and install two utility tools that claim to be able to undelete files that were accidentally deleted (see Figure 12-28). Prepare a practice file on a USB drive if one is available; otherwise use the hard drive, but set up a separate folder for your experiment. Delete the file (make sure it is not the only copy of the file if it contains data you need to keep). Before you perform any other file management tasks on the same disk, use the undelete utility tools to try to recover the deleted file. Do the undelete utilities perform as advertised? Compare the results and ease-of-use of the two utilities. Write a brief report on your experiment and your experience with the undelete utilities.

Activity 12-8

Add a feature to print a directory listing. Support specialists frequently need to print a directory listing of the files in a folder on a disk. Recent versions of Windows do not include a feature to easily obtain a printout of a directory listing. Research whether a utility tool is available to print a directory listing. If so, describe the steps to download and install a solution to this problem. Is there more than one way to provide this capability?

Activity 12-9

Research a computer virus warning. A user received the following text in an email message:

Subject: READ IMMEDIATLY AND PLEASE CIRCULATE

NO JOKE...

READ AND PASS ON TO EVERYONE YOU KNOW. Someone is sending out a very cute screensaver of the Budweiser® Frogs.

If you download it, you will lose everything! Your hard drive will crash and someone from the Internet will get your screen name and password! DO NOT DOWNLOAD IT UNDER ANY CIRCUMSTANCES!

It just went into circulation yesterday. Please distribute this message. This is a new, very malicious virus and not many people know about it. This information was announced yesterday morning from Microsoft. Please share it with everyone that might access the Internet.

Press the forward button on your email program and send this notice to EVERYONE you know. Let's keep our email safe for everyone.

The end user wants to know what he should do as a result of receiving this message. Please research the problem and write a response to the user.

Activity 12-10

Perform a disk clean operation. On a PC to which you have authorized access, use a system information utility of your choosing to discover the amount of free space available on the hard disk (see Figure 12-31). Then use the Windows disk cleanup utility (or use a similar utility of your choosing) to free up disk space by deleting files that are no longer needed. Use the system information utility to again measure the amount of free space on the cleaned disk. How much free space was gained by the procedure?

Write a brief report on the results of the disk clean operation, including a description of the options the tool offers. In addition, explain any options you would not advise a typical user to choose, and explain why. If possible, perform another disk cleanup operation on the same PC, but with a different utility. Did the second tool free up any additional disk space? Explain which tool you would recommend for use by end users.

Activity 12-11

Benchmark a PC's Internet connection. Use the Bandwidth Speed Test tool described in this chapter (see Figure 12-23) or a similar tool to run benchmark tests on the download and upload speeds on a PC to which you have access. Run the test at least 10 times at different times of the day on the same computer. Keep a record of the results of the bandwidth test in a spreadsheet program.

Are the test results consistent? Explain why or why not. Use the spreadsheet to analyze the download and upload speeds and quality of service ratings. Find the range (high and low) for each measure. Also compute the average download, upload, and quality of service measures. How much variation in the times did you observe? Use the chart feature in the spreadsheet program to prepare a graph to illustrate your results.

Activity 12-12

Locate forgotten user passwords on a PC. Download and install a password cracker utility, such as John the Ripper (see Figure 12-37). Run the utility only on a PC to which you have authorized access. Prepare a brief report on the features of John the Ripper and describe the type of user passwords it was able to recover. Explain any concerns you have about the use of password cracker utilities.

Activity 12-13

Get experience with a suite of utility tools. Advanced SystemCare is a package of several utility programs that perform a variety of diagnosis, maintenance, optimization, and repair functions (see Figure 12-30). Download and install the free version of Advanced SystemCare on a PC to which you have authorized access. Learn about its features.

Prepare a document designed for end users that describes several functions available in Advanced SystemCare, including the utility's primary features and why an end user would want to use each feature. Finally, list any utility functions that are not currently included in Advanced SystemCare that you would like to see added in the next version. When this activity is completed, you may remove the Advanced SystemCare utility from the PC.

Case Projects

1. Content Filtering Software for the Library

Some organizations that provide public Internet access, such as schools, libraries, and churches, may want to make sure that Web pages displayed or downloaded from the Internet have appropriate content for their clients, including young children. As a user support specialist at the local library, you need to learn about software utility programs that are available to filter Internet content. Research this category and then write a memo to the head librarian that explains how content filtering software works. In your memo, describe the pros and cons of using content filter utilities as a tool in a library.

2. Preventive Maintenance Checklist for BizNet Systems

Kai Edmonds is a manager of client support services for BizNet Computer Systems, a vendor that sells computer networks to small organizations. She is aware that a number of BizNet's customers have very little experience with the tasks associated with keeping a network system up and running. Kai spends considerable time on the telephone answering questions. The top three kinds of questions she gets relate to the following topics:

- Security threats
- Media backups
- Disk performance

Kai thinks BizNet needs a document to provide to its customers when they take delivery of their office network. The document Kai has in mind would address the three concerns she hears most often from customers. Assume that BizNet sells Windows desktop clients that are attached to a Windows or Novell NetWare server (or make any other assumptions that are consistent with the kind of network environment with which you are familiar).

First, develop a preventive maintenance checklist of tasks that a small business organization could use to manage their systems for maximum performance and reliability.

Next, if time permits, Kai would like to expand the checklist to provide clients with a brief explanation of how to perform each step on the checklist. If time is short, your instructor or trainer may ask you to pick one of the three categories above to work on.

586

As you write your preventive maintenance checklist and explanation of how to perform each step, remember that BizNet clients are not computer professionals.

3. How to Manage Spam Email at Columbia Watercraft

Columbia Watercraft is a manufacturing and distribution facility for fiberglass pleasure boats. Several workers at Columbia who have Internet access on their desktop computers have complained recently in a computer user's group meeting about the amount of unwanted email they receive. CEO Lucy Falk wants you to research some ways to deal with the excessive number of unwanted email messages as a way to improve worker productivity—the fewer the spam email messages received, the less time Columbia's workers have to spend reading and deleting them.

- First, research whether any spam management tools exist in the email system that Columbia uses, which happens to be the same email software you use.

- Second, research whether any software utility programs are available at no or low cost that Columbia's workers could use to help filter out spam email messages.

- Write a one- to two-page document targeted at end users at Columbia Watercraft that responds to their need to reduce or eliminate spam messages.

4. Prepare a Training Session on a Utility Tool for Your Colleagues

Select a utility tool with which you have experience. You might choose a tool you learned about in another activity in this chapter. Prepare a 20-minute training session on the use of the utility you select. Design the training as if the target audience is a group of user support workers or trainees, such as your school or work colleagues. Your training session could include elements such as:

- An explanation of the purpose and major features of the tool

- A demonstration of its use

- A description of any problems you encountered while using the tool

- Your personal evaluation of how useful the tool would be to support workers

- A handout on the steps to use the tool in support situations

Use the ideas you learned about in Chapter 11 to prepare and present your training session, either in a one-to-one environment or to a larger group of your colleagues.

5. Retrieve Software Product Keys at Paulina Specs

Paulina Specs is a regional chain of stores that sells eyeglasses and other accessories. The Director of Computer Services at Paulina Specs received the following email from a user in one of the stores.

From: PatW@PaulinaSpecs.net

To: CompSvcs@PaulinaSpecs.net

I have just taken delivery of a new Windows PC for use in the Optical Sales Department in our store. I'm in the process of transferring the software from the old PC to its replacement. I have the CD we used to install the original Office suite on the old PC, but I can't find the case that the installation CD came in. I need it to find the product key code to reinstall the Office suite on the new PC. If I can't locate the product key, we'll have to purchase another copy of the software in order to get a new product key code. Is there any way to find the product key code used when the Office suite was originally installed on the old PC? I figure it must be buried in there somewhere.

Thanks for your help,

Pat

Research the problem and write a response to Pat with information you found about the possibility of locating the original product key code.

Answers to Check Your Understanding Questions

This appendix lists the answers to the end-of-chapter Check Your Understanding questions.

Chapter 1		Chapter 2	
1.	True	1.	True
2.	d. all of these	2.	personal communication style
3.	environment, software use, features used, relationship	3.	a. greeting
		4.	d. Therapeutic
4.	Information Technology (IT), Information Services (IS)	5.	a. Discriminative
		6.	c. Talk to fill awkward silences.
5.	d. 1990s	7.	eye contact, gestures, distance, voice quality
6.	b. worker in an organization	8.	True
7.	False	9.	False
8.	Ergonomics	10.	c. We
9.	c. an invasion of privacy	11.	b. the support agent's own words
10.	graphical user interface (GUI)	12.	True
11.	True	13.	False
12.	True	14.	greet a caller, transfer a call, terminate a call
13.	d. any of the above		
14.	c. Outsourcing uses expertise a company may not have.	15.	True
		16.	c. Agree to any demand a client makes.
15.	a. increase	17.	d. Never admit that you are not sure.
16.	needs analysis, needs assessment	18.	False

(continues)

(continued)

Chapter 1	Chapter 2
17. Support standards	19. False
18. c. operates a large-scale computer	20. organization, format
19. documentation, documents, user manual	21. thread
20. knowledge, skills, and abilities (KSAs)	
21. d. chat session	
22. False	

Chapter 3	Chapter 4
1. False	1. d. All of these are difficult problems.
2. reference sheet, handout	2. False
3. False	3. False
4. c. tutorial manual	4. b. active listening
5. True	5. b. critical thinking
6. a. online help systems	6. decision making
7. False	7. False
8. analogy	8. Escalation
9. b. 2 – 4 – 3 – 1	9. metacognition
10. True	10. probe
11. True	11. c. knowledge base
12. a. complete	12. True
13. True	13. a. Look for a simple, obvious fix.
14. c. 10-12th grade	14. d. an opportunity to look at other alternatives
15. style sheet	15. "You don't see any text or colors on your display?"
16. False	
17. drive error, disk error	16. contradiction
18. Brainstorming	17. b. verification
19. a. reference format	18. False
20. False	19. virtual private network (VPN)
21. False	20. variables
	21. social media

Chapter 5

1. False
2. a burn-in test
3. a. at the time a component is purchased and installed
4. False
5. c. hard drive
6. d. configuration problem
7. conflict
8. False
9. d. new version
10. workaround
11. False
12. False
13. c. both hardware and software problems
14. True
15. Quick start behavior
16. Written reminder note, save password in operating system, reference sheet, script, checklist
17. False
18. d. a service pack
19. a. incompatible
20. Automatic update
21. Registry

Chapter 6

1. True
2. c. *level 1*: incident screener; *level 2*: product specialist; *level 3*: technical support; *level 4*: support manager
3. Incident management (or call management)
4. False
5. c. 1 – 3 – 4 – 2
6. False
7. b. a problem
8. a. first in, first out (FIFO)
9. d. escalation
10. queue
11. False
12. True
13. False
14. automatic call distributor (ACD)
15. False
16. False
17. Job stress
18. end users, help desk agents, support managers
19. c. on a support Web site
20. Changes in off-shore outsourcing; employer demand for certified workers; acceptance of telecommuting work style; industry best practices; pressure to reduce support costs; Web support portals; quantitative metrics, resources for security; help desk software integration
21. a. a set of industry best practices
22. True

Chapter 7

1. True
2. False
3. b. justify the value and expense of help desk services
4. False
5. b. help desk fees for services

Chapter 8

1. False
2. True
3. Product standards
4. False
5. Acceptable use policies
6. Trial, evaluation, demonstration

(*continues*)

(continued)

Chapter 7	Chapter 8
6. performance appraisal	7. False
7. d. an Erlang	8. False
8. True	9. benchmark
9. True	10. d. weighted point method
10. False	11. request for proposal (RFP)
11. a. computer adaptive test	12. b. industry standard products
12. b. behavioral question	13. b. B – D – A – C
13. code of ethical conduct	14. Subjective criteria
14. d. a nondirected question	15. True
15. Noisy interview environment; interruptions; multiple interviews; overly technical questions	16. d. any of these
	17. extraneous variable
16. a. increase	18. c. user preferences
17. budget	19. Vendor literature, market information, Web sites and user manuals; demonstration and evaluation products; product review articles; industry expert opinion; colleague opinion
18. a. a user satisfaction survey	
19. d. abandonment rate	
20. professional association	20. True

Chapter 9	Chapter 10
1. False	1. a. anticipate possible installation problems
2. d. purchase	2. footprint
3. False	3. True
4. c. technological feasibility	4. c. down slightly
5. True	5. Ergonomics
6. d. 4 – 3 – 1 – 2	6. False
7. True	7. False
8. True	8. power strip, surge protector, surge suppressor
9. Build-versus-buy decision	9. True
10. c. model	10. b. with an LED tester
11. deliverable	11. b. fluorescent light
12. True	12. True
13. False	13. c. multiple systems installed in an office or training facility
14. True	
15. a. acquisition cost	14. b. reduce the risk of damage to computer components

(continued)

Chapter 9	Chapter 10
16. project plan, charter	15. Plug and Play
17. flowchart	16. False
18. True	17. license, site license
19. d. predecessor task	18. disaster recovery, contingency plan
20. d. all of these	19. d. an uninterruptible power supply
	20. False

Chapter 11	Chapter 12
1. True	1. d. all of these
2. False	2. False
3. Concepts level	3. False
4. c. perform	4. license agreement, software license, EULA
5. True	5. False
6. False	6. d. a burn-in utility
7. c. expertise	7. a. System Information
8. b. 2 – 4 – 1 – 3	8. b. Back up the Registry onto a hard drive
9. Multimedia	9. b. an autoruns utility
10. False	10. False
11. a. classes	11. True
12. d. problem solve	12. audit
13. True	13. True
14. a. The development cost is high, but the cost per user is low.	14. c. an uninstaller utility
15. handouts, reference sheets	15. Heavy packet volumes, external denial-of-service attacks, processor or memory overload, contention for disk accesses
16. False	16. False
17. d. training evaluation surveys	17. d. any of these
18. Learning styles	18. defrag, defragmentation
19. Role play, role playing	19. virus
20. False	20. Defragment disks, clean Registry, manage startup applications, analyze and repair disk and file errors, optimize Windows configuration and settings
	21. True

HelpSTAR® Student Edition

In this appendix, you will learn about:

◎ The features of HelpSTAR, a commercial help desk software package

◎ How to install HelpSTAR on a PC

◎ How several organizations use HelpSTAR

◎ How to access HelpSTAR's online materials and demonstrations

◎ How to use some basic features of HelpSTAR

The purpose of this appendix is to give you some hands-on experience with a representative commercial help desk software package similar to those you might encounter in a help desk position. Chapter 6 provided an overview of help desk software tools and the HelpSTAR package. This appendix contains additional information about HelpSTAR and provides you with an opportunity to use the software.

A CD packaged with this book includes the HelpSTAR Student Edition software, a product of Help Desk Technology International Corporation. The Student Edition is a 180-day trial version of the HelpSTAR commercial edition. The trial period should give you an opportunity to learn as much as you would like about the product. The Student Edition includes full access to online tutorials, demonstrations of HelpSTAR, and video interviews with HelpSTAR's users.

Install HelpSTAR Student Edition

To install the Student Edition of HelpSTAR, you must have:

- HelpSTAR Student Edition installation CD (packaged with this book)
- Windows XP/Vista/7 operating system
- Windows Installer version 4.5 or later
- Minimum of 1 gigabyte of RAM
- Approximately 1.5 gigabyte of available disk space
- Internet access (broadband connection)

The installation process takes approximately 20 to 30 minutes, depending on the speed of the PC on which HelpSTAR is being installed. In addition to HelpSTAR, other software packages will be installed on the PC (unless they are already installed), including Microsoft's .NET 3.5 framework and Microsoft's SQL Server (2005 Express edition). The .NET framework contains a library of support software that HelpSTAR needs to operate. SQL Server is the database software in which HelpSTAR information is stored.

Reinstalling HelpSTAR deletes any changes you made to the sample database that is included with the software. If you reinstall HelpSTAR in order to start over with the original sample database, the reinstallation process will only take about 10 minutes because .NET and SQL do not have to be installed again.

To install HelpSTAR, complete the following steps:

1. Insert the HelpSTAR CD into the CD/DVD drive. (If the CD AutoPlay feature is operational on the PC, you may skip Steps 2, 3, and 4 below.)
2. Click the desktop icon **Computer** (or **My Computer**, depending on your operating system), or click **Start** and then click **Computer** on the Start menu.
3. The CD should appear in the Computer window as "HelpSTAR 2012 SE".

4. Double-click the **HelpSTAR 2012 SE** CD icon, and then, if necessary, double-click autorun.exe; a welcome screen for the Student Edition is displayed.

5. Depending on the operating system, Window's User Account Control (UAC) may request permission for HelpSTAR to be installed on the system. If necessary, enter an Admin password, and then click **Yes**.

6. An InstallShield Wizard will guide you through the installation process. (See Chapters 5 and 10 for more information about installation utilities such as InstallShield.) Click **Next**.

7. The License Agreement for HelpSTAR Student Edition is displayed. Read the license agreement carefully. Among other provisions, paragraph 1 of the agreement says that the Student Edition is limited to 180 days for the purpose of testing and evaluation. Paragraph 3 indicates that you can install and use the software on more than one PC, such as a school or work system and a home system. If you agree to the terms displayed on the screen, click to accept the license agreement, and then click **Next**.

Your license agreement is with Help Desk Technology International Corporation (HDTIC), the company that developed and sells HelpSTAR, and not with the publisher or author of this book.

8. Click **Next** to verify the installation destination folder. During installation, InstallShield copies HelpSTAR to the default folder C:\Program Files\HelpSTAR Student Edition\. (Note that in 64-bit versions of Windows, HelpSTAR installs in the 32-bit folder, C:\Program Files (x86)\HelpSTAR Student Edition\.) In addition to HelpSTAR, the .NET and SQL Server packages described above are installed. Click **Next** to accept the default folder location.

   As part of the installation, HelpSTAR installs a shortcut to the program on the PC's desktop. The executable program is named WinI.exe in the \HelpSTAR Student Edition\ folder.

9. When all files have been installed, HelpSTAR displays a successful installation message. Click **Finish.**

10. Next, InstallShield configures the HelpSTAR package.

11. When the configuration is complete, you will be required to register the software with HelpSTAR. Enter your name (first name is sufficient) and email address. Your school name, course number, and telephone number are optional entries. Click **Register** when finished.

12. When using the Student Edition, you will log in as a help desk support representative named Beth Markham. After you register the software, a login screen for Beth Markham will be displayed. Click the **Login** button to view HelpSTAR's workspace. Beth's password is *helpstar*.

13. To exit HelpSTAR, click **Exit Helpstar** on the *File* tab, or click the **X** (Close) button in the upper-right corner of the window, and then click **Yes**.

The Student Edition of HelpSTAR does not include technical support for installation or operational problems. In case of problems, contact your instructor. Please do not contact Help Desk Technology International Corporation, the author, or the publisher, Course Technology (Cengage Learning), about any installation or operational problems.

Getting Started Learning About HelpSTAR

HelpSTAR includes a variety of online audio/visual interviews and demonstrations to help you get started learning about the software. These resources can be accessed on HelpSTAR's Web site and in the HelpSTAR software. Because the Web-based HelpSTAR learning resources are data intensive, they should be accessed on a high-speed, broadband Internet connection.

ON THE WEB

If you would like to view HelpSTAR's online product information without installing the software, follow these links:

- Client Interviews (videos): **www.helpstar.com**, then click the **Testimonials** tab

- HelpSTAR Evaluator's Guide (a product overview): **www.helpstar.com/quickeval/quickEvalGuide2012.pdf**

- Product Feature Demos (videos): **www.helpstar.com/help-desk-resources/feature-demos.asp**

After HelpSTAR is installed, you can access additional information in the program's help system.

- On the ribbon, in the upper-right corner of the HelpSTAR screen, click the Help (**?**) button, and then click **HelpSTAR Help**, or press the F1 function key. A table of contents for HelpSTAR help is in the left pane. Note that the help system is for the 2010 version of HelpSTAR; some menus and screens appear somewhat differently in the 2012 version.

Client Interviews

To hear from some help desk staff about why they chose HelpSTAR software and to learn more about how it is used in a variety of business, educational, and government organizations, go to HelpSTAR's Web site (**www.helpstar.com**) and click the **Testimonials** tab. The comments of help desk workers, managers, and network technicians provide several perspectives on using the software. Note the following information about viewing these videos:

- Adobe Flash Player is required to view the video testimonials.
- To play a testimonial, click the play button in the center of the video.
- To stop a video, click the pause button or click outside the video screen.

Feature Demos

The HelpSTAR Web site also includes videos that describe HelpSTAR product features. These videos are designed as sales tools, and are not primarily tutorial demonstrations. Click the **Feature Demos** link on the right side of the Web site to view short videos on the following HelpSTAR features:

- Intuitive User Interface
- Business Rules
- Auto Discovery
- Email Inbox
- User-Defined Fields
- Project Templates
- Web Portal
- Active Directory
- Reporting and Data Analysis
- Role-Based Access Control

The material in these product demos includes descriptions of how HelpSTAR solves a variety of help desk and user support problems. Some of these features are covered in greater depth in the tutorial steps below.

HelpSTAR Terminology

Part of learning to use a new software package is adapting to its vocabulary. Some HelpSTAR terminology is similar to key terms defined elsewhere in this book; other terms are unique to HelpSTAR. HelpSTAR provides a glossary of terms as part of its online help system. To access a glossary within the software, press the **F1** function key, and then click the **Glossary of Terms** item in the *Help* menu. Figure B-1 lists some key terms—and their definitions—that you are likely to encounter as you use HelpSTAR. The glossary of terms in HelpSTAR expands on the definitions in Figure B-1 and includes definitions of other terms that you are not likely to encounter as you work through the HelpSTAR tutorial in this appendix.

599

- **alert**—A HelpSTAR-generated message to a support rep that is triggered by an event (such as a request being closed) or by the application of a business rule.

- **asset**—An inventory item, such as a PC, server, network gateway, or software package.

- **auto discovery**—A tool to scan the hardware and software on a network to locate new or unauthorized devices or audit for compliance with the terms of software license agreements.

- **Best Solutions**—HelpSTAR's knowledge base of resolved service requests and support articles.

- **business rule**—An *if-then* rule used to automate tasks in HelpSTAR; when a condition has been met (such as when a service request with a critical priority is not handled within 30 minutes), an action is triggered (for example, the service request is escalated or an email is sent).

- **category**—A way to classify each service request according to the nature of the problem.

- **dashboard**—A brief management report (statistics and charts) on the performance of a help desk.

- **organizational unit**— Within an organization, a department or other structure (such as a sub-department) that can generate service requests.

- **query**—Criteria used to search for or filter (select) information in a database.

- **reference number**—A unique number HelpSTAR automatically assigns to each new request.

- **reminder**—A message—initiated by an end user, agent, or manager—to prompt a user to take some action, such as make a follow-up phone call.

- **requester**—Any user of the HelpSTAR system; requesters can submit service requests.

- **SLA (service level agreement)**—A contract between end users and a service provider that defines a specified level of help desk services; for example, an SLA may specify maximum help desk response and resolution times. Provisions of a service level agreement are often defined as business rules in HelpSTAR.

- **service request**—An incident, phone call, or email from a user to a help desk or service facility.

- **support rep**—A help desk agent or user support specialist who handles service requests.

- **user**—Anyone who uses the HelpSTAR system, including end users, help desk staff, and managers (the latter two groups are *privileged* users because they have access to features that end users do not).

- **workflow**—A process during which a service request passes through various stages (sometimes called a life cycle) from receipt to dispatch, prioritization, assignment, escalation, resolution, documentation, and finally to termination; similar to the steps in incident management.

Figure B-1   Key terms used in HelpSTAR software

HelpSTAR's Workspace

Launch HelpSTAR by double-clicking the desktop program icon, or click **HelpSTAR 2012 Student Edition** in the Windows Start menu. The initial screen shows the login screen, with Beth Markham's name and password (*helpstar*) already entered. Click the **Login** button to display the main HelpSTAR window or workspace, shown in Figure B-2. The window contains the following elements (numbered descriptions below correspond to the numbered bullets in the figure):

1. **Ribbon interface**—A ribbon menu appears across the top of each HelpSTAR window; this menu style is common to Windows software such as the Microsoft Office 2007 or 2010 suites.

2. **HelpSTAR menu**—In the left pane of the workspace, HelpSTAR displays shortcuts to six of the software's most popular tools:

   - **HelpSTAR Today**—Displays a user's workspace, which includes announcements, the user's calendar, and action items—such as service requests that need attention

   - **Service Requests**—Displays a detailed list of service requests (in priority order) that have been assigned to the agent

   - **Emails, Communications**—Displays an inbox of communications sent to an agent from end users, help desk staff, and managers

   - **Calendar**—Displays the agent's online calendar of events, which can be edited

   - **Documents**—Displays a list of documents stored in the HelpSTAR system to which users have access

   - **Assets/Configuration**—Provides a portal into the asset and workstation configuration database

3. **Support Rep's status**—At the bottom of each screen is a status bar. The status bar in Figure B-2 shows links to various alerts, messages, reminders, and queues that are part of Beth Markham's HelpSTAR desktop workspace. Beth's workspace consists of all the HelpSTAR services to which she has authorized access.

4. **Close button**—To exit from HelpSTAR, click the **Close** (X) button in the upper-right corner of the window.

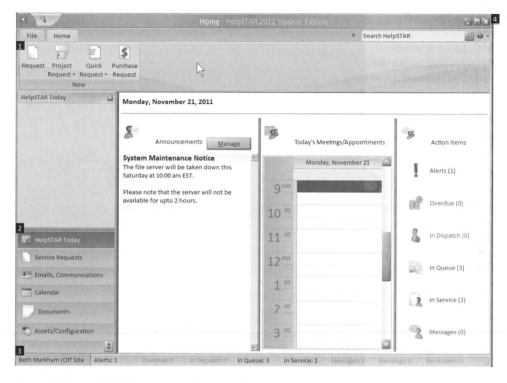

Figure B-2   HelpSTAR home page for Beth Markham

A Case Study Tutorial Using HelpSTAR

HelpSTAR is an extensive commercial help desk system with many features. The purpose of this case study tutorial is to give you an introductory experience with HelpSTAR, as an example of a help desk system used in real businesses. The case study tutorial is not designed or intended to be a complete guide to all of HelpSTAR's software features. In addition, the question of whether HelpSTAR is appropriate for a specific organizational use is beyond the scope of this text.

Ocean House Case Study

Ocean House is a company that designs and programs custom Web sites for other companies. The company is organized into several departments, including Administration, Development, Facilities Management, Human Resources, Sales, and Tech Support. Ocean House wants to offer its clients the ability to add interactive maps to their Web sites, and has recently hired George Friedman, a GIS (Geographical Information Systems) technician with experience in Web-based map software. Beth Markham, a help desk representative, has been assigned to get George set up in Ocean House's HelpSTAR system.

This case study tutorial assumes you have installed HelpSTAR on your PC. The Student Edition of HelpSTAR is distributed with a sample database that includes a few users, assets, service requests, solutions, and other information, some of which will be used in this case study tutorial.

The tutorial below does not detail each keystroke or mouse click. It assumes that you are generally familiar with the use of the Windows GUI interface and that you have viewed several of the demonstrations on the HelpSTAR Web site described above. The entire tutorial of 18 steps takes 2 to 3 hours to complete.

Step 1: Start HelpSTAR

- Double-click the **HelpSTAR** icon on your desktop or choose HelpSTAR from the Windows Start menu, and log in as Beth Markham.

In HelpSTAR, users often find they have multiple windows open. Any time you want to return to the HelpSTAR main menu, click the **Close** button in the upper-right corner to close the top window, or click the **HelpSTAR Today** button in the left pane.

Step 2: Update the Company Information

Before entering George as a user in HelpSTAR, you can get some experience with basic information entry by updating the information for the company, Ocean House.

- On the ribbon menu on the *HelpSTAR Today* screen, click the **File** tab.
- In the *File* menu, click the **Setup/Administration** button (on the left side). Then click the **HelpSTAR Objects** tab at the top of the *Setup/Administration* window.
- On the *HelpSTAR Objects* tab, click the **Manage Companies** icon. In the list of companies, click **Ocean House**. In the *Manage* command group, click **Update**. Enter the following information about Ocean House into the *Edit Company* form:
- *Name*: **Ocean House**
- *Company Type*: **Manufacturer**
- *Telephone*: **905-960-0000**
- *Street 1*: **101 Foothills Street**
- *Street 2*: **Suite 300**
- *City*: **Newmarket**
- *State*: **ON**
- *Code*: **L3X 4G0**

- *Country*: **Canada**

- When you have completed the *Edit Company* form for Ocean House, save the entry by clicking the **Save** button on the Quick Access toolbar, or press the **Ctrl+S** keys.

- To review the company information you entered, click **Ocean House** in the list, and then click the **Company Properties** icon on the ribbon to view the information about Ocean House. When finished, click the **Close** button (upper-right corner of the window).

- If you made a mistake in the entry, click the **Update** command again, and make any necessary corrections.

To delete a company from the list of companies, click its name to highlight it, and then click **De-Activate** in the ribbon's *Manage* group.

Step 3: Enter a New Group as an Organizational Unit

Since George is the first GIS Technician in Ocean House, Beth needs to add GIS as a group into HelpSTAR's database. A group is a type of organizational unit (OU) in HelpSTAR. Each organizational unit generates a queue (folder) of service requests for help desk agents. The new GIS group will be part of the Development Department.

- On the ribbon menu on the *HelpSTAR Today* screen, click the **File** tab. In the *File* menu, click the **Setup/Administration** button. Then click the **HelpSTAR Objects** tab at the top of the *Setup/Administration* window.

- On the *HelpSTAR Objects* tab, click the **Manage Organizational Hierarchy** icon. Look over the existing departments in Ocean House. Click **Development** to make that department the active organizational unit.

- On the ribbon, click the **New** button in the *Organizational Hierarchy* group, and then click **Organizational Unit** from the drop-down menu. Enter the following information about the GIS group on the form:

  - *Queue Name*: **GIS Group**

  - For the *Queue Type*, click **Generic OU/Folder**

- When you have entered the information for the GIS Group, save the entry by clicking the **Save** button on the Quick Access toolbar or pressing the **Ctrl+S** keys. GIS Group should now appear in the list of available organizational units in the Development department.

To delete an organizational unit from the list of available units, click its name to highlight it, and then click **De-Activate** in the ribbon's *Organizational Hierarchy* group.

Step 4: Enter a New User

Beth's next task is to add George Friedman's user information into HelpSTAR's database of users. To do so, complete the following steps:

- On the *HelpSTAR Today* screen, click the **File** tab. In the *File* menu, click the **Setup/Administration** button. Then click the **HelpSTAR Objects** tab at the top of the *Setup/Administration* window.

- On the *HelpSTAR Objects* tab, click the **Manage Users** icon. On the ribbon, click the **Create New User** icon, and then enter the following information about George on the *New User* form:

  - On the *Main* tab:

    - *User Type*: **Internal Staff**

    - *Name*: **George Friedman**

      - Click the option button to indicate George is an internal user.

    - *Organizational Unit*: **GIS Group**

    - *Telephone*: **905-960-0000**

    - *Extension*: **777**

    - *Location*: **Newmarket**

    - *Workstation ID*: **PC-0123**

  - On the *Logins/Email* tab:

    - *Logins*: **Enabled**

    - *Email*: **Enabled**

    - *Email Address*: **GFriedman@oceanhouse.local**

  - Leave other fields on the *New User* form blank.

- When you have entered the above information, save the entry by clicking the **Save** icon at the top of the form or by pressing the **Ctrl+S** keys. Respond **No** to questions about granting access and adding another user. George should now appear in the list of users.

- Click the **Refresh** button on the Quick Access toolbar. In the list of users, click **George Friedman**, and then click the **User Properties** icon on the ribbon to display the User Properties window shown in Figure B-3.

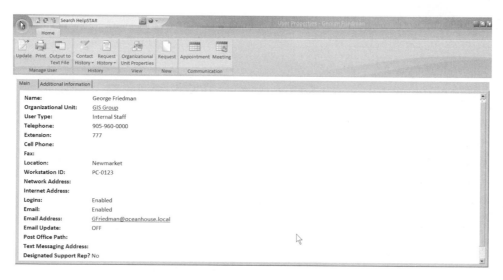

Figure B-3 HelpSTAR entry for user George Friedman

- If you made any mistakes when entering George's information, click **Update** on the ribbon, and make any necessary corrections.

> To delete a user from the list, right-click their name and choose **De-Activate**.

Step 5: Add an Asset

Ocean House purchased a new laptop computer for George to use. Beth needs to add information about George's laptop into HelpSTAR's asset database.

- On the *HelpSTAR Today* screen, click the **File** tab. In the *File* menu, click the **Setup/Administration** button, and then click the **HelpSTAR Objects** tab at the top of the *Setup/Administration* window.

- In the *HelpSTAR Objects* tab, click the **Manage Assets** icon. On the ribbon, click the **Create New Asset** icon, and then enter the following information about George's laptop on the form:

  ◆ *Asset Type*: **Workstation**

  ◆ *Asset Name*: **Lenovo ThinkPad Edge 15**

  ◆ *Identification Tag*: **PC-0123**

  ◆ *Serial Number*: **FGR5152645**

  ◆ *Allocated to*: **User (George Friedman)**

- *Cost*: **799.99**

- *Acquisition Date*: **9/16/2011**

- *Quantity*: **1**

- *Memo*: **Windows 7 laptop is for George's use in GIS development projects.**

- Leave the other fields on the asset form blank.

- When you have finished entering the information for George's laptop, save the entry by clicking the **Save** icon at the top of the *New Asset* form, or pressing the **Ctrl+S** keys. Click **OK** in the window to confirm that the asset was added.

- Close the *Find an Asset* window. On subsequent asset screens, the Lenovo laptop should be listed.

- Verify that George's laptop has been added as an asset.

 To delete an asset from the list, right-click its name and choose **De-Activate**.

Step 6: Set Up a Service Request Category

On his first day on the job, George called Beth to say that he was getting settled into his office, but was having difficulty connecting his Lenovo laptop to the Ocean House network. He reported that his laptop could not find a wireless network to connect to. Beth explained to George that his office area does not currently have wireless access. However, Beth mentioned that a wired Ethernet connection was available as a temporary workaround. She asked if George had an Ethernet cable to use to connect. He didn't, so Beth entered a service request ticket and told George that she would have a cable delivered to his office. In HelpSTAR, Beth quickly discovered that there was no category for Network Connectivity problems. She decided to create a new category called Network Connectivity under Network problems.

- On the *HelpSTAR Today* screen, click the **File** tab. In the *File* menu, click the **Setup/Administration** button. Then click the **HelpSTAR Objects** tab at the top of the *Setup/Administration* window.

- On the *HelpSTAR Objects* tab, click the **Manage Categories** icon. In the list of categories in the left pane, click the + in front of *Network* to see its current subcategories.

- Click the **Network** category to make it active. Then click the **New Category** command on the ribbon. In the *New Category* form, enter **Network Connectivity** as a generic category, and press the **Ctrl+S** keys to save.

- When you are finished, *Network Connectivity* should appear as a subcategory under *Network*. If *Network Connectivity* ended up in the wrong place, you can drag it to the place in the category list where you want it.

Step 7: Enter a Service Request

With an appropriate service request category defined, Beth was able to enter a service request so George could get an Ethernet cable.

- On the *HelpSTAR Today* screen, click the **Home** tab, and then click **Request** on the ribbon menu to open the New Service Request window.

- Begin in the *General Information* box:

  - *Request Type:* **Request for Service**

  - *Requester:* **George Friedman**

    - (*Hint*: Click [**Find User ...**])

  - *Category:* **Ocean House\Network\Network Connectivity**

    - (*Hint*: Using the drop-down menu, select **+ Network**, and then click the subcategory **Network Connectivity**.)

  - *Title:* **Needs Ethernet cable to connect**

- In the *Asset box:*

  - *Asset:* **Lenovo ThinkPad Edge 15 [Asset]**

    - (*Hint*: Click the [**...**] button to find George's laptop in the list of assets; in the Assets By Allocation list, double-click **Ocean House**, double-click **GIS Group**, and then double-click **George Friedman**. Finally, click **Lenovo ThinkPad Edge 15**, and click **OK**.)

- In the *Importance* box:

  - *User* Urgency: **High**

- In the *Current Location* box:

  - *Current* Location: **Dispatch - [Dispatch]**

- In the *Memo* box:

  - *Memo:* **George Friedman needs a 12 foot Ethernet cable in his office to connect his laptop to the network.**

- Leave the other fields in the service request form blank.

After you have completed these steps, the service request will look like the example in Figure B-4.

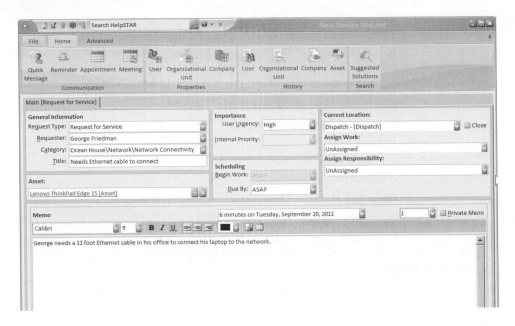

Figure B-4   HelpSTAR entry for a new service request

- Press **Ctrl+S** to save the request, and click **OK** to confirm.

When you save a new service request, HelpSTAR automatically assigns a 5-digit reference number to the form (in this example, 10059).

Step 8: Assign a Service Request to a Support Rep

A little later, Beth headed from the help desk office in the direction of George's office to perform another task. Before she left the help desk office, she checked on the status of George's request for an Ethernet cable.

- On the *HelpSTAR Today* screen, click **Service Requests** in the left pane. The Service Requests navigation folders are located above the *HelpSTAR Today* button in the left pane. Note that Beth can look at several queues in the HelpSTAR system.

- Click the **In Service** queue. The *In Service* folder is a list of service requests that have been assigned to Beth. Beth does not find George's request in her list.

- Click the **In Dispatch** queue. Find the service request from George Friedman.

- In the *Dispatch* queue workspace list, click George Friedman's cable request to highlight it. Then click the **Assign** command in the *Update Request* group on the ribbon menu. In the *Assign* dialog box, click the *Work* drop-down menu; then click **MySelf** to assign the request to Beth. When prompted, click **Inbox\Beth Markham** and then click **OK** to send a notice of the assignment to Beth's Inbox. Finally, click **OK** to exit the *Assign* form.

- In the Service Requests list click **Inbox\Beth Markham.** When HelpSTAR asks if you want to save the changes to the service request, click **Yes**. Then click **In Service** in the Service Requests list to verify that the request was assigned to Beth. (If you wish, you can also verify that George's service request is no longer in the *Dispatch* queue.) By double-clicking service request 10059, Beth can display the details of the request.

When these steps are completed, George Friedman's service request for an Ethernet cable is reassigned from *In Dispatch* to Beth Markham's queue. Double-click the George Friedman service request in the Workspace List pane to see the request details (see Figure B-5). Beth can view a complete history of the service request in the lower part of the same screen (see Figure B-6).

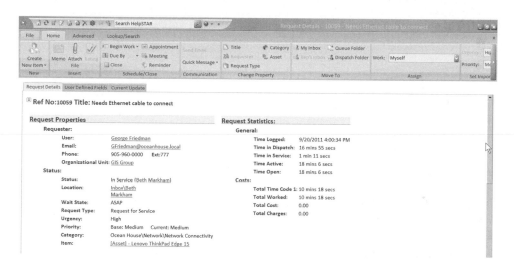

Figure B-5   George Friedman's service request is now assigned to Beth Markham's queue

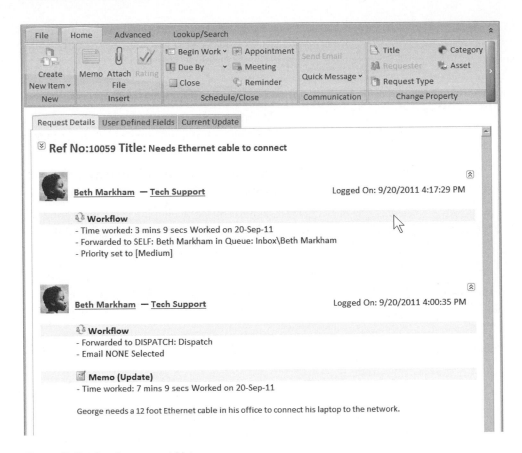

Figure B-6   Service request history

Using HelpSTAR menu choices, Beth can move pending service requests to her queue (*In Service*), to another queue, to another support rep's queue, or back to *In Dispatch;* she can also choose to *Close* a request. Whether a support rep can perform some or all of these service request assignment tasks depends on a company's policies and the privileges set for each agent in HelpSTAR. For example, senior support reps can be assigned privileges that entry-level agents don't have, and supervisors or team leaders can be assigned an even wider array of privileges. These privileges can be set for individual agents or based on their roles (such as dispatcher, help desk agent, technical support agent, supervisor, and so on).

Step 9: Close a Service Request

Beth delivered the Ethernet cable to George and got him connected to the office network. When she returned to her office, she closed the service request.

- On the *HelpSTAR Today* screen, click **Service Requests** in the left pane. Find the Service Requests navigation folders above the *HelpSTAR Today* menu in the left pane. Click the **In Service** queue.

- In the list of the service requests assigned to Beth, click George's request for the Ethernet cable.

- In the *Update Request* command group on the ribbon menu, click the **Schedule/Close** command, and then choose **Close** from the drop-down menu.

- Click **Memo** on the ribbon. In the *memo* field, write a notation: **Delivered cable to George and got him connected.**

- When prompted to save the memo, click **OK,** and then press the **Ctrl+S** keys to save the memo.

- Click the **Refresh** button on the Quick Access toolbar (or press **F5**) to refresh the screen and verify that George's request has been closed.

You can review the entire history of any service request by right-clicking it in any list and then clicking **View Request Details**.

Step 10: Find a Service Request

Beth would like to verify that the HelpSTAR record for George's service request was completed. She uses the *Find* option in the *File* menu to locate the service request.

- On the *HelpSTAR Today* screen, click the **File** tab. In the *File* menu, click **Find** to view the list of HelpSTAR objects that a user can search for.

- For example, to search for service requests for George Friedman, click **Requester** in the *Request* group.

- In the *Requester* box, enter **George** and click the **Find** button. Or use the drop-down menu to select a user from the list. An agent can further narrow the search by date in the *Requester* box.

The *Find* option permits very flexible searches for objects in the HelpSTAR database, such as service requests (by number, title, or category), users, departments, companies, assets, or support reps.

Step 11: Find a Solution to a Problem

Beth was the agent assigned to Ocean House's Help Desk hotline telephone when she received a call from George Friedman. George thanked her again for her help with the Ethernet cable. He reported that he would like to be able to connect to the company's virtual private network (VPN) as a security precaution when he is working at home. Beth followed Step 7 above to enter a service request. Then she searched HelpSTAR's Best Solutions database for information about the company's VPN to see if documentation was available she could send to George.

- On the *HelpSTAR Today* screen, click the **File** tab. In the *File* menu, click **Find** to view a list of many of the objects in HelpSTAR's database that a user can search for.

- In the list of objects you can search for in HelpSTAR, use the *Best Solution* option and click **Search Phrase.** In the Search Criteria section, enter **VPN**, and then press the **Enter** key.

611

- Double-click the search result to display instructions on VPN connections, as shown in Figure B-7. Although the instructions were for an earlier version of Windows, Beth copied the instructions and sent them as a Quick Message in HelpSTAR to George.

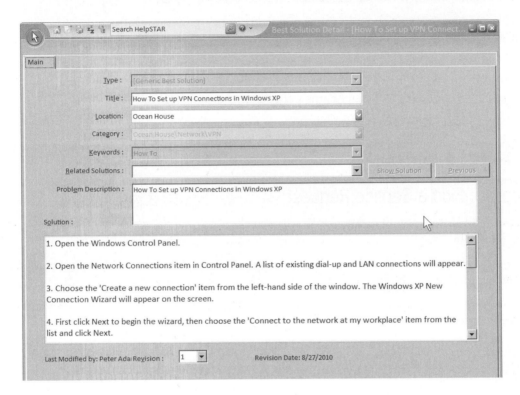

Figure B-7   Best Solution knowledge base entry in HelpSTAR for VPN connection

The Best Solutions knowledge base in the sample database distributed with HelpSTAR Student Edition is just an example, but over time, an organization such as Ocean House can build an extensive collection of problem resolutions, documentation, Web links, articles, and notes for their help desk agents and users to access.

Step 12: Escalate a Service Request

Beth reviewed service requests in various queues when one particular item caught her eye—Ref# 10041, a request from Stacy Warner regarding a problem accessing email at home over the weekend. Beth checked the Best Solutions database, but found no specific entries that referred to email problems outside the office network. Beth knew that Peter Adams would normally handle service requests related to email, since Peter is the email expert on the Network Support team.

- To move request 10041 into Peter Adams's queue, find request #10041 and double-click the listing for it. (*Hint:* Ref# 10041 is currently in the folder *Tech Support/Support/North America/Tech Level 1*. You can also locate it by clicking the **File** tab, and then clicking **Find.** Enter 10041 in the # input box.)

- Click **Ref# 10041** to highlight it, and then, on the ribbon menu, in the *Update Request* command group, click **Assign.**

- In the *Work* box, use the drop-down menu and click to expand the *Assigned Users* list and find Peter Adams's name. Click his name, and then click **OK**.

- Finally, click the **Save** button on the Quick Access Toolbar, or press **Ctrl+S** to save the changes to Ref#10041 (Stacy's email problem).

- Note that service request Ref# 10041 has been updated to show that Beth Markham moved the request into Peter Adams's queue, as shown in Figure B-8.

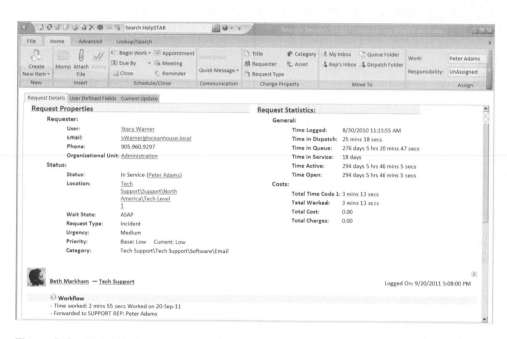

Figure B-8   Beth Markham assigns a service request to another agent

- To verify the current status of a service request by number, use the *Find* option in HelpSTAR's *File* menu. In the *#* box, enter the number of the service request (e.g., 10041), and press the **Enter** key, or search by user name or other characteristic.

- You can also check Peter Adams's queue by clicking **Service Requests** on the left side of the HelpSTAR screen to display an *Other Views* tab on the ribbon. In the *Active Requests* group on the *Other Views* tab, click **Other Workspaces**. In the list of agents, double-click **Peter Adams** to view Peter's queue of service requests.

- Click the **X** close button in the upper-right corner to close the view of Peter's queue.

Beth was able to move a request from *In Dispatch* to Peter Adams's queue because that privilege is assigned to her in HelpSTAR's user database.

Step 13: Draft a New Best Solution

Beth's supervisor at Ocean House asked her to write a new Best Solution in HelpSTAR's knowledge management system on how to use HelpSTAR's online help system. Beth reviewed the features of the help system and then wrote a draft of an article for a Best Solution.

- On the *HelpSTAR Today* screen, click the **File** tab. In the *File* menu, click **Knowledge Management**, and then click **Create New Best Solution**.

- In the *Title* box, enter **HelpSTAR help system**.

- In the *Category* drop-down menu, click **Tech Support**; within the *Tech Support* category, select the subcategory **Tech Support**, and finally, click **Software**. (To expand any category that is collapsed, click the plus (+) sign in front of the category name.)

- Click the **Add** button to the right of the *Keywords* box, and then at the top of the *Keywords* box, click the **New** button (the key symbol), or press **Ctrl+N**.

- Enter **HelpSTAR** and then click **OK**.

- From the *Available Keywords* list in the left pane, click **HelpSTAR**, and click the **Add** button.

- Repeat these steps to add two more keywords: **online** and **help**. Then click **Save**. Click **OK** to close the *Find Category* dialog box.

- Verify that *HelpSTAR*, *online*, and *help* are listed as keywords for this Best Solution. (You will need to use the drop-down arrow to see all three keywords.)

- In the *Problem Description* box, enter: **Support Reps need to be able to use HelpSTAR's online help system to locate information about features.**

- In the *Solution* box, enter the following text:

  To access HelpSTAR's online help system, click the question mark button next to the HelpSTAR button, or press F1.

  On the help system page, which is displayed in your Web browser, click the Contents tab at the top of the page to view the table of contents in the left pane.

  The help topics that are most relevant to beginning support reps are:

  - A Brief Lesson in How HelpSTAR Works

  - HelpSTAR Home Page

  - Service Request

  - Configuration Management

  - Knowledge Management

  The help system's Search tab is also useful, and the Glossary tab can provide definitions of unfamiliar terms.

- Click the **Save** button at the bottom of the window to save the Best Solution draft. Then click **OK** in the confirmation dialog box.

- To publish the draft Best Solution on HelpSTAR's help system, click the **File** tab. In the *File* menu, click **Knowledge Management**, and then click **Best Solutions Listing**.

- Find the draft article in the list. Right-click the article, and select the **Publish Internally** option from the drop-down menu.

- To find your solution, select **Knowledge Management** on the *File* tab again, and click **Find Best Solutions**. In the *Search Phrase* box, enter **help**, and press the **Enter** key.

Note that the Find option can locate the Best Solution you wrote using the keyword *help*, but it cannot locate the same solution using the keyword *glossary* (even though *glossary* appears in the Best Solution text) unless you click the **Resolution** box on the search form.

The draft Best Solution that Beth wrote is shown in Figure B-9.

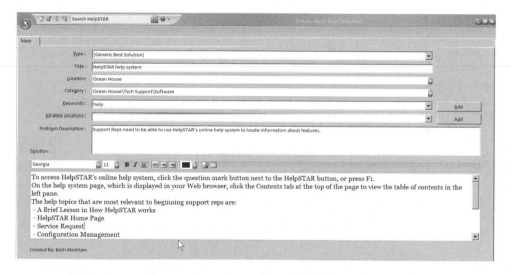

Figure B-9 Best Solution knowledge base draft article on HelpSTAR's help system

Step 14: Update a Service Request

Beth noticed that one of the service requests in the *Tech Support/Support/North America/Tech Level 1* queue is a message from Frank Catton reporting that he received an email that his antivirus software needed to be updated. Since Beth regularly deals with software updates, she looked at the service request and responded to it.

- In Beth Markham's service request queue, find **Ref# 10042** from Frank Catton. Double-click the request to display it.

- In the *Insert* command group on the ribbon, click **Memo**.

- In the *Create a New Memo* window, enter the following:

Frank -

I updated the image of the antivirus software on our network server today. I also scheduled a reimage of the software on each PC tonight at 2AM.

Thanks for reporting this problem# and please call me if you get future messages from the antivirus software.

Beth

- Click the **OK** button in the upper-left corner of the *Create a New Memo* window (shown in Figure B-10) to add this response as a memo to Frank's service request. Then press **Ctrl+S** to save the changes to Frank's service request.

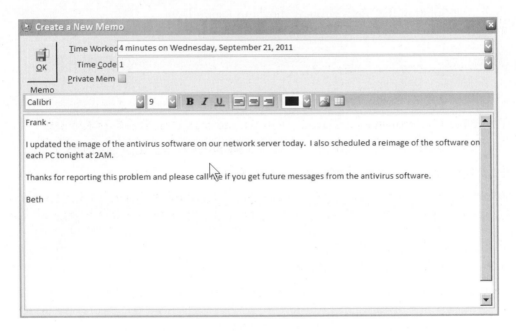

Figure B-10 Beth added a memo to Frank's service request

Step 15: Set a Reminder

Beth wants to call Frank the next day to verify that the antivirus software was actually updated. She used HelpSTAR's reminder system to help her remember to make the call.

- Locate Frank's service request, **Ref# 10042**, and double-click the service request to select it.

- In the *Schedule/Close* group, click the **Reminder** button.

- In the *Reminder* window, click the **Myself** check box to send the reminder.

- In the *Settings* section, use the drop-down list to set the time to a few minutes in the future (as a test of this feature). In a real situation, Beth would probably set the reminder time to 24 hours.

- In the *Memo* box, enter: **Call Frank to verify antivirus utility on his PC was updated as scheduled**. Click **Save**. Then click the **Close** button to return to HelpSTAR's screen.

- Check the *Reminders* button on the status bar at the bottom of the HelpSTAR window in a few minutes to verify that Beth received the reminder you set. The *Reminders* button indicates the number of reminders waiting for Beth's attention.

- Click the **Reminders** button on the status bar at the bottom of the screen to view Beth's list of reminders.

- Locate the reminder message in the list. To delete the reminder, right-click the reminder in the list and click the **Dismiss** option.

Step 16: Create a Standard Report

Beth would like to view a listing of the Best Solution topics currently in Ocean House's knowledge database. The listing of topics is predefined as a standard report in HelpSTAR. To access the report, follow these steps:

- In HelpSTAR's *File* menu, click **Data Analysis**, and then click **Standard Reports**.

- On the *Standard Reports* ribbon menu, click **Best Solution** in the *Listing* group.

- In the *Reports List* pane on the left, click **Best Solutions**.

The report of current Best Solution topics is displayed. Click the ➤ button at the top of the report window to view subsequent pages. Does the online help system topic that you added in Step 13 appear in the list?

Step 17: Create a Query Report

The Ocean House Human Resources supervisor asked Beth how many pending service requests the help desk had from new hires. To get a list, Beth used the data analysis tools in HelpSTAR to construct a query and prepare a report.

- On HelpSTAR's ribbon menu, click the **File** tab. In the *File* menu, click **Data Analysis**, and then click **Queries.**

- On the ribbon menu in the *Query* window, click **New Request Query**. Take a moment to study the layout of the *Query Designer* window. Note that in the left pane, you can select fields to be queried. In the right pane, you can specify the criteria for the query and see a preview of the results.

- Locate the *Request Field Selection* section in the left pane. Begin with all boxes in the list of fields unchecked, except the box in front of the *Service Request* field. Verify that no design criteria are listed in the *Design and Preview* pane on the right.

618

- In the *Request Field Selection* pane, click the + in front of *Service Request* to expand the list of service request types. Then click the box in front of *Service Request Type* to select it; in the *Selection Criteria* window that appears, click the box in front of the *New Employee Request* type, and then click **OK**. These steps narrow the query to service requests from new employees. When you have completed this step, the *Design and Preview* pane on the right should contain the query criteria, *Service Request Type Equal To "New Employee Request".*

- Go back to the *Request Field Selection* pane on the left and check the boxes in front of *Ref#, Title,* and *Status.* These three fields should now appear in the *Design and Preview* pane on the right. When you are finished with this step, the *Design and Preview* pane should show four fields, including the three you just added. No selection criteria are needed for these three fields; they will just be listed on the query report. (Although, if you want to limit the search results, you could click the **Criteria** box for the *Status* field and narrow the search for *In Dispatch* or *In Queue*.)

- Click the **Preview Query Results** tab to see a list of pending requests from new hires.

Once Beth has prepared the criteria for this database query report, she can use commands on the ribbon to save the query to run it again in the future, print a report of the query results, or export the query results to Excel.

Step 18: Display a Performance Dashboard

If Beth wants to quickly check on the performance of Ocean House's user support team, she can do so by using HelpSTAR's dashboard feature, which displays a customizable, one-page summary of various performance indicators. (Because the sample database included in the HelpSTAR Student Edition is small, these statistics are for illustration only.)

- On HelpSTAR's ribbon menu, click the **File** tab. In the *File* menu, click **Dashboard**.

- In the upper-right corner of the dashboard display, Beth noticed a report on the frequency of help desk incident calls for each Ocean House department.

- Click in the upper-right pane. Then click the **View Full Screen** icon on the ribbon. Beth observes that the column chart shows that Human Resources had the highest number of incidents in the period covered by the report.

- Click the **Human Resources** bar to drill-down to the list of requests from that department. When you are finished, click **Close (X)** button for the window to return to the dashboard view.

- To view other dashboard charts, click the **Restore Screen** button in the *Chart Actions* group. Then, repeat the previous two steps for the chart you want to view. To learn about other dashboard options, click the **Design** icon on the Dashboard ribbon.

This tutorial emphasized common and frequent activities to give you a brief introduction to the tasks support reps perform in HelpSTAR every day. However, HelpSTAR is an extensive software package with many features for help desks and other business applications. These tutorial steps have just scratched the surface of the software's capabilities. We have not covered many useful HelpSTAR features, such as:

- purchase order processing

- business rules to automate HelpSTAR tasks and communications

- links to email and pagers

- user-defined fields to customize HelpSTAR

- advanced data analysis and reporting features

- assignment of access privileges based on the roles HelpSTAR users perform

- use of HelpSTAR as a Web portal

Make good use of the 180-day student edition to explore these and other features of the software. Many support organizations use HelpSTAR or a similar package to automate help desk recordkeeping.

Hands-On Activities

Activity B-1

Add another new user. Follow the steps in the tutorial above to add another user, Rahim Waleed, to the GIS Group in the Development. Enter the following information about Rahim:

- On the *Main* tab:

  - *User Type*: **Internal Staff**

  - *Name:* **Rahim Waleed**

    - Click the button to indicate Rahim is an internal user.

  - *Organizational Unit:* **GIS Group**

  - *Telephone:* **555-555-5555**

  - *Extension:* **222**

  - *Location:* **DEV-22**

  - *Workstation ID:* **PC-0127**

- On the *Logins/Email* tab:

  - *Logins:* **Enabled**

  - *Email:* **Enabled**

  - *Email Address:* **RWaleed@OceanHouse.local**

- Leave other fields blank, and don't add access privileges for Rahim at this time.

Verify that Rahim has been added as a user. If this activity is for a class assignment, display and print Rahim's user information.

Activity B-2

Enter a service request. Follow the steps in the tutorial above to add a service request for Rahim. Enter the following information about Rahim's service request:

- In the *General Information* box:
    - *Request Type*: **Service Request**
    - *Requester*: **Rahim Waleed**
    - *Category*: **Ocean House\Technical Support\Software\Microsoft\Word**
    - *Title*: **MS Word Installation**
- In the *Importance* box:
    - *User Urgency*: **Low**
- In the *Current* Location box:
    - *Current* Location: **Dispatch**
- In the *Memo* box:
    - *Memo*: **Would like to have MS Office 2010 installed with Ocean House templates.**
- Leave the other fields in the service request form blank.

Verify that the service request has been entered correctly. If this activity is for a class assignment, display and print the service request.

Activity B-3

Find a service request. Use the *Find* option in the *File* menu to locate the service request you created in Activity B-2 (or use any other service request in the database as an example). Write short descriptions for three different ways you could find a service request using HelpSTAR's *Find* feature. Which of the three methods do you prefer? Explain why.

Activity B-4

Enter a new vendor/manufacturer. Search the Web to locate contact information for user support at Lenovo US, which supplies laptop computers to Ocean House. Use the *Setup/Administration* button on HelpSTAR's *File* menu to enter information into the database for Lenovo. Verify that the vendor contact information has been entered correctly. If this activity is for a class assignment, display and print the vendor information for Lenovo US.

Activity B-5

Find the service request categories that are defined for Ocean House. Locate a list of the service request categories currently defined in HelpSTAR. Add a new category under *Tech Support\Software* for service requests that are related to *Engineering* software. Verify that the new category for *Engineering* software has been added to the service request category list. If you enter a new service request now, does *Tech Support\ Software\Engineering* appear as a category in the *General Information* section? If this activity is for a class assignment, display and print the list of *Tech Support* categories and subcategories.

Activity B-6

Add an attachment to a service request. Use HelpSTAR's help system to research how to add an attachment to a service request. Then use the service request from Rahim in Activity B-2 (or any other service request) to add an attachment.

- Verify that the attachment has been added to the service request. If this activity is for a class assignment, display and print the service request to show that the attachment was added.

- Write a short description of the steps in HelpSTAR to add an attachment to a service request. Write your description so that other new HelpSTAR support reps could follow the procedure.

Activity B-7

Write a draft of a Best Solution. Follow the procedure in tutorial Step 13 above to write a Best Solution for a technical support problem with which you are familiar. The problem could be one you wrote about for an end-of-chapter activity earlier in this book. Your Best Solution should describe the problem and how you solved it.

Which keywords did you use to describe the best solution you wrote about? What is the difference between a draft best solution and a published one in HelpSTAR? If this activity is for a class assignment, display and print the best solution report you prepared.

Activity B-8

Audit the hardware and software on your workstation. Use HelpSTAR's tools to audit the hardware and software on your PC. On HelpSTAR's *Home* tab, click **Assets/Configuration**. Click the **Auto Discovery** tab, and then click the **Current Workstation** button. Prepare a report on the hardware and software for the PC you are using. Write a brief report that describes the kinds of information available on the audit report. If this activity is for a class assignment, display and print the Summary page of the audit for your workstation.

Does HelpSTAR remember the audit information for your PC? If so, how can you redisplay the information after the original audit report is closed?

Activity B-9

Prepare a report based on a query. Follow the procedure described in tutorial Step 17 above to prepare a query report listing the *Ref#* and *Title* for all service requests for which the *Current Priority* is equal to *Critical*. List the reference numbers for the service requests that are currently defined as critical.

To which support reps are the critical service requests assigned? How would you find out using the query tool?

Case Projects

1. Create a Help Desk Solution for Willamette Planning.

Willamette Planning is a local company that performs urban planning and land use studies for local business and government agencies. It has a small research and design department as well as a management team. Willamette Planning relies heavily on computer technology, and expects to grow; therefore, they hired Beth Markham as a help desk support rep, and have decided to adopt HelpSTAR as a help desk platform.

Your task in this assignment is to play the role of Beth Markham and set up HelpSTAR for Willamette Planning. Use the information in the table below to enter the Willamette Planning employees as new users in HelpSTAR. (You may make any reasonable assumptions or use any fictitious information you feel is appropriate for the purposes of this case study.)

User	Department	Ext	Email	Workstation	ID
Aaron Rupp	Management	10	a.rupp@wp.net	Lenovo Laptop	WS0018
Chris North	Management	14	c.north@wp.net	Lenovo Laptop	WS0023
Rakhi Windsor	Design	11	r.windsor@wp.net	Dell Laptop	WS0019
Walter Willis	Design	12	w.willis@wp.net	Dell Laptop	WS0020
Chris Green	Design	13	c.green@wp.net	Dell Laptop	WS0021
Beth Markham	Help Desk	15	b.markham@wp.net	Lenovo Laptop	WS0022

After adding all of the users in the table, enter the following service requests into HelpSTAR.

User	Service Request
Chris Green	I am unable to connect to the server from my workstation (WS0021).
Chris Green	I need to install the latest version (10.0) of the GIS software package.
Aaron Rupp	I can no longer print from my workstation.
Rakhi Windsor	The battery in my laptop now lasts less than 60 minutes when I am out of the office.

Prepare a report that lists the open service requests by user.

Challenge activity: Since Beth Markham is currently the only help desk support rep at Willamette Planning, research how to write a HelpSTAR business rule that automatically assigns service requests from *In Dispatch* to *In Queue* for Beth.

2. Perform a Feasibility Study for a Help Desk.

If you work or volunteer at a help desk, training lab facility, or instructional computer lab, assemble a small group of your colleagues to work as an assessment team to perform a feasibility study to implement HelpSTAR in your facility. You may want to view some of the client videos available on HelpSTAR's Web site to learn more about how various organizations use HelpSTAR. For additional background information, download and read a HelpSTAR Evaluator's Guide (**www.helpstar.com/quickeval/quickEvalGuide2012.pdf**), which contains an overview of HelpSTAR features.

Use your team's knowledge of the operation of the facility to prepare a feasibility study that addresses the following issues:

- Which features in HelpSTAR could be used to implement a help desk or instructional lab service request tool in the facility? Your team should use its knowledge of the facility and consider features in HelpSTAR for problem management, knowledge management, asset management, purchase order processing, and data analysis and reporting.

- Which features in HelpSTAR would probably not be of immediate use in this facility, and why not?

- Review the material on feasibility studies in Chapter 9 in this book. Include a section in your report that briefly evaluates economic, operational, technological, and timeline feasibility.

- Conclude your report with a recommendation to the management of your facility about whether HelpSTAR is a suitable help desk package for the facility.

3. Research Ways to Reset the Windows Administrator Password

One of the most common incident reports a help desk receives is, *"I forgot my password."* Your task in this case project is to research ways to reset the administrator password on a Windows 7 PC. Try out some methods until you find one that is reliable. Then write a Best Solutions knowledge base article in HelpSTAR aimed at other help desk agents that explains how to perform this task. Is this a task end users should be able to perform themselves, or could the steps you describe create even greater problems?

User Support Presentations and Meetings

In this appendix, you will learn about:

◎ How to design and develop effective presentations

◎ How to prepare for and participate effectively in support team meetings

Two aspects of work as a support specialist are introduced in this appendix. First, support workers often need to develop presentations. Some presentations, such as user training modules and reports on the findings and recommendations of a needs assessment project, are targeted to end users. Other presentations, such as training sessions for other support workers or progress reports on special projects, are aimed at support colleagues or managers. In all of these examples, the goal of a support specialist is to prepare an effective, professional presentation of information.

Second, support workers are often participants in or conveners of meetings. These meetings may include end users, work colleagues, and managers. The purpose of a meeting may be to gather or report on information related to special project work, or a periodic team meeting to discuss and make decisions about the activities of a support work group. In every meeting in which a support worker participates, the goal is to be an effective contributor, whether in the role of meeting convener or participant.

The purpose of this appendix is to describe some ways in which a support specialist can improve their performance related to presentations and meetings.

Introduction to Presentation Software

This appendix focuses on presentation software used as a tool to design and deliver effective presentations. For many support workers, Microsoft PowerPoint is the presentation software tool of choice, if for no other reason than it is installed and available in so many training and work environments. However, several other good presentation software tools are available, including some products that can be used at no cost. Popular examples include Zoho Show, Google Docs presentations, and OpenOffice Impress. Corel's WordPerfect Office Suite includes a tool with many of PowerPoint's features named Corel Presentations, which is only available as part of the Corel Suite, and IBM's Lotus Symphony suite includes a Presentations tool.

ON THE WEB

For information about free and open source presentation tools, which offer varying degrees of compatibility with PowerPoint, visit one or more of these sites:

- **show.zoho.com**—Zoho's Show is a Web-based presentation tool; free registration is required.

- **www.google.com/google-d-s/presentations**—Google Docs' presentations feature is a Web-based tool; free registration is required.

- **www.openoffice.org/product/impress.html**—Impress is a presentation tool that can be downloaded and installed without charge on a PC as part of the OpenOffice suite.

The purpose of this appendix is to provide information about how to design an effective presentation, rather than to serve as a user's manual or tutorial on presentation software. Tutorial introductions and other learning resources on these tools are available elsewhere, as described in Figure C-1.

Presentation Tool	Learning Resources
Microsoft PowerPoint	• **www.gcflearnfree.org/powerpoint2010**; introduction to the 2010 version • **office.microsoft.com/en-us/powerpoint-help/CL010370721.aspx**; links to several training modules for the 2010 version • **www.guidesandtutorials.com/powerpoint-2007-window.html**; introduction to the 2007 version • **www.fgcu.edu/support/office2007/ppt/index.asp**; covers 2007 version • *Illustrated Course Guide: Microsoft PowerPoint 2010 Advanced* by David Beskeen (Course Technology, 2011); editions covering the 2003 and 2007 versions are also available by the same author
Zoho Show	• **wiki.itap.purdue.edu/display/INSITE/Zoho+Show09#ZohoShow09-III.HowtouseZohoShow** • *Zoho 4 Everyone* by Nancy Conner (Que, 2009); one chapter on Show in a book that covers several Zoho tools
Google Docs presentations	• **www.msigeek.com/2472/how-to-create-an-online-powerpoint-presentation-with-google-docs** • *Google Docs 4 Everyone* by Steven E. Holzner (Que, 2009); two chapters on Google presentations in a book covering several Google Docs tools
OpenOffice Impress	• **wiki.services.openoffice.org/wiki/Documentation/OOo3_User _Guides/Impress_Guide** • **www.learnopenoffice.org/contents.htm** • **presentationsoft.about.com/od/openofficeimpress/tp/071021openoffice_beginguide.htm** • *OpenOffice.org 3 IMPRESS Guide* by OOoAuthorsTeam (CreateSpace, 2009); also available online (**documentation.openoffice.org/manuals/userguide3/0500IG3-ImpressGuideOOo3.pdf**)
Lotus Symphony Presentations	• **www-03.ibm.com/software/lotus/symphony/idcontents/tutorial/en/presentations_tutorial/frameset.html**

Figure C-1   Tutorials on selected presentation software tools

To learn the basic features of presentation software tools, start with a PowerPoint tutorial; Zoho Show, Google Docs presentations, and OpenOffice Impress have many of the same features as PowerPoint. All three can also read and write PowerPoint (PPT) slideshow files.

Steps to Design and Develop a Presentation

Most support workers follow a sequence of basic steps when they design and develop a presentation, no matter what the purpose. These steps are summarized in Figure C-2.

- **Plan the presentation**
    1. Define the audience, topic, and purpose
    2. Learn about the presentation location and delivery media
    3. Outline the major points
- **Design the presentation**
    4. Select a slide design
    5. Select a slide background and color scheme
- **Create the presentation slides**
    6. Choose a slide layout
    7. Prepare the text for each slide
    8. Add other objects to selected slides, such as sound, photos, charts, tables, movies, maps, and diagrams
- **Organize the slides into a slideshow**
    9. Decide on the sequence of slides
    10. Add transitions or animation
- **Generate handout materials**
    11. Create speaker notes
    12. Create handouts
- **Present the presentation**

Figure C-2   Basic steps to design and prepare a presentation

As with other lists of steps in this textbook, the set of steps in Figure C-2 should be considered a starting point, to which a support specialist will add, subtract, and modify as the specifics of a presentation warrant. The sections that follow provide guidelines for each of these steps.

Plan the Presentation

Step 1: Define the Audience, Topic, and Purpose

The chapters on training (Chapter 11) and technical writing (Chapter 3) emphasized the importance of (1) identifying the target audience, (2) clarifying the topic, and (3) focusing on the purpose of a presentation. These strategies apply equally to planning a presentation.

Characteristics of the audience that need to be identified include whether they are novice users, sophisticated users, user support staff, or managers. The technical experience of the audience makes a difference in the amount of technical detail, jargon terms, and acronyms that can be used in a presentation.

Without a clear definition of the presentation topic, a presenter may include material that strays from the central point. The topic definition should also identify what the presentation will *not* cover, as a way to focus on the central topic. A good presenter prepares each slide with an important question in mind: *"What information do I want the audience to take away from viewing this slide?"*

Finally, a presenter should define the purpose of the presentation—whether to inform, convince, or entertain. Since most user support presentations are not primarily entertainment, the choice is usually between an informational presentation (such as a training module) and one that tries to convince the audience to take some action or reach a decision (such as a recommendation at the conclusion of a user needs assessment project). It is also important to consider whether the presentation will be presented one time or at several events (for example, a product information presentation might be presented multiple times). Presentations that are offered on more than one occasion or that will be available for an extended period on the Web may require more time and effort to polish. In any case, a presentation represents both the presenter and the organization, and should be the most professional product that can be prepared in the time allocated to it.

Step 2: Learn About the Presentation Location and Delivery Media

During the presentation planning stage, a preparer should identify the location where the presentation will be delivered. Location is important for a variety of reasons. A presenter should determine, for instance, whether the presentation room will be brightly or dimly lit. In brightly lit rooms, darker slides can be used for visibility, but lighter slides should be used in a dimly lit room.

It is also important to identify the equipment that will be available to host the presentation. Some presentations occur in a meeting room equipped with a computer, projector, and screen. If a computer-equipped meeting room is available, does the projector include a handheld remote unit that can control the computer's mouse? Is the projector or computer enabled for sound? Or, lacking a computer projection system, will the presentation need to be printed on overhead slides for an older projection system?

Other presentations are targeted for audience access via the Web or as printed handouts. If Web access is the delivery medium, will sound or animation or both be used to augment the informational slides? If a presentation will be distributed as a printed handout, will the material include color pages, black and white, or grayscale? How many printed pages can be included in the handout?

Step 3: Outline the Major Points

With a clear definition of a presentation's audience, topic, purpose, location, and delivery medium, a preparer can begin to outline the major points in a presentation. Each major point will probably translate into one or more slides.

Many first-time presenters try to include too much information in their slideshows. Remember that in most presentations, a slideshow is a visual presentation method that should augment and emphasize a presenter's verbal message. Rarely should a slideshow presentation contain all the information the audience members need. Except in stand-alone slideshows designed for presentation at tradeshows or on the Web, the presenter is the star of the show. Slides that contain too much text or that make excessive use of format features (such as color, fonts, animation, and photos) may distract from the presenter and from the central message of the presentation.

Chapter 3 on writing end-user documents contains additional suggestions for developing an outline of a presentation.

Design the Presentation

Step 4: Select a Slide Design

Presentation software packages include a large number of predefined slide themes, sometimes called slide masters or templates, from which a preparer can choose. The purpose of a standard master slide design is to give a slideshow a consistent, professional appearance. Generally, simpler master slide designs that do not distract from the information content are more effective than flashy designs (unless the target audience is younger people who may prefer more colorful, creative designs). Many of the format features on a master slide can be modified to create a custom appearance that can be part of a presenter's unique signature.

Other slide design elements are optional, and are probably best omitted, unless specific reasons require their inclusion. Footers fall into this category—they should not be included in a slide master design just because the feature to create them is available in the presentation software. A slide number may be a useful tool to keep the presenter on track, and a copyright notice is useful when the material is proprietary. Other footer features should be used judiciously.

Step 5: Select a Slide Background and Color Scheme

The background and color scheme, font selection, and other aspects of a slide's appearance can either contribute to or detract from the effectiveness of a presentation. Avoid using a photo or a pattern as a slide background because they tend to overshadow the information content on a slide. Plain backgrounds or ones with simple logos or designs are preferable. Muted colors are often more effective than bright hues that seem to jump off the screen. Simpler fonts (ones that avoid handwriting, scripts, and stylized fonts) keep the focus on the content.

The general design principle here is that anything that draws the attention of audience members away from the central message on a slide should be avoided. As a presenter, do you want the audience to remember how unusual or fancy or entertaining your slides were, or remember the message you want to communicate?

The selection of design and format elements is an important decision. When in doubt, get a second opinion. Show some design options to a few colleagues you trust and get their feedback.

Create the Presentation Slides

Step 6: Choose a Slide Layout

Slide layouts give a presenter control over the arrangement of information on each slide. A slide layout is a combination of one or more of (1) a title, (2) contents, (3) objects, and (4) optional footer. Presentation software provides a variety of slide layout options. Each slide layout contains placeholders—a blank space such as a textbox to which a presenter will add content, as shown in Figure C-3. Some placeholders are designed to hold titles for the slideshow; others provide space for text information. Some placeholders are designed to present comparisons between two or more side-by-side content areas. Still other placeholders are arranged to include media objects, such as photos, tables, charts, sound, video clips, diagrams, and maps.

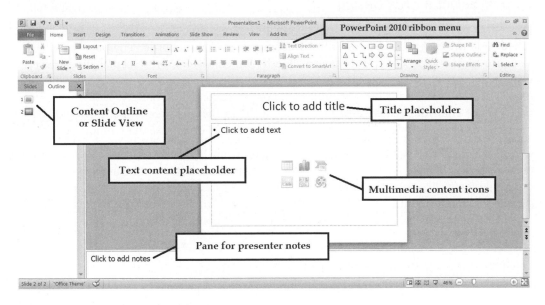

Figure C-3 PowerPoint 2010 slide layout with content placeholders

Slide layouts that use several of these layout elements (or placeholders) should be used with care. Audience members must take time to read a title and text contents, and view other media objects when several design elements are included on a single slide. During the time an audience member is absorbing all of the information content on a slide, they are not focusing their attention on you, the presenter.

Step 7: Prepare the Text for Each Slide

Most slides consist of at least some text information. Here are some guidelines for the preparation of text on a slide:

- Keep text information short; avoid lengthy passages. Information items can be a word or a phrase, rather than a complete sentence. Let white space be the dominant feature of each slide. (A presenter should speak in complete sentences, but the slides don't necessarily have to include full sentences.)

If you find yourself continually reducing the font size on a slide in order to make the information fit, you have probably included too many points. Split a slide when the information becomes too large to fit.

- If a title or phrase extends over more than a single line, help the viewer by using natural breaking points between the lines. Use the title of this chapter as an example and consider various ways to break a title into two meaningful lines.

- Keep the number of bullets on a slide to a reasonable number (three to four points is plenty—never more than seven).

- When they view a slide, audience members notice *differences*. Changes in font sizes, different font colors, changes from normal to bold or italic, and differences in alignment or spacing all invite the audience to ask why the differences appear and what the differences mean. Avoid differences for variety's sake, or changes just to make the text fit in the content space.

- To highlight important content on a slide, use a different font size or color, or use the drawing toolbar to add a callout or textbox. But don't overdo the use of these elements to call attention to important content—an audience will tire of looking at information, all of which appears to be of special importance. In other words, use differences in design elements to help your audience figure out what is really important.

- Vary the length of each slide's information content. Avoid creating several slides in a sequence with the same slide layout and with the same number and length of bulleted items.

- Always check the spelling of slideshow content, and if possible, ask a colleague to proofread the content. A proofreader who is not a subject matter expert can often help identify gaps in content as well as mechanical problems.

Step 8: Add Other Objects to Selected Slides, such as Sound, Photos, Charts, Tables, Movies, Maps, and Diagrams

Multimedia objects can certainly add interest to a slideshow. However, many beginning presenters make the mistake of thinking that each slide must contain something of interest beyond its text content. When used sparingly, multimedia objects embedded in a slideshow presentation can highlight important information or supplement that provided by the presenter. Photos, graphics, sound, color, clip art, maps, and other attention-getting devices are most effective at the beginning of a presentation to grab attention; they may become a distraction if used extensively in the heart of the presentation.

 An exception to this guideline applies to slideshows that are specifically designed to be stand-alone presentations, such as those intended for the Web. Stand-alone slideshows can often benefit from more multimedia material because, without a presenter, the slideshow must carry the entire weight of the presentation.

Especially when adding sound, photos, movie clips, and other multimedia materials to a slideshow, a presenter must observe copyright laws and cite the source of materials that are not the presenter's own work.

ON THE WEB

Guy Kawasaki, a venture capitalist, formulated a 10-20-30 rule for slide design. You can view a short video clip of Guy discussing his rule (**www.youtube.com/watch?v=liQLdRkOZiw**).

Organize the Slides into a Slideshow
Step 9: Decide on the Sequence of Slides

Presentation software permits a designer to copy, move, and delete slides easily using a slide sorter or other tools. As part of the normal presentation editing process, it is often necessary to move slides around, split some, and combine others.

Step 10: Add Transitions or Animation

Use of slide transitions and animation is tricky. Often, nothing is wrong with a transition that simply replaces a slide with the next one in sequence with little or no transition between them. This guideline follows the principle that the mechanical features of a slideshow should not detract from the information content. However, some presenters use simple transitions, such as a rapid fade, to add interest to the presentation. If so, keep the transitions simple, smooth, and consistent throughout the slideshow—in a word: unobtrusive. If an audience member is wondering from which direction the next slide will fly in, or whether the presenter has an even trickier dissolve planned for a future slide, they are likely not focusing on the message.

Presenters should avoid transitions between bulleted items on a slide, where the presenter must click to reveal each new bulleted item. Let audience members view the slide's entire contents, and avoid the distraction of transitions between bullets.

Generate Handout Materials

Step 11: Create Speaker Notes

Most presentation packages include a feature to add speaker notes to a slide. See the bottom of Figure C-3 as an example. These notes do not appear during a presentation or in handout materials, but are reminders to the presenter to discuss additional information or ask the audience a question to see whether they are following the presentation.

Step 12: Create Handouts

Because training sessions, project team reports, and other presentations are usually one-time events, many presenters choose to prepare and distribute handouts of the slideshow to participants. Handouts can consist of a reduced-size version of each slide and, optionally, space for audience members to take notes next to each slide.

Present the Presentation

Presenters may want to review the suggestions for trainers in Chapter 11, especially the 10 guidelines listed in Figure 11-6 and described on the pages that follow the figure. These suggestions apply equally to any presentation in which a slideshow is featured. If you have followed the discussion in this appendix, you know that successful presenters design slideshow materials that are simple, rather than elaborate; that are short, rather than lengthy; and that supplement the presenter, rather than steal the show. Figure C-4 contains some additional tips on slideshow presentations.

- Stand to one side of the screen instead of directly in front of it; don't cross in front of the screen frequently to switch sides.
- Face the audience; don't turn your back to the audience to read what is on a slide.
- Don't insult the intelligence of your audience by reading either the content of your slides or the speaker's notes. Use your slides as an outline of your presentation, which you talk about, rather than read.
- Give audience members time to read and study each slide, especially one with a lot of material or an image. A pause in the presentation is preferable to talking while the audience is trying to read.
- Use your abilities as a presenter, rather than elaborate slides, to make your presentation interesting. Make eye contact with your audience. Use your hands and arms to gesture to your slides for emphasis (rather than standing stiffly).
- Don't use a laser pointer unless the speaker's position is naturally in the back of the room, behind the audience. Use hands and arms to point to slide information instead of a pointer.
- Avoid the temptation to deliver your presentation as rapidly as possible in order to be finished quickly. It is preferable to speak too slowly than to speak too fast.
- Don't sound like a *presenter*. A presenter in this context speaks in a stilted, rapid, professional voice. Better to aim for the kind of relaxed, conversational speech you would use around a water cooler than to sound too much like a scripted, professional presenter.
- When not using your hands for gesturing, practice letting them hang naturally at your side, or folded in front. Don't put your hands in your pocket, or fold them in back.
- Review the guidelines for training session presentations in Chapter 11.

Figure C-4   Tips on slideshow presentations

In summary, important aspects of a presentation are, in order:

1. The audience
2. The information content of the presentation
3. The presenter
4. The contents of each slide
5. The layout or arrangement of each slide
6. The design elements and format features of the slideshow

Don't let items 5 and 6 in this list overwhelm the first three items. With this list of priorities in mind, and based on the discussion in this appendix, compare the two example slides in Figure C-5. Which slide do you think is more effective in presenting the material in the first part of this appendix? Which guidelines in this appendix are violated in each slide?

STEPS TO DESIGN AND DEVELOP A PRESENTATION

- Plan the Presentation by defining the audience, topic and purpose, location and delivery media; then outline the major points
- Design the Presentation by selecting an effective slide design, background color and color scheme
- Create the Presentation Slides by choosing a slide layout and preparing the text for each slide; then add object to each slide, such as sound, photos, charts, tables, etc., etc., etc.
- Organize the Slides into a Slideshow by deciding on the sequince of slides, and add transitions or animation
- Generate Handout Material – create speaker notes and handouts

A Guide to Computer User Support for Help Desk & Support Specialist, Fifth Edition   1

Steps to
Design and Develop a Presentation

- **Plan**
  Audience → Topic → Purpose → Location → Medium
  Outline major points
- **Design**
  Slide design → Background → Color scheme
- **Create**
  Slide layout → Text → Objects
- **Organize**
  Sequence → Transitions
- **Generate**
  Speaker notes → Handouts
- **Present**

A Guide to Computer User Support for Help Desk & Support Specialist, Fifth Edition   2

Figure C-5   Alternate slides designed to cover material in the first part of this appendix

ON THE WEB

To view a collection of slides that illustrate several poorly designed slides along with suggested improvements, visit **www.slideshare.net/garr/sample-slides-by-garr-reynolds**.

Figure C-6 lists some additional online and print resources for presenters.

- **Online resources**
  - "Guidelines for Creating Accessible PowerPoint Presentations" by the Association for Education and Rehabilitation of the Blind and Visually Impaired offers advice on preparation of PowerPoint materials with assistive strategies (**www.aerbvi.org/downloads/8/0/06%20AER%20PowerPoint%20Guidelines.doc**)
  - "Guidelines for Developing PowerPoint Lectures" by the University of Connecticut (**library.uchc.edu/copyright/docs/guidelines.pdf**)
  - "PowerPoint Presentation Advice" by Mike Splane (**www.cob.sjsu.edu/splane_m/PresentationTips.htm**)
  - "Using PowerPoint to Design Effective Presentations" by Rice University (**www.owlnet.rice.edu/~cainproj/presenting.ppt**)
- **Books**
  - *The Cognitive Style of PowerPoint: Pitching Out Corrupts Within, Second Edition* by Edward R. Tufte (Graphics Press, 2006)
  - *Presentation Zen: Simple Ideas on Presentation Design and Delivery* by Garr Reynolds (New Rider's Press, 2008)
  - *Slide:ology: The Art and Science of Creating Great Presentations* by Nancy Duarte (O'Reilly Books, 2008)
  - *Why Most PowerPoint Presentations Suck—And How You Can Make Them Better* by Rick Altman (Harvest Books, 2007)

Figure C-6   Additional resources for presentation presenters

Improving User Support Meeting Performance

Meetings with end users, support team colleagues, and managers are common in most support situations. Meetings are frequently necessary to obtain information from a group of users, such as when a support specialist interviews users as part of a needs assessment project. Similarly, the results of a needs assessment project are often presented to users, colleagues, and managers at a meeting. Support specialists often meet as a team to discuss operational issues, such as how to support a new product or new version of an existing product. And special project teams may meet periodically to assess progress on a project or troubleshoot problems that have arisen. Some groups of support staff, such as team leaders, may meet regularly to discuss operational or personnel issues within a support department.

The challenge for support workers, of course, is to make meetings as productive for themselves and team members as possible. Professionals who study meetings held in corporations, nonprofit organizations, government agencies, and educational institutions provide many suggestions for improving the productivity of attendees and the usefulness of meetings. The purpose of this section of the appendix is to offer some strategies and tools for productive meetings.

 Some organizations, in an attempt to encourage short, productive meetings, have designed meeting rooms where participants stand at four-foot-high tables during a meeting. The tables permit participants to take notes, but few meetings where participants must stand are likely to last very long.

Figure C-7 lists some strategies and tools for successful meetings.

Avoid Regularly Scheduled Meetings

Meetings that are scheduled on a periodic basis frequently pose challenges. Often these meetings lack a purpose; rather they occur simply because the meeting time popped up on attendees' calendars. Productive meetings are those that occur for a specific purpose, as you will see below, rather than because they are driven by a calendar.

- Avoid regularly scheduled meetings
- Focus the purpose of a meeting
- Prepare a meeting agenda
- Distribute materials prior to the meeting
- Refine the list of attendees
- Define the roles of attendees
- Manage meeting time
- Manage the agenda
- Manage interruptions and distractions
- Prepare meeting minutes

Figure C-7 Strategies and tools for effective meetings

Focus the Purpose of a Meeting

Less productive meetings are those that have agenda items such as: call to order, approval of minutes, approval of a financial report, announcements, additions to the agenda, routine project status reports, refreshment breaks, discussion of new topics, topics for the next meeting, for-the-good-of-the-order announcements, set the next meeting time, and adjournment. Notice that few of these agenda items contribute directly to the productivity of the attendees; some only add to the length of the meeting and to the poor reputation meetings often have.

For-the-good-of-the-order announcements are informal comments from attendees that are usually only indirectly related to agenda items; they may be announcements about the accomplishments of attendees (e.g., promotions, awards), personal events (e.g., new baby, vacation report), or other, similar comments that often add length, but not substance, to a meeting.

The primary purpose of any meeting should be to enable participants to perform tasks that cannot be accomplished individually or in smaller work teams. In most cases, meetings should be designed to brainstorm ideas; analyze the pros and cons of alternatives; reach a consensus, decision, or recommendation; and assign follow-up action tasks to attendees. Here are some specific ways to help focus the purpose of a meeting and improve its usefulness:

- Distribute minutes of the previous meeting via email and ask for any suggested corrections or additions via email or text message.

- Make announcements via email (i.e., eliminate this agenda item completely).

- Do not permit additions to a meeting's preset agenda (record ideas for worthwhile new topics for a follow-up meeting).

- Solicit suggested agenda topics for the next meeting via email or text.

- Assign the task of setting a next meeting date and time to the convener, use a calendaring system, or use a free, Web-based tool such as **www.doodle.com**.

- Reduce or eliminate social activities, refreshments, routine reports, good-of-the-order announcements, corporate or personal bragging, rumors, gossip, etc.

The measure of each item on a meeting's agenda should be: is this a task which must be accomplished at this meeting, or can this task be accomplished in some other way that uses fewer resources?

Under normal circumstances, a meeting should not be so long that a mid-meeting break is required.

Prepare a Meeting Agenda

An agenda is a description of a meeting that answers basic questions: *when*, *where*, *who*, and *what is the purpose* of the meeting. A meeting that does not have a preset agenda is an open invitation to one that will last too long and wander off topic. A meeting's convener can prepare an agenda based on emailed topic suggestions received from participants. But the convener should filter suggested topics by considering whether other ways to deal with a topic can be found besides using time and resources in a meeting. Figure C-8 describes an example outline of the agenda of a typical meeting.

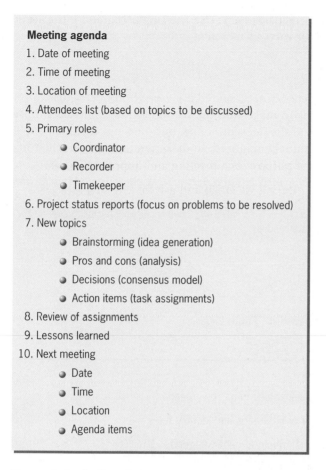

Meeting agenda

1. Date of meeting
2. Time of meeting
3. Location of meeting
4. Attendees list (based on topics to be discussed)
5. Primary roles
   - Coordinator
   - Recorder
   - Timekeeper
6. Project status reports (focus on problems to be resolved)
7. New topics
   - Brainstorming (idea generation)
   - Pros and cons (analysis)
   - Decisions (consensus model)
   - Action items (task assignments)
8. Review of assignments
9. Lessons learned
10. Next meeting
    - Date
    - Time
    - Location
    - Agenda items

Figure C-8   Outline of typical meeting agenda

Many items on the agenda outline in Figure C-8 are self-explanatory or will be described in detail below. Item 9, "Lessons learned," can be used to provide an opportunity for meeting participants to share whether problems identified in project status reports or in the discussion of new topics reveal any conclusions about what has been learned by participants or by the organization that should be recorded in the meeting summary. This is a short topic, but one that can contribute to an organization's knowledge about itself and how it operates.

Distribute Materials Prior to the Meeting

In addition to the preparation and distribution of an agenda, as well as a summary of the previous meeting, other pre-meeting activities include distribution of materials participants need to study as the basis for discussion of new topics. Each participant should commit to read and study the background materials prior to the meeting so that valuable meeting time is not spent reading reports, drafts of proposals, problem descriptions, and so on. Meetings go faster and are more productive when participants come to a meeting prepared for the agenda with relevant issues already identified for each agenda item.

Refine the List of Attendees

Attending a meeting at which your presence is not required is a very unproductive use of your time. One role of a meeting convener is to make sure the list of attendees includes those whose participation is needed to address the decision items, but does not include people who are not required, or are only tangentially required, to make decisions about the topics under discussion. Avoid situations, such as, *"We should invite Joe to the meeting. He rarely participates, but he has always attended these meetings and may feel left out if we don't invite him."*

Organizations that take meeting productivity very seriously may bring in certain participants only for the portion of the meeting for which they are needed.

Define the Roles of Attendees

Four important meeting roles are described in Table C-1.

Role	Responsibilities
Convener (also called chair, coordinator, or facilitator)	• Collect and filter topics to narrow agenda • Prepare a list of attendees and identify roles • Prepare and distribute a meeting agenda • Allocate time to discuss topics • Start the meeting on time • Follow the preset agenda • Coordinate a targeted discussion of topics • Encourage participation • Help participants identify when a consensus has been reached • Identify topics for next meeting
Recorder (also called secretary or recording secretary)	• Prepare and distribute a summary of decisions made and lessons learned

Table C-1 Roles of meeting participants (*continues*)

(continued)

Role	Responsibilities
Timekeeper	• Monitor time allocated for topic discussion
	• Alert convener and participants when time is exceeded
Participants	• Contribute suggested agenda items
	• Read summary of previous meeting for errors and omissions
	• Read distributed, preset agenda
	• Study background materials to prepare for discussion
	• Identify issues relating to each topic that need attention
	• Arrive on time and ready to begin meeting
	• Engage in active listening
	• Participate in discussions and decisions
	• Move the discussion toward a consensus on a decision
	• Avoid grandstanding, bragging, rumors, and gossip
	• Contribute to lessons learned
	• Read summary of meeting
	• Follow up on assigned tasks

Table C-1   Roles of meeting participants

Many meeting participants assume that the most important role in any meeting is that of convener. It's an important role; however, count the number of responsibilities in Table C-1 for the convener and for the participants. Who has the longest list of responsibilities?

Manage Meeting Time

Managing meeting time to increase productivity is a joint responsibility. The convener obviously has a responsibility to follow the agenda, keep the discussion on topic, quickly identify when the discussion gets off-topic, encourage participation, and help the participants identify when a consensus on a topic or decision has been reached. As noted in Table C-1, some groups use a timekeeper to monitor the time spent on each topic and to alert the convener and participants when the time allocated has been reached. (By consensus, consideration of a topic whose allocated time has expired can continue for a short period—but the timekeeper helps by saying, *"Time has come to wrap up this topic and move on to others."*) Meeting participants can help to manage meeting time by arriving on time, being well-prepared for the discussion, participating in the discussion, and helping to move the discussion toward a consensus.

Some groups rotate convener responsibilities (perhaps monthly or quarterly) to give every participant an opportunity to develop their meeting planning, participation, and leadership skills. Serving in the role of convener often gives attendees a new perspective on meeting mechanics that helps them be better participants.

Manage the Agenda

Managing the agenda is also a joint responsibility, which begins when participants contribute agenda items to the convener for consideration. It requires a commitment from participants that they will refrain from getting off-topic, monopolizing the discussion, grandstanding, bragging, and other unproductive meeting behaviors. Grandstanding occurs when participants offer opinions on issues, whether or not they have anything important or new to contribute. One way to identify a tendency to grandstand is when a participant expresses a belief (perhaps to him or herself), *"I haven't said anything for a while—it is time to make myself heard."*

When meeting participants recognize a topic or aspect of a problem as off-the-point, the person taking the minutes can make a note to suggest the topic for a future meeting.

Manage Interruptions and Distractions

Interruptions and distractions in meetings are another form of unproductive participation. Interruptions are sometimes tolerated simply because they become part of an organizational meeting culture. Interruptions can occur when a work colleague enters a meeting room to talk with a participant on a topic that "just can't wait," when a cell phone goes off during a meeting, or when a participant with a laptop, tablet, or smartphone spends time replying to email or text messages. Productive meetings occur when participants commit to help the convener and other participants reduce or eliminate interruptions and distractions; with a group effort, these behaviors can be discouraged.

A convener can help reduce interruptions by reminding participants to turn off electronic devices at the start of a meeting.

Prepare Meeting Minutes

One of the onerous jobs associated with meetings is that of the recorder. No one wants to "take minutes." The job is considered onerous partly because meeting minutes are misunderstood or misused in many situations. The term "minutes" itself implies a blow-by-blow account of everything that happened during each *minute* of a meeting. No wonder few want the recorder job, or want to read the lengthy minutes that result, for that matter.

Serving as a meeting recorder is an excellent way for a support specialist to build their technical writing skills and to use the writing tools you learned in Chapter 3. Capturing the results of a one-hour meeting on a single sheet of paper takes skill—a skill worth building, and one your colleagues will appreciate and admire.

Meeting minutes are probably more appropriately titled a meeting summary because in most cases (legal discussions are an important exception), a summary of decisions made and lessons learned is the appropriate content of meeting minutes. Effective minutes do not relate all aspects of the discussion; their purpose is to briefly record decisions made and lessons learned. Minutes can simply state when, where, who, what was decided, what follow-up assignments were made, and what lessons were learned. The most effective meeting summaries are less than a page. That's about all anyone wants to read, anyway.

This appendix has described some guidelines designed to encourage effective and productive meetings. Meetings serve many purposes for an organization beyond simply providing a vehicle for decision making. Many meetings include a team-building, collegiality, motivational, or social dimension that was not emphasized above. Organizational culture determines which guidelines in this appendix are followed to the letter, and which get a reduced emphasis. The point of these guidelines is to increase the effectiveness of meetings for participants and organizations and to present some lessons learned from those who have sought ways to make many kinds of meetings more productive. Use these guidelines to influence the meeting culture where you attend school or work.

Figure C-9 provides some additional resources for meeting participants.

- **Online resources**
  - "Effective Meeting Management: 12 Tips to Improve Meeting Productivity" by Nick McCormick (**ezinearticles.com/?Effective-Meeting-Management:-- 12-Tips-to-Improve-Meeting-Productivity&id=406722**)
  - *"The Makings of a Good Meeting"* by Kevin Wolf & Associates (**www.dcn.davis.ca.us/go/kjwolf/manual.html**)
  - Find other useful suggestions about meetings in these articles:
    - "Seven Steps to More Productive Meetings" (**www.entrepreneur.com/article/207490**)
    - "Six Tips for More Effective Meetings" (**www.effectivemeetings.com/meetingbasics/6tips.asp**)
- **Books**
  - *Great Meetings! Great Results* by Dee Kelsey (Hanson Park Press, 2004)
  - *Meeting Excellence: 33 Tools to Lead Meetings that Get Results* by Glenn M. Parker (Jossey-Bass, 2006)
  - *Successful Meetings: How to Plan, Prepare, and Execute Top-Notch Business Meetings* by Shri L. Henkel (Atlantic Publishing Company, 2007)

Figure C-9   Resources for effective meetings

Hands-On Activities

Activity C-1

Examine poorly designed slides along with some suggested improvements. Garr Reynolds has written and presented extensively on slideshow design. He assembled a collection of slides that illustrate poor design. For each slide, he provides a version to show how the slide could be improved to communicate more effectively. View the collection (**www.slideshare.net/garr/sample-slides-by-garr-reynolds**). Then select several of the slides in the Reynolds collection. Using guidelines from this appendix, or based on your own experience, write a paragraph that describes the difference between the poor example and Reynolds's version.

Activity C-2

Critique an example slideshow. The Web has thousands of examples of slideshows that can be used to learn more about the differences between good and poor slideshow design. An example intended to promote a discussion of slideshow design is available at **www.shkaminski.com/Classes/Samples/haitema.pdf**. Assemble a small group of work or school colleagues to view and critique the slideshow. Although the example is not related to user support, it provides an opportunity to apply what you have learned in this chapter and in your previous experience. Be sure to understand the stated purpose of the slideshow, which is included on the first slide, before you begin your critique. Prepare a brief report on your conclusions.

Activity C-3

Evaluate examples of meetings. View four short examples of meetings on YouTube listed below. As you view each video clip, make a list of guidelines to increase meeting productivity.

- *How NOT to Conduct a Meeting* (**www.youtube.com/watch?v=KRk4DHF8sr8**)

- *No Bull* (**www.youtube.com/watch?v=u5MoWq-5xrM**)

- *Meeting from Hell!* (**www.youtube.com/watch?v=xQW1fEwYZVA**)

- *How to Avoid Meetings that Suck* (**www.youtube.com/watch? v=BVHIMxW6D8w&NR=1**)

Prepare a short report on guidelines you can use to make meetings more productive. Better yet, design and prepare a short slideshow of your guidelines to present to your colleagues.

Activity C-4

Prepare and conduct a meeting on project meetings. If you belong to a project group or team at work or school, prepare and conduct a meeting on how to make meetings of that group more useful. Develop an agenda and a list of attendees; assign the roles of convener, recorder, and timekeeper. The primary purpose of the meeting is to identify some lessons learned and best practices for future meetings of the group. Use the meeting as an example of a well-run meeting. Use the minutes of the meeting to record the group's lessons learned and agreed-upon best practices for future meetings.

Activity C-5

Use activities in previous chapters to get more experience with presentations and meetings. Several hands-on activities and case projects in prior chapters provide an opportunity to get additional experience with presentations and meeting productivity tools. Some of these end-of-chapter exercises ask you to make presentations on various topics. Other exercises ask you to organize or participate in a meeting. Use the table below to locate one or more exercises that you can build upon to further develop your presentation and meeting skills.

Presentation Exercises

Chapter	Exercise	Activity
1	Case 1	Prepare a slide presentation to present the results of the total cost of ownership of a PC.
5	Case 1	Prepare a slide presentation to communicate information about Internet error messages.
5	Case 3	Prepare a slideshow on a topic related to problem solving.
6	Activity 6-8	Prepare a slideshow for support staff on job stressors.
7	Case 3	Prepare a slide presentation on employee retention strategies.
9	Activity 9-3	Prepare a slideshow that explains the costs and benefits of a home PC.
10	Activity 10-10	Prepare a slideshow on local recycling options.
11	Cases 2 & 4	Prepare a slide presentation as part of a training activity.

Meeting Exercises

Chapter	Exercise	Activity
8	Activity 8-6	Prepare an agenda for a meeting to set product standards.
9	Case 1	Participate in a meeting to perform a feasibility study.

Index